Juvenile
DELINQUENCY

SIXTH EDITION

Clemens Bartollas

University of Northern Iowa

Boston | New York | San Francisco
Mexico City | Montreal | Toronto | London | Madrid | Munich | Paris
Hong Kong | Singapore | Tokyo | Cape Town | Sydney

President: Nancy Forsyth	Composition and Prepress Buyer: Linda Cox
Editor-in-Chief: Karen Hanson	Manufacturing Buyer: Chris Marson
Series Editor: Jennifer Jacobson	Cover Administrator: Linda Knowles
Editorial Assistant: Elizabeth Lee	Interior Designer: Carol Somberg
Senior Marketing Manager: Judeth Hall	Photo Researcher: Katharine S. Cook
Editorial-Production Administrator: Anna Socrates	Illustrations: Omegatype Typography, Inc.
Editorial-Production Service: Matrix Productions	Electronic Composition: Omegatype Typography, Inc.

For related titles and support materials, visit our online catalog at www.ablongman.com.

Library of Congress Cataloging-in-Publication Data

Bartollas, Clemens.
    Juvenile delinquency / Clemens Bartollas.—6th ed.
      p.;cm.
    Includes bibliographical references and indexes.
    ISBN 0-205-36102-1
    1. Juvenile delinquency—United States.   2. Juvenile justice, Administration of—United States.   3. Juvenile delinquency—United States—Prevention.   4. Juvenile delinquents—Rehabilitation—United States.   I. Title.

HV9104 .B345   2001
364.36'0973—dc21

                                  2002020662

Printed in the United States of America

10 9 8 7 6 5 4 3 2 1   CIN   07 06 04 03 02

To Kristin Bartollas Polatty,
a beautiful daughter

Contents

part two THE CAUSES OF DELINQUENCY 65

chapter 3
INDIVIDUAL CAUSES OF DELINQUENCY 66

chapter 4
SOCIAL STRUCTURAL THEORIES 94

chapter **5**

SOCIAL PROCESS THEORIES 124

chapter **6**

SOCIAL REACTION THEORIES 157

part four PREVENTION, DIVERSION, AND TREATMENT   351

part five SOCIAL CONTROL OF DELINQUENCY 379

chapter 13

AN OVERVIEW OF THE JUVENILE JUSTICE PROCESS 380

chapter 14

THE POLICE AND THE JUVENILE 405

chapter 15

The Juvenile Court   432

chapter 16

Community-Based Corrections   471

chapter **17**

INSTITUTIONS FOR JUVENILES 500

Foreword

We know from philosophers no less notable than Socrates and Aristotle that some of the youths in the ancient Greece of their time loathed work; were disobedient of and disrespectful to others; engaged in crime, vandalism, and deviant conduct; and frustrated their parents and teachers. This litany—that the young are an aggravation to a decent and sober society—is almost as old as recorded history.

Through four or more millenia, all sorts of explanations have been offered for the phenomenon of delinquency. Disruptive, deviant, and delinquent youths were thought to be—in loose chronological order—evil (in a religious and moral sense); biologically defective; intellectually impaired; psychologically sick; and, more recently, the products of sociocultural forces, especially poverty, family breakdown and abuse, and weakened community controls. There has never been a shortage of seemingly plausible explanations for the problems of that often stormy and violent period in the life cycle called adolescence. Nor, indeed, has there been any shortage of recommended panaceas. The prevailing interventions have invariably fit the status of children in the society. When children were not valued and were a burden economically, treatment was harsh and even cruel. When children were thought to be the wave of the future, as during the dreadful plagues and wars that swept across Europe over and over again, treatment of children improved dramatically. Western society has never quite come to terms with its young. They hover somewhere between the products of original sin and pure innocence, and closer to one pole or another, depending on the social terrain. Nevertheless, it is safe to argue that all social interventions have gone beyond punishment, beyond psychological insight, and beyond behavior modification and have focused on three variables: work, education, and discipline.

In a speech delivered in June 1984, Chief Justice Warren Burger called for a full workweek for all prisoners (including juveniles, I presume) as a necessary element in their rehabilitation. The speech was greeted with enthusiasm, the idea was hailed as novel. In fact, such pleas are recurrent. Once again, the youth population has become a burden on the economic system, and youths are restricted to activities other than full labor market participation. Little wonder, then, that crime in the United States is disproportionately youth crime. A significant percentage of the crimes for which arrests are made involve juveniles. The good news is that arrests of individuals under the age of eighteen for property crimes have fallen; the bad news is that juveniles, with their deadly trilogy of guns, gangs, and drugs, are killing each other with reckless abandon.

In an attempt to reduce youth crime, the usual reaction has been to get tougher on juvenile predators by increasing the penalties and reducing the correctional alternatives such as probation and community care. On the other end of the delinquency spectrum, status offenders (noncriminals by adult statutes) who are school truants, incorrigibles, and runaways have been virtually eliminated from the juvenile justice system to make room for serious and dangerous delinquents. Pressured by the public on one side and reformers on the other, the juvenile justice system is in shambles. The emergent system will most likely manage delinquent juveniles as a junior version of adult criminals, emphasizing due process, harm, intent, and punishment.

It is always an event of some importance to the field of criminology and criminal justice when Professor Clemens Bartollas publishes a new book or an updated version of an earlier edition. The sixth edition of *Juvenile Delinquency* is no exception. It is comprehensive, factual, and readable—and is a fair reflection of what is new (and not so new) in our discipline. Clemens Bartollas is genuinely interested in delinquents and in all those who work with and have contact with delinquents. This book reflects Professor Bartollas's abiding intellectual and emotional commitment to understanding and reducing delinquency, as well as to ameliorating the personal and social ills that generate the massive delinquency problems not only in the United States but also in nearly all modern industrial nations. The reader cannot help but feel Professor Bartollas's empathy with the actors in the system, an empathy that is displayed both in his interviews with them and in his descriptions of their interactions and roles. There is a palpable and healthy tension between the author as the detached and analytical observer of the juvenile justice scene on the one hand and as a once active participant in institutional work on the other. Professor Bartollas was a cottage leader and later a wing director in a top-of-the-line training school for hard-core, habitual, and aggressive delinquents (jobs that he held with distinction). He is still remembered by old-time personnel in this overcrowded (which institutions are not?), 240-bed training school as a sensitive and effective incumbent in these positions. His occasional visit to the "joint" has some of the elements of a class reunion—something that is rare in institutional work.

Of late, Professor Bartollas has channeled his interpersonal skills, knowledge, and empathy into research on juvenile gangs. In the early 1990s he was involved with a group of Black Gangster Disciples and designed and implemented a gang prevention model for a local community. In the mid 1990s he developed relationships with chiefs and leaders of the major Chicago gangs. This fieldwork and gang control policy analysis is evident in his chapter on gangs, which contains a history of the evolution of gang organization, goals, activities, leadership, and focal concerns from the 1950s to the present. This chapter also presents the theories of gang development and survival, from Frederick Thrasher's classic study of more than 1,300 gangs in Chicago, published in 1927, through the work of urban sociologists, ethnographers, and criminologists who have studied this phenomenon in the intervening years. Thanks largely to the advent of the crack cocaine problem, the modern gang, which is organized along racial and ethnic lines as before, has transformed itself into a local business organization that monopolizes the neighborhood market and vies with other similar groups, using as much force and violence as necessary for economic dominance in this outside-the-law marketplace. This chapter offers some of the finest, most perceptive analyses of 1990s gangs to be found in any textbook.

This sixth edition continues several important traditions established in the original textbook: the focus on the life histories of representative delinquents, which helps to pinpoint the problems in their lives, tracing their early involvement in delinquency and their progression as delinquents; the social organization and interactional emphases; the historical context of delinquency; the changing legal environment, including major court decisions that have transformed the juvenile justice system; and descriptions and discussions of juvenile delinquency prevention and control programs.

Once again, it is fair to say that Professor Bartollas has done us all a service—those who teach no less than those who learn. This textbook is a job well done.

Simon Dinitz
The Ohio State University

Preface

Juvenile delinquency—crimes committed by young people—constitutes, by recent estimates, nearly one-third of the property crimes and one-fifth of the crimes against persons in the United States. The high incidence of juvenile crime makes the study of juvenile delinquency vital to an understanding of American society today.

The sixth edition of this book examines juvenile delinquency, as previous editions have, from a sociological perspective. This perspective is used to examine the explanations of juvenile delinquency, the environmental influences on delinquent behavior, the efforts of society to prevent juvenile delinquency, an evaluation of the justice system's effectiveness in controlling juvenile delinquency, the review of recent legislation and court rulings on the rights of youthful offenders, and the rights of adolescents in general.

Several approaches enrich the sociological analysis of delinquency in this book. First, there is a continued focus on context. Five contexts receive attention: historical, sociocultural, legal, political, and economic. In addition, when studies are available, contextual analysis is used in an examination of particular aspects of juvenile delinquency.

Contextual analysis, as an analytical tool, was developed first by the Chicago School of Sociology in the 1920s and 1930s and has been rediscovered in the 1980s and 1990s. Contextual analysis attempts to determine how the interrelationships of various contexts affect the social phenomenon under examination.

This text also emphasizes the importance of the interpretation and meaning that delinquents themselves bring to their social world. Thus, this book gives value to the life experiences leading up to delinquent behavior, to the external and internal influences on the delinquent, and to the choices that lead to a life of crime. The stories of real delinquents illustrate the text.

Voices of Delinquency, available as a companion to the textbook, is a further resource for the student who is interested in the life experiences of delinquents. The stories in this book range from those of delinquents who quickly turned their behaviors around during or subsequent to their adolescent years and who have lived exemplary lives as adults to those of delinquents who committed murders following their institutional confinement and who are serving life without parole or are on death row. These fascinating stories also reveal how the theoretical explanations in the text apply to life experiences of delinquents.

A policy-oriented analysis has been used in this book. In the midst of a great deal of discouragement about juvenile crime, nearly every chapter presents policy recommendations. I feel that a major challenge for all of us is to design recommendations that provide helpful direction for dealing more effectively with all adolescents in this society, not only delinquents.

Major restructuring has taken place in the sixth edition of this text. Chapter 1 places greater emphasis on the adolescent process than in previous editions. Chapter 2 no longer discusses group relations, for this section has been moved to the gang chapter. Chapter 3 includes new materials on developmental theory and temperament. Chapter 4 gives more attention to ecology than in previous editions. Chapter 7, Female Delinquency: Gender, Class, and Race, has been moved to the section on environmental influences. It places a much greater emphasis on gender than before. Chapter 10 includes peers in the discussion of youth gangs in the United States. Chapter 12 is a new chapter, focusing on prevention, diversion, and treatment. Chapter 13 includes new materials on intermediate sentencing, on the influence of the 1994 Juvenile Justice and

Delinquency Prevention Act, and on the philosophy of punishing juveniles. Chapter 15, on the juvenile court, has been expanded to include more materials on sentencing. Chapter 16 has new materials on juvenile probation, and Chapter 17, on Juvenile Institutions, has been reorganized to include only long-term placements for juveniles.

In addition to the major structural reorganization and the addition of new topics in nearly every chapter, the references have been updated throughout the text, and many new tables and figures have been added. Another new feature is that the boxes have been greatly increased in number and are divided into Theory and Research, Social World of the Delinquent, Juvenile Law , and Treatment Intervention.

The text is divided into five parts: The Nature and Extent of Delinquency; The Causes of Delinquency; Environmental Influences on Delinquency in the United States; Prevention, Diversion, and Treatment of Delinquency; and the Social Control of Delinquency. Part One explores how delinquent behavior affects the larger society and measures the nature and extent of delinquency by examining the available statistical tools. Part II examines four explanations of delinquent behavior: (1) individual causes, ranging from free will to biological and psychological positivism; (2) social structural factors; (3) social process factors; and (4) social reaction theories. Part III examines the relationship between delinquency and gender; problems in the family, such as child abuse; experiences in the school; peers and gang delinquency; and drug abuse. Part IV examines primary, secondary, and tertiary prevention of delinquency. In discussing the social control of delinquency, Part V includes an overview of the justice process, police–juvenile relations, the juvenile court, community-based corrections, and institutions for juveniles.

A study of delinquency in the United States is a blend of both theory and research, of the views of softliners and hardliners, of the concerns of victims and the justifications of youths, of the choices of treatment or protection of society, and of both disillusionment about past failures and increased motivation to find more effective answers. *Juvenile Delinquency* is designed to give the student a thorough overview of the subject by explaining the major studies and statistical sources, by examining delinquency in its wider social context, and by recommending policy directions to handle delinquents in American society more effectively.

Acknowledgments

Several individuals have made invaluable contributions to this text. Foremost was Linda Dippold Bartollas. She conducted interviews with youthful offenders and practitioners in the juvenile justice system, edited and conceptualized materials throughout the manuscript, and wrote materials in several chapters, including Chapter 8, on the family, and Chapter 10, on the gang. Allison Abele, Diane Kaufman, Megan Johnson, Jamie Donaldson, Jerome Van Daele, and Lucas Bee assisted in the preparation of this text in a number of ways. I am grateful to the criminologists, participants in the juvenile justice system, present and former gang leaders, and delinquents who consented to be interviewed. My gratitude to Simon Dinitz is never ending; he wrote the foreword and has been associated in one way or another with most of the books I have written. I thank Betty Heine for all the tasks that she and her staff performed to keep the manuscript moving without interruption. In preparing for the sixth edition, I would like to thank the following reviewers for their helpful critiques: Anne-Victoria Lawrence-Robinson, Kean University; Tom Cook, Wayne State College; Helen T. Greene, Old Dominion University; Yolander G. Hurst, Southern Illinois University; and Kevin M. Thompson, North Dakota State University. Finally, I am grateful to Jennifer Jacobson, my editor at Allyn and Bacon, who has been supportive and helpful throughout the process of this revision.

Welcome to a preview of the new edition of

Juvenile DELINQUENCY

by **Clemens Bartollas.**

This is the most exciting revision to date! The author continues to provide a comprehensive overview of all aspects of juvenile delinquency with a sociological focus.

A NEW LOOK AND A NEW PRICE!

Students and instructors will rejoice in the new large-format paperback design at a lower price that save students more than $15 compared to other comprehensive books in this market.

part two

THE CAUSES OF DELINQUENCY

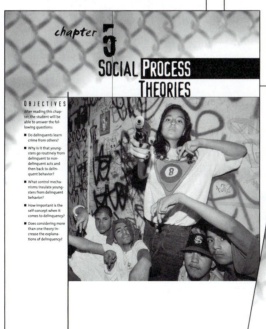

chapter **5**

SOCIAL PROCESS THEORIES

OBJECTIVES

After reading this chapter, the student will be able to answer the following questions:

■ Do delinquents learn crime from others?

■ Why is it that youngsters go routinely from delinquent to non-delinquent acts and then back to delinquent behavior?

■ What control mechanisms insulate youngsters from delinquent behavior?

■ How important is the self-concept when it comes to delinquency?

■ Does considering more than one theory increase the explanations of delinquency?

CHAPTER 4 OUTLINE

SOCIAL DISORGANIZATION THEORY
Shaw and McKay
THEORY AND RESEARCH 4.1 The Ecological Foundations of Delinquency
TREATMENT INTERVENTION 4.2 The Chicago Area Projects
HOW CULTURAL DEVIANCE THEORY IS RELATED TO DELINQUENCY
Miller's Lower-Class Culture and Delinquent Values
HOW STRAIN AFFECTS DELINQUENT BEHAVIOR
Merton's Theory of Anomie
Cohen's Theory of Delinquent Subcultures
THEORY AND RESEARCH 4.3 Interview with Albert K. Cohen
Cloward and Ohlin's Opportunity Theory
THE RELATIONSHIP BETWEEN SOCIAL STRATIFICATION AND DELINQUENCY
THE SOCIAL POLICY IMPLICATIONS OF STRUCTURAL EXPLANATIONS OF DELINQUENCY
SUMMARY
KEY TERMS
CRITICAL THINKING QUESTIONS
WEB DESTINATIONS
NOTES

Sam, an institutionalized delinquent, made this statement shortly before he left an end-of-the-line training school:

You know I never had a father or, at least, I didn't know him. I have a good mother, but she has had a hard life. At times, we barely have enough food to eat. The last time I was released from Fairfield, I made up my mind to stay out of trouble. My friends kept coming around with their schemes, and I told them to get out of my face. Then, my mother needed surgery, and there wasn't any money. My friends wanted to hit [rob] a liquor store, and I went along. But we got caught, and I ended up here.

I've grown a lot lately. It hasn't been the institution and the silly-ass rules. It has been people like John and you. You've given me respect. I want to make something of myself now. I'm eighteen, and I've got my high school diploma. I want to make a contribution to my people. Blacks have been held down too long.

But I know it won't be easy to stay out of trouble. I've got to go back to the same old neighborhoods, the same old buddies. Street life will always be there for me. I know it will be prison next time, and I don't want to spend the rest of my life in and out of places like this.¹

NEW FEATURES REINFORCE FIVE IMPORTANT THEMES IN EVERY CHAPTER

Newly reorganized boxed feature program highlights high interest enriched content in five key areas: "Theory and Research," "Treatment Intervention," "Social Policy," "Social World of the Delinquent," and "Juvenile Law."

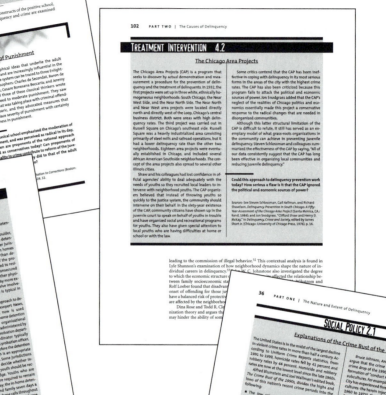

FIGURES and TABLES are easier to read, and PHOTOS are more effective in getting students' attention.

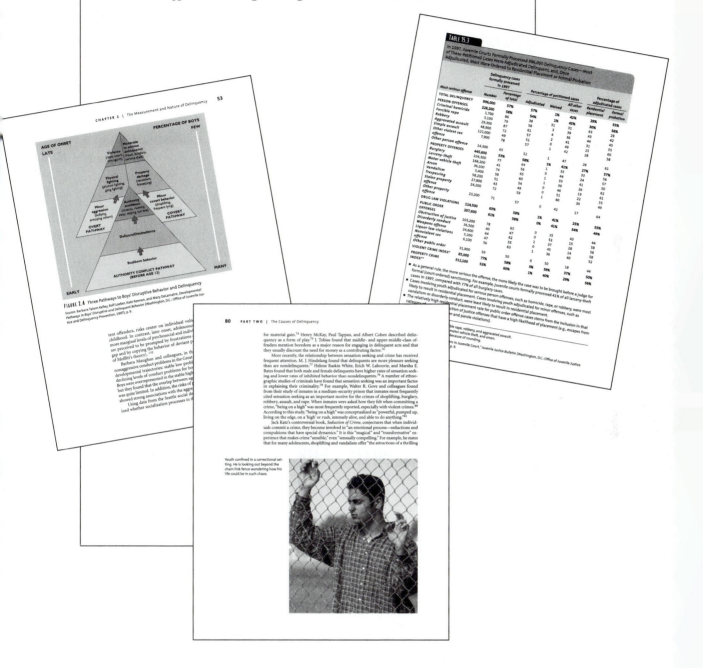

IN THE BARTOLLAS TRADITION, VOICES OF REAL PEOPLE ARE INTEGRATED THROUGHOUT THE BOOK!

*Many of the chapters start out with **case examples of real delinquents** to give the reader a glimpse of what it feels like to be viewed and processed as a delinquent. The author excels at communicating a sense of the real delinquent in the boxed feature, "Social World of the Delinquent."*

Sam, an institutionalized delinquent, made this statement shortly before he left an end-of-the-line training school:

You know I never had a father or, at least, I didn't know him. I have a good mother, but she has had a hard life. At times, we barely have enough food to eat. The last time I was released from Fairfield, I made up my mind to stay out of trouble. My friends kept coming around with their schemes, and I told them to get out of my face. Then, my mother needed surgery, and there wasn't any money. My friends wanted to hit [rob] a liquor store, and I went along. But we got caught, and I ended up here.

I've grown a lot lately. It hasn't been the institution and the silly-ass rules. It has been people like John and you. You've given me respect. I want to make something of myself now. I'm eighteen, and I've got my high school diploma. I want to make a contribution to my people. Blacks have been held down too long.

But I know it won't be easy to stay out of trouble. I've got to go back to the same old neighborhoods, the same old buddies. Street life will always be there for me. I know it will be prison next time, and I don't want to spend the rest of my life in and out of places like this.[1]

95

Social World of the Delinquent 6.1
"I Became What They Said about Me."

John remembers that a teacher came to his home at the end of the last day of his first school year.

The first grader sat in an overstuffed chair, and listened, seemingly unnoticed, as his mother and his teacher talked in the living room. The teacher said, "John has not done very well in school this year. He seems to be a slower learner. He is also an agitator."

The first grader thought to himself, "I wonder what an agitator is. I bet it is a troublemaker." He went back to listening to the two adults.

"I think," the teacher said, "we had better hold John back a year. Let him repeat first grade next year. If we do that, he may be able to make it through most of high school."

The first grader listened to the two adults sealing his fate. He thought to himself, "I have flunked first grade. I am also dumb and a troublemaker. I am always going to have trouble with school. School is such a pain."

True to his label, John had problems in school. Every year he came close to failing, and teachers regarded him as the major troublemaker in his class. He was also known as the worst kid in town because he

became involved in a number of illegal activities. At one point, he was nearly sent to training school.

At the end of his sophomore year in high school (he failed two subjects his freshman year), he was called to the principal's office. John remembers that the principal said, "We just got the IQ scores back. When I look at yours, I cannot understand why such a smart kid would do so poorly in school. Do you know you rank absolutely last in your class?"

John responded, "Well, at least it is a small class. I think we only have fifty-two in it."

The principal did not laugh.

School was an arena of total defeat for John until his junior year of high school, when he had a major turning point and decided to go into the ministry. He finished third in his class in the final two years of high school, was an honors student in college, and finished his academic work at Princeton Theological Seminary.

How much do you think what the teacher said in first grade actually influenced John? Could one comment be that significant to a person's life?

MORE OPPORTUNITIES FOR CRITICAL THINKING!

New Critical Thinking Questions have been added to the end of each chapter to provide instructors and students with an opportunity for in-depth analysis and mastery of chapter content. Chapter-ending pedagogy includes a chapter summary, key terms, author-recommended websites, and chapter notes.

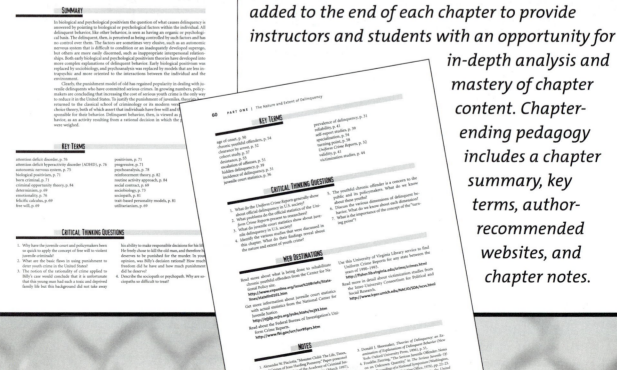

CHAPTER 3 | Individual Causes of Delinquency   89

SUMMARY

In biological and psychological positivism the question of what causes delinquency is answered by pointing to biological or psychological factors within the individual. All delinquent behavior, like other behavior, is seen as having an organic or psychological basis. The delinquent, then, is perceived as being controlled by such factors and has no control over them. The factors are sometimes very elusive, such as an autonomic nervous system that is difficult to condition or an inadequately developed superego, but others are more easily discerned, such as inappropriate interpersonal relationships. Both early biological and psychological positivism theories have developed into more complex explanations of delinquent behavior. Early biological positivism was replaced by sociobiology, and psychoanalysis was replaced by models that are less intrapsychic and more oriented to the interactions between the individual and the environment.

Clearly, the punishment model of old has regained popularity in dealing with juvenile delinquents who have committed serious crimes. In growing numbers, policymakers are concluding that increasing the cost of serious youth crime is the only way to reduce it in the United States. To justify the punishment of juveniles, theorists have returned to the classical school of criminology or its modern version, rational choice theory, both of which assert that individuals have free will and thus are responsible for their behavior. Delinquent behavior, then, is viewed as purposeful behavior, as an activity resulting from a rational decision in which the pros and cons were weighed.

KEY TERMS

attention deficit disorder, p. 76
attention deficit hyperactivity disorder (ADHD), p. 76
autonomic nervous system, p. 75
biological positivism, p. 71
born criminal, p. 71
criminal opportunity theory, p. 84
determinism, p. 69
emotionality, p. 76
felicific calculus, p. 69
free will, p. 69

positivism, p. 71
progressive, p. 71
psychoanalysis, p. 78
reinforcement theory, p. 82
routine activity approach, p. 84
social contract, p. 69
sociobiology, p. 73
sociopath, p. 81
trait-based personality models, p. 81
utilitarianism, p. 69

CRITICAL THINKING QUESTIONS

1. Why have the juvenile court and policymakers been so quick to apply the concept of free will to violent juvenile criminals?
2. What are the basic flaws in using punishment to deter youth crime in the United States?
3. The notion of the rationality of crime applied to Billy's case would conclude that it is unfortunate that this young man had such a toxic and deprived family life but this background did not take away

his ability to make responsible decisions for his life. He freely chose to kill the old man, and therefore he deserves to be punished for the murder. In your opinion, was Billy's decision rational? How much freedom did he have and how much punishment did he deserve?
4. Describe the sociopath or psychopath. Why are sociopaths so difficult to treat?

---

60 PART ONE | The Nature and Extent of Delinquency

KEY TERMS

age of onset, p. 50
chronic youthful offenders, p. 54
clearance by arrest, p. 32
cohort study, p. 37
desistance, p. 55
escalation of offenses, p. 51
hidden delinquency, p. 39
incidence of delinquency, p. 31
juvenile court statistics, p. 36

prevalence of delinquency, p. 31
reliability, p. 41
self-report studies, p. 39
specialization, p. 54
turning point, p. 58
Uniform Crime Reports, p. 32
validity, p. 41
victimization studies, p. 44

CRITICAL THINKING QUESTIONS

1. What do the Uniform Crime Reports generally show about official delinquency in U.S. society?
2. What problems do the official statistics of the Uniform Crime Reports present to researchers?
3. What do juvenile court statistics show about juvenile delinquency in U.S. society?
4. Identify the various studies that were discussed in this chapter. What do their findings reveal about the nature and extent of youth crime?

5. The youthful chronic offender is a concern to the public and its policymakers. What do we know about these youths?
6. Discuss the various dimensions of delinquent behavior. What do we know about each dimension?
7. What is the importance of the concept of the "turning point"?

WEB DESTINATIONS

Read more about what is being done to rehabilitate chronic youthful offenders from the Center for National Policy site.
http://www.cnponline.org/issue%20Briefs/State-
lines/stateline0101.htm

Get more information about juvenile court statistics with actual statistics from the National Center for Juvenile Justice.
http://ojjdp.ncjrs.org/pubs/stats/ncj93.htm

Read about the Federal Bureau of Investigation's Uniform Crime Reports.
http://www.fbi.gov/ucr/ucr95prs.htm

Use this University of Virginia Library service to find Uniform Crime Reports for any state between the years of 1990–1993.
http://fisher.lib.virginia.edu/crime/crimes.html

Read more in detail about victimization studies from the Inter-University Consortium for Political and Social Research.
http://www.icpsr.umich.edu/NACJD/SDA/ncvs.html

NOTES

1. Alexander W. Pisciotta, "Monster Child: The Life, Times, and Crimes of Jesse Harding Pomeroy," Paper presented at the Annual Meeting of the Academy of Criminal Justice Sciences in Boston, Massachusetts (March 1997).

3. Donald J. Shoemaker, Theories of Delinquency: an Examination of Explanations of Delinquent Behavior (New York: Oxford University Press, 1996), p. 31.
4. Franklin Zimring, "The Serious Juvenile Offender: Notes on an Unknown Quantity," in The Serious Juvenile Offender: Proceedings of a National Symposium (Washington, D.C.: U.S. Government Printing Office, 1978), pp. 22–23.
5. Federal Bureau of Investigation, Crime in the United States: Uniform Crime Reports (Washington, D.C.:

THE NATURE AND EXTENT OF DELINQUENCY

chapter 1

ADOLESCENCE AND DELINQUENCY

OBJECTIVES

After reading this chapter, the student will be able to answer the following questions:

- What does it mean to be an adolescent in American society?

- Are adolescents treated the same now as in the past?

- What are the problem behaviors in adolescence?

- How can delinquency be defined?

- What is a status offense?

- How have delinquents been handled through the history of the United States?

- What are the major themes of this text?

A college student reflects on her adolescence and why she acted as she did:

I was a real mess as a teenager. I got into the party crowd in high school. My mother is a doctor, and I ran around with lawyers' and doctors' kids. We were looked upon as rich kids. But I had such low self-esteem at the time that I would do just about anything to make friends.

Fourteen was a big turning point for me. I had my first beer, my first cigarette, had sex for the first time, and started to do drugs. I would sleep with guys just to make myself feel like I was liked. We would get high before school or skip classes and get high. It started out with marijuana, but by my junior year I started to do acid. We drank a lot. We got drunk every weekend and sometimes during the week. A lot of people I hung out with did cocaine, but I pretty much stayed away from it.

I never got into the crime thing. I think the reason for this was I was a good student. I went to a Catholic school, made good grades, and didn't have to put any effort into it. I did run away from home my junior year and stayed with an abusive boyfriend for a week. I almost got kicked out of school for that.

I came from the classic dysfunctional family. My father is an alcoholic. He controlled every aspect of my life. My father is incapable of loving anyone but himself. The turning point for me was when my parents divorced my senior year in high school.

I got rid of my abusive boyfriend. I started to grow up and realize that I am not totally worthless. Now, I am a senior in college. It has been two years since I've done drugs. I have a boyfriend who loves me and wants to marry me. I've learned so much by everything I've been through. It makes me appreciate what I have and what I am now.[1]

What does her statement that she has learned so much by everything she has been through mean? Why is her self-concept so important to what happens in her life? In what ways can you relate to her adolescent years?

The period of adolescence, as this college student so aptly reports, is sometimes a period of struggle. She had conflict with her father and drove her mother to despair. In this time of experimenting with the new and departing from the old, she tells how she would do almost anything to gain acceptance from peers. She drank, smoked, and did drugs on a regular basis. She was sexually active and became involved in an abusive relationship. She ran away from home and was truant from school. She looks back to her adolescent years and considers herself fortunate that she was able to survive this turbulent time.

Adolescence is a term that defines the life interval between childhood and adulthood. The term has been used in the last few decades to mark a new stage of human growth and development, but there is no way to pinpoint this period chronologically or to restrict it within physiological boundaries. For the purposes of discussion in this chapter, however, adolescence is considered to be the years between twelve and eighteen. Within this transitional period, youngsters experience many biological changes and develop new attitudes, values, and skills to guide them through their young adult years.

Delinquency, as well as other problem behaviors, increases during the adolescent years for several reasons. First, these years bring increasing freedom from parental scrutiny, and with this freedom come more opportunities to be involved in socially unacceptable behavior. New tastes, often expensive ones, are also acquired for such things as stereos, clothing, automobiles, and alcohol, yet legitimate means for satisfying these desires are often not available. The lengthening of adolescence in U.S. culture has further increased the crises and struggles of this life period, thereby increasing the chance of problems with the law, the school, and the home. Fourth, there is often a mismatch between adolescents' needs and the opportunities provided them by their social environment.[2] Finally, in some cases, the unmet needs and frustrations of early childhood fester into socially unacceptable behavior in later years.

How the Treatment of Adolescents Has Changed in the United States

Adolescence, as a stage of human growth and development, evolved out of the modern notion of childhood. The concept of childhood, as reflected in today's child-centered culture, is a relatively recent phenomenon.[3] Much of recorded history reveals abuse and indifference to be the fate of many children. Lloyd de Mause depicts childhood historically as a time when children were "killed, abandoned, beaten, terrorized, and sexually abused"; he prefaces this statement by saying, "the history of childhood is a nightmare from which we have only recently begun to awaken."[4]

The end of child labor was one of the watersheds in the development of modern adolescence. Throughout history, children have worked, but until the Industrial Revolution their work was usually done within or around the house, often out-of-doors. As work moved from the home to the factory, children were considered a source of cheap labor. It was not unusual for them to work in the worst of conditions for sixteen hours a day, six days a week.[5] Until the child labor laws were actually enforced, children as young as four and five worked in the mines, mills, and factories. But with advancing technology and mechanization, children and adolescents were no longer needed in the labor market, and by 1914, every state but one had passed laws prohibiting the employment in industry of children under a certain age, generally fourteen.

Another important stage in the development of modern adolescence was compulsory public schooling. As Chapter 9 discusses, nineteenth-century U.S. schools were violent and chaotic places in which teachers attempted to maintain control over unmotivated and unruly children, sometimes using brutal disciplinary methods. The Progressive education movement arose partly because of the dissatisfaction of some elements of society with the schools. The influence of John Dewey and other Progressive educators encouraged individualism and personal growth in the classroom. Compulsory education laws also evolved from early-twentieth-century social and religious views, which held that adolescents should be kept in school because they needed guidance and control.

A further stage in the development of modern adolescence was the twentieth-century belief that raising children was less one of conquering their spirits than one of training and socializing them. Parents in the United States, especially since the 1940s, have emphasized a helping relationship, attempting to meet their children's expanding needs in a democratic and supportive environment.[6]

An additional stage in this development took place in the 1960s and 1970s when special legal protections for juveniles were granted, highlighting the perception of adolescents as needing special attention, guidance, and support.[7] Psychologist Eric H. Erickson has observed, "Childhood . . . is the model of all oppression and enslavement, a kind of inner colonization, which forces grown ups to accept inner repression and self-restriction."[8] A chief reason for the repression of childhood, according to Erickson and others, is the lack of rights given to young people. The children's rights movement, which encompasses a spectrum of approaches, became popular in the 1970s as a means to compensate for young people's lack of rights. Consensus also increased on what is needed for an adolescent to achieve responsible adulthood:

- The search for self-identity
- The search for a personal set of values
- The acquisition of competencies necessary for adulthood, such as problem solving and decision making
- The acquisition of skills necessary for social interaction
- The attainment of emotional independence from parents

- The ability to negotiate between the need for personal achievement and the need for peer acceptance
- The need to experiment with a wide variety of behaviors, attitudes, and activities[9]

In sum, the concept of adolescence is a social construction that emerged during the late nineteenth and twentieth centuries. This social construction has had the result of further removing young people from the employment world and the mainstream of society. The process of lengthening childhood and delaying adult responsibilities was strongly influenced not only by humanitarian considerations, but also by the major economic, social, and political forces in society.

Youth at Risk Today

Nanette J. Davis contends that there is a youth crisis today. This crisis, according to Davis, ranges from "the personal to the global, from the specific to the general, and from the material to the symbolic levels."[10] She adds that an important feature of this crisis is that much of it is invisible. Invisible crises lurk beneath the surface of many adults' everyday lives, and they may choose not to see them. Yet youths caught in crises are involved in such "structural" arrangements as the discrimination and humiliations of racism, the hazards and deprivations of poverty, the culture of violence, and the ever-present temptation of drugs and alcohol. It is the consequence of these crises that has led to nationwide expansion of youth gangs, nearly two million homeless young persons, drop-out rates of 50 percent in inner-city schools, wide experimentation with various forms of dangerous drugs, and increased numbers of youths sentenced to adult prisons.[11]

Davis rejects the notion that it is the youths who are the problem. Instead of the problems resting with this aged cohort, Davis argues that the problems are found within society. It is her thesis that institutions of the United States are contributing in major ways to this youth crisis.[12] See Social Policy 1.1.

SOCIAL POLICY 1.1

Risks of Living in American Society

The term "manufactured risk" best distills the reality of the current youth crisis. American institutions—our economy, political order, schools, families, communities, and even churches—have made life more difficult, often impossible, much less welcoming, and certainly far less nurturing for those growing up today. Young people are not suffering because it is in the nature of the age group—their biology or stage of life. Instead, the extraordinarily large numbers of young people in America succumbing to permanent social and economic disadvantage, victimhood, deviance, or criminal lifestyles mark the end of the American dream, as generations of us have known it. Add to this the unproductive punitive "warehousing" approach to juvenile delinquents, and the trends take

on greater clarity. Without transforming changes, the American public appears to be settling in for a debilitating epoch of increased numbers of wasted lives.

Do you agree with Davis's perhaps overstated position that American culture and institutions have made life so difficult for young people? Is her statement more true for some adolescents than for others? There are others who state that we, as a society, do not like kids. Is this true?

Source: Nanette J. Davis, *Youth Crisis: Growing Up in the High-Risk Society* (Westport, Conn.: Praeger, 1999), p. xiii.

High-Risk Behaviors

Researchers have identified several important insights into adolescence and problem behaviors. First, high-risk youths often experience multiple difficulties. They are frequently socialized in economically stressed families and communities, more often than not have histories of physical abuse and sexual victimization, typically have educational and vocational skill deficits, and are prone to become involved in alcohol and other drug abuse and forms of delinquency.[13] The more of these problem behaviors that are present, the more likely it is that a youth will become involved in socially undesirable behaviors.[14] Second, adolescent problem behaviors—especially delinquency, drug and alcohol abuse, failing in or dropping out of school, and unprotected sex—are interrelated. An involvement in one problem behavior is generally indicative of some participation in other socially undesirable behaviors. Finally, a common factor may underlie all problem behaviors. The pursuit of this general tendency is generating considerable excitement among those interested in adolescent research.[15]

The Pittsburgh Youth Study, the Denver Youth Survey, and the Rochester Youth Development Study examined the co-occurrence or overlap of serious delinquency with drug use, problems in school, and mental health problems. Across all three study sites, the prevalance of persistent problem behaviors was usually consistent. Twenty to thirty percent of males were serious delinquents; 7 to 22 percent had school problems; 14 to 17 percent used drugs; and 7 to 14 percent had mental health problems (See Figure 1.1).[16]

John E. Donovan and Richard Jessor not only corroborated the interrelationships among high-risk behaviors in a study on adolescent drinking but also suggested that a common factor of "unconventionality" underlies all of these behaviors. This factor of unconventionality is measured by lower religiosity, tolerance of deviance, approval of drug abuse, peer approval of deviant behavior, more liberal views, and poor school performance.[17]

Travis Hirschi explains the relationship between drug abuse and delinquency by suggesting that the two are not merely influenced by the same factors but "are manifestations

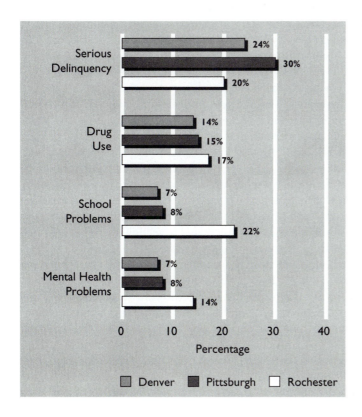

FIGURE 1.1 Prevalence of Persistent Problem Behaviors Among Males

Source: David Huizinga, Rolf Loeber, Terence P. Thornberry, and Lynn Cothern, *Co-Occurrence of Delinquency and Other Problem Behaviors* (Washington, D.C.: Office of Juvenile Justice and Delinquency Prevention, 2000), p. 3.

Status offenses involve acts that are illegal only because of a person's age, such as smoking, drinking, or running away from home. Underage drinking is a status offense, but driving under the influence of alcohol is a criminal offense. Very few youths who commit only status offenses come into contact with the juvenile justice system.

of the same thing." This "thing" is criminality, which Hirschi defines as "the tendency or propensity of the individual to seek short-term, immediate pleasure," which provides "money without work, sex without courtship, revenge without court delays."[18] In their 1990 publication, *A General Theory of Crime,* Michael R. Gottfredson and Travis Hirschi define lack of self-control as the common factor underlying problem behaviors.[19]

Yet researchers tend to be dubious about accepting this "generality of deviance hypothesis." Helene Raskin White suggests that several factors challenge the acceptability of a total generality of deviance hypothesis.[20] First, she states that "the low correlations among problem behaviors indicate that the majority of the variance in one behavior is not shared with the others.[21] Second, "various problem behaviors," according to White, "follow different developmental paths, for example, delinquency peaks between ages 15 and 17 and then declines, whereas polydrug use increases through adolescence into young adulthood.[22] White's longitudinal study of males and females also revealed that the constellation of problems varied by gender and that the associations among problem behavior over time were unstable.[23] Third, White reports that the "data indicate that problem behaviors do not cluster together in one homogeneous group of adolescents and the degree of overlap among problems is often low.[24] Finally, she claims that "there are several independent influences on each behavior."[25]

Of the twenty-seven million adolescents in the United States in 1999, approximately one in four was at high risk of engaging in multiple problem behaviors. These behaviors, particularly committing delinquent acts and abusing drugs and alcohol, quickly bring adolescents to the attention of the juvenile justice system. This means that almost seven million adolescents living primarily in disadvantaged neighborhoods are in dire need of assistance. Although minority adolescents have higher prevalence rates, the majority of these youths with multiple problems are white and male. Nearly another seven million youngsters, making up 25 percent, practice risky behavior but to a lesser degree and, consequently, are less likely to experience negative consequences. It is estimated that thirteen and a half million, or half the adolescent population, are not currently involved in high-risk behaviors.[26] See Figure 1.2 for the risk factors involved in adolescent problem behaviors.

Delinquency is one of the problem behaviors with which all but low-risk adolescents become involved from time to time (see Chapter 2). *Delinquency* is a legal term initially used in 1899 when Illinois passed the first law on juvenile delinquent behavior. Juvenile delinquency is typically defined as an act committed by a minor that violates

Risk Factors	Substance Abuse	Delinquency	Teenage Pregnancy	School Dropout	Violence
Availability of drugs	✔				
Availability of firearms		✔			✔
Community laws and norms favorable toward drug use, firearms, and crime	✔	✔			✔
Media portrayals of violence					✔
Transitions and mobility	✔	✔		✔	
Low neighborhood attachment and community organization	✔	✔			✔
Extreme economic deprivation	✔	✔	✔	✔	✔
Family history of the problem behavior	✔	✔	✔	✔	
Family management problems	✔	✔	✔	✔	✔
Family conflict	✔	✔	✔	✔	✔
Favorable parental attitudes and involvement in the problem behavior	✔	✔			✔
Early and persistent antisocial behavior	✔	✔	✔	✔	✔
Academic failure beginning in elementary school	✔	✔	✔	✔	✔
Lack of commitment to school	✔	✔	✔	✔	
Rebelliousness	✔	✔		✔	
Friends who engage in the problem behavior	✔	✔	✔	✔	✔
Favorable attitudes toward the problem behavior	✔	✔	✔	✔	
Early initiation of the problem behavior	✔	✔	✔	✔	✔
Constitutional factors	✔	✔			✔

Adolescent Problem Behaviors

FIGURE 1.2 Adolescent Problem Behaviors

Data Source: J. D. Hawkins and R. F. Catalano, *Risk-Focused Prevention: Using the Social Development Strategy* (Seattle: Developmental Research and Programs, 1995).

Source: J. C. Howell, ed., *Guide for Implementing the Comprehensive Strategy for Serious, Violent, and Chronic Juvenile Offenders.* (Washington, D.C.: Office of Juvenile Justice and Delinquency Prevention, U.S. Department of Justice, May 1995).

the penal code of the government with authority over the area in which the act occurs. The age at which an individual is considered a minor varies among states, but it is sixteen or seventeen and younger in most states.

Some evidence indicates that delinquency in U.S. society is changing. Beginning in the late 1980s and extending even more throughout the 1990s, adolescents participated widely in street gangs, some of which provided a base for trafficking narcotics; had rising rates of murder from 1989 through 1993; were more likely to own and use firearms than ever before; and were becoming increasingly involved in various forms of hate crimes.

Yet the average U.S. delinquent is far more likely to shoplift, commit petty theft, use marijuana, violate liquor laws, or destroy property than to commit a violent or serious crime. In 2000, juveniles between the ages of ten and seventeen were arrested for 345,731 property crimes, compared with 65,910 arrests for violent crimes. In other words, juveniles were arrested for committing more than five times more property crimes than violent crimes.[27]

Besides committing the same crimes as adults, juveniles are also arrested for truancy, incorrigibility, curfew violations, and runaway behavior. Such offenses are called **status offenses*** because they would not be defined as criminal if adults committed them. The legal separation between status offenders and delinquents is important because of the large number of arrests each year for acts such as truancy, disobeying parents, and running away from home. The *Uniform Crime Reports* (see Chapter 2) reveals that in 2000, three times as many youths were arrested for committing status offenses as violent crimes. This ratio between status offenses and violent crimes would be even greater if the *Uniform Crime Reports* included truancy and incorrigibility, two of the most common status offenses.[28]

How the Juvenile Court Codes Affect the Definitions of Delinquent Behavior

Juvenile court codes, which exist in every state, specify the conditions under which the state can legitimately intervene in a juvenile's life. State juvenile codes, as part of the *parens patriae,* or rehabilitative, philosophy of the juvenile court, were enacted to eliminate the arbitrary nature of juvenile justice beyond the rights afforded juveniles by the U.S. Constitution and to deal with youths more leniently because they were seen as not fully responsible for their behavior. The *In re Poff* (1955) decision aptly expresses the logic of this argument:

> The original Juvenile Court Act enacted in the District of Columbia . . . was devised to afford the juvenile protections in addition to those he already possessed under the Federal Constitution. Before this legislative enactment, the juvenile was subject to the same punishment for an offense as an adult. It follows logically that in the absence of such legislation the juvenile would be entitled to the same constitutional guarantees and safeguards as an adult. If this is true, then the only possible reason for the Juvenile Court Act was to afford the juvenile safeguards in addition to those he already possessed. The legislative intent was to enlarge and not diminish those protections.[29]

Juvenile court codes usually specify that the court has jurisdiction in relation to three categories of juvenile behavior: delinquency, dependency, and neglect. First, the courts may intervene when a youth has been accused of committing an act that would be a misdemeanor or felony if committed by an adult. Second, the courts may intervene when a juvenile commits certain status offenses. Third, the courts may intervene in cases involving dependency and neglect. If a court determines that a child is being deprived of needed support and supervision, it may decide to remove the child from the home for his or her own protection. The problem with these broad categories is that they lack precise criteria for determining the types of behavior that qualify as juvenile delinquency.

An examination of the various juvenile court codes, or statutes, shows the diverse definitions of delinquent behavior that have developed. Some statutes define a "delin-

---

*Key terms appear in boldface type when first used in the text. They are also listed at the end of each chapter.

quent youth" as one who has committed a crime or violated probation; others define a "delinquent child" in terms of such behaviors as "associating with immoral or vicious persons" (West Virginia) or "engaging in indecent or immoral conduct" (Connecticut).[30] A particular juvenile, then, could be considered a delinquent under some juvenile codes and not under others. Juvenile Law 1.2 lists behaviors that have been defined as delinquent.

Some controversy surrounds the issue of how long juveniles should remain under the jurisdiction of the juvenile court. The age at which a youthful offender is no longer treated as a juvenile ranges from sixteen to eighteen. In thirty-seven states and the District of Columbia, those persons under eighteen years of age charged with a law violation are considered juveniles. In ten states the upper limit of juvenile court jurisdiction is sixteen years and in three states, the upper limit is fifteen years (See Figure 1.3 for the upper age of juvenile court jurisdiction.)[31]

What Is a Status Offense?

In various jurisdictions, status offenders are known as MINS (minors in need of supervision), CHINS (children in need of supervision), JINS (juveniles in need of supervision), CHINA (children in need of assistance), PINS (persons in need of supervision), CHIPS (children in need of protection and services), or members of FINS (families in need of supervision). They may also be termed *predelinquent, incorrigible, beyond control, ungovernable,* or *wayward* children. What these terms and acronyms have in common is that they view the status offender as being in need of supervision or assistance.

There are three important questions about **status offenders:** Why do they behave the way they do? Do status offenders differ in offense behavior from delinquents? How should society handle their behavior?

Juvenile Law 1.2

Various Definitions of Delinquency in Juvenile Codes

- Violates any law or ordinance
- Violates juvenile court order
- Associates with criminal or immoral persons
- Engages in any calling, occupation, or exhibition punishable by law
- Frequents taverns or uses alcohol
- Wanders the streets in the nighttime
- Grows up in idleness or breaks curfew
- Enters or visits a house of ill repute
- Is habitually truant
- Is habitually disobedient or refuses to obey reasonable and proper (lawful) orders of parents, guardians, or custodians
- Engages in incorrigibility or ungovernability
- Absents himself or herself from home without permission
- Persists in violating rules and regulations of school

- Endangers welfare, morals, and/or health of self or others
- Uses vile, obscene, or vulgar language (in a public place)
- Smokes cigarettes (around a public place)
- Engages in dissolute or immoral life or conduct
- Wanders about railroad yards or tracks
- Jumps a train or enters a train without authority
- Loiters, sleeps in alleys
- Begs or receives alms (or is in the street for that purpose)

Which of these definitions is most surprising to you? Do you sense any class favoritism in these definitions?

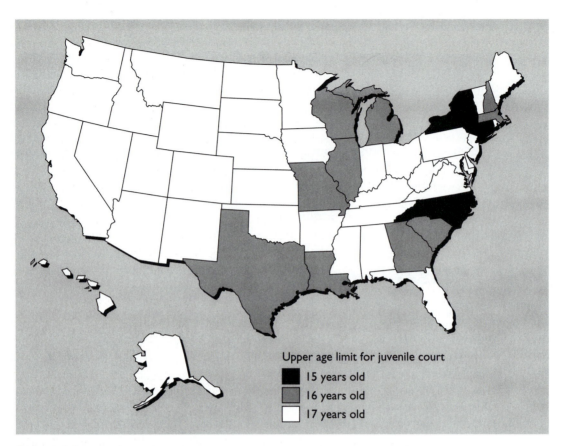

FIGURE 1.3 Upper Age Limit for Defendants in Juvenile Court, 1995

Sources: Howard Snyder and Melissa Sickmund, *Juvenile Offenders and Victims: A National Report,* Office of Juvenile Justice and Delinquency Prevention, NCJ-153569, 1995, p. 73, and Patricia Torbert et al., *State Responses to Serious and Violent Juvenile Crime.* Office of Juvenile Justice and Delinquency Prevention, 1996, p. 3.

Explanations for Status Offense Behavior

Status offenders, many of whom come from single-parent homes, generally place the blame for their problems on parental figures in the home. They believe that fulfilling their need for a warm, accepting, and loving relationship with their parents is not possible. They want to be loved by a parent who may not have the capacity to provide that love. Although their needs for sustenance and shelter may have been met, some have been physically and sexually abused. At the least, they feel rejected and neglected. They become resentful and angry with their parents, who may have problems in expressing physical affection, setting reasonable and consistent limits, and showing acceptance to their children. Many of these parents were abused as children, have limited parenting skills, or evince immature behaviors themselves.

The parents, in turn, often view status offenders as defiant, demanding, and obnoxious. Parents usually believe that they have no control over their children, who will not accept restrictions or limitations on their behavior. A power struggle results. The consequences often climax in verbal altercations and physical violence erupting from the child's striking or pushing the parent. As a result, parents call the police to intervene with such abusive or unmanageable children. Sometimes, a parent asks police to act because the youngster stays out very late, associates with older youngsters or delinquent friends, or responds to the parent with rage.

School officials and teachers tend to view status offenders, some of whom have had conflicts with teachers since kindergarten, as resistant to authority. Besides refusing to accept the limits placed on their behavior, status offenders also tend to be disruptive, disrespectful, belligerent, emotionally withdrawn or explosive, and unfocused or unconcerned. Many have been psychologically tested and found to be hyperactive or to have attention deficit disorder. They are then prescribed varying doses of medication, typically imipramine or Ritalin®, to help them focus and control their emotional difficulties.

In addition to these psychological explanations, others argue that society's response to status offenders, especially female status offenders, is a major contributing factor in defining who belongs to this legal status. Society believes that young males should behave in a certain way, typically granting leniency for the right of boys to "be boys." Society's expectations for young females, however, are still based on the maxim "Sugar and spice and everything nice, that's what little girls are made of." Meda Chesney-Lind found from her examination of the judicial handling of female status offenders that the juvenile justice system discriminates against girls because of the fear of sexual activity.[32] According to Chesney-Lind, a double standard exists between male and female adolescents because society believes it must protect adolescent girls from the potential consequences of their sexual desires. The juvenile justice system, then, becomes a moral chastity belt for adolescent females. The unfair labeling of female adolescents continues when they are victims of violence and sexual abuse at home. If they run away from these abusive environments, they are regarded as runaways and processed as status offenders. Their cycle of victimization continues as they are forced to engage in panhandling, petty theft, and occasional prostitution to survive.[33]

Offense Behavior of Status Offenders and Delinquents

Charles W. Thomas challenges the notion that status offenders are merely incorrigible youths with family problems. In a randomly selected sample of 2,589 juveniles who appeared before one of two juvenile courts in Virginia, he found that many juveniles who appeared in court for charges involving status offenses had previously appeared for more serious charges and that those juveniles whose first appearance involved a status offense were more likely to be returned to court than were those who had first been charged with a misdemeanor or felony. Thomas contends, based on these data, that status offenders not only differ very little in offense behavior from delinquent offenders, but also tend to progress from status to delinquent offenses.[34]

Maynard L. Erickson found that those who commit only status offenses represent a very small proportion of all youths who come into contact with the juvenile justice system. Most adolescents who are brought to court for status offense behavior, he adds, are mixed offenders who have, at one time or another, been involved in misdemeanors and felonies as well as status offenses.[35]

Researchers have generally agreed, however, that the majority of status offenders do differ in offense behavior from delinquents. For example, Solomon Kobrin, Frank R. Hellum, and John W. Peterson, evaluating data from a national study of status offenders, identified three groups of such offenders: the "heavies," who were predominantly serious delinquent offenders; the "lightweights," who committed misdemeanors as well as status offenses, and the "conforming youths," who occasionally became involved in status offenses. The meaning of "status offenses," according to this study, differed for each group. For heavies, a status offense was likely to be an incidental event. For lightweights, the pattern was one of minor and intermittent delinquent acts as well as status offenses. Conforming youths were likely to restrict themselves to multiple status offenses, perhaps as an outburst of rebellion against adult authority.[36]

This national study further found that most youths who received a citation for a status offense had no official record of a prior offense of any kind. These youths were principally between the ages of thirteen and sixteen, equally distributed between males and females, and more likely to be white than nonwhite. Significantly, of those with no prior status or delinquent offenses, 83.1 percent remained free of subsequent offenses of any kind.[37]

J. G. Weis and associates found that juveniles "who began their offender careers engaging in status offenses only" (or in petty illegal behavior) were not likely to graduate into more serious crime.[38] Joseph H. Rankin and L. Edward Wells, whose longitudinal study followed more than 2,000 adolescent males, also found little evidence of escalation; indeed, about two-thirds remained status offenders or never committed another offense.[39] Moreover, Thomas Kelley's analysis of the offense patterns of status offenders who appeared before a large urban court drew the following conclusions: (1) Status offenders are less prone to recidivism than are delinquent offenders; (2) their offense careers are not as long; and (3) the process of referring status offenders to the juvenile court appears to result in more serious delinquent acts.[40]

Randall G. Shelden, John A. Horvath, and Sharon Tracy's data from a longitudinal study of juvenile court referrals further revealed that the majority of youths whose first referral was a status offense did not become serious delinquents. Yet, according to these researchers, significant differences existed between male and female status offenders and among those referred for various status offenses. Male, much more than female, status offenders' behavior was likely to escalate, and those who were referred to the court for violations of liquor laws, truancy, and curfew were much more likely to commit more serious offenses than were runaways and incorrigibles.[41]

In sum, although the studies generally concluded that status offenders differ in offense behavior from delinquents and that status offenders are not likely to escalate to more serious behaviors, one-third of the status offenders in Kobrin and colleagues' study had committed delinquent offenses and continued to commit such offenses.[42] Furthermore, Shelden and colleagues found that gender and types of status offense behavior affected the likelihood of escalation into serious forms of delinquent behavior.[43]

Social Control and the Status Offender

The handling of status offenders, one of the most controversial issues in juvenile justice, has focused on two questions: Should status offenders be institutionalized with delinquents, and should the juvenile court retain jurisdiction over status offenders?

In the 1970s, the policy of confining status offenders with delinquents came under increased criticism. One disturbing finding was that before their dispositional hearing, status offenders were more likely to be detained or treated more harshly than delinquents.[44] Studies of juvenile institutionalization also show that status offenders stayed longer in training schools than did delinquents, were vulnerable to victimization in these settings, and found institutionalization with delinquents to be a destructive experience.[45]

The passage of the 1974 **Juvenile Justice and Delinquency Prevention Act** and its various modifications served as the impetus for the deinstitutionalization of status offenders (no longer to confine them in secure detention facilities or secure correctional facilities with delinquents). This act also limits the placement of juveniles in adult jail facilities.[46] The effectiveness of this federal mandate is seen in that fewer status offenders were held in secure public facilities in 1992 than in 1975. For example, in 1975 an estimated 143,000 status offense cases involved detention; in 1992 the figure was 24,300.[47]

The **Deinstitutionalization of Status Offenders Project (DSO),** funded by the Office of Juvenile Justice Delinquency Prevention (OJDP), evaluated the effects of deinstitutionalization in eight local sites. Overall, the evaluations revealed that these programs did reduce the number of white status offenders held in secure detention, but the detention of African American status offenders actually increased after the DSO project was implemented. There also was little evidence that the recidivism rate was reduced by the deinstitutionalization of status offenders.[48]

A majority of states in the 1990s were in compliance with the DSO mandate and appeared to be committed to its purposes. A 1992 monitoring report indicated that five states and three territories had achieved full compliance, and twenty-nine states were in full compliance, with minimal exceptions.[49] The chronic status offender presents a stumbling block to some states' compliance with the DSO mandate. Chronic status offenders who are runaways and those who have emotional and behavioral problems are typically the least amenable to community-based intervention strategies. As a result, some juvenile judges and juvenile justice officials view losing the option to hold these youth as losing the opportunity to help them.[50]

Juvenile court personnel have the option of manipulating jurisdictional categories in terms of status offenders. They may label downward as dependent or neglected youths, upward as delinquent youths, or laterally into private mental health facilities.[51] Thus, the juvenile court still can institutionalize status offenders in states that strongly support de-institutionalization by redefining them as delinquents or as requiring mental health services. A truant may be charged with a minor delinquent offense and be institutionalized in a private facility, or school attendance may be required as a condition of probation and further truance is then defined as a delinquent offense.[52] This permits the "invisible" institutionalization of status offenders in either private or public institutions.

The juvenile court's jurisdiction over status offenders, an equally volatile issue, faces several challenges. Critics argue that the status offender statute's lack of clarity often makes them blatantly discriminatory, especially in regard to gender. It is further argued that governmental bodies have no legitimate interest, or right to intercede, in many of these behaviors. Other critics contend that the juvenile court's intervention promotes rather than inhibits status offense behaviors. Many insist that status offenders represent a special class that must be treated differently from delinquents.[53]

Juvenile court judges, not surprisingly, challenge the movement to strip the court of jurisdiction over status offenders (which is called "divestiture"). They charge that status offenders will have no one to provide for or protect them if they are removed from the court's jurisdiction. This argument is reinforced every time a status offender is victimized or commits a serious crime. For example, following a murder of a runaway girl in 1993, the Washington legislature reinstated police and court authority to hold status offenders in secure facilities for up to five days.[54]

Several states, including Maine, New York, and Washington, have decriminalized status offenses, thus removing them from the juvenile court's jurisdiction. The most broad-based movement to strip the juvenile court of jurisdiction over status offenders has taken place in New York State, heralded by the passage of the 1985 PINS Adjustment Services Act. A central goal of this legislation was to displace the family court as the institution of first choice for minor family-related matters. The PINS legislation also has constructed an innovative system of its own that operates as formally as the family court. Children whose families are receptive are referred to the Designated Assessment Service (DAS), which in turn refers these youths to a community-based agency for long-term services. As long as youths are responsive to the rehabilitative programs designed for them, the legal proceedings are suspended.[55]

In sum, the conservative agenda in juvenile justice continues to take a dim view of stripping the juvenile court of jurisdiction over status offenders. Thus, it is unlikely that many more states in the near future will remove status offenders from the juvenile court's jurisdiction. Indeed, between 1988 and 1996, the juvenile court's formal status offense caseload more than doubled.[56.] The status offense legislation in Maine and Washington also was partly repealed to give the juvenile courts jurisdiction, especially over abandoned, runaway, or seriously endangered children.[57]

How Juvenile Delinquents Have Been Handled in the United States

Many sociological interpretations of delinquency lack a sense of history. Indeed, attempts to account for the origins and emergence of typical patterns of delinquency rarely locate those origins in a historical context. Such ahistorical approaches to understanding delinquency have a serious shortcoming, because the history of how law-violating juveniles have been dealt with is important in understanding how delinquent youths are handled today. The philosopher Santayana reminds us that "those who cannot remember the past are condemned to repeat it."[58]

The history of handling the juvenile delinquent in the United States can be divided into seven periods: colonial, houses of refuge, juvenile court, juvenile rights, the reform agenda of the late 1970s, social control and juvenile crime in the 1980s, and delinquency and U.S. society in the 1990s.

The Colonial Period (1636–1823)

The history of juvenile justice in the United States actually began in the colonial period. The colonists believed that the family was the source and primary means of social control of children. In colonial times, the law was uncomplicated, and the family was the cornerstone of the community.[59] Town fathers, magistrates, sheriffs, and watchmen were the only law enforcement officials, and the only penal institutions were jails for prisoners awaiting trial or punishment.

Juvenile lawbreakers did not face a battery of police, probation, or parole officers, nor would the juvenile justice system try to rehabilitate them. Young offenders were sent back to their families for punishment. If they were still recalcitrant after harsh whippings and other forms of discipline, they could be returned to community officials for more punishment, such as public whippings, dunkings, the stocks, or, in more serious cases, expulsion from the community or even capital punishment.

The Houses of Refuge Period (1824–1898)

Later reformers became disillusioned with the family and looked for a substitute that would provide an orderly, disciplined environment similar to that of the "ideal" Puritan family.[60] **Houses of refuge** were proposed as the solution; there, discipline was to be administered firmly and harshly. These facilities were intended to protect wayward children from "weak and criminal parents," "the manifold temptations of the streets," and "the peculiar weakness of [the children's] moral nature."[61] Houses of refuge reflected a new direction in juvenile justice, for no longer were parents and family the first line of control for children. The family's authority had been superseded by that of the state, and wayward children were placed in facilities presumably better equipped to reform them.

Houses of refuge flourished for the first half of the nineteenth century, but by the middle of the century reformers were beginning to suspect that these juvenile institutions were not as effective as had been hoped. Some had grown unwieldy in size; discipline, care, and order had disappeared from most. Reformers were also aware that many youth were being confined in institutions—jails and prisons—that were filthy, dangerous, degrading, and ill-equipped to manage juveniles effectively. A change was in order, and reformers proposed the juvenile court as a way to provide for more humane care of law-violating youths.

The Juvenile Court Period (1899–1966)

First created in Cook County, Illinois, the juvenile court was a new court for children based on the legal concept of *parens patriae*. This medieval English doctrine sanctioned the right of the Crown to intervene in natural family relations whenever a child's welfare was threatened. The concept was explained by the committee of the Chicago Bar Association that created the new court:

> The fundamental idea of the juvenile court law is that the state must step in and exercise guardianship over a child found under such adverse social or individual conditions

as to encourage the development of crime. . . . The juvenile court law proposes a plan whereby he may be treated, not as a criminal, or legally charged with crime, but as a ward of the state, to receive practically the care, custody, and discipline that are accorded the neglected and dependent child, and which, as the act states, "shall approximate as nearly as may be that which should be given by its parents."[62]

Proponents of the juvenile court promised that it would be flexible enough to give individual attention to the specific problems of wayward children. These reformers believed that once the causes of deviance were identified accurately, specific problems could be treated and cured; juveniles would be kept out of jails and prisons, thereby avoiding corruption by adult criminals.

The juvenile court period did not see radical change in the philosophy of juvenile justice, because the family continued to be subservient to the state and children still could be institutionalized. What differed was the viewpoint that children were not altogether responsible for their behavior. They were seen as victims of a variety of factors, including poverty, the ills of city life, and inadequate families, schools, and neighborhoods. No longer regarded as criminals, youthful violators were defined as children in need of care, protection, moral guidance, and discipline. Accordingly, the juvenile court was established as another official agency to aid in controlling wayward children. Juvenile delinquents would continue to be under the control of the state until they were either rehabilitated or too old to remain under the jurisdiction of juvenile authorities.

Society extended its control over the young in several other ways. Police departments established juvenile bureaus. The notion of treating juveniles for their specific problems was evidenced by the implementation in the first part of the twentieth century of both probation and parole (aftercare) agencies. Commitment to a training or industrial school, a carryover from the nineteenth century, was reserved for those whose needs became secondary to the protection of society.

The Juvenile Rights Period (1967–1975)

The criticism of the juvenile court continued to mount until, by the 1960s, the court was widely accused of dispensing capricious and arbitrary justice. The U.S. Supreme Court responded to this criticism with a series of decisions that changed the course of juvenile justice: *Kent v. United States,* 1966; *In re Gault,* 1967; *In re Winship,* 1970; *McKeiver v. Pennsylvania,* 1971; and *Breed v. Jones,* 1975.[63] The *In re Gault* decision, a landmark case, stated that juveniles have the right to due process safeguards in proceedings in which a finding of delinquency could lead to confinement and that juveniles have the rights to notice of charges, counsel, confrontation and cross-examination, as well as privilege against self-incrimination. The intent of the Court decisions was to ensure that children would have due process rights in the juvenile justice system.[64]

Reformers also believed that inconsiderate treatment by the police, five-minute hearings in juvenile courts, and degrading and sometimes brutal treatment in training schools fostered rather than reduced juvenile crime. Lower-level federal courts responded to the curbstone justice that resulted from police decisions and repressive justice in training schools by handing down numerous decisions that brought more due process rights to juveniles at the time they were arrested and taken into custody and more humane conditions during their time of confinement.

Community-based programs received an enthusiastic response in the late 1960s and early 1970s as more and more states began a process of deinstitutionalization under which only hard-core delinquents were sent to long-term training schools. Enthusiasm for community-based corrections was so widespread in the early 1970s that many observers believed that training schools would soon become extinct.

The children's rights movement also gathered momentum during the 1960s. Interest groups began to examine children's special needs, and in the 1970s the rights of children were litigated in the courts. Progress was made in the areas of custody in divorce cases, guardianship for foster children, protection of privacy rights, independent access to medical care, and legislation on child abuse.

The Reform Agenda of the Late 1970s

The reform agenda of the mid to late 1970s emphasized reducing the use of juvenile correctional institutions, diverting minor offenders and status offenders from the juvenile justice system, and reforming the juvenile justice system. The major purpose of this reform agenda was to divert status offenses from a criminal to a noncriminal setting. Status offenders received such an emphasis because of the mandate of the federal Juvenile Justice and Delinquency Prevention Act of 1974, discussed earlier. The principal objectives of this act were to promote the deinstitutionalization of status offenders as dependent, neglected, and abused children; to encourage the elimination of the practice of jailing juveniles; and to encourage the development of "community-based alternatives to juvenile detention and correctional facilities."[65]

However, this liberal agenda made a major political blunder in paying insufficient attention to the problem of serious juvenile crime. For example, less than 10 percent of the nearly $120 million in discretionary funds given out by the Office of Juvenile Justice and Delinquency Prevention between 1975 and 1980 was targeted for the population of violent and serious juvenile offenders.[66] Significantly, at a time when public concern about serious juvenile crime was at a fever pitch, the federal government not only was insensitive to the issue but also emphasized an essentially different agenda.[67] In 1978, Lloyd Ohlin correctly predicted that the failure to address violent youth crime and repeat offenders could prove to be "the Achilles' heel of a reform process."[68] The inability of reformers during the 1970s to provide meaningful programs and policies aimed at serious youth offenders contributed to the wave of "get tough" legislation that subsequently swept across the United States.[69]

Social Control and Juvenile Crime in the 1980s

The public, alerted by the media to the chilling realities of youth crime, became increasingly alarmed in the early 1980s and wanted something done to curb the serious problem of juvenile delinquency in U.S. society. Ronald Reagan was in the White House, and the formerly muted criticisms of the hard-liners suddenly became public policy. The new federal agenda attacked the Juvenile Justice and Delinquency Prevention Act as being "antifamily" and called for cracking down on juvenile law violators. Alfred S. Regnery, administrator in the Office of Juvenile Justice and Delinquency Prevention, communicated this new federal perspective in a speech delivered on December 2, 1984:

> In essence, we have changed the outlook of the office from emphasizing the lesser offender and the nonoffender to one emphasizing the serious juvenile offender. We have placed less emphasis on juvenile crime as a social problem and more emphasis on crime as a justice problem. In essence, the office now reflects the general philosophy of President Reagan and his administration rather than that of President Carter and his administration.[70]

In 1984, the National Advisory Committee for Juvenile Justice and Delinquency Prevention (NAC) also stated that "the time has come for a major departure from the existing philosophy and activity of the federal government in the juvenile justice field."[71] The NAC recommended that the "federal effort in the area of juvenile delinquency should focus primarily on the serious, violent, or chronic offender."[72] The committee also recommended that federal initiatives be limited to research, carefully designed and evaluated demonstration projects, "dissemination of information," and providing "training and technical assistance."[73] It rejected basic components of the Juvenile Justice and Delinquency Prevention Act, such as the continued provision of grants to accomplish deinstitutionalization of status offenders and the removal of juveniles from jail.[74]

Several factors led to this reassessment of the soft-line, or least restrictive, approach to minor offenders and status offenders. First, young people seemed to be clearly out of control in U.S. society. Drug and alcohol abuse were viewed as serious problems, teenage pregnancy had reached epidemic proportions, and teenage suicide was also increasing at an alarming rate.[75] Second, the spirit of the times was one of "getting tough." Nationwide, politicians assured their constituency that the answer to youth problems was to get tough on all levels. Third, "Tough Love" and other such movements showed a growing acceptance of the notion that parents must be stricter with their children. Finally, the Reagan administration made a concerted effort to show that the soft-line approach had had disastrous consequences in children's lives. For example, it was shown that increasing numbers of middle-class runaway girls had ended up as prostitutes.

The major thrusts of the Reagan administration's crime control policies for juveniles, then, were to get tough on serious and violent juvenile crime and to withdraw from the reform efforts of the 1970s. This federal mandate encouraged the development of five trends throughout the nation: (1) preventive detention; (2) transfer of violent juveniles to the adult court; (3) mandatory and determinate sentencing for violent juveniles; (4) increased confinement of juveniles; and (5) enforcement of the death penalty for juveniles who commit brutal and senseless murders.[76] These trends are described and evaluated later in this text.

Even though the public favored a more punishment-oriented response to juvenile delinquents, the juvenile court continued throughout the 1980s to have three approaches to juvenile lawbreakers (see Figure 1.4). On one end of the spectrum, the *parens patriae* doctrine is used with status offenders and minor offenders. As in the past, these youths are presumed to need treatment rather than punishment, because their offenses are seen as being caused by internal psychological or biological conditions or by sociological factors in their environment.

On the other end of the spectrum, juveniles who commit serious crimes or continue to break the law are presumed to deserve punishment rather than treatment because they possess **free will** and know what they are doing. Their delinquencies are

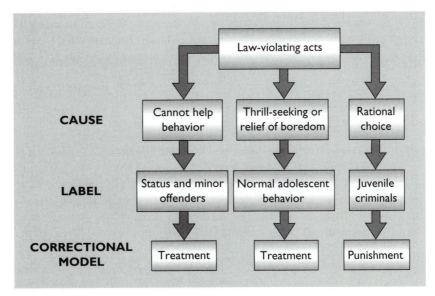

FIGURE 1.4 Three Approaches to Delinquency Control

viewed as purposeful activities resulting from rational decisions in which the pros and cons are weighed and the acts that promise the greatest potential gains are performed.[77] Their behavior is seen as being bad rather than sick and as arising from a rational decision-making process. In other words, youths in this group were to be treated by the juvenile justice system more like adults than juveniles.

Between these two groups fall youths who see crime as a form of play and commit delinquent acts because they enjoy the thrill of getting away with illegal behavior or because they want to relieve their boredom. Although criminologists usually conclude that the crimes these juveniles commit represent purposeful activity, the youths in this middle group are not considered as bad as the serious delinquents. It is reasoned that these youths may be exercising free will but that their behavior is mischievous rather than delinquent. The juvenile court continues to excuse middle-class youths for such mischievous behavior.

Delinquency and U.S. Society in the 1990s

Several interrelated social factors in the 1980s influenced delinquency in U.S. society in rather dramatic ways in the 1990s. In the mid 1980s, crack cocaine became widely available in urban areas. There was soon a large demand for this drug—some even referred to it as a crack epidemic—and this led to the recruitment of young people into the market to sell crack. By 1988 and 1989 the crack epidemic became a major impetus for the development and spread of drug-trafficking street gangs across the nation. Indeed, by the end of the decade, street gangs were found in nearly every city and many communities across the nation. One of the consequences of this illegal marketplace was that young people used guns to protect themselves from being robbed of the "valuable goods" they were carrying. Significantly, by the early 1990s the use of guns had spread from individuals involved in drug transactions to larger numbers of young people. The availability and use of guns, the spread of the drug market, and the skyrocketing growth of street gangs all contributed to a dramatic rise in murder rates among young people.[78] Finally, beginning in the 1980s and continuing in the 1990s, young people became increasingly involved in various forms of hate crimes.

This changing nature of delinquency, as well as increased media coverage of violent juveniles who carry weapons and are typically involved in gangs, began to harden public attitudes toward the juvenile delinquent. The resulting "get tough" attitude toward the violent juvenile led to a number of juvenile justice initiatives in the 1990s that went beyond those implemented in the 1980s. The urgency with which states responded is seen in the fact that nearly every state in the 1990s enacted legislation changing the way juvenile delinquents are handled.[79] This legislation led to nine state initiatives in juvenile justice: (1) curfews, (2) parental responsibility laws, (3) combating street gangs, (4) the movement toward graduated sanctions, (5) juvenile boot camps, (6) youth and guns, (7) juvenile proceedings and records, (8) juvenile transfer to criminal courts, and (9) expanded sentencing authority.

CURFEW   Curfews have recently reemerged as a popular means to control delinquent behavior. Georgia, Minnesota, Ohio, Tennessee, and Texas have recently enacted curfew ordinances.[80] A December 1995 survey of 1,000 cities with populations of more than 30,000 reported that 70 percent of the responding 387 cities have a curfew ordinance in place. In addition, 6 percent, or 23 cities, were considering adopting curfew legislation.[81] Most curfews restrict minors to their homes between 11 P.M. and 6 A.M., with some jurisdictions allowing later hours on weekends and during the summer months.[82]

PARENTAL RESPONSIBILITY LAWS   In 1995, Susan and Anthony Provenzino of St. Clair Shores, Michigan were each fined one hundred dollars and ordered to pay an additional one thousand dollars in court fees because they were convicted of violating the parental accountability ordinance. This case brought national attention to the growing

Anthony and Susan Provenzino were convicted of violating a parental responsibility ordinance when their sixteen-year-old son was charged with breaking and entering and possession of marijuana. Such ordinances make parents liable for the actions of their dependent children.

trend at both local and state levels to combat youth crime by making parents criminally responsible for the delinquent behavior of their children. Parents have been civilly responsible for their children's actions for a long time. What is new are the recent laws that make parents criminally liable for their children's actions.[83] At least thirty-six states have mandated some type of responsibility provision for parents beyond civil liability for their children's actions.[84]

COMBATING STREET GANGS   In the mid and late 1990s, some communities developed a variety of gang prevention and control strategies incorporating grassroots community involvement and providing services to gang youth. But more typically, the basic approaches to gang control involved repressive methods. The word *combating,* then, aptly portrays such antigang measures as harsher penalties for gang leaders convicted of drug dealing; increased penalties for gang-related violence, such as drive-by shootings; and enhanced penalties for any criminal act committed by a gang member.[85]

MOVEMENT TOWARD GRADUATED SANCTIONS   The development of graduated, or accountability-based, sanctions is one means that states are using to ensure that youths who are adjudicated delinquent receive an appropriate disposition by the juvenile court. Underlying this philosophy of graduated sanctions is "the notion of providing swift and appropriate punishment to youthful offenders based on the gravity of their offense and an assessment of the potential risk for reoffending, coupled with appropriate treatment to reduce the risk of reoffending."[86]

JUVENILE BOOT CAMPS   First started in Georgia in 1983, adult boot camps soon spread across the United States. Indeed, more than seventy adult boot camp programs are now operating in thirty states. It did not take long for a "get tough" climate to urge their implementation in juvenile justice, and juvenile boot camps are currently operating in ten states.[87]

YOUTH AND GUNS   In the midst of a continuing debate over gun control in the United States, there is consensus about the need to maintain and strengthen current laws restricting the possession, storage, licensing, and transfer of guns to juveniles and to enact new laws regarding juveniles who bring guns to school.[88] The school shootings in recent years have added urgency to the public's desire to get guns out of the hands of juveniles.

JUVENILE PROCEEDINGS AND RECORDS   In addition to the public's concern about juvenile crime, government agencies, school officials, and victims want more information about juvenile offenders. An increasing number of states are responding to this need by broadening access to juvenile records, allowing public access to and victim participation in juvenile proceedings, altering expungement laws for juvenile records, and fingerprinting and photographing youthful offenders.[89]

JUVENILE TRANSFER TO CRIMINAL COURT   In the 1990s, states expanded the legislation passed in the 1980s allowing for prosecution of juveniles in adult court. This trend has increased to permit transfer of younger offenders for a larger number of offenses. The three mechanisms used to transfer juvenile offenders to adult court are judicial waiver, statutory exclusion, and direct file. The extensiveness of this movement of juvenile transfer is seen in the fact that in 1995, seventeen states expanded or amended their waiver sanctions.[90]

EXPANDED SENTENCING AUTHORITY   Several states have created blended sentencing structures for cases involving repeat and serious juvenile delinquents as a mechanism for holding these juveniles accountable for their offenses. This expanded sentencing authority allows criminal and juvenile courts to impose either juvenile or adult sentences, or at times both, in cases involving juveniles.[91]

In sum, an examination of the history of the past two hundred years reveals that juveniles constitute the only age group required to obey special laws, that juveniles receive less punishment than adults who commit the same offenses, that contemporary juveniles are viewed as committing more frequent and serious offenses than juveniles have in the past, and that juvenile justice policies are consistently blamed for the high rates of juvenile crime because these policies are viewed as either too lenient or too harsh. The failure of juvenile justice policies gives rise to a cycle of juvenile justice, in which harsh punishments are replaced with lenient punishments when harsh punishments are blamed for high rates of juvenile crime. In turn, lenient punishments are replaced with harsh punishments when lenient punishments are blamed for a "juvenile crime wave."[92]

The Themes Used to Examine the Study of Delinquency

A focus on social context, the interrelationships of adolescent behaviors, individual and social construction, and a policy-oriented analysis are four themes that are used repeatedly in this text to examine delinquency in the United States.

Focus on Social Context

A major thread woven throughout this book is that the definition of delinquency, the portrayal of delinquent events, the reform and punishment of delinquents, and policy decisions about delinquency occur in a particular social setting. This social setting is shaped by at least five contexts: historical, legal, sociocultural, economic, and political.

The historical context defines how juvenile delinquents were handled in the past and influences how they are perceived and handled in the present. A study of history also enables us to perceive previous cycles of juvenile justice and to understand the emergence and the eventual decline of the philosophies governing these cycles.[93]

The legal context establishes the definition of delinquent behavior and status offense behavior. Within this context, the role and jurisdiction of the juvenile court are determined. This context also determines the legal basis of juvenile court decisions and the constitutional procedure for dealing with youths in trouble.

The sociocultural context examines the relationship between societal institutions and the delinquent, including the family, the school, and the church or synagogue. It investigates the extent to which peer groups, neighborhoods, urbanization, and industrialization contribute to delinquent behavior. Sociocultural forces also shape society's norms and values, including its attitudes toward youth crime.

The economic context examines the conditions under which delinquents live and investigates to what extent economic factors contribute to delinquent behavior. This context cannot be ignored in U.S. society because so many attitudes and behaviors are influenced by success goals and the means to achieve them. The economic context gains in importance in fiscally hard times, as high unemployment and tight budgets affect all institutions in society, including those for youth.

Finally, within the political context, local, national, and policy decisions are made that deal with youth crime. It is in this context, then, that decisions are made to toughen or soften the approach to juvenile crime. The influence of political factors on juvenile justice agencies is examined in this context. The mood of reform may begin in the wider society, but it is in the political context that the philosophy of reform is designed and the procedures for reform are implemented.

This focus on context, which goes back to the Chicago School of Sociology, has a long history in sociology in the United States.[94] Andrew Abbott's recent assessment has noted the Chicago School's emphasis on context in understanding social life:

> [According to the Chicago School], one cannot understand social life without understanding the arrangements of particular social actors in particular social times and places. . . .
>
> No social fact makes any sense abstracted from its context in social (and often geographic) space and social time.[95]

Some studies of delinquency use contextual analysis to understand how much the interrelationships of various contexts affect the interpretation and handling of delinquency. Interest in doing contextual analysis in examinations of delinquency increased during the 1980s and 1990s. When appropriate, this text will refer to these studies of contextual analysis.

Interrelationships of Adolescent Behaviors

Another theme of this text is that juvenile problem behaviors are interrelated and therefore causation theories and prevention interventions should be directed toward the common antecedents of these behaviors rather than at the separate manifest behaviors.[96]

One of the implications of the interrelated nature of adolescent behaviors is that causation theories must be integrated to improve their explanatory power. An examination of the causation theories of delinquency readily leads to the conclusion that no single theory can be used to explain all delinquent behavior. Indeed, most of the major explanations of delinquency contain an element of truth, and so a proportion—in some cases, only a small proportion—of delinquent behavior can be accounted for by a particular explanation. Each of the main theories about the causes of delinquency, then, provides a small piece of the puzzle, but combined they are even more helpful in understanding youth crime in the United States. The task is to increase the explanatory power of these theories by building on the strengths of each. Future chapters provide some building blocks that will be useful in providing a greater synthesis of the various explanations of delinquent behavior.

A further implication of the interrelated nature of problem behaviors is that prevention and treatment intervention strategies must be integrated to improve their effectiveness. As recommended in later chapters, multidimensional approaches centering on family, school, and community are needed. For example, J. David Hawkins and colleagues' integrated social development model calls for three kinds of interventions to help high-risk children: (1) creating opportunities for positive involvement with families, schools, communities, and peers; (2) helping youngsters acquire the social, cognitive, and behavioral skills to participate successfully in those social units; and (3) making reinforcement available through consistent rewards for prosocial behavior.[97]

Individual and Social Construction

Moreover, this text relates to the importance of the interpretation and meaning that delinquents themselves bring to their social world. Delinquent behavior is not merely the product or consequence of societal and community forces, it is also the creation of symbol-using, self-reflexive human beings. The likelihood of a young person committing a delinquent act is largely determined by four contexts: structural, situational, interactional, and personal. The structural context pertains to the sociocultural, economic, legal, and political factors on a societal level that affect all adolescents. The situational context is defined by such matters as the support systems available in the neighborhood, experiences in the school, and the family situation of each youth. The interactional context determines how youngsters develop shared symbols and derive meaning as they become involved in social interaction with others. Finally, the personal context refers to the way in which individual youngsters translate what happens to them in the other contexts through their own experiences and assumptions concerning life. Certainly, their biological and psychological traits, as well as the social situations impinging on them, influence their behaviors and actions. Some youngsters are more influenced by external contexts than others, but all seek to make sense of their lives and to decide on behavior that is appropriate for their perception of life. (Figure 1.5 depicts this process.)

Social construction is found in the study of delinquency in such varied subjects as the social construction of childhood and adolescence, the definition and conception of delinquency, child-saving activities and the creation of the juvenile court, the importance of class in the treatment of juveniles, and the disproportionate placement of minorities in juveniles facilities. Social construction is further found in the various crime control models, influencing how law-violating juveniles are treated. In addition, there is social construction reflected in the rules and regulations that juveniles face on probation and aftercare, in residential programs, and in juvenile facilities.

FIGURE 1.5 Contexts Affecting Decision Making among Adolescents

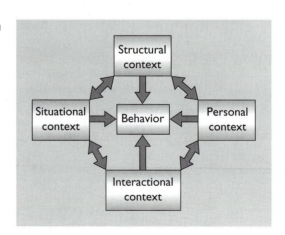

Policy-Oriented Analysis

There is much to be discouraged in the approach to handling juveniles in general and law-violating juveniles in particular in this society. Far too many children are homeless. Far too many are physically and sexually abused and neglected, are suspended or drop out of school, are involved in gang activities, are addicted to drugs or alcohol, are involved in delinquent behaviors, and go on to adult crime. Despite landmark U.S. Supreme Court decisions that grant juveniles many of the same due process and procedural safeguards accorded to adults, despite the enactment of the Juvenile Justice and Delinquency Prevention Act of 1974, despite class action lawsuits that attack the conditions under which juveniles are confined, and despite exposure in the media, widespread abuses in the juvenile justice system continue to exist.

The pressing and exciting challenge for all of us is to design recommendations that provide helpful directions for dealing more effectively with adolescents in general and delinquency in particular.

SUMMARY

This chapter has placed delinquent behavior within the wider context of adolescent problem behaviors. Those adolescents most likely to become delinquent are high-risk youths who are involved in multiple problem behaviors. These problem behaviors include school failure and dropout, teenage pregnancy and fatherhood, drug use, and delinquency. About one in every four adolescents is at high risk of engaging in multiple problem behaviors.

A focus on context will be used to help understand juvenile delinquency in the United States as we enter the twenty-first century. The history of dealing with juvenile misbehavior in this nation has been one of taking authority away from the family and at the same time becoming increasingly dissatisfied with the State's means of handling juvenile crime.

The legal context for dealing with delinquency stems from the *parens patriae* philosophy, through which the juvenile court becomes a substitute parent for wayward children. The task of the juvenile court is to reconcile the best interest of the child with the protection of society. In addition to committing the same crimes as adults, juveniles are arrested for status offenses, which would not be defined as criminal if adults committed them.

Delinquency in the United States occurs in a social context that has become more and more child centered, but the least restrictive approach to youth problems traditionally has been reserved largely for middle- and upper-class youths. Lower-class youngsters are often viewed differently and, accordingly, receive more punitive sanctions from the juvenile court.

At the same time that the public is child centered, there is an increased concern that we need to get tough on juvenile crime. Nearly every society since the dawn of history has looked on youth crime as a serious problem, and our society is no different. The present focus is on the serious and repeat juvenile criminal, and both the public and its policymakers want to be certain that these offenders are held accountable and face tough sanctions for their violent crimes.

Nevertheless, the story at the beginning of the chapter, as well as countless other accounts of youthful offenders, make us question what can be done to reduce the problem of juvenile delinquency in U.S. society. Although the tangible and intangible costs of delinquency today are staggering, equally important to U.S. society is the cost of letting vast numbers of young people grow up without realizing their potential. One of the goals of this text is to propose the means by which youngsters in our society can realize their potential and lead productive and satisfying lives.

KEY TERMS

Deinstitutionalization of Status Offenders Project (DSO), p. 14
houses of refuge, p. 16
free will, p. 19
Juvenile Justice and Delinquency Prevention Act, p. 14

parens patriae, p. 10
status offenders, p. 11
status offenses, p. 10

CRITICAL THINKING QUESTIONS

1. How has the role of the family changed throughout the history of juvenile justice in the United States?
2. Define the concept of *parens patriae*. Why is it important in understanding juvenile delinquency?
3. What are the three categories in which the juvenile court has jurisdiction over youths?

4. What are some of the factors that make juvenile delinquency a serious problem in U.S. society?
5. How have the juvenile justice initiatives of the 1990s affected how delinquents are handled?

WEB DESTINATIONS

Find out more about the court cases dealing with *parens patriae* on the Barefoot's World site.
http://www.barefootsworld.net/parensp.html

Read from the Legal Information Institute what the United States code says about the Juvenile Justice and Delinquency Prevention Act.
http://www4.law.cornell.edu/uscode/42/5601.html

Find out more about status offenders and status offenses from the National Center for Juvenile Justice site.

www.ncjrs.org/html/ojjdp/jjbul2000_10_3/page6.html

Get juvenile court statistics regarding status offenses from the Office of Juvenile Justice and Delinquency Prevention.
http://ojjdp.ncjrs.org/pubs/juvctstats/estim-pet.html

NOTES

1. Interviewed in September 1995.
2. Jacquelynne S. Eccles, Carol Midgley, Allan Wigfield, Christy Miller Buchanan, David Reuman, Constance Flanagan, and Douglas MacIver, "Development during Adolescence: The Impact of Stage-Environment Fit on Young Adolescents' Experiences in Schools and in Families," *American Psychologist* (February 1993), p. 90.
3. The concept of childhood is usually identified as beginning in the early decades of the twentieth century. For a good discussion of the social construction of adolescence, see Barry C. Feld, *Bad Kids: Race and the Transformation of the Juvenile Court* (New York: Oxford Press, 1999), pp. 19–31.
4. Lloyd de Mause, ed., *The History of Childhood* (New York: Psycho-History Press), 1974, p. 1.

5. George Henry Payne, *The Child in Human Progress* (New York: G. P. Putnam, 1969), p. 324.
6. Gerald R. Adams and Thomas Gullotta, *Adolescent Life Experiences* (Monterey, Calif.: Brooks/Cole Publishing, 1983), p. 6.
7. Adams and Gullotta, *Adolescent Life Experiences*, pp. 7–8.
8. Eric H. Erikson and Huey P. Newton, *In Search of Common Ground* (New York: W. W. Norton, 1973), p. 52.
9. Joy G. Dryfoos, *Adolescents at Risk: Prevalence and Prevention* (New York: Oxford University Press, 1990), p. 25.
10. Nanette J. Davis, *Youth Crisis: Growing Up in the High-Risk Society* (Westport, Conn.: Praeger, 1999), p. 3.
11. Ibid., pp. 4–5.
12. Ibid., p. iii.
13. Richard Dembo, Linda Williams, Jeffrey Fagan, and James Schmeidler, "Development and Assessment of a

Classification of High-Risk Youths," *Journal of Drug Issues* 24 (1994), p. 26.

14. Marc Le Blanc, "Family Dynamics, Adolescent Delinquency and Adult Criminality." Paper presented at the Society for Life History Research Conference, Keystone, Colorado (November 1990).

15. Richard Jessor and S. L. Jessor, *Problem Behavior and Psychosocial Development: A Longitudinal Study of Youth* (New York: Academic Press, 1977). See also Richard Jessor, John E. Donovan, and Francis M. Costa, *Beyond Adolescence: Problem Behavior and Young Adult Development* (New York: Cambridge University Press, 1991).

16. David Huizinga, Rolf Loeber, Terence P. Thornberry, and Lynn Cothern, *Co-Occurrence of Delinquency and Other Problem Behaviors* (Washington, D.C.: Office of Juvenile Justice and Delinquency Prevention, 2000), p. 1

17. John E. Donovan and Richard Jessor, "Structure of Problem Behavior in Adolescence and Young Adulthood," *Journal of Consulting and Clinical Psychology* 53 (1985), pp. 890–904. See also D. Wayne Osgood, Lloyd D. Johnston, Patrick M. O'Malley, and Jerald G. Bachman, "The Generality of Deviance in Late Adolescence and Early Adulthood," *American Sociological Review* 53 (1988), pp. 81–93.

18. Travis Hirschi, "A Brief Commentary on Akers' 'Delinquent Behavior, Drugs and Alcohol: What Is the Relationship,' " *Today's Delinquent* 3 (1984), pp. 49–52.

19. Michael R. Gottfredson and Travis Hirschi, *A General Theory of Crime* (Stanford, Calif.: Stanford University Press, 1990), pp. 90–91.

20. Helene Raskin White, "Early Problem Behavior and Later Drug Problems," *Journal of Research in Crime and Delinquency* 29 (November 1992), p. 414.

21. For this position, see also D. Wayne Osgood, "Covariation among Adolescent Problem Behaviors." Paper presented at the Annual Meeting of the American Society of Criminology, Baltimore, Md. (November 1990); and Helene R. White, "The Drug Use–Delinquency Connection in Adolescence," in *Drugs, Crime and the Criminal Justice System*, edited by Ralph Weisheit (Cincinnati, Ohio: Anderson, 1990), pp. 215–256.

22. See also Delbert S. Elliott, David Huizinga, and Scott Menard, *Multiple Problem Youth: Delinquency, Substance Use and Mental Health Problems* (New York: Springer-Verlag, 1989).

23. White, "Early Problem Behavior and Later Drug Problems," p. 412.

24. See also Jeffrey Fagan, Joseph G. Weis, Y.–T. Cheng, and John K. Watters, *Drug and Alcohol Use, Violent Delinquency and Social Bonding: Implications for Theory and Intervention* (San Francisco: URSA Institute, 1987).

25. See also Delbert S. Elliott et al., *Multiple Problem Youth*; and Denise B. Kandel, Ora Simcha-Fagan, and Mark Davies, "Risk Factors for Delinquency and Illicit Drug Use from Adolescence to Young Adulthood," *Journal of Drug Issues* 16 (1986), pp. 67–90.

26. Dryfoos, *Adolescents at Risk*, pp. 245–246.

27. Federal Bureau of Investigation, *Crime in the United States: Uniform Crime Reports, 2000* (Washington, D.C.: U.S. Government Printing Office, 2001), p. 226.

28. Ibid.

29. *In re Poff*, 135 F. Supp. 224 (C.C.C. 1955).

30. Barry Krisberg and James Austin, *The Children of Ishmael: Critical Perspectives on Juvenile Justice* (Palo Alto, Calif.: Mayfield Publishing, 1978), p. 60.

31. Carol J. DeFrances, *Juveniles Prosecuted in State Criminal Courts* (Washington, D.C.: Office of Juvenile Justice and Delinquency Prevention, U.S. Department of Justice, 1997), p. 1.

32. Meda Chesney-Lind, *The Female Offender: Girls, Women, and Crime* (Thousand Oaks, Calif.: Sage, 1997), pp. 65–67.

33. See Chesney-Lind on the feminist theory of delinquency in Chapter 7.

34. Charles W. Thomas, "Are Status Offenders Really So Different," *Crime and Delinquency* 22 (1976), pp. 438–455.

35. Maynard L. Erickson, "Some Empirical Questions Concerning the Current Revolution in Juvenile Justice," in *The Future of Childhood and Juvenile Justice*, edited by LaMar Empey (Charlottesville: University of Virginia Press, 1979).

36. Solomon Kobrin, Frank R. Hellum, and John W. Peterson, "Offense Patterns of Status Offenders," in *Critical Issues in Juvenile Delinquency*, edited by David Shichor and Delos H. Kelley (Lexington, Mass.: Heath, 1980), p. 211.

37. Ibid., pp. 230–231.

38. J. G. Weis, Karleen Sakumoto, John Sederstrom, and Carol Zeiss, *Jurisdiction and the Elusive Status Offender: A Comparison of Involvement in Delinquent Behavior and Status Offenses* (Washington, D.C.: U.S. Government Printing Office, 1980), p. 96.

39. Joseph H. Rankin and L. Edward Wells, "From Status to Delinquent Offense Escalation," *Journal of Criminal Justice* 13 (1985), pp. 171–180.

40. Thomas Kelley, "Status Offenders Can Be Different: A Comparative Study of Delinquent Careers," *Crime and Delinquency* 29 (1983), pp. 365–380.

41. Randall G. Shelden, John A. Horvath, and Sharon Tracy, "Do Status Offenders Get Worse? Some Clarifications on the Question of Escalation," *Crime and Delinquency* 35 (April 1989), pp. 214–215.

42. Solomon Kobrin et al., "Offense Patterns of Status Offenders," p. 213.

43. Shelden et al., "Do Status Offenders Get Worse? Some Clarifications on the Question of Escalation," p. 215.

44. See Chris E. Marshall, Ineke Haen Marshall, and Charles W. Thomas, "The Implementation of Formal Procedures in Juvenile Court Processing of Status Offenders," *Journal of Criminal Justice* 11 (1983), pp. 195–211.

45. See Clemens Bartollas, Stuart J. Miller, and Simon Dinitz, *Juvenile Victimization: The Institutional Paradox* (New York: Halsted Press, 1976).

46. U.S. Congress, Senate, Committee on the Judiciary Subcommittee to Investigate Juvenile Delinquency, 1973, *The Juvenile Justice and Delinquency Prevention Act—S.3148 and S.821*. 92d Cong., 2d sess.; 93d Cong., 1st sess.

47. National Council on Juvenile Justice, *National Juvenile Court Case Records 1975–1992* (Pittsburgh, Pa.: NCJJ, 1994).

48. M. A. Bortner, Mary Sutherland, and Russ Winn, "Race and the Impact of Juvenile Institutionalization," *Crime and Delinquency* 31 (1985), pp. 35–46; and Anne L. Schneider, *The Impact of Deinstitutionalization on*

Recidivism and Secure Confinement of Status Offenders (Washington, D.C.: U.S. Department of Justice, 1985).

49. Gwen A. Holden and Robert A. Kapler, "Deinstitutional-izing Status Offenders: A Record of Progress," *Juvenile Justice* 2 (Fall/Winter, 1995), p. 5.

50. Ibid., p. 8.

51. Barry Feld, *Bad Kids*, p. 178.

52. Thomas J. Bernard, *The Cycle of Juvenile Justice* (New York: Oxford University Press, 1992), p. 28.

53. Thomas, "Are Status Offenders Really So Different," pp. 440–442.

54. Feld, *Bad Kids*, p. 178.

55. Martin Rouse, "The Diversion of Status Offenders, Crim-inalization, and the New York Family Court." Revised pa-per presented at the Annual Meeting of the American Society of Criminology, Reno, Nevada (November 1989), pp. 1, 2, 10–11.

56. Howard N. Snyder and Melissa Sickmund, *Juvenile Of-fenders and Victims: 1999 National Report* (Washington, D.C.: Office of Juvenile Justice and Delinquency Preven-tion, 2000), p. 166.

57. Feld, *Bad Kids*, p. 179.

58. George Santayana, *The Life of Reason* (London: Consta-ble, 1905), p. 284.

59. David J. Rothman, *The Discovery of the Asylum* (Boston: Little, Brown, 1971), pp. 46–53.

60. Ibid., pp. 225–227.

61. Bradford Kinney Peirce, *A Half Century with Juvenile Delinquents* (Montclair N.J.: Patterson Smith, 1969 [1869]), p. 41.

62. Roscoe Pound, "The Juvenile Court and the Law," *Na-tional Probation and Parole Association Yearbook* 1 (1944), p. 4.

63. *Kent v. United States*, 383 U.S. 541, 86 S. Ct. 1045, 16 L. Ed. 2d 84 (1966); *In re Gault*, 387 U.S. 1, 18 L. Ed. 368 (1970); *McKeiver v. Pennsylvania*, 403 U.S. 528, 535 (1971); *In re Barbara Burrus*, 275 N.C. 517, 169 S.E. 2d 879 (1969); and *Breed v. Jones*, 421 U.S. 519, 95 S. Ct. 1779 (1975).

64. *In re Gault.*

65. U.S. Congress, *The Juvenile Justice and Delinquency Pre-vention Act.*

66. National Advisory Committee for Juvenile Justice and Delinquency Prevention, *Serious Juvenile Crime: A Redi-rected Federal Effort* (Washington, D.C.: U.S. Department of Justice, 1984), p. 18.

67. Ira M. Schwartz, *(In)justice for Juveniles: Rethinking the Best Interests of the Child* (Lexington, Mass.: Lexington Books, 1989), p. 118.

68. R. B. Coates, A. D. Miller, and L. E. Ohlin, *Diversity in a Youth Correctional System: Handling Delinquents in Mass-achusetts* (Cambridge, Mass.: Ballinger Publishing, 1978), p. 190.

69. Barry Krisberg et al., "The Watershed of Juvenile Justice Reform," *Crime and Delinquency* 32 (January 1986), p. 30.

70. Alfred S. Regnery, "A Federal Perspective on Juvenile Jus-tice Reform," *Crime and Delinquency* 32 (January 1986),

p. 40. For an extensive examination of crime control in the 1980s, see Ted Gest, *Crime and Politics: Big Govern-ment's Erratic Campaign for Law and Order:* (New York: Oxford, 2001). pp. 41–62.

71. National Advisory Committee for Juvenile Justice and Delinquency Prevention (NAC), *Serious Juvenile Crime: A Redirected Federal Effort*, p. 9.

72. Ibid., pp. 9, 11.

73. Ibid., p. 11.

74. Krisberg et al., "Watershed of Juvenile Justice Reform," p. 7.

75. Schwartz, *(In)justice for Juveniles*, p. 132.

76. Krisberg et al., "Watershed of Juvenile Justice Reform," p. 9; Barry C. Feld, "Legislative Policies toward the Seri-ous Juvenile Offender," *Crime and Delinquency* 27 (Octo-ber 1981), p. 500.

77. Edward Cimler and Lee Roy Bearch, "Factors Involved in Juvenile Decisions about Crime," *Criminal Justice and Behavior* 8 (September 1981), pp. 275–286.

78. For the development of these trends, see the interview with Alfred Blumstein in *Law Enforcement News* 21 (April 30, 1995), pp. 1–2 and 11–12.

79. National Criminal Justice Association, *Juvenile Justice Re-form Initiatives in the States: 1994–1996* (Washington, D.C.: Office of Juvenile Justice and Delinquency Preven-tion, 1997), p. 9.

80. Ibid, p. 13.

81. "Cities with Curfews Trying to Meet Constitutional Test," *Washington Post*, December 26, 1995.

82. National Criminal Justice Association, *Juvenile Justice Re-form Initiatives in the States*, p. 13.

83. Ibid., p. 18.

84. Ibid., p. 20.

85. Ibid., p. 24.

86. Ibid., p. 27.

87. Ibid., p. 29.

88. Ibid., p. 33.

89. Ibid., p. 36.

90. Donna Lyons, "National Conference of State Legislatures, State Legislature Report," *Juvenile Crime and Justice State Enactments* 9 (November 1995), pp. 13–14.

91. National Criminal Justice Association, *Juvenile Justice Re-form Initiatives in the States*, p. 46.

92. Bernard, *The Cycle of Juvenile Justice*, pp. 21–22.

93. Ibid., p. 64.

94. Andrew Abbott, "Of Time and Space: The Contempo-rary Relevance of the Chicago School," *Social Forces* 75 (1997), pp. 1149–1182. Quoted in James F. Short Jr., "The Level of Explanation Problem Revisited—The American Society of Criminology 1997 Presidential Address," *Criminology* 36 (1998), p. 6.

95. Abbott, "Of Time and Space," p. 1152.

96. Dryfoos, *Adolescents at Risk*, p. 7.

97. J. David Hawkins and Joseph G. Weis, "The Social Devel-opment Model: An Integrated Approach to Delinquency Prevention," *Journal of Primary Prevention* 6 (1985), pp. 73–97.

chapter 2

THE MEASUREMENT AND NATURE OF DELINQUENCY

OBJECTIVES

After reading this chapter, the student will be able to answer the following questions:

- What do official and unofficial statistics tell us about the extent of juvenile delinquency?

- Why is juvenile violent crime decreasing in the United States?

- What do such social factors as gender, race and ethnic background, and social class contribute to understanding delinquency?

- What other dimensions of offending are important in understanding delinquent behavior?

- Why do the majority of juvenile offenders exit from delinquent acts by the end of their adolescent years?

Alexander W. Pisciotta tells about one of the nineteenth century's most notorious youthful criminals:

Jesse Harding Pomeroy was one of nineteenth-century America's most infamous criminals. His crimes—a series of sadistic sexual tortures of children (1871–1872) and two horrifying murders (1874), committed in Massachusetts when he was just fourteen years old—captured headlines across the country. Newspapers characterized him as the "Young Demon," the "Young Monster," or more commonly, the "Boy Fiend." One late-nineteenth-

century writer stated that this "love for cruel deeds and inordinate thirst for human blood stand without precedent in history." Another described his trial and punishment as the "most remarkable case in the history of crime or criminal law." In 1917 the Boston Daily Globe *reported that he was "the most noted life prisoner in the United States." When Jesse Pomeroy died in 1932, the New York Times described him as the "nation's most famous convict."*

. . . Primary and secondary sources reveal that the crimes, arrest, trial, and punishment of the "Boy Fiend" did, indeed, shock the collective conscience of the country. This case sparked a national debate regarding the nature and causes of crime and delinquency, the limits of criminal responsibility and the use of the insanity defense, the role of expert testimony in the courtroom, concepts of childhood and the legal distinction between adult and juvenile offenders, and the use of the death penalty for minors. It also raised questions about the criminal justice system's fundamental ideological balance between punishment, reform, and social defense.[1]

> **How many Jesse Pomeroys do you think there are today in the United States? What punishment do you believe such a juvenile criminal deserves?**

Today, Jesse Pomeroy would take his place in a long line of those perceived as juvenile monsters, or "superpredators." The nation's newspapers testify nearly daily to the senseless killings and rapes committed by youth. The prevalence of juvenile violent crime has contributed to the growing perception that something is seriously wrong with U.S. society. Citizens, especially those who have been victims of youthful thugs, are uneasy about their own safety, have modified their behavior to decrease their vulnerability to crime, and have called for stronger measures to address violent youth crime.[2]

This chapter examines some of the public's most pressing questions concerning juvenile delinquency. Is juvenile crime more serious than it was in the past? Is it increasing? Why are juvenile homicides decreasing in the United States? Are there more juvenile "monsters" now than before? What do we know about violent and chronic delinquents? Is a major juvenile crime wave in our foreseeable future? To determine answers to these questions, it is necessary to examine the various means of measuring the extent of delinquent behavior, the social factors related to delinquency, and the dimensions of delinquent behavior.

The *Uniform Crime Reports,* juvenile court statistics, cohort studies, self-report studies, and victimization surveys are the major sources of data used to measure the extent and nature of delinquent behavior. A knowledge of the prevalence as well as the incidence of delinquency is necessary to understand the extent of youth crime. **Prevalence of delinquency** has to do with the proportion of a cohort or specific age category that has committed delinquent acts by a certain age in life.[3] **Incidence of delinquency** refers to the frequency of offending, or the number of delinquent events.

The Contributions Uniform Crime Reports Have Made to Understanding Delinquency

New York, Massachusetts, and Maine were the first states to collect crime statistics, but for the most part, record keeping by state and locality during the early years of U.S. history was haphazard or nonexistent. Federal record keeping was authorized in 1870 when Congress created the Department of Justice. Initially, the states and local police establishments largely ignored the task of record keeping because of either indifference or fear of federal control, but this tendency began to reverse in the early part of the twentieth century when the International Association of Chiefs of Police created a committee on **Uniform Crime Reports.** In 1930 the attorney general designated the Federal Bureau of Investigation to serve as the national clearinghouse for data collected by the Uniform Crime Reports program.

An examination of the *Uniform Crime Reports* indicates that juveniles are arrested for the same kinds of offenses as adults, as well as for some in which adults are seldom involved. For example, although both adults and juveniles are arrested for such serious offenses as murder and aggravated assault and for such less serious offenses as simple assault and carrying weapons, only juveniles can be taken into custody for running away, violating curfew, or truancy from school.

The crimes for which the FBI collects information are divided into two classes, Part I and Part II offenses. Part I offenses, also known as index offenses, are subdivided further into crimes against the person, such as murder, rape, robbery and aggravated assault, and crimes against property, such as burglary, larceny, auto theft, and arson. Juveniles who are arrested for the violent Part I offenses are more likely to be held for trial as adults, whereas those arrested for less serious offenses usually are processed by juvenile authorities. The exceptions to this general rule are those juveniles who have lengthy records of crime, including violent offenses, and those who are held over for trial in adult courts because they are believed to be threats to society.

Each month, police departments across the United States report to the FBI the number of offenses that come to their attention and the number of offenses that the police are able to clear by arrest. **Clearance by arrest** indicates that a person is arrested because he or she confesses to an offense or is implicated by witnesses or by other criminal evidence of having committed an offense. These monthly reports are summarized in year-end reports, which constitute our major official source of information about crime in the United States. The data are subdivided into many different statistical categories, including the backgrounds of alleged offenders and the types of crimes for which they are arrested.

The *Uniform Crime Reports'* data pose a number of problems, but one of the most serious complaints is that the police can make arrests only when crimes come to their attention. Many crimes are hidden or are not reported to the police; therefore the *Uniform Crime Reports* vastly underestimate the actual amount of crime in the United States. Some also charge that because the police arrest only those who violate important laws and ignore most of the other offenses committed by juveniles, these statistics tell us more about official police policy and practice than about the amount of crime. Moreover, youthful offenders may be easier to detect in the act of committing a crime than older offenders, with a resulting inflation of the rates for youths.[4] Finally, there is the issue that the local police departments often manipulate the statistics that are reported to the FBI. The intent may be to make the problem appear worse or better depending on the reporting agency's agenda.

Crime by Age Groups

The *Uniform Crime Reports* examine the extent of juvenile crime; compares youth crime to adult crime; considers gender and racial variations in youth crime; and presents city, suburban, and rural differences in youth crime. The chief findings of the *Uniform Crime Reports* as they relate to juveniles are as follows:

1. Youth crime is widespread in U.S. society. The *Uniform Crime Reports* revealed that in 2000 there were 1,560,289 juveniles under eighteen arrested. Juveniles between the ages of ten and seventeen constituted about 25 percent of the population, and youths in this age group were arrested for 16 percent of the violent crimes and 32 percent of all arrests.

2. Juveniles are arrested for committing some offenses more frequently than they are for others. As Figure 2.1 indicates, the percentage of total arrests involving juveniles is highest in curfew and loitering, running away, vandalism, arson, burglary, motor vehicle theft, and larceny-theft.

3. Juveniles are arrested for serious property offenses as well as violent offenses. Juveniles were arrested for 33 percent of all burglary arrests, 25 percent of robbery arrests, 24 percent of weapon arrests, 9 percent of murder arrests, and 14 percent of aggravated assault arrests in 2000.

4. Juvenile murder rates increased substantially between 1987 and 1993. In the peak year of 1993, there were about 3,800 juvenile arrests for murder. But between 1993 and 2000, juvenile arrests for murder declined, with the number of arrests in 2000 (806) about one-fifth of that in 1993.

5. Juveniles were involved in 13 percent of all drug arrests in 2000. Between 1991 and 2000, juvenile arrests for drug abuse violations increased 145 percent.

6. Twenty-eight percent of juvenile arrests in 2000 were arrests of females. Law enforcement agencies made 431,760 arrests of juvenile females.

7. The racial composition of the juvenile population in 2000 was 79 percent white, 15 percent African American, and 5 percent other races, with most Hispanics classified as white. In contrast, 55 percent of juvenile arrests for violent crimes involved white youths and 42 percent African American youths.[5]

Youth Crime Trends

The *Uniform Crime Reports* also provide one indicator of the rise and fall of youth crime. According to these official statistics, between 1971 and 2001 the percentage of

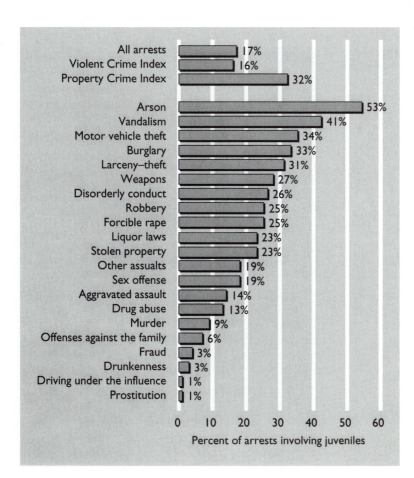

FIGURE 2.1 Juvenile Property Crime Arrests Exceed Their Violent Crime Arrests

In 2000, juveniles were involved in fewer than 1 in 6 arrests for a violent crime, 1 in 3 arrests for a property offense, and 1 in 4 arrests for a weapons law violation.

Note: Running away from home and curfew violations are not presented in this figure because, by definition, only juveniles can be arrested for these offenses.

Data source: Crime in the United States 2000 (Washington, DC: U.S. Government Printing Office, 2001), table 38, p. 226.

All arrests 17%
Violent Crime Index 16%
Property Crime Index 32%

Arson 53%
Vandalism 41%
Motor vehicle theft 34%
Burglary 33%
Larceny–theft 31%
Weapons 27%
Disorderly conduct 26%
Robbery 25%
Forcible rape 25%
Liquor laws 23%
Stolen property 23%
Other assualts 19%
Sex offense 19%
Aggravated assault 14%
Drug abuse 13%
Murder 9%
Offenses against the family 6%
Fraud 3%
Drunkenness 3%
Driving under the influence 1%
Prostitution 1%

Percent of arrests involving juveniles

Part I arrests involving juveniles under the age of eighteen declined from 45 percent to 27.5 percent. In those years the percentage of violent arrests declined from 22 percent to 15.9 percent, and the percentage of property crimes declined from 51 to 32 percent.[6]

The most pressing question concerning youth crime trends is whether there will be a youth crime wave in the next ten to fifteen years. Alfred Blumstein provides bad news about the trends in youth crime. The bad news, according to Blumstein, "makes for a grim, chilling picture. Between 1995 and 2010, this population cohort will grow by some 30 percent, and many of them will have grown up in poverty to single mothers."[7]

Blumstein contends that the crime rate changed dramatically in 1985 with the introduction of crack cocaine, especially in urban areas. This "gave rise to a large demand for crack, and the recruitment of lots of people, particularly young people, into the market to sell crack."[8] Young people soon began carrying guns, adds Blumstein,

> to protect themselves because they were carrying lots of valuable stuff; they were in no position to call the police if somebody set upon them. The more kids started carrying guns, the more the incentive for the other kids to start carrying.
>
> This gave rise to an escalating arms race out in the streets among the kids. Kids are not very good at resolving disputes verbally, as most middle-class folks are. When you look in school yards, we're always seeing pushing and shoving. When the guns are around, that pushing and shoving and fighting escalate into shooting. That's really contributed to what has been the most dramatic growth of homicide by young people of young people.[9]

Blumstein is arguing that a long-term decline in the rates of homicide by young people depends on both getting the guns out of the hands of the young and addressing the issue that we will have an increasing number of youths who are being socialized in high-risk settings.

Two people exchange (a hundred dollar bill, a handgun) on a street. Studies show that violent crimes committed by juveniles are directly linked to the availability of handguns.

James Alan Fox also sees a grim picture in the future concerning increased juvenile violence. He states that "there are now 39 million children in the country who are under the age of ten, more children than we've had for decades."[10] The critical problem, according to Fox, is that millions of these children are at high risk, live in poverty, and lack full-time supervision at home and that "by the year 2005, the number of teens, ages 14–17, will increase by 20 percent, with a larger increase among blacks in this age group (26 percent)."[11] Fox projects that "even if the per-capita rate of teen homicide remains the same, the number of 14–17 year-olds who will commit murder should increase to nearly 5,000 annually because of changing demographics."[12]

John J. DiIulio Jr. adds that the United States is "sitting on a demographic crime bomb."[13] By the year 2000, DiIulio predicts that there will be an additional 500,000 youngsters between 14 and 17. He contends that this "large population of seven-to-10-year old boys now growing up fatherless, Godless, and jobless, and surrounded by deviant, delinquent, and criminal adults, will give rise to a new and more vicious group of predatory street criminals than the nation has ever known."[14] He adds that "we must therefore be prepared to contain the explosion's force and limit its damage."[15]

William Bennett, John DiIulio Jr., and John Walters further argue that a new generation of juvenile criminals is emerging that is far worse than in the past. In referring to this new generation of juvenile criminals as "superpredators," they state that "today's bad boys are far worse than yesteryear's, and tomorrow's will be even worse than today's."[16] The result is that "America is now home to thicker ranks of juvenile's 'super-predators'—radically impulsive, brutally remorseless youngsters, including ever more preteenage boys who murder, assault, rob, burglarize, deal deadly drugs, join gun-toting gangs, and create serious communal disorders."[17] The underlying cause of the super-predator phenomenon, they assert is "moral poverty—children growing up without love, care, and guidance from responsible adults."[18]

In the midst of this prediction of a violent juvenile crime wave, Franklin E. Zimring as well as Philip J. Cook and John Laub represent dissenting voices as to whether this violent juvenile crime wave will materialize. Zimring argues that "using demographic statistics to project how many kids are going to commit homicide [has] extremely limited utility."[19] He adds that " . . . the overall incidence of homicide, which is variable and cyclical, is still a much better predictor of future violence than assumptions based on demographic shifts."[20]

Cook and Laub's explanation for why the epidemic of youth gun violence peaked in 1993 and has rapidly declined since then represents another dissenting voice.[21] They propose that a change in context rather than the "moral poverty" explanation makes far more sense of the reduced juvenile homicides between 1993 and 1997. This changing context, especially in terms of limiting the availability of guns, according to Cook and Laub, will continue to depress rather than to escalate youth homicide in the immediate future.[22]

In a 1998 publication, Blumstein and Richard Rosenfeld abandoned somewhat their earlier prophecy of gloom about the prospects of a juvenile crime wave. They agree that the reduction in arrests of juveniles for homicides can be attributed in a large part to the reduced use of handguns by young people. But Blumstein and his colleague warn that "no one can be certain when the next upturn in homicide [with juveniles] will occur, but the present reductions cannot continue indefinitely."[23] See Social Policy 2.1 for explanations about the "crime bust of the 1990s."

In sum, the early support for a violent juvenile crime wave, especially from such recognized scholars as Blumstein, Fox, and DiIulio, has given way to the realization that youth homicide rates have been declining since 1994 and that the reduced use of handguns by minority young people in large cities has been a chief contributor to this decline. There is no reason to believe that this downturn will change in the immediate future, even with an upsurge over the next decade or so in the numbers of young people in the United States.

SOCIAL POLICY 2.1

Explanations of the Crime Bust of the 1990s

The United States is in the midst of the largest decline in violent crime rates in more than half a century. According to Uniform Crime Reports statistics, from 1991 to 1999, homicide rates fell by 41 percent and robbery rates by 44 percent. Homicide and robbery rates are now at the lowest level since the late 1960s.

Alfred Blumstein and Joel Wallman's edited book, *The Crime Bust of the 1990s,* divides the highs and lows of this nation's recent crime periods into the following:

- The *low crime period,* from 1946 to 1960, is marked by low and stable crime rates;
- The *crime boom period,* from 1961 to 1973, is marked by rapidly increasing crime rates;
- The *crime plateau period,* from 1974 to 1990, is marked by fluctuating but consistently high crime rates;
- The *crime bust period,* from 1991 to 1999, is marked by steep declines in crime.

In *The Crime Drop in America,* which is the first major book aimed at explaining the 1990 crime bust, most of the analysis and discussion of crime data is limited to homicide, and, to a lesser extent, to robbery trends.

In Blumstein's chapter, he shows that the entire increase in homicides during the crime boomlet of the mid-1980s can be attributed to rising handgun use among young adults under twenty years of age. These patterns were especially pronounced for young African American men and for big cities. The theme that is developed in greater depth in individual chapters from other authors that follow is that the crime boomlet of the mid-1980s and the crime bust of the 1990s are tied mostly to handgun use among juveniles and young adults under twenty-five years old who were participating in the crack cocaine market.

Bruce Johnson, Andrew Golub, and Eloise Dunlap argue that the crime rise of the mid-1980s and the crime drop of the 1990s can be explained by a transformation of "conduct norms" within successive drug subcultures. For example, since World War II, New York City has experienced three relatively distinct drug subcultures: the heroin injection era (which peaked from 1960 to 1973), the cocaine/crack era (which peaked from 1984 to 1989), and the marijuana/blunts era (which started in 1990). The timing of violent crime trends, according to these authors, is closely related to the relative strength of these three drug subcultures. Accordingly, the rise of the cocaine/crack subculture coincided with the violent crime increase that began in the mid-1980s and the rise of the marijuana/blunts subculture took place at the same time as the 1990s decline in violent crime rates.

Other authors argue in their chapters that the 1990s drop in violent crime was also related to more effective gun policies, increased levels of incarceration, more effective policing, growing availability of services for abused women, and decline in percentage of residents in crime-prone, age–gender–race categories.

Do you agree that the decline of violence in both adult and juvenile crime in the 1990s is related in large part to the decline of the crack cocaine markets? Beyond this, what else do you think contributed to the bust of violent crime in the 1990s?

Source: Alfred Blumstein and Joel Wallman, *The Crime Drop in America* (Boston: Cambridge University Press, 2000) and Gary Lafree, "Explaining the Crime Bust of the 1990s," *The Journal of Criminal Law and Criminology* 91 (2001), pp. 269–305.

Juvenile Court Statistics

Most information about the number of children appearing before the juvenile court each year comes from the *Juvenile Court Statistics.* In 1926 the Juvenile Court Statistics Project was inaugurated by the Children's Bureau of the Department of Labor. One of the most important objectives of compiling **juvenile court statistics** was "to furnish an index of the general nature and extent of the problems brought before the juvenile court."[24]

The reporting procedures, content, and project objectives of the annual reports of juvenile court statistics have been modified since the project was implemented. Initial reports included analyses of trends in delinquency based on factors such as sex, race, home conditions, reasons for referral, place of detention care, and disposition. Then, in 1952, the amount of information requested from jurisdictions was limited to a summary account of delinquency, dependency, neglect, and traffic cases, and cases involving special proceedings. The responsibility for collecting the *Juvenile Court Statistics* was shifted from the Department of Health, Education and Welfare to the Law Enforcement Assistance Administration (LEAA). Under a grant awarded by LEAA in 1975, the National Center for Juvenile Justice was given the responsibility for maintaining the series.

The *Juvenile Court Statistics,* like the *Uniform Crime Reports,* have some serious limitations. First, the usual time lag in these statistics lessens their usefulness. Second, these cases make up only a small percentage of the total number of juvenile offenses. Third, the data collected by the National Institute of Juvenile Justice and Delinquency Prevention represent only an estimate of juvenile crimes that come to the attention of the juvenile court. Still, these national statistics, as well as statistics of local juvenile courts, provide a means by which researchers can examine the characteristics of referred juveniles and the emerging trends in juvenile justice.

The number of children appearing before the juvenile court significantly increased from the late 1950s until the mid-1970s, when it began to level off. In the late 1970s and throughout the 1980s the estimated number of delinquency cases decreased slightly. An estimated 1,348,000 cases were disposed of in 1981, 1,304,000 in 1984, and 1,156,000 in 1988.[25] However, by 1997 the number of cases had increased to 1,755,000.[26] Drug offenses, especially for nonwhites, showed a dramatic increase between 1987 and 1997.[27] (See Table 2.1 for delinquency cases by most serious offense, 1997.)

Caseloads of the juvenile court generally increased between 1988 and 1997 across the four major offense categories (see Figure 2.2). Juveniles ages fifteen and older made up 63 percent of the delinquency caseload of the court in 1997, juveniles ages thirteen and fourteen were involved in 26 percent of delinquency cases, and juveniles age twelve and younger accounted for 10 percent.[28] The number of delinquency cases involving females rose 83 percent between 1988 and 1997, compared with 39 percent increase for males.[29]

The Contributions of the Cohort Studies

Juvenile delinquency has been studied from a wide variety of perspectives and with an equally wide variety of research methods. The longitudinal method has recently gained popularity, and the **cohort study** is a specific example of the longitudinal method. In the cohort study, a group of people who have something in common—they were born in the same year, graduated from high school in the same year, or were first arrested in the same year—are studied over a period of time.[30]

Delinquency cohort studies usually include all people born in a particular year in a city or county who are followed through part or all of their lives. This procedure is extremely costly but permits researchers to determine, through a year-by-year search of police files and community records, interviews, and self-report studies, which individuals in a cohort were arrested and which were not. Offenders can be identified early, followed throughout their lives, and compared with nonoffenders, thereby giving a picture of their criminal careers and how they progressed.

Cohort studies, like all forms of criminal statistics, have a number of problems. One major difficulty is that their findings cannot be generalized confidently beyond the individuals in the cohort. Such studies also are very expensive and time-consuming. Keeping track of a sample of youths even up to age thirty-five is next to impossible because names and addresses change, some people die, and others simply drop out of sight; the same holds true for researchers and their assistants. Finally, to provide a true picture of the national crime rate would require that a sample be taken each year in every area of the country. Still, even with these drawbacks, cohort studies remain an accepted and

TABLE 2.1

Youths were charged with a property offense in nearly half the delinquency cases handled by juvenile courts in 1997

Most serious offense	Number of cases	Percentage of total cases	Percent change 1988–97	Percent change 1996-97
TOTAL DELINQUENCY	**1,755,100**	**100%**	**48%**	**0%**
PERSON OFFENSES	**390,800**	**22**	**97**	**2**
Criminal homicide	2,000	<1	31	−17
Forcible rape	6,500	<1	48	−5
Robbery	33,400	2	55	−11
Aggravated assault	67,900	4	66	−18
Simple assault	248,800	14	124	11
Other violent sex offense	10,200	1	59	8
Other person offense	22,000	1	72	3
PROPERTY OFFENSES	**841,800**	**48**	**19**	**−3**
Burglary	135,900	8	2	−4
Larceny-theft	401,600	23	23	−4
Motor vehicle theft	48,800	3	−11	−6
Arson	9,300	1	44	4
Vandalism	114,800	7	41	−4
Trespassing	65,100	4	28	1
Stolen property offense	33,800	2	5	0
Other property offense	32,800	2	60	0
DRUG LAW VIOLATIONS	**182,400**	**10**	**125**	**4**
PUBLIC ORDER OFFENSES	**340,100**	**19**	**67**	**4**
Obstruction of justice	132,600	8	78	4
Disorderly conduct	92,300	5	107	3
Weapons offense	38,500	2	74	−6
Liquor law violation	11,100	1	−31	0
Nonviolent sex offense	11,100	1	−4	7
Other public order	54,600	3	56	17
VIOLENT CRIME INDEX*	**109,800**	**6**	**61**	**−15**
PROPERTY CRIME INDEX**	**595,300**	**34**	**14**	**−4**

- Person offense cases accounted for 22% of all delinquency cases handled by juvenile courts in 1997. Cases involving a Violent Crime Index offense accounted for 6% of all delinquency cases.
- Ten percent of all delinquency cases involved drug law violations as the most serious charge.
- Although much of the growth in court referrals is related to arrests, changes in juvenile court caseloads also depend on other forces. Between 1988 and 1997, the overall growth in juvenile court cases (48%) was greater than the growth in arrests of persons under age 18 (35%). Violent Crime Index arrests rose 49%, arrests for Property Crime Index offenses rose 1%, and drug arrests rose 125%.

*Includes criminal homicide, forcible rape, robbery, and aggravated assault.
**Includes burglary, larceny-theft, motor vehicle theft, and arson.
Note: Detail may not add to totals because of rounding. Percent calculations are based on unrounded numbers.

Source: Melissa Sickmund, "Offenders in Juvenile Court, 1997," *Juvenile Justice Bulletin* (Washington, D.C.: Office of Juvenile Justice and Delinquency Prevention, 2000), p. 2.

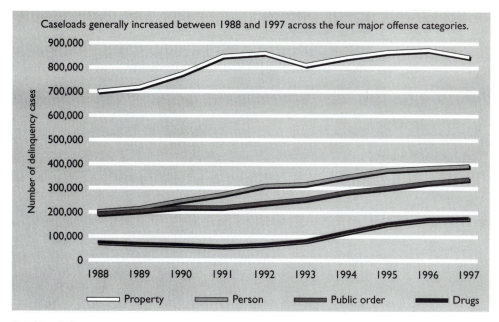

FIGURE 2.2 Juvenile Court Caseloads, 1988–1997

Source: Melissa Sickmund, "Offenders in Juvenile Court, 1997," *Juvenile Justice Bulletin* (Washington, D.C.: Office of Juvenile Justice and Delinquency Prevention, 2000), p. 3.

useful addition to other official and nonofficial statistics in illuminating the problem of delinquency and crime.

Findings of cohort studies based on official data and conducted in Philadelphia; London, England; Racine, Wisconsin; and Columbus, Ohio, have been useful in filling out the picture of youth crime. The four cohort studies agreed far more than they disagreed. (Table 2.2 compares the four cohort studies.) The most significant findings on which they agree are that lower-class, minority males committed the most serious offenses, that a few offenders committed the majority of serious property and violent offenses, and that punishments by the juvenile justice system tended to encourage rather than discourage future criminality. There was general agreement that males committed more offenses and more serious offenses than did females, that youth crimes progressed from less serious to more serious, and that the probability of becoming an adult offender increased for individuals with a record of juvenile delinquency.[31]

How Self-Report and Official Statistics Compare

In the late 1950s and 1960s the use of delinquency studies that relied on official statistics on incarcerated populations declined, whereas self-report surveys using community or school samples rapidly increased.[32] **Self-report studies,** like other forms of measurements, have shortcomings, but criminologists generally consider them to be helpful tools in measuring and understanding delinquent behavior. The main justifications for self-report surveys are that a large proportion of youthful offenders are never arrested and that a large amount of **hidden delinquency** is not contained in official arrest statistics.

New national interview data that became available in the 1970s and 1980s have led to improved self-report studies. The National Youth Survey (NYS) involves a probability sample of seven birth cohorts in a panel design. The sample of 1,725 adolescents aged

TABLE 2.2

Comparison of Four Cohort Studies

	Philadelphia Cohorts	London Cohort	Racine Cohorts	Columbus Cohort
SAMPLE	Males born in 1945 and males and females born in 1958	Males born between 1951 and 1954	Males and females born in 1942, 1949, and 1955	Males and females born between 1956 and 1960
DELINQUENT POPULATION	32.6 percent in first cohort and 34.9 percent in second cohort	About one-third of the cohort	90 percent of males and 65 to 70 percent of females in each cohort	1,138 youths born during these years committed a violent offense
GENDER	Females not as delinquent	N.A.	White females had least involvement with the police	Males outnumbered females by almost 6 to 1
RACE	Nonwhites committed more serious crimes and were more likely to be recidivists	N.A.	African American males had more police contacts and committed more serious crimes	African Americans were more likely to commit violent offenses than were whites
CHRONIC OFFENDERS	6.3 percent of first cohort and 7.5 percent of males in second cohort	6 percent; 23 boys of the 396 had 6 or more convictions	N.A.	Nearly one-third of the violent offenders were arrested 5 or more times
PATTERNS OF DELINQUENT BEHAVIOR	Reasonably constant	Chronics exhibited high and stable recidivism rates through sixth involvement of 72 percent	Declining seriousness and discontinuation after teenage period	Did not progress from less to more serious crimes
IMPACT OF INTERVENTION BY JUSTICE SYSTEM	Profitable if early in a delinquent career	Early discrimination and treatment of persisters can help prevent adult criminality	Increase in seriousness and involvement following sanctions	Length of time outside an institution between arrests reduced after each commitment

eleven to seventeen was selected to be a representative sample of U.S. youths born in the years 1959 through 1965. This youth panel has been interviewed nine times: during the calendar years of 1977–1981 (waves 1 to 5); in 1984 (wave 6); in 1987 (wave 7); in 1990 (wave 8); and in 1993 (wave 9).[33]

The logic of self-report studies is based on the fundamental assumption of survey research, "If you want to know something, ask."[34] Researchers have gone to juveniles themselves and asked them to admit to any illegal acts they have committed. Self-report studies, however, have been criticized for three reasons: their research designs have often been deficient, resulting in the drawing of false inferences; the varied nature of social settings in which the studies have been undertaken makes it difficult to test hypotheses; and their reliability and validity are questionable.[35]

The most serious questions about self-report studies relate to their reliability and validity. In terms of **validity,** how can researchers be certain that juveniles are telling the truth when they fill out self-report questionnaires? Short and F. Ivan Nye argue that items can be built into questionnaires to "catch the random respondent, the overconformist, and the individual who is out to impress the researcher with his devilishness, the truth notwithstanding."[36] Yet Michael J. Hindelang and colleagues contend that self-report studies are likely to underestimate the illegal behavior of the seriously delinquent youth, because the juvenile who has committed frequent offenses is less likely to answer the questions truthfully than is the youth who is less delinquent.[37] Stephen A. Cernkovich and colleagues, in using both a youth sample in the community and an institutional sample, add that "institutionalized youth are not only more delinquent than the 'average kid' in the general youth population, but also considerably more delinquent than the *most delinquent* youth identified in the typical self-report survey."[38]

Reliability is related to the consistency of a questionnaire or an interview; that is, whether repeated administration of a questionnaire or an interview will elicit the same answers from the same juveniles when they are questioned two or more times. The examination of the reliability of self-report studies by Hindelang and colleagues concluded that "reliability measures are impressive, and the majority of studies produce validity coefficients in the moderate to strong range."[39]

Austin L. Porterfield conducted the first study of hidden delinquency in the 1940s when he asked several hundred college students whether or not they had ever engaged in delinquent acts.[40] Although all of the students reported that they had engaged in delinquent acts, few of them had been brought to police or court attention. But it was Short and Nye in the late 1950s who pioneered the first self-report study of a delinquent population.[41] After their first study of a training school population, they conducted a self-report study with members of three Washington communities, with students in three midwestern towns, and with delinquents in training schools in Washington State.[42] In their findings from these two studies, as well as in other published papers, Short and Nye concluded that delinquency was widespread throughout the adolescent population, that the seriousness and frequency of delinquent behavior were major factors determining the actions taken against juvenile lawbreakers, and that no relationship could be found between delinquency and social class.[43]

Self-report studies also commonly agree that almost every youth commits some act of delinquency. David Huizinga and Delbert S. Elliott, using information from the National Youth Survey, *Uniform Crime Reports,* and other sources, concluded that only 24 percent of juveniles who committed offenses for which they could have been arrested were in fact arrested.[44] Franklyn W. Dunford and Elliott's analysis of self-report data from a national youth panel wave and seven birth cohorts of youths age eleven to seventeen also reported that arrest data reflected only a small fraction of the delinquent activity occurring in U.S. society.[45] Of course, offenders who commit violent or predatory crimes are more likely than minor offenders to be arrested and referred to the juvenile court. Yet Dunford and Elliott found that 207, or 86 percent, of the 242 self-reported career offenders had no record of arrest during a three-year period when they were involved in frequent and serious delinquent offenses.[46] (Figure 2.3 is an example of a self-report study.)

More recently, self-report studies conducted in Denver, Colorado; Rochester, New York; and Pittsburgh, Pennsylvania, showed that a surprisingly large proportion of juveniles committed violent acts.[47] By the time they were tenth or eleventh graders, 58 percent of the Rochester youths and 54 percent of the Denver juveniles reported that they had been involved in a violent crime at some time in their lives. Chronic violent offenders, constituting 14 percent of the sample in Denver and 15 percent in Rochester, accounted for 82 percent of the violent offenses in Denver and 75 percent of the violent

---

Please indicate how often you have done each of the following in the last 12 months.

> If you *have not* engaged in a particular activity, put ___0___ and go to the next.
> If you *have*, put the number of times.

REMEMBER: YOUR ANSWERS ARE PRIVATE SO YOU CAN ANSWER HONESTLY.

During the last 12 months, how many times did you:

1. Break into a place to do something illegal? _____
2. Take something from a store on purpose without paying for it (shoplifting)? _____
3. Steal something worth more than $100 (not counting shoplifting)? _____
4. Steal something worth less than $100 (not counting shoplifting)? _____
5. Beat up or hurt someone on purpose? _____
6. Get into any fistfights or brawls (not counting the times you beat up or hurt someone on purpose)? _____
7. Ruin, break, or damage someone else's property on purpose? _____
8. Take a car without the owner's permission? _____
9. Take money or something by threatening someone with a weapon (gun, knife, etc.)? _____
10. Take money or something by threatening someone without a weapon? _____

FIGURE 2.3 Example of a Self-Report Questionnaire

Source: Excerpted from a high school survey used in research by M. L. Erickson, J. P. Gibbs, and G. F. Jensen as part of a National Institutes of Mental Health Study titled "Community Tolerance and Measures of Delinquency."

offenses in Rochester. According to these self-report studies, a large proportion of those who became involved in violent behavior at an early age later became chronic violent offenders. In Denver, chronic violent offenders reported a total of 4,134 violent crimes, an average of 33.6 per person. In Rochester, chronic violent offenders reported 5,164 violent acts, an average of 51.7 per person.[48] See Theory and Research 2.2 for more extensive findings from these three longitudinal self-report studies.

The desire to uncover the true rate of delinquency and greater recognition that official statistics on juvenile delinquency have serious limitations have led to a growing reliance on the use of self-report studies. These studies reveal the following conclusions:

1. There is considerable undetected delinquency, and police apprehension is low, probably less than 10 percent.
2. Both middle- and lower-class juveniles are involved in considerable illegal behavior.
3. Not all hidden delinquency involves minor offenses; a significant number of serious crimes are committed each year by juveniles who elude apprehension by the police.
4. Lower-class youths appear to commit more frequent delinquent acts, especially in their early years, and are more likely to be chronic offenders than are middle-class youths.
5. African Americans are more likely than whites to be arrested, convicted, and institutionalized even though both have committed offenses of similar seriousness.
6. Females commit more delinquent acts than official statistics indicate, but males still appear to commit more delinquent acts and to commit more serious crimes than females do.
7. Alcohol and marijuana are the most widely used drugs among adolescents, but other drug use has decreased in recent years.

Youth Crime Trends

The use of national samples enables self-report studies to shed more light on youth crime trends. For example, the Monitoring the Future study, an annual national survey

THEORY AND RESEARCH 2.2

Highlights from Denver, Pittsburgh, and Rochester Youth Surveys

DENVER

The Denver study follows 1,527 boys and girls from high-risk neighborhoods in Denver who were 7, 9, 11, 13, and 15 years old in 1987. In exploring the changes in the nature of delinquency and drug use from the 1970s to the 1990s, the Denver study's findings are as follows:

- Overall, there was little change in the prevalence rates of delinquency, including serious delinquency and serious violence. However, the prevalence rate of gang fights among males doubled (from 8 percent to 16 percent).
- The level of injury from violence offenses increased substantially.
- The prevalence of drug use decreased substantially: alcohol, from 80 percent to 50 percent; marijuana, from 41 percent to 18 percent; and other drug use, from 19 percent to 4 percent.
- The relationship between drug use and delinquency has changed in that a smaller percentage (from 48 percent to 17 percent) of serious delinquents are using hard drugs other than marijuana, and a greater percentage (from 27 percent to 48 percent) of hard drug users are serious offenders.
- More than half (53 percent) of the youth in the study ages 11 through 15 in 1987 were arrested over the next 5 years.

PITTSBURGH

The Pittsburgh study, a longitudinal study of 1,517 inner-city boys, followed three samples of boys for more than a decade to advance knowledge about how and why boys become involved in delinquency and other problem behaviors. Its chief findings are as follows:

- There were no differences between African American and white boys at age 6, but differences gradually developed, the prevalence of serious delinquency at age 16 reaching 27 percent for African American boys and 19 percent for white boys.
- As prevalence increased, so did the average frequency of serious offending, which rose more rapidly for African American boys than for white boys.
- The onset of offending among the boys involved in serious delinquency occurred by age 15, when 51 percent of African American boys and 28 per-

cent of white boys had committed serious delinquent acts.
- The boys generally developed disruptive and delinquent behavior in an orderly, progressive fashion, with less serious problem behaviors preceding more serious problem behaviors.
- Three groups of developmental pathways were identified that displayed progressively more serious problem behaviors:

Authority Conflict. Youths on this pathway exhibit stubbornness prior to age 12, then move on to defiance and avoidance of authority.
Covert. This pathway includes minor acts, such as lying, followed by property damage and moderately serious delinquency.
Overt. This pathway includes minor aggression followed by fighting and violence.

ROCHESTER

The Rochester study, a longitudinal study of 1,000 urban adolescents, investigates the causes and consequences of adolescent delinquency and drug use by following a sample of high-risk urban adolescents from their early teenage years through their early adult years. Its chief findings are as follows:

- Attachment and involvement were both significantly related to delinquency. Children who were more attached to and involved with their parents were less involved in delinquency.
- The relationship between family process factors and delinquency was bidirectional—poor parenting increased the probability of delinquent behavior and delinquent behavior further weakened the relationship between parent and child.
- The impact of family variables appeared to fade as adolescents became older and more independent from their parents. Weak school commitment and poor school performance were associated with increased involvement in delinquency and drug use.
- Associating with delinquent peers was strongly and consistently related to delinquency, in part because peers provided positive reinforcements for delinquency. There was a strong relationship between gang membership and delinquent behavior, particularly serious and violent delinquency.

(continued)

What do the findings of these three studies have in common? How do they differ?

Sources: Katharine Browning, Terence P. Thornberry, and Pamela K. Porter, "Highlights of Findings from the Rochester Youth Development Study," *OJJDP Fact Sheet* (Washington, D.C.: Office of Juvenile Justice and Delinquency Prevention, 1999);

Katharine Browning and Rolf Loeber, "Highlights from the Pittsburgh Youth Study," *OJJDP Fact Sheet* (Washington, D.C.: Office of Juvenile Justice and Delinquency Prevention, 1999); and Katharine Browning and David Huizinga, "Highlights from the Denver Youth Survey," *OJJDP Fact Sheet* (Washington D.C.: Office of Juvenile Justice and Delinquency Prevention, 1999).

of high school seniors conducted by the University of Michigan's Institute for Social Research, provides an adequate base for the study of time trends. This study, which includes large samples for the past twenty-two years (1975–1996), shows that some offenses increased during this period but others did not. It can be concluded that crime trends, especially in the population of seventeen- to twenty-three-year-olds, failed to indicate any increased tendency toward criminality.[49]

Self-report studies have been particularly useful in estimating the prevalence and incidence of drug use among adolescents in the United States. They reveal how drug use among adolescents reached epidemic proportions in the late 1960s and into the 1970s, appeared to peak sometime around 1979, and decreased into the 1990s. As revealed in the Monitoring the Future survey and the National Household Survey on Drug Abuse, marijuana use among adolescents began a dramatic increase in 1992 and continued to increase through 1996.[50] (See Chapter 11 for a more extensive discussion of drug use among adolescents.)

The Contribution of Victimization Surveys

In 1972 the Census Bureau began **victimization studies** to determine as accurately as possible the extent of crime in the United States. These surveys involve three different procedures. The largest component of the program is the National Crime Panel, which oversees the interviewing of a national sample of approximately 125,000 people in 60,000 households every six months for up to three and one-half years. Data from these individuals are used to estimate the national frequency of the crimes found in the FBI's Crime Index (except for murder).[51]

The Census Bureau also interviewed the owners, managers, and clerks of 42,000 business establishments selected as a sample to provide an estimate of robbery and burglary rates for businesses. This portion of the survey ended in 1976.

Finally, the Census Bureau conducts victimization surveys in twenty-six major cities. Housing units in the central area of each city are randomly selected, and each member in the household age twelve years or older is questioned about his or her experiences, if any, as a victim of crime. In addition, one-half of the respondents are asked about their perception of crimes, the extent of their fears, and other attitudes about criminal activities.

Victimization surveys have several limitations. Information on status offenses is not included, nor is information on so-called victimless crimes, such as drug abuse, prostitution, and drunkenness. Information on white-collar crime is difficult to gain from victim surveys. Information on age is always questionable because victims must guess offenders' ages. Also, victims may give inaccurate information. Victims may forget the victimization they have experienced, may deliberately exaggerate or fail to admit victimization, or may state that a specific crime took place within the research year when it actually occurred before or after that period.[52] Nevertheless, victimization surveys are an important supplement to official statistics and self-report surveys, adding to what is known about crime and delinquency in the United States.

The National Crime Victimization Survey reported that during 2000, individuals who were twelve and older experienced nearly 26 million violent victimizations. Violent crime rates fell 15 percent between 1999 and 2000, which resulted in the greatest annual percentage decline and the lowest rates of violent crime recorded since the inception of the NCVS in 1973. The overall violent crime rate decline took place because of a decrease in simple assault and rape/sexual assault coupled with a slight fall in aggravated assault during 2000. Property crime rates also fell between 1999 and 2000 due to a decline in theft and a slight decline in motor vehicle theft. [53]

Males were more likely than females to be victims of violent crime, but females were many times more likely than men to be victims of rape or sexual assault. African Americans were more likely than whites to be victims of violent crimes. In simple assault, which shows the greatest racial difference in victimization, African Americans were victimized at rates greater than those of whites. In addition, Hispanics were twice as likely as non-Hispanics to be victimized by robbery. (See Table 2.3 for the rates of violent crime and personal theft, by sex, age, race, and Hispanic origin, 2000).[54]

Victimization studies have revealed that the experience of being victimized increases the likelihood of offending.[55] Nicholas Anderson and Orlando Rodriguez found

TABLE 2.3

Rates of violent crime and personal theft, by gender, age, race, and Hispanic origin, 2000

Characteristic of victim	Population	Victimizations per 1,000 persons age 12 or older						Personal theft
		Violent crimes						
			Rape/ sexual assault	Robbery	Assault			
		All			Total	Aggravated	Simple	
GENDER								
Male	109,816,970	32.9	0.1*	4.5	28.3	8.3	19.9	1.0
Female	116,987,650	23.2	2.1	2.0	19.0	3.2	15.8	1.4
AGE								
12–15	16,064,090	60.1	2.1	4.2	53.8	9.9	43.9	1.8
16–19	16,001,650	64.3	4.3	7.3	52.7	14.3	38.3	3.0
20–24	18,587,790	49.4	2.1	6.2	41.2	10.9	30.3	1.1*
25–34	37,757,070	34.8	1.3	3.9	29.5	6.8	22.7	1.5
35–49	64,927,820	21.8	0.8	2.7	18.4	4.7	13.7	0.9
50–64	40,764,000	13.7	0.4*	2.1	11.1	2.8	8.4	0.5*
65 or older	32,702,210	3.7	0.1*	0.7*	2.9	0.9	2.0	1.2
RACE								
White	189,308,050	27.1	1.1	2.7	23.3	5.4	17.9	1.1
Black	27,978,180	35.3	1.2	7.2	26.9	7.7	19.2	1.9
Other	9,518,390	20.7	1.1*	2.8	16.7	5.2	11.5	1.8*
HISPANIC ORIGIN								
Hispanic	24,513,290	28.4	0.5*	5.0	23.0	5.6	17.4	2.4
Non-Hispanic	200,294,810	27.7	1.2	3.0	23.5	5.7	17.8	1.1

Note: The National Crime Victimization Survey includes as violent crime rape, sexual assault, robbery, and assault. Because the NCVS interviews persons about their victimizations, murder and manslaughter cannot be included.

*Based on 10 or fewer sample cases

Source: Callie Marie Rennisoln, *Criminal Victimization 2000: Changes 1999–2000 with Trends 1993–2000* (Washington, D.C.: National Crime Victimization Survey, 2001), p. 6.

that adolescents in high-crime neighborhoods joined gangs in response to or in anticipation of victimization.[56] Victimization rates also increased through association with delinquent peers. Moreover, juveniles' participation in delinquency lead to exposure to victimization.[57]

Simon I. Singer's examination of the interaction between individuals' experiences as victims and as offenders in the follow-up example of Wolfgang and colleagues' Cohort I study found that offenders had higher rates of victimization than did nonoffenders. For whites, 23 percent of the offenders were victims, compared with 14 percent of the nonoffenders; for nonwhites, 46 percent of the offenders were victims, compared with 19 percent of the nonoffenders. Furthermore, offenders using weapons were more likely than those not using weapons to be victimized for both violent and property offenses.[58]

Victimization surveys have not been as widely used in analyzing delinquency as have the *Uniform Crime Reports, Juvenile Court Statistics,* cohort studies, and self-report studies, but they do add to what is known about crime in the United States. Some of the principal findings of victimization surveys are as follows:

1. Much more crime is committed than is recorded, but the discrepancy between the number of people who say they have been victimized and the number of crimes known to the police varies with the type of offense.
2. The rank order of serious offenses reported by victims, with the exception of vehicle theft, is identical to that of the *Uniform Crime Reports.*
3. The probability of being victimized varies with the kind of crime and where one lives. The centers of cities are more probable sites of violent crimes.
4. The most frequent crimes experienced, according to victims, are thefts of property worth less than $250.
5. Juveniles are more likely to commit crimes, especially property offenses, than any other age group: Juveniles are also more likely to be victimized than any other age group.
6. African Americans are over-represented as perpetrators and victims in serious personal crimes. Official arrest data indicate that a somewhat greater proportion of African American offenders are involved in forcible rape, aggravated assault, and simple assault than the victimization data indicate.
7. In 2000, 48 percent of violent crimes and 36 percent of property crimes were reported to the police. Females and African Americans were more likely to report a crime to police than were males and whites.
8. From 1999 to 2000, violent crime rates fell for almost every demographic group considered: males, females, whites, African Americans, non-Hispanics, and 12- to 24-year-olds. Violent crime against Hispanics also fell somewhat during this period.[59]

The Most Important Social Factors Related to Delinquency

An examination of gender, racial and ethnic relations, and social class reveals much about the social factors affecting delinquency in U.S. society. The importance of gender on delinquency is examined in Chapter 7; the relationship of social class and delinquency is considered in Chapter 4; and disproportionate handling of racial and ethnic groups is a major concern throughout the chapters on juvenile justice.

Gender and Delinquent Behavior

Official arrest statistics, victimization data, and self-report studies show that adolescent females are involved in less frequent and less serious delinquent acts than are adolescent males. The *Uniform Crime Reports* documented in 1999 that males were arrested for seven times more drug violations, more than five times more violent crimes, and more than three times more property crimes than females. The male-to-female ratios were much closer in some offenses, averaging about two to one in larceny-theft, forgery, fraud, and embezzlement. The overall ratio between adolescent male and female arrests in 1999 was about three to one (females had 27 percent of the total arrests).[60]

Adolescent males are far more likely to be arrested for possession of stolen property, vandalism, weapons offenses, and other assaults. In contrast, adolescent females are more likely to be arrested for running away from home and prostitution; indeed, arrests for running away from home account for nearly one-fifth of all female arrests.[61]

Longitudinal research adds that males are arrested for more serious charges than females are. In Cohort II of the Philadelphia cohort, the ratio for male/female arrests was almost 9:1 for index crimes and 14:1 for violent offenses.[62] Furthermore, males are more likely than females to begin their careers at an early age and to extend their delinquent careers into their adult lives.[63]

Self-report studies indicate that female delinquency is more prevalent and more similar to male delinquency than official arrest statistics suggest.[64] For example, David C. Rowe, Alexander T. Vazsonyi, and Daniel J. Flannery found that the correlates of delinquency were similar for both adolescent males and females. In examining whether such variables as impulsivity, rebelliousness, and deceitfulness could explain the sex differences in delinquency, they found that the mean differences in delinquent behavior between boys and girls arise largely because boys are more exposed to criminogenic factors than are girls.[65]

Victimization data reveal that adolescent females are more likely to be victims than are adolescent males, and that their victimization is shaped by their gender, race, and social class.[66] Meda Chesney-Lynd has found that many adolescent females become victimized by "multiple marginality," in that their gender, race, and class place them at the economic periphery of society.[67] (See Chapter 7 for a more extensive development of this thesis.) The gender differences in child sexual abuse are particularly pronounced. According to David Finkelhor and Larry Baron, studies reveal that about 71 percent of the victims of child sexual abuse are females.[68]

Racial/Ethnic Background and Delinquent Behavior

Studies based on official statistics have reported that African Americans are overrepresented in arrest, conviction, and incarceration with respect to their population base. In contrast, most studies using self-report measures have found that African Americans are more likely to be officially delinquent, but not significantly worse than whites in their prevalence or frequency of offending.[69]

The earlier self-report studies revealed less relationship between race and crime than have more recent studies. William J. Chambliss and Richard H. Nagasawa, in comparing questionnaire responses of high school boys in a high-delinquency area with official records obtained from the juvenile court, found that the arrest rate for African Americans was substantially higher than that for whites. But on examination of the students' self-reported delinquent behavior, little difference in involvement was found between African Americans and whites.[70] Leroy C. Gould's self-report data on all seventh-grade boys in two junior high schools in Seattle found that race was strongly related to official delinquency but not to self-reported delinquent activity.[71] Travis Hirschi also found that the differences in offense behavior between African Americans and whites were much less in self-report accounts.[72] Huizinga and Elliott's examination of the National Youth Survey concludes that "there are few if any substantial and consistent differences between the delinquency involvement of different racial groups."[73] They suggest that differences in official responses to offenders, rather than differences in delinquent behavior, explain the differentials in arrest, conviction, and incarceration figures.[74]

Two national studies found that whites and African Americans reported involvement in seventeen delinquent behaviors with similar frequencies, but when the seriousness of delinquency was tallied, it was found that the seriousness of self-reported delinquency was slightly greater for African American males than for white males.[75] Furthermore, when Suzanne S. Ageton and Elliott analyzed the ratio of African Americans to whites for the total number of offenses, they found that it was nearly two to one. They concluded that this difference was due primarily to the greater involvement of African Americans in serious property offenses, especially a large number of multiple, or chronic, African American offenders.[76]

Race also affects the relationship between gender and delinquent behavior: official statistics document that African American females violate the law more frequently and seriously than white females do. Self-report studies indicate that African American females were much more likely than white females to admit committing the theft of fifty dollars or more or the offenses of auto theft, aggravated assault, and robbery, whereas both groups were about equally involved in burglary. African American females had a higher rate of involvement than white males for robbery, and the two were about equal for aggravated assault.[77]

Gary Jensen and Raymond Eve's study in Richmond, California, found that for two major property offenses, theft of fifty dollars or more and auto theft, African American females were twice as likely as white females to admit to the theft of fifty dollars or more, but both groups were equally likely to admit to auto theft.[78] Cernkovich and Giordano discovered that the acts predominately committed by African American females were attacking someone with fists, using a weapon to attack someone, engaging in gang fights, extortion, and carrying a weapon. The acts committed mostly by white females included disobeying or defying parents, drinking alcohol, using drugs, driving while intoxicated (DWI), property destruction (under ten dollars), and disturbing the peace.[79]

Furthermore, race affects the rates of victimization between white and African American females. African American females, regardless of age, are more likely than white females to be victimized by violent crime. In fact, the victimization rate for violent offenses of twelve- to fifteen-year-old African American females is equal to the rate for white males. For crimes of theft, adolescent white females report more property victimization than either African American adolescent males or females and are victimized at a rate nearly equivalent to that of adolescent white males.[80] See Table 2.4 for violent victimizations by age, sex, and race of victim, 1992-1996.

Social Class and Delinquency

Decades of debate still have not achieved consensus on the true relationship between social class and delinquency. Common sense tells us if a child comes from a neighborhood where crime prevails, from a poverty-stricken family in which the parent is unable to provide basic needs, or from an environment where friends are involved and arrested for delinquent acts, there is not much hope that the child will avoid delinquent activity. Consistent with this reasoning, we know that juvenile arrest rates are highest in economically deprived and socially disorganized communities. Yet the empirical reality is that available research data still do not consistently support a relationship between social class and delinquency.

One of the most startling findings of the self-report studies is that middle- and upper-class juveniles are as delinquent as their lower-class peers.[81] J. R. Williams and Martin Gold, in their national study of thirteen- to sixteen-year-old boys and girls, forcefully make this point: "In no case is the relationship between social status and delinquent behavior strong."[82] Travis Hirschi's survey of 4,000 junior and senior high school students in Richmond, California, states that little association existed between self-reported delinquencies and income, education, and occupation, except that the sons of professionals and executives committed fewer delinquent acts.[83] Johnson, in redefining social class as underclass and earning class, concludes: "The data provide no

TABLE 2.4

Violent victimizations, by age, sex, and race of victim, 1992–1996

	Percent of violent victimizations				
Victim age/sex	All races	American Indian	White	Black	Asian
Total	100.0%	100.0%	100.0%	100.0%	100.0%
12–17	24.2%	20.4%	23.8%	26.8%	24.0%
18–24	23.6	31.5	23.4	24.0	21.7
25–34	23.6	23.5	23.6	23.2	26.3
35–44	17.0	18.0	17.1	16.6	18.3
45–54	7.5	4.7	7.8	6.1	7.3
55 or older	4.1	1.9	4.3	3.3	2.4
Male	57.4%	58.9%	58.4%	50.5%	62.6%
Female	42.6	41.1	41.6	49.5	37.4
Number of violent victimizations	10,784,826	149,614	8,880,083	1,570,386	184,743

Source: Lawrence A. Greenfeld and Steven K. Smith, *American Indians and Crime* (Washington, D.C.: Bureau of Justice Statistics, 1999), p. 5.

firm evidence that social class, no matter how it is measured, is a salient factor in generating delinquent involvement."[84] Charles Tittle, Wayne Villemez, and Douglas Smith's review of thirty-five studies examining the relationship between class and crime concluded that very little support exists for the contention that delinquency is basically a lower-class phenomenon.[85]

Critics charge that self-report studies overload their questionnaires with trivial offenses. Thus, when middle- and upper-class youths record their participation in such offenses as swearing or curfew violations, they are found to be as delinquent as lower-class youth. Ageton and Elliott's national study found that a different pattern emerged when juveniles were asked how many times they had violated the law during the previous year. They found that the average number of delinquent acts reported by lower-class youngsters exceeded that reported by working-class or middle-class youths. The average number of crimes against persons reported by lower-class juveniles was one and one-half times greater than that reported by the working-class group and nearly four times greater than that reported by the middle-class group. The average number of reported crimes against property was also slightly higher for lower-class than for working-class or middle-class youth.[86]

Elliott and Huizinga applied to a national probability sample of adolescents a new self-report measure deemed to be more representative of the full range of official acts for which juveniles could be arrested. They found class differences in how widespread youth crime is in society (prevalence) and in the frequency of delinquent acts for serious offenses (incidence). Their study also revealed class differences in the incidence of nonserious offenses. Class differences, according to these researchers, are more pervasive and stronger when using an incidence as opposed to a prevalence measure.[87]

Margaret Farnworth and colleagues, in examining the first four waves of data from the Rochester Youth Development Study (RYDS), found that the "strongest and most consistent class-crime associations are found between measures of continuing underclass status and sustained involvement in street crimes."[88] Their article also explores the possibility that "inadequate measurement may explain past findings indicating no relationship between class and delinquency."[89]

Bradley R. Wright and colleagues found that socioeconomic status (SES) has both a negative and a positive indirect effect upon delinquency but that these negative and positive effects coexist and cancel each other out. As a result, they conclude that there

Angry skinhead lashes out during a demonstration. How do you explain the power that racist groups such as the Ku Klux Klan hold over their members? Are irrational thinking and intense emotion key ingredients for leaders to manipulate?

are many causal links between socioeconomic status and delinquency but little overall correlation.[90] In Theory and Research 2.3, Marvin E. Wolfgang adds to this discussion on the relationship between class and delinquency.

The Dimensions of Delinquent Behavior

The age of onset, escalation of offenses, specialization of offenses, chronic offending, and desistance from crime are important dimensions of delinquent behavior. The age of onset dimension is concerned with when delinquent behavior started. The escalation of offenses dimension focuses on whether future offenses are more serious than previous ones. The specialization of offenses dimension investigates whether delinquents specialize in the type of offenses they commit, and examines the chronic offender through background and predictors of future offending. Finally, the desistance from crime dimension considers why some delinquents cease to commit youthful offenses in their later teenage years.

Age of Onset

Several studies have related the **age of onset** to the number of offenses in subsequent years. Marvin E. Wolfgang, Terence P. Thornberry, and Robert M. Figlio, in following a 10 percent sample of Cohort I to the age of thirty, found that those who began their criminal careers at age ten or younger would be arrested an average of seven times. Those who began their careers at ages eleven or twelve, however, would be arrested an average of ten times, the highest average number for any age-of-onset category. For those who began their careers after the age of thirteen, the average number of offenses tended to decline nearly uniformly as their age of onset increased.[91]

Patrick H. Tolan, in a reanalysis of three waves of the National Youth Survey data, categorizes subjects aged eleven to thirteen in the first wave into three onset groups: early onset (thirteen or before), late onset (after thirteen), and no onset. He concludes that early-onset delinquents tend to engage in more delinquent behavior, exhibit more serious offenses, are more likely to persist in their offending behavior, and are more likely to have more arrests.[92]

Blumstein, David P. Farrington, and Soumyo Moitra also showed that one of the factors predicting those who became chronic offenders was offending at an early age.[93]

THEORY AND RESEARCH 2.3

Interview with Marvin E. Wolfgang

Question: The Philadelphia Cohort study is considered a classic in terms of understanding juvenile crime in this nation. How do you reconcile your findings in the first and second cohort studies concerning socioeconomic status with the self-report studies?

Wolfgang: In a follow-up sample of 567 males age 25 to 26 in Cohort I, we asked a series of questions at the end of the interview that contained self-reports on 22 offenses ranging from criminal homicide to minor offenses like disorderly conduct. Dr. Paul Tracy, from our Center, has conducted special studies comparing the self-report offense frequency and type among nondelinquents, delinquents, one-time offenders, recidivists and chronic offenders. He further delineated these groups by socioeconomic status and found that there is considerable correlation between the self-admitted commission of offenses and arrests, both by type and frequency. The chronic lower SES delinquents admitted committing many more and many more serious violent offenses for which they had never been arrested than did delinquents in any other category or nondelinquents. This finding holds across race as well. Moreover, some of the more sophisticated self-reports studies, such as the work done by the late Michael Handelang, indicate that the previously reported disparity between self-report and arrests by SES is considerably reduced when looking at a variety of sources, including victimization surveys. The reduced disparity holds mostly for serious offenses and less for the trivial ones. Thus, although all of the delinquents in both Cohorts I and II were so designated as having an official police contact, we in general maintain that the SES differences by frequency of delinquency contact are real.

Wolfgang is making two important points. He says that lower-class youngsters in the two Philadelphia cohort studies committed the more serious and more frequent delinquent acts and that the more sophisticated self-report studies have also found that lower-class juveniles commit more serious and frequent crimes than higher class ones. Why is class so important in understanding delinquent behavior?

Source: The late Marvin E. Wolfgang was widely acknowledged as one of the top criminologists in the United States. Interviewed in May 1984 and used with permission.

Farrington found that those who were first convicted at the earliest age (ten to twelve) offended consistently at a higher rate and for a longer period than did those first convicted at later ages.[94]

Ronald L. Simons and colleagues, in examining four waves of data on 177 adolescent boys, found that early and late starters had different paths to delinquent behavior. For early starters, the quality of parenting predicted oppositional/defiant behavior, but for late starters, quality of parenting predicated affiliation with deviant peers, which was associated in turn with involvement with the justice system.[95]

The Office of Juvenile Justice and Delinquency Prevention's Program funded three longitudinal studies (Denver, Colorado; Rochester, New York; and Pittsburgh, Pennsylvania) that have led to important insights on serious, violent, and chronic juvenile careers. In the Rochester study, of those who initiated violent offenses at age nine or younger, 39 percent became chronic violent offenders during their adolescent years. But among those who began committing violent offenses between ages ten and twelve, 30 percent became violent offenders.[96] The Denver findings were even more striking. Of those who began committing violent behavior at age nine or younger, 62 percent became chronic violent offenders.[97]

Escalation of Offenses

The findings on **escalation of offenses** are more mixed than those on age of onset. Official studies of delinquency have generally found that the incidence of arrest accelerates at age thirteen and peaks at about age seventeen, but this pattern is not so clearly evident in self-report studies. Using the *Uniform Crime Reports* for 1982, Farrington calculated the peak years of arrest for males and females. He found that nonviolent crime rates for males peaked at age seventeen, with 6.4 offenses per 100 population, whereas violent crime rates peaked at age eighteen, with 1.3 per 100. For females, nonviolent crime rates peaked at age sixteen, with 1.5 offenses per 100 population, and violent crime rates peaked at age twenty, with 0.13 per 100. Therefore it appears that the peak age for violent crimes is slightly later than the peak age for nonviolent crimes.[98]

Jay R. Williams and Martin Gold's self-report study found that older juveniles were more frequently and seriously delinquent than were younger ones.[99] Yet in their national study, Ageton and Elliott found that the incidence of some offenses, such as assault and robbery, increased with age, while that of others peaked between ages thirteen and fifteen.[100] Elliott and Huizinga, combining data from three cohorts, provide information not only about the prevalence of different kinds of offending at each age but also about the percentage of individuals initiating and terminating their involvement in criminal activity. They concluded that initiation peaked at thirteen to fifteen, prevalence at sixteen to seventeen, and termination at eighteen to nineteen.[101]

Wolfgang, Figlio, and Sellin's findings from Cohort I revealed that the average seriousness of offenses was reasonably constant during the juvenile years but then increased during the young adult years.[102] In the follow-up to age thirty of Cohort I, Wolfgang, Thornberry, and Figlio concluded that "for both the whites and nonwhites, the average number of offenses committed at each age is relatively constant from ages 10 to 30."[103] Pamela Tontodonato's examination of the data from Cohort II found that offenders who had three arrests by the age of fifteen had higher transition rates to additional arrests than did juveniles who accumulated arrests more slowly. Juveniles who were members of minorities, she found, showed a higher rate of movement to injury and theft offenses than did whites.[104] In contrast, in the older two of Lyle W. Shannon's Racine cohorts, the average seriousness of offenses decreased steadily with age.[105] Furthermore, Katherine T. Van Dusen and Sarnoff A. Mednick found in their replication of the Philadelphia cohort study in Copenhagen that the average seriousness of offenses decreased with age, reaching a minimum level at age seventeen to eighteen, and then increased again.[106]

Rolf Loeber and colleagues' longitudinal study on the development of antisocial and prosocial behavior in 1,517 adolescent males found a number of correlates of escalation in offending among the three samples. The across-age effects were low educational achievement and low school motivation. The age-specific effects were physical aggression, untrustworthiness, unaccountability, truancy, negative attitude toward school, school suspension, positive attitude to problem behavior, single parenthood, and negative caretaker–child relation.[107] Using data from two community samples of boys, Loeber and colleagues identified three developmental pathways to a delinquent career:

1. An early Authority Conflict Pathway, which consists of a sequence of stubborn behavior, defiance, and authority avoidance;
2. A Covert Pathway, which consists of minor covert behaviors, property offenses, and moderate to serious forms of delinquent behavior; and
3. An Overt Pathway, which consists of fighting, aggression, and violence.[108]

They found that these pathways are interconnected; that is, youths may embark on two or three paths simultaneously. An implication of this research is that youths' behavior may escalate as they become involved in more than one developmental pathway. See Figure 2.4 for these three pathways to boys' disruptive behavior and delinquency.[109]

Terrie Moffitt and colleagues have proposed a developmental taxonomy differentiating the small group of early onset, persistent offenders from the much larger category of "adolescence-limited" delinquent males. They found that these two groups differ both in age-related profiles of offending and in patterns of early risk. For persis-

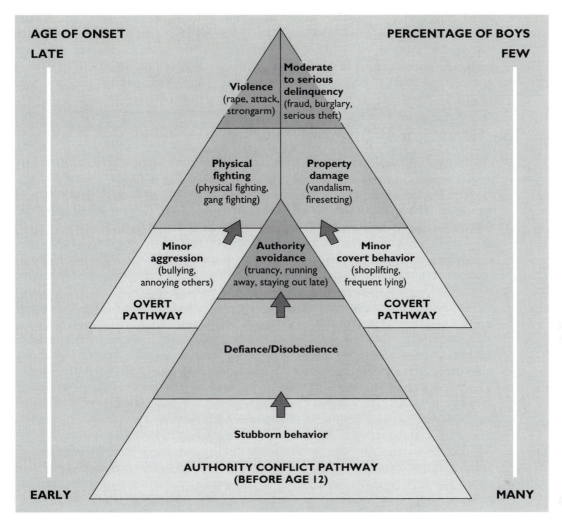

FIGURE 2.4 Three Pathways to Boys' Disruptive Behavior and Delinquency

Source: Barbara Tatem Kelley, Rolf Loeber, Kate Keenan, and Mary DeLamatre, *Developmental Pathways in Boys' Disruptive and Delinquent Behavior* (Washington, D.C.: Office of Juvenile Justice and Delinquency Prevention, 1997), p. 9.

tent offenders, risks center on individual vulnerabilities that were evident early in childhood. In contrast, later onset, adolescence-limited groups are characterized by more marginal levels of psychosocial and individual risks. Their adolescent difficulties are perceived to be prompted by frustrations associated with an adolescent maturity gap and by copying the behavior of deviant peers (see Chapter 3 for more discussion of Moffitt's theory). [110]

Barbara Maughan and colleagues, in their longitudinal study of aggressive and nonaggressive conduct problems in the Great Mountain Study of Youth, identified three developmental trajectories: stable low problem levels, stable high problem levels, and declining levels of conduct problems for both aggressive and nonaggressive behaviors. Boys were overrepresented in the stable high trajectory class on the aggressive trajectory, but they found that the overlap between aggressive and nonaggressive trajectory classes was quite limited. In addition, the risks of police contact and arrest in early adolescence showed strong associations with the aggressive and nonaggressive trajectory classes. [111]

Using data from the Seattle social develpment project, Todd I. Herrenkohl examined whether socialization processes in the social development model predict violence in late adolescence (age 18) for childhood initiators of violence (age 10-11) and adolescent initiators of violence (ages 12–16). Their analysis of a panel of children since they entered the fifth grade in 1985 revealed "that during adolescence, socialization pathways leading to violence at age 18 were similar for those who initiated violence in childhood and those who initiated violence in adolescence." They concluded that the same preventive interventions might be effective for individuals in both groups.[112]

Specialization of Offenses

The findings on **specialization** reach a greater consensus than those on escalation. Farrington and colleagues, in examining juvenile court statistics, found "a small but significant degree of specialization in offending superimposed on a great deal of versatility."[113] Specialization was identified among nearly 20 percent of the offenders, and the most specialized offenses were running away, burglary, motor vehicle theft, drinking liquor, incorrigibility, violating curfew, truancy, and using drugs. Farrington and colleagues further reported that the degree of specialization tended to increase with successive referrals, which was due to more versatile offenders dropping out. Moreover, they concluded that more serious offenses such as robbery, aggravated assault, and motor vehicle theft tended to escalate in frequency with the number of referrals, whereas less serious offenses, such as running away and being truant, tended to decrease.[114]

Wolfgang and colleagues' Cohort I study showed no specialization from one age to the next and showed no specialization from one arrest to the next. But the probability of an index offense being followed by no offense declined steadily with age (from ten to sixteen).[115] Donna Martin Hamparian and colleagues also reported no specialization among the violent offenders in Columbus. In fact, nonviolent offenses constituted nearly 70 percent of their official delinquent behaviors.[116]

Susan K. Datesman and Michael Aickin, in examining a sample of status offenders who had been referred to the family court in Delaware during a three-year period, found that specialization was much more typical of status offenders. The majority of status offenders, regardless of sex and race, were referred to court within the same offense category 50 to 70 percent of the time. Females, particularly white females, specialized in official offense behavior to a greater extent than did males; 35.2 percent of the white females were referred to court for the same offense, a sizable proportion of them for running away. The findings of this study further suggest that no evidence exists of escalation in seriousness of offense as the offense career lengthens.[117]

Chronic Offending

Chronic offending is drawing increased attention for several reasons. It is perceived that **chronic youthful offenders** constitute a majority of the active offenders. The finding that a small number of chronic juvenile offenders account for a disproportionate share of all crimes also contributes to their increased attention. Furthermore, it is commonly believed that these offenders are treated much more leniently than are their older colleagues.[118] An examination of their social backgrounds, violence and drug use, and predictors of chronic offending is helpful in understanding this population.

SOCIAL BACKGROUNDS   The cohort studies consistently report that chronic offenders are more frequently involved in violence than are other juvenile offenders. They are also more likely than other youthful offenders to use crack cocaine or other hard-core drugs or to traffick drugs to other juveniles at school and in the neighborhood.[119] Furthermore, they generally assume leadership roles in drug-trafficking gangs and, as they become adults, are more likely to continue their gang involvement. Finally, they frequently are involved in gang assaults and drive-by shootings.[120]

The vast majority of chronic offenders are identified by most cohort studies as coming from the ever-growing minority underclass that finds itself permanently trapped. These youths are marginal to the social order and perceive crime as representing the best option they have. They have no stake in the system and are not easily amenable to measures designed to rehabilitate them by making them employable or to deter them from delinquent or criminal conduct. Contributing to the hopelessness among African American males is the realization that they are several times more likely to be victims of homicides than any other demographic group and that they finish last in nearly every socioeconomic category, from the high school dropout rate to unemployment. Indeed, a 1990 study found that one in four college-age African Americans is in prison or on parole.[121]

PREDICTIONS OF CHRONIC OFFENDING One of the most important but controversial issues is whether chronic juvenile offending can be predicted. Blumstein and colleagues identified three population groups in their study: a group of "innocents" never involved with law enforcement, a group of "amateurs" with a relatively low recidivism probability, and a group of "persisters" with a relatively high recidivism probability. They found that seven factors distinguished the chronics, or persisters, from other convicted offenders: (1) conviction for crime before age thirteen; (2) low family income; (3) troublesome rating by teachers and peers at ages eight to ten; (4) poor public school performance by age ten; (5) psychomotor clumsiness; (6) low nonverbal IQ; and (7) convicted sibling.[122]

Farrington and J. David Hawkins's examination of the Cambridge Study in Delinquent Development found that persistence in crime between ages twenty-one and thirty-two was predicted "by low paternal involvement with the boy in leisure activities, a low degree of commitment to school and low verbal IQ at ages eight to ten years" and by heavy drinking and unemployment during the adolescent years.[123] Kimberly L. Kempf's analysis of Cohort II found that "delinquents who became adult offenders by the age of twenty-six were somewhat more likely than other delinquents to have had more seriously offensive adolescent careers."[124]

A more alarming approach is the popular assumption that childhood factors, some of which are crime-related, can be used to predict chronic delinquency and adult criminality and that intervention is justified based on these predicted factors. Peter Greenwood—as well as Paul Tracy, Wolfgang, Figlio and Blumstein, Farrington, and Moitra—claimed that a group of chronic offenders who are responsible for a disproportionate share of crime can be identified.[125] Although Greenwood argues that he has developed a calculus that can predict who adult chronic offenders will be and can produce estimates of crime reduction that would be achieved through their imprisonment,[126] this selective incapacitation policy has been soundly dismissed by a host of researchers.[127]

In sum, the research literature gives us extensive documentation of the lower-class and deprived backgrounds of chronic offenders, of their sociopathic attitudes, and of the seriousness and violence of their offending. What is debatable is whether it is possible to predict their chronic offending.

Desistance from Crime

Desistance, or the age of termination, is a recent consideration of researchers. One of the problems of establishing desistance is the difficulty of distinguishing between a gap in a delinquent career and true termination. It is reasonable to conclude that there will be crime-free periods in the middle of delinquent careers. Long-term follow-up is clearly required to establish the age of termination.[128]

Desistance appears to be strongly related to the maturation process as youths become aware of either the desirability of pursuing a conventional lifestyle or the undesirability of continuing with unlawful activities. Sheldon and Eleanor Glueck drew this conclusion from the follow-up of juvenile delinquent careers: "With the passing of the years there was . . . both a decline in criminality and a decrease in the seriousness of the offenses of those who continued to commit crimes."[129] Edward Mulvey and John LaRosa found that desistance was linked to a cognitive process taking place in the late teens when delinquents realized that they were "going nowhere" and that they better make changes in their lives if they were going to be successful as adults.[130] James Q. Wilson and Richard Herrnstein contend that the relatively minor gains from crime lose their power to reinforce deviant behavior as juveniles mature and develop increasing ties to conventional society. Another aspect of this maturation process, according to Wilson and Herrnstein, is the ability to delay gratification and forgo the immediate gains that delinquent or criminal acts bring.[131] Furthermore, Alicia Rand's longitudinal study of delinquent youths found that those who chose a more conventional lifestyle marked by marriage and military service were the most likely to desist from criminal careers.[132]

Barry Glassner and colleagues' study of youths in a medium-size city in New York State reported that these youths curtailed involvement in delinquent activities at age sixteen because they feared being jailed if they were apprehended as adults.[133] Farrington also noted that the severity of the adult system appeared to be a deterrent with this population.[134] The chronic offenders with whom the author interacted for several years stated that they were "going to walk away from crime" for three basic reasons: They had spent enough time in the justice system ("I am fed up with the system messing over me"); they had brought enough embarrassment to their families ("I want to make up for the disappointments I've brought my family"); and they feared the adult system and punishment ("I do not want to go on to the adult system" and "I do not want to spend the rest of my life in prison").[135]

Loeber and colleagues' Pittsburgh longitudinal study found several correlates of desistance in offending for the three samples. The age-specific effects of the youngest sample were positive attitude to school and two-parent family. The age-specific effects of the middle sample were good communication with parents about the child's activities and negative attitude to delinquency. The age-specific effects of the oldest sample were positive attitude to school, low depression, and good supervision. The across-age effects included low physical aggression, good educational achievement, low school suspension, low peer delinquency, and negative attitude to problem behavior.[136] Social World of the Delinquent 2.4 presents a remarkable account of desistance.

Why Some Juvenile Offenders Go On to Adult Crime

Wolfgang, Thornberry, and Figlio, in a follow-up to age thirty of a 10 percent sample of Cohort I, selected a random sample of 975 subjects. They were able to locate and interview 567 of these subjects when they were twenty-six and thirty years of age. Of the 567 members of the follow-up sample, the probability of being arrested by age thirty was 0.47, an increase over the 0.35 probability observed up to age eighteen. Significantly, for the subjects who were members of minorities the probability of ever being arrested before age thirty was 0.69, compared with 0.38 for the white subjects.[137]

Wolfgang and colleagues identified three groups in this follow-up study: offenders only during their juvenile years, offenders only during their adult years, and persistent offenders during both periods. Of the 459 offenders, 170 (37 percent) were juvenile delinquents only, 111 (24.2 percent) were adult offenders only, and 178 (38.8 percent) were persistent offenders. A comparison of the frequency of violations showed that the juvenile and adult offenders committed an average of slightly over two offenses. The persistent offenders, however, committed an average of 8.9 offenses; furthermore, the offenses became more serious as their careers developed, and the offenses committed during adulthood were much more serious than those committed during the juvenile years.[138]

Social World of the Delinquent 2.3

Interview with Sam Dillon

Question: Tell me about your former leadership position in the Black P-Stone Nation.

Dillon: I was a member of the main "twenty-one" of the Blackstone Rangers. We later became the Black P-Stone Nation. The main "twenty-one" were the enforcers of the Black P-Stone Nation. If someone violated or stepped out of line, they had to deal with us. I was responsible for controlling the North Side and parts of Woodlawn.

Question: I understand that you were pretty "bad."

Dillon: I've been shot and stabbed on different occasions, and this tended to make me very ruthless. Life became very cheap for me. As I look back on the things I used to do, it sometimes frightens me.

Question: You did time in prison. How did that come about?

Dillon: I was sentenced to fourteen to twenty years for murder. I did nine years and three months. I was released and continued my involvement with the gang. A year later I was charged with a double homicide, and I went on the run for eight years. I even made the television show "America's Most Wanted."

Question: What turned you around? What was your turning point?

Dillon: My faith in God. I had a religious experience and came to know that God was indeed real. I also realized that the list of people who needed to be dealt with became too long.

Question: Did gangs provide any positive contributions to you? What is your evaluation of gangs today?

Dillon: Gangs are based on raw power. Gangs are an indigenous creation of the people on the street. Gangs are people who claim power for people who have no power. But gangs have gotten out of control. Kids can't be kids. The children are normally the future of the nation, but gangs destroy children. Therefore they destroy a nation.

Question: Tell me about your work with gangs now.

Dillon: I have developed a gang model that is designed to make kids think about their actions. This model is specifically designed for gang kids....

I teach kids about the realities of gang life. I try to warn children not to make the mistakes I have and to come the way I have. I've wasted over half of my life in jails and prisons, and I try to prevent that from happening to kids today.

Source: Interviewed in June 1995, Sam Dillon, a graduate student in sociology at the University of Northern Iowa, is writing an autobiography. For the three years Sam worked at the Boys Training School at Eldora, Iowa all the gang kids at the training school were required to take his course to be released. In the late 1990s and early 2000s, Sam has worked with gang kids in an urban high school in Chicago.

Hamparian and colleagues expanded the analysis of a cohort of violent juvenile offenders and followed them into early adulthood, the period ending in the mid-twenties. Tracking the adult criminal involvement of 1,222 persons who had been arrested for at least one violent or assaultive offense as juveniles, they found that almost 60 percent of them were arrested at least once as a young adult for a felony offense, that the first adult arrest generally took place before age twenty, and that there is a clear continuity between juvenile and adult criminal careers.[139]

Katherine S. Ratcliff and Lee N. Robins, using data on a cohort of 233 African American males who grew up in St. Louis, concluded that the relationship between childhood and adult criminal behavior showed that (1) serious antisocial behavior in adults rarely takes place without high levels of childhood antisocial behavior—70 percent of highly antisocial adults were highly antisocial children, (2) only about half of very antisocial children became antisocial adults, and (3) the number of antisocial behaviors in childhood is the best indicator of severe antisocial behavior in adults. They also found that having an antisocial father is the best predictor of severe antisocial behavior in adulthood among mildly antisocial children; that being placed away from both parents and having few childhood years with parents of both sexes in the home are predictors of antisocial behavior as adults; and that being subjected to severe poverty in childhood is a predictor of severe antisocial behavior as adults.[140]

Michael Gottfredson and Hirschi's *A General Theory of Crime* concluded that "competent research regularly shows that the best predictor of crime is prior criminal behavior."[141] Wilson and Herrnstein also observed that "the offender offends not just because of immediate needs and circumstances but also because of enduring personal characteristics, some of whose traces can be found in his behavior from early childhood on. . . . [142] Both of these works draw on a vast literature that shows a positive association between delinquency and adult criminality and such factors as poor parental supervision, parental rejection, parental criminality, delinquent sibling, and low IQ.[143]

Daniel S. Nagin and Raymond Paternoster, in examining the relationship between delinquency and adult criminality, suggest two interpretations of this relationship. The first is that "prior participation has a genuine behavioral impact on the individual. Prior participation may, for example, reduce inhibitions against engaging in delinquent activity."[144] They refer to such an effect as "state dependence." Another explanation is that individuals have a different propensity to delinquency and that this "propensity is persistent over time." This second explanation is similar to the findings of Gottfredson and Hirschi and of Wilson and Herrnstein.[145] Nagin and Paternoster, in using a three-wave panel set, found that the positive association between past and future delinquency is due to a state-dependence influence.[146]

Robert J. Sampson and Laub sought to explain both the continuity of delinquency into adult criminality and noncriminality, or change, in adulthood for those who were delinquent as children. Their basic thesis is threefold:

1. structural context mediated by informal family and school social control explains delinquency in childhood and adolescence;
2. in turn, there is continuity in antisocial behavior from childhood through adulthood in a variety of life domains; and
3. informal social bonds in adulthood to family and employment explain changes in criminality over the life span despite early childhood propensities.[147]

Using life-history data drawn from the Gluecks' longitudinal study of 1,000 men, Laub and Sampson found that although adult crime is connected to childhood behavior, both incremental and abrupt changes still take place through changes in adult social bonds. The emergence of strong bonds to work and family among adults deflects early, established behavior trajectories. They also argue that the events that trigger the formation of strong adult bonds to work and family commonly occur by chance or luck.[148]

The concept of a **turning point** is one of the fascinating contributions of Laub and Sampson's research. A turning point involves a gradual or dramatic change and may lead to "a modification, reshaping, or transition from one state, condition, or phase to another."[149] In seeking to unravel the mechanisms that operate at key turning points to turn a risk trajectory to a more adaptive path, Laub and Sampson found that stable employment and a good marriage, or changing roles and environments, can lead to investment of social capital or relations among persons.[150] "Social capital," according to James S. Coleman, "is productive, making possible the achievements of certain ends that in its absence would not be possible."[151] (See Chapter 4 for discussion of the development of social capital theory.)

More recently, Raymond Paternoster, Robert Brame, and David P. Farrington, using data from the Cambridge Study in Delinquent Development, investigated the relationship between adolescent and adult involvement in criminal behavior. In opposition to Sampson and Laub, Paternoster and colleagues found that adult offending "is not systematically related to events and experiences after adolescence." They are suggesting that variation in adult offending is consistent with a random process and, accordingly, it is impossible to conclude that relatively simple explanations, such as employment and marriage, can explain complex life-course decisions. They propose that much further study is needed to further clarify the relationship between adolescent delinquent acts and adult criminal behaviors.[152]

In sum, considerable consensus exists concerning the dimensions of delinquent behavior. Youths who begin offending early tend to have long delinquent careers. Delinquents generally show a great deal of versatility, rather than specialization, in committing offenses. Desistance, or terminating delinquent behavior, is strongly related to the maturation process. In the midst of the continuity of childhood antisocial behavior, some adults experience turning points, or change, usually related to such matters as stable jobs or a satisfying marriage or family life.

SUMMARY

Official and unofficial statistics have contributed a number of important findings about youth crime in U.S. society:

- Juveniles under the age of eighteen commit a disproportionate number of property and violent offenses.
- Juveniles are committing more violent crimes than they have in the past. But juvenile rates of homicide have been decreasing since 1994.
- Juveniles are carrying far more guns than they have in the past. The good news is that law enforcement efforts in large urban areas in the mid to late 1990s have had some success in reducing juveniles' use of guns.
- Most youths are involved in delinquent behavior, and more than 90 percent of delinquent acts are undetected.
- Lower-class youths are involved in more frequent and more serious offenses than middle-class youths are; indeed, serious youth crime is primarily focused among lower-class youths.
- Nonwhites commit more frequent and more serious offenses than whites.
- Males commit more frequent and more serious offenses than females do.
- Urban youths commit more frequent and more serious offenses than suburban or rural youths do.
- A small group of youthful offenders, primarily lower-class minority males, commits half or more of the serious offenses in urban areas.
- Interventions by the juvenile justice system frequently make youths' behavior worse rather than better.
- Some evidence exists that youthful offenders progress to increasingly serious forms of delinquent behavior.

These various forms of statistics on juvenile delinquency, which have far more agreement than disagreement, answer some pressing questions about juvenile delinquency. They suggest that the rates of delinquency in the United States have either leveled off or are declining. Indeed, since 1993, the rates of juvenile homicides have been declining rather dramatically, and the dreaded violent juvenile crime wave is probably unlikely to materialize in the near future. Some juvenile violent offenders and gang members, as the media have been quick to inform the public, do commit vicious and brutal crimes, but little or no evidence exists that there are more juvenile "monsters" than in the past.

This chapter does a better job of answering questions about the extent of juvenile delinquency than about its nature. In future chapters, as the social context and personality variables are examined, more clarity will emerge about such baffling public concerns as: Why are kids from decent backgrounds killing classmates in school? Are female delinquents any different than they were in the past? Why have youth gangs become a serious problem, and what can be done about them? What social policy is needed to prevent and control juvenile delinquency more effectively in the United States?

KEY TERMS

age of onset, p. 50
chronic youthful offenders, p. 54
clearance by arrest, p. 32
cohort study, p. 37
desistance, p. 55
escalation of offenses, p. 51
hidden delinquency, p. 39
incidence of delinquency, p. 31
juvenile court statistics, p. 36

prevalence of delinquency, p. 31
reliability, p. 41
self-report studies, p. 39
specialization, p. 54
turning point, p. 58
Uniform Crime Reports, p. 32
validity, p. 41
victimization studies, p. 44

CRITICAL THINKING QUESTIONS

1. What do the *Uniform Crime Reports* generally show about official delinquency in U.S. society?
2. What problems do the official statistics of the *Uniform Crime Reports* present to researchers?
3. What do juvenile court statistics show about juvenile delinquency in U.S. society?
4. Identify the various studies that were discussed in this chapter. What do their findings reveal about the nature and extent of youth crime?
5. The youthful chronic offender is a concern to the public and its policymakers. What do we know about these youths?
6. Discuss the various dimensions of delinquent behavior. What do we know about each dimension?
7. What is the importance of the concept of the "turning point"?

WEB DESTINATIONS

Read more about what is being done to rehabilitate chronic youthful offenders from the Center for National Policy site.
http://www.cnponline.org/issue%20Briefs/State-lines/statelin0101.htm

Get more information about juvenile court statistics with actual statistics from the National Center for Juvenile Justice.
http://ojjdp.ncjrs.org/pubs/stats/ncj93.htm

Read about the Federal Bureau of Investigation's Uniform Crime Reports.
http://www.fbi.gov/ucr/ucr95prs.htm

Use this University of Virginia Library service to find Uniform Crime Reports for any state between the years of 1990–1993.
http://fisher.lib.virginia.edu/crime/crimes.html

Read more in detail about victimization studies from the Inter-University Consortium for Political and Social Research.
http://www.icpsr.umich.edu/NACJD/SDA/ncvs.html

NOTES

1. Alexander W. Pisciotta, "Monster Child: The Life, Times, and Crimes of Jesse Harding Pomeroy." Paper presented at the Annual Meeting of the Academy of Criminal Justice Sciences in Boston, Massachusetts (March 1997), p. 1. For citations from newspapers and other sources in this quoted passage, see his excellent paper.
2. Donna Martin Hamparian et al., *The Young Criminal Years of the Violent Few* (Cleveland, Ohio: Federation for Community Planning, 1984), p. 1.
3. Donald J. Shoemaker, *Theories of Delinquency: an Examination of Explanations of Delinquent Behavior* (New York: Oxford University Press, 1996), p. 51.
4. Franklin Zimring, "The Serious Juvenile Offender: Notes on an Unknown Quantity," in *The Serious Juvenile Offender: Proceedings of a National Symposium* (Washington, D.C.: U.S. Government Printing Office, 1978), pp. 22–23.
5. Federal Bureau of Investigation, *Crime in the United States 2000: Uniform Crime Reports* (Washington, D.C.:

U.S. Government Printing Office, 2001), pp. 220, 226, 230, 235.

6. Ibid., p. 226.

7. Marie Simonetti Rosen, "A LEN Interview with Professor Alfred Blumstein," *Law Enforcement News,* John Jay College of Criminal Justice, New York City, 21 (April 30, 1995), p. 10.

8. Ibid.

9. Ibid.

10. James Alan Fox, *Trends in Juvenile Violence: A Report to the United States Attorney General on Current and Future Rates of Juvenile Offending.* Prepared for the Bureau of Justice Statistics (March 1996), executive summary, p. 19.

11. Ibid.

12. Ibid.

13. John J. DiIulio Jr., "Arresting Ideas: Tougher Law Enforcement Is Driving Down Urban Crime," *Policy Review* (Fall 1995), p. 15.

14. Ibid.

15. Ibid.

16. William J. Bennett, John J. DiIulio, and John P. Walters, *Body Count: Moral Poverty and How to Win America's War against Crime and Drugs* (New York: Simon and Schuster, 1996).

17. Cited in Philip J. Cook, "The Epidemic of Youth Gun Violence," *Perspectives on Crime and Justice: 1997–1998* (Washington, D.C.: The National Institute of Justice, 1998), pp. 110–111.

18. Ibid., p. 111.

19. Franklin E. Zimring, Presentation at National Criminal Justice Association Annual Meeting (May 30, 1996).

20. Franklin E. Zimring, "Crying Wolf Over Teen Demons," *L.A. Times,* August 19, 1996, p. A17.

21. Philip J. Cook and John Laub, "The Unprecedented Epidemic in Youth Violence," in *Crime and Justice,* edited by Mark H. Moore and Michael Tonry (Chicago: University of Chicago Press, 1998), pp. 101–138.

22. Cook, "The Epidemic of Youth Gun Violence," p. 111.

23. Alfred Blumstein and Richard Rosenfeld, "Assessing the Recent Ups and Downs in U.S. Homicide Rates," *National Institute of Justice Journal,* Issue No. 237 (October 1998), pp. 10–11.

24. I. R. Perlman, "Juvenile Court Statistics," *Juvenile Court Judges Journal* 16 (1965), p. 1–3.

25. Howard N. Snyder et al., *Juvenile Court Statistics 1984* (Pittsburgh, Pa.: National Center for Juvenile Justice, 1987), p. 7; and Howard N. Snyder et al., *Juvenile Court Statistics 1988* (Pittsburgh, Pa.: National Center for Juvenile Justice, 1988, p. 11.

26. Melissa Sickmund, "Offenders in Juvenile Court, 1997," *Juvenile Justice Bulletin* (Washington, D.C.: Office of Juvenile Justice and Delinquency Prevention, 2000), p. 2.

27. Ibid.

28. Ibid., p. 3.

29. Ibid, p 4.

30. Randall G. Shelden, "The Chronic Delinquent: Gender and Racial Differences." Paper presented at the Annual Meeting of the American Society of Criminology, Montreal, Canada (November 1987), p. 2.

31. For the Philadelphia cohort study, see Marvin E. Wolfgang, Robert M. Figlio, and Thorsten Sellin, *Delinquency in a Birth Cohort* (Chicago: University of Chicago Press, 1972). For the London, England, cohort, see Alfred Blumstein, David P. Farrington, and Soumyo Moitra, "Delinquency Careers: Innocents, Amateurs, and Persisters," in *Crime and Justice: An Annual Review* 6, edited by Michael Tonry and Norval Morris (Chicago: University of Chicago Press, 1985), pp. 187–220. For the Racine, Wisconsin, cohort, see Lyle W. Shannon, *Assessing the Relationships of Adult Criminal Careers to Juvenile Careers: A Summary* (Washington, D.C.: U.S. Government Printing Office, 1982). For the Columbus cohort, see Donna Martin Hamparian et al., *The Violent Few: A Study of Dangerous Juveniles* (Lexington, Mass.: Lexington Books, 1980).

32. Stephen A. Cernkovich, Peggy C. Giordano, and Meredith D. Pugh, "Chronic Offenders: The Missing Cases in Self-Report Delinquency," *Journal of Criminal Law and Criminology* 76 (1985), p. 705.

33. Cynthia Jakob-Chien provided this information on the National Youth Survey.

34. Michael J. Hindelang, Travis Hirschi, and Joseph G. Weis, *Measuring Delinquency* (Beverly Hills, Calif.: Sage, 1981), p. 22.

35. Ibid., p. 86.

36. James F. Short Jr. and F. Ivan Nye, "Reported Behavior as a Criterion of Deviant Behavior," *Social Problems* 5 (Winter 1957–1958), p. 211.

37. Hindelang et al., *Measuring Delinquency,* p. 295.

38. Cernkovich et al., "Chronic Offenders," p. 706. For other efforts to include frequent and serious offenders, see Ross Matsueda, Rosemary Gartner, Irving Piliavin, and Michael Polakowski, "The Prestige of Criminal and Conventional Occupations: A Subcultural Model of Criminal Activity," *American Sociological Review* 57 (1992), pp. 752–770; and James Inciardi, Ruth Horowitz, and Anne Pottieger, *Street Kids, Street Drugs, Street Crime: An Examination of Drug Use and Serious Delinquency in Miami* (Belmont, Calif.: Wadsworth Publishing, 1993).

39. Hindelang et al., *Measuring Delinquency,* p. 126. For the reliability of self-report studies, see also David H. Huizinga and Delbert S. Elliot, *A Longitudinal Study of Drug Use and Delinquency in a National Sample of Youth: An Assessment of Causal Order* (A Report of the National Youth Survey. Boulder, Colo.: Behavioral Research Institute, 1981); Beatrice A. Rouse, Nicholas J. Kozel, and Louise G. Richards, eds., *Self-Report Methods of Estimating Drug Use: Meeting Current Challenges to Validity,* NIDA Research Monograph 57 (Rockville, Md.: National Institute on Drug Abuse, 1985).

40. Austin L. Porterfield, "Delinquency and Its Outcome in Court and College," *American Journal of Sociology* 49 (November 1943), pp. 199–208.

41. James F. Short Jr., "A Report on the Incidence of Criminal Behavior, Arrests, and Convictions in Selected Groups," *Research Studies of the State College of Washington* 22 (June 1954), 110–118.

42. James F. Short Jr. and F. Ivan Nye, "Extent of Unrecorded Juvenile Delinquency: Tentative Conclusions," *Journal of Criminal Law, Criminology and Police Science* 49 (November-December 1958), pp. 296–302.

43. Short and Nye, "Reported Behavior as a Criterion of Deviant Behavior," pp. 207–213.

44. David H. Huizinga and Delbert S. Elliott, "Juvenile Offenders: Prevalence, Offender Incidence, and Arrest Rates by Race," *Crime and Delinquency* 33 (April 1987), pp. 208, 210.

45. Franklyn W. Dunford and Delbert S. Elliott, "Identifying Career Offenders Using Self-Reported Data," *Journal of Research in Crime and Delinquency* 21 (February 1984), pp. 57–82.

46. Ibid.

47. David H. Huizinga, Rolf Loeber, and Terence P. Thornberry, *Urban Delinquency and Substance Abuse: Initial Findings* (Washington, D.C.: U.S. Department of Justice, Office of Juvenile Justice and Delinquency Prevention, 1994).

48. Cited in *Guide for Implementing the Comprehensive Strategy for Serious, Violent, and Chronic Juvenile Offenders* (Washington, D.C.: Office of Juvenile Justice and Delinquency Prevention, 1995), p. 3.

49. Jerald G. Bachman and Patrick M. O'Malley, *A Continuing Study of American Youth (12th-Grade Survey, 1996)* (Ann Arbor, Mich.: Institute for Social Research, 1998).

50. Ibid., and Office of Applied Statistics, *National Household Survey on Drug Abuse: Population Estimates 1997* (Washington, D.C.: Department of Health and Human Services, 1998).

51. Cheryl Ringel, *Criminal Victimization 1996: Changes 1995–1996 with Trends 1993–1996* (Washington, D.C.: U.S. Department of Justice, Bureau of Justice Statistics, 1997), p. 1.

52. Leonard D. Savitz, Michael Lalli, and Lawrence Rosen, *City Life and Delinquency-Victimization: Fear of Crime and Gang Membership* (Washington, D.C.: U.S. Government Printing Office, 1977), p. 11.

53. Callie Marie Rennisoln, *Criminal Victimization 2000: Changes 1999-2000 with Trends 1993-2000* (Washington, D.C.: National Crime Victimization Survey, 2001), p. 6.

54. Ibid., p. 6.

55. Jeffrey Fagan, Elizabeth S. Piper, and Yu-Teh Cheng, "Contributions of Victimization to Delinquency in Inner Cities," *Journal of Criminal Law and Criminology* 78 (1987), p. 587.

56. Nicholas Anderson and Orlando Rodriguez, "Conceptual Issues in the Study of Hispanic Delinquency," *Research Bulletin* 7 (Hispanic Research Center, Fordham University) (1984), pp. 2–5.

57. Fagan et al., "Contributions of Victimization to Delinquency in Inner Cities," p. 593.

58. Simon I. Singer, "Victims in a Birth Cohort," in *From Boy to Man, from Delinquency to Crime*, pp. 174, 176, 178.

59. Rennisoln, *Criminal Victimization, 2000.*

60. Ibid.

61. Snyder, "Juvenile Arrests 1999."

62. Peter E. Tracy, Marvin E. Wolfgang, and Robert M. Figlio, *Delinquency in Two Birth Cohorts: Executive Summary* (Washington, D.C.: U.S. Department of Justice, 1985).

63. Meda Chesney-Lind and Randall G. Shelden, *Girls: Delinquency and Juvenile Justice* (Pacific Grove, Calif.: Brooks/Cole, 1992), p. 20.

64. For a review of these studies, see Chesney-Lind and Shelden, *Girls*, pp. 14–18.

65. David C. Rowe, Alexander T. Vazsonyi, and Daniel J. Flannery, "Sex Differences in Crime: Do Means and Within-Sex Variation Have Similar Causes," *Journal of Research in Crime and Delinquency* 32 (February 1995), pp. 84–100.

66. Chesney-Lind and Shelden, *Girls*, p. 24.

67. Meda Chesney-Lind, *The Female Offender: Girls, Women, and Crime* (Thousand Oaks, Calif.: Sage Publications, 1997), p. 4.

68. David Finkelhor and Larry Baron, "Risk Factors for Child Sexual Abuse," *Journal of Interpersonal Violence* 1 (1986), pp. 43–71.

69. David P. Farrington, Rolf Loeber, Magda Stouthamer-Loeber, Welmoet B. Van Kammen, and Laura Schmidt, "Self-Reported Delinquency and a Combined Delinquency Seriousness Scale Based on Boys, Mothers, and Teachers: Concurrent and Predict Validity for African Americans and Caucasians," *Criminology* 34 (November 1996), p. 495.

70. William J. Chambliss and Richard H. Nagasawa, "On the Validity of Official Statistics: A Comparative Study of White, Black and Japanese High-School Boys," *Journal of Research in Crime and Delinquency* (January 1969), pp. 71–77.

71. Leroy C. Gould, "Who Defines Delinquency: A Comparison of Self-Reported and Officially Reported Indices of Delinquency for Three Racial Groups," *Social Problems* (Winter 1969), pp. 325–336.

72. Travis Hirschi, *Causes of Delinquency* (Berkeley: University of California Press, 1969), Table 14.

73. Huizinga and Elliott, "Juvenile Offenders," p. 215.

74. Ibid., p. 219.

75. Jay R. Williams and Martin Gold, "From Delinquent Behavior to Official Delinquency," *Social Problems* 20 (1972); and Martin Gold and David J. Reimer, *Changing Patterns of Delinquent Behavior among Americans 13 to 16 Years Old.*

76. Suzanne S. Ageton and Delbert S. Elliott, *The Incidence of Delinquent Behavior in a National Probability Sample of Adolescents* (Boulder, Colo.: Behavioral Research Institute, 1978).

77. Michael J. Hindelang et al., *Measuring Delinquency.*

78. Gary Jensen and Raymond Eve, "Sex Differences in Delinquency," *Criminology* 13 (1976), pp. 427–448.

79. Steven A. Cernkovich and Peggy Giordano, "A Comparative Analysis of Male and Female Delinquency," *Sociological Quarterly* 20 (1979), pp. 131–145.

80. Chesney-Lind and Shelden, *Girls*, pp. 24–25.

81. F. I. Nye, *Family Relationships and Delinquent Behavior* (New York: John Wiley and Sons, 1958); Short and Nye, "Extent of Unrecorded Juvenile Delinquency," pp. 296–302; Robert A. Dentler and Lawrence J. Monroe, "Social Correlates of Early Adolescent Theft," *American Sociological Review* 26 (October 1961), pp. 733–743; Ronald L. Akers, "Socio-Economic Status

and Delinquent Behavior: A Retest," *Journal of Research in Crime and Delinquency* (January 1964), pp. 38–46; W. L. Slocum and C. L. Stone, "Family Culture Patterns and Delinquent-Type Behavior," *Journal of Marriage and Family Living* 25 (1963), pp. 202–208; LaMar T. Empey and Maynard L. Erickson, "Hidden Delinquency and Social Status," *Social Forces* 44 (June 1966), pp. 546–554; Travis Hirschi, *Causes of Delinquency;* Williams and Gold, "From Delinquent Behavior to Official Delinquency"; D. H. Kelly and W. T. Pink, "School Commitment, Youth Rebellion, and Delinquency," *Criminology* 10 (1973), pp. 473–485.

82. Williams and Gold, "From Delinquent Behavior to Official Delinquency," p. 217.

83. Hirschi, *Causes of Delinquency,* p. 75.

84. Richard E. Johnson, "Social Class and Delinquent Behavior: A New Test," *Criminology* 18 (May 1980), p. 91.

85. Charles Tittle, Wayne Villemez, and Douglas Smith, "The Myth of Social Class and Criminality: An Empirical Assessment of the Empirical Evidence," *American Sociological Review* 43 (1978), pp. 643–656.

86. Ageton and Elliott, *The Incidence of Delinquent Behavior.*

87. Elliott and Huizinga, "Social Class and Delinquent Behavior in a National Youth Panel," *Criminology* 21 (May 1983), pp. 149–177. For a discussion about whether different definitions of class are likely to produce different results on social class and delinquency, see Margaret Farnworth, Terence P. Thornberry, Alan J. Lizotte, and Marvin D. Krohn, "Social Background and the Early Onset of Delinquency: Exploring the Utility of Various Indicators of Social Class Background" (Albany, N.Y.: Rochester Youth Development Study, June 1990).

88. Margaret Farnworth, Terence P. Thornberry, Marvin D. Krohn, and Alan J. Lizotte, "Measurement in the Study of Class and Delinquency: Integrating Theory and Research," *Journal of Research in Crime and Delinquency* 31 (1994), p. 32.

89. Ibid.

90. Bradley R. Entner Wright, Avshalom Caspi, Terrie Moffitt, Richard A. Miech, and Phil A. Silva, "Reconsidering the Relationship between SES and Delinquency: Causation but Not Correlation," *Criminology* 37 (February 1999), pp. 175, 190.

91. Marvin E. Wolfgang, Terence P. Thornberry, and Robert M. Figlio, *From Boy to Man, from Delinquency to Crime* (Chicago: University of Chicago Press, 1987), pp. 37, 39.

92. Patrick H. Tolan, "Age of Onset and Delinquency Patterns, Legal Status, and Chronicity of Offending." Paper presented at the Annual Meeting of the American Society of Criminology, Montreal, Canada (November 1987), p. 44.

93. Alfred Blumstein, David P. Farrington, and Soumyo Moitra, "Delinquency Careers, Innocents, Desisters, and Persisters," in *Crime and Justice: An Annual Review* 6, edited by Michael Tonry and Norval Morris (Chicago: University of Chicago Press, 1985).

94. David P. Farrington, "Offending from 10 to 25 Years of Age," in *Prospective Studies of Crime and Delinquency,* edited by K. T. Van Dusen and S. A. Mednick (Boston: Kluwer-Nijhoff, 1983).

95. Ronald L. Simons, Chyi-In Wu, Rand D. Conger, and Frederick O. Lorenz, "Two Routes to Delinquency: Differences between Early and Late Starters in the Impact of Parenting and Deviant Peers," *Criminology* 32 (1994), p. 247.

96. Cited in Barry Krisberg, *Guide for Implementing the Comprehensive Strategy for Serious, Violent, and Chronic Juvenile Offenders* (Washington, D.C.: Office of Juvenile Justice and Delinquency Prevention, 1995), pp. 3–4.

97. Ibid., p. 4.

98. David P. Farrington, "Age and Crime," in *Crime and Justice: An Annual Review* 7, edited by Michael Tonry and Norval Morris (Chicago: University of Chicago Press, 1986), p. 194.

99. Williams and Gold, "From Delinquent Behavior to Official Delinquency," p. 215.

100. Ageton and Elliott, *The Incidence of Delinquent Behavior in a National Probability Sample of Adolescents.*

101. Elliott and Huizinga, "Social Class and Delinquent Behavior in a National Youth Panel," pp. 149–177.

102. Marvin E. Wolfgang, Robert M. Figlio, and Thorsten Sellin, *Delinquency in a Birth Cohort* (Chicago: University of Chicago Press, 1972).

103. Wolfgang et al., *From Boy to Man,* p. 41.

104. Pamela Tontodonato, "Explaining Rate Changes in Delinquent Arrest Transitions Using Event History Analysis," *Criminology* 26 (1988), p. 454.

105. Lyle W. Shannon, *Assessing the Relationships of Adult Criminal Careers to Juvenile Careers: A Summary* (Washington, D.C.: U.S. Government Printing Office, 1982), p. v.

106. Cited in Farrington, "Age and Crime," p. 224.

107. Rolf Loeber, Magda Stouthamer-Loeber, Welmoet Van Kammen, and David P. Farrington, "Initiation, Escalation and Desistance in Juvenile Offending and Their Correlates," *Journal of Criminal Law and Criminology* 82 (1991), p. 37.

108. Rolf Loeber, Phen Wung, Kate Keenan, Bruce Giroux, Magda Stouthamer-Loeber, and Welmoet B. Van Kammen, "Developmental Pathways in Disruptive Child Behavior," *Development and Psychopathology* 5 (Winter-Spring, 1993), pp. 103–133.

109. See Barbara Tatem Kelley, Rolf Loeber, Kate Keenan, and Mary DeLamatre, *Developmental Pathways in Boys' Disruptive and Delinquent Behavior* (Washington, D.C.: Office of Juvenile Justice and Delinquency Prevention, 1997).

110. T. E. Moffitt, "Adolescent-Limited and Life-Course Persistent Antisocial Behavior: A Developmental Taxonomy," *Psychological Review* 100 (1993), pp. 674–701. For one of the studies that is highly supportive of Moffitt's taxonomy of offending behavior, see Paul Mazerolle, Robert Brame, Ray Paternoster, Alex Piquero, and Charles Dean, "Onset Age, Persistence, and Offending Versatility: Comparisons across Gender," *Criminology* 38 (November 2000), pp. 1143-1172.

111. Barbara Maughan, Andrew Pickles, Richard Rowe, E. Jane Costello, and Adrian Angold, "Developmental Trajectories of Aggressive and Non-aggressive Conduct Problems," *Journal of Quantitative Criminology* 16 (2000), p. 199.

112. Todd I. Herrenkohl, Bu Huang, Rick Kosterman, J. David Hawkins, Richard F. Catalano, and Brian H. Smith, "A Comparison of Social Development Processes Leading to Violent Behavior in Late Adolescence for Childhood Initiators and Adolescent Initiators of Violence," *Journal of Research in Crime and Delinquency* 38 (February 2001), p. 45.

113. David P. Farrington, Howard N. Snyder, and Terrence A. Finnegan, "Specialization in Juvenile Court Careers," *Criminology* 26 (August 1988), p. 461.

114. Ibid.

115. Wolfgang, et al., *Delinquency in a Birth Cohort.*

116. Hamparian et al., *The Young Criminal Years of the Violent Few.*

117. Susan K. Datesman and Michael Aickin, "Offense Specialization and Escalation among Status Offenders," *Journal of Criminal Law and Criminology* 75 (1984), pp. 1260–1273.

118. Peter Greenwood, "Differences in Criminal Behavior and Court Responses among Juvenile and Young Adult Defendants," in *Crime and Justice: An Annual Review,* edited by Michael Tonry and Norval Morris (Chicago: University of Chicago Press, 1986), p. 153.

119. For an investigation of gang involvement in crack cocaine sales, see Malcolm W. Klein, Cheryl L. Maxson, and Lea C. Cunningham, " 'Crack,' Street Gangs, and Violence," *Criminology* 29 (1991), pp. 623–650.

120. Information derived from interviews and interactions with these youth in 1990–1991.

121. Isabel Wilkerson, "Facing Grim Data on Young Males: Blacks Grope for Ways to End Blight," *New York Times,* July 17, 1990, p. A14.

122. Blumstein, Farrington, and Moitra, "Delinquency Careers: Innocents, Amateurs, and Persisters."

123. David P. Farrington and J. David Hawkins, "Predicting Participation, Early Onset and Later Persistence in Officially Recorded Offending," *Criminal Behaviour and Mental Health* 1 (1991), p. 1.

124. Kimberly L. Kempf, "Crime Severity and Criminal Career Progression," *Journal of Criminal Law and Criminology* (1988), p. 537.

125. Peter Greenwood, *Selective Incapacitation* (Santa Monica, Calif.: Rand, 1982); Paul Tracy, Marvin Wolfgang, and Robert Figlio, *Delinquency in Two Birth Cohorts;* and Blumstein, Farrington, and Moitra, "Delinquent Careers."

126. Greenwood, *Selective Incapacitation.*

127. See Scott H. Decker and Barbara Salert, "Predicting the Career Criminal: An Empirical Test of the Greenwood Scale," *Journal of Criminal Law and Criminology* 77 (1986), p. 219.

128. Farrington, "Age and Crime," pp. 221–222.

129. Sheldon Glueck and Eleanor Glueck, *Juvenile Delinquents Grown Up* (New York: Commonwealth Fund, 1940), p. 89.

130. Edward Mulvey and John LaRosa, "Delinquency Cessation and Adolescent Development: Preliminary Data,"

American Journal of Orthopsychiatry 56 (1986), pp. 212–224.

131. James Q. Wilson and Richard Herrnstein, *Crime and Human Nature* (New York: Simon and Schuster, 1985), pp. 126–147.

132. Alicia Rand, "Transitional Life Events and Desistance from Delinquency and Crime," in *From Boy to Man, from Delinquency to Crime* edited by Marvin Wolfgang, Terence Thornberry, and Robert Figlio, pp. 134–163.

133. Barry Glassner, Margaret Ksander, and Bruce Berg, "A Note on the Deterrent Effect of Juvenile vs. Adult Jurisdiction," *Social Problems* 31 (December 1983), p. 221.

134. Farrington, "The Age of Crime," p. 224.

135. Representative statements made by these older youth before they left the maximum-security institution.

136. Loeber et al., "Initiation, Escalation and Desistance in Juvenile Offending and Their Correlates," p. 72.

137. Wolfgang et al., *From Boy to Man,* p. 20.

138. Ibid., p. 21.

139. Hamparian et al., *The Young Criminal Years of the Violent Few,* pp. 3, 12.

140. Katherine S. Ratcliff and Lee N. Robins, "Risk Factors in the Continuation of Childhood Antisocial Behaviors into Adulthood," *International Journal of Mental Health* 7 (1979), pp. 96–116.

141. Michael Gottfredson and Travis Hirschi, *A General Theory of Crime* (Palo Alto, Calif.: Stanford University Press, 1990), p. 107.

142. Wilson and Herrnstein, *Crime and Human Nature,* p. 209.

143. Daniel S. Nagin and Raymond Paternoster, "On the Relationship of Past to Future Participation in Delinquency," *Criminology* 29 (May 1991), p. 165.

144. Ibid., p. 163.

145. Ibid., p. 163.

146. Ibid., p. 163.

147. Robert J. Sampson and John H. Laub, *Crime in the Making: Pathways and Turning Points through Life* (Cambridge: Harvard University Press, 1993), p. 7. For further support of life-course theory, see Ronald L. Simons, Christine Johnson, Rand D. Conger, and Glen Elder, Jr., "A Test of Latent Trait versus Life-Course Perspectives on the Stability of Adolescent Antisocial Behavior," *Criminology* 36 (May 1998), pp. 217–243.

148. John H. Laub and Robert J. Sampson, "Turning Points in the Life Course: Why Change Matters to the Study of Crime," *Criminology* 31 (August 1993), pp. 301–320.

149. Ibid., p. 309.

150. Ibid., p. 310.

151. James S. Coleman, "Social Capital in the Creation of Human Capital," *American Journal of Sociology* 94 (1988), p. 98.

152. Raymond Paternoster, Robert Brame, and David P. Farrington, "On the Relationship Between Adolecsent and Adult Conviction Frequencies." *Journal of Quantitative Criminology* 17 (2001), pp. 201, 222.

part two

THE CAUSES
OF DELINQUENCY

chapter 3

INDIVIDUAL CAUSES OF DELINQUENCY

OBJECTIVES

After reading this chapter, the student will be able to answer the following questions:

- What role does free will have in the classical school's understanding of criminal or delinquent behavior?

- What are the main forms of positivism? How does each form explain delinquent behavior?

- How does rational choice theory differ from positivism?

- What type of delinquencies are more likely to be determined?

- Which type of delinquents are more likely to be responsible for their actions?

John Conrad tells the sad story of Billy, one of the many stories of juveniles whose lives ended early:

A seventeen-year-old whom *I shall call Billy was one of a fairly large family of Appalachian antecedents living on the margins of the economy. His parents had been more often on welfare than not. Poor managers, they had been unable to provide their children with more than subsistence. Love and harmony were rarely manifest in a home chiefly remarkable for violence. Billy recalled having been beaten with electric cords, straps, belts, sticks, broom handles, and boards from early childhood. This type of discipline went on until one day, when he was fourteen, his mother came at him in a fury, armed with a plank with which she was going to beat him. He knocked her out. From that time on he was mostly on his own.*

School had been an arena of defeat. He had great difficulty in reading and was eventually found to be dyslexic—neurologically impaired so that letters did not arrive in his brain in intelligible order for words to be made out of

*them. He learned to think of himself as a dummy, the word that other kids ap-
plied to him. School records noted that by the time he was nine, he had taken
to sniffing glue, which certainty did not improve his nervous system. When he
was fourteen, he dropped out, perhaps because of his unrelieved scholastic failures, perhaps because of his assault on his mother.*

*He took to hanging around, sometimes in the company of an uncle four-
teen years older who introduced him to homosexual practices. It was not long
before he was earning $20 a trick as a prostitute. A large portion of his earn-
ings was spent on various uppers and downers and marijuana. He does not
seem to have used "heavy stuff."*

*One of his customers was the old man who was to become a victim on the
Fourth of July weekend last summer. Billy and his uncle spent the holiday at
the old man's apartment. They drank heavily and smoked pot. As they became
more and more drunk, conviviality turned into acrimony. They ran out of beer,
and the old man told Billy to go out and get some more, calling him a dummy
and a punk as he issued the order. The police account alleged that in a rage
Billy attacked him with his fists, knocked him flat, and then stomped him until
the old man succumbed. The pathologist's report showed that the alcoholic content of his blood was so high that death would have been imminent anyway.[1]*

**Why do you believe Billy committed the crime he did? When did he start to go
wrong? If your mother had attacked you with a large board when you were an adolescent, what would you have done? How rational was the murder he committed?**

Billy stood accused of the most serious of crimes, the murder of another human being. His background and personal situation inspired no confidence at all in his ability
to change. To argue that he was not dangerous was to dismiss the horrible affair on the
Fourth of July, a record of violent family relations, and a life without adult control for
the previous three years.[2]

The public defender was concerned whether Billy, a slight youngster with chestnut
blond hair, could survive in prison. He had scored well above average on an IQ test but
spoke haltingly and seemed painfully childish. He intended, if he got out of his trouble,
to go to Florida and find work as a deep-sea fisherman. His dreams of a fisherman's life
were never realized. The juvenile court decided to transfer Billy over for trial in the adult
court. Three weeks later, Billy hanged himself with a sheet in his cell.

Billy was a real defendant caught in the grip of the justice system. His seventeen years
are a tragic story of neglect, abuse, and violence. His decisions to make money from sex
and to use drugs eventually led him to a final choice of taking his life. Billy was like many
other youngsters who come into contact with the juvenile and adult justice systems.
Their lives reflect many tragic dimensions that make simple answers hard to find.

This chapter, the first of four on causation, focuses on the individual causes of juvenile delinquency. Juvenile delinquency, according to the classical school of criminology and rational choice theory, is rational behavior; that is, juvenile crime is the
outcome of the offender's broadly rational choices and decisions. Ronald V. Clarke and
Derek B. Cornish suggest that crime is caused not by factors beyond the offender's control but by "the conscious thought processes that give purpose to and justify conduct,
and the underlying cognitive mechanisms by which information about the world is selected, attended to, and processed."[3]

A second theoretical position discussed in this chapter is that delinquents cannot help committing their socially unacceptable behavior. They are controlled by either biological or psychological factors, or traits, that cause them to become involved in delinquent behavior. The delinquent act, then, is determined by a preexisting and underlying biological or psychological condition. Yet this notion of partial or total **determinism** is in conflict with the concept of legal responsibility, for if an adolescent's delinquent act is determined or predisposed by antecedent conditions, then the adolescent cannot be held responsible for this behavior. Taken to its logical conclusion, **determinism** denies the relevance of the legal and punishment process.[4]

The Contribution of the Classical School to the Understanding of Delinquency

The association between criminal behavior and the rationality of crime has roots in the eighteenth-century classical school of criminology. Cesare Beccaria and Jeremy Bentham, this school's founders, viewed humans as rational creatures who are willing to surrender enough liberty to the state so that society can establish rules and sanctions for the preservation of the social order.[5]

In 1764, Cesare Bonesana, Marquis of Beccaria, then only twenty-six and just out of law school, published a slim volume titled *On Crime and Punishments.* This essay, which appeared anonymously because Beccaria feared reprisals if its authorship were known, was read avidly and translated into all the languages of Europe.[6] Beccaria based the legitimacy of criminal sanctions on the **social contract.** The authority of making laws rested with the legislator, who should have only one view in sight: "the greatest happiness of the greatest number." Beccaria also saw punishment as a necessary evil, and suggested that "it should be public, immediate, and necessary; the least possible in the case given; proportioned to the crime; and determined by the laws."[7] He then defined the purpose and consequences of punishment as being "to deter persons from the commission of crime and not to provide social revenge. Not severity, but certainty and swiftness in punishment best secure this result."[8]

In 1780, the Englishman Jeremy Bentham published *An Introduction to the Principles of Morals and Legislation,* which further developed the philosophy of the classical school. Believing that a rational person would do what was necessary to achieve the most pleasure and the least pain, Bentham contended that punishment would deter criminal behavior, provided it was made appropriate to the crime. He stated that punishment has four objectives: (1) to prevent all offenses if possible, (2) to persuade a person who has decided to commit an offense to commit a less rather than a more serious one, (3) "to dispose [a person who has resolved upon a particular offense] to do no more mischief than is necessary to his purpose," and (4) to prevent the crime at as cheap a cost to society as possible.[9]

The basic theoretical constructs of the classical school of criminology were developed from the writings of Beccaria and Bentham: First, human beings were looked on as rational creatures who, being free to choose their actions, could be held responsible for their behavior. This doctrine of **free will** was substituted for the widely accepted concept of theological determinism, which saw humans as predestined to certain actions. Second, punishment was justified because of its practical usefulness, or **utilitarianism.** No longer was punishment acceptable on the grounds of vengeful retaliation or as expiation on the basis of superstitious theories of guilt and repayment. The aim of punishment was the protection of society, and its dominant theme was deterrence. Third, the human being was presumed to be a creature governed by a **felicific calculus** oriented toward obtaining a favorable balance of pleasure and pain. Fourth, a rational scale of punishment was proposed that should be painful enough to deter the criminal from further offenses and to prevent others from following his or her example of crime. Fifth, sanctions should be proclaimed in advance of their use; these sanctions should be proportionate to the offense and should outweigh the rewards of crime. Sixth, equal justice should be offered to everyone. Finally, proponents of the classical school urged that individuals should be judged by the law solely for their acts, not for their beliefs.

According to the principles of the classical school, then, juveniles (such as Billy) who commit serious crimes or continue to break the law are presumed to deserve punishment rather than treatment, because they possess free will and know what they are doing. Their delinquencies are viewed as purposeful activity resulting from rational decisions in which the pros and cons are weighed and the acts that promise the greatest potential gains are performed.[10] See Theory and Research 3.1 for the influence of the Classical School in the moderation of punishment.

The Insights Positivism Offers to the Understanding of Delinquency

Beginning with a brief introduction to the theoretical constructs of the positive school, the biological and psychological explanations of delinquency and crime are examined in this section.

THEORY AND RESEARCH 3.1

The Classical School and the Moderation of Punishment

Until the eighteenth century, punishments were very severe. About two hundred crimes were punishable by death. It was not unusual for rulers who felt that their nation was under attack by internal dissidents to order mass executions. Mass executions could also be used when particular crimes seemed to be a problem. For example, during the reign of Henry VIII in England, more than 72,000 thieves were hanged. During the reign of Elizabeth I, "vagabonds were strung up in rows, as many as three or four hundred at a time."

The Enlightenment was an eighteenth-century European philosophical movement characterized by rationalism, skepticism in social and political thought, an impetus toward learning, and moderation in punishment. During the Enlightenment, the explanations of crime based on sin and demons were being replaced by explanations focusing on rationality, individual responsibility, and free choice. Philosophers were advocating the primacy of the rights of the individual over those of the state. Enlightenment thinkers were particularly indignant at the injustice of the criminal law in its widespread use of torture, corporal punishment, and the death penalty. They blamed these brutal measures on authorities' lack of regard for human life.

The philosophical ideas that underlie the adult justice system and are increasingly influential in the juvenile justice system can be traced to three Enlightenment philosophers: Charles de Secondat, Baron de Montesquieu; Cesare Bonesana Beccaria; and Jeremy Bentham. All three of these classical thinkers wrote about the need to moderate punishment. They saw much of what was taking place with criminal offenders as barbaric, and they advocated measures that would replace severity of punishment with certainty and swiftness in punishment.

If the classical school emphasized the moderation of punishment, and was perceived as radical in its day, why then are proponents of the rational approach viewed as conservatives today? Can proponents of rationality in crime contribute to reform of the juvenile justice system as they did to that of the adult system three centuries ago?

Source: Clemens Bartollas, *Invitation to Corrections* (Boston: Allyn and Bacon, 2002), pp. 28–29, 32.

Development of Positivism

According to positivism, human behavior is but one more facet of a universe that is part of a natural order, but human beings can study behavior and discover how natural laws operate. Two positions diverge at this point of natural law. One view states that, since a natural order with its own laws exists, changing human behavior is impossible. The other view is that, just as laws operate in the medical, biological, and physical sciences, laws govern human behavior, and these laws can be understood and used. The causes of human behavior, once discovered, can be modified to eliminate or ameliorate many of society's problems. This second position is the one most scientists accept. The concept, as it applies to juvenile justice, is called **positivism.**

Positivism became the dominant philosophical perspective of juvenile justice at the time the juvenile court was established at the beginning of the twentieth century. During the Progressive Era (the period from about 1890 to 1920), the wave of optimism that swept through U.S. society led to the acceptance of positivism. The doctrines of the emerging social sciences assured reformers that through positivism their problems could be solved. The initial step was to gather all the facts of the case. Equipped with these data, reformers were then expected to analyze the issues in scientific fashion and discover the right solution.[11]

Armed with these principles, reformers set out to deal with the problem of delinquency, confident that they knew how to find its cause. **Progressives** looked first to environmental factors, pinpointing poverty as the major cause of delinquency. Some progressives were attracted also to the doctrine of eugenics and believed that the biological limitations of youthful offenders drove them to delinquency. But eventually the psychological origins of delinquency came to be more widely accepted than either the environmental or biological origins.[12]

Positivism is based on three basic assumptions.[13] First, the character and personal backgrounds of individuals explain delinquent behavior. Positivism, relegating the law and its administration to a secondary role, looks for the cause of deviancy in the actor.

Second, the existence of scientific determinism is a critical assumption of positivism. Delinquency, like any other phenomenon, is seen as determined by prior causes; it does not just happen. Because of this deterministic position, positivism rejects the view that the individual exercises freedom, possesses reason, and is capable of choice.

Third, the delinquent is seen as fundamentally different from the nondelinquent. The task then is to identify the factors that have made the delinquent a different kind of person. In attempting to explain this difference, positivism has concluded that wayward youths are driven into crime by something in their physical makeup, by aberrant psychological impulses, or by the meanness and harshness of their social environment.[14]

Early Theories of Biological Positivism

The belief in a biological explanation for criminality has a long history. Physiognomy, which suggests that one's physical appearance betrays a predisposition toward brutality or crime, was developed by the ancient Greeks. Indeed, a physiognomist charged that Socrates had a face that reflected a brutal nature.[15]

The attention given to **biological positivism** in the United States may be divided into two periods. The first period was characterized by the nature–nurture debate during the latter part of the nineteenth century and the early twentieth century. Lombroso's theory of physical anomalies, genealogical studies, and theories of human somatotypes, or body types, represent early approaches relating crime and delinquency to biological factors.

LOMBROSO AND BIOLOGICAL POSITIVISM   Cesare Lombroso frequently regarded as the founder of biological positivism, is best known for the theory of the atavistic criminal. According to Lombroso, the atavistic, or **born criminal,** was a reversion to an earlier evolutionary form or level; that is, the characteristics of primitive men periodically reappeared in certain individuals.[16] Lombroso claimed that he discovered the secret of criminal behavior when he was examining the skull of the notorious criminal Vihella:

> This was not merely an idea, but a flash of inspiration. At the sight of that skull, I seemed to see all of a sudden, lighted up as a vast plain under a flaming sky, the problem of the nature of the criminal—an atavistic being who reproduces in his person the ferocious instincts of primitive humanity and the inferior animals. Thus were explained anatomically the enormous jaws, high cheek bones, prominent superciliary arches, solitary lines in the palms, extreme size of the orbits, handle-shaped or sensile ears found in criminals, savages, and apes, insensibility to pain, extremely acute sight, tattooing, excessive idleness, love of orgies, and the irresistible craving for evil for its own sake, the desire not only to extinguish life in the victim, but to mutilate the corpse, tear its flesh, and drink its blood.[17]

Initially, Lombroso insisted that all criminals or delinquents were born criminals, but study of several thousand criminals led him to modify his theory. In 1897, by the time of the fifth edition of his book *L'Uomo Delinquente,* he had reduced his estimate of the percentage of born criminals to 40 percent. He eventually concluded that environment was more responsible for crime than was atavism. He also identified a continuum of "criminaloids"—individuals who fell between atavistic and other types of criminals.[18]

Lombroso's theory of the atavistic criminal has not stood the test of scientific investigation. Enrico Ferri, one of Lombroso's students, found that 63 percent of Italian soldiers showed some of the same physical signs of degeneration.[19] Furthermore, Charles Goring, in a study of 3,000 English convicts, along with students and sailors serving as controls, concluded that his results did not confirm Lombroso's assertions concerning the atavistic, or biologically inferior, criminal.[20]

Yet Lombroso did make two significant contributions to the study of juvenile delinquency. He provided the impetus to study the individual offender rather than the crimes committed by the person. His manner of studying the criminal, which involved control groups and a desire to have his theories tested impartially, also influenced the development of the scientific method.

GENEALOGICAL STUDIES AND DELINQUENCY   In 1877, Richard Dugdale did a detailed genealogical study of the Jukes family, covering some 1,200 individuals and spanning nearly a century. He documented an extensive theory of "pauperism, prostitution, exhaustion, disease, fornication, and illegitimacy."[21] In 1913, Henry H. Goddard conducted another now well-known genealogical study in a training school in New Jersey for "feebleminded" boys and girls. On investigating the family history of one of the wards, Deborah Kallikak, Goddard discovered that she was a descendant of a brief union between a Revolutionary War soldier and a feebleminded girl. He was able to locate 484 descendants of this union, of whom 143 were feebleminded and several were alcoholics and prostitutes. Impressed by these findings, Goddard concluded that "bad stock" was the cause of feeblemindedness and that such persons should not be permitted to reproduce.[22]

 These recommendations received little support, but Goddard's finding that at least half of all juvenile delinquents were mentally defective sparked intense debate for over a decade.[23] William Healy and Augusta Bronner were supporters of the correlation between low intelligence and delinquent behavior. In 1926 they tested a group of delinquents in Chicago and Boston and concluded that delinquents were five to ten times more likely to be mentally deficient than were nondelinquents.[24] But the findings of John Slawson and Edwin Sutherland discouraged future investigations of the correlation between intelligence and delinquency. Slawson, studying 1,543 delinquent boys in New York City, found that delinquents were about normal in mechanical aptitude and nonverbal intelligence and lower in abstract verbal intelligence. He also found that no relationships existed among the number of arrests, the types of offenses, and IQ.[25] Edwin Sutherland, evaluating IQ studies of delinquents and criminals, concluded that the lower IQs of offenders were related more to testing methods and scoring than to the offenders' actual mental abilities.[26]

BODY TYPE THEORIES OF DELINQUENCY   Ernst Kretscher, a German, first developed the theory that there are two body types, the cyclothyme and the schizothyme. Schizothymes are strong and muscular, and they are more likely to be delinquent than are cyclothymes, who are soft-skinned and lack muscle.[27]

William Sheldon, author of *Varieties of Delinquent Youth*, was the first U.S. researcher to examine the relationship between body type and delinquent behavior. Sheldon described three body types: *endomorphic* (soft, round, and fat); *mesomorphic* (bony, muscular, and athletic); and *ectomorphic* (tall, thin, and fragile). Sheldon postulated that these somatotypes had temperamental correlates. He investigated with great thoroughness 200 delinquent boys whose ages ranged from fifteen to twenty-four years. He found that the delinquents were more likely to be mesomorphic and less likely to be ectomorphic. The temperamental correlations with mesomorphy pertained to such characteristics as social assertiveness, lesser submissiveness to authority, and less-inhibited motor responses.[28]

Sheldon's work came under intense criticism soon after its publication. He was criticized for numerous flaws in his research, including sampling defects and lack of reliability in the assignment of youths to the three groups. Critics also charged that using photographs was too subjective to inspire confidence in its accuracy. But perhaps most damaging was that Sheldon's definition of delinquency—which he vaguely defined as "disappointingness"—made its measurement nearly impossible.

Sheldon Glueck and Eleanor T. Glueck's *Physique and Delinquency* was the result of comprehensive research into persistent delinquency. They studied the causes of delinquency through a comparison of 500 persistent delinquents and 500 nondelinquents. Their comparison indicated marked and significant differences in their somatotypes (60.1 percent of the delinquents were mesomorphic as compared to 30.7 percent of the nondelinquents). "Among the delinquents, mesomorphy is far and away the most dominant component," they found, "with ectomorphic, endomorphic, and balanced types about equally represented but in relatively minor strength."[29]

Juan B. Cortes and Florence M. Gatti drew on body type theory to develop a biopsychosocial theory of delinquency. Yet they criticized the Gluecks' study for the following reason: All the delinquents studied were committed to correctional institutions; accordingly, the results may apply to institutionalized delinquents but not necessarily to delinquents in general. They also questioned the reliability of the methods used to estimate the somatotype. Furthermore, the age of the 500 delinquents ranged from nine to seventeen years, with an average age of fourteen years and six months; the problem with somatotyping youths this age is the general acceleration of growth and morphological changes.[30]

Sociobiology, or Contemporary Biological Positivism

Sociobiology stresses the interaction between the biological factors within an individual and the influence of the particular environment. Supporters claim that what produces delinquent behavior, like other behaviors, is a combination of genetic traits and social conditions. Recent advances in experimental behavior genetics, human population genetics, the biochemistry of the nervous system, experimental and clinical endocrinology and neurophysiology, and other related areas have led to more sophisticated knowledge of the way in which the environment and human genetics interact to affect the growth, development, and functioning of the human organism.[31]

The relationship between twins and adoption, intelligence, physique, neuropsychological and learning and behavioral disabilities are examined in the following section.

TWINS AND ADOPTIONS   The role of genetic influences has been suggested by a number of twins and adoption studies.[32] The comparison of identical (MZ—monozygotic) and same-sex fraternal (DZ—dizygotic) twins provides the most comprehensive data for exploring genetic influences on human variation. Identical twins develop from a single fertilized egg that divides into two embryos; hence their genes are the same. Fraternal twins develop from two separate eggs that were both fertilized during the act of conception; hence about half their genes are the same. Early in the twentieth century, it was reasoned that with the studies of twins, hereditary influences on behavior could be accurately determined by comparing concordance rates of behavior (concordance refers to the agreement in behavior outcome between pairs of individuals) of identical and fraternal twins. If heredity influences behavior more than environment, identical twins should have higher concordance rates than fraternal twins do.[33]

Karl O. Christiansen reported on a sample of 3,586 twin pairs from the Danish Twin Register, a complete listing of twins born in Denmark between 1870 and 1920. The subset used by these researchers included almost all the twins born between 1881 and 1910 in a certain region of Denmark. Criminal justice statistics turned up 926 offenses for the 7,172 twins, coming from 799 twin pairs. The probability of finding a criminal twin when the other twin was a criminal was .5 for MZ twins and .21 for DZ (same sex) twins. Although the concordances (i.e. both twins showing the same trait) in this study were lower than in earlier surveys, they were still significant and indicated a genetic contribution to criminal behavior.[34]

Thomas Bouchard Jr. examines three large data sets to determine what is known about the heritability of five basic personality traits: extroversion, neuroticism, agreeableness, conscientiousness, and openness.[35] He found that a common environment explained very little variance in these studies, but that the genetic inheritance explained 51 percent of the variance in these early twin studies and 42 percent and 46 percent in the two other studies. According to Bouchard, the conclusion is straightforward: "The similarity we see in the personality between biological relatives is almost entirely genetic in origin."[36]

In another recent article, Robert Plomin, Michael Owen, and Peter McGuffin summarize the relationship between identical and nonidentical twins exhibiting medical disorders, behavioral disorders, and different abilities. They conclude that a strong genetic component appears to be present with a wide range of disorders and abilities and that a wide variation in the importance of genetics also seems to be evident among the disorders and abilities considered.[37]

The largest systematic adoption study of criminality is one based on all nonfamilial adoptions in Denmark from 1924 to 1947. This sample included 14,427 male and female adoptees and their biological and adoptive parents. After exclusions—because criminal records or other kinds of demographic information were missing—the analysis involved no fewer than 10,000 parents in the four parental categories (i.e., biological/adoptive, mother/father) and more than 13,000 adoptees. The parents were counted as criminal if either the mother or father had a criminal conviction. Of those boys who had neither adoptive nor biological criminal parents, 13.5 percent had at least one conviction. The percentage rose slightly to 14.7 if adoptive (but not biological) parents were criminal; if biological (but not adoptive) parents were criminal, 20 percent of the boys had at least one conviction. Boys with both adoptive and biological criminal parents had the highest proportion, 24.5 percent. Christiansen concluded that criminality of the biological parents is more important than that of the adoptive parents, a finding that suggests genetic transmission of some factor or factors associated with crime.[38]

In sum, the evidence of these and other studies of twins and adoptions is impressive. However, the twin method does have a number of weaknesses. The differences in MZ and DZ twin similarity tell us about genetic involvement only to the extent that the MZ–DZ difference is not related to environmental differences; the small number of twin pairs make adequate statistical comparisons difficult; it is not always easy to determine if twins are monozygotic or dizygotic; and official definitions of crime and delinquency, with all their limitations, are exclusively used.[39]

INTELLIGENCE　　With the growing acceptance of sociobiology in the 1960s and 1970s, intelligence was again examined as a factor in delinquent behavior. D. J. West and D. P. Farrington, in conducting a longitudinal study of 411 English boys, found that those who later became criminals were characterized by lower IQs than were those who did not. The authors concluded that intelligence is a meaningful predictive factor of future delinquency.[40] Lis Kirkegaard-Sorensen and Sarnoff A. Mednick also conducted a longitudinal study on the value of adolescent intelligence test scores for the prediction of later criminality. They found that adolescents who committed criminal acts later had a lower tested intelligence score than their more law-abiding peers.[41] Robert A. Gordon, in comparing delinquency prevalence rates and delinquency incidence rates, concluded that minority juvenile males had higher arrest rates and court appearance rates than white males or females, regardless of any specific geographical location, rural or urban. He proposed that differences in IQ may provide the greatest explanation of these persistent differences in unlawful behavior.[42] In another paper, Gordon stated that lower "IQ was always more successful in accounting for the black–white differences [in crime] than income, education, or occupational status."[43]

Travis Hirschi and Michael Hindelang reexamined a number of research studies— Hirschi's 1969 data from California, Marvin Wolfgang and associates' Philadelphia data, and Joseph Weis's data from the state of Washington—and found that "the weight of evidence is that IQ is more important than race and social class" for predicting delinquency. These researchers also rejected the contention that IQ tests are race- and class-biased in that they favor middle-class whites and are therefore invalid means of comparing lower- and middle-class youths. They concluded that low IQ affects school performance, resulting in an increased likelihood of delinquent behavior.[44] James Q. Wilson and Richard J. Herrnstein further contended that there is an inverse relationship between intelligence and certain types of adult criminality.[45]

Sociologists thought that the IQ issue was dead in the mid 1930s, when the studies consistently challenged the relationship between IQ and delinquency, but recent studies have resurrected the issue. Unquestionably, whatever the correlation between IQ and delinquency, the association is strengthened by other environmental factors, such as school performance.[46]

NEUROPSYCHOLOGICAL FACTORS AND DELINQUENCY　　Some neuropsychological factors appear to be more directly related to delinquent behavior than others. Studies by Hans Eysenck on the autonomic nervous system have received wide attention. Eysenck's theory of the **autonomic nervous system,** like body type theory, has its origins in the earlier attempts to understand the relationship between constitutional factors and delinquency. But his sociobiological theory goes one step further in noting the interaction of both biological and environmental factors. Eysenck contends that some children are more difficult to condition morally than others because of the inherited sensitivity of their autonomic nervous systems. He argues that types of individuals range from those in whom it is easy to excite conditioned reflexes and whose reflexes are difficult to inhibit to those whose reflexes are difficult to condition and easy to extinguish. Yet the moral conditioning of the child also depends on the quality of the conditioning the child receives within the family.[47]

Individuals whose autonomic nervous systems are more difficult to condition tend to be extroverts rather than introverts. Extroverts are much more likely, according to Eysenck, to welcome involvement in delinquent behavior. He sees extroverts as people who crave excitement, take chances, act on the spur of the moment, and frequently are impulsive. He also believes that extroverts tend to be aggressive and lose their temper quickly, are unable to keep their feelings under control, and are not always reliable.[48] Eysenck's theory has come under extensive criticism, especially his research techniques, but the research on the organic sources of behavioral disorders appears to be much more promising.[49]

Diana H. Fishbein and Robert W. Thatcher argue that electroencephalographic (EEG) abnormalities have been significantly correlated with individuals who are at risk for antisocial and aggressive behavior.[50] R. R. Monroe found abnormal EEGs in 41 percent of aggressive recidivists, whereas the general population has an incidence of 10 to 15 percent.[51] W. W. Surwillo claimed that abnormal EEGs are found in 48 to 70 percent of aggressive psychopaths.[52]

Fishbein and Thatcher report that computerized electroencephalographic equipment can now measure the adequacy of neural processing. They contend that an examination of EEG measures provides the hope of early detention and intervention for children with abnormal EEGs before behavioral problems develop. The dynamic interaction among physiology, biochemistry, environment, and behavior, then, can be identified by factors that have negative effects on brain development and functioning.[53]

Terrie E. Moffitt, Donald R. Lynam, and Phil A. Silva, in their examination of the neuropsychological status of several hundred New Zealand males between the ages of thirteen and eighteen, found that poor neuropsychological scores "were associated with early onset of delinquency" but were "unrelated to delinquency that began in adolescence."[54] Moffitt's developmental theory views delinquency as proceeding along two developmental paths. On one path, children develop a lifelong path of delinquency and crime at an age as early as three. They may begin to bite and hit at age 4, shoplift and be truant at age 10, sell drugs and steal cars at age 16, rob and rape at age 22, and commit fraud and child abuse at age 30.[55] These "life-course-persistent" (LCP) delinquents, according to Moffitt, continue their illegal acts throughout the conditions and situations they face. During childhood, they may also exhibit such neuropsychological problems as deficit disorders or hyperactivity and learning problems in schools.[56]

On the other path, the majority of delinquents begin offending during the adolescent years and desist from delinquent behaviors around the eighteenth birthday. Moffitt refers to these youthful offenders as "adolescent-limited" (AL) delinquents. The early and persistent problems found with members of the LCP group are not found with the AL delinquents. Yet the frequency of offending and even the violence of offending during the adolescent years may be as high as the LCP. Moffitt notes that the AL antisocial behavior is learned from peers and sustained through peer-based rewards and reinforcements. ALs continue in delinquent acts as long as such behaviors appear profitable or rewarding to them, but they have the ability to abandon those behaviors when prosocial styles become more rewarding.[57] See Theory and Research 3.2 for an interview with Terrie E. Moffitt.

Numerous studies have found that violent criminal offenders may have neuropsychological impairments.[58] An underlying contention of these studies, according to Elizabeth Kandel and Sarnoff A. Mednick, is that developmental deficits, in turn, may "predispose affected children to aggressive or violent behavior."[59] There is some evidence that pregnancy and birth complications may result in fetal brain damage, predisposing a child to impulsive and aggressive behavior.[60] For example, Kandel and Mednick's study of a Danish birth cohort found that "delivery events predicted adult violent offending, especially in high-risk subjects and recidivistically violent offenders."[61]

TEMPERAMENT A child's temperament is hard to define but can more easily be identified by the behaviors associated with it. Activity and emotionality are two of these behaviors. Activity refers to gross motor movements, such as the movement of arms and legs, crawling, or walking. Children who exhibit an inordinate amount of movement compared with peers are sometimes labeled "hyperactive" or having an **attention deficit disorder** (usually referred to as **attention deficit hyperactivity disorder** or **ADHD**). **Emotionality** ranges from very little reaction to intense emotional reactions that are out of control.

The hyperactive child remains a temperamental mystery. This child's three behaviors are inattention (is easily distracted and does not want to listen), impulsivity (shifts quickly from one activity to another), and excessive motor activity (cannot sit still, runs about, is talkative, and noisy). Educators note that ADHD children have difficulty stay-

THEORY AND RESEARCH 3.2

Interview with Terrie E. Moffitt

Question: What do you feel are the best features of developmental theory as you and colleagues have developed it?

Moffitt: We proposed that people who engage in delinquent and offending behavior should be viewed as falling into two main patterns, life-course persistent and adolescence-limited. I think one of the main advantages of this two-group approach is that it accounts for the known "big facts" about antisocial behavior's relations with age, sex, and social class. The two-group approach also explains why some correlates of antisocial behavior appear, disappear, and reappear across the life-course. For example, low social class, reading difficulties, and genetic risk are all strong correlates of antisocial behavior during childhood and adulthood, but not during adolescence. Conversely, peer influences on antisocial behavior are strong during adolescence, but not during childhood and adulthood. If two different kinds of people take part in antisocial behavior at different developmental stages, that would explain these curious "disappearing" findings. Finally, the two-group approach focuses attention on different intervention plans needed to prevent early-onset versus late-onset delinquency.

Question: Do you see any areas that need to be expanded or reformulated?

Moffitt: One aspect that clearly needs to be expanded is the number of offender groups. The original theory proposed only two, life-course persistent and adolescence-limited. But subsequently researchers have tested for the correct number of groups needed to account for the delinquent activity in representative samples. From this work a third group of offenders has emerged: the "low-level chronics." In my own longitudinal study this group was highly aggressive in childhood, but then was only minimally involved in delinquency during adolescence. As adults, the group emerged as steady low-level chronic offenders. They are very unusual males, because they are socially isolated, have many fears and phobias, lack friendships or female partners, and have low intelligence and low-status jobs, or no jobs. David Farrington's London longitudinal study finds the same low-level chronic offenders who are poorly functioning social isolates. We need to know more about them.

Question: How did you come to be involved in the formulation of this theory?

Moffitt: I was taught an important lesson by the birth cohort of 1000 young New Zealanders we followed as they grew up. In the 1980's, when the cohort were children, my students and I found there were not many antisocial study members, but their antisocial behavior had many strong correlates, such as difficult temperament, harsh parenting, and low IQ. We published lots of papers about this. When we recontacted the cohort in the 1990's at age 15 to collect more data from them, we found many more study members had taken up antisocial behavior. We were pleased about that because we now had more delinquents to study. However, we found that all the former correlates of antisocial behavior had suddenly dropped to non-significance. What a surprise! Because we had nothing to publish, we had to find an explanation for these disappearing findings! This motivated me to brainstorm about why more participants in delinquency would be associated with disappearing correlates of delinquency. While thinking about this puzzle, I remembered my own experience of school. In my primary school, there were some really bad kids that my good-student friends and I were afraid of, but by junior high school, many of us began to hang out with those bad kids and got into a fair amount of serious trouble ourselves. After high school, my good-student friends and I have moved on to be more successful. I wondered if this small-town story applied to young people more widely, and apparently it does.

Question: Have you been encouraged or discouraged by the response that the theory has received?

Moffitt: I am delighted that so many people have found this simple two-group theory worthy of their attention, and I am even overwhelmed by this. This taxonomy of childhood versus adolescent onset antisocial behavior is codified in the American Psychiatric Association's guidelines for diagnosing conduct disorders (DSM-IV, 1994), and has been invoked in the National Institute of Mental Health Factsheet on Child and Adolescent Violence (2000) and the Surgeon General's report on Youth Violence (2001). The original paper that proposed the two prototypes and their different etiologies appeared about ten years ago (Moffitt, 1993) and in the seven years since it has been cited by readers more than 600 times in their own papers, which is a high compliment. Several research

(continued)

teams in nine countries have tested hypotheses put forward from the theory. Most of the research teams have reported findings that are consistent with the theory, but some have pointed to important issues that need to be resolved. For example, a Baltimore study found that the theory fit young African American men better than young white men, but a California study found the theory did not fit African American men at all. Obviously, this needs more work! It is exciting that the theory is stimulating so much research activity and debate, and I'm pleased that it can make this contribution. Most criminologists now think about human development, and this is quite gratifying to me.

What new insights about developmental theory are found in this interview? What does it mean to think in terms of human development? How do you evaluate Moffitt and colleagues' developmental theory?

Source: Terrie E. Moffitt is professor of psychology at the University of Wisconsin. She does lifespan longitudinal research with large samples in field settings. Her research topics include (1) natural history of antisocial behavior from childhood to adulthood, (2) etiology of conduct disorder, juvenile delinquency, and antisocial personality disorder, (3) interactionist approaches to psychopathology, (4) longitudinal research methodology, (5) neuropsychological assessment, and neurobehavioral disorders. Interviewed in February 2002.

ing on task, sustaining academic achievement in the school setting, remaining cognitively organized, and maintaining control over their behavior.[62]

Psychological Positivism

Psychological factors have long been popular in the study of juvenile delinquency because the very nature of the *parens patriae* philosophy requires treatment of wayward youth. Psychoanalytic theory was first most widely used with delinquents, but more recently other behavioral and humanistic schools of psychology have been applied to the problem of youth crime.

PSYCHOANALYTIC EXPLANATIONS OF DELINQUENT BEHAVIOR   Sigmund Freud, in developing **psychoanalysis,** contributed three insights that have shaped the handling of juvenile delinquents: (1) the personality is made up of three components; (2) all normal children pass through three psychosexual stages of development; and (3) a person's personality traits are developed in early childhood.

Freud's theory of the personality involves the id, the ego, and the superego. The id has to do with the person's raw instincts and primitive drives; it wants immediate gratification of its needs and therefore tends to be primitive and savage. The ego and superego, the other two components, have the express purpose of controlling the primitive drives of the id. The ego mediates between the id and superego and is important in the socialization of the child. The superego, or the conscience, internalizes the rules of society. Thus as a child develops, he or she learns to distinguish socially acceptable behavior from socially unacceptable behavior.[63]

Freud identified the oral, anal, and phallic stages as the life stages that shape personality development. The first stage, the oral one, is experienced by the newborn infant. Pleasure is experienced in this stage through eating, sucking, and chewing. In the anal stage, which takes place between one and three years of age, urinary and bowel movements replace sucking as the basic source of pleasure for the child. During the phallic stage, which takes place in normal children between the ages three to six, the child receives pleasure from the genitals. Each stage brings increased social demands on the child and affects the way in which he or she deals with basic, innate drives. The sexual and aggressive drives, in particular, create tensions that a child must learn to resolve in socially acceptable ways.[64]

Freud also argued that by age five, all the essential ingredients of a child's adult personality are determined. What a child has experienced emotionally by the age of five affects that child for the rest of his or her life. Emotional traumas experienced in childhood are likely to cause lifelong psychological problems.[65] Delinquency across the life course, according to this position, is continually affected by what a person has experienced as a young child.

Freud's followers have identified four ways in which emotional problems that develop in childhood might lead to delinquent behavior.[66] First, delinquent behavior is related to neurotic development in the personality. Freud established a relationship between desire and behavior; that is, everything is integrated in the subconscious drives of the organism. A youth may feel guilty about a socially unacceptable desire and, as a result, seek out self-defeating behaviors.

Second, Freudians attribute delinquent behavior to a defective superego. The failure to develop a normally functioning superego can result in the inability to feel guilt, to learn from experience, or to feel affection toward others.[67] Such individuals, sometimes called sociopathic or psychopathic, may constantly express aggressive and antisocial behavior toward others.

Third, violent delinquent behavior is sometimes explained by the tendency of children with an overdeveloped superego to repress all negative emotional feelings throughout childhood to the degree that these repressed feelings explode in a violent act in adolescence. So-called model adolescents occasionally become involved in violent crimes toward parents and neighbors, sometimes horribly mutilating their victims.[68]

Fourth, delinquent involvements can be related to a search for compensatory gratification. According to Freud, individuals who were deprived at an early age of development later seek the gratification they missed. An adolescent may become an alcoholic to satisfy an oral craving or may become sadistic because of poor toilet training received during the anal period.

A number of individuals have taken the insights of psychoanalysis and applied them to the situations of delinquents. William Healy's particular adaptation of psychoanalytic theory focused on mental conflicts that originated in unsatisfactory family relationships. Healy pioneered the establishment of psychiatric child guidance clinics in several U.S. cities under the auspices of the Commonwealth Fund Program for the Prevention of Delinquency. Although Healy specified that such mental conflicts originated in the child's family relationships, he also realized the importance of the community in modifying delinquent behavior.[69]

August Aichhorn, another proponent of psychoanalytic theory, also worked extensively with youths in trouble. Aichhorn thought that delinquents had considerable hatred toward their parents because of the conflictual nature of the family relationship and that they transferred this hatred toward parents to other authority figures. He believed that institutionalized delinquents, exposed to the love and acceptance of a therapeutic relationship, would learn to trust one adult figure and, in turn, would learn to respond more appropriately to other adults.[70]

Kate Friedlander provided another psychoanalytic approach to treating delinquents. She focused on the development of antisocial characteristics in the personality, such as selfishness, impulsiveness, and irresponsibility, which she defined as the results of disturbed ego development in early childhood. According to Friedlander, delinquency is an alternative way to fulfill desires the youth is unwilling to express directly.[71]

SENSATION SEEKING AND DELINQUENCY   Sensation seeking can be defined "as an individual's need for varied, novel and complex sensations and experiences and the willingness to take physical and social risks for the sake of such experience."[72] Derived from optimal arousal theory, this construct assumes that organisms are driven or motivated to obtain an optimal level of arousal.[73]

Other observers have also noted that delinquency is an enjoyable activity. Frederick Thrasher thought that a "sport motive" was more important in stealing than a desire for material gain.[74] Henry McKay, Paul Tappan, and Albert Cohen described delinquency as a form of play.[75] J. Tobias found that middle- and upper-middle-class offenders mention boredom as a major reason for engaging in delinquent acts and that they usually discount the need for money as a contributing factor.[76]

More recently, the relationship between sensation seeking and crime has received frequent attention. M. J. Hindelang found that delinquents are more pleasure seeking than are nondelinquents.[77] Helene Raskin White, Erich W. Labouvie, and Marsha E. Bates found that both male and female delinquents have higher rates of sensation seeking and lower rates of inhibited behavior than nondelinquents.[78] A number of ethnographic studies of criminals have found that sensation seeking was an important factor in explaining their criminality.[79] For example, Walter R. Gove and colleagues found from their study of inmates in a medium-security prison that inmates most frequently cited sensation seeking as an important motive for the crimes of shoplifting, burglary, robbery, assault, and rape. When inmates were asked how they felt when committing a crime, "being on a high" was most frequently reported, especially with violent crimes.[80] According to this study, "being on a high" was conceptualized as "powerful, pumped up, living on the edge, on a 'high' or rush, intensely alive, and able to do anything."[81]

Jack Katz's controversial book, *Seduction of Crime*, conjectures that when individuals commit a crime, they become involved in "an emotional process—seductions and compulsions that have special dynamics." It is this "magical" and "transformative" experience that makes crime "sensible," even "sensually compelling." For example, he states that for many adolescents, shoplifting and vandalism offer "the attractions of a thrilling

Youth confined in a correctional setting. He is looking out beyond the chain link fence wondering how his life could be in such chaos.

melodrama," because "quite apart from what is taken, they may regard 'getting away with it' as a thrilling demonstration of personal competence, especially if it is accomplished under the eyes of adults."[82]

Katz is arguing that instead of approaching criminal or delinquent behavior from the traditional focus on background factors, what needs more consideration are the foreground or situational factors that directly precipitate antisocial acts and reflect crimes' sensuality. According to Katz, offenders' immediate social environment and experiences encourage them to construct crimes as sensually compelling.[83]

PERSONALITY AND CRIME   **Trait-based personality models** in recent years have gained popularity as an essential personality construct.[84] Traits represent characteristics of individuals that are relevant to a wide variety of behavioral domains, including delinquency and criminality.[85]

Glueck and Glueck's study *Unraveling Juvenile Delinquency* examined a sample of 500 juvenile offenders and 500 nonoffenders in an effort to discover significant distinctions in the personality traits of the two groups. The Gluecks found that the delinquents were more defiant, ambivalent about authority, extroverted, fearful of failure, resentful, hostile, suspicious, and defensive than the nondelinquents. The Rorschach test (which is used to determine personality structure through subjects' interpretations of ink blots) was used as the basis of the Gluecks' assessment.[86]

J. J. Conger and W. C. Miller, in a longitudinal study of male delinquents using all the boys entering the tenth grade in Denver, Colorado public schools in 1956, found that by the age of fifteen, delinquents could be differentiated from nondelinquents either by the standard personality tests or by teacher evaluations. Delinquents, on the average, were characterized as emotionally unstable, impulsive, suspicious, hostile, given to petty expressions of irritation, egocentric, and typically more unhappy, worried, and dissatisfied than their nondelinquent counterparts.[87]

Eysenck found that crime could be associated with extreme individual values on the personality factors of extroversion, neuroticism, and psychoticism.[88] Marvin Zuckerman contended that offenders are high on a factor he calls "P-ImpUSS," which is characterized by lack of responsibility, impulsivity, and aggressiveness.[89] In addition, C. Robert Cloninger contended that individuals high in novelty seeking and low in harm avoidance and reward dependence are likely to be delinquents today and criminals tomorrow.[90]

Avshalom Caspi and colleagues recently examined the personality traits of youthful offenders in New Zealand and Pittsburgh and found that "the personality correlates of delinquency were robust in different nations, in different age cohorts, across gender, and across race."[91] They added that "greater delinquent participation was associated with a personality configuration characterized by high Negative Emotionality and weak Constraint."[92] They concluded that "negative emotions may be translated more readily into antisocial acts when Negative Emotionality (the tendency to experience aversive affective states) is accompanied by weak Constraint (difficulty in impulse control)."[93]

Joshua D. Miller and Donald Lynam, in their meta-analytic analysis of the basic models of personality, identified certain personality traits that are more characteristic of antisocial personalities. These traits are hostility, self-centeredness, spitefulness, jealousy, and indifference to others. These antisocial individuals also typically lack ambition, perseverance, and motivation; hold nontraditional and unconventional values and beliefs (i.e., are low in Conscientiousness) and have difficulty controlling their impulses.[94]

THE PSYCHOPATH   The psychopath (also known as the **sociopath**, antisocial personality, person with a conduct disorder, and a host of other names) is acknowledged as the personality of the hard-core juvenile delinquent. The claim is made that these are chiefly the unwanted, rejected children, who grow up but remain undomesticated "children" and never develop trust in or loyalty to other adults.[95] Hervey Cleckley gave the most complete clinical description of this type of personality. He indicated that the psychopath is charming and of good intelligence; is not delusional or irrational; is unreliable; is insecure and can not be trusted; lacks shame and remorse; will commit all kinds of misdeeds for astonishingly small stakes, and sometimes for no reason at all; has poor judgment; never learns from experience; will repeat over and over again patterns of self-defeating behavior; has no real capacity for love; lacks insight; does not respond to consideration, kindness, or trust; and shows a consistent inability to make or follow any sort of life plan.[96]

The continuity between childhood symptoms of emotional problems and adult behavior emerged in L. N. Robins's thirty-year follow-up of 526 white childhood patients in a St. Louis, Missouri guidance clinic in the 1920s. Robins was looking for clues of the adult "antisocial personality," or "sociopathy."[97] Excluding cases involving organic brain damage, schizophrenia, mental retardation, or symptoms that appeared only after heavy drug or alcohol use, she found that the adult sociopath is almost invariably an antisocial child grown up. In fact, she found no case of adult sociopathy without antisocial behavior before the age of eighteen. Over 50 percent of the sociopathic males showed an onset of symptoms before the age of eight.[98]

Linda Mealey argues that there are two kinds of sociopaths: primary sociopaths and secondary sociopaths. *Primary sociopaths* have inherited traits that predispose them to illegal behavior; that is, they have a genotype that predisposes them to antisocial behavior. *Secondary sociopaths,* in contrast, are constitutionally normal but are influenced by such environmental factors as poor parenting. Thus, she argues that one type of sociopathic behavior has a genetic basis and the other is environmentally induced.[99]

REINFORCEMENT THEORY James Q. Wilson and Richard Herrnstein's *Crime and Human Nature* combines biosocial factors and psychological research with rational choice theory to redevelop reinforcement theory.[100] Wilson and Herrnstein consider potential causes of crime and of noncrime within the context of **reinforcement theory,** that is, the theory that behavior is governed by its consequent rewards and punishments, as reflected in the history of the individual.

The rewards of crime, according to Wilson and Herrnstein, are found in the form of material gain, revenge against an enemy, peer approval, and sexual gratification. The consequences of crime take place with pains of conscience, disapproval of peers, revenge of the victim, and, most important, the possibility of punishment. The rewards of crime tend to be more immediate, whereas the rewards of noncrime generally are realized in the future. The authors are quick to dismiss evidence that is inconsistent with their theoretical framework, but, as few have done in the field of criminology, they are able to show how gender, age, intelligence, families, schools, communities, labor markets, mass media, drugs, as well as variations across time, culture, and race greatly influence the propensity to commit criminal behavior, especially violent offenses.[101]

Wilson and Herrnstein's theory does have serious flaws. Most important, their theory consistently shows a disdain for the social context in which crime occurs. What Wilson and Herrnstein do, in effect, is factor society out of their considerations of crime. Instead of examining criminal behavior as part of complex social mechanisms and attempting to understand the connection, they typically conclude that no conclusion is possible from the available data, and therefore no programs for reducing criminality among groups perceived as major sources of crime are worth their costs.[102]

In sum, psychologists present an abundance of qualitative evidence that delinquents are psychologically different. But it is difficult to substantiate on paper-and-pencil tests that personality differences actually exist between delinquents and nondelinquents.[103] What appears to be a reasonable position is that most delinquents have psychological traits within the normal adolescent range but that some delinquents do have acute emotional problems. Table 3.1 summarizes the biological, sociobiological, and psychological theories of delinquency.

TABLE 3.1

Summary of Biological, Sociobiological, and Psychological Theories of Crime

Theory	Proponents	Causes of Crime Identified	Supporting Research
Atavistic, or born, criminal	Lombroso	The atavistic criminal is a reversion to an earlier evolutionary form	Weak
Genealogical studies	Dugdale Goddard	Criminal tendencies are inherited	Weak
Body type	Sheldon Glueck and Glueck Cortes and Gatti	Mesomorphic body type	Weak
Twins and adoption	Christiansen Mednick	Positive correlations between identical and fraternal twins and criminality show a genetic influence	Moderately strong
Intelligence	Hirschi Hindelang	IQ is a meaningful factor in criminal behavior when combined with environmental factors	Moderately strong
Autonomic nervous system	Eysenck	Insensitivity of the autonomic nervous system, as well as faulty conditioning by parents	Weak
Psychoanalytic theory	Freud	Unconconscious motivations resulting from early childhood experiences	Weak
Psychopathic personality	Cleckley	Inner emptiness as well as biological limitations	Moderately strong
Reinforcement theory	Wilson and Herrnstein	Several key constitutional and psychological factors	Weak

Contemporary Approaches to the Rationality of Crime

In the 1970s and 1980s a variety of academic disciplines, including the sociology of deviance, criminology, economics, and cognitive psychology, began to view crime as the outcome of rational choices and decisions.[104] The ecological tradition in criminology and the economic theory of markets, especially, have applied the notion of rational choice to crime.

Ecological researchers have inferred from the distribution of particular crimes that offenders make rational choices. For example, findings from several studies have revealed that homes on the borderline of affluent districts are at most risk of burglary. Paul J. Brantingham and Patricia L. Brantingham suggested that burglars preying on such districts select the nearest of the suitable targets because escape is easier and they prefer to operate where they feel least conspicuous.[105]

Economic analysis of criminal behavior argues that criminals and noncriminals share the properties of being active, rational decision makers who respond to incentives and deterrents. In economic models of criminal decision making, crime is assumed to involve rational calculation and is viewed essentially as an economic transaction or a question of occupational choice.[106]

Rational Choice Theory

Rational choice theory, borrowed primarily from the utility model in economics, is one of the hottest topics in the 1990s in criminology, sociology, political science, and law.[107] Rational choice theory in its pure form can be seen, at least in part, as an extension of the deterrence doctrine found in the classical school, which includes incentives as well as deterrents and focuses on the rational calculation of payoffs and costs before delinquent and criminal acts are committed.[108]

Philip J. Cook, in using a market perspective, has developed what he calls **criminal opportunity theory.** He claims that "criminals tend to be somewhat selective in choosing a crime target and are most attracted to targets that appear to offer a high payoff with little effort or risk of legal consequence."[109] He sees the interaction between potential offenders who respond to the net payoff of crime and potential victims who take actions to modify the payoff of crime as akin to the interaction between buyers and sellers in a marketplace. Thus, in using the market perspective to examine the interaction between potential victims and offenders, criminal opportunity theory emphasizes individual choice guided by the perceived costs and benefits of criminal activity.[110]

Lawrence E. Cohen and Marcus Felson, guided by ecological concepts and the presumed rationality of offenders, developed a **routine activity approach** for analyzing crime rate trends and cycles. This approach links the dramatic increase in crime rates since 1960 to changes in the routine activity structure of U.S. society and to a corresponding increase in target suitability and a decrease in the presence of "guardians" such as neighbors, friends, and family. The decline of the daytime presence of adult caretakers in homes and neighborhoods is partly the result of a trend toward increased female participation in the labor force. Cohen and Felson believe that the volume and distribution of predatory crime are related to the interaction of three variables relating to the routine activities of U.S. life: the availability of suitable targets, the absence of capable guardians, and the presence of motivated offenders.[111]

Steven F. Messner and Kenneth Tardiff, in using the routine activities approach to help interpret patterns of homicides in Manhattan (New York City), found that the routine activity approach does indeed provide a useful framework for interpreting the social ecology involved in urban homicides. They found that people's lifestyles affected their chances of being victimized. People who were victimized by strangers tended to go out more often, while those who preferred to stay at home were more likely to be killed by someone they knew.[112]

D. Wayne Osgood and colleagues, in analyzing within-individual changes in routine activities and deviance across five waves of data from a national sample, extended routine activity's situational analysis of crime to a broad range of deviant behaviors.[113] They found that "unstructured socializing with peers in the absence of authority figures presents opportunities for deviance. In the presence of peers," they add, "deviant acts will be easier and more rewarding; the absence of authority figures reduces the potential for social control responses to deviance; and the lack of structure leaves time available for deviant behavior."[114]

Ronald L. Akers's examination of rational choice theory led him to conclude that a key issue is whether or not the rational choice perspective proposes a purely "rational man" theory of criminal behavior. He questions: Does it argue for a direct resurrection of classical criminology in which each person approaches the commission or noncommission of a crime with a highly rational calculus? Is rational choice theory essentially free of all constraining elements? Does it propose that each individual chooses, with full free will and knowledge, to commit or not to commit a crime, taking into account a carefully reasoned set of costs and benefits?[115]

Akers answers these questions by saying that current rational choice models emphasize "limitations and constraints on rationality through lack of information, structural constraints, values, and other 'non-rational' influences. Indeed," Akers adds, "the rational choice models in the literature . . . paint a picture of partial rationality with all kinds of situational and cognitive constraints and all kinds of positivistic and deterministic notions of causes."[116]

Derek B. Cornish and Ronald V. Clarke's *The Reasoning Criminal* is probably the most frequently cited source on rational choice and crime. Yet in both the preface and introductory essay, Cornish and Clarke say that the starting assumption of their model is that

> offenders seek to benefit themselves by their criminal behavior; that this involves the making of decisions and choices, however rudimentary on occasion these processes might be; and that these processes exhibit a measure of rationality, albeit constrained by limits of time and ability and the availability of relevant information."[117]

They perceive offenders as "reasoning decision makers" based on the assumption that criminals or delinquents "exercise some degree of planning and foresight."[118]

Raymond Paternoster also presents what he labels a "deterrence/rational choice model" to examine a youth's decision to participate in, continue with, or to desist from delinquent acts. Rational choice, according to Paternoster, recognizes that there are "choice structuring" variables and that the choices do not require complete information or rational analytic methods.[119] For an interview with a proponent of such a deterrence/rational choice model, see Theory and Research 3.3.

In sum, rational choice theory in criminology has recently moved away from the strictly rational, reasoning model of behavior to a more limited and constrained role for rational thought. Rational choice theory does not even assume that all or even most delinquent or criminal acts result from clear, planned, well-informed, and calculated choices.[120] It can still be argued, of course, that the rational choice model places more emphasis on rationality and free will than do other theories of delinquent behavior.[121] We consider the question of whether delinquency is rational behavior in the next section.

Is Delinquency Rational Behavior?

An analysis of delinquent behavior leads to the conclusion that antisocial behavior often appears purposeful and rational. Some youthful offenders clearly engage in delinquent behavior because of the low cost or risk of such behavior. The low risk comes from the *parens patriae* philosophy, being based on the presumption of innocence for the very young, as well as of reduced responsibility for those up to their midadolescence. Therefore in early adolescence, the potential costs of all but the most serious forms of delinquent behavior are relatively slight.[122]

Juveniles are also protected from punishment by the existence of enormous probation caseloads in large cities, the confidentiality of juvenile court records, and the increased costs of long-term training schools. Youths on probation, then, can sometimes repeatedly violate the law and suffer no real consequences. According to a delinquent testifying before the New York State Select Committee at a hearing on assault and robbery against the elderly:

> If you're 15 and under you won't go to jail. . . . That's why when we do a "Rush and Crib"—which means you rush the victim and push him or her into their apartment, you let the youngest member do any beatings. See, we know if they arrest him, he'll be back on the street in no time.[123]

Furthermore, offenders may decide that the risks of continued delinquent behavior are not justified by the rewards. Howard J. Parker found that many in a group of adolescents gave up shoplifting and opportunistic theft of car radios when increased police

THEORY AND RESEARCH 3.3

Interview with Ernest van den Haag

In this interview, Ernest van den Haag, who is acknowledged as one of the leading spokespersons for the utilitarian punishment model, talks about the role of punishment with juvenile lawbreakers. Professor van den Haag also indicates why he feels punishment will be a more effective deterrent than the present way juveniles are handled by the juvenile justice system.

Question: What can we do to reduce the extent of juvenile crime in the United States?

Van den Haag: If you or I committed a crime, we might be irrational, because we stand a great deal to lose and relatively little to gain. But most of the people who commit crime have very little to lose and a lot to gain. They know that the chances of being punished are very small, so crime for them is perfectly rational.

Let me conclude by saying that currently crime pays. Crime pays for adults. It pays even more for juveniles. [Juveniles will] take things seriously only when crime stops paying. Hard-core juvenile offenders know that the chances of being punished are very small, so crime for them is perfectly rational. We must make crime irrational. It is not the criminal who is irrational; it is society.

Question: Is it possible to put enough cost on juveniles to deter delinquent behavior?

Van den Haag: Oh yes! I think that what we have done now is to make their crimes costless. We have given them an immunity from punishment and then we are astonished that they would commit crime. I would abolish tomorrow all juvenile courts because they have been a terrible failure. I believe that anyone over thirteen should be dealt with in the adult court. A youth's attorney, of course, is free to maintain that the youth didn't have *mens rea* and could not form intention. The court in some cases may accept the argument and in some cases it may not.

On an individual basis, I would certainly agree that juveniles quite often don't know what they are doing. But I don't think that one should say in general that a fourteen-year-old doesn't know what he is doing.

That is nonsense! If you say it, the fourteen-year-old is encouraged. He or she, in effect, is told he can do what he wants with impunity.

Now I don't think that punishment is the only factor that influences the crime rate. There are many, many other factors, but they are much harder to manipulate. For instance, religion may be very desirable and better family upbringing is certainly desirable. But I don't quite know how to produce either. I do know how to impose punishment. It is simply the one thing that society can do directly, therefore, I am in favor of it.

Question: What role does rationality play in your position?

Van den Haag: My position is based more on incentives and disincentives than on the rationality of behavior. Whether a person is a juvenile or an adult, I think you can have disincentives for certain types of behavior and incentives for other types of behavior. Obviously, the purpose of the criminal law is to give disincentives strong enough to discourage criminal and delinquent behavior.

There is one complication though. You are not only trying to influence the behavior of the person being punished, but also you are trying to influence the behavior of others. General deterrence, which is what we mean by influencing the behavior of others, does require sufficient rationality to infer that when person X suffers punishment Y for doing act A, then if I do A, I may also experience punishment Y. So in this sense rationality is required, but it still plays a minor role in criminal activity.

Do you agree that we have been as soft on juveniles as Professor van den Haag suggests? What disincentives that we are not using now can we give juveniles to discourage them from committing delinquencies? Are you in favor of punishment?

Source: Interviewed in 1983.

activity resulted in some of their number being apprehended and placed in custody.[124] W. Gordon West's study of the careers of young thieves provides similar evidence of the rational nature of their decisions to desist.[125]

Even more to the point, most persistent offenders appear to desist from crime as they reach their late teens or early twenties. They claim that continued criminality is incompatible with the demands of holding a full-time job or settling down to marriage and a family.[126] Desistance from crime, or maturing out of crime, as was previously mentioned, is a process of deciding that the benefits of crime are less than the advantages of continuing to commit crime.

Yet there are important qualifications in assuming too much rationality in delinquent behavior. Rationality is based on the notion that delinquent behavior is planned. Planning has to do with formulating a scheme or a procedure for doing something before doing it or having an intention of acting. It has to do with assessing the possible alternative courses of actions available, choosing a particular course, and constructing a complex set of acts to achieve the intended results.[127] But studies of delinquency have reported that most delinquent behavior is not planned; spur-of-the-moment decision making most frequently characterizes juvenile wrongdoing.[128] Michael Hindelang's study did reveal that planning was most evident when events were serious and profit-oriented.[129]

The concept of rationality also assumes that individuals have free will and are not controlled by their emotions. But many youngsters do not appear to have such control. Youths who are mentally ill or who engage in obsessive-compulsive acts such as compulsive arsonists, kleptomaniacs, or sex offenders, seem to be held in bondage by their emotions.

Furthermore, in examining the actual process of rationality, it is apparent that there are degrees of freedom for all juveniles and that rationality is contextually oriented with juveniles. The notion of the degrees of freedom proposes, then, that delinquents "are neither wholly free nor completely constrained but fall somewhere between."[130] The contextual nature of rationality suggests that in most situations, delinquents do have some control over their acts, but in other situations they may have little or no control.

Robert Agnew's examination of hard and soft determinism led him to conclude that freedom of choice varies from one individual to another. It is dependent on factors such as biological, psychological, or social nature, that exist previous to the choice process itself. One individual, for example, may be able to choose between two different alternatives, but another may have six different alternatives. The latter, Agnew suggests, has more freedom of choice.[131] For an examination of rationality in one delinquent, see Social World of the Delinquent 3.4.

In sum, although some youths' involvement in delinquency may be largely related to cost-benefit decisions and to a rational process, for other youngsters, delinquent behavior arises without much forethought as they interact with their environment. Experiencing an intense emotional reaction to a situation or deep involvement in a peer group seem to lead them to bypass any rational process.

Policy Recommendations for Rational Choice Theories

The conservative model seems to be based on the notion that we have a great deal of crime because there are insufficient curbs on the appetites or impulses impelling individuals toward criminal behavior.[132] This is why Ernest van den Haag and others want to increase the cost of criminal behavior. The conservative model proposes that we

Social World of the Delinquent 3.4

Patrick and Rationality

Question: "Did you know your victim?"

Answer: "We grew up together."

Question: "You mean you killed your friend?"

Answer: "Were we friends? In some ways we had nothing in common. He hated school and came from people with no aspirations. He had mostly raised himself. He was much more streetwise than I am. I pretend, but he survived because of his street experience. Deep down, I felt a bond with him because our mothers were both junkies. Strange, both their sons made a living from selling drugs."

Question: "How can you distance yourself like this? You killed someone you'd known your whole life."

Answer: "It's because I still can't believe it. It was a simple transaction in a car. I had done it hundreds of times. I couldn't believe he was sitting in the back seat. I wanted to say to him, 'Man, what are you doing back there? That's real dangerousness.' I saw it was a set up. I thought he was my friend. But there he was, ready to rob me. Then everything happened fast. I can't believe he pulled his gun. And I can't believe I fired mine. Through the car seat. To warn him. And now he's dead."

Question: "Do you feel responsible?"

Answer: I am so sorry. I wish I could live that one day over. I had to face his family at the funeral. They had heard that I did it, but I hadn't been arrested yet. It's the first time I used a gun. I didn't mean to kill anyone. I keep having nightmares where my terror in the front seat of that car is all jumbled up with my horror of seeing him hit."

How much rationality is there in the murder that Patrick committed? How much freedom of choice did he have in this incident? He had never been in trouble before and was a college bound student. What punishment should he receive for his actions?

Source: Marty Beyer, *Delinquency Case Book.* Privately distributed. For copies of these true stories of nine delinquents, contact martbeyer@aol.com

increase the levels of punishment to the degree that crime is no longer a choice for the reasonable person.

Conservative writers go on to point the finger at the family, the school, and American culture in general for failing to encourage the virtues of sobriety, self-restraint, and the curbing of appetites. The theme of insidious moral decline or moral downfall, this position continues, has corroded social life and is expressed in the triumph of "self-expression over self-control as a core human value," to "exalt rights over duties, spontaneity over loyalty, tolerance over conformity, and authenticity over conventions."[133] The conservative model proposes that teaching morals and responsibility in the family, churches/synagogues, and schools, will encourage individuals to delay immediate gratifications found in property crimes, to avoid the anger outbursts expressed in violent offenses, and to resist the temptations involved in the use of drugs.

There are, of course, many examples of youths who emerge from the ashes of lack of parental guidance, of the influence of drugs and alcohol around them, of poverty in the home and neighborhood, and of delinquent peers and perhaps even family members. They go on to live responsible lives and to make outstanding contributions to their communities. But the fact is that this conservative agenda of moral reliance and of stiffer dosages of punishment has not worked with the vast majority of high-risk youths. They may be affected to some degree by rational decision making in their delinquent behaviors, but they see very little reason to have any stake in the system. They experience poverty at home, rejection at school, boredom at church, and social injustice from officials of the justice system.

SUMMARY

In biological and psychological positivism the question of what causes delinquency is answered by pointing to biological or psychological factors within the individual. All delinquent behavior, like other behavior, is seen as having an organic or psychological basis. The delinquent, then, is perceived as being controlled by such factors and has no control over them. The factors are sometimes very elusive, such as an autonomic nervous system that is difficult to condition or an inadequately developed superego, but others are more easily discerned, such as inappropriate interpersonal relationships. Both early biological and psychological positivism theories have developed into more complex explanations of delinquent behavior. Early biological positivism was replaced by sociobiology, and psychoanalysis was replaced by models that are less intrapsychic and more oriented to the interactions between the individual and the environment.

Clearly, the punishment model of old has regained popularity in dealing with juvenile delinquents who have committed serious crimes. In growing numbers, policymakers are concluding that increasing the cost of serious youth crime is the only way to reduce it in the United States. To justify the punishment of juveniles, theorists have returned to the classical school of criminology or its modern version of rational choice theory, both of which assert that individuals have free will and therefore are responsible for their behavior. Delinquent behavior, then, is viewed as purposeful behavior, as an activity resulting from a rational decision in which the pros and cons were weighed.

KEY TERMS

attention deficit disorder, p. 76
attention deficit hyperactivity disorder (ADHD), p. 76
autonomic nervous system, p. 75
biological positivism, p. 71
born criminal, p. 71
criminal opportunity theory, p. 84
determinism, p. 69
emotionality, p. 76
felicific calculus, p. 69
free will, p. 69

positivism, p. 71
progressive, p. 71
psychoanalysis, p. 78
reinforcement theory, p. 82
routine activity approach, p. 84
social contract, p. 69
sociobiology, p. 73
sociopath, p. 81
trait-based personality models, p. 81
utilitarianism, p. 69

CRITICAL THINKING QUESTIONS

1. Why have the juvenile court and policymakers been so quick to apply the concept of free will to violent juvenile criminals?
2. What are the basic flaws in using punishment to deter youth crime in the United States?
3. The notion of the rationality of crime applied to Billy's case would conclude that it is unfortunate that this young man had such a toxic and deprived family life but this background did not take away his ability to make responsible decisions for his life. He freely chose to kill the old man, and therefore he deserves to be punished for the murder. In your opinion, was Billy's decision rational? How much freedom did he have and how much punishment did he deserve?
4. Describe the sociopath or psychopath. Why are sociopaths so difficult to treat?

WEB DESTINATIONS

Check this Crime Theory website to learn more about the classical school of criminology.
www.crimetheory.com/Theories/classical.htm

Read more about utilitarianism as described by John Stuart Mill.
http://www.utilitarianism.com/mill1.htm

Learn more about positivism at this Cornell University site.
http://trochim.human.cornell.edu/kb/positivism.htm

Learn more about sociobiology at this site.
www.ship.edu/~cgboeree/sociobiology.html

Learn more about Ernest van den Haag at this web site.
http://www.pbs.org/wgbh/pages/frontline/angel

Read more about the Reinforcement Theory from the Eberly College of West Virginia.
http://www.as.wvu.edu/~sbb/comm221/chapters/rf.htm

Read more about a specific sociopath, "Bugsy" Segal (the infamous gangster), from the Crime Library site.
http://www.crimelibrary.com/gangsters/bugsy/bugsymain.htm

NOTES

1. John P. Conrad, "The Hoodlum in the Helpless Society." Unpublished paper.
2. The account of Billy is contained in Conrad, "The Hoodlum in the Helpless Society."
3. Ronald V. Clarke and Derek B. Cornish, "Modeling Offenders' Decisions: A Framework for Research and Policy," in *Crime and Justice* 6, edited by Michael Tonry and Norval Morris (Chicago: University of Chicago Press, 1985), p. 147.
4. Michael Phillipson, *Understanding Crime and Delinquency* (Chicago: Aldine Publishing, 1974), p. 18.
5. Cesare Bonesana Beccaria, *On Crimes and Punishments*, translated by H. Paolucci (1764; reprint ed., Indianapolis: Bobbs-Merrill, 1963); Jeremy Bentham, *An Introduction to the Principles of Morals and Legislation* (1823; reprint ed., New York: Hafner Publishing, 1948).
6. Beccaria, *On Crimes and Punishments.*
7. Ysabel Rennie, *The Search for Criminal Man: A Conceptual History of the Dangerous Offender* (Lexington, Mass.: Lexington Books, 1978), p. 15.
8. Beccaria, *On Crimes and Punishments*, p. 179.
9. Rennie, *The Search for Criminal Man*, p. 22.
10. Edward Cimler and Lee Roy Bearch, "Factors Involved in Juvenile Decisions about Crime," *Criminal Justice and Behavior* 8 (September 1981), pp. 275–286.
11. This section on the Progressive Era and the influence of positivism is largely adapted from David J. Rothman, *Conscience and Convenience: The Asylum and Its Alternatives in Progressive America* (Boston: Little, Brown, 1980), p. 32.
12. Ibid., pp. 43–60.
13. David Matza, *Delinquency and Drift* (New York: Wiley, 1964), p. 5.
14. Donald C. Gibbons, "Differential Treatment of Delinquents and Interpersonal Maturity Level: A Critique," *Social Services Review* 44 (1970), p. 68.
15. James Q. Wilson and Richard J. Herrnstein, *Crime and Human Nature* (New York: Simon and Schuster, 1985), p. 71.
16. Ian Taylor, Paul Walton, and Jock Young, *The New Criminology: For a Social Theory of Deviance* (New York: Harper and Row, 1973), pp. 41–42.
17. Cesare Lombroso, introduction to Gina Lombroso-Ferrero, *Criminal Man, according to classification of Cesare Lombroso* (Montclair, NJ: Patterson Smith, 1972).
18. Gina Lombroso-Ferrero, *Criminal Man* (New York: Putnam, 1911) p. xiv.
19. M. F. A. Montagu, "The Biologist Looks at Crime," *Annals of the American Academy of Political and Social Science* 217 (1941), pp. 46–57.
20. Charles Goring, *The English Convict: A Statistical Study* (Montclair, N.J.: Patterson Smith, 1972).
21. Saleem A. Shah and Loren H. Roth, "Biological and Psychophysiological Factors in Criminality," *Handbook of Criminology*, edited by Daniel Glaser (Chicago: Rand McNally, 1974), p. 107.
22. Henry H. Goddard, *Efficiency and Levels of Intelligence* (Princeton: Princeton University Press, 1920).
23. Ibid.
24. William Healy and Augusta Bronner, *Delinquency and Criminals: Their Making and Unmaking* (New York: Macmillan, 1926).
25. John Slawson, *The Delinquent Boys* (Boston: Budget Press, 1926).
26. Edwin Sutherland, "Mental Deficiency and Crime," in *Social Attitudes*, edited by Kimball Young (New York: Henry Holt, 1973).
27. William Sheldon, *Varieties of Delinquent Youth* (New York: Harper and Row, 1949).
28. Ibid.
29. Sheldon Glueck and Eleanor Glueck, *Physique and Delinquency* (New York: Harper and Row, 1956), p. 9.

30. Juan B. Cortes with Florence M. Gatti, *Delinquency and Crime: A Biopsychosocial Approach: Empirical, Theoretical, and Practical Aspects of Criminal Behavior* (New York: Seminar Press, 1972), pp. 18–19.

31. Shah and Roth, "Biological and Psychophysiological Factors in Criminality," p. 101.

32. Karl O. Christiansen, "A Preliminary Study of Criminality among Twins," in *Biosocial Bases of Criminal Behavior*, edited by S. A. Mednick and K. O. Christiansen (New York: Gardner, 1977) pp. 89–108; D. R. Cloninger et al., "Predisposition to Petty Criminality: II. Cross-Fostering Analysis of Gene-Environment Interaction," *Archives of General Psychiatry* 39 (November 1982), pp. 1242–1247; R. Crowe, "An Adoptive Study of Psychopathy: Preliminary Results from Arrest Records and Psychiatric Hospital Records," in *Genetic Research in Psychiatry*, edited by R. Fieve et al. (Baltimore: Johns Hopkins University Press, 1975); William F. Gabrielli and Sarnoff A. Mednick, "Urban Environment, Genetics, and Crime," *Criminology* 22 (November 1984), pp. 645–652; S. Sigvardsson et al., "Predisposition to Petty Criminality in Swedish Adoptees: III. Sex Differences and Validation of Male Typology," *Archives of General Psychiatry* 39 (November 1982), pp. 1248–1253.

33. Donald J. Shoemaker, *Theories of Delinquency: An Examination of Explanations of Delinquent Behavior*, 3d ed. (New York: Oxford University Press, 1996), pp. 27–28.

34. Christiansen, "A Preliminary Study of Criminality among Twins," pp. 89–108.

35. Thomas Bouchard, Jr., "Genes, Environment, and Personality," *Science* 264 (1994), pp. 1700–1701.

36. Ibid., p. 1701.

37. Robert Plomin, Michael Owen, and Peter McGuffin, "The Genetic Basis of Complex Behaviors," *Science* 264 (1994), pp. 1733–1739.

38. Christiansen, "A Preliminary Study of Criminality among Twins," pp. 89–108.

39. Edwin H. Sutherland and Donald R. Cressey, *Criminology*, 10th ed. (New York: Lippincott, 1978).

40. D. J. West and D. P. Farrington, *Who Becomes Delinquent?* (London: Heinemann, 1973).

41. Lis Kirkegaard-Sorensen and Sarnoff A. Mednick, "A Prospective Study of Predictors of Criminality: Intelligence," in *Biosocial Basis of Criminal Behavior*, edited by Sarnoff A. Mednick and Karl O. Christiansen (New York: Gardner Press, 1977).

42. Robert A. Gordon, "Prevalence; The Rare Datum in Delinquency Measurement and Its Implications for the Theory of Delinquency," in *The Juvenile Justice System*, edited by Malcolm Klein (Beverly Hills, Calif.: Sage, 1976), pp. 201–284.

43. Robert A. Gordon, "IQ—Commensurability of Black-White Differences in Crime and Delinquency." Paper presented at the Annual Meeting of the American Psychological Association (Washington, D.C.: August 1986), p. 1.

44. Travis Hirschi and Michael Hindelang, "Intelligence and Delinquency: A Revisionist Review," *American Sociological Review* 42 (1977), pp. 471–486.

45. James Q. Wilson and Richard J. Herrnstein, *Crime and Human Nature*, pp. 166–167.

46. For a study that supported the school performance model over the IQ/LD connection, see David A. Ward and Charles R. Tittle, "IQ and Delinquency: A Test of Two Competing Explanations," *Journal of Quantitative Criminology*, 10 (1994), pp. 189–200.

47. Hans Eysenck, "The Technology of Consent," *New Scientist* 26 (June 1969), p. 689.

48. Hans Eysenck, *Fact and Fiction in Psychology* (Harmondsworth, England: Penguin, 1965), pp. 260–261.

49. See Diana H. Fishbein, "Biological Perspectives in Criminology," *Criminology* 28 (1990), p. 27–72.

50. Diana H. Fishbein and Robert W. Thatcher, "New Diagnostic Methods in Criminology: Assessing Organic Sources of Behavioral Disorders," *Journal of Research in Crime and Delinquency* 23 (August 1986), pp. 240–241.

51. R. R. Monroe, *Brain Dysfunction in Aggressive Criminals* (Lexington, Mass.: D.C. Heath, 1987).

52. W. W. Surwillo, "The Electroencephalogram and Childhood Aggression," *Aggressive Behavior* 6 (1980), pp. 9–18.

53. Fishbein and Thatcher, "New Diagnostic Methods in Criminology," pp. 252–259.

54. Terrie E. Moffitt, Donald R. Lynam, and Phil A. Silva, "Neuropsychological Tests Predicted Persistent Male Delinquency," *Criminology* 32 (May 1994), p. 277.

55. Terrie E. Moffitt, "Adolescent-Limited and Life-Course-Persistent Antisocial Behavior: A Developmental Taxonomy," *Psychological Review* 100 (1993), p. 679.

56. Terrie E. Moffitt, "The Neuropsychology of Conduct Disorder," *Development and Psychopathology* 5 (1993); and Terrie E. Moffitt, Avshalom Caspi, N. Dickson, Phil A. Silva, and W. Stanton, "Childhood-Onset Versus Adolescent-Onset Antisocial Conduct Problems in Males: Natural History from Ages 3 to 18," *Development and Psychopathology* 8 (1996), pp. 399–424.

57. Ibid.

58. F. A. Elliott, "Neurological Aspects of Antisocial Behavior," in *The Psychopath*, edited by W. H. Reid (New York: Bruner/Mazel, 1978); V. E. Krynicki, "Cerebral Dysfunction in Repetitively Assaultive Adolescents," *Journal of Nervous and Mental Disease* 166 (1978), pp. 59–67; F. Spellacy, "Neuropsychological Differences between Violent and Nonviolent Adolescents," *Journal of Clinical Psychology* 33 (1977), pp. 966–969; F. Spellacy, "Neuropsychological Discrimination between Violent and Nonviolent Men," *Journal of Clinical Psychology* 34 (1978), pp. 49–52.

59. Elizabeth Kandel and Sarnoff A. Mednick, "Perinatal Complications Predict Violent Offending," *Criminology* 29 (1991), p. 519.

60. S. Litt, "Perinatal Complications and Criminality." In *Proceedings*, 80th Annual Convention of the American Psychological Association in Washington, D.C. (1972); D. Mungas, "An Empirical Analysis of Specific Syndromes of Violent Behavior," *Journal of Nervous and Mental Disease* 17 (1983), pp. 354–361.

61. Kandel and Mednick, "Perinatal Complications Predict Violent Offending," p. 519.

62. Curt R. Bartol and Anne M. Bartol, *Delinquency and Justice: A Psychosocial Approach*, 2nd ed. (Upper Saddle River, N.J.: Prentice-Hall, 1998), p. 89.

63. Sigmund Freud, *An Outline of Psychoanalysis,* translated by James Strachey (1940; reprint, New York: W. W. Norton, 1963).

64. Ibid.

65. Ibid.

66. LaMar T. Empey, *American Delinquency: Its Meaning and Construction* (Homewood, Ill.: Dorsey Press, 1982), pp. 172–173.

67. Hervey Cleckley, *The Mask of Sanity,* 3d ed. (St. Louis: Mosby, 1955), pp. 382–417.

68. See Kathleen M. Heide, "Parents Who Get Killed and the Children Who Kill Them," *Journal of Interpersonal Violence* 8 (December 1993), pp. 531–544.

69. William Healy, *Twenty-Five Years of Child Guidance,* Studies from the Institute of Juvenile Research, Series C. no. 256 (Chicago: Illinois Department of Public Welfare, 1934), pp. 14–15.

70. August Aichhorn, *Wayward Youth* (New York: Viking Press, 1963).

71. Kate Friedlander, *The Psychoanalytic Approach to Juvenile Delinquency* (London: Routledge and Kegan Paul, 1947).

72. Marvin Zuckerman, *Sensation Seeking Beyond the Optimal Level of Arousal* (Hillsdale, N.J.: Lawrence Eribaum, 1979), p. 10.

73. Ibid.

74. Frederick Thrasher, *The Gang* (Chicago: University of Chicago Press, 1936).

75. Henry D. McKay, "The Neighborhood and Child Conduct," *Annals of the American Academy of Political and Social Science* 261 (1949), pp. 32–41; P. Tappan, *Juvenile Delinquency* (New York: McGraw-Hill, 1949), and A. Cohen, "The Delinquent Subculture," in *The Sociology of Crime and Delinquency*, 2d ed., edited by M. Wolfgang, L. Savitz, and N. Johnston (New York: Wiley, 1970).

76. J. J. Tobias, "The Affluent Suburban Male Delinquent," *Crime and Delinquency* 16 (1970), pp. 273–279.

77. M. J. Hindelang, "The Relationship of Self-Reported Delinquency to Scales of the CPI and MMPI," *Journal of Criminal Law, Criminology and Police Science* 63 (1972), pp. 75–81.

78. Helene Raskin White, Erich W. Labouvie, and Marsha E. Bates, "The Relationship between Sensation Seeking and Delinquency: A Longitudinal Analysis," *Journal of Research in Crime and Delinquency* 22 (August 1985), pp. 195–211.

79. Paul F. Cromwell, James N. Olson, and D'Aunn Wester Avary, *Breaking and Entering: An Ethnographic Analysis of Burglary* (Newbury Park, Calif.: Sage, 1991); and Jack Katz, *Seductions of Crime: Moral and Sensual Attractions in Doing Evil* (New York: Basic Books, 1988).

80. Walter R. Gove, "Why We Do What We Do: A Biopsychosocial Theory of Human Motivation," *Social Forces* 73 (1994), pp. 374–375.

81. Ibid., p. 388.

82. Katz, *Seductions of Crime,* p. 9.

83. Bill McCarthy, "Not Just 'For the Thrill of It': An Instrumentalist Elaboration of Katz's Explanation of Sneaky Thrill Property Crimes," *Criminology* 33 (November 1995), p. 519. For other studies that have identified the importance of sensual experience, see S. Lyng, "Edgework: A Social Psychological Analysis of Voluntary Risk Taking," *American Journal of Sociology* 95 (1990), pp. 851–856; and William J. Miller, "Edgework: A Model for Understanding Juvenile Delinquency." A paper presented at the Academy of Criminal Justice Sciences Annual Meeting in Albuquerque, New Mexico (March 1998).

84. Avshalom Caspi, Terrie E. Moffitt, Phil A. Silva, Magda Stouthamer-Loeber, Robert F. Krueger, and Pamela S. Schmutte, "Are Some People Crime-Prone? Replications of the Personality-Crime Relationships Across Countries, Genders, Races, and Methods," *Criminology* 32 (1994), p. 165. See also Douglas T. Kenrick and David C. Funder, "Profiting from Controversy: Lessons from the Person-Situation Debate," *American Psychologist* 43 (1988), pp. 23–34.

85. Caspi et al., "Are Some People Crime-Prone?" p. 165.

86. Sheldon Glueck and Eleanor Glueck, *Unraveling Juvenile Delinquency* (Cambridge: Harvard University Press for the Commonwealth Fund, 1950).

87. J. J. Conger and W. C. Miller, *Personality, Social Class, and Delinquency* (New York: Wiley, 1966).

88. The following studies on personality and crime are found in Caspi, et al., "Are Some People Crime-Prone?" pp. 164–165; Hans J. Eysenck, *Crime and Personality* (London: Routledge and Kegan Paul, 1977).

89. Marvin Zuckerman, "Personality in the Third Dimension: A Psychobiological Approach," *Personality and Individual Differences* 10 (1989), pp. 391–418.

90. C. Robert Cloninger, "A Systematic Method for Clinical Description and Classification of Personality Variants," *Archives of General Psychiatry* 44 (1987), pp. 573–588.

91. Avshalom Caspi et al., "Are Some People Crime-Prone?" p. 163.

92. Ibid.

93. Ibid.

94. Joshua D. Miller and Donald Lynam, "Structural Models of Personality and Their Relation to Antisocial Behavior: A Meta-Analytic Review," *Criminology* 39 (2001), p. 780.

95. Richard L. Jenkins, "Delinquency and a Treatment Philosophy," in *Crime, Law and Corrections*, edited by Ralph Slovenko (Springfield, Ill.: Charles C. Thomas, 1966), pp. 135–136.

96. Cleckley, *The Mask of Sanity,* pp. 382–417.

97. L. N. Robins, *Deviant Children Grown Up: A Sociological and Psychiatric Study of Sociopathic Personality* (Baltimore: Williams and Wilkins, 1966), p. 256.

98. L. N. Robins et al., "The Adult Psychiatric Status of Black Schoolboys," *Archives of General Psychiatry* 24 (1971), pp. 338–345.

99. Linda Mealey, "The Sociobiology of Sociopathy: An Integrated Evolutionary Model," *Behavioral and Brain Sciences* 18 (1995), pp. 523–540.

100. Wilson and Herrnstein, *Crime and Human Nature.*

101. Ibid.

102. Edgar Z. Friedenberg, "Solving Crime," *Readings: A Journal of Reviews* (March 1986), p. 21.

103. For a study that concluded it was impossible to determine significant differences between criminal and noncriminal

personalities, see Karl Schuessler and Donald Cressey, "Personality Characteristics of Criminals," *American Journal of Sociology* 55 (1955), pp. 476–484. For an investigation that found statistical differences in 81 percent of the studies, see Gordon Waldo and Simon Dinitz, "Personality Attributes of the Criminal: An Analysis of Research Studies 1950–1965," *Journal of Research in Crime and Delinquency* 4 (1967), pp. 185–201. The latter study does warn that these studies are full of methodological weaknesses. For a study that replicated Waldo and Dinitz's study and found that between the years 1966 and 1975, 80 percent of the personality tests showed significant differences between criminals and noncriminals, see David J. Tennenbaum, "Personality and Criminality: A Summary and Implications of the Literature," *Journal of Criminal Justice* 5 (1977), pp. 225–235.

104. Anne Campbell, *Girl Delinquents* (New York: St. Martin's Press, 1981), p. 149.

105. Paul J. Brantingham and Patricia L. Brantingham, "The Spatial Patterning of Burglary," *Howard Journal of Penology and Crime Prevention* 14 (1975), pp. 11–24.

106. Clarke and Cornish, "Modeling Offenders' Decisions," p. 156.

107. Derek B. Cornish and Ronald V. Clarke, eds., *The Reasoning Criminal: Rational Choice Perspectives on Offending* (New York: Springer, 1986); Kirk R. Williams and Richard Hawkins, "The Meaning of Arrest for Wife Assault," *Criminology* 27 (1989), pp. 163–181; Irving Piliavin, Craig Thornton, Rosemary Gartner, and Ross L. Matsueda, "Crime, Deterrence, and Rational Choice," *American Sociological Review* 51 (1986), pp. 101–119; Raymond Paternoster, "Decisions to Participate in and Desist from Four Types of Common Delinquency: Deterrence and the Rational Choice Perspective," *Law and Society Review* 23 (1989), pp. 7–40; Raymond Paternoster, "Absolute and Restrictive Deterrence in a Panel of Youth: Explaining the Onset, Persistence/Desistance, and Frequency of Delinquent Offending," *Social Problems* 36 (1989), pp. 289–309; Marcus Felson, "Predatory and Dispute-Related Violence: A Social-Interactionist Approach," in *Routine Activity and Rational Choice: Advances in Criminological Theory*, Vol. 5, R. V. Clarke and M. Felson, eds. (New Brunswick, N.J.: Transaction Books, 1993); Marcus Felson, *Crime and Everyday Life: Insight and Implications for Society* (Thousand Oaks, Calif.: Pine Forge Press, 1994).

108. Ronald L. Akers, "Deterrence, Rational Choice, and Social Learning Theory: The Path Not Taken." Paper presented to the Annual Meeting of the American Society of Criminology, Reno, Nevada (November 1989), pp. 2–3.

109. Philip J. Cook, "The Demand and Supply of Criminal Opportunities," in *Crime and Justice* 7, edited by Michael Tonry and Norval Morris (Chicago: University of Chicago Press, 1986), p. 2.

110. Ibid, pp. 2–3.

111. Lawrence E. Cohen and Marcus Felson, "Social Change and Crime Rate Trends: A Routine Activity Approach," *American Sociological Review* (August 1979), pp. 588–609. For more recent expressions of the routine activity approach, see Felson, *Crime and Everyday Life*.

112. Steven F. Messner and Kenneth Tardiff, "The Social Ecology of Urban Homicides: An Application of the 'Routine Activities' Approach," *Criminology* 23 (1985), pp. 241–267.

113. D. Wayne Osgood, Janet K. Wilson, Patrick M. O'Malley, Jerald G. Bachman, and Lloyd D. Johnson, "Routine Activities and Individual Deviant Behavior," *American Sociological Review* 61 (1996), p. 635.

114. Ibid.

115. Ronald L. Akers, "Deterrence, Rational Choice, and Social Learning Theory," p. 8.

116. Ibid., pp. 8–9.

117. Cornish and Clarke, *The Reasoning Criminal*, pp. 1–2.

118. Ibid., p. 13.

119. Paternoster, "Absolute and Restrictive Deterrence in a Panel of Youth" and "Decisions to Participate in and Desist from Four Types of Common Delinquency."

120. Akers, "Deterrence, Rational Choice, and Social Learning Theory," p. 12.

121. Akers, however, questions this in his paper, "Deterrence, Rational Choice, and Social Learning Theory," p. 11.

122. David F. Greenberg, "Delinquency and the Age Structure of Society," *Contemporary Crisis* 1 (1977), p. 209.

123. Ibid., p. 210.

124. Howard J. Parker, *View from the Boys: A Sociology of Down-Town Adolescents* (Newton Abbot, England: David and Charles, 1974).

125. W. Gordon West, "The Short-Term Careers of Serious Thieves," *Canadian Journal of Criminology* 20 (1978), pp. 169–190.

126. D. F. Greenberg, "Delinquency and the Age Structure of Society," pp. 189–223; Gordon B. Trasler, "Delinquency, Recidivism, and Desistance," *British Journal of Criminology* 19 (1979), pp. 314–322.

127. Gove, "Why We Do What We Do," p. 370.

128. Marvin E. Wolfgang, Terence P. Thornberry, and Robert M. Figlio, *From Boy to Man: From Delinquency to Crime* (Chicago: University of Chicago Press, 1987), p. 125. See also James F. Short, Jr., and Fred L. Strodtbeck, *Group Process and Gang Delinquency* (Chicago: University of Chicago Press, 1965), pp. 248–265; and Charles W. Thomas and Donna M. Bishop, "The Effect of Formal and Informal Sanctions on Delinquency: A Longitudinal Comparison of Labeling and Deterrence Theories," *Journal of Criminal Law and Criminology* 75 (1984), p. 1244.

129. Michael J. Hindelang, *Situational Influences on the Delinquent Act* (Rockville, Md.: National Institutes of Mental Health, 1972).

130. David Matza, *Delinquency and Drift*, p. 27. See also Silvan S. Tomkins, *Affect, Imagery, Consciousness: The Positive Affects* (New York: Springer, 1962), pp. 108–109.

131. Robert Agnew, "Determinism, Indeterminism, and Crime: An Empirical Exploration," *Criminology* 33 (1995), pp. 87–88.

132. Elliott Currie, *Confronting Crime: An American Challenge* (New York: Pantheon Books, 1985), p. 23.

133. Ibid.

chapter **4**

SOCIAL STRUCTURAL THEORIES

OBJECTIVES

After reading this chapter, the student will be able to answer the following questions:

- How is cultural deviance theory related to lower-class delinquency?

- What is the relationship between socially disorganized communities and delinquent behavior?

- How does strain propel juveniles into delinquent behavior?

- What delinquent behavior explains homelessness among youth?

- How do social structural theories explain middle-class delinquency?

Sam, an institutionalized delinquent, made this statement shortly before he left an end-of-the-line training school:

You know I never had *a father or, at least, I didn't know him. I have a good mother, but she has had a hard life. At times, we barely have enough food to eat. The last time I was released from Fairfield, I made up my mind to stay out of trouble. My friends kept coming around with their schemes, and I told them to get out of my face. Then, my mother needed surgery, and there wasn't any money. My friends wanted to hit [rob] a liquor store, and I went along. But we got caught, and I ended up here.*

I've grown a lot lately. It hasn't been the institution and the silly-ass rules. It has been people like John and you. You've given me respect. I want to make something of myself now. I'm eighteen, and I've got my high school diploma. I want to make a contribution to my people. Blacks have been held down too long.

But I know it won't be easy to stay out of trouble. I've got to go back to the same old neighborhoods, the same old buddies. Street life will always be there for me. I know it will be prison next time, and I don't want to spend the rest of my life in and out of places like this.[1]

> **What is Sam saying here? If he were really determined, why would returning home be such a fearful experience?**

Sam was a special person. He was intelligent and verbally articulate. He wrote poetry and was reflective about his past and his future. Still, he had spent five years in juvenile institutions, had robbed people and carried a firearm, had used hard drugs, and was afraid that he would be unable to walk away from crime.

This chapter and the next two examine sociological explanations of delinquent behavior. So many of the social structure theories examined in this chapter were found in Sam's life. He came from a socially disorganized society and, as a lower-class youth, was part of a culture that had little stake in the system. He felt considerable strain and, indeed, it was the pressure of not having money for his mother's surgery that was the determining factor in his returning to crime.

The basic flaw of explanations based on the individual, according to social structural theorists, is that such interpretations fail to come to grips with the underlying social and cultural conditions giving rise to delinquent behavior. These theorists add that the overall crime picture reflects conditions requiring collective social solutions and that therefore social reform, not individual counseling, must be given the highest priority in efforts to reduce crime problems.[2]

The setting for delinquency, as suggested by social structural theorists, is the social and cultural environment in which adolescents grow up or the subcultural groups in which they choose to become involved. Social structural theorists, typically using official statistics as their guide, claim that such forces as cultural deviance, social disorganization, status frustration, and social mobility are so powerful that they induce lower-class youths to become involved in delinquent behavior.

Social Disorganization Theory

Social disorganization can be defined "as the inability of a community structure to realize the common values of its residents and maintain effective social control."[3] Social disorganization theory suggests that macrosocial forces (e.g., migration, segregation, structural transformation of the economy, and housing discrimination) interact with community-level factors (concentrated poverty, family disruption, residential turnover) to impede social organization. This sociological viewpoint focuses attention on the structural characteristics and mediating processes of community social organization that help explain crime, while also recognizing the larger historical, political, and social forces that shape local communities.[4]

The intellectual antecedents of **social disorganization** theory can be traced to the work of Emile Durkheim; William I. Thomas and Florian Znaniecki; Robert E. Park, Ernest W. Burgess, and Roderick D. McKenzie; S. P. Breckinridge and Edith Abbott; and Frederick M. Thrasher. In Durkheim's view, anomie or "normlessness" resulted from society's failure to provide adequate regulation of its members' attitudes and behaviors. Deregulation was particularly likely when society and its members experienced rapid change, and laws did not keep pace.[5] To Thomas and Znaniecki, social disorganization reflected the influences of an urban, industrial setting on the ability of immigrant subcultures, especially parents, to socialize and effectively control their children.[6] From Park, Burgess, and McKenzie came the idea of the ecological processes of invasion, dominance, and succession in the development of the city.[7] Breckinridge and Abbott contributed the idea of plotting "delinquency maps."[8] Thrasher viewed the gang as a substitute socializing institution whose function was to provide order (social organization) where there was none (social disorganization).[9]

Shaw and McKay

Social disorganization theory was developed by Clifford R. Shaw and Henry D. McKay during the first half of the twentieth century. Shaw and McKay were farm boys who came to Chicago to undertake graduate work in sociology at the University of Chicago. Both were born and brought up in rural areas of the Midwest. Shaw was from an Indiana crossroads that barely constituted a town, and McKay hailed from the prairie regions of South Dakota.[10] The rural settings from which they came made Shaw and McKay acutely aware of the importance of community life in which "people were brought together by certain ties of long acquaintance and friendship" and "by certain common beliefs and interests."[11] In this social setting, people would join together "to meet a crisis or disaster when the occasion arose."[12]

Jon Snodgrass suggests that perhaps the glaring contrast between the order of their home communities and the disorder of Chicago during the early decades of the twentieth century so intrigued Shaw and McKay that they spent their careers examining the effects of social disorganization on delinquency. Snodgrass adds that Shaw's method of delinquency prevention was "actually an effort to create numerous replicas of his agrarian home community in the urban environs of Chicago."[13]

Shaw and McKay extended social disorganization theory by focusing specifically on the social characteristics of the community as a cause of delinquency.[14] Their pioneering investigations established that delinquency varied in inverse proportion to the distance from the center of the city, that it varied inversely with socioeconomic status, and that delinquency rates in a residential area persisted regardless of changes in racial and ethnic composition of the area.[15]

SOCIAL DISORGANIZATION AND THE COMMUNITY　Shaw and McKay viewed juvenile delinquency as resulting from the breakdown of social control among the traditional primary groups, such as the family and the neighborhood, because of the social disorganization of the community. Rapid industrialization, urbanization, and immigration processes contributed to the disorganization of the community. Delinquent behavior, then, became an alternative mode of socialization through which youths who were part of disorganized communities were attracted to deviant lifestyles.[16] The delinquent values and traditions, replacing traditional ones, were passed from one generation to the next.

Shaw and McKay turned to ecology to show this relationship between social disorganization and delinquency. Park and Burgess had earlier used the concept of ecology in explaining the growth of cities. Burgess, for example, suggested that cities do not merely grow at their edges, but rather have a tendency to expand radially from their centers in patterns of concentric circles, each moving gradually outward.[17] Figure 4.1 is a diagram of the growth zones as Burgess envisioned them. See Theory and Research 4.1 for the ecological foundations of delinquency.

In 1929, Shaw reported that marked variations in rates of school truancy, juvenile delinquency, and adult criminality existed among different areas in Chicago. These rates varied inversely with the distance from the center of the city; that is, the nearer a given locality was to the center of the city, the higher its rates of delinquency and crime. Shaw also found that areas of concentrated crime maintained their high rates over a long period, even when the composition of the population changed markedly.[18] In a study Shaw and McKay performed for the National Commission on Law Observance and Enforcement, they reported that this basic ecological finding was true for a number of other cities also.[19]

In 1942, Shaw and McKay published their classic work, *Juvenile Delinquency and Urban Areas,* which developed these ecological insights in greater scope and depth.[20] What Shaw and McKay had done was to study males brought into the Cook County Juvenile court on delinquency charges in 1900–1906, 1917–1923, and 1927–1933. They discovered that, over this thirty-three-year period, the vast majority of the delinquent

FIGURE 4.1 The Growth of the City

Source: This material appears in Ernest W. Burgess, "The Growth of the City," in *The City,* edited by Robert E. Park, Ernest W. Burgess, and Roderick D. McKenzie (Chicago: University of Chicago Press, 1928), p. 51.

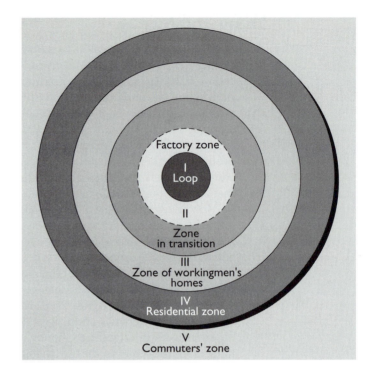

boys came from either an area adjacent to the central business and industrial areas or along two forks of the Chicago River. Then, applying Burgess's concentric zone hypothesis of urban growth—that urban areas grow in concentric circles—they constructed a series of concentric circles, like the circles on a target, with the bull's-eye in the central city. Measuring delinquency rates by zone and by areas within the zones, they found that in all three periods the highest rates of delinquency were in Zone I (the central city), the next highest in Zone II (next to the central city), and so forth, in progressive steps outward to the lowest in Zone V. Significantly, although the delinquency rates changed from one period to the next, the relationship among the different zones remained constant, even though in some neighborhoods the ethnic compositions of the population had changed totally. During the first decade of the century, the largest portion of the population was German or Irish, but thirty years later, it was Polish and Italian.[21]

Shaw and McKay, in analyzing the official data, found that several factors were related to high rates of delinquency. First, buildings were allowed to deteriorate in anticipation of the expansion of industry. Second, as a result of the anticipated displacement of residential dwellings by industry, the population began to decrease. Third, the percentage of families in the area that received financial aid from the United Charities and the Jewish Charities increased. Fourth, lower-class African Americans and foreign-born individuals were attracted to these inner-city areas.[22]

OPPORTUNITY STRUCTURE AND DELINQUENCY Shaw and McKay eventually refocused their analysis from the influence of social disorganization of the community to the importance of economics on high rates of delinquency. They found that the economic and occupational structure of the larger society was more influential in the rise of delinquent behavior than was the social life of the local community. They concluded that the reason members of lower-class groups remained in the inner-city community was less a reflection of their newness of arrival and their lack of acculturation to American institutions than it was a function of their class position in society.[23]

The consequence of this **differential opportunity structure** led to a conflict of values in local communities, as some residents embraced illegitimate values while others main-

THEORY AND RESEARCH 4.1

The Ecological Foundations of Delinquency

Ernest W. Burgess and Robert E. Park joined the sociology faculty at the University of Chicago in 1914. The two were office mates and had little in common except their love of sociology and their work-intensive habits. Burgess, who was 22 years younger than Park, was slight in stature and rarely left his office. A lifelong bachelor who lived with his father and sister, he was totally caught up in his work. Park, a former newspaper reporter, was the prototypical absent-minded professor. With unruly and wild-looking white hair, he at times appeared before his classes with traces of shaving soap on his face. He often wore wrinkled and disheveled clothes.

Park was fascinated with theories of plant ecology and their applications to humans, especially to the study of urban life. For example, he believed that the process of invasion, dominance, and succession that was demonstrated by plant species in taking over regions of the world had relevance to population growth in urban areas. He eventually framed a theory of "human ecology," speculating that the city was a superorganism, with its physical structure, people, and institutions making up separate and interlocking parts.

Burgess was intrigued with Park's theory. To test it, the two set out to gather as much information as they could about the city of Chicago. They encouraged students to observe and systematically record phenomena of the city. Within a short period of time, the department was accumulating large sets of data, both descriptive and quantified. The Chicago School became well known for its "urban ecological" focus.

Researchers of the ecological school quickly discovered that extremes in poverty, illness, and crime were found disproportionately in particular parts of Chicago. Both male and female delinquents lived and operated in certain locations and were less conspicuous in others.

Why would the findings of ecological studies in Chicago be important in the study of delinquency? What seems to be true about this approach in terms of relating delinquent behavior to where youths live? How is this approach not true?

Sources: Harold Finestone, *Victims of Change: Juvenile Delinquents in American Society* (Westport, CT.: Greenwood Press, 1976) and Curt R. Bartol and Anne M. Bartol, *Delinquency and Justice: A Psychological Approach,* 2nd ed. (Upper Saddle River, N.J.: Prentice-Hall, 1999), pp. 212–13.

tained allegiance to conventional ones. Delinquent groups were characterized by their own distinctive standards, and Shaw and McKay became increasingly involved in examining the process through which delinquents came to learn and to pass on these standards.[24]

CULTURAL TRANSMISSION THEORIES   Shaw and McKay also elaborated on social disorganization theory in arguing that delinquent behavior became an alternative mode of socialization through which youths who were part of disorganized communities were attracted to deviant life-styles.[25] This became known as the cultural deviance component of social disorganization theory.

Shaw and McKay further contended that delinquent values and traditions, which replaced traditional ones, were not the property of any one ethnic or racial group, but were culturally transmitted from one generation to the next.[26] As evidence of **cultural transmission theory,** these researchers found that certain inner-city areas continued to have the highest delinquency rates in Chicago, despite shifts of nearly all of these areas' populations.

Shaw and McKay assumed that juvenile and adult gangs in these areas accounted for the transmission of this tradition of delinquency. See Figure 4.2 for the theoretical constructs of Shaw and McKay's social disorganization theory.

FIGURE 4.2 Shaw and McKay's Theory

EVALUATION OF SHAW AND MCKAY'S DISORGANIZATION THEORY Few studies in the area of delinquency have been as influential in the development of research, theory, and social action as those of social disorganization theory. This theory lost much of its vitality as a prominent criminological theory in the late 1960s and the 1970s because theory and research focused primarily on individual rather than group and community characteristics.[27] In conjunction with this shift in orientation, W. R. Arnold and T. M. Brungardt flatly dismiss social disorganization as a theory of crime causation since "it is not even a necessary condition of criminality, let alone a sufficient one."[28] R. N. Davidson also argues that social disorganization "should be seen as a descriptive convenience rather than a model of criminogenic behavior."[29] Despite these and other criticisms, social disorganization in the 1980s experienced "a quiet, but significant revival."[30]

Shaw and McKay's studies have been so influential in the development of criminological theory because their work addressed the problem of crime in terms of multiple levels of analysis. They shifted attention away from individual characteristics of delinquents and nondelinquents to group traditions in delinquency and to the influence of the larger community. Thus Shaw and McKay's analysis provides a theoretical framework bridging sociological and social psychological explanations.[31]

The fact that Shaw and McKay's model incorporates specific images of the delinquent in each stage of development permits such bridging. They viewed delinquents as disaffiliated in the social disorganization stage, for delinquents were part of disorganized communities and, as such, were alienated from the values and norms of the larger society. They viewed delinquents in the functionalist stage as "frustrated social climbers," primarily because these youths were poor and longed for the cultural goals that could be achieved only through illegitimate means. Shaw and McKay viewed delinquents in the third, or interactionist, stage as "aggrieved citizens." Delinquents were faced with cultural groups in their own communities, which provided social acceptance but also involved them in socially unacceptable behavior. To gain acceptance among peers, then, meant rejection by the larger society and punishment from its social control agencies.[32]

Shaw and McKay's social disorganization tradition has also contributed to a rediscovery of the importance of macrolevels and the community in understanding delinquency. This rediscovery has led to the conclusion that an adequate understanding of the causes of illegal behavior required an examination of the social structure, the individual, and other social contexts, such as primary groups, that mediated between the individual and that structure.[33]

This contextual analysis is found in Ora Simcha-Fagan and Joseph E. Schwartz's analysis of the formal and informal networks of control within a set of neighborhoods in New York City.[34] Data were collected from a stratified random sample of urban adolescent males from twelve New York City neighborhoods. Four variables were considered in investigating the effects of community characteristics: community residential stability, community economic level, level of organization participation, and level of disorder–criminal culture. The manner in which social disorganization, cultural deviance, and labeling theories jointly or distinctly affected various aspects of delinquency was further examined. Tending to support social disorganization theory, Simcha-Fagan and Schwartz's analysis of the data revealed that two neighborhood-level factors were important: the community level of organizational participation and the extent of disorder and criminal subculture. They also found that the salience of these contextual effects varied for different forms of delinquency.[35]

Robert J. Sampson and W. Byron Grove's article testing social disorganization theory in two surveys conducted in Great Britain found support for Shaw and McKay's original model.[36] The general hypothesis of the contextual analysis found in this study was that low economic status, ethnic heterogeneity, residential mobility, and family disruption would lead to community disorganization, which would increase the rates of crime and delinquency. Results from both surveys established that "communities characterized by sparse friendship networks, unsupervised teenage peer groups, and low organization participation had disproportionately high rates of crime and delinquency."[37]

Within the social disorganization tradition, Robert J. Sampson later proposed "dynamic contextualization as a promising paradigm for future criminological inquiry."[38] With dynamic contextualism Sampson attempts to recognize and join "developmental and historical insights, event structures and community context, qualitative narratives and causal explanation, and ultimately, time and place."[39] He essentially focuses on the "unfolding of human lives in particular contexts," but argues that "one must also come to grips with social change and the simultaneous—sometimes asynchronous—changing of lives and macrolevel forces (e.g., community, societal)."[40] Sampson sees that such contextual analysis has the advantage of not only examining the "main effects of community structure on individual behavior, but the interaction of community and individual/familial characteristics."[41]

The Project on Human Development in Chicago Neighborhoods is tracing how criminal behavior develops from birth to age 32 in the 11,000 individuals in the study. The initial analysis of this longitudinal study reveals that the structural characteristics of a community, as well as neighborhood cohesion and informal social control, most affect the levels of crime.[42]

Shaw and McKay further contributed important insights on gang formation. They saw the delinquent gang as responding normally to the slum conditions and the social deprivations of local environments. Shaw and McKay regarded delinquent behavior as an understandable choice given the lack of legitimate opportunity for lower-class families in the inner city. In developing the **Chicago Area Projects,** Shaw and McKay were able to persuade former delinquents to become involved as leaders of neighborhood groups working with youths, primarily because they viewed these former delinquents not as being different from nondelinquents but as being individuals who had made normal choices to deal with life in a deprived social environment.[43] See Treatment Intervention 4.2.

The significance of Shaw and McKay's theory is also seen in the recent resurgence of interest in examining how people and institutions adapt to their environment.[44] In the 1980s, several studies examined the relationship between ecological change and crime and delinquency rates in Cleveland and San Diego,[45] Baltimore,[46] and Racine, Wisconsin.[47] Janet L. Heitgerd and Robert J. Bursik Jr. examined the effect on local delinquency rates of racial change in areas adjoining a community.[48] In a 1997 article, Paul E. Bellair found that occasional social interaction among neighbors had an effect on reducing burglary, motor vehicle theft, and robbery.[49] Fred Markowitz and colleagues, building on social disorganization research, found from three waves of the British Crime Survey that decreases in neighborhood cohesion increase crime and disorder, which increase fear and in turn further decrease cohesion.[50] D. Wayne Osgood and Jeff M. Chambers, in their examination of 264 nonmetropolitian counties of four states, reported that juvenile violence was associated with rates of family disruption, residential instability, and ethnic heterogeneity.[51]

Moreover, recent examination of the social disorganization perspective has opened up exciting new avenues of research inquiry that to some extent has gone beyond Shaw and McKay's original work. One area that has received extensive examination concerns the effects of neighborhood contexts on motivational processes

TREATMENT INTERVENTION 4.2

The Chicago Area Projects

The Chicago Area Projects (CAP) is a program that seeks to discover by actual demonstration and measurement a procedure for the prevention of delinquency and the treatment of delinquents. In 1932, the first projects were set up in three white, ethnically homogeneous neighborhoods: South Chicago, the Near West Side, and the Near North Side. The Near North and Near West area projects were located directly north and directly west of the Loop, Chicago's central business district. Both were areas with high delinquency rates. The third project was carried out in Russell Square on Chicago's southeast side. Russell Square was a heavily industrialized area consisting primarily of steel mills and railroad operations, but it had a lower delinquency rate than the other two neighborhoods. Eighteen area projects were eventually established in Chicago, and included several African American Southside neighborhoods. The concept of the area projects also spread to several other Illinois cities.

Shaw and his colleagues had lost confidence in official agencies' ability to deal adequately with the needs of youths so they recruited local leaders to intervene with neighborhood youths. The CAP organizers believed that instead of throwing youths so quickly to the justice system, the community should intervene on their behalf. In the sixty-year existence of the CAP, community citizens have shown up in the juvenile court to speak on behalf of youths in trouble and have organized social and recreational programs for youths. They also have given special attention to local youths who are having difficulties at home or school or with the law.

Some critics contend that the CAP has been ineffective in coping with delinquency in its most serious forms in the areas of the city with the highest crime rates. The CAP has also been criticized because this program fails to attack the political and economic sources of power. Jon Snodgrass added that the CAP's neglect of the realities of Chicago politics and economics essentially made this project a conservative response to the radical changes that are needed in disorganized communities.

Although this latter structural limitation of the CAP is difficult to refute, it still has served as an exemplary model of what grass-roots organizations in the community can achieve in preventing juvenile delinquency. Steven Schlossman and colleagues summarized the effectiveness of the CAP by saying, "All of our data consistently suggest that the CAP has long been effective in organizing local communities and reducing juvenile delinquency."

Could this approach to delinquency prevention work today? How serious a flaw is it that the CAP ignored the political and economic sources of power?

Sources: See Steven Schlossman, Gail Aellman, and Richard Shavelson, *Delinquency Prevention in South Chicago: A Fifty-Year Assessment of the Chicago Area Project* (Santa Monica, CA.: Rand, 1984); and Jon Snodgrass, "Clifford Shaw and Henry D. McKay," in *Delinquency, Crime and Society,* edited by James Short Jr. (Chicago: University of Chicago Press, 1976), p. 16.

leading to the commission of illegal behavior.[52] This contextual analysis is found in Lyle Shannon's examination of how neighborhood dynamics shape the nature of individual careers in delinquency.[53] John W. C. Johnstone also investigated the degree to which the economic structure of a youth's community affected the relationship between family socioeconomic status and delinquency.[54] Per-Olof H. Wikstrom and Rolf Loeber found that disadvantaged neighborhoods have a direct impact on the late onset of offending for those juveniles who score high on protective factors or who have a balanced risk of protective and risk factors. These well-adjusted juveniles, then, are affected by the neighborhood in terms of becoming juvenile delinquents.[55]

Dina Rose and Todd R. Clear's study is set within the framework of social disorganization theory and argues that "an overreliance on incarceration as a formal control may hinder the ability of some communities to foster other forms of control because

According to Cohen, destruction of property is a product of reaction formation, in which lower-class youths respond to the strain of living in a middle-class culture. But what about middle-class youths who commit such acts? Does Cohen's theory hold for them, or can their acts be attributed to pure sensation seeking?

they weaken family and community structures." They add that "at the ecological level, the side effects of policies intended to fight crime by controlling individual behavior may exacerbate the problems they are intended to address." As a result, communities experience more, not less, social disorganization.[56]

Bursik's evaluation of social disorganization theory concludes that this perspective has received several main criticisms. It has been assumed generally that the aggregate nature of group or neighborhood findings does not lead to predictions concerning individual behavior. Shaw and McKay's analysis of delinquent behavior was also based on official statistics, and as previous chapters have indicated, official rates of delinquency tend to distort the extent and nature of delinquent behavior. Furthermore, the conceptual lack of clarity in this perspective has led to confusion and rejection. For example, critics charge that classic social disorganization theories have often used delinquency rates as "both an example of disorganization and something caused by disorganization."[57] In addition, critics assert that Shaw and McKay assumed stable ecological structures that no longer exist in urban settings. Finally, the failure to take seriously the importance of power in community organization appears to many to be insensitive to the current realities of political and social life.[58]

Nevertheless, as the recent reemergence of interest in social disorganization theory shows, the work of Shaw and McKay has had an enduring impact on the study of delinquency in the United States.

How Cultural Deviance Theory Is Related to Delinquency

Cultural deviance theories generally view delinquent and criminal behavior as an expression of conformity to cultural values and norms that are in opposition to those of the larger society. According to Ruth Rosner Kornhauser, the necessary and sufficient cause of delinquency in cultural deviance models "is socialization to subcultural values condoning as right conduct what the controlling legal system defines as crime."[59]

Miller's Lower-Class Culture and Delinquent Values

In his version of **cultural deviance theory,** the anthropologist Walter B. Miller argued that the motivation to become involved in delinquent behavior is endemic to lower-class culture:

> The cultural system which exerts the most direct influence on [delinquent] behavior is that of the lower-class community itself—a long-established, distinctively patterned tradition with an integrity of its own—rather than a so-called "delinquent subculture" which has arisen through conflict with middle-class culture and is oriented to the deliberate violation of middle-class norms.[60]

FOCAL CONCERNS OF LOWER-CLASS CULTURE   Miller argued that a set of **focal concerns of the lower class** characterizes this socioeconomic group. These concerns command widespread attention and a high degree of emotional involvement. They are trouble, toughness, smartness, excitement, fate, and autonomy.[61]

Miller contended that staying out of trouble represents a major challenge for lower-class citizens and that personal status is therefore often determined in light of this law-abiding/nonlaw-abiding dimension. But which of the two qualities is valued depends largely on the individual and his or her circumstances. An overt commitment may be made to abiding by the law, while a covert commitment is given to breaking the law. Miller adds that membership in adolescent gangs may be contingent on a commitment to the law-violating alternative.

Physical prowess, as demonstrated by strength and endurance, is valued in lower-class culture; the tough guy who is hard, fearless, undemonstrative, and a good fighter is, in the eyes of lower-class boys, the ideal man. Miller contended that the intense concern over toughness is directly related to a significant proportion of lower-class males being reared in matriarchal households; therefore, a nearly obsessive concern with masculinity is found in these youths.

The capacity to outsmart, outfox, outwit, con, dupe, and "take" others is valued in lower-class culture; one must also be able to avoid being outwitted, "taken," or duped himself. Smartness is also necessary to achieve material goods and personal status without physical effort.

The search for excitement or a thrill is another of the focal concerns of lower-class life. The widespread use of alcohol by both sexes and gambling of all kinds spring from this quest for excitement. Going out on the town is the most vivid expression of the search for a thrill, but, of course, pursuits of this nature frequently lead to trouble. Between periods of excitement, lower-class life is characterized by long periods of inaction or passivity.

Lower-class individuals, according to Miller, often feel that their lives are subject to a set of forces over which they have little control; they may accept the concept of destiny, meaning that their lives are guided by strong spiritual forces. They believe that getting lucky or being in luck might rescue the individual from lower-class life; this belief in fate, in fact, encourages the lower-class person to gamble.

The desire for personal independence is an important concern, partly because the lower-class individual feels controlled so much of the time. A consequence of this desire for autonomy is the inability to deal with controlled environments such as those found in schools or correctional facilities.

In sum, Miller contended that the lower-class has a distinctive culture of its own. Its focal concerns, or values, make lower-class boys more likely to become involved in delinquent behavior. These boys want to demonstrate that they are tough and are able to outwit the cops. The pursuit of crime is viewed as a thrill. Yet lower-class youths believe that if an individual is going to get caught, there is nothing he or she can do about it. Crime, then, permits one to show personal independence from the controls placed on him or her. Crime also provides an avenue by which one can gain material goods and personal status with a minimum of physical effort.

MEMBERSHIP IN ONE-SEX PEER GROUP   The one-sex peer group, according to Miller, is a significant structural form in the lower-class community. This group is a reaction to female-dominated homes, wherein the male parent is absent from the household, is present only occasionally, or, when present, is only minimally involved in the support and rearing of children. The male-oriented peer group, then, represents the first real opportunity for lower-class boys to learn the essential aspects of the male role in the context of peers facing similar problems of sex-role identification. The desire to prove their masculinity, Miller reasoned, is what attracts lower-class boys to these one-sex peer groups. Miller saw delinquent behavior as the lower-class boy's attempt to prove that he is grown up and no longer tied to his mother's apron strings. Delinquent offenses are motivated primarily by the desire to achieve ends, status, or qualities valued within the youth's most significant cultural milieu.[62] See Figure 4.3 for the theoretical constructs of Miller's theory.

EVALUATION OF MILLER'S THESIS OF LOWER-CLASS CULTURE   Miller's theory appears most plausible when applied to the behavior of lower-class gang delinquents. These gang cultures appear to establish their own values and norms, distinct from the values and norms of the larger culture. In addition, Marvin E. Wolfgang and Franco Ferracuti argue that a subculture of violence among young males in the lower social classes legitimates the use of violence in various social situations.[63]

Miller's contention that the lower classes have distinctive values has been widely criticized. Some critics argue that the evidence shows that lower-class youths hold to the same values as those of the larger culture. For example, Travis Hirschi has found that little disagreement exists among youngsters from different classes concerning their attachment to the social bond.[64] As discussed later in this chapter, Albert K. Cohen as well as Richard A. Cloward and Lloyd E. Ohlin claimed that lower-class youths have internalized middle-class values and that their delinquent acts are a reflection of these middle-class values.[65]

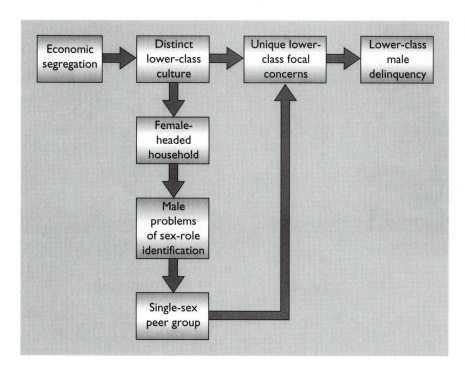

FIGURE 4.3 Miller's Theory

How Strain Affects Delinquent Behavior

Strain theorists view delinquency as a consequence of the frustration individuals feel when they are unable to achieve the goals they desire. Merton, Cohen, and Cloward and Ohlin all have contributed variations of **strain theory.**

Merton's Theory of Anomie

Merton has made an important contribution to understanding how deviant behavior is produced by different social structures. According to Merton,

> Socially deviant behavior is just as much a product of social structure as conformist be-havior. . . . Our primary aim is to discover how some social structures exert a definite pressure upon certain persons in the society to engage in nonconforming rather than conforming behavior.[66]

In *Social Theory and Social Structure,* Merton considered two elements of the so-cial and cultural systems. The first is the set of "**culturally defined goals,** purposes, and interests held out as legitimate objectives for all or for diversely located members of the society." These are the goals that people feel are worth striving for; they may be considered cultural goals. A second important aspect "defines, regulates, and controls the acceptable means of reaching out for these goals." Although a specific goal may be attained by a variety of means, the culture does not sanction all of these means. The acceptable method is referred to as the **institutionalized means.** Merton contended that the two elements must be reasonably well integrated if a culture is to be stable and run smoothly. If individuals believe that a particular goal is important, they should have a legitimate means to attain it. When a culture lacks such integration, then a state of normlessness, or anomie, occurs. Merton further asserted that contemporary U.S. culture seemed to "approximate the polar type in which great emphasis upon certain success-goals occurs without equivalent emphasis upon institutional means."[67] The lower classes are asked to orient their behavior toward the prospect of accumu-lating wealth, while they are largely denied the means to do so legitimately. The op-position of the cultural emphasis and the social structure creates intense pressure for deviation.

Merton developed a typology of the modes of adaptation that can be used when an individual is confronted with anomie. Table 4.1 lists five types of individual adaptation: a plus (+) signifies acceptance, a minus (−) signifies rejection, and a plus-or-minus (±) signifies a rejection of the prevailing values and a substitution of new ones. These modes of adaptation are used to explain how deviant behavior in general is produced by the social structure, but they can also be applied specifically to juvenile lawbreaking.[68]

TABLE 4.1

Merton's Theory of Anomie

Modes of Adaptation	Cultural Goal	Institutional Means
1. Conformity	+	+
2. Innovation	+	−
3. Ritualism	−	+
4. Retreatism	−	−
5. Rebellion	±	±

Source: This material appears in Robert K. Merton, "Social Structure and Anomie," *American Sociological Review* 3 (1938), p. 676.

CONFORMITY   If a society is well integrated and therefore anomie is absent, conformity both to cultural goals and to institutionalized means will be the most common and most widely found adaptation. Conforming juveniles accept the cultural goal of society as well as the institutional means of attaining it; they work hard in legitimate ways to become a success.

INNOVATION   When adolescents accept the cultural goal but reject the institutional means of attaining it, they may pursue other paths that frequently are not legitimate in terms of cultural values. Merton expressed the opinion that innovation resulting in deviant behavior is especially likely to occur in a society that offers success as a goal for all but at the same time withholds from a segment of the population the legitimate means of attaining that goal. For example, lower-class youths who have accepted the cultural goal of success are likely to steal if they are denied legitimate opportunities to achieve the goal they have internalized.[69] Unable to "make it" in socially acceptable ways, they tend to pursue the success goal in law-violating ways.

RITUALISM   Although they may have abandoned the cultural goals, some juveniles will continue to abide by the acceptable means for attaining them. Ritualism consists of "individually seeking a private escape from the dangers and frustrations . . . inherent in the competition for major cultural goals by abandoning these goals and clinging all the more closely to the safe routines and institutional norms."[70] For example, some of these youngsters, while keeping their behavior within the confines of the law, stop trying to achieve in school. They go through the motions of attending classes and studying but abandon the goal of success.

Whereas innovation is a mode of adaptation typical of the lower class, ritualism is encountered more frequently in the lower-middle class because parents of lower-middle-class children exert continuous pressure on them to abide by the moral mandates of society.

RETREATISM   When individuals have rejected both the goals of the culture and the institutionalized means of attaining them, they have, in effect, retreated from their society. Drug addicts have divorced themselves from the cultural goal of success and must break the law to obtain and use their drugs. Yet, even though they have none of the rewards held out by society, these socially disinherited persons face few of the frustrations involved in continuing to seek those rewards.

REBELLION   Rebellion consists of rejecting the values and institutions of one's culture and substituting for them a new set of values and institutions. The rebellious juvenile, for example, may commit himself or herself to a political ideology, such as Marxism, that is intent on establishing a new social order that has a "closer correspondence between merit, effort, and reward."[71]

Merton argued that his theory of anomie "is designed to account for some, not all, forms of deviant behavior customarily described as criminal or delinquent."[72] Thus instead of attempting to explain all the behaviors prohibited by criminal law, Merton focused attention on the pressure or strain resulting from the discrepancy between culturally induced goals and the opportunities inherent in the social structure.[73]

Evaluation of Merton's Strain Theory

Merton's revision of anomie theory has been called "the most influential single formulation in the sociology of deviance in the last 25 years and . . . possibly the most frequently quoted single paper in modern sociology."[74] This theory's influence on the later theoretical contributions of Cohen and Cloward and Ohlin demonstrates its importance to delinquency theory.[75]

One of Merton's main emphases—which has been largely ignored—is that he proposed "a theory of societal 'anomie,' not of individually felt strain."[76] Velmer S. Burton Jr. and Francis T. Cullen added that Merton's theoretical purpose is fundamentally sociological: to explain rates of deviance/crime across the social structure, not to explain which individuals feel the pressure to engage in such wayward activities. . . . Here he is true to his Durkheimian roots and portrays crime as rooted in the breakdown of normative control."[77]

Strain theory dominated criminology in the 1960s before labeling theory gained acceptance in the late 1960s and early 1970s. A major reason for the wide acceptance of strain theory in the sixties was that its central thesis of **blocked opportunity** resonated with the growing concern of Americans over equal opportunity and with the fear of liberals that injustice has serious costs. Strain theory also "did not require a broad rejection of the social order."[78]

Strain theory met increased criticism in the 1970s. Many commentators at the time argued that strain theory had little empirical support and needed to be abandoned as a causal explanation of crime.[79] Strain theory survived those attacks, but now plays a more limited role in explaining crime/delinquency.[80] In the 1980s, Thomas J. Bernard defended strain theory as not having been tested adequately.[81]

Margaret Farnworth and Michael J. Leiber's analysis of a self-report study of 1,614 delinquents revealed that the appropriate operationalization of strain theory is to measure the disjunction between economic aspirations and educational expectations.[82] "Strain" would result, then, "when a person is strongly committed to making a lot of money, but views college as beyond attainment."[83] They further stated that "strain is a better predictor of delinquency than financial goals alone when commitment is operationalized in a way that is consistent with a strain perspective."[84] They contended that the failure of strain theory in recent empirical study has more to do with inappropriate operationalization than the empirical invalidity of its basic postulates.[85]

Robert Agnew's revised strain theory of delinquency points to another source of frustration and strain: the blockage of pain-avoidance behavior.[86] Agnew argued that when juveniles are compelled to remain in painful or aversive environments, such as family and school, the ensuing frustration is likely to lead to escape attempts or anger-based delinquent behavior. His examination of data from the Youth in Transition survey revealed that a juvenile's location in aversive environments in the school and family "has a direct effect on delinquency and an indirect effect through anger."[87]

Additionally, Agnew has developed a "general strain theory of crime and delinquency" that distinguishes three different sources of strain: "failure to achieve positively valued goals," "the removal of positively valued stimuli from the individual," and "the presentation of negative stimuli." He then presented guidelines, or a strategy, for measuring strain and explored under what conditions strain is likely to result in "nondelinquent and delinquent coping."[88] Timothy Brezina built on Agnew's general strain theory by exploring the ways in which delinquency may enable adolescents to cope with strain. Brezina found that "delinquency enables adolescents to minimize the negative emotional consequences of strain," and delinquency, then, becomes an adaptive response to aversive environments.[89]

Raymond Paternoster and Paul Mazerolle conducted a comprehensive test of general strain theory with a longitudinal sample of adolescents and found that several dimensions of strain are positively related to a wide range of delinquent involvements. "Strain," according to Paternoster and Mazerolle's findings, "has both a direct effect on delinquency and indirect effects by weakening the inhibitions of the social bond and increasing one's involvement with delinquent peers."[90] They concluded that "general strain theory makes an important contribution to delinquency theory."[91]

Lisa M. Broidy's test of general strain theory included measures of negative emotions, including anger, and legitimate coping mechanisms. She found that strain, negative emotions, and legitimate coping are all related, but not always in the expected direction. The nature of the link among these three variables and criminal/delinquent outcomes are shaped by the types of strain and negative affect that individuals experience.[92]

The general strain theory focuses on the individual level of analysis, whereas the institutional anomie theory (IAT) is in the process of reforming the macrolegal elements of Merton's theory.[93] In a testing of cross-national data sets, Jukka Savolainen finds support for the institutional anomie theory. In this study, the positive effects of economic inequality on the level of lethal violence are limited to nations characterized by weak collective institutions of social protection.[94]

Scott Menard developed a rigorous test of anomie theory for a national sample of adolescents (National Youth Survey) in their early, middle, and late adolescence.[95] He found that such a test of Merton's anomie theory explained 17 to 23 percent of the variance in the frequency of minor delinquency, 8 to 14 percent of index offending, 14 to 30 percent of marijuana use, and 2 to 18 percent of polydrug use. He concluded that "the predictive power of strain theory in general and of Merton's anomie theory in particular" has been seriously underestimated.[96]

Cohen's Theory of Delinquent Subcultures

Cohen's thesis in his book *Delinquent Boys: The Culture of the Gang* was that lower-class youths are actually protesting against the goals of middle-class culture, but they experience **status frustration,** or strain, because they are unable to attain these goals. This strain explains their membership in delinquent gangs and their nonutilitarian, malicious, and negativistic behavior.[97]

THE DELINQUENT SUBCULTURE   The social structure in American society, Cohen claimed, has an immense hold on citizens; even twelve- or thirteen-year-old children know about the class system.[98] This class system defines the middle-class values and norms children are expected to aspire to and to achieve:

> These norms are, in effect, a tempered version of the Protestant ethic which has played such an important part in the shaping of American character and American society. In brief summary, this middle-class ethic prescribes an obligation to strive, by dint of rational, ascetic, self-disciplined, and independent activity, to achieve in worldly affairs. A not irrebuttable but common corollary is the presumption that "success" is itself a sign of the exercise of these moral qualities.[99]

Status at school especially is measured by these middle-class standards. First, the teacher is hired to foster the development of middle-class personalities. Second, the teacher is likely to be a middle-class person, who values ambition and achievement and quickly recognizes and rewards these virtues in others. Third, Cohen pointed out, the educational system itself favors "quiet, cooperative, 'well-behaved' pupils" who make the teacher's job easier. It greets with disapproval the "lusty, irrepressible, boisterous youngsters who are destructive of order, routine, and predictability in the classroom."[100]

A pivotal assumption in Cohen's theory is that lower-class males internalize middle-class norms and values but then are unable to attain middle-class goals. Status frustration occurs, and the mechanism of **reaction formation** is used to handle it. On the one hand, according to Cohen, the delinquent claims that the middle-class standards do not matter, but, on the other hand, he directs irrational, malicious, unaccountable hostility toward the norms of the respectable middle-class society.[101]

The delinquent subculture offers the lower-class male the status he does not receive from the larger culture. But, of course, the status offered by the delinquent subculture is status only in the eyes of his fellow delinquents. According to this theory, the same middle-class value system in America is instrumental in generating both respectability and delinquency.[102]

Cohen added that the delinquent subculture is nonutilitarian because delinquents commit crimes "for the hell of it," without intending to gain or profit from their crimes. Cohen also claimed that malice is evident in the crimes of the delinquent subculture, that delinquents often display an enjoyment in the discomfort of others and a delight in the defiance of taboos. Further, the delinquent's conduct is right by the standards of the subculture precisely because it is wrong by the norms of the larger culture.[103]

Moreover, the delinquent subculture demonstrates versatility in its delinquent acts; members of this subculture do not specialize, as do many adult criminal gangs and "solitary" delinquents. The delinquent subculture is characterized by "short-run hedonism." It has little interest in planning activities, setting long-term goals, budgeting time, or gaining knowledge and skills that require practice, deliberation, and study. Instead, gang members hang around the corner waiting for something to turn up. A further characteristic of this subculture is its emphasis on group autonomy, which makes it intolerant of any restraint except the informal pressures of the gang itself.[104] See Figure 4.4 for the theoretical constructs of Cohen's theory.

Cohen, along with James F. Short, Jr., refined the original theory a few years later in defining five adaptations of the delinquent subculture. See Theory and Research 4.3 for an even more recent update of Cohen's theory.[105]

1. *Parent male subculture.* This refers to the negativistic subculture identified in *Delinquent Boys.*
2. *Conflict-oriented subculture.* A large gang culture that becomes involved in collective violence.
3. *Drug-addict subculture.* Groups of adolescents whose lives revolve around the trafficking and use of narcotics.
4. *Semiprofessional theft.* Youths who rob or steal for monetary gain.
5. *Middle-class subculture.* Delinquent groups that develop because of the strain of living in middle-class environments.[106]

EVALUATION OF COHEN'S THEORY OF DELINQUENT SUBCULTURES Cohen's theory, as well as the issues and controversies raised by this theory, have done much to spark the development of delinquency theory. James F. Short Jr. and Fred L. Strodtbeck used it to develop their research design to study youth gangs.[107] Cloward and Ohlin's later subcultural theory profited from Cohen's earlier discussion.[108]

Cohen's theory is also important because it views delinquency as a process of interaction between the delinquent youth and others rather than as the abrupt and sudden product of strain or anomie, as proposed by Merton's theory. Cohen contended that delinquency arises during a continuous interaction process whereby changes in the self result from the activities of others.[109]

Numerous criticisms have been leveled at Cohen's theory. Travis Hirschi questioned the feasibility of using status frustration as the motivational energy to account for delinquency, because most delinquent boys eventually become law-abiding, even though their lower-class status does not change. Therefore, because the lower-class boy's posi-

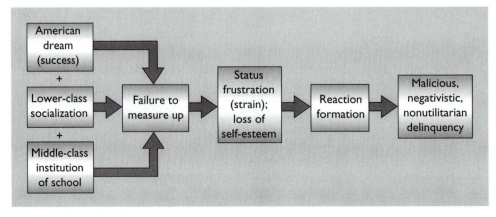

FIGURE 4.4 Cohen's Theory

THEORY AND RESEARCH 4.3

Interview with Albert K. Cohen

Question: Let's begin with the thesis that you expressed in *Delinquent Boys* thirty years ago. Would you express it any differently today?

Cohen: I don't know what form it would take, except that it would be different. It has been subject to a lot of criticisms, and I have developed some of my own reservations about it, which have not necessarily been embodied in the public criticism in the literature. It obviously would have to be rethought.

But I think in certain respects my own thinking has not been altered—the notion that most delinquent activity, like most human activity, consists of actions that people do more or less together, or that are at least oriented to other people, is still true. The motivation to engage in those activities always is to some extent the function of a person's relationships to other people and one's participation in those activities is in some sense instrumental to the promotion of satisfying relationships with others. This, I think, is the fundamental premise of the whole book; it's a basic premise, I think, to the whole idea of sociology.

What has bothered me most in the years since the publication of that book is not so much the declining influence of acceptance of some of the ideas specific to that particular interpretation of delinquency, but rather the decline of this general perspective on human conduct as applied to delinquency. I think it is a safe generalization that, in the past fifteen years or so, the literature is coming to focus more and more on the nature, the character, and the individual circumstances of persons. Thus, rather than seeing the delinquent act as something that occurs in an interactive situation and is the product of an interaction, the delinquent's actions are interpreted through that person's personality and background.

Delinquency needs to be perceived and treated as events performed in company of others or oriented to others, guided somehow by the norms, expectations, and beliefs that are derived from and are sustained by one's communication with other people. The delinquent act is an event in a matrix of interaction, and in that matrix there are a number of people. One of the persons will be the person to whom the act will be accredited. Amongst all the people there is one person whom we point the finger at and we say, "That's the person who did it!" But if you are trying to explain the action or the event, you don't explain it by saying, "This person did it," and then look at that person and try to find out what's special about that person, because the event was a product of the whole context in which it was embedded. What was going on at the time will include all the contributions by all the participants.

I think there is a very fundamental kind of linkage between the sociological and the psychological level. But having answered the psychological question, you are still left with the sociological question. I think *Delinquent Boys* was in a way quintessentially sociological. That doesn't make it superior to Hirschi or other studies of delinquency. The sociological question is not any more legitimate than the psychological question. But this book was addressed to the sociological question. By this I mean, it looked at certain kinds of events, in this case delinquency. It located these events in a certain space and that space was within the social system. It raised such questions as: What's going on in this society? Where does it happen? On what scale? And why?

Source: Albert K. Cohen, professor emeritus of sociology at the University of Connecticut, is the author of the classic study *Delinquent Boys: The Culture of the Gang.* He is also the author of *Deviance and Control* and edited the *Sutherland Papers* and *Prison Violence.* Interviewed in November 1983.

tion in the economic structure is relatively fixed, his eventual reform cannot be attributed to changes in the conditions that originally drove him into delinquency.[110]

David Matza challenged Cohen's radical distinction between the delinquent and the conventional actor. Matza, who sees the values of the delinquent as largely in harmony with those of the larger culture, rejected the oppositional viewpoint between delinquent and conventional values.[111] David F. Greenberg argued that the choice of target may be more rational than Cohen allows because, rather than engaging only in nonutilitarian activities, some delinquent youths can be seen as rational and committing crime for profit or gain.[112] Furthermore, while Cohen's theory may apply to a small population of delinquent boys who commit destructive acts, it fails to explain the delinquent behavior of many American adolescents who drift in and out of delinquency during their teenage years.[113] In addition, it ignores those youths who commit delinquent acts on their own. Finally, Cohen does not offer any empirical evidence to support his theory, and the vagueness of such concepts as reaction formation and lower-class internalization of middle-class values make it difficult to test his theory.

Yet Cohen's *Delinquent Boys* made a seminal contribution to the delinquency literature, and much of the delinquency research since its publication has built on its findings.

Cloward and Ohlin's Opportunity Theory

Cloward and Ohlin sought to integrate the theoretical contributions of Merton and Cohen with the ideas of Sutherland. Although Merton argued that lower-class youths strive for monetary success and Cohen contended that they strive for status, Cloward and Ohlin conceptualized success and status as separate strivings that can operate independently of each other. Cloward and Ohlin portrayed delinquents who seek an increase in status as striving for membership in the middle class, whereas other delinquent youths try to improve their economic post without changing their class position.[114]

Cloward and Ohlin proposed four basic categories of delinquent youths; these categories are Type I, Type II, Type III, and Type IV. Contesting Cohen's argument, they claimed that boys of Type I and Type II, who are striving to increase their status and whose values are consistent with those of the middle class, do not constitute the major group of delinquents. They also argued that Type IV youths, who may incur criticism from middle-class authorities for their "lack of ambition," usually avoid trouble with the law because they tend to avoid middle-class institutions and authorities as much as possible.[115]

Cloward and Ohlin contended that the most serious delinquents are Type III youths, who are oriented toward conspicuous consumption. Of the four groups, type III youths experience the greatest conflict with middle-class values, since they "are looked down upon both for what they do want (i.e., the middle-class style of life) and for what they do not want (i.e., 'crass materialism')."[116] Cloward and Ohlin use Merton's theory to explain the particular form of delinquency that Type III youths commit. They assume that these youths have no legitimate opportunities to improve their economic position and therefore that they will become involved in one of three specialized gang subcultures: "criminal," "conflict," and "retreatist."[117]

THE CRIMINAL SUBCULTURE   The criminal subculture is primarily based on criminal values. Within this subculture, such illegal acts as extortion, fraud, and theft are accepted as means to achieve economic success. This subculture provides the socialization by which new members learn to admire and respect older criminals and to adopt their lifestyles and behaviors. As new members master the techniques and orientations of the criminal world through criminal episodes, they become hostile and distrust representatives of the larger society, whom they regard as "suckers" to be exploited whenever possible.[118]

THE CONFLICT SUBCULTURE   Violence is the key ingredient in the conflict subculture, whose members pursue status, or "rep," through force or threats of force. Warrior youth gangs exemplify this subculture. The "bopper," the basic role model, fights with weapons to win respect from other gangs and to demand deference from the adult world. The bopper's role expectation is to show great courage in the face of personal danger and always to defend his personal integrity and the honor of the gang.[119]

A reputation for toughness, the primary goal of fighting gangs, ensures respect from peers and fear from adults and provides a means of gaining access to the scarce resources for pleasure and opportunity in underprivileged areas. Relationships with the adult world are typically weak because gang members are unable to find appropriate adult role models who offer a structure of opportunity leading to adult success.[120]

THE RETREATIST SUBCULTURE   The consumption of drugs is the basic activity of the retreatist subculture. Feeling shut out from conventional roles in the family or occupational world, members of this subculture have withdrawn into an arena where the ultimate goal is the "kick." The "kick" may mean alcohol, marijuana, hard drugs, sexual experiences, hot music, or any combination of these, but whatever is chosen, the retreatist is seeking an intense awareness of living and a sense of pleasure that is "out of this world."[121]

The retreatist subculture generates a new order of goals and criteria of achievement. But instead of attempting to impose their system of values on the world of the "straights," retreatists are content merely to strive for status and deference within their own subculture.[122]

Cloward and Ohlin noted that although these subcultures exhibit essentially different orientations, the lines between them may become blurred. For example, a subculture primarily involved with conflict may on occasion become involved in systematic theft. Members of a criminal subculture may sometimes become involved in conflict with a rival gang.[123] Figure 4.5 reveals the main theoretical constructs of Cloward and Ohlin's theory.

EVALUATION OF CLOWARD AND OHLIN'S OPPORTUNITY THEORY   Cloward and Ohlin's **opportunity theory** is important because of the impact it has had on the development of public policy and criminological theory. Delbert S. Elliot and Harwin L. Voss used variables drawn from Cloward and Ohlin's study to design their influential study of school dropouts.[124] Mobilization for Youth, a delinquency prevention program in New York City, was based on the premise that youths who do not have legitimate avenues to success will pursue illegitimate ones. The 1960s War on Poverty welfare programs likewise were influenced by Cloward and Ohlin's thesis that lower-class individuals will pursue illegitimate opportunities if they are not provided legitimate ones.[125]

Irving Spergel, examining Cloward and Ohlin's theoretical construct that different patterns of delinquency are found in neighborhoods with varying opportunity

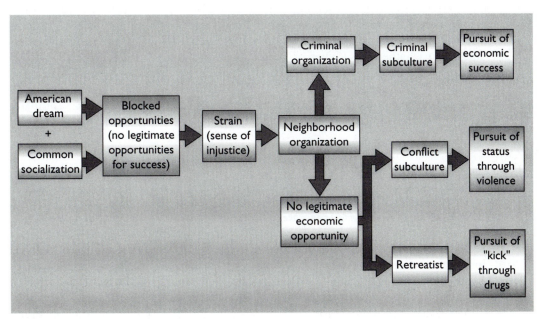

FIGURE 4.5 Cloward and Ohlin's Theory

structures, supported this construct when they identified three subcultural neighborhoods in New York City, each of which had an opportunity structure consistent with the socioeconomic status of the neighborhood.[126] Erdman B. Palmore and Phillip E. Hammond's study of children in the Aid to Families with Dependent Children welfare program also found that delinquency was more common in sections of the city where family and neighborhood disorganization were present; delinquency rates were lower in areas exhibiting stable family patterns and low disorganization.[127]

The research of James F. Short Jr. and associates offered mixed support for Cloward and Ohlin's opportunity theory. On one hand, they found discrepancies between juveniles' aspirations and their expectations for fulfillment by legitimate means. But Short and colleagues also found that although African Americans experienced the greatest discrepancy between aspirations and achievement expectations, they were the least delinquent.[128]

The findings of several studies disagree sharply with the assumptions of Cloward and Ohlin's opportunity theory. Gwynn Nettler has charged that the two key concepts in the theory are aspiration and opportunity and that neither term is defined very clearly.[129] A number of studies have failed to find evidence in gang delinquents of the particular kind of thought processes suggested by Cloward and Ohlin.[130] Ruth Kornhauser, in reviewing the empirical research on aspirations and expectations of delinquents, claims it shows that delinquency is consistently associated with both low expectations and low aspirations; delinquents may not expect to get much, but they do not want much either. Thus, Kornhauser challenged the strain aspect of opportunity theory.[131]

Cloward and Ohlin's theory has been further criticized because it portrays gang delinquents as talented youth who have a sense of injustice about the lack of legitimate opportunities available to them. In contrast, many studies have found that gang delinquents have limited social and intellectual abilities.[132] Cloward and Ohlin's concept of the criminal, conflict, and retreatist gangs is further challenged because of a lack of empirical adequacy. Studies simply have not found the existence of these three lower-class types of male gangs.[133]

On balance, strain theory explains that juveniles are "pushed" into delinquency as a result of a lack of access to opportunities for the realization of a set of success goals. In other words, those who are denied legitimate achievement of their success goals often turn to delinquency as a means of reaching desired goals or of striking back at an unfair system.[134] The role of blocked opportunity, whether found in Merton or Cloward and Ohlin, has received considerable attention in the sociological analysis of male delinquency. Cloward and Ohlin add that it is the Type III youths who have no legitimate opportunities to improve their economic position and therefore are likely to become involved in criminal, conflict, or retreatist gang subculture. There is considerable question about whether these types of gang subcultures actually exist, especially the retreatist gang subculture. Yet Cloward and Ohlin's theory was designed to explain the behavior of seriously delinquent urban male gang members, and studies that focus on these youths have produced strong support for opportunity theory. Table 4.3 compares the structural and cultural theories of delinquency.

The Relationship Between Social Stratification and Delinquency

Social structure explanations of delinquency relate delinquent behavior to the structural and cultural characteristics of youth in the United States. A youth may become delinquent because he or she lives in a disorganized community, because he or she is unable to achieve middle-class standards, because he or she becomes part of a delinquent subculture due to status frustration, or because of the lower-class values of the subculture to which he or she belongs.

TABLE 4.3

Summary of Social Structure and Cultural Theories of Crime

Theory	Cause of Crime Identified in the Theory	Supporting Research
CULTURAL DEVIANCE THEORIES		
Shaw and McKay	Delinquent behavior becomes an alternative mode of socialization through which youths who are part of disorganized communities are attracted to delinquent values and traditions	Moderate
Miller	Lower-class culture has a distinctive culture of its own, and its focal concerns, or values, make lower-class boys more likely to become involved in delinquent behavior	Weak
Wolfgang and Ferracuti	Subcultures of violence exist among lower-class males and legitimize the use of violence	Moderate
STRAIN THEORIES		
Merton	Social structure exerts pressure on those individuals who cannot attain the cultural goal of success to engage in nonconforming behavior	Weak
Cohen	Lower-class boys are unable to attain the goals of middle-class culture, and therefore they become involved in nonutilitarian, malicious, and negative behavior	Weak
OPPORTUNITY THEORY		
Cloward and Ohlin	Lower-class boys seek out illegitimate means to attain middle-class success goals if they are unable to attain them through legitimate means, usually through one of three specialized gang contexts	Moderate

These theories ultimately rest on the importance of class as a significant variable in the explanation of delinquent behavior. But, as previously indicated, recently the relationship between social class and delinquency has been deemphasized in delinquency research. Self-report studies show that delinquent behavior is widespread through all social classes.[135] Charles Tittle and associates, for example, flatly declare that the relationship between social class and delinquency is a myth.[136]

However, Elliott and Huizinga's national sample revealed that class differences among males are found in the prevalence and incidence of all serious offenses and in the incidence of nonserious and total offenses. Among females, the only significant and persistent class differences involved felony assault and public disorder offenses.[137] A survey by John Braithwaite also found that research tends to support higher offense rates among lower-class juveniles. He added that studies not reporting those higher rates are particularly susceptible to methodological criticism. Braithwaite concluded: "The sociological study of crime does not need to 'shift away from class-based theories' as Tittle, et al. [advocate]. What we require are class-based theories which explain why certain types of crimes are perpetuated disproportionately by the powerless, while other forms of crime are almost exclusively the prerogative of the powerful."[138]

Social capital theory, developed by James S. Coleman in the late 1980s, suggests that one of the reasons lower-class individuals have higher rates of crime and delinquency is that they lack social capital. Coleman defines social capital as "the resources that reside in the social structure itself—norms, social networks and interpersonal relationships that contribute to a child's growth."[139]

Coleman, in a subsequent paper, adds that "just as physical capital is created by making changes in materials so as to form tools and facilitate production, human capital is created by changing persons so as to give them skills and capabilities that make them able to act in new ways."[140] An important consideration is how parents use the social capital of the family to create the capabilities and skills that become the human capital of their children.

Coleman explains that the social capital needed to create human capital includes more than the family:

> Beyond the family, social capital in the community exists in the interest, and even the intrusiveness, of one adult in the activities of someone else's child. Sometimes that interest takes the form of enforcing norms imposed by parents or by the community; sometimes it takes the form of lending a sympathetic ear to problems not discussable with parents; sometimes volunteer youth group leadership, or participation in other youth-related activities.[141]

Coleman goes on to suggest how social capital found in effective, functioning, intact nuclear and extended families, as well as well-integrated neighborhoods and communities, can achieve more effective crime control in the United States.[142] For example, he notes that "effective norms that inhibit crime in a city make it possible for women to walk freely outside at night and for old people to leave their homes without fear."[143]

Bill McCarthy and John Hagan, in combining insights from Coleman's work on social capital, Sutherland's theory of differential association, and Granovetter's research on embeddedness, suggest that "embeddedness in networks of deviant associations provides access to tutelage relationships that facilitate the acquisition of criminal skills and attitudes, assets that we call 'criminal capital.' "[144] In testing this hypothesis with a sample of homeless youth who were involved in drug selling, theft, and prostitution, they found that embeddedness in criminal networks does enhance exposure to tutelage relationships, resulting in increased rates of delinquency.[145]

Hagan and McCarthy's prize-winning book, *Mean Streets: Youth Crime and Homelessness,* addressed the issue of the lack of social capital in the lives of homeless youths. Using observational, survey, and interview data gathered in Toronto and Vancouver, they documented the family and school histories, living conditions, and criminal experiences of youth who were living on the streets. The homeless population they studied was about two-thirds male and one-third female, and the males were a little older than the females (18.1 versus 17.1 years old). Between a quarter and a third came from families that experienced frequent unemployment. Less than a third of these youths lived with both biological parents at the time they left home. Most had experienced physical abuse (87 percent) and neglect. Also common was parental use of alcohol and drugs.[146] One youth told why he left home at sixteen:

> My parents threw me out. . . . They're drug addicts. Hash, weed, coke, crack—everything. I didn't want to leave but they just threw me out. I had a huge fight with my dad. We'd fight 'cause I'd go, "quit drugs," and he would go "no." . . . I'd go, "quit drinking." He'd say "no." So we just argued about that most of the time. And one day he goes, "I think its about time you leave, get on your own." So I just left.[147]

The Social Policy Implications of Structural Explanations of Delinquency

Two important policy implications of structural explanations of delinquency are the consequences of the reduced capital that lower-class children have and the importance of disorganized communities in affecting the decisions that lower-class children make.

Lower-class youngsters often lack access to areas that are vitally important in allowing them to realize their potential. They may be forced to struggle to meet their basic survival needs. Economic deprivation is first felt at home, and the squalor of their home experiences is what drives many youths to the streets.[148] Mothers and fathers cannot make do on a day-to-day basis when they live on the edge of economic survival. Not surprisingly, frequently the father leaves, children are neglected and abused, and the mother is gone much of the time simply trying to make ends meet. The harsh reality of a lack of food, clothing, and a warm home may lead a youth to conclude that "you have to learn to hustle at an early age if you want to make it."[149]

Lower-class children further encounter the difficulty of coping in constructive ways when they are unable to meet the success goals of society. This inability to meet the success goals usually becomes evident at school. Both lower- and middle-class youths may respond to lack of success with disruptive behavior, truancy, and crime. The inability to find a job or to compete in the marketplace encourages these adolescents to pursue illegitimate means. Robert Gillespie's survey of fifty-seven studies shows considerable support for a relationship between unemployment and property crime. He found that the relationship is most evident in studies using such variables as class, crime, and delinquency in a methodologically sophisticated manner.[150] Stephen W. Baron and Timothy F. Hartnagel's recent study of 200 homeless male street youths found that lengthy unemployment and a lack of income, as well as anger, increase their criminal activities.[151] However, Steven F. Messner and colleagues, in using national data for 1967–1998, found that child poverty is positively related to arrests, but unemployment yields a negative effect on youth offending.[152]

In addition, lower-class youngsters must deal with the impact of disorganized communities on their attitudes and worldview. Learning to adapt to a disorganized community may easily lead adolescents to an acceptance of cultural patterns that are conducive to delinquent behavior. For youths who experience economic deprivation at home, the streets offer the promise of attaining goods and services that their parents could never afford. In these disorganized communities, youth gangs typically are well-established; in many communities youngsters may feel required to join a gang for safety. Disorganized communities also offer drugs of every type, frequent contact with adult criminals, and ongoing exposure to violence. Mary E. Pattillo's study of an African American middle-class neighborhood in Chicago found that this neighborhood was closer to high poverty and high-crime areas than were white middle-class neighborhoods and, as a result, had more problems with gang members and drug dealers.[153]

Thomas J. Bernard's "Angry Aggression among the 'Truly Disadvantaged' " explained the high levels of anger and aggression among members of the underclass.[154] He theorized that three social factors—urban environments, low social position, and racial and ethnic discrimination—increased the likelihood that the "truly disadvantaged" will react with frequent or intense physiological arousal. Social isolation, a fourth social factor, concentrated the effects of the first three factors through multiple feedback loops. The end result, according to Bernard's theory, is a "peak" of angry aggression that is comparable to learned helplessness.[155]

This theory begins with an individual level that considers the physiological and cognitive bases of angry aggression in the context of this person's biological and psychological characteristics. Then an aggregate-level theory is developed about the distribution of crime rates among social groups in such circumstances as the "truly disadvantaged" life. The individual-level theory predicts that individuals who live under such circumstances will demonstrate high levels of angry aggression even if they have normal biological and psychological characteristics. The third level of theory construction considers individuals' abnormal biological and psychological characteristics that, the theory predicts, will intensify and increase the degree of angry aggression. Existing research, according to Bernard, has found that each of these theoretical postulates is associated with increased rates of violence and delinquency.[156]

Thus, recent evidence appears to support a relationship between social class, disorganization of the community, and delinquency. The type of informal community controls found in the Chicago Area Projects during the 1930s and 1940s perhaps offers one of the most hopeful means to reduce the rates of delinquency in high crime areas. In their innovative work on neighborhoods and crime, Robert Sampson and colleagues developed the notion of "collective efficacy" which relates to informal social control and cohesion, or mutual trust, found among neighborhoods that most effectively control youth crime.[157] This collective efficacy is what characterized the most effective Chicago Area Projects' communities and is found in present-day low crime urban communities. The task of policymakers is to provide the structure or framework from which neighborhood solidarity and grass-roots community organization can arise (see Chapter 10 for more development of the grassroots community organization concept).

SUMMARY

This chapter describes some of the best-known theories in sociology. Shaw and McKay, members of the Chicago School, showed the ecological importance of where a young person lives. The closer youths live to the inner city, the more likely they are to become involved in delinquency. But the explanation for the delinquency in these areas goes beyond that of social disorganization, for a cultural tradition passes these criminogenic norms from one generation to the next. Merton's social structure and anomie theory states that the social structure of a society influences the behavior that occurs in that society. Youths who are caught in anomie or normlessness are more likely to become deviant or delinquent than those who are not. Cohen's theory of lower-class gang cultures, derived from Merton's work as well as that of others, contends that lower-class youths aspire to middle-class values, but their inability to attain them causes them to invert these values and become involved in negativistic, malicious, and nonutilitarian behaviors. Cloward and Ohlin argue that lower-class gang youths aspire to middle-class values but become involved in illegitimate pursuits because they are unable to attain these pursuits legitimately. Yet Miller contends that lower-class youths do not aspire to middle-class values because they have their own lower-class values, or focal concerns, and these focal concerns encourage involvement in delinquent behavior.

The context of all these theories relates to the structure of society, and these structural theories see delinquency as a response to inequalities. They vary in the mechanisms they describe as mediating the impact of inequalities, but their focus is still to identify a channel through which the pressure toward delinquency flows. Social structural theories propose that structural and cultural disorder results in high rates of crime, unsafe and disruptive living conditions, and the breeding ground for a subculture of unsocialized individuals who strike out at their society. Yet this structural equation requires another element, namely, the social process involved in an individual's becoming a delinquent. The next chapter discusses the process of becoming a delinquent.

KEY TERMS

Chicago Area Projects, p. 101
blocked opportunity, p. 108
cultural deviance theory, p. 104
cultural transmission theory, p. 99
culturally defined goals, p. 106
differential opportunity structure, p. 98
focal concerns of the lower class, p. 104

institutionalized means, p. 106
opportunity theory, p. 113
reaction formation, p. 109
social capital theory, p. 115
social disorganization, p. 96
status frustration, p. 109
strain theory, p. 106

CRITICAL THINKING QUESTIONS

1. According to Shaw and McKay, what is the relationship among ecology, social disorganization, and transmission of deviant culture?
2. Which of the theories in this chapter impressed you as being most logical? Why?
3. Should poverty exclude a youngster from responsibility for delinquent behavior? Why or why not?
4. Do you believe that lower-class youngsters aspire to middle-class values? Or do they have their own values?
5. How important does poverty appear to be from the stories that you read in *Voices of Delinquency?*
6. According to the stories found in *Voices of Delinquency,* what seemed to be present for poor youths to walk away from a delinquent lifestyle?
7. Several of the individuals in *Voices of Delinquency* were middle-class but became involved in delinquent behavior. What structural explanations of delinquency most likely explain middle-class delinquency?

WEB DESTINATIONS

Read about Opportunity and Strain Theory in greater detail from the Hewett School of Norwich, Norfolk, UK.

http://www.hewett.norfolk.sch.uk

Find many links on peer influence and crime on the Juvenile Justice Clearinghouse site.

http://www.criminology.fsu.edu/jjclearinghouse/ jj13.html

Go to Hewett's Crime and Deviance Home page for links to Durkheim and Anomie, Merton's Strain Theory, Cloward and Ohlin's Differential Opportunity Theory, Sykes and Matza's Techniques of Neutralization, and Labeling Theories.

http://www.hewett.norfolk.sch.uk/curric/soc/crime/ crim.htm

NOTES

1. Interviewed in April 1987.
2. Edwin Schur, *Our Criminal Society* (Englewood Cliffs, N.J.: Prentice-Hall, 1969), p. 15.
3. Robert J. Sampson and W. B. Groves, "Community Structure and Crime: Testing Social-Disorganization Theory," *American Journal of Sociology* 94 (1989), pp. 774–802.
4. Robert J. Sampson and William Julius Wilson, "Toward a Theory of Race, Crime, and Urban Equality," in *Crime and Inequality,* edited by John Hagan and Ruth D. Peterson (Stanford, California: Stanford University Press, 1995), p. 49.
5. See Emile Durkheim, *Suicide,* translated by John A. Spaulding and George Simpson (New York: Free Press of Glencoe, 1893).
6. William I. Thomas and Florian Znaniecki, *The Polish Peasant in Europe and America,* 5 volumes (New York: Knopf, 1927). For an excellent review of Thomas and Znaniecki's five-volume work on the Polish peasant, see Randall Collins and Michael Makowsky, *The Discovery of Society,* 4th ed. (New York: Random House, 1989), pp. 189–190.
7. Robert E. Park, Ernest W. Burgess, and Roderick D. McKenzie, eds., *The City* (Chicago: University of Chicago Press, 1967 [1925]).
8. S. P. Breckinridge and Edith Abbott, *The Delinquent Child and the Home* (New York: Arno Press, 1970).
9. Frederick M. Thrasher, *The Gang: A Study of 1,313 Gangs in Chicago* (Chicago: University of Chicago Press, 1927).
10. Jon Snodgrass, "Clifford R. Shaw and Henry D. McKay, Chicago Criminologists," *British Journal of Criminology* 16 (January 1976), pp. 1–19.
11. Clifford R. Shaw, *The Natural History of Delinquent Careers* (Chicago: University of Chicago Press, 1931), pp. 69–70.
12. Ibid.
13. Jon Snodgrass, *The American Criminological Tradition: Portraits of the Men and Ideology in a Discipline.* Ph.D. dissertation, University of Pennsylvania, 1972.
14. There is a cultural deviance component to Shaw and McKay's perspective, but Ruth Rosner Kornhauser claims it is an unnecessary aspect of their social disorganization theory. See Ruth Rosner Kornhauser, *Social Sources of Delinquency: An Appraisal of Analytic Models* (Chicago: University of Chicago Press, 1978), p. 79.
15. Albert J. Reiss, Jr., "Settling the Frontiers of a Pioneer in American Criminology: Henry McKay," in *Delinquency, Crime and Society,* edited by James F. Short Jr. (Chicago: University of Chicago Press, 1976), p. 79.
16. Harold Finestone, *Victims of Change: Juvenile Delinquents in American Society* (Westport, Conn.: Greenwood Press, 1976), p. 90.

17. George B. Vold and Thomas J. Bernard, *Theoretical Criminology,* 3d ed. (New York: Oxford University Press, 1986), p. 163.

18. Clifford R. Shaw, *Delinquency Areas* (Chicago: University of Chicago Press, 1929), pp. 198-203.

19. Clifford R. Shaw and Henry D. McKay, *Social Factors in Juvenile Delinquency; Report on the Causes of Crime,* Vol. II (Washington, D.C.: National Commission on Law Observance and Enforcement, 1931), p. 60.

20. Clifford R. Shaw and Henry D. McKay, *Juvenile Delinquency and Urban Areas* (Chicago: University of Chicago Press, 1942).

21. Ysabel Rennie, *The Search for Criminal Man* (Lexington, Mass.: Lexington Books, 1978), p. 129.

22. Finestone, *Victims of Change,* pp. 83–84.

23. Ibid., p. 92.

24. Ibid., p. 99.

25. Finestone, *Victims of Change,* p. 90.

26. Shaw and McKay, *Juvenile Delinquency and Urban Areas,* pp. 38–39.

27. Rodney Stark, "Deviant Places: A Theory of the Ecology of Crime," *Criminology* 25 (1987), p. 894.

28. W. R. Arnold and T. M. Brungardt, *Juvenile Misconduct and Delinquency* (Boston: Houghton Mifflin, 1983), p. 113.

29. R. N. Davidson, *Crime and Environment* (New York: St. Martin's Press, 1981), p. 89.

30. Robert J. Bursik Jr., "Ecological Stability and the Dynamics of Delinquency," in *Communities and Crime,* Vol. 8, edited by Albert J. Reiss, Jr., and Michael Tonry (Chicago: University of Chicago Press, 1986), p. 36.

31. John Laub, *Criminology in the Making: An Oral History* (Boston: Northeastern University Press, 1983), p. 10.

32. James F. Short Jr., introduction to *Delinquency, Crime and Society,* edited by James F. Short Jr. (Chicago: University of Chicago Press, 1976), p. 3.

33. Robert J. Bursik Jr., "Social Disorganization and Theories of Crime and Delinquency: Problems and Prospects," *Criminology* 26 (November 1988), p. 522.

34. Ora Simcha-Fagan and Joseph E. Schwartz, "Neighborhood and Delinquency: An Assessment of Contextual Effects," *Criminology* 24 (1986), pp. 667–704.

35. Ibid.

36. Robert J. Sampson and W. Byron Groves, "Community Structure and Crime: Testing Social-Disorganization Theory," *American Journal of Sociology* (January 1989), pp. 774–802.

37. Ibid., p. 704. For an article that examines how neighborhood factors influence rates of delinquency among African American youths, see Faith Peeples and Rolf Loeber, "Do Individual Factors and Neighborhood Context Explain Ethnic Differences in Juvenile Delinquency?" *Journal of Quantitative Criminology* 10 (1994), pp. 141–157.

38. Robert J. Sampson, "Linking Time and Place: Dynamic Contextualism and the Future of Criminological Inquiry," *Journal of Research in Crime and Delinquency* 30 (November 1993), p. 426.

39. Ibid.

40. Ibid.

41. Ibid., p. 435.

42. Robert J. Sampson and Stephen W. Raudenbush, *National Institute of Justice Research in Brief,* "Disorder in Urban Neighborhoods—Does It Lead to Crime?" (Washington, D.C.: U.S. Department of Justice, 2001), p. 2.

43. For how Shaw influenced the Chicago Area Projects, see Ernest Burgess, Joseph Lohman, and Clifford Shaw, "The Chicago Area Project," *Yearbook* (National Probation Association, 1937), pp. 8–10; Steven Schlossman and Michael Sedlak, "The Chicago Area Project Revisited," *Crime and Delinquency* (July 1983), pp. 398–460; and Steven Schlossman, Gail Zellman, and Richard Shavelson, *Delinquency Prevention in South Chicago: A Fifty-Year Assessment of the Chicago Area Project* (Santa Monica, Calif.: Rand, 1984).

44. Bursik, "Social Disorganization and Theories of Crime and Delinquency," pp. 519–551; James M. Byrne and Robert J. Sampson, eds., *The Social Ecology of Crime* (New York: Springer-Verlag, 1986); Reiss and Tonry, *Communities and Crime;* Stark, "Deviant Places," pp. 893–909.

45. Dennis W. Roncek, "High Schools and Crime: A Replication," *Sociological Quarterly* 26 (1985), pp. 491–505; Dennis W. Roncek and Antoinette LoBosco, "The Effect of High Schools on Crime in their Neighborhoods," *Social Science Quarterly* 64 (1983), pp. 598–613.

46. Jeanette Covington and Ralph B. Taylor, "Neighborhood Revitalization and Property Crime." Paper presented at the Annual Meeting of the American Sociological Association (Atlanta, 1988).

47. Lyle W. Shannon, *The Relationship of Juvenile Delinquency and Adult Crime to the Changing Ecological Structure of the City.* Executive Report submitted to the National Institute of Justice, 1982; and Lyle W. Shannon, *The Development of Serious Criminal Careers and the Delinquent Neighborhood.* Executive Report submitted to the National Institute of Justice and Delinquency Prevention, 1984.

48. Janet L. Heitgerd and Robert J. Bursik Jr., "Extracommunity Dynamics and the Ecology of Delinquency," *American Journal of Sociology* 92 (January 1987), pp. 775–787.

49. Paul E. Bellair, "Social Interaction and Community Crime: Examining the Importance of Neighbor Networks," *Criminology* 35 (1997), pp. 677–703.

50. Fred E. Markowitz, Paul E. Bellair, Allen E. Liska, and Jianhong Liu, "Extending Social Disorganization Theory: Modeling the Relationships between Cohesion, Disorder, and Fear," *Criminolgy* 39 (2001), p. 293.

51. D. Wayne Osgood and Jeff M. Chambers, "Social Disorganization Outside the Metropolis: An Analysis of Rural Youth Violence," *Criminology* 38 (February 2000), p. 81.

52. Bursik, "Social Disorganization and Theories of Crime and Delinquency," p. 539.

53. Shannon, *The Relationship of Juvenile Delinquency and Adult Crime to the Changing Ecological Structure of the City;* Shannon, *The Development of Serious Criminal Careers and the Delinquent Neighborhood.*

54. John W. C. Johnstone, "Social Class, Social Areas, and Delinquency," *Sociology and Social Research* 63 (1978), pp. 49–77.

55. Per-Olof H. Wikstrom and Rolf Loeber, "Do Disadvantaged Neighborhoods Cause Well-Adjusted Children to Become Adolescent Delinquents? A Study of Male Juve-

nile Serious Offending, Individual Risk and Protective Factors, and Neighborhood Context," *Criminology* 38 (November 2000), p. 1109.

56. Dina R. Rose and Todd R. Clear, "Incarceration, Social Capital, and Crime: Implications for Social Disorganization Theory," *Criminology* 36 (1998), p. 441.

57. Stephen J. Pfohl, *Images of Deviance and Social Control* (New York: McGraw Hill, 1985), p. 167.

58. Bursik, "Social Disorganization and Theories of Crime and Delinquency," pp. 521–538.

59. Kornhauser, *Social Sources of Delinquency,* p. 25. For a review of the decline of cultural deviance theory, see J. Mitchell Miller, Albert K. Cohen, and Kevin M. Bryant, "On the Demise and Morrow of Subculture Theories of Crime and Delinquency," *Journal of Crime and Justice* 20 (1997), pp. 167–178.

60. Walter B. Miller, "Lower-Class Culture as a Generation Milieu of Gang Delinquency," *Journal of Social Issues* 14 (1958), pp. 9–10.

61. Ibid., pp. 11–14.

62. Ibid., pp. 14–16.

63. Marvin E. Wolfgang and Franco Ferracuti, *The Subculture of Violence* (London: Tavistock, 1957). For a study that challenges the black subculture of violence thesis, see Liqun Cao, Anthony Adams, and Vickie J. Jensen, "A Test of the Black Subculture of Violence Thesis: A Research Note," *Criminology* 35 (May 1997), pp. 367–379.

64. Travis Hirschi, *Causes of Delinquency* (Berkeley: University of California Press, 1969).

65. Richard A. Cloward and Lloyd E. Ohlin, *Delinquency and Opportunity: A Theory of Delinquent Boys: The Culture of the Gang* (Glencoe, Ill.: Free Press, 1955).

66. The following analysis of social structure and anomie is adapted from Robert K. Merton, *Social Theory and Social Structure,* 2d ed. (New York: Free Press, 1957), pp. 131–132.

67. Morton Deutsch and Robert M. Krauss, *Theories in Social Psychology* (New York: Basic Books, 1965), p. 198.

68. Merton, *Social Theory and Social Structure,* pp. 139–152.

69. Cloward and Ohlin, *Delinquency and Opportunity.*

70. Merton, *Social Theory and Social Structure,* p. 151.

71. Ibid., p. 155.

72. Ibid.

73. For Merton's recent thoughts about the emergence and present status of strain theory, see Robert K. Merton, "Opportunity Structure: The Emergence, Diffusion, and Differentiation of a Sociological Concept, 1930s–1950s," in *The Legacy of Anomie Theory: Advances in Criminological Theory,* Vol. 6, edited by Freda Adler and William S. Laufer (New Brunswick, N.J.: Transaction Publishers, 1995), pp. 3–78.

74. Marshall B. Clinard, "The Theoretical Implications of Anomie and Deviant Behavior," in *Anomie and Deviant Behavior,* edited by Marshall B. Clinard (New York: Free Press, 1964), p. 10.

75. Albert K. Cohen, *Delinquent Boys: The Culture of the Gang* (Glencoe, Ill.: Free Press, 1955); and Cloward and Ohlin, *Delinquency and Opportunity.*

76. Velmer S. Burton Jr. and Francis T. Cullen, "The Empirical Status of Strain Theory," *Journal of Crime and Justice* 15 (1992), p. 5.

77. Ibid.

78. Ibid., pp. 2–3.

79. Travis Hirschi, *Causes of Crime* (Berkeley: University of California Press, 1969); and Ruth Kornhauser, *Social Sources of Delinquency.*

80. Robert Agnew, "Foundations for a General Strain Theory of Crime and Delinquency," *Criminology* 30 (February 1992), p. 47.

81. Thomas J. Bernard, "Control Criticisms of Strain Theory: An Assessment of Theoretical and Empirical Adequacy," *Journal of Research in Crime and Delinquency* 21 (1984), pp. 353–372; Thomas J. Bernard, "Testing Structural Strain Theories," *Journal of Research in Crime and Delinquency* 24 (1987), pp. 262–280.

82. Margaret Farnworth and Michael J. Leiber, "Strain Theory Revisited: Economic Goals, Educational Means, and Delinquency," *American Sociological Association* 54 (1989), pp. 259–279.

83. Ibid., p. 264.

84. Ibid., p. 272.

85. Ibid.

86. Agnew, "A Revised Strain Theory of Delinquency," pp. 151–167.

87. Ibid., p. 151.

88. Agnew, "Foundations for a General Theory of Crime and Delinquency," pp. 47–87. See also Robert Agnew, "Building on the Foundation for a General Strain Theory." Paper presented to the Annual Meeting of the American Society of Criminology, Washington, D.C. (November 1998); and John P. Hoffman and Alan S. Miller, "A Latent Variable Analysis of General Strain Theory," *Journal of Quantitative Criminology* 14 (1998), pp. 83–110.

89. Timothy Brezina, "Adapting to Strain: An Examination of Delinquent Coping Responses," *Criminology* 34 (1996), p. 39.

90. Raymond Paternoster and Paul Mazerolle, "General Strain Theory and Delinquency: A Replication and Extension," *Journal of Research in Crime and Delinquency* 31 (August 1994), p. 235.

91. Ibid.

92. Lisa M. Broidy, "A Test of General Strain Theory," *Criminology* 39 (February 2001), pp. 9–10. For another test of general strain theory, see John P. Hoffmann and Alan S. Miller, "A Latent Variable Analysis of General Strain Theory," *Journal of Quantitative Criminology* 14 (1998), pp. 83–110.

93. See Steven F. Messner and Richard Rosenfeld, *Crime and the American Dream* (Belmont, CA: Wadsworth/Thompson Learning, 2001; and Mitchell B. Chamlin and John K. Cochran, "Assessing Messner and Rosenfeld's Institutional Anomie Theory: A Partial Test." *Criminology* 33 (1995), pp. 411–29.

94. Jukka Savolainen, "Inequality, Welfare State, and Homicide: Further Support for the Institutional Anomie Theory," *Criminology* 38 (November 2000), p. 1021.

95. Scott Menard, "A Developmental Test of Mertonian Anomie Theory," *Journal of Research in Crime and Delinquency* 32 (May 1995), pp. 136–166.

96. Ibid., p. 169.

97. Cohen, *Delinquent Boys,* p. 25.

98. Ibid., p. 82.

99. Ibid., p. 87.

100. Ibid., pp. 113–114.

101. Ibid., p. 133.

102. Ibid., p. 137.

103. Ibid., p. 28.

104. Ibid., pp. 26–31.

105. Albert Cohen and James F. Short, "Research on Delinquent Subcultures," *Journal of Social Issues* 14 (1958), pp. 25–31.

106. Ibid.

107. James F. Short Jr. and Fred L. Strodtbeck, *Group Process and Gang Delinquency* (Chicago: University of Chicago Press, 1965).

108. Cloward and Ohlin, *Delinquency and Opportunity.*

109. Albert K. Cohen, "The Sociology of the Deviant Act: Anomie Theory and Beyond," *American Sociological Review* 30 (1965), p. 9.

110. Hirschi, *Causes of Delinquency.*

111. David Matza, *Delinquency and Drift* (New York: Wiley, 1964).

112. David F. Greenberg, "Delinquency and the Age Structure of Society," *Contemporary Crises* 1 (1977), p. 199.

113. But Cohen does deal with middle-class delinquency in the article "Middle-Class Delinquency and the Social Structure," in *Middle-Class Delinquency,* edited by E. W. Vaz (New York: Harper and Row, 1967), pp. 207–221.

114. Vold and Bernard, *Theoretical Criminology,* p. 196.

115. Cloward and Ohlin, *Delinquency and Opportunity.*

116. Vold and Bernard, *Theoretical Criminology,* p. 197.

117. Cloward and Ohlin, *Delinquency and Opportunity,* p. 97.

118. Ibid., p. 20.

119. Ibid., p. 23.

120. Ibid., p. 24.

121. Ibid., p. 25.

122. Ibid., pp. 25–26.

123. Ibid., p. 27.

124. Delbert S. Elliott and Harwin L. Voss, *Delinquency and Dropout* (Lexington, Mass.: Lexington Books, 1974).

125. Cloward and Ohlin, *Delinquency and Opportunity.*

126. Irving Spergel, *Racketville, Slumtown, Haulber* (Chicago: University of Chicago Press, 1964).

127. Erdman B. Palmore and Phillip E. Hammond, "Interacting Factors in Juvenile Delinquency," *American Sociological Review* 29 (December 1964), pp. 848–854.

128. James F. Short, Jr., Ramon Rivera, and Ray Tennyson, "Perceived Opportunities, Gang Membership and Delinquency," *American Sociological Review* 30 (1965), p. 56–57.

129. Gwynn Nettler, *Explaining Crime,* 3d ed. (New York: McGraw-Hill, 1984), pp. 228–230.

130. Hagan, *Modern Criminology,* p. 196.

131. Ruth Rosner Kornhauser, *Social Sources of Delinquency,* pp. 139–180.

132. Nettler, *Explaining Crime,* pp. 212–218.

133. Vold and Bernard, *Theoretical Criminology,* p. 200.

134. Merton, "Social Structure and Anomie," and Cloward and Ohlin, *Delinquency and Opportunity.*

135. See Chapter 2 for the findings of these self-report studies.

136. Charles R. Tittle, Wayne J. Villemez, and Douglas A. Smith, "The Myth of Social Class and Criminality: An Empirical Assessment of the Empirical Evidence," *American Sociological Review* 43 (October 1978), pp. 643–656. See also Joseph Weis, "Social Class and Crime," in *Positive Criminology,* edited by Michael Gottfredson and Travis Hirschi (Newbury Park, Calif.: Sage, 1987); and Gary Jensen and Kevin Thompson, "What's Class Got to Do with It? A Further Examination of Power-Control Theory," *American Journal of Sociology* 95 (1990), pp. 1009–1023.

137. Delbert S. Elliott and David Huizinga, "Social Class and Delinquent Behavior in a National Youth Panel," *Criminology* 21 (May 1983), p. 49.

138. John Braithwaite, "The Myth of Social Class and Criminality Reconsidered, *American Sociological Review* 46 (February 1981), p. 49.

139. James S. Coleman, "Social Capital in the Development of Human Capital: The Ambiguous Position of Private Schools." Paper presented at the Annual Conference of the National Association of Independent Schools in New York (February 25–26, 1988), pp. 1, 5.

140. James Coleman, *Foundations of Social Theory* (Cambridge: Harvard University Press, 1990), p. 304.

141. Coleman, "Social Capital in the Development of Human Capital," pp. 7–8. For an examination of social capital among twelve- to fourteen-year-old African American males, see Joseph B. Richardson, "Social Capital and Delinquency among Young African American males." Paper presented to the Annual Meeting of the American Society of Criminology, Washington, D.C. (November 1998).

142. John Hagan, *Crime and Disrepute* (Thousand Oaks, Calif.: Pine Forge Press, 1994), pp. 68–69.

143. Coleman, *Foundations of Social Theory,* p. 310.

144. Bill McCarthy and John Hagan, "Getting into Street Crimes: The Structure and Process of Criminal Embeddedness," *Social Science Research* 24 (1995), p. 63.

145. Ibid.

146. John Hagan and Bill McCarthy, *Mean Streets: Youth Crime and Homelessness* (Cambridge: Cambridge University Press, 1997), pp. 23–25.

147. Ibid., p. 25.

148. For articles that examine children's poverty, see Greg J. Duncan, "Has Children's Poverty Become More Persistent?" *American Sociological Review* 56 (August 1991), pp. 538–550; and David J. Eggebeen and Daniel T. Lichter, "Race, Family Structure, and Changing Poverty among American Children," *American Sociological Review* 56 (December 1991), pp. 801–817.

149. Interviewed in 1987.

150. Robert Gillespie, "Economic Factors in Crime and Delinquency: A Critical Review of the Empirical Evidence," *Hearings, Subcommittee on Crime of the Committee of the Judiciary, House of Representatives,* 95th Congress, serial 47 (Washington, D.C.: U.S. Government Printing Office, 1978), pp. 601–625.

151. Stephen W. Baron and Timothy F. Hartnagel, "Attributions, Affect, and Crime: Street Youths' Reactions to Unemployment," *Criminology* 35 (August 1997), p. 409. However, another study challenges this relationship between employment and reduced rates of delinquency: see Matthew Ploeger, "Youth Employment and Delin-

quency: Reconsidering a Problematic Relationship," *Criminology* 35 (November 1997), pp. 659–675.

152. Steven F. Messner, Lawrence E. Raffalovich, and Richard McMillan, "Economic Deprivation and Changes in Homicide Arrest Rates for White and Black Youths, 1967–1998: A National Time-Series Analysis," *Criminology* 39 (August 2001), 591.

153. Mary E. Pattillo, "Sweet Mothers and Gangbangers: Managing Crime in a Black Middle-Class Neighborhood," *Social Forces* (March 1998), pp. 747–774.

154. Thomas J. Bernard, "Angry Aggression among the 'Truly Disadvantaged,' " *Criminology* 28 (1990), pp. 73–96. See also William Julius Wilson, *The Truly Disadvantaged* (Chicago: University of Chicago Press, 1987).

155. Ibid., p. 74.

156. Ibid.

157. Robert J. Sampson, Jeffrey D. Morenoff, and Felton Earls, "Beyond Social Capital: Spatial Dynamics of Collective Efficacy for Children," *American Sociological Review* 64 (1999), 633–660.

chapter 5

SOCIAL PROCESS THEORIES

OBJECTIVES

After reading this chapter, the student will be able to answer the following questions:

- Do delinquents learn crime from others?

- Why is it that youngsters go routinely from delinquent to non-delinquent acts and then back to delinquent behavior?

- What control mechanisms insulate youngsters from delinquent behavior?

- How important is the self-concept when it comes to delinquency?

- Does considering more than one theory increase the explanations of delinquency?

An individual who grew up in California tells about the beginning of his delinquent career:

I went out with this dude one night. He said he would be back in a minute and went in and robbed this store while I was in the car. He came out and we took off. As he was pulling all of this money out of a sack and giving me my share, I said, "What the hell is going on? Why are you giving me this?" He said, "You were out in the car and you were the driver." He then said that he had done his share, and now it was my turn. I had never robbed anyone in my life. He gave me this gun to use; I think it was a .38 special. It was one of those long ones. I stuck it in my belt and walked into this place. I really didn't want to rob anybody. Hell, I was scared to death. I went back to get a Twinkie and that *became my name—the cupcake bandit. So I gave it to the guy who was as young as I was, and he asked me if there was anything else. He was acting real nervous. I guess I was acting real hardassed. I said, "Naw, just put it in the bag." He was getting change out because I gave him a dollar. I said to put it all in a bag. I meant the change. I wasn't going to rob him; I had changed my mind. The guy just started filling up the bag with money. When he started doing that, I got bold and told him to put the other till [money from the other cash register] in the bag too. That was my first robbery, and after that, it was easy.*[1]

Why does it get easy after you have once participated in deviant behavior? Is this the same for minor and serious forms of delinquency?

Social process theories, the focus of this chapter, examine the interactions between individuals and their environments that influence them to become involved in certain behaviors—in this case, delinquency. In the above quotation, the interaction between this young man and his companion influenced him to pursue a life of crime. Differential association, drift, and social control theories became popular in the 1960s because they provided a theoretical mechanism for the translation of environmental factors into individual motivations. Differential association theory examines how delinquents learn crime from others. Drift theory proposes that any examination of the **process of becoming deviant** must take seriously both the internal components of the individual and the influence of the external environment. Social control theory provides an explanation of why youths do not become delinquent as well as why they do become delinquent. In addition to these three social process theories, this chapter also describes and evaluates four integrated theories.

Differential Association Theory

Edwin H. Sutherland's formulation of **differential association theory** proposes that delinquents learn crime from others. His basic premise was that delinquency, like any other form of behavior, is a product of social interaction. In developing the theory of differential association, Sutherland contended that individuals are constantly being changed as they take on the expectations and points of view of the people with whom they interact in small, intimate groups.[2] Sutherland began with the notion that criminal behavior is to be expected of individuals who have internalized a preponderance of definitions that are favorable to law violations.[3] In 1939, he first developed the theory in his text *Principles of Criminology,* and he continued to revise it until its final form appeared in 1945. Theory and Research 5.1 gives background information on how Sutherland discovered his own theory.

Propositions of Differential Association

Sutherland's theory of differential association is outlined in these nine propositions:

1. Criminal behavior, like other behavior, is learned from others. That is, delinquent behavior is not an inherited trait but rather an acquired one.
2. Criminal behavior is learned through a youth's active involvement with others in a process of communication. This process includes both verbal and nonverbal communication.

THEORY AND RESEARCH 5.1

Background of Edwin H. Sutherland

Edwin H. Sutherland had much in common with Clifford R. Shaw and Henry D. McKay. All were born before the turn of the century and hailed from small Midwestern towns. They all did their graduate work at the University of Chicago during the early decades of the twentieth century. They knew one another personally and frequently responded to each other's work.

McKay and Sutherland, especially, were very good friends. They corresponded regularly and got together each year during the summer. Their friendship was not surprising, because the two men were so alike in ancestry, geography, demeanor, and character. It was also McKay who first identified the theory of differential association in the second edition of Sutherland's 1934 criminology textbook.

In a conversation with Sutherland in 1935, McKay referred to the "Sutherland theory." Sutherland sheepishly inquired what the "Sutherland theory" was. McKay responded that he should read pages 51 and 52 of his own criminology text. Sutherland quickly located the pages and was surprised to find the statement "The conflict of cultures is the fundamental principle in explanations of crime." In helping Sutherland discover his own theory in his own book, McKay actually stimulated the evolution of differential association theory.

Source: Derived from Jon Snodgrass, *The American Criminological Tradition: Portraits of the Men and Ideology in a Discipline.* Ph.D. dissertation, The University of Pennsylvania, 1972.

3. The principal learning of criminal behavior occurs within intimate personal groups. The meanings that are derived from these intimate relationships are far more influential for adolescents than is any other form of communication, such as movies and newspapers.

4. When criminal behavior is learned, the learning includes techniques of committing the crime, which are sometimes very simple, and the specific direction of motives, drives, rationalizations, and attitudes. For example, a youth might learn how to hotwire a car from a delinquent companion with whom he is involved; he also acquires from the other boy the attitudes or mind-set that will enable him to set aside the moral bounds of the law.

5. The specific direction of motives and drives is learned from definitions of legal codes as favorable and unfavorable. Adolescents come into contact both with people who define the legal codes as rules to be observed and with those whose definitions of reality favor the violation of the legal codes. This creates culture conflict; the next proposition explains how this conflict is resolved.

6. A person becomes delinquent because of an excess of definitions that are favorable to violation of law over definitions that are unfavorable to violation of law. This proposition expresses the basic principle of differential association. A person becomes delinquent, then, because he or she has more involvement with delinquent peers, groups, or events than with nondelinquent peers, groups, or events. Both an excess of contacts with delinquent definitions and isolation from antidelinquent patterns are important.

7. Differential associations may vary in frequency, duration, priority, and intensity. The impact that delinquent peers or groups have on a young person depends on the frequency of the social contacts, the time period over which the contacts take place, the age at which a person experiences these contacts, and the intensity of these social interactions.

8. The process of learning criminal behavior by association with criminal and anticriminal patterns involves all the mechanisms that are involved in any other learning. The learning of delinquent behavior is not restricted to mere imitation of others' behavior.

9. Though criminal behavior is an expression of general needs and values, it is not explained by those general needs and values, because noncriminal behavior is an expression of the same needs and values. The motives for delinquent behavior are different from those for conventional behavior because they are based on an excess of delinquent definitions learned from others.[4]

These nine propositions of differential association theory consist of three interrelated concepts—normative (culture) conflict, differential association, and differential social organization. The interrelated concepts operate at two levels of explanation: society or the group and the individual.[5]

Sutherland assumes that delinquents must be taught antisocial behavior. Those who do not engage in socially unacceptable behavior have been socialized or enculturated to conventional values, but those who become involved in delinquent behavior do so because they have been taught other values. Sutherland developed a quantitative metaphor, in which conventional and criminal value systems are composed of elementary units called "definitions." Each unit can be weighted by the modalities of frequency, priority, duration, and intensity of contact. Thus, delinquency or criminality is determined by the algebraic sum of these weighted units.[6] Figure 5.1 depicts Sutherland's explanation of differential association. Donald R. Cressey, who was the spokesperson for differential association theory after Sutherland's death, explains this theory further in Theory and Research 5.2.

Evaluation of Differential Association Theory

Sutherland's differential association theory represented a watershed in criminology. Criminology was under heavy criticism before this theory was developed because it lacked a general theoretical perspective to integrate findings and guide research.[7] In addition to providing this theoretical perspective, differential association theory retains an important place in the study of delinquent behavior because it is difficult to reject the argument that juveniles learn crime from others. Needless to say, juveniles learn their basic values, norms, skills, and perception of self from others; accordingly, the idea that they also learn crime from significant others seems irrefutable. Learning crime from those who have a greater number of definitions that are favorable to law violations appears to be particularly true of juveniles because of their extreme vulnerability to the influence of the group.

Differential association theory also has appeal in that it is seen as positive. It does not reduce delinquency to psychological and biological models, which postulate that personal inadequacies cannot be penetrated by outside influence. Instead, Sutherland

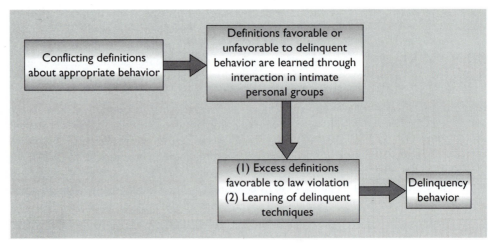

FIGURE 5.1 Sutherland's Theory

THEORY AND RESEARCH 5.2

Interview with Donald R. Cressey

Question: What do you feel are the best features of differential association theory and do you see any areas that need to be reformulated?

Cressey: The strongest characteristic of differential association theory is its orientation to the scientific method and thus to empiricism. This means that its users do not assume that human behavior is prompted by deeply hidden "pushers," whether they be biological, psychological, or social. On the contrary, the theory is based on an assumption that every social scientist used to make, namely, that human events are as natural as physical and biological events. Put more specifically, down deep under differential association theory is an assumption that humans come into the world as complex but unprogrammed computers. Then, during the course of their lives, they get programmed to behave in certain ways. The programming is not systematic or consistent, as it is when a technician programs a real computer. Still, various rules for behavior are fed into us, and we behave accordingly. No behavior that has not been programmed into a person will ever show up in the person's actions. Nowadays a lot of people object to that scientific assumption. They want the human to be more dignified and majestic than other animals, so they give us a soul, a psyche, a mind, or a will. But because such pushers are not observable or measurable, differential association theory assumes that we must look elsewhere for explanations of why people behave as they do.

So starting with the assumption, all the differential association theory says is that if people are programmed to behave in a certain way, they will act that way. If you are programmed to know only that "honesty is the best policy," then you will be honest. If you are programmed to know only that it is all right to steal, then you will steal. But the matter is not so simple because, starting when we are at our mothers' knees, we are programmed in both ways. What the theory says, then, is that whether you will steal or not depends on the *ratio* of these two kinds of behavior patterns that have been put into the computer which is you.

Now that's a great oversimplification of what differential association theory says about human learning. If you start to explore the process seriously and in detail, it gets very complicated in a hurry. The biggest problem I see with the theory is the idea that the effects of behavior patterns—whether favorable to crime or unfavorable to it—are cumulative. It isn't that behavior patterns are not observable.

At least hypothetically, one can measure the ratio of the two kinds of behavior patterns a person has learned.

But no one has shown how behavior patterns presented at one time in a person's life link up with behavior patterns presented at a later time, if indeed they do.

The strength of differential association is that it makes good sense of the so-called "factors" that are correlated with high crime and delinquency rates. Indeed, the theory makes better sense of the sex ratio, the age ratio, and the social class ratio in crime and delinquency than does any other theory. Consider poverty. Street crimes are clearly associated with poverty, and a popular theory is that poverty causes crime and delinquency. But if you think about the relationship for a moment, it will dawn on you that poverty doesn't grab people by the shoulders, kick them in the butt, and make them commit crime. Girls living in ghetto areas are in equal poverty with boys, but their delinquency rates are much lower than the rates for boys. So something else is at work. The "something else" that accounts for the differences in the rates is associated with the behavior patterns unfavorable or favorable to delinquent behavior.

Differential association theory is often misinterpreted. Some think it refers to association with delinquents or criminals, but it doesn't. It refers to association with criminal *behavior patterns,* which often are presented by mothers, fathers, and others who are not criminals. The idea that differential association is a theory about criminality in general also is an error. The error stems from the way the theory is presented, but if you think about it for a while, it's clear that differential association is really a theory about specific kinds of crime. For example, if you have an excess of associations favorable to shoplifting sweaters from local department stores, as teenaged girls are likely to do, that doesn't mean you have an excess of associations favorable to burglary, robbery, or stealing hubcaps. People don't become criminals in general. They are programmed to believe that committing only some kinds of crime is "really" bad, indecent, immoral, or otherwise unacceptable.

Does differential association theory makes sense to you? What types of delinquents do you think it most applies to; which ones appear to be explained least by this learning theory?

Source: The late Donald R. Cressey was acknowledged as one of the top criminologists in the United States. He is the author of books such as *Other People's Money* and *Theft of the Nation* and coauthor of the classic text *Criminology* (with Edwin H. Sutherland) and of such books as *Social Problems* and *Justice by Consent.* Interviewed in November 1983.

sees individuals as changeable and as subject to the opinions and values of others. The chief task in delinquency prevention, then, becomes one of effecting change in small groups in which adolescents are involved, rather than attempting to change an entire society.[8]

Some support for the differential association theory can be found in the literature. James F. Short Jr. tested an institutional sample of 126 boys and 50 girls and found that a consistent relationship existed between delinquent behavior and delinquent associations and that such associations were significant for both boys and girls.[9] Albert J. Reiss Jr. and A. Lewis Rhodes, using a sample of 378 white males, also found that a youth's chance of committing a delinquent act depended on whether other members of his friendship group committed the same act.[10] Craig Reinarman and Jeffrey Fagan, using data from a three-year follow-up study of 130 serious juvenile offenders, found overall that differential association variables were the strongest predictors of delinquency. But they "were unable to demonstrate that this predictive efficacy varied significantly by the delinquents' social class."[11] Elton F. Jackson and colleagues' study found that the differential association process appears to be similar over a wide range of offenses and that this theory may explain other forms of deviance besides crime.[12] John Paul Wright and Francis T. Cullen's analysis of a sample of high school seniors revealed that work-related delinquency is affected both by underlying antisocial propensities as well as contact with delinquent coworkers on the job.[13]

Ross L. Matsueda and Karen Heimer found from their Richmond Youth Project data that differential association is a better explanation of self-report delinquency than such social control factors as broken homes and attachment to parents.[14] William E. Thompson and colleagues also concluded that differential association theory is a better explanation of delinquent behavior than is social control theory. This study administered questionnaires to 724 male and female high school students and found that the existence of delinquent companions was substantially more associated with delinquency than were such social control factors as conventional attitudes and attachment to parents, school, and peers.[15]

Brenda S. Griffin and Charles T. Griffin tested differential association theory in two studies of drug use among adolescents and found that the findings generally supported Sutherland's theory.[16] A study by Richard E. Johnson and colleagues of 768 students in a private western high school revealed that differential association theory and variables, particularly peer associations, were more strongly related to drug use and delinquency than were attachments or beliefs. Nevertheless, they contended that a combination of differential association theory and social control theory will produce an even better explanation of delinquency.[17] Delbert S. Elliot and his colleague's integration of strain, control, and social learning theories further appears to support differential association theory over strain and control theories. In examining the relationship between drug use and delinquency, they found that the extent of "bonding" to delinquent and nondelinquent peers is by far the most important predictor of delinquency and mediates the influence on delinquency of control and strain variables.[18]

The enduring impact of the differential association theory on the study of juvenile delinquency is apparent in the attempts to revise this theory. Melvin DeFleur and Richard Quinney, in reformulating the nine propositions of differential association theory, argued that the theory could be formally tightened if it were based on the concepts of symbolic interaction and attitude formation.[19] Daniel Glaser's modification of differential association theory applied the interactionist concept of the self and is called **differential identification theory.** The theory of differential identification is stated as follows: "A person pursues criminal behavior to the extent that he identifies himself with real or imaginary persons from whose perspective his criminal behavior seems acceptable."[20] Glaser subsequently incorporated the concepts of role-taking and commitment and generalized his explanation to differential anticipation.[21] Glaser's revision allowed for human choice and stressed the importance of motives existing in the wider culture independent of direct intimate association.

Robert J. Burgess Jr. and Ronald L. Akers's differential reinforcement theory proposed a step-by-step restatement of differential association according to such ideas as reinforcement and punishment (operant conditioning). This reformulation, now known as social learning theory, contended that criminal or delinquent behavior is learned primarily "in those groups which comprise the individual's major source of reinforcements."[22] Behavior not only is shaped by social and, to a lesser extent, nonsocial consequences but can also be acquired through imitation or modeling. The probability of deviant behavior, according to social learning theory, is determined by the balance of rewards and punishments for, and definitions that are favorable and unfavorable toward, deviant behavior compared with those for alternate behaviors.[23]

Marvin D. Krohn's network approach to delinquent behavior incorporates some of the elements of differential association theory. *Network analysis* refers to sets of groups or organizations linked by the web of social relationships. Krohn suggests that the three most important concepts in personal social networks are focal concerns (the organization or purpose around which people are oriented), degree of multiplexity (whether members of the network are jointly engaged in a number of contexts), and density (the degree to which members are friends with one another). Krohn added that the most important concept in accounting for delinquency is multiplexity. If members of a social network participate jointly in a number of activities, they are likely to influence the behavior of actors within the network.[24]

The criticisms of the differential association theory can be grouped into four areas. First, Ruth R. Kornhauser's reduction of differential association to a cultural deviance perspective has been widely accepted in the field.[25] This criticism has influenced many researchers either to reject differential association theory outright in favor of a social control theory or to place it with a version of integrated theory.[26] However, Matsueda's rebuttal of Kornhasuer's position suggests that she has forced differential association into a cultural deviance model, because she fails to "appreciate two principles followed by Sutherland: logical abstraction, and differentiation of levels of explanation."[27]

Second, the terms of differential association theory are so vague that it is nearly impossible to test the theory empirically.[28] For example, how can excess of definitions toward criminality be measured statistically? How can frequency, duration, priority, and intensity be studied? How can the learning process be more clearly specified?[29] What defines an intimate personal group? What exact techniques, motives, and rationalizations are learned from others?

Third, differential association theory has been accused of proposing a view that does not deal with several critical questions relating to the process of learning crime from others. For example, why does one youth succumb to delinquent definitions and another does not? Why do youths who are exposed to delinquent definitions still engage in conforming behavior most of the time? How did the first "teacher" learn delinquent techniques and definitions to pass on? Why do most youths desist from delinquent behavior at the age of seventeen or eighteen? Why do youths frequently continue delinquent behavior even after the removal of the aversive stimuli (delinquent peers)? Finally, what is the effect of punishment on delinquents?

Fourth, critics point out that differential association theory has no room for human purpose and meaning, because it ultimately reduces the individual to an object that merely reacts to the bombardment of external forces and cannot reject the material being presented.[30] The delinquent, then, is viewed as a passive vessel into which various definitions are poured, and the resultant mixture is something over which he or she has no control.[31]

On balance, although differential association theory has been under sharp attack in recent years, it remains one of the best-known and most enduring theories of delinquent behavior. Matsueda's favorable analysis of differential association theory proposes that research is needed to specify "the concrete elements of the theory's abstract principles," especially "identifying the content of definitions favorable to crime."[32]

How Drift Theory Is Related to Delinquency

The process of becoming a delinquent, Matza says, begins when a juvenile neutralizes himself or herself from the moral bounds of the law and drifts into delinquency. Drift, according to Matza, means that "the delinquent transiently exists in limbo between convention and crime, responding in turn to the demands of each, flirting now with one, now the other, but postponing commitment, evading decision. Thus he drifts between criminal and conventional action."[33]

Matza's concept of drift and differential association have many assumptions in common, but Matza's **drift theory** does place far greater importance than differential association theory on the exercise of juveniles' choices and on the sense of injustice that juveniles feel about the discriminatory treatment they have received.

Matza, having established that the delinquent is one who drifts back and forth between convention and deviancy, then examines the process by which legal norms are neutralized. But fundamental to his analysis is the contention that delinquent youths remain integrated into the wider society and that a violation of legal norms does not mean surrendering allegiance to them:[34]

> There are millions of occasions during which a delinquency may be committed. Except for occasions covered by surveillance, virtually every moment experienced offers an opportunity for offense. Yet delinquency fails to occur during all but a tiny proportion of these moments. During most of the subcultural delinquent's life he is distracted and restrained by convention from the commission of offenses. Episodically, he is released from the moral bind of conventional order. This temporary though recurrent release from the bind of convention has been taken for compulsion or commitment. It is, instead, almost the opposite. During release the delinquent is not constrained to commit an offense; rather, he is free to drift into delinquency. Under the condition of widely available extenuating circumstances, the subcultural delinquent may choose to commit delinquencies.[35]

Delinquency, then, becomes permissible when responsibility is neutralized. According to a well-known article by Gresham M. Sykes and Matza, neutralization provides a means of understanding how delinquents insulate themselves from responsibility for wrongdoing. Sykes and Matza claim that there are five techniques of neutralization, or justifications, of delinquent behavior that precede delinquent behavior and make such behavior possible by defining it as acceptable.[36]

- Denial of responsibility ("I didn't mean it.")
- Denial of injury ("I didn't hurt anyone.")
- Denial of the victim ("They had it coming to them.")
- Condemnation of the condemners ("Everyone is picking on me.")
- Appeal to higher loyalties ("I didn't do it for myself.")[37]

The sense of responsibility, then, is the immediate condition of drift. But other conditions of drift include the sense of injustice, the primacy of custom, and the assertion of tort. Matza claims that subcultural delinquents are filled with a sense of injustice because they depend on a memory file that collects examples of inconsistency. The primacy of custom relates to the male delinquent's observation of the virtues of his subculture; these virtues stress the "traditional precepts of manliness, celebrating as they do the heroic themes of honor, valor, and loyalty." In the group setting, the delinquent must demonstrate valor and loyalty when faced with dare, challenge, and insult. The assertion of tort, which has to do with a private transaction between the accused and the victim, occurs when the subcultural delinquent considers a harmful wrong to be a tort instead of a crime. Subcultural delinquents frequently believe that the justice process cannot be invoked unless the victim is willing to file a complaint.[38]

Matza concludes that "the breaking of the moral bind to law arising from neutralization and resulting in drift does not assure the commission of a delinquent act."[39] The missing element that provides "the thrust or impetus by which the delinquent act is realized is *will.*"[40] The will is activated both on mundane occasions and in extraordinary situations.[41] But the subcultural delinquent is not likely to have the will to repeat an old offense if he or she has failed in the past: "Few persons—clowns and fools are among them—like to engage in activities they do badly."[42] Desperation, reasons Matza, also can activate one's will to commit infractions. Matza sees desperation intertwined with the mood of fatalism; that is, because the delinquent feels pushed around, he or she needs to make something happen to restore the mood of humanism. Crime then enables the subcultural delinquent to see himself or herself as cause rather than as effect.[43]

Matza developed the drift theory to account for the majority of adolescents who, from time to time, engage in delinquent behavior. But in *Becoming Deviant,* he introduces the concepts of will, commitment, and conversion. Using nonempirical terms that are traditionally reserved for the theologian or the philosopher, Matza suggested that delinquents' will must be captured by deviant influences before they are committed to a delinquent way of life. When delinquents permit their will to be captured, then a type of conversion experience happens. The former nondelinquent becomes a different kind of person and is willing to stand up for this new way of life.[44] Figure 5.2 presents Matza's explanation of delinquent behavior.

Evaluation of Drift Theory

Drift theory has been largely ignored in subsequent analyses of delinquency, which is unfortunate because it does have several strengths. Drift theory builds on the assumption that delinquent behavior is a learning process that takes place in interactions with others. It examines the influence of the group in encouraging youths to release themselves from the moral binds of the law. Drift theory also can be used to account for the fact that the majority of adolescents commit occasional delinquent acts but then go on to accept roles as law-abiding adults. Matza's explanation for delinquency declining as adolescents approach adulthood is that such individuals were not committed to delinquent norms in the first place.

Drift theory is additionally helpful in understanding the situational aspects of delinquent behavior. Matza views the delinquent as one who is pressured by a specific situational context and the norms of that context to engage in delinquent behavior. Matza rightly contends that youths are influenced by group processes to commit behaviors that they may not otherwise commit.

Moreover, Matza's *Delinquency and Drift* challenges the notion that delinquents are "constrained" to engage in delinquency. He contends that hard determinism predicts far too much delinquency and that a soft determinism much more accurately explains delinquent behavior.[45] This argument for soft determinism found in drift theory is

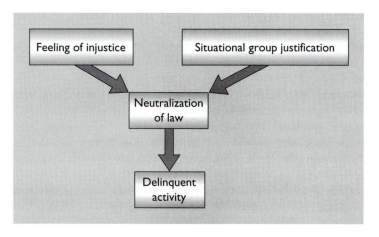

FIGURE 5.2 Matza's Drift Theory

similar to various later versions of soft determinism or indeterminism found in control theory,[46] rational choice theory,[47] social learning theory,[48] and conflict theory.[49]

Another important conjecture of drift theory is that the attitudes of delinquents and nondelinquents toward unlawful behaviors are basically the same. Robert Regoli and Eric Poole's study revealed that delinquents possibly do drift into and out of delinquent behavior, since the attitudes of delinquents and nondelinquents were very similar.[50] But in two studies, Michael J. Hindelang found that those who had engaged in unlawful acts were more approving of delinquency than those who had not. He went on to question whether delinquents do in fact subscribe to the same moral code as do nondelinquents.[51]

It can be argued that hate crime is a good example of drift theory. Skinheads who commit hate crime believe that their violence is aimed at a higher loyalty, protecting the "American way of life" or their Aryan heritage. They may attend school and be good students and be looked upon as fine Christian young men, but still they are capable of spontaneous outbursts of violence against those whom they perceive as "different."

Finally, John Hagan shows how drift can be integrated with social control theory and a life course conceptualization to study cultural stratification. He found that "adolescents adrift from parental and educational control are more likely than those with more controls to develop mild or more seriously deviant subcultural preferences" and that "among males with working-class origins, identification with the subculture of delinquency has a negative effect on trajectories of early adult status attainment."[52]

Yet what has been examined much more extensively in the development of delinquency theory are the techniques of neutralization, better known as **neutralization theory.** John E. Hamlin suggests that neutralization theory has come to occupy a central place in delinquency theory because it has contributed to two broad traditions: learning theory and control theory.[53] Akers's learning theory implies that delinquency must neutralize moral prescriptions before unlawful acts are committed.[54] Control theory also uses the assumptions of neutralization theory.[55]

Neutralization theory has received mixed support.[56] Richard A. Ball developed and used a neutralization attitude scale with a sample of youth at the Fairfield School for Boys in Lancaster, Ohio, and with a sample of core-city high school boys. He found that delinquents tended to give more excuses for various offenses than did nondelinquents. These differences were used for both personal and property offenses. Ball concluded that delinquents accept the influence of neutralization more readily than do nondelinquents.[57] However, Ball later found no significant differences in neutralization scores between less delinquent "rurban" sixth grade girls and more delinquent "rural" sixth grade boys,[58] and Ball and J. Robert Lilly found no significant differences in neutralization scores between "rurban" sixth graders and a sample of institutionalized delinquents.[59]

Robert Agnew's analysis of data from the second and third waves of the National Youth Survey revealed that neutralization is more likely to be present with violent behaviors than with nonviolent behaviors. He found that although only a small percentage of youths approved of violence, a large percentage of youths accepted neutralization and justified the use of violence in particular situations. According to Agnew, neutralization was most likely to lead to violence among those who disapproved of violence and associated with delinquent peers.[60]

Walter C. Reckless and Shlomo Shoham developed another theory of neutralization that they called *norm erosion.* As the opposite of norm retention, norm erosion is a process of "give" in moral and ethical resistance; norm erosion can be applied to behavior that is embraced even when it is in violation of the moral norms that the delinquent or criminal originally internalized.[61]

In sum, Sykes and Matza's neutralization theory has been influential in the development of delinquency theory, but it appears to apply to some delinquent behaviors more than others. Even though Matza's drift theory has received less attention than neutralization theory, it still is one of the most useful expressions of the dynamics of why individuals become involved in delinquent behavior. In Theory and Research 5.3 Matza updates some of his thoughts on drift and neutralization theories.

THEORY AND RESEARCH 5.3

Interview with David Matza

Question: Has your thinking changed concerning the process of becoming a delinquent since you wrote *Delinquency and Drift*?

Matza: Not too much but some. I would now place more emphasis on racial oppression and the class correlates of racial oppression. The underlying social and political basis for the sense of injustice is left too implicit in *Delinquency and Drift*. Partly that was because the usual theories in the early sixties were based on class injustice and such theories were not very firmly based in fact, as I tried to point out in sections of the book and in *Becoming Deviant*. In my opinion, the thesis of racial injustice is based much more securely in the known facts of American history and social structure and very accurately reflected in the composition of prison and juvenile correctional populations.

Question: Are you as convinced that most subcultural delinquents adhere to societal norms as you were when you wrote *Delinquency and Drift*?

Matza: I am not as convinced, yet I still believe that even in rebellion against a morality whose application is unjust, a belief in the truth of an uncorrupted morality is asserted. When Frederick Douglass asserted that to be free, the slave was compelled to break most, if not all of the rules of the oppressor, he was not by that statement breaking with the idea of society or with the belief in morality. Increasingly, I have come to think that what we call juvenile delinquency is, in part, the behavior of the youthful section of what traditionally has been termed the dangerous classes. The nineteenth century ideas of the dangerous classes are today lodged in the writings of Edward Banfield. Without understanding the oppressive context of social life among oppressed populations, the dangerous behavior of youth is likely to be misconceived as deriving from biological factors, a tendency which is once again rampant in criminology and sociology thanks to ideologues like Banfield and his followers.

Question: Commitment to delinquency is one concept in your publications which has been widely debated. What is your reaction to this concept today?

Matza: I still do not think that very many youngsters are committed to delinquency. I am not sure how fruitful the debate is since "commitment" is a very slippery term. Commitment to an institution is a much firmer basis for subsequent juvenile delinquency than anything so intangible as an attudinal commitment.

Question: In a 1971 interview, you indicated that *Delinquency and Drift* is a "confused jumbling of conservative, liberal, and radical views" and that "*Becoming Deviant* is sort of liberal and radical, maybe a little conservative too." What did you mean by these comments?

Matza: I meant to imply that I was quite disappointed if not angry at the way criminal justice systems were already beginning to twist much of the writings of the sixties toward their punitive and correctional ends. I guess I thought and still think that if my writing was unclear enough to appeal to conservatives, I must have been pretty confused. I was being critical of myself and perhaps others of similar perspective for having presented material so easily absorbed by an establishment which between 1970 and 1984 abandoned and then turned against improving or at least reforming the penal system. I also meant that I was not very happy about my work, that a deeper formulation of the phenomenon would eliminate some of the philosophical ambiguity.

Question: Interest and research in the attributes, motivations, and socialization of youthful offenders have largely waned today. Instead, theorists are discussing the neoclassical revival, biosociological focus, radical, or critical, criminology, and the labeling perspective. What is your reaction to this current emphasis? Does this take us further away from the real delinquent?

Matza: I think the emphasis is intellectually and scientifically repressive, taking us very far from the actual person caught breaking the rules. My reaction is to continue being critical of such tendencies in my classroom teaching and perhaps awaiting the opportunity to propose more realistic theories of practice when the population finally realizes the conservative fringe has led absolutely nowhere with regard to the problems of poverty, injustice, and crime. Even talking about crime to students over the past fifteen years has been difficult. Under the conservative mentality the study of crime is not really possible, not in any deep scientific or intellectual sense.

Question: What other thoughts about the prevention and control of delinquency in American society would you like to add?

(continued)

Matza: Delinquency cannot be controlled when government is hostile to poor and working people. Delinquency can only be prevented by a just and peaceful social order.

Do you agree with Matza that "delinquency can only be prevented by a just and peaceful social order?"

What new direction does Matza seem to be taking his theory of delinquency and drift?

David Matza is professor of sociology at the University of California, Berkeley. He is the author of *Delinquency and Drift* and *Becoming Deviant* and coauthor of "Techniques of Neutralization." Interviewed in April, 1984, and used with permission.

The Relationship between Social Control and Delinquent Behavior

The core ideas of **control theory** have a long history, going back at least to the nineteenth century. Control theorists agree on one fundamental point: human beings must be held in check, or somehow controlled, if delinquent tendencies are to be repressed. Control theorists also generally agree that delinquency is the result of a deficiency in something. Juveniles commit delinquency because some controlling force is absent or defective.[62]

Early versions of control theory include Albert J. Reiss Jr.'s theory of personal and social controls and F. Ivan Nye's family-focused theory of social control. Reiss described how the weak egos of delinquents lacked the personal controls to produce conforming behavior.[63] Nye added that the problem for the theorist was not to find an explanation for delinquent behavior; rather, it was to explain why delinquent behavior is not more common.[64] Walter C. Reckless's containment theory and Travis Hirschi's social control theory are the most developed examples of control theory, and we examine them extensively.

Containment Theory

Reckless developed **containment theory** in the 1950s and 1960s to explain crime and delinquency. Containment theory, which can explain both conforming behavior and deviancy, has two reinforcing elements: an inner control system and an outer control system. The assumption is that strong inner containment and reinforcing external containment provide insulation against deviant behavior. But Reckless noted that containment theory does not explain the entire spectrum of delinquent behavior. It does not account for delinquency that emerges from strong inner pushes, such as compulsions, anxieties, and personality disorders, or from organic impairments, such as brain damage.[65]

ELEMENTS OF CONTAINMENT THEORY   Reckless defines the ingredients of inner containment as self-components, such as self-control, positive self-concept, well-developed superego, ego strength, high frustration tolerance, high resistance to diversions, high sense of responsibility, ability to find substitute satisfactions, goal orientations, and tension-reducing rationalizations.

Outer containment, or external regulators, represents the structural buffers in the person's immediate social world or environment that are able to hold him or her within bounds. External controls consist of such items as the presentation of a consistent moral front to the person; institutional reinforcement of his or her norms, goals, and expectations; effective supervision and discipline; provision for a reasonable scope of activity, including limits and responsibilities; and opportunity for acceptance, identity, and belongingness.

Internal pushes consist of the drives, motives, frustrations, restlessness, disappointments, rebellion, hostility, and feelings of inferiority that encourage a person to become involved in socially unacceptable behavior. Environmental pressures are those associated with poverty or deprivation, conflict and discord, external restraint, minority group status, and limited access to success in an opportunity structure. Finally, the pulls of the environment consist of distractions, attractions, temptations, patterns of deviancy, carriers of delinquent patterns, and criminogenic advertising and propaganda in the society.

RELATIONSHIP OF CONTAINMENT AND DELINQUENCY   If a youth has a weak outer containment, the external pressures and pulls need to be handled by the inner control system. If the youth's outer buffer is relatively strong and effective, his or her inner defense does not have to play such a critical role. Similarly, if the youth's inner controls are not equal to the ordinary pushes, an effective outer defense may help to hold him or her within socially acceptable behavior. But if the inner defenses are in good working order, the outer structure does not have to come to the rescue. Juveniles who have both strong external and internal containment, then, are much less likely to become delinquent than those who have only either strong external containment or strong internal containment. Youths who have both weak external and internal controls are the most prone to delinquent behavior, although weak internal controls appear to result in delinquent behavior more often than do weak external controls.

THE SELF-CONCEPT AS AN INSULATION AGAINST DELINQUENCY   Containment theory involves both outer and inner containment, but inner containment, or self-concept, has received far more attention than has outer containment. Reckless, Simon Dinitz, and their students spent over a decade investigating the effects of self-concept on delinquent behavior. The subjects for this study were sixth-grade boys living in the area of Columbus, Ohio, that had the highest white delinquency rate. Teachers were asked to nominate those boys who, in their point of view, were insulated against delinquency. In the second phase of the study, teachers in the same area schools were asked to nominate sixth-grade boys who appeared to be heading toward delinquency. Both the "good boy" group and the "bad boy" group were given the same battery of psychological tests; the mothers of both groups were interviewed.[66]

Reckless and Dinitz concluded from these studies that one of the preconditions of law-abiding conduct is a good self-concept. This insulation against delinquency may be viewed as an ongoing process reflecting an internalization of nondelinquent values and conformity to the expectations of significant others—parents, teachers, and peers. Thus, a good self-concept, the product of favorable socialization, steers youths away from delinquency by acting as an inner buffer or containment against delinquency.

In the 1960s, Reckless and Dinitz undertook a four-year intervention project that involved seventh-grade boys in all of the Columbus junior high schools and was designed to improve the self-concept of potential delinquents. But the follow-up data indicated that the special classes had no appreciable impact.[67]

Several other studies have examined the efficacy of a positive self-concept in insulating adolescents from delinquent behavior. E. D. Lively and colleagues, who investigated self-concept in teenagers of various ethnic groups in Akron, Ohio, found that self-concept appeared to improve as subjects moved away from the inner city.[68] In another study in Hawaii, Gary F. Jensen examined specific variables of self-concept and their relationship to "inner containment." He found that the greater the self-esteem, the less likely a youth was to become involved in delinquent behavior.[69] The result of a study of delinquency by Franco Ferracuti and colleagues in San Juan, Puerto Rico, also supported the relationship of poor self-concept to delinquent behavior.[70]

Timothy J. Owens, using the Youth in Transition study, compares the reciprocal interrelationships of self-deprecation (negative self-evaluation), positive self-worth (positive self-evaluation), and global self-esteem (including both positive and negative evaluations) on high school grades, delinquency, and depression. With regard to delinquency, he found that "a sense of self-worth and an absence of feeling worthless (as indicated by high global self-esteem, high positive self-worth, or low self-deprecation) reduced delinquent behavior." Yet "delinquency has virtually no impact on any aspect of self-worth examined."[71]

L. Edward Wells and Joseph R. Rankin, using self-report data from a national panel survey, concluded that self-esteem has little direct effect on delinquent acts.[72] John D. McCarthy and Dean R. Hoge also found that the effect of self-esteem on subsequent delinquent activity is weak.[73] Reckless and colleagues based their theory on white males, and Jensen's data suggested that contact with officials is more detrimental for white youths' self-concept than for that of African Americans.[74] W. E. Thompson and R. A. Dodder further found that containment theory offered little explanation for delinquency among African Americans.[75]

Other researchers have argued that people behave in a fashion designed to maximize their self-esteem, and therefore youngsters adopt deviant reference groups for the purpose of enhancing self-esteem.[76] Delinquent behavior then becomes a coping strategy to defend against negative self-evaluation. H. B. Kaplan found that some students did become involved in particular activities with new membership groups to enhance self-esteem with those groups, and if they had negative experience with nondeviant groups, they would turn to delinquent-oriented groups to achieve a positive self-experience.[77] Florence R. Rosenberg and Morris Rosenberg found that lower-class boys are most likely to align themselves with deviant groups to restore their damaged self-esteem.[78]

The major flaw of inner containment, or self-concept, theory is the difficulty of defining self-concept in such a way that researchers can be certain they are accurately measuring the key variables of this concept.[79] Michael Schwartz and Sandra S. Tangri also proposed that a poor self-concept might have other outcomes besides vulnerability to delinquency. They further disputed the adequacy of Reckless and Dinitz's measures of self-concept and questioned the effects of labeling on the subsequent behavior of both the "good" and "bad" boys.[80]

Social Control or Bonding Theory

Travis Hirschi is the theorist most closely identified with **social control theory,** or bonding theory. In *Causes of Delinquency,* Hirschi linked delinquent behavior to the quality of the bond an individual maintains with society, stating that "delinquent acts result when an individual's bond to society is weak or broken."[81] Hirschi is indebted to Emile Durkheim for recognition of the importance of the social bond to society and accepts the view of Thomas Hobbes, Puritan theologians, and Sigmund Freud that humans are basically antisocial and sinful. In Hirschi's words, "We are all animals and thus all naturally capable of committing criminal acts."[82] Hence, he argues that humans' basic impulses motivate them to become involved in crime and delinquency unless there is reason for them to refrain from such behavior. Instead of the standard question, "Why do they do it?" Hirschi asserts that the most important question becomes, "Why don't they do it?"[83]

Hirschi theorized that individuals who are most tightly bonded to social groups such as the family, the school, and peers are less likely to commit delinquent acts.[84] The **social bond,** according to Hirschi, is made up of four main elements: attachment, commitment, involvement, and belief.

An individual's attachment to conventional others is the first element of the social bond. The sensitivity toward others, argues Hirschi, relates to the ability to internalize norms and to develop a conscience.[85] Attachment to others also includes the ties of affection and respect children have to parents, teachers, and friends. The stronger the attachment to others, the more likely that an individual will take this into consideration when and if he or she is tempted to commit a delinquent act.[86] The attachment to parents is the most important variable insulating a child against delinquent behavior. Even if a family is broken by divorce or desertion, the child needs to maintain attachment to one or both parents. "If the child is alienated from the parent," Hirschi asserts, "he will not develop an adequate conscience or superego."[87]

Commitment to conventional activities and values is the second element of the bond. An individual is committed to the degree that he or she is willing to invest time, energy, and himself or herself in conventional activities, such as educational goals, property, or reputation. When a committed individual considers the cost of delinquent behavior, he or she uses common sense and thinks of the risk of losing the investment already made in conventional behavior.[88] Hirschi contended that if juveniles are committed to these conventional values and activities, they develop a stake in conformity and will refrain from delinquent behavior.

Involvement also protects an individual from delinquent behavior. Because time and energy are limited, involvement in conventional activities leaves no time for delinquent behavior. "The person involved in conventional activities is tied to appointments, deadlines, working hours, plans, and the like," reasoned Hirschi, "so the opportunity to commit deviant acts rarely arises. To the extent that he is engrossed in conventional activities, he cannot even think about deviant acts, let alone act out his inclinations."[89]

The fourth element is belief. Delinquency results from the absence of effective beliefs that forbid socially unacceptable behavior.[90] Respect for the law and for the social norms of society are important components of belief. This respect for the values of the law and legal system is derived from intimate relations with other people, especially parents. Hirschi developed a causal chain "from attachment to parents, through concern for the approval of persons in positions of authority, to belief that the rules of society are binding on one's conduct."[91]

The family can provide all the necessary elements of a strong social bond: attachment, commitment, involvement, and belief. According to social control theorists, a child's attachment to and respect for his or her parents is the most important variable in preventing delinquency.

Hirschi tested his theory by administering a self-report survey to 4,077 junior high and high school students in Contra Costa County, California. He also used school records and police records to analyze the data he received on the questionnaires. His analysis yielded data on the basic elements of the social bond.

Hirschi analyzed attachment of respondents in the sample to parents, to the school, and to peers. The greater the attachment to parents, he found, the less likely the child was to become involved in delinquent behavior. But more than the fact of communication with the parents, the quality or the intimacy of the communication was the critical factor. The more love and respect found in the relationship with parents, the more likely that the child will recall the parents when and if a situation of potential delinquency arose.[92]

Hirschi also found that in terms of attachment to the school, students with little academic competence and those who performed poorly were more likely to become involved in delinquent behavior. Significantly, he found that students with weak affectional ties to parents tended to have little concern for the opinions of teachers and to dislike school.[93]

The attachment to peers, Hirschi added, did not imply lack of attachment to parents. The respondents who were most closely attached to and respectful of their friends were least likely to have committed delinquent acts. Somewhat surprisingly, delinquents were less dependent on peers than nondelinquents. Hirschi theorized from his data "that the boy's stake in conformity affects his choice of friends rather than the other way around."[94]

In terms of commitment, Hirschi found that if a boy claimed the *right* to smoke, drink, date, and drive a car, he was more likely to become involved in delinquency. The automobile, like the cigarette and bottle of beer, indicated that the boy had put away childish things. Also, the more a boy was committed to academic achievement, the less likely he was to become involved in delinquent acts. Hirschi further reported that the higher the occupational expectations of boys, the less likely it was that they would become involved in delinquent behavior.[95]

Hirschi found that the more a boy was involved in school and leisure activities, the less likely he was to become involved in delinquency. In other words, the more that boys in the sample felt that they had nothing to do, the more likely they were to become involved in delinquent acts. Hirschi theorized that lack of involvement and commitment to school releases a young person from a primary source of time structuring.[96]

Moreover, he found that the less boys believed they should obey the law, the less likely they were to obey it. He added that delinquents were relatively free of concern for the morality of their actions and therefore they were relatively amoral and differed significantly in values from nondelinquents. Additionally, the data in this study failed to show much difference between lower- and middle-class young people in terms of values.[97] In Theory and Research 5.4, Hirschi expresses some more recent thoughts about social control theory. Figure 5.3 depicts the relationship of the main constructs of Hirschi's theory.

Evaluation of Social Control Theory

Social control theory has received wide support. Barbara J. Costello and Paul R. Vowell, in reanalyzing the Richmond data, challenge Matsueda's finding that social disorganization theory is supported over control theory. Costello and Vowell report that the social bond and friends' delinquency retain important direct effects on delinquent behavior and that these effects are greater than those of definitions favorable to law violations.[98] Charles R. Tittle also agrees that lack of control can lead to deviant behavior, but he asserts that overcontrol (a control plus) can lead to exploitation, plunder, and decadence. Referring to his theory as **"control balance theory,"** Tittle contends that the amount of control to which an individual is subject relative to the amount of control the individual can exercise affects both the probability that the person will engage in a deviant act and the specific form or type of deviance.[99]

THEORY AND RESEARCH 5.4

Interview with Travis Hirschi

Question: If you were to rewrite *Causes of Delinquency,* would you reformulate control theory in any way?

Hirschi: Control theory as I stated it can't really be understood unless one takes into account the fact that it was attached to a particular method of research. When I was working on the theory, I knew that my data were going to be survey data; therefore, I knew I was going to have mainly the perceptions, attitudes, and values of individuals as reported by them. So I knew the theory had to be stated from the perspective of individuals committing or not committing delinquent acts. Had I data on other people, or on the structure of the community, I would have stated the theory in a quite different way. There are lots of control theories, but the major differences among them stem from differences in the vantage point of the theorists, not from differences in their understanding of the theory.

For example, I was aware at the time I wrote my theory that it was well within the social disorganization tradition. I knew that, but you have to remember the status of social disorganization as a concept in the middle 1960s when I was writing. I felt I was swimming against the current in stating a social control theory at the individual level. Had I tried to sell social disorganization at the same time, I would have been in deep trouble. So I shied away from that tradition. As a result, I did not give social disorganization its due. I went back to Durkheim and Hobbes and ignored an entire American tradition that was directly relevant to what I was saying. But I was aware of it and took comfort in it. I said the same things the social disorganization people had said, but since they had fallen into disfavor I had to disassociate myself from them. Further, as Ruth Kornhauser so acutely points out, social disorganization theories had been associated with the cul-

tural tradition. That was the tradition I was working hardest against; so in that sense, I would have compromised my own position or I would have introduced a lot of debate I didn't want to get into had I dealt explicitly with social disorganization theory. Now, with people like Kornhauser on my side, and social disorganization back in vogue, I would emphasize my roots in this illustrious tradition.

Question: Can control theory be expanded? What would be the main propositions and underpinnings of this expanded control theory?

Hirschi: Jack Gibbs mentioned the other day that, traditionally, the problem with social control as a concept is that it tends to expand until it becomes synonymous with sociology, and then it dies. It dies because then there is nothing unique or distinct about it. This danger is present even when the concept is limited initially to delinquency. I enjoy papers that apply my theory to areas other than delinquency, such as Watergate and white collar crime, but I recognize the risk. Because of it, generality is not something I would move toward. Instead, I would try to focus on the theory's image of criminality and ask how far that might take us. I think I've generally worked with a too restrictive image of delinquency. I did this because I thought the field had made a mistake by bringing things into delinquency that were not delinquency. If, for example, smoking and drinking are part of delinquency, they cannot be causes of delinquency. I thought that was a mistake because I wanted to use those kinds of behaviors as independent variables. I now believe that smoking and drinking are delinquency.

Source: Travis Hirschi is professor emeritus of sociology at the University of Arizona. He is the author of *Causes of Delinquency* and most recently is coauthor of *A General Theory of Crime.* Interviewed in 1984.

Michael Wiatrowski, David Griswold, and Mary K. Roberts explored the degree to which the four dimensions of the social bond are mutually independent, as well as the direct and indirect effect of socioeconomic class. Using self-reports of 2,213 tenth-grade boys, they concluded that items that are considered to be indicators of attachment to school, parents and peers, future occupational commitment, and school involvement are mutually independent predictors of moderate delinquent behaviors.[100] Krohn and James L. Massey also found a moderate relationship between a wide range of delinquent behaviors and social bond measures.[101] Yet both of these studies concluded that social bond factors tell only a partial story; other factors also are needed to understand delinquent

FIGURE 5.3 Hirschi's Social Control Theory

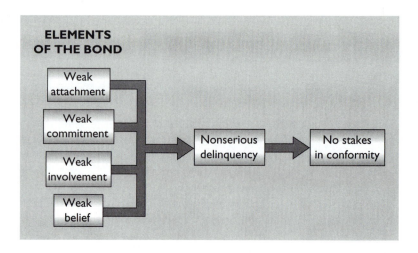

behavior.[102] Hindelang, using as subjects sixth through twelfth graders in a New York State school system, essentially supported Hirschi's social control findings. The attachment to peers was the major difference between his study and Hirschi's, for Hindelang found, as have many other researchers, that identification with peers was directly related to delinquent involvements.[103] Finally, several studies have found that social control variables are at least as powerful as structural variables, if not more so, in explaining delinquency.[104]

Krohn and Massey's examination of data drawn from a sample of 3,065 adolescents, however, found that the bonding perspective offers a more powerful explanation of the less serious forms of delinquency than of the more serious forms.[105] Elliott and colleagues, using data from the National Youth Survey, found that the control variables in their analysis did not have a direct effect on delinquency and, with certain exceptions, had only small indirect effects.[106] Rankin's investigation of social control theory failed to find support for this theory, especially in terms of conformity.[107] Agnew, in reconceptualizing the measures in the National Youth Survey to more accurately reflect Hirschi's social bond theory, found weak longitudinal effects of social control theory across age groups. For example, the effect of the bond was stronger for younger and less serious offenders.[108] Randy L. LaGrange and Helene Raskin White also found that the effect of the social bond is stronger for fifteen-year olds than among other juveniles.[109] Kimberly Kempf Leonard and Scott H. Decker, using data from the Richmond Youth Project, found that "the social control model was unable to distinguish delinquency very well" and that "the elements of the bond work differently for pre-teens than for their older counterparts."[110] Robert L. Gardner and Donald J. Shoemaker's investigation of a population of rural and urban youths generally supported social control theory but did find that this theory was a stronger explanation of delinquency among rural than urban youth.[111]

Control theory has several strengths. Significantly, control theory is amenable to empirical examination. Unlike other theorists discussed in this unit, Hirschi was able to test his theory with a population of adolescents. The basic theoretical constructs of control theory—terms such as *attachment to parents, involvement in school,* and *commitment to conventional activities*—are clearly defined.

Social control theory also has provided valuable insights into delinquent behavior. For example, the importance of the intrafamily relationship has been substantiated. The relationship between the school and delinquency is another important area that social control theory addresses. Hirschi explored such areas as aspirations, achievement, affection toward teachers, time spent on homework, and influence of class on school performance. Furthermore, he examined peer relationships in perhaps greater depth than any other researcher, and although his findings about peers and delinquency may be questioned, the issues he raised are extremely helpful in understanding these relationships. In addition, Hirschi discussed the importance of work, occupational aspiration, use of the automobile, leisure-time activities, and religious affiliation, among other factors, all of which have significantly increased our knowledge of delinquent behavior.

Social control theory cannot explain all acts of delinquency, but it still has more empirical support today than any other explanation of delinquency. Especially valid is the proposition that attachments and commitments to societal institutions (the social bond) are associated with low rates of delinquency. Moreover, researchers are increasingly using this theory to develop integrated explanations of delinquent behavior.[112]

But Hirshi's theory does have limitations. He used a limited array of items to evaluate the dimensions of the social bond, and the questionnaire items that he used to measure delinquency listed only a few relatively minor behavior problems.[113] This means that Hirschi's theory may adequately explain delinquency in juveniles who are involved only in relatively trivial offenses, but whether or not its findings apply as well to serious delinquents is questionable. Social control theory also fails to describe the chain of events that weaken the social bond, and it divides delinquents into either socialized and unsocialized youths. In addition, the importance of other factors in the explanation of delinquency is indicated by the amount of delinquent behavior that is not explained by social control variables.[114] Finally, greater attention must be given to the operational definitions of the elements of the social bond before the theoretical merits of social control theory can be ascertained.[115] Table 5.1 presents a summary of social process theories.

How Integrated Theory Explains Delinquency

The theoretical development of integrated explanations of delinquency has been one of the most highly praised concepts in criminology.[116] Theory integration generally implies the combination of two or more existing theories on the basis of their perceived commonalities. According to Steven Messner, Marvin Krohn, and Allen Liska, the two main types of theoretical integration are propositional and conceptual. They also suggest that a "middle range," including both conceptual and propositional integration, might be useful.[117] The overarching purpose of theoretical integration is the development of a new theory that improves on the constituent theories from which the reformulated theory is derived. The ultimate goal of theory integration, then, is the advancement of our understanding of crime and delinquency.[118]

TABLE 5.1

Summary of Social Process Theories of Crime

Theory	Proponents	Cause of Crime Identified in the Theory	Supporting Research
Differential association	Edwin Sutherland	Criminal behavior is expected of those individuals who have internalized a preponderance of definitions favorable to law violations	Moderate
Drift	David Matza	Juvenile neutralizes himself or herself from the moral bounds of the law and drifts into delinquent behavior	Moderate
Containment	Walter Reckless	Strong inner and reinforcing external containment provide an insulation against criminal behavior	Moderate
Social control	Travis Hirschi	Criminal acts result when individual's bond to society is weak or broken	Strong

Hirshi has developed a typology that is a useful means of summarizing propositional integration.[119] He has identified three types or forms that theoretical integration may take: side-by-side or parallel integration, end-to-end or sequential integration, and up-and-down or deductive integration.[120] Side-by-side integration refers to the dividing of the subject matter into constituent types or forms; the most common expression of side-by-side integration is offender typologies. End-to-end integration, perhaps the most widely used today, refers to placing causal variables in a temporal order so that the independent variables of some theories are used to become the dependent variables of the integrated theory. The process of integrating macro-level causes with micro-level causes is another common use of the end-to-end approach.[121] For example, as Mark Colvin and John Pauly argue, the macro-level of social class is linked to delinquency indirectly through the micro-level factor of parenting.[122] Up-and-down integration is the process of consolidating into one formulation the ideas of two or more theories by identifying a more abstract or general perspective from which at least parts of the theories can be deducted. This strategy is not frequently used because of the difficulty in compromising different assumptions.[123]

Attempts to combine theoretical explanations of delinquency into a coherent sequence of connecting events and outcomes give rise to several issues and concerns. First, because the specific form of delinquent behavior to be explained may vary from one theory to another, variations will likely be present in the power and utility of the integrated theory with respect to different types of delinquent activity. Social control, or bonding, theory, for example, tends to be a more useful explanation for the less serious rather than the more serious forms of delinquency.[124]

Also, when theoretical expressions of delinquency are mixed, the question of which factors to use as a representation of theories utilized in the model becomes an issue. Differential association illustrates this second issue. It is divided into nine propositions and even further subcategories. The question then becomes, which proposition or propositions should be used as representative of differential association theory? The same is true for social control or social bonding theory. Which of the four major components should be representative of the theory?[125]

Moreover, in regard to synthesis efforts, an issue sometimes arises about the generalizability of the theory to all segments of the population. For example, most delinquency theories focus on lower-class adolescent males, but these theories may or may not apply to lower-class adolescent females or to middle- or upper-class adolescent males and females.[126]

Finally, another concern is the different basic assumptions that included theories may make with respect to motivations, attitudes, and the specific contributing factor to delinquency. Interdisciplinary theories, especially, offer opposing views on feelings and attitudes of delinquents, but it is not uncommon for structural or process sociological theories to have widely divergent views on delinquents' attitudes and motivations or the effects of stimuli.[127]

Despite these daunting challenges, several integrated theories for delinquent behavior have been developed.[128] Four of the most important are Michael R. Gottfredson and Hirschi's general theory of crime, Elliott's integrated social process theory, Terence P. Thornberry's interactional theory, and J. David Hawkins and Joseph G. Weis's social development theory.[129]

Gottfredson and Hirschi's General Theory of Crime

Researchers are beginning to inquire whether a common factor underlies all problem behavior. John E. Donovan and Richard Jessor not only corroborated the interrelationships among high-risk behaviors in a study on adolescent drinking but also suggested that a common factor of "unconventionality" underlies all these behaviors. This factor of unconventionality is measured by lower religiosity, tolerance of deviance, approval of drug abuse, peer approval of deviant behavior, more liberal views, and poor school performance.[130]

Hirschi explains the relationship between drug abuse and delinquency by suggesting that the two are not merely influenced by the same factors but "are manifestations of the same thing."[131] This "thing" is criminality, which Hirschi defines as "the tendency or propensity of the individual to seek short-term, immediate pleasure," which provides "money without work, sex without courtship, revenge without court delays."[132]

In their 1990 publication, *A General Theory of Crime*, Gottfredson and Hirschi define lack of self-control as the common factor underlying problem behaviors.[133]

> People who lack self-control will tend to be impulsive, insensitive, physical (as opposed to mental), risk-taking, short-sighted, and nonverbal, and they will tend therefore to engage in criminal and analogous acts [which include smoking, drinking, using drugs, gambling, having children out of wedlock, and engaging in illicit sex]. Since these traits can be identified prior to the age of responsibility for crime, since there is considerable tendency for these traits to come together in the same people, and since the traits tend to persist through life, it seems reasonable to consider them as comprising a stable construct useful in the explanation of crime.[134]

Thus, self-control is the degree to which an individual is "vulnerable to the temptations of the moment."[135] The other pivotal construct in this theory of crime is crime opportunity, which is a function of the structural or situational circumstances encountered by the individual. In combination, these two constructs are intended to capture the simultaneous influence of external and internal restraints on behavior.[136]

Gottfredson and Hirschi propose that only their theory of self-control explains the facts revolving around the stability of differences in individuals' propensity to crime. Self-control accounts for all variations by culture, gender, age, and circumstances and "explains all crime, at all times, and, for that matter, many forms of behavior that are not sanctioned by the state."[137] Individuals with high self-control are "substantially less likely at all periods of life to engage in criminal acts."

Ineffective or incomplete socialization, according to Gottfredson and Hirschi, causes low self-control. Parents are able to socialize their children into self-control by being attached to them, by supervising them closely, by recognizing their lack of self-control, and by punishing deviant acts. Once self-control is formed in childhood, they add, it remains relatively stable throughout life.[138] See Figure 5.4.

EVALUATION OF GENERAL THEORY   More than two dozen studies have been conducted on general theory, and the vast majority have been largely favorable.[139] Indeed,

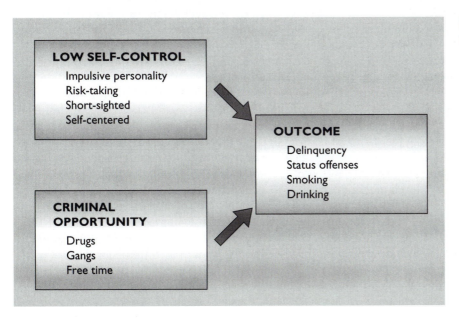

FIGURE 5.4 The General Theory of Crime

LOW SELF-CONTROL

Impulsive personality
Risk-taking
Short-sighted
Self-centered

OUTCOME

Delinquency
Status offenses
Smoking
Drinking

CRIMINAL OPPORTUNITY

Drugs
Gangs
Free time

A General Theory of Crime ranks second in citations of all criminal and criminal justice books in the 1990s.[140] It has been found that self-control is related to self-reported crime among college students, juveniles, and adults; tends to predict future criminal convictions and self-reported delinquency; and is related to social consequences other than crime.[141] Teresa C. LaGrange and Robert A. Silverman found partial support for the general theory revealing measures of self-control and delinquency among 2,000 Canadian secondary school students that varied by magnitude across gender and for different offense types.[142] Raymond Paternoster and Robert Brame, using data from the Cambridge Study in Delinquent Development, found that self-control explains any association that exists between involvement in criminal activity and involvement in analogous behaviors.[143] Another finding is that attitudinal and behavioral measures of self-control have effects on crime, even when a range of social factors is controlled.[144] Dennis M. Giever and colleagues further found that "parenting does seem to matter in the socialization of children to delay gratification and consider the long term consequences of actions."[145] Carter Hay, in using a sample of high school students, found some support for self-control theory in that "monitoring discipline significantly affects low self-control, and low self-control significantly affects delinquency and partially mediates the effects of monitoring-discipline."[146]

Gottfredson and Hirschi's theory of self-control is part of a trend that pushes the causes of crime and delinquency farther back in the life course into the family. In some respects it is a return to the emphasis found in the works of Sheldon and Eleanor Glueck and also resembles the important themes in James Q. Wilson and Richard Herrnstein's reinforcement theory. This emphasis on early childhood socialization as the cause of crime, of course, departs from the emphasis on more proximate causes of crime found in rational choice theory and in most sociological theories.[147] Gottfredson and Hirschi's focus on a unidimensional trait also departs from the movement toward multidimensional and integrated theories of crime.[148]

Criticisms of general theory have focused largely on its lack of conceptual clarity.[149] Some argue that key elements of the theory remain to be tested,[150] that the theory does not have the power to explain all forms of delinquency and crime,[151] and that "questions remain regarding the ubiquity of self-concept."[152] Nevertheless, despite these criticisms, general theory will likely continue to spark continued interest and research.

Elliott and Colleagues' Integrated Social Process Theory

Elliott and colleagues offer "an explanatory model that expands and synthesizes traditional strain, social control, and social learning perspectives into a single paradigm that accounts for delinquent behavior and drug use."[153] They argue that all three theories are flawed in explaining delinquent behavior. Strain theory is able to account for some initial delinquent acts but does not adequately explain why some juveniles enter into delinquent careers while others avoid them. Control theory is unable to explain prolonged involvement in delinquent behavior in light of there being no reward for this behavior, and learning theories portray the delinquent as passive and susceptible to influence when confronted with delinquency-producing reinforcements.[154]

Integrating the strongest features of these theories into a single theoretical model, Elliott and colleagues contended that the experience of living in socially disorganized areas leads youths to develop weak bonds with conventional groups, activities, and norms. High levels of strain, as well as weak bonds with conventional groups, lead some youth to seek out delinquent peer groups. These antisocial peer groups provide both positive reinforcement for delinquent behavior and role models for this behavior. Consequently, Elliott and colleagues theorize, there is a high probability of involvement in delinquent behavior when bonding to delinquent groups is combined with weak bonding to conventional groups.[155]

The model was tested on a national probability sample of more than 1,700 U.S. eleven- to seventeen-year-olds, who were interviewed three times between 1977 and 1979. Elliott and colleagues found that their integrated theory was generally supported, with the major exception that some youths reported developing both strong bonds to delinquent peers and acceptance of the values of conventional society. Their interpretation of this finding was that youths living in a disorganized area may not have conventional groups that they can join.[156]

Elliott and colleagues did not attempt to integrate this theoretical perspective at the macrosociological level. Instead, the integration occurs at an individual level as it provides an explanation for how youngsters become involved in delinquent acts. Although the model initially was conceived to explain the causes of delinquent behavior, it was developed more fully and used to explain drug-using behavior as well.[157] See Figure 5.5.

EVALUATION OF INTEGRATED SOCIAL PROCESS THEORY   This theory represents a pure type of integrated theory. It can be argued that general theory and interactional theory are not fully integrated theories but rather are elaborations of established theories. In contrast, there is no question that integrated social process theory is an integrated theory.

Examinations of this theory have generally been positive. Yet some question has been raised about its application to various types of delinquent behaviors. Questions have even been raised about its power and utility with different types of drug activity. For example, integrated social process theory explained 59 percent of the variation in marijuana use but only 29–34 percent of the distribution of hard drug use.[158]

Thornberry's Interactional Theory

In Thornberry's interactional theory of delinquency the initial impetus toward delinquency comes from a weakening of the person's bond to conventional society, represented by attachment to parents, commitment to school, and belief in conventional

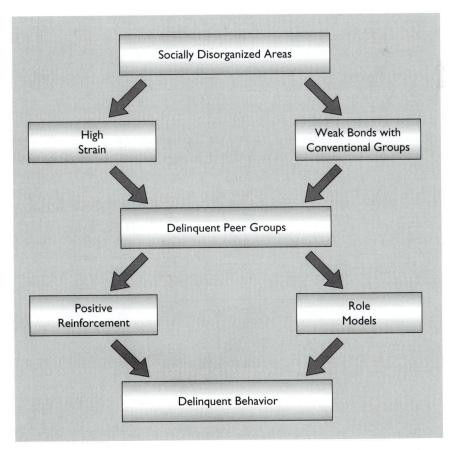

FIGURE 5.5 Elliott and Colleagues' Integrated Social Process Theories

values. Associations with delinquent peers and delinquent values make up the social setting in which delinquency, especially prolonged serious delinquency, is learned and reinforced. These two variables, along with delinquent behavior itself, form a mutually reinforcing causal loop that leads toward increasing delinquency involvement over time.[159]

Moreover, this interactive process develops over the person's life cycle. During early adolescence the family is the most influential factor in bonding the youngster to conventional society and reducing delinquency. But as the youth matures and moves through middle adolescence, the world of friends, school, and youth culture becomes the dominant influence over behavior. Finally, as the person enters adulthood, commitment to conventional activities, and to family especially, offers new avenues to reshape the person's bond to society and involvement with delinquent behavior.[160]

Finally, interactional theory holds that these process variables are systematically related to the youngster's position in the social structure. Class, minority-group status, and the social disorganization of the community all affect the initial values of the interactive variables as well as the behavioral trajectories. It is argued that youths from the most socially disadvantaged backgrounds begin the process least bonded to conventional society and most exposed to the world of delinquency. The nature of the process increases the chances that they will continue on to a career of serious criminal involvement; on the other hand, youths from middle-class families enter a trajectory that is oriented toward conformity and away from delinquency.[161] See Figure 5.6.

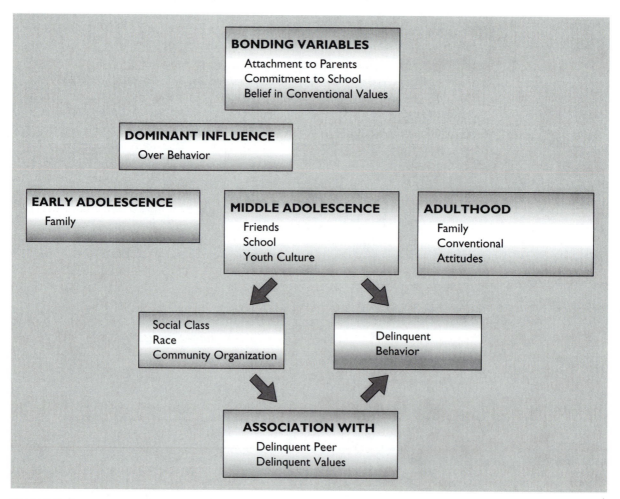

FIGURE 5.6 Thornberry's Interactional Theory

EVALUATION OF INTERACTIONAL THEORY   Thornberry's theory essentially views delinquency as the result of events that occur in a developmental fashion. Delinquency is not viewed as the end product, but instead it leads to the formation of delinquent values, which then contribute to disconnections in social bonds, more attachments to antisocial peers, and additional involvement in delinquent behavior. As found in other developmental theories, some variables affect unlawful behavior at certain ages and other factors at other ages.[162]

Thornberry and colleagues offer some support for interactional theory in the Rochester Youth Development Study. In this longitudinal study, they found that weakened bonds to parents and school contributed to delinquency, but that delinquent behavior also contributed to further weakening of these bonds.[163] Another examination of these data reported that peer influences were of primary importance in developing delinquent behavior patterns, delinquent beliefs, and interactions among these variables.[164]

Interactional theory has several shortcomings. Most important, interactional theory fails to address the presence of middle-class delinquency and basically ignores race and gender issues. Also, its viewpoint that delinquency will persist throughout adolescence and into adulthood leaves little room for short-term discontinued or permanent termination of illegal behavior patterns.[165]

The most positive feature of interactional theory is that it is consistent with social settings in which individuals live and interact with others. This feature largely explains its popularity among delinquency researchers as well as those doing interdisciplinary research. Another attractive feature is that the Rochester Youth Development Project, which uses interactional theory as its theoretical design, has been very favorably received.[166]

Hawkins and Weis's Social Development Model

In terms of developing a new strategy, Weis and Hawkins's **social development model** offers an integrated approach to delinquency prevention that could have long-range consequences for dealing with youth crime in American society.[167]

The social development model is based on the integration of social control theory and cultural learning theory. According to social control theory, the weakening, absence, or breakdown of social controls leads to delinquency.[168] Cultural learning, or cultural deviance, theory emphasizes the role of peers and the community in the rise of delinquency. In disorganized communities, then, youths are at greater risk of delinquency.[169]

Social control theory focuses on the individual characteristics that lead to delinquent behavior and the impact of the major socializing institutions on delinquency, whereas cultural learning theory examines the role of the community context in the process of learning criminal and delinquent attitudes and behaviors. Social control theory theorizes that youths become delinquent because of inadequate social controls; cultural learning theory adds that juveniles become socialized to delinquency in disorganized communities.

The social development model proposes that the development of attachments to parents will lead to attachments to school and a commitment to education, as well as a belief in and commitment to conventional behavior and the law. Learning theory describes the process by which these bonds develop. If juveniles are given adequate opportunities for involvement in legitimate activities and are able to acquire the necessary skills with a consistent reward structure, they will develop the bonds of attachment, commitment, and belief. Figure 5.7 presents a diagram of the social development model.

Thus, as a foundation for delinquency prevention, the social development model implies that families, schools, and peer groups are appropriate objects for intervention, depending on the child's developmental stage. Interventions that seek to increase the likelihood of social bonding to the family are appropriate from early childhood through early adolescence. Interventions that seek to increase the likelihood of social bonding to school are appropriate throughout the years of school attendance and are especially important as juveniles approach and enter adolescence.[170] The social development model provides an empirically grounded theoretical basis for designing, implementing, and assessing delinquency prevention programs.

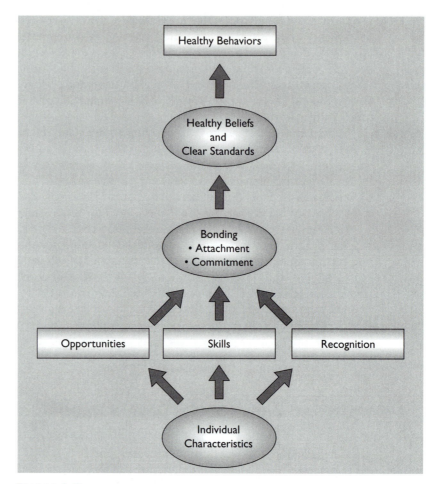

FIGURE 5.7 Social Development Model

Source: James C. Howell, ed. *Guide for Implementing the Comprehensive Strategy for Serious, Violent, and Chronic Juvenile Offenders* (Washington, D.C.: Office of Juvenile Justice and Delinquency Prevention, 1995), p. 23.

Bu Huang and colleagues, in examining the fit of the social development model to predict violent behavior at age 18, used construct measures at ages 10, 13, 14, and 16. They found that the social development model adequately predicts the likelihood of violence at age 18 and is able to mediate much of the effect of prior violence.[171] Yet a disorganized community with high rates of delinquency and crime reduces the potential of delinquency prevention, because the socializing institutions are weakened by higher rates of family disorganization, inadequate educational facilities, few material and social resources, and less respect for the law. Consequently, those youths who are not receiving adequate support and direction from their families and who are not experiencing success in school are most vulnerable to delinquency.[172]

Policy Implications of Social Process Theories

The theories discussed in this chapter focus on process. Delinquency, like other processes, starts at a particular point and either ceases or continues. If delinquency continues, it may eventually become a career, a way of individuals seeing themselves. Career delinquents focus much more on antisocial activities than casual delinquents or delinquents in drift. They generally commit the majority of their serious juvenile crimes in a particular jurisdiction. Career delinquents are typically called chronic or serious youthful offenders. These juvenile offenders call attention to themselves. The most liberal juvenile judge and the most conservative juvenile justice official tend to join together to administer punishment to these offenders.

The adult court is a sad setting for families of youthful offenders who have been sentenced to long prison terms, to life-without-parole, or to the death penalty. Mothers are horrified to realize that their children may be spending the rest of their lives in prison. But typically in that courtroom will be victims' families. They have lost mothers and fathers, sisters and brothers, or grandparents because of the act of the juvenile on trial. They see the scenario unfolding before them in a much different way. The juvenile is a murderer who has taken a loved one from them forever.

Curbing the crime of violent and chronic juvenile delinquents is a major challenge of today's society. In the 1990s, the Office of Juvenile Justice and Delinquency Prevention began a major emphasis to provide prevention and treatment programs to high-risk juveniles before or early in the establishment of their delinquent lifestyles. This active emphasis has been quite different from merely waiting for these youngsters to explode in violent acts and then punishing them severely. This effort of the Office of Juvenile Justice and Delinquency Prevention needs to be expanded and broadened, so that society begins to think more of meeting the needs and responding to the challenges of high-risk juveniles.

SUMMARY

Each of the social process theories in this chapter contributes to an understanding of how adolescents become delinquent. Differential association theory suggests that individuals learn from their association with small groups; if they are involved in antisocial groups, they are more likely to accept antisocial conduct norms or definitions. Social control theory adds that the more strongly attached adolescents are to the social bond, the more likely it is that they will refrain from delinquent behavior. Containment theory states that positive experiences in the home, in the school, and in the community will lead to good self-concepts, thereby insulating individuals from crime and delinquency.

The strength of social process theories rests in their analyses of the individual level of the delinquent. The process of bonding to significant others, drifting in and out of delinquent behavior, and developing the self-concept are key concepts in these theories. The picture offered of the delinquent, particularly by drift and social control theories, emphasizes the decision-making process.

Although the strength of these theories is found in their microanalysis of the meaning, behavior, and interactions of the individual delinquent, their major flaw lies in terms of macroanalysis. These theories fail to place sufficient emphasis on the impact of the larger political and economic systems on the delinquent. As the major weakness in the social structural explanations of delinquency lies in their ignoring the level of the individual delinquent, the major limitation of social process theories is their preoccupation with that level of analysis. But together, these two types of sociological analysis can provide a much stronger explanation for why delinquency occurs and persists in U.S. society. Most delinquent theories now use both structural and process components.

KEY TERMS

containment theory, p. 136
control balance theory, p. 140
control theory, p. 136
differential association theory, p. 126
differential identification theory, p. 130
drift theory, p. 132

neutralization theory, p. 134
process of becoming deviant, p. 126
social bond, p. 138
social control theory, p. 138
social development model, p. 149

CRITICAL THINKING QUESTIONS

1. Why is differential association theory called a "learning" theory?
2. Self-concept, according to containment theory, is vitally important in affecting behavior. Do you agree?
3. Matza and Hirschi proposed different interpretations of the degree to which delinquents identify with the norms and values of society. Define the position of each theorist and explain which position you find more credible.
4. Which of the four integrated theories make the most sense to you? What are the advantages of integrated theory? What are its disadvantages?

5. Does Matza's drift theory seem to be present in the lives of those in *Voices in Delinquency?* What forces seem to set in motion the drift toward delinquency?
6. Matza also talked about commitment to delinquency. Did you find much evidence of commitment in the stories you read?
7. As suggested by differential association, did those individuals in *Voices of Delinquency* seem to be influenced by others to commit delinquent acts? Was this as true for delinquent acts as it was for drug offenses?
8. How important was control in the lives of those individuals in *Voices of Delinquency?*

WEB DESTINATIONS

Read more about Differential Association Theory on the Florida State University site.
http://www.criminology.fsu.edu/crimtheory/ sutherland.html

Read more about the Drift and Neutralization Theory from the Hewett School of Norwich, Norfolk UK.
http://www.hewett.norfolk.sch.uk/curric/soc/crime/ sykes_ma.htm

Learn more about Social Control Theory from the University of Washington site.
http://faculty.washington.edu/bridges/soc271/ tutorials/tutorial6

Go to this University of Minnesota Duluth site to look at an overall powerpoint presentation of Gottfredson and Hirschi's General Theory of Crime.
www.d.umn.edu/~jmaahs/Deviance/Over-heads%20and%20Powerpoint/general_theory.p

Go to this University at Albany site to learn more about Thornberry's Interactional Theory.
www.albany.edu/scj/faculty/thornbry.html

Go to this Drug Prevention site to learn more about Hawkins and Weis's Social Development Theory.
http://www.drugsprevention.net/default.asp?s= E&d=E9

NOTES

1. Interview conducted in April 1987.
2. For this symbolic interactionist perspective, see Charles H. Cooley, *Human Nature and the Social Order* (1902); reprint ed. (New York: Schocken Books, 1964); George H. Mead, *Mind, Self and Society* (Chicago: University of Chicago Press, 1934.)
3. Edwin H. Sutherland, "A Statement of the Theory," in *The Sutherland Papers,* edited by Albert Cohen, Alfred Lindesmith, and Karl Schuessler (Bloomington: Indiana University Press, 1956), p. 9.
4. Edwin H. Sutherland, *Principles of Criminology* (Philadelphia: J. B. Lippincott, 1947).
5. Ross L. Matsueda, "The Current State of Differential Association Theory," *Crime and Delinquency* 34 (July 1988), p. 280.
6. Harold Finestone, *Victims of Change: Juvenile Delinquents in American Society* (Westport, Conn.: Greenwood Press, 1976), p. 157.
7. Matsueda, "The Current State of Differential Association Theory," pp. 277–278.
8. LaMar T. Empey, *American Delinquency: Its Meaning and Construction* (Homewood, Ill.: Dorsey Press, 1982), p. 218.
9. James F. Short Jr. "Differential Association as a Hypothesis: Problems of Empirical Testing," *Social Problems* 8 (1960), pp. 14–25.
10. Albert J. Reiss Jr. and A. Lewis Rhodes, "The Distribution of Delinquency in the Social Class Structure," *American Sociological Review* 26 (1961), p. 732.
11. Craig Reinarman and Jeffrey Fagan, "Social Organization and Differential Association: A Research Note from a Longitudinal Study of Violent Juvenile Offenders," *Crime and Delinquency* 34 (July 1988), p. 307.
12. Elton F. Jackson, Charles R. Tittle, and Mary Jean Burke, "Offense-Specific Models of the Differential Association Process," *Social Problems* 33 (1986), pp. 335–356.

13. John Paul Wright and Francis T. Cullen, "Juvenile Delinquency in Occupational Delinquency," *Criminology* 38 (August 2000), p. 863.

14. Ross L. Matsueda, "Testing Control Theory and Differential Association: A Causal Modeling Approach," *American Sociological Association* 47 (1982), pp. 489–504; Ross L. Matsueda and Karen Heimer, "Race, Family Structure, and Delinquency," *American Sociological Review* 52 (1987), pp. 826–840. See also Raymond Paternoster and Ruth Triplett, "Disaggregating Self-Reported Delinquency and Its Implications for Theory," *Criminology* 25 (1987), pp. 591–620.

15. William E. Thompson, Jim Mitchell, and Richard A. Doddler, "An Empirical Test of Hirschi's Control Theory of Delinquency," *Deviant Behavior* 5 (1984), pp. 11–22.

16. Brenda S. Griffin and Charles T. Griffin, "Marijuana Use among Students and Peers," *Drug Forum* 7 (1978), pp. 155–165.

17. Richard E. Johnson, Anastasios C. Marcos, and Stephen J. Bahr, "The Role of Peers in the Complex Etiology of Adolescent Drug Use," *Criminology* 25 (1987), pp. 323–340.

18. Delbert S. Elliott, David Huizinga, and Suzanne S. Ageton, *Explaining Delinquency and Drug Use* (Beverly Hills, Calif.: Sage, 1985).

19. Melvin DeFleur and Richard Quinney, "A Reformulation of Sutherland's Differential Association Theory and a Strategy for Empirical Verification," *Journal of Research in Crime and Delinquency* 3 (January 1966), pp. 1–11.

20. Daniel Glaser, "Criminality Theory and Behavioral Images," *American Journal of Sociology* 61 (1956), pp. 433–444.

21. Daniel Glaser, "Differential Association and Criminological Prediction," *Social Problems* 8 (1960), pp. 6–14.

22. Robert J. Burgess Jr. and Ronald L. Akers, "A Differential Association-Reinforcement Theory of Criminal Behavior," *Social Problems* 14 (1966), pp. 128–147. See also Ronald L. Akers, *Deviant Behavior: A Social Learning Approach*, 3d ed. (Belmont, Calif.: Wadsworth, 1985), p. 41.

23. Marvin D. Krohn et al., "Social Learning Theory and Adolescent Cigarette Smoking: A Longitudinal Study," *Social Problems* 32 (June 1985), pp. 455–474.

24. Don C. Gibbons and Marvin D. Krohn, *Delinquent Behavior*, 5th ed. (Englewood Cliffs, N.J.: Prentice-Hall, 1991), pp. 212–213.

25. Ruth R. Kornhauser, *Social Sources of Delinquency* (Chicago: University of Chicago Press, 1978).

26. Matsueda, "The Current State of Differential Association Theory," p. 289.

27. Ibid., p. 292.

28. For those who see little value in a theory such as differential association that cannot be tested, see Jack P. Gibbs, "The State of Criminology Theory," *Criminology* 25 (1987), pp. 821–840; Sheldon Glueck, "Theory and Fact in Criminology," *British Journal of Criminology* 7 (1956), pp. 92–109; and Travis Hirschi, *Causes of Delinquency* (Berkeley: University of California Press, 1969). For a defense of the testability of differential association theory, see James D. Orcutt, "Differential Association and Marijuana Use: A Closer Look at Sutherland (with a Little Help from Becker)," *Criminology* 25 (1987), pp. 341–358.

29. Ronald L. Akers, "Is Differential Association/Social Learning Cultural Deviance Theory?" *Criminology* 34 (1996), p. 230.

30. Steven Box, *Deviance, Reality and Society* (New York: Holt, Rinehart and Winston, 1971), p. 21.

31. C. R. Jeffery, "An Integrated Theory of Crime and Criminal Behavior," *Journal of Criminal Law, Criminology and Police Science* 49 (1959), pp. 533–552.

32. Matsueda, "The Current State of Differential Association Theory," p. 295.

33. David Matza, *Delinquency and Drift* (New York: Wiley, 1964), p. 28.

34. Ibid., p. 49.

35. Ibid., p. 69.

36. Gresham M. Sykes and David Matza, "Techniques of Neutralization: A Theory of Delinquency," *American Sociological Review* 22 (December 1957), pp. 664–666.

37. Ibid.

38. Matza, *Delinquency and Drift*, p. 156.

39. Ibid., p. 181.

40. Ibid.

41. Ibid., p. 184.

42. Ibid., p. 185.

43. Ibid., p. 188–189.

44. David Matza, *Becoming Deviant* (Englewood Cliffs, N.J.: Prentice-Hall, 1969).

45. Matza, *Delinquency and Drift*. See also Robert Agnew, "Determinism, Interdeterminism, and Crime: An Empirical Exploration," *Criminology* 33 (February 1995), p. 83.

46. Travis Hirschi, "On the Compatibility of Rational Choice and Social Control Theories of Crime," in *The Reasoning Criminal*, Derek B. Cornish and Ronald V. Clarke, eds. (New York: Springer-Verlag, 1986); Michael R. Gottfredson and Travis Hirschi, eds., *Positive Criminology* (Newbury Park, Calif.: Sage, 1987); Michael R. Gottfredson and Travis Hirschi, *A General Theory of Crime* (Palo Alto, Calif.: Stanford University Press, 1990).

47. See John S. Goldkamp, "Rational Choice and Determinism," in *Positive Criminology*.

48. Ronald L. Akers, "Rational Choice, Deterrence, and Social Learning in Criminology: The Path Not Taken," *Journal of Criminal Law and Criminology* 81 (1990), p. 666.

49. Ian Taylor, Paul Walton, and Jack Young, *The New Criminology* (New York: Harper and Row, 1973).

50. Robert Regoli and Eric Poole, "The Commitment of Delinquents to Their Misdeeds: A Reexamination," *Journal of Criminal Justice* 6 (1978), pp. 261–269.

51. Michael J. Hindelang, "The Commitment of Delinquents to Their Misdeeds: Do Delinquents Drift?" *Social Problems* 17 (1970), pp. 50–59; Michael J. Hindelang, "Moral Evaluation of Illegal Behaviors," *Social Problems* 21 (1974), pp. 370–385.

52. John Hagan, "Destiny and Drift: Subcultural Preferences, Status Attainments, and the Risks and Rewards of Youth," *American Sociological Review* 56 (1991), p. 567.

53. John E. Hamlin, "The Misplaced Role of Rational Choice in Neutralization Theory," *Criminology* 26 (1988), p. 426.

54. Ronald L. Akers, *Deviance Behavior: A Social Learning Approach*, 2d ed. (Belmont, Calif.: Wadsworth, 1977).

55. Hirschi, *Causes of Delinquency*, pp. 207–208.

56. Robert Agnew and Ardith A. R. Peters, "The Techniques of Neutralization: An Analysis of Predisposing and Situational Factors," *Criminal Justice and Behavior* 13 (1986), pp. 81–97; Roy L. Austin, "Commitment, Neutralization, and Delinquency," in *Juvenile Delinquency: Little Brother Grows Up,* Theodore N. Ferdinand, ed. (Beverly Hills, Calif.: Sage, 1977); William W. Minor, "Techniques of Neutralization: A Reconceptualization and Empirical Examination," *Journal of Research in Crime and Delinquency* 18 (1981), pp. 295–318; and Quint C. Thurman, Craig St. John, and Lisa Riggs, "Neutralization and Tax Evasion: How Effective Would a Moral Appeal Be in Improving Compliance to Tax Laws?" *Law and Policy* 6 (1984), pp. 309–327.

57. Richard A. Ball, "An Empirical Exploration of Neutralization Theory," *Criminologia* 4 (1966), pp. 22–32. See also Richard Allen Ball, "A Report to the Ohio Youth Commission and Columbus Public Schools" based on Ph.D. dissertation, Ohio State University, 1965.

58. Richard A. Ball, "Emergent Delinquency in a Rurban Area," in *Juvenile Delinquency: Little Brother Grows Up.*

59. Richard A. Ball and J. Robert Lilly, "Juvenile Delinquency in a Rurban County," *Criminology* 9 (1971), pp. 69–85.

60. Robert Agnew, "The Techniques of Neutralization and Violence," *Criminology* 32 (November 1994), p. 555.

61. Walter C. Reckless and Shlomo Shoham, "Norm Containment Theory as Applied to Delinquency and Crime," *Excerpta Criminologica* 3 (November-December 1963), pp. 637–644.

62. Donald J. Shoemaker, *Theories of Delinquency: An Examination of Explanations of Delinquent Behavior,* 3d. ed.(New York: Oxford University Press, 1996), p. 157.

63. Albert J. Reiss Jr., "Delinquency as the Failure of Personal and Social Controls," *American Sociological Review* 16 (1951), pp. 196–207.

64. F. Ivan Nye, *Family Relationships and Delinquent Behavior* (New York: John Wiley, 1958), p. 5.

65. The principles of containment theory are adapted from Walter C. Reckless, "A New Theory of Delinquency and Crime," *Federal Probation* 24 (December 1961), pp. 42–46.

66. Simon Dinitz and Betty A. Pfau-Vicent, "Self-Concept and Juvenile Delinquency: An Update," *Youth and Society* 14 (December 1982), pp. 133–158.

67. Walter C. Reckless and Simon Dinitz, *The Prevention of Juvenile Delinquency: An Experiment* (Columbus: Ohio State University Press, 1972).

68. E. D. Lively, Simon Dinitz, and Walter C. Reckless, "Self-Concept as a Prediction of Juvenile Delinquency," *American Journal of Orthopsychiatry* 32 (1962), pp. 159–168.

69. Gary F. Jensen, "Inner Containment and Delinquency," *Criminology* 64 (1973), pp. 464–470.

70. Franco Ferracuti, Simon Dinitz, and E. Acosta de Brenes, *Delinquents and Nondelinquents in the Puerto Rican Slum Culture* (Columbus: Ohio State University Press, 1975).

71. Timothy J. Owens, "Two Dimensions of Self-Esteem: Reciprocal Effects of Positive Self-Worth and Self-Deprecations on Adolescent Problems," *American Sociological Review* 59 (1994), pp. 391, 405.

72. L. Edward Wells and Joseph R. Rankin, "Self-Concept as a Mediating Factor in Delinquency," *Social Psychology Quarterly* 46 (1983), p. 19.

73. John D. McCarthy and Dean R. Hoge, "The Dynamics of Self-Esteem and Delinquency," *American Journal of Sociology* 90 (1984), p. 396.

74. Gary F. Jensen, "Delinquency and Adolescent Self Conceptions: A Study of the Personal Relevance of Interactions," *Social Problems* 20 (Fall 1972), pp. 84–101.

75. W. E. Thompson and R. A. Dodder, "Juvenile Delinquency Explained? A Test of Containment Theory," *Youth and Society* 15 (December 1983), pp. 171–194.

76. Florence R. Rosenberg and Morris Rosenberg, "Self-Esteem and Delinquency," *Journal of Youth and Adolescence* 7 (1978), p. 280.

77. H. B. Kaplan, *Deviant Behavior in Defense of Self* (New York: Academic Press, 1980).

78. Rosenberg and Rosenberg, "Self-Esteem and Delinquency," p. 289. See also Morris Rosenberg, Carmi Schooler, and Carrie Schoenbach, "Self-Esteem and Adolescent Problems," *American Sociological Review* 54 (1989), pp. 1004–1018.

79. Dinitz and Pfau-Vicent, "Self-Concept and Juvenile Delinquency," p. 155.

80. Michael Schwartz and Sandra S. Tangri, "A Note on 'Self-Concept as an Insulator against Delinquency'," *American Sociological Review* 30 (1965), pp. 922–926.

81. Hirschi, *Causes of Delinquency,* p. 16.

82. Ibid., p. 31.

83. Ibid., p. 34.

84. Ibid., pp. 16–34.

85. Ibid., p. 18.

86. Ibid., p. 83.

87. Ibid., p. 86.

88. Ibid., p. 20.

89. Ibid., p. 22.

90. Ibid., p. 198.

91. Ibid., p. 200.

92. Ibid., p. 108.

93. Ibid., pp. 110–134.

94. Ibid., pp. 135–161.

95. Ibid., pp. 162–185.

96. Ibid., pp. 187–196.

97. Ibid., pp. 197–224.

98. Barbara J. Costello and Paul R. Vowell, "Testing Control Theory and Differential Association: A Reanalysis of the Richmond Youth Project Data," *Criminology* 37 (November 1999), p. 815.

99. Charles R. Tittle, *Control Balance: Toward a General Theory of Deviance* (Boulder, Colo: Westview, 1995). For a recent attempt to test Tittle's control balance theory, see Alex R. Piquero and Matthew Hickman, "An Empirical Test of Tittle's Control Balance Theory," *Criminology* 37 (May 1999), pp. 319–341.

100. Michael D. Wiatrowski, David D. Griswald, and Mary R. Roberts, "Social Control Theory and Delinquency," *American Sociological Review* 46 (1981), pp. 525–541.

101. Marvin D. Krohn and James L. Massey, "Social Control and Delinquent Behavior: An Examination of the Elements of the Social Bond" (unpublished paper, 1980). See also Marvin D. Krohn, James L. Massey, and William F. Skinner, "Social Bonding Theory and Minor Deviant Behavior: A Longitudinal Analysis of Adolescent Cigarette Smoking." Paper presented at the Annual Meeting

of the American Society of Criminology, Toronto, Canada (November 1982).

102. Richard Salem, "Commitment and Delinquency: Social Attachments and Behavioral Change in Group Homes." Paper presented at the Annual Meeting of the Wisconsin Sociological Association, October 22, 1982, p. 5.

103. Michael J. Hindelang, "Causes of Delinquency: A Partial Replication and Extension," *Social Problems* 20 (Spring 1973), pp. 471–487.

104. Steven A. Cernkovich, "Evaluating Two Models of Delinquency Causation: Structural Theory and Control Theory," *Criminology* 25 (1987), pp. 335–352; Raymond A. Eve, "A Study of the Efficacy and Interactions of Several Theories for Explaining Rebelliousness among High School Students," *Journal of Criminal Law and Criminology* 69 (1978), pp. 115–125.

105. Marvin D. Krohn and James L. Massey, "Social Control and Delinquent Behavior: An Examination of the Elements of the Social Bond," *Sociological Quarterly* 21 (August 1980), p. 542.

106. Elliott, *Explaining Delinquency and Drug Use.*

107. Joseph H. Rankin, "Investigating the Interrelations among Social Control Variables and Conformity," *Journal of Criminal Law and Criminology* 67 (1977), pp. 470–480.

108. Robert Agnew, "Social Control Theory and Delinquency: A Longitudinal Test," *Criminology* 23 (1985), pp. 47–61.

109. Randy L. LaGrange and Helene Raskin White, "Age Differences in Delinquency: A Test of Theory," *Criminology* 23 (1985), pp. 19–45.

110. Kimberly Kempf Leonard and Scott H. Decker, "Theory of Social Control: Does It Apply to the Very Young," *Journal of Criminal Justice* 22 (1994), p. 89.

111. Robert L. Gardner and Donald J. Shoemaker, "Social Bonding and Delinquency: A Comparative Analysis," *The Sociological Quarterly* 39 (1989), p. 481.

112. Shoemaker, *Theories of Delinquency,* p. 182.

113. Salem, "Commitment and Delinquency," p. 3.

114. Shoemaker, *Theories of Delinquency,* p. 180–181.

115. Leonard and Decker, "Theories of Social Control, " p. 89.

116. Among the growing number of works citing the advantages of integrated theory are Richard Johnson, *Juvenile Delinquency and Its Origins: An Integrated Theoretical Approach* (Cambridge: Cambridge University Press, 1979); Elliot, Huizinga, and Ageton, *Explaining Delinquency and Drug Use;* Steven Messner, Marvin Krohn, and Allen Liska, eds., *Theoretical Integration in the Study of Deviance and Crime: Problems and Prospects* (Albany: State University of New York at Albany Press, 1989); and John Hagan and Bill McCarthy, *Mean Streets: Youth Crime and Homelessness* (Cambridge: University Press, 1997).

117. Messner, Krohn, and Liska, *Theoretical Integration in the Study of Deviance and Crime.* Cited in Thomas J. Bernard and Jeffrey B. Snipes, "Theoretical Integration in Criminology," in *Crime and Justice: A Review of Research,* Volume 20, edited by Michael Tonry (Chicago and London: The University of Chicago Press, p. 306.)

118. Margaret Farnworth, "Theory Integration Versus Model Building," in *Theoretical Integration in the Study of Deviance and Crime,* p. 93.

119. Barnard and Snipes, "Theoretical Integration in Criminology," p. 307.

120. Travis Hirschi, "Separate and Equal Is Better," *Journal of Research in Crime and Deliquency* 16 (January 1979), pp. 34–37.

121. Ibid.

122. Mark Colvin and John Pauly, "A Critique of Criminology: Toward an Integrated Structural-Marxist theory of Deliquency Production," *American Journal of Sociology* 89 (November 1983), pp. 513–551.

123. Hirshi, "Separate and Equal is Better, pp. 34–37.

124. Shoemaker, *Theories of Delinquency,* pp. 253–254.

125. Ibid., p. 254.

126. Ibid., p. 255.

127. Ibid., p. 256.

128. For other integrated theories, see James Q. Wilson and Richard J. Herrnstein, *Crime and Human Nature* (New York: Simon and Schuster, 1985), which is discussed in Chapter 3; Robert J. Sampson and John H. Laub, *Crime in the Making: Pathways and Turning Points through Life* (Cambridge, Mass.: Harvard University Press, 1993), which is discussed in Chapter 2; Colvin and Pauly, "A Critique of Criminology," pp. 513–551, which is discussed in Chapter 6; John Hagan, A. R. Gillis, and John Simpson, "The Class Structure of Gender and Delinquency: Toward a Power-Control Theory of Common Delinquent Behavior," *American Journal of Sociology* 90 (1985), pp. 1151–1178, which is discussed in Chapter 6; John Hagan and Bill McCarthy, *Mean Streets: Youth Crime and Homelessness* (Cambridge: University Press, 1997), which is discussed in Chapter 4.

129. Michael R. Gottfredson and Travis Hirschi, *A General Theory of Crime* (Palo Alto, Calif.: Stanford University Press, 1990); Elliot et al., *Explaining Delinquency and Drug Use;* Delbert S. Elliot, Suzanne S. Ageton, and Rachelle J. Canter, "An Integrated Theoretical Perspective on Delinquent Behavior," *Journal of Research in Crime and Delinquency* 16 (1979), pp. 3–27; Terence P. Thornberry, "Toward an Interactional Theory of Delinquency," *Criminology* 25 (1987), pp. 862–891; and Terence P. Thornberry, Alan J. Lizotte, Marvin D. Krohn, Margaret Farnworth, and Sung Joon Jang, "Testing Interactional Theory: An Examination of Reciprocal Causal Relationships among Family, School, and Delinquency," *Journal of Criminal Law and Criminology* 82 (1991), pp. 3–35. J. David Hawkins and Joseph G. Weis, "The Social Development Model: An Integrated Approach to Delinquency Prevention," *Journal of Primary Prevention* 6, (Winter 1985) pp. 77–78.

130. John E. Donovan and Richard Jessor, "Structure of Problem Behavior in Adolescence and Young Adulthood," *Journal of Consulting and Clinical Psychology* 53 (1985), pp. 89–904. See also D. Wayne Osgood, Lloyd D. Johnston, Patrick M. O'Malley, and Jerald G. Bachman, "The Generality of Deviance in Late Adolescence and Early Childhood," *American Sociological Review* 53 (1988), pp. 81–93.

131. Travis Hirschi, "A Brief Commentary on Akers' 'Delinquent Behavior, Drugs and Alcohol: What Is the Relationship?'," *Today's Delinquent* 3 (1984), pp. 49–52.

132. Ibid.

133. Gottfredson and Hirschi, *A General Theory of Crime.*

134. Ibid., pp. 90–91.

135. Ibid., p. 87.

136. Douglas Longshore, Susan Turner, and Judith A. Stein, "Self-Control in a Criminal Sample: An Examination of Construct Validity," *Criminology* 34 (1996), p. 209.

137. Gottfredson and Hirschi, *A General Theory of Crime*, p. 117.

138. Ibid.

139. Dennis Giever, "Empirical Testing of Gottfredson and Hirschi's General Theory of Crime." Paper presented to the Annual Meeting of the American Society of Criminology in San Diego, California (November 1997), p. 15.

140. Travis C. Pratt and Francis T. Cullen, "The Empirical Status of Gottfredson and Hirschi's General Theory of Crime: A Meta-Analysis," *Criminology* 38 (August 2000), p. 931.

141. For a review of these studies, see T. David Evans, Francis T. Cullen, Velmer S. Burton Jr., R. Gregory Dunaway, and Michael L. Benson, "The Social Consequences of Self-Control: Testing the General Theory of Crime," *Criminology* (1997), pp. 476–477.

142. Teresa C. LaGrange and Robert A. Silverman, "Low Self-Control and Opportunity: Testing the General Theory of Crime as an Explanation for Gender Differences in Delinquency," *Criminology* 37 (February 1999), p. 41.

143. Raymond Paternoster and Robert Brame, "On the Association among Self-Control, Crime, and Analogous Behaviors," *Criminology* 38 (August 2000), p. 971.

144. David Brownfield and Marie Soreson, "Self-Control and Juvenile Delinquency: Theoretical Issues and an Empirical Assessment of Selected Elements of a General Theory of Crime," *Deviant Behavior* 4 (1993), pp. 243–264; and Alex Piquero and Stephen Tibbetts, "Specifying the Direct and Indirect Effects of Low Self-Control and Situational Factors in Decision-Making: Toward a More Complete Model of Rational Offending," *Justice Quarterly* 13 (1996), pp. 481–510.

145. Dennis M. Giever, Dana C. Lynskey, and Danette S. Monnet, "Gottfredson and Hirschi's General Theory of Crime and Youth Gangs: An Empirical Test on a Sample of Middle-School Students." Unpublished paper sent to author, 1998.

146. Carter Hay, "Parenting, Self-Control, and Delinquency: A Test of Self-Control Theory," *Criminology* 39 (August 2001), p. 726.

147. Harold G. Grasmick, Charles R. Tittle, Robert J. Bursik Jr., and Bruce J. Arneklev, "Testing the Core Empirical Implications of Gottfredson and Hirschi's General Theory of Crime," *Journal of Research in Crime and Delinquency* 30 (February 1993), p. 5.

148. For other criticisms of this general theory of crime, see Ronald L. Akers, "Self-Control as a General Theory of Crime," *Journal of Quantitative Criminology* 7 (1991), pp. 291–211; Michael L. Benson and Elizabeth Moore, "Are White-Collar and Common Offenders the Same? An Empirical and Theoretical Critique of a Recently Proposed General Theory of Crime," *Journal of Research in Crime and Delinquency* 29 (August 1992), pp. 251–272; Bruce J. Arneklev, Harold G. Grasmick, Charles R. Tittle, and Robert J. Bursik Jr., "Low Self-Control and Imprudent Behavior," *Journal of Quantitative Criminology* 9 (1993), pp. 225–247; Susan L. Miller and Cynthia Burack, "A Critique of Gottfredson and Hirschi's General Theory of Crime: Selective

(In)Attention to Gender and Power Positions," *Women and Criminal Justice* 4 (1993), pp. 115–133; and Michael Polakowski, "Linking Self- and Social Control with Deviance: Illuminating the Structure Underlying a General Theory of Crime and Its Relation to Deviant Activity," *Journal of Quantitative Criminology* 10 (1994), pp. 41–78.

149. Shoemaker, *Theories of Delinquency*, p. 252.

150. Giever, "Empirical Testing of Gottfredson and Hirschi's General Theory of Crime," p. 16.

151. Michael Polakowski, "Linking Self- and Social Control with Deviance: Illuminating the Structure Underlying a General Theory of Crime and Its Relation to Deviant Activity," *Journal of Quantitative Criminology* 10 (1994), pp. 41–77.

152. Ibid., p. 41.

153. Elliott et al., "An Integrated Theoretical Perspective on Delinquent Behavior," p. 11.

154. Ibid., p. 3–27.

155. Ibid.

156. Elliott et al., *Explaining Delinquency and Drug Use.*

157. Ibid. For a more recent extension of this model, see Cynthia Chien, "Testing the Effect of the Key Theoretical Variable of Theories of Strain, Social Control and Social Learning on Types of Delinquency." Paper presented to the Annual Meeting of the American Society of Criminology, Baltimore, Maryland (November 1990).

158. Shoemaker, *Theories of Delinquency*, p. 254.

159. Thornberry, "Toward an Interactional Theory of Delinquency," p. 886. See also Terence P. Thornberry, "Reflections on the Advantages and Disadvantages of Theoretical Integration," in *Theoretical Integration in the Study of Deviance and Crime: Problems and Prospects* (Albany: State University of New York Press, 1989), pp. 51–60.

160. Ibid., p. 886.

161. Ibid.

162. This evaluation of interactional theory is largely derived from Shoemaker, *Theories of Delinquency*, pp. 161–163.

163. Thornberry et al., "Testing Interactional Theory," pp. 19–25.

164. Terence P. Thornberry, Alan J. Lizotte, Marvin D. Krohn, Margaret Farnworth, and Sung Joon Jang, "Delinquency Peers, Beliefs, and Delinquent Behavior: A Longitudinal Test of Interactional Theory, " p. 74.

165. Shoemaker, *Theories of Delinquency*, p. 263.

166. Ibid., p. 262–263.

167. J. David Hawkins and Joseph G. Weis, "The Social Development Model: An Integrated Approach to Delinquency Prevention," *Journal of Primary Prevention* 6 (Winter 1985), pp. 77–78.

168. Hirschi, *Causes of Delinquency.*

169. Clifford R. Shaw, *Delinquent Areas* (Chicago: University of Chicago Press, 1929); Clifford Shaw and Henry D. McKay, *Juvenile Delinquency in Urban Areas* (Chicago: University of Chicago Press, 1942).

170. Hawkins, et al., *Typology of Cause-Focused Strategies.*

171. Bu Huang, Rick Kosterman, Richard F. Catalano, J. David Hawkins, and Robert D. Abbott, "Modeling Mediation in the Etiology of Violent Behavior in Adolescence: A Test of the Social Development Model," *Criminology* 39 (February 2001), p. 75.

172. See Shaw, *Delinquent Areas;* and Shaw and McKay, *Juvenile Delinquency in Urban Areas.*

chapter 6

SOCIAL REACTION THEORIES

OBJECTIVES

After reading this chapter, the student will be able to answer the following questions:

- How important is the label in generating future behavior?

- What about those youngsters who become more determined to succeed because they have been labeled?

- Does peer evaluation affect some youngsters more than others?

- How much does class actually affect the system's response to a troublesome youth?

Walter, an ex-offender, talks about how poverty influenced the social reaction of the justice system:

All the trouble I caused as a kid was tied into being poor. We lived in housing projects that were run down. I didn't have things that other kids had. I found or stole most of the toys I played with. My folks went to the local bar and drank the little money we had. My folks used to send me to buy horse meat for hamburger because they were too embarrassed to do it themselves.

As I got into my teens, I saw that the law treated me different than the rich kids. We'd be driving along, and the cops would pull us over, shake us down, *and harass us. I remember one time this rich kid and I went out booting [stealing] tires. He went for the thrill, but I went because I needed the tires. We got stopped and, when the cops discovered the tires in the trunk, they took me to jail and let the rich kid go. Another time we went to this beach party in La Jolla [California], where there was a lot of rich kids. All of us got noisy. They let the rich kids go and took us to jail. They booked me for vagrancy.*

When I was in the "joint" in the late 1960s and early 1970s, they [the inmates] were talking about how we were being held as political prisoners. We had a riot in San Quentin over that stuff. I knew at the time that prisoners, especially blacks and Chicanos, were taking advantage of the political talk to improve prison conditions. But I also knew that we were all poor and down and out. We were in the joint because we didn't have nothing. We used to say at the time that if you're rich, you ride; if you're poor, you walk. If you're rich, you do the crime and get away with it; if you're poor, you do the crime and end up doing the dime [time].[1]

—Walter

Are rich youngsters really treated differently from poor ones? Do you believe that you are as quick to be labeled by the system today as was true in Walter's day?

This man's life depicts in many ways the social reaction to delinquency theories. He had spent a total of eighteen years in the California State Prison at San Quentin. After his release he was incarcerated for three additional years for a drug (heroin) conviction. On his return to the community, he decided to kick his heroin habit and attend community college. He did well, continued his schooling, and received his undergraduate degree. He found employment in a group home for male delinquents. In analyzing his childhood and delinquent behavior, he talked frequently about the labels he was given and how he tried to live up to these labels. He also contended that economic inequality, oppressiveness of the law, and social injustice were key factors in his becoming delinquent and continuing to adult crime.[2]

This chapter evaluates labeling theory, symbolic interactionist theory, and conflict theory. All three of these theories are social reaction theories in that they focus on the role that social and economic groups and institutions have in producing delinquent behavior. The labeling theory discusses how the creation and enforcement of the rules of society play an important role in determining the nature and extent of delinquency. The symbolic interactionist theory further considers the process by which deviant or delinquent behavior is influenced by reference groups and peers. Conflict theorists see delinquency as a product of the conflict that results when groups or classes with differing power and interests interact with each other. Marxist criminology, one of the expressions of conflict criminology, contends that crime and delinquency in capitalist society emerge because of the efforts of the powerful to maintain their power at all costs, with the result that the working class is exploited.

How Labeling Theory Explains Delinquency

During the 1960s and 1970s, the labeling perspective was unquestionably one of the most influential approaches to understanding crime and delinquency.[3] The **labeling** perspective, sometimes called the *interactional theory of deviance* or the *social reaction perspective*, is based on the premise that society creates deviants by labeling those who are apprehended as different from other individuals, when in reality they are different only because they have been tagged with a deviant label. Accordingly, labeling theorists focus on the processes by which individuals become involved in deviant behavior and stress the part played by social audiences and their responses to the norm violations of individuals.

The view that formal and informal social reactions to criminality can influence criminals' subsequent attitudes and behaviors has been recognized for some time. Frank Tannenbaum, Edwin M. Lemert, and Howard Becker, three of the chief proponents of the labeling perspective, focus on the process by which formal social control agents change the self-concept of individuals through these agents' reactions to their behavior. Recent work in labeling theory is also discussed in this section.

Frank Tannenbaum: The Dramatization of Evil

Frederick M. Thrasher's 1927 study of juvenile gangs in Chicago was one of the first to suggest that the consequences of official labels of delinquency were potentially negative.[4] In 1938, Tannenbaum developed the earliest formulation of labeling theory in his book *Crime and the Community.* Tannenbaum examined the process whereby a juvenile came to the attention of the authorities and was labeled as different from other juveniles. Tannenbaum theorized that this process produced a change in both how those individuals were then handled by the justice system and how they came to view themselves:

> The process of making the criminal, therefore, is a process of tagging, defining, identifying, segregating, describing, emphasizing, making conscious and self-conscious; it becomes a way of stimulating, suggesting, emphasizing, and evoking the very traits that are complained of.[5]

Tannenbaum called this process the *dramatization of evil*. He wrote that the process of tagging a juvenile resulted in the youth's becoming involved with other delinquents and that these associations represented an attempt to escape the society that was responsible for negative labeling. The delinquent then became involved in a deviant career, and regardless of the efforts of individuals in the community and justice system to change his or her "evil" behavior, the negative behavior became increasingly hardened and resistant to positive values. Tannenbaum proposed that the less the evil is dramatized, the less likely youths are to become involved in deviant careers.[6]

Edwin Lemert: Primary and Secondary Deviation

The social reaction theory developed by Edwin H. Lemert provided a distinct alternative to the social disorganization theory of Shaw and McKay, the differential association notion of Edwin H. Sutherland, and the social structural approach of Merton. Lemert focused attention on the interaction between social control agents and rule violators and on how certain behaviors came to be labeled *criminal, delinquent,* or *deviant*.[7]

Lemert's concept of primary and secondary deviation is regarded as one of the most important theoretical constructs of the labeling perspective. According to Lemert, **primary deviation** consists of the individual's behavior, and **secondary deviation** is society's response to that behavior. The social reaction to the deviant, Lemert charged, could be interpreted as forcing a change in status or role; that is, society's reaction to the deviant resulted in a transformation in the individual's identity.[8] The social reaction to the deviant, whether a disapproving glance or a full-blown stigmatization, is critical in understanding the progressive commitment of a person to a deviant mode of life.

Lemert observed this **process of becoming deviant** as having the following stages:

> The sequence of interaction leading to secondary deviation is roughly as follows: (1) primary deviation; (2) social penalties; (3) further primary deviation; (4) stronger

penalties and rejection; (5) further deviation, perhaps with hostilities and resentment beginning to focus upon those doing the penalizing; (6) crisis reached in the tolerance quotient, expressed in formal action by the community stigmatizing of the deviant; (7) strengthening of the deviant conduct as a reaction to the stigmatizing and penalties; (8) ultimate acceptance of deviant social status and efforts at adjustment on the basis of the associated role.[9]

The social reaction to deviance is expressed in this process of interaction. *Social reaction* is a general term that summarizes both the moral indignation of others toward deviance and the action directed toward its control. This concept also encompasses a social organizational perspective. As an organizational response, the concept of social reaction refers to the capacity of control agents to impose such constraints on the behavior of the deviant as are reflected in terms such as *treat, correct,* and *punish.*[10]

Howard Becker and the Deviant Career

Howard Becker, another major labeling theorist, conceptualized the relationship between the rules of society and the process of being labeled as an outsider:

> Social groups create deviance by making the rules whose infraction constitutes deviance, and by applying those rules to particular people and labeling them as outsiders. From this point of view, deviance is not a quality of the act the person commits, but rather a consequence of the application by others of rules and sanctions to an "offender." The deviant is one to whom that label has successfully been applied; deviant behavior is behavior that people so label.[11]

Becker argued that once a person is caught and labeled, that person becomes an outsider and gains a new social status, with consequences for both the person's self-image and his or her public identity. The individual is now regarded as a different kind of person.[12] Although the sequence of events that leads to the imposition of the label of "deviant" is presented from the perspective of social interaction, the analytical framework shifts to that of social structure once the label is imposed. In other words, before a person is labeled, he or she participates in a process of social interaction, but once labeling has occurred the individual is assigned a status within a social structure.[13] For the relationship among the theoretical constructs of labeling theory, see Figure 6.1.

New Developments in the Effects of Labeling

These early versions of labeling theory came under serious attack for theoretical flaws and lack of support.[14] The two most damaging criticisms of this perspective were the charges that "labeling theorists had grossly exaggerated the role of labeling by suggesting that it is the only factor responsible for persistent deviance and by implying that it always increases the likelihood of subsequent rule breaking."[15] The influence of these and other criticisms is seen in the fact that the theory was seriously challenged by 1980 and, as Raymond Paternoster and Leeann Iovanni observe, was "pronounced dead by 1985."[16]

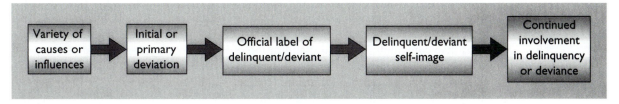

FIGURE 6.1 Generic Assumptions of Labeling Theory

The labeling perspective has enjoyed a resurgence in recent years because of its more sophisticated application.[17] Ruth Ann Triplett and G. Roger Jarjoura developed "a number of new avenues for exploring the effects of labeling."[18] They separated labeling into formal and informal labeling. Formal labels, the emphasis of early labeling theorists, are the reactions by official agents of the justice system to illegal behaviors. In contrast, an informal label is "an attempt to characterize a person as a given 'type' . . . by persons who are not acting as official social control agents, and in social situations that are not formal social control 'ceremonies.' "[19] Informal labels, especially, are given by parents, neighbors, and friends. John Braithwaite's examination of shaming in the family is a relatively recent example of informal labels. His study showed that the family uses shaming, or reintegrative shaming, to bring the offender back into line with the family's beliefs.[20]

Triplett and Jarjoura also divided labels into subjective and objective labels. An audience's reaction illustrates an objective label, whereas an actor's interpretation of the reaction is a subjective label. Although the importance of subjective labels has always been emphasized in symbolic interactionism, one of the important roots of labeling theory, it has remained largely unexplored in the theory and research of labeling.[21] Triplett, in using the four waves of Elliott's National Youth Survey, concluded that the informal labels of significant others (parents) affect delinquent behavior both directly and indirectly for whites but that informal or subjective labels of significant others have no consistent direct or indirect effect on delinquent behavior for nonwhites.[22]

Moreover, Triplett and Jarjoura separated labels into exclusive and inclusive social reactions. J. D. Orcutt refers to these two types of reactions in his research on small-group reactions to deviance:

> Inclusive reactions will designate those attempts at social control which are premised on the assumption that the rule-breaker is and will continue to be an ordinary member of the community. . . . This form of social reaction attempts to control rule-infractions by bringing the present or future behavior of the rule-breaker into conformity with the rules without excluding him from it. Exclusive reactions are those attempts at social control which operate to reject the rule-breaker from the group and revoke his privileges and status as an ordinary member.[23]

Several studies have found that the consequences of official or legal punishment instead of being uniform depend on such individual characteristics as employment and marital status.[24] These studies suggest that under certain circumstances, "official punishment appears to increase the likelihood of subsequent deviance as suggested by labeling theory."[25] In addition, Francis Polymeria, Francis T. Cullen, and Joanne C. Gersten found that the formal reaction to delinquency affects the likelihood of subsequent delinquent behavior but that these effects are related to the types of reaction and the types of deviance.[26] Anthony Matarazzo, Peter J. Carrington, and Robert D. Hiscott, in investigating the relationship between prior and current youth court disposition, found support for social-reaction theory because prior juvenile court dispositions exerted a significant impact on current disposition, even with the control of relevant variables.[27]

Labeling theory has further examined the effects of societal reaction on areas of an individual's life other than that to which the label refers. Bruce Link and colleagues have found that the indirect effects of labeling have been largely ignored. In a series of articles dealing with mental disorders, Link and colleagues demonstrated that deviant labels sometimes resulted in a host of problematic conditions, such as job loss, social rejection, and reduced access to social support. The inability to adjust to these problematic conditions then contributed to the destabilization of the subjects' mental disorders.[28]

Moreover, the possible effects of labeling on risk factors related to crime and delinquency have received some attention. In their call for a "revitalization" of the labeling theory of juvenile delinquency, Paternoster and Iovanni contend that labeling may create problems of adjustment, encouraging further delinquency.[29] Robert J. Sampson and John H. Laub have used insights from labeling theory with social control theory to analyze the developmental process leading to adult crime.[30] The negative effects of criminal records at a young age affected later job prospects, which interfered with the establishment of strong family bonds. According to these researchers, the two structural factors of employment and family ties, especially marriage, are critical risk factors for adult criminality.[31] See Social World of the Delinquent 6.1, "I Became What They Said about Me."

Evaluation of the Labeling Perspective

The labeling perspective has consistently received mixed responses. Gary F. Jensen found that official labels are strongly related to the self-definition of a delinquent and that white youths are more affected by official labels than are African American youths.[32] Susan Ageton and Delbert Elliott also found from a longitudinal study that the self-concepts of white youths declined after they had police contact.[33] Merry Morash found that individual and peer group characteristics that suggest to the police that adolescents are delinquent or a threat to others increase a youth's chances of arrest.[34] Malcolm W. Klein tested the components of the labeling perspective in an experimentally controlled police diversion project and found support for some of the labeling theory's propositions but not for others.[35] Melvin C. Ray and William R. Downs's investigation of drug use among adolescent males and females partially supported labeling theory propositions for males but not females.[36]

Social World of the Delinquent 6.1

"I Became What They Said about Me."

John remembers that a teacher came to his home at the end of the last day of his first school year.

The first grader sat in an overstuffed chair, and listened, seemingly unnoticed, as his mother and his teacher talked in the living room. The teacher said, "John has not done very well in school this year. He seems to be a slower learner. He is also an agitator."

The first grader thought to himself, "I wonder what an agitator is. I bet it is a troublemaker." He went back to listening to the two adults.

"I think," the teacher said, "We had better hold John back a year. Let him repeat first grade next year. If we do that, he may be able to make it through most of high school."

The first grader listened to the two adults sealing his fate. He thought to himself, "I have flunked first grade. I am also dumb and a troublemaker. I am always going to have trouble with school. School is such a pain."

True to his label, John had problems in school. Every year he came close to failing, and teachers regarded him as the major troublemaker in his class. He was also known as the worst kid in town because he became involved in a number of illegal activities. At one point, he was nearly sent to training school.

At the end of his sophomore year in high school (he failed two subjects his freshman year), he was called to the principal's office. John remembers that the principal said, "We just got the IQ scores back. When I look at yours, I cannot understand why such a smart kid would do so poorly in school. Do you know you rank absolutely last in your class?"

John responded, "Well, at least it is a small class. I think we only have fifty-two in it."

The principal did not laugh.

School was an arena of total defeat for John until his junior year of high school, when he had a major turning point and decided to go into the ministry. He finished third in his class in the final two years of high school, was an honors student in college, and finished his academic work at Princeton Theological Seminary.

How much do you think what the teacher said in first grade actually influenced John? Could one comment be that significant to a person's life?

Jack Foster, Simon Dinitz, and Walter Reckless, however, found that labeling by the juvenile justice system during an early stage of processing did not produce either changes in self-concept or increased delinquent behavior.[37] Stuart J. Miller examined the effect of labeling during the institutional process and also concluded that such labels as *emotionally disturbed* or *aggressive behavior* had very little predictive power in determining the future behavior of hard-core delinquents.[38] John R. Hepburn, in comparing the self-concepts and attitudes of 105 nondelinquent males and 96 arrested delinquent males, found that an arrest record had no direct effect on a youngster's self-concept or delinquent identification.[39]

More recently, some research has provided evidence in support of labeling theory. Howard B. Kaplan and associates, in their analysis of negative labeling in their longitudinal study, found that negative reactions from others expressed in school expulsions, run-ins with authority figures, and referrals to psychiatrists or psychologists seemed to have adverse effects on youngsters. Some of these adverse effects were self-rejection, a propensity toward deviance, associations with deviant peers, drug use, and delinquent behavior.[40] Ross L. Matsueda, using data from the National Youth Survey, found that negative labeling from parents is strongly connected with negative self-appraisals and with delinquent behavior. But this researcher suggests that this process is bidirectional: The negative labels from parents may come from delinquency on the part of a youth, which leads to more delinquent behavior.[41]

Labeling theory has several strengths. First, it provides an explanation for why youths who become involved in the juvenile justice process frequently continue delinquent acts until the end of their adolescent years. The official labeling process has identified them as different from other adolescents, and they continue to live up to their reputations.

Second, labeling theory emphasizes the importance of rule making and power in the creation of deviance. Considering the broader contexts of the labeling process lifts the focus of delinquency from the behavior of an individual actor to the interactions of an actor and his or her immediate and broader influences. Because society is emphasized as contributing to the process of becoming deviant, the rules made and the enforcement of those rules are critical in understanding the phenomenon of delinquency.

Third, as part of a larger symbolic interactionist perspective, labeling theory points out that individuals do take on the roles and self-concepts that are expected of them; this means that they are indeed victims of self-fulfilling prophecies. A student who is reinforced typically attempts to seek more reinforcement; likewise, the student who is put down by a teacher often is discouraged and begins engaging in negative or self-defeating behaviors.

Fourth, the more sophisticated application of the labeling perspective in the past decade has moved this explanation of delinquent behavior from a unidimensional (one-directional) basis to one that examines more contingencies of labeling effects, including both direct and indirect effects of labeling. The increased complexity of labeling findings seems to capture more adequately the process and effects of human interaction than most other explanations of delinquent behavior.

The theoretical basis of the labeling approach has been widely criticized. Jack Gibbs charged that the labeling approach lacks clear-cut definitions, fails to produce a coherent set of interrelated propositions and testable hypotheses, and therefore ought not to be considered a theory in any sense.[42] Gibbs also said that the labeling approach raises major questions:

> But the new conception has left at least four crucial questions unanswered. First, what elements in the scheme are intended to be definitions rather than substantive theory? Second, is the ultimate goal to explain behavior or to explain reactions to deviation? Third, is deviant behavior to be identified exclusively in terms of reaction to it? Fourth, exactly what kind of reaction identifies behavior as deviant?[43]

The labeling perspective has also been criticized because it fails to answer a number of critical questions raised by the assumptions it makes: Are the conceptions that we have of one another correct? Whose label really counts? When is a personal identity changed and by whose stigmatizing effort? Does a bad name cause bad action? Is social response to crime generated more by the fact of the crime or by the legally irrelevant social characteristics of the offender? If official labels are so important, why do so many youths mature out of delinquency during their later adolescent years?[44]

The labeling perspective is further faulted for excusing the delinquent's behavior. Critics charge that this approach fails to take seriously the delinquent's motivation for such behavior. This becomes particularly important when dealing with actors who are aware of the high probability of apprehension for their behavior.[45] Finally, David Bordua suggested that the labeling perspective lacks empirical verification.[46] Other social researchers have added that this perspective has not clarified its basic assumptions to the point at which they can be tested.[47]

In sum, delinquency is clearly related to factors other than official labels. It is extremely questionable to ascribe too much significance to the labeling process in terms of influencing adolescents' subsequent identities and behavior.[48] Nevertheless, the resurgence of labeling theory in the late 1980s and 1990s does prove that it remains alive and well. The recent theoretical advances in labeling theory (i.e., formal and informal labels, subjective and objective labels, and exclusive and inclusive social reactions) promise to be fruitful avenues to examine delinquent behavior in the future.

The Contributions of Symbolic Interactionist Theory to the Understanding of Delinquency

In a number of publications, Matsueda and Karen Heimer have developed a symbolic interactionist theory of delinquency.[49] This perspective was developed to specify a theory of the self that explains delinquent behavior.[50] As Matsueda states, the interactionist perspective "presupposes that the special order is the product of an ongoing process of social interaction and communication."[51] What is "of central importance is the process by which shared meanings, behavioral expectations, and reflected appraisals are built up in interaction and applied to behavior."[52] This interactionist perspective, according to Heimer, also has the "potential for illuminating the dynamic relationship among gender inequality, racial inequality, and law violation."[53]

The intellectual roots of symbolic interactionism lie in the tradition of the Scottish moral philosophies (e.g., Smith, Hume), and in the tradition of American pragmatism (e.g., Dewey, James, Cooley, and G. H. Mead). By the mid-20th century, symbolic interactionism had achieved a dominant position among sociological theories through a number of scholars who became known as the Chicago School of Sociology. For symbolic interactionism, individuals, groups, social systems, and situations constitute an ongoing social process, mutually influencing one another and merging imperceptibly in the web of daily interactions. The work of George Herbert Mead was especially influential in the development of this theoretical tradition. Mead's analysis of the social act is the basis of most versions of contemporary symbolic interactionism.[54]

Role-Taking and Delinquency

Matsueda and Heimer built on the social act as the unit of analysis. They begin with the immediate situation of delinquent behavior which is made up of a social interaction between two or more individuals.[55] The situation can influence delinquency in two ways: first, the specific situation that juveniles encounter may present opportunities for delinquent behavior, and, second, and more importantly, the immediate situation influences delinquent behavior through its effects on the content and direction of social interaction.[56]

In analyzing social interaction, symbolic interactionists define the unit of analysis as the transaction that takes place in interaction between two or more individuals.[57] The important mechanism by which interactants influence each other is role-taking, which Mead viewed as the key to social control.[58] According to Matsueda, role-taking consists of

> projecting oneself into the role of other persons and appraising, from their standpoint, the situation, oneself in the situation, and possible lines of action. With regard to delinquency, individuals confronted with delinquent behavior as a possible line of action take each other's roles through verbal and nonverbal communication, fitting their lines of action together into joint delinquent behavior.[59]

The transaction is built up through this process of reciprocal role-taking, in which one person initiates a lawful or unlawful action and a second takes the role of the other and responds. The first person then reacts to the response, which continues until a jointly developed goal is reached, a new goal is substituted, or the transaction is ended. Through such reciprocal role-taking, individual lines of action are coordinated and concerted action is taken toward achieving the goal. This means that the initiated delinquent act of one juvenile might elicit a negative response from another juvenile, perhaps contributing to the group searching for another, more suitable alternative. (See Figure 6.2 for a model of reflected appraisals and behavior.) Matsueda goes on to suggest that "Whether or not a goal is achieved using unlawful means is determined by each individual's contribution to the direction of the transaction; those contributions, in turn, are determined by the individual's prior life experience or biography."[60]

This process by which role-taking can lead to delinquent behavior, according to Matsueda, can be illustrated by several classic studies of delinquency. Scott Briar and Irving Piliavin's study found that gang youth who are committed to nonconventional lines of action are often incited into delinquent behavior by "situationally induced motives," which are verbal motives presented by other youth. Free from considering how conventional others would react, they can take the role of each other, presenting delinquent motives and adopting delinquent behavior.[61] James F. Short Jr. and Fred L. Strodtbeck noted that a youth's willingness to join a gang fight frequently revolved around the risk of losing status with the gang. In taking the role of the group and considering the group's negative reactions, these gang youth would join in for fear of losing status.[62] Donald Gibbons's study of delinquent boys further found that one result of group interaction was the emergence of novel shades of norms and values that influenced the direction of joint behavior.[63]

Matsueda concludes that this discussion of risk-taking implies four features of a theory of the self and delinquent behavior. First, the self is formed by how an individual perceives that others view him or her and thus is rooted in symbolic interaction. Sec-

FIGURE 6.2 Alternative Models of Reflected Appraisals

Source: Ross L. Matsueda, "Reflected Appraisals, Parental Labeling, and Delinquency: Specifying a Symbolic Interactionist Theory," *American Journal of Sociology* 97 (May 1992), p. 1585. Reprinted with permission of the University of Chicago.

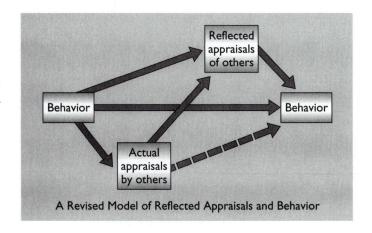

A Revised Model of Reflected Appraisals and Behavior

ond, the self is an object that "arises partly endogenously within situations, and partly exogenously from prior situational self being carried over from previous experience." Third, the self as an object becomes a process that has been determined by the self at a previous point in time and by prior resolutions of problematic situations. Fourth, delinquent behavior takes place partly because of the formation of habits and partly because the stable perception of oneself is shaped by the standpoint of others.[64]

Using classic symbolic interactionist theory, Matsueda talks about the self as a consistent "me" that is relatively stable across situations. This self, which is called "a looking-glass self" by Charles H. Cooley[65] or the "self as an object" by George H. Mead,[66] is a process that consists of three components: how others actually see us (others' actual appraisals); how we perceive the way others see us (reflected appraisals); and how we see ourselves (self-appraisals)."[67] One's self, then, is made up in part by a "reflected appraisal" of how significant others appraise or evaluate one.[68]

Matsueda used a sample from the National Youth Survey to test his theory. His findings supported a symbolic interactionist conceptualization of reflected appraisals and delinquency in a number of ways. Juveniles' reflected appraisals of themselves from the standpoint of parents, friends, and teachers "coalesced into a consensual self, rather than remaining compartmentalized as distinct selves."[69] This remained true whether the reflected appraisals were found in rule violators or socialized youth. In agreement with labeling theory, parental labels of youths as rule violators were more likely among nonwhites, urban dwellers, and delinquents. Delinquent youths' "appraisals of themselves are also strongly influenced by their parents' independent appraisals of them."[70] Moreover, prior delinquent behavior, both directly and indirectly, reflected appraisals of self. In addition, reflected appraisals as a rule violator exerted a large effect on delinquent behavior and mediated much of the effect of parental appraisals as a rule violator on delinquent behavior. Finally, age, race, and urban residence exerted significant effects on delinquency, most of which worked indirectly through prior delinquency and in part through the rule-violator reflected appraisal.[71]

INTERACTIONIST PERSPECTIVE ON GENDER, RACE, AND DELINQUENCY

Heimer argues that "structural conflict gives rise to gender and race differences in motivations to break to law."[72] From the vantage point of the interactionist perspective, then, racial and gender inequality are consequential for law violation because they restrict the positions of minorities and females and therefore constrain communication networks and power needed to influence others.[73] She goes on to say:

> Hence, these forms of structural inequality influence definitions of situations because they partially determine the significant others and reference groups considered in the role-taking process. Through shaping definitions of situations, gender and racial inequality contribute to the patterning of crime and delinquency. Thus, consistent with the tradition of differerential association in criminology, an interactionist theory of delinquency argues that there will be differences across groups in definitions of situations and the law to the extent that communication networks vary.[74]

Evaluation of Symbolic Interactionist Theory and Delinquency

This approach to understanding delinquency has several advantages. First, it builds on symbolic interactionist theory, a great tradition in sociology in the United States. This tradition has identified the locus of social control in the process of taking the role of the other and of linking the broader social organization through the concepts of role commitment, generalized others, and reference groups.[75]

Second, symbolic interactionist theory builds on and adds further insights to labeling theory. At a time in which labeling is being reformulated and is emerging in a more sophisticated form, the insights that Matsueda and colleagues provide in their relating symbolic interactionism and delinquency promise to further enrich labeling's contributions to understanding delinquent behavior.[76]

Third, the symbolic interactionist theory of delinquent behavior is insightful about how both law-abiding and delinquent youths form their conception of themselves and how this perception influences their decision making. This theory contributes helpful insights about the influence of delinquent peers and the group context in forming self-appraisal.

In sum, an evaluation of this theory may be premature because it has been tested by Matsueda, Heimer, and colleagues in only a few settings. Bartusch and Matsueda used this interactionist model to examine the gender gap in delinquent behavior.[77] Heimer also expanded this model to explain the relationship between gender and racial inequality and law violation with delinquents.[78] Stacy De Coster and Heimer further employed an interactionist analysis to examine the relationship between law violation and depression.[79] At this point, it is uncertain how much delinquency it explains, even among group delinquents. Indeed, so much of the criticism addressed to labeling theory applies also to this theory, but symbolic interactionist theory is still a promising new attempt to explain delinquent behavior. For additional insights about symbolic interactionist theory and delinquency, see Theory and Research 6.2, Interview with Karen Heimer.

How Conflict Theory Explains Crime and Delinquency

The development of the conflict model is indebted to the concept of "dialectics." This concept, like that of order, can be traced back to the philosophers of ancient Greece. In antiquity the term *dialectics* referred to the art of conducting a dispute or bringing out the truth by disclosing and resolving contradictions in the arguments of opponents.[80]

Georg F. Hegel used this concept of dialectical thinking to explain human progress and social change. A prevailing idea, or "thesis," according to Hegel, would eventually be challenged by an opposing idea, or "antithesis." The resultant conflict usually would result in the merging of the two, or "synthesis." The synthesis gradually would be accepted as the thesis, but then would be challenged by a new antithesis and so forth throughout history.[81] Karl Marx, rather than applying the method to ideas as Hegel did, applied the concept to the material world. Marx's theory became one of dialectical materialism, as he contended that the conflict was one of competing economic systems, in which the weak must ward off exploitation by the strong or powerful in society.[82]

Georg Simmel, a twentieth-century conflict theorist, argued that unity and discord are inextricably intertwined and together act as an integrative force in society. Simmel added that "there probably exists no social unity in which convergent and divergent currents among its members are not inseparably interwoven."[83] Simmel's notion of dialectics thus acknowledged the existence of tendencies for order and disorder.

More recently, Rolf Dahrendorf contended that functionalists misrepresented reality by being overconcerned with order and consensus. Dahrendorf argued that functionalists present a description of a utopian society—a society that never has existed and probably never will. Dahrendorf proposed that social researchers would be wise to opt for the conflict model because of its more realistic view that society is held together by constraint rather than consensus, not by universal agreement but by the coercion of some people by others.[84]

The conflict perspective views social control as an outcome of the differential distribution of economic and political power in society; laws are seen as created by the powerful for their own benefit.[85] Richard Quinney argued, for example, that criminal law is a social control instrument of the state "organized to serve the interests of the

THEORY AND RESEARCH 6.2

Interview with Karen Heimer

Question: What do you feel are the best features of symbolic interactionist theory?

Heimer: One of the strengths of symbolic interactionist approaches is that they locate the individual within the social situation. These approaches share an emphasis on the general idea that people come to know the world around them and themselves through taking the perspectives of others. Consistent with some other interactionist theories of crime, differential social control theory focuses on how the *role-taking process* can lead to delinquency or crime. More specifically, differential social control posits that the following five key elements of interactions are consequential for law violation: (1) identities or reflected appraisals of self; (2) anticipated reactions to law violation from significant others (including family and peers); (3) definitions of the law and morality; (4) influence of delinquent peers; and (5) habitual or scripted responses to opportunities to break the law. All of these influence law violation through role-taking in situations. I think that an important strength of differential social control theory, therefore, is the specification of the mechanisms through which situations affect delinquency and crime. We have attempted to elaborate the theory to show how the link between changes over the life course and offending might be better understood, how gender differences in delinquency emerge, and how delinquency and depression are linked.

Question: Do you see any areas that need to be expanded or reformulated?

Heimer: There are several areas of the theory that need further refinement and elaboration. For example, there likely are dimensions of role-taking in situations other than those we have identified that are important for crime and delinquency. I hope that future research will uncover some of these. In addition, I would like to see research on the theory attempt to further elaborate the ways in which social structural circumstances constrain or facilitate interactions that lead to law violations. In our published work to date, we have shown how disadvantaged social circumstances increase the chances that individuals will associate with delinquent youths and criminal adults, and thereby become more likely to see themselves as deviant, perceive that others would not strongly disapprove of law violations, and adopt delinquent attitudes and beliefs. But the ways in which social structures can influence role-taking are certainly more complex and diverse. I would like to see this part of the theory elaborated more fully in future work. Finally, I think that our recent work on an interactionist view of the connections between delinquency and depression opens the door to exploring how a variety of "deviant" outcomes might be linked via similar role-taking mechanisms.

Question: How did you come to be involved in the formulation of the theory?

Heimer: My early education in graduate school was in psychological social psychology. When I began my graduate work in sociology, I took a course on sociological social psychology in which I learned about the richness of theory and research on symbolic interactionism. So my interest in working on a symbolic interactionist approach to crime and delinquency can be traced to my early intellectual history.

Question: Have you been encouraged or discouraged by the response that the theory has received?

Heimer: I am very pleased that the differential social control perspective has come to gain recognition within criminology. I hope that future work will chart new territory by elaborating and extending the theory, especially along the lines of the areas that I mention above. I think that the theory has much promise for integrating a variety of theoretical approaches to crime and delinquency, as we argued in our 1994 paper. I also think that attention to the ways that social interactions lead to law violation is essential for understanding law violation more fully. For these reasons, I think that the theory offers a fruitful avenue for future work.

Why do you think Karen Heimer refers to this theory as "differential social control perspective?" What do you believe that this theory contributes to understanding delinquent behavior?

Source: Interview in February of 2002.

dominant economic class, the capitalist ruling class."[86] William Bonger earlier made this same point: "in every society which is divided into a ruling class and a class ruled, penal law has been principally constituted according to the will of the former."[87]

A more humane social order is the vision of some radical criminologists.[88] The goals of this ideal society are reduced inequality, reduced reliance on formal institutions of justice, and reduced materialism. The social relations of this social order are committed to developing self-reliance, self-realization, and mutual aid.[89] This peaceful society can be attained by using compromise and negotiation on a community level to defuse violent social structures. Communities must organize themselves in such a way as to prevent crime and to help victims without punishing offenders when crime does occur.[90] See Social Policy 6.3 for an examination of peacemaking in criminology.

Dimensions of Conflict Criminology

A great deal of variation exists among the ideas of conflict criminologists. Some theories emphasize the importance of socioeconomic class, some focus primarily on power and authority relationships, and others emphasize group and cultural conflict.

SOCIOECONOMIC CLASS AND MARXIST CRIMINOLOGY Even though Marx wrote very little on the subject of crime as the term is used today, he inspired a new school of criminology that emerged in the early 1970s. This school is variously described as radical, Marxist, critical, Socialist, left-wing, or new. Marx was concerned both with deriving a theory of how societies change over time and with discovering how to go about changing society. This joining of theory and practice is called "praxis."[91]

Marx saw the history of all societies as the history of class struggles and crime as a result of these class struggles.[92] He wrote in the *Communist Manifesto*:

Freeman and slave, patrician and plebian, lord and serf, guildmaster and journeyman, in a word, oppressor and oppressed, stood in constant opposition to one another, car-

---

SOCIAL POLICY 6.3

Peacemaking in Criminology

Peacemaking in criminology is based on spiritual humanistic critique of Western civilization. Peacemaking criminologists Harold Pepinsky and Richard Quinney want to replace making war on crime with the idea of making peace on crime. Like crimes, penal sanctions are intended harms and this position suggests that we need to reject the idea that those who cause injury or harm to others should suffer severance of the common bonds of respect and concern that bind members of a community. They also relinquish the notion that it is acceptable to try to get rid of another person, whether through execution, banishment, or caging away people about whom we do not care. These criminologists argue that instead of escalating the violence in our already violent society by responding to violence and conflict with state violence and conflict in the form of penal sanctions, such as death and prison, we need to de-escalate violence by responding to it through forms of conciliation, mediation, and dispute settlement. That is, the only path to peace is peace itself. Punishment merely adds heat. Relief from violence requires people to indulge in democracy, in making music together. By democracy, Pepinsky means a genuine participation by all in decisions about our lives that is only achieveable in decentralized, nonhierarchical social sturcture.

Why do you think that these ideas have met with considerable criticism? Are there some who cannot be stopped by others "being nice" to them? What room is there for peacemaking when it comes to working with juvenile delinquents?

Source: Mark Lanier and Stuart Henry, *Essential Criminology* (Boulder, Colorado: Westview Press, 1998), p. 288.

ried on an uninterrupted, now hidden, now open fight, a reconstruction of society at large, or in the common ruin of the contending classes.[93]

Emerging with each historical period, according to Marx's theory, is a new class-based system of ranking. Marx contended that with **capitalism,** "society as a whole is more and more splitting up into two great classes directly facing each other—bourgeoisie [capitalist class] and proletariat [working class]."[94] The relations between the bourgeoisie and the proletariat become increasingly strained as the ruling class or bourgeoisie comes to control more and more of the society's wealth and the proletariat is increasingly pauperized. In this relationship between the oppressive bourgeoisie and the pauperized proletariat lie the seeds of the demise of capitalism.[95]

In the Marxist perspective, the state and the law itself are ultimately tools of the ownership class and reflect mainly the economic interests of that class. Capitalism produces egocentric, greedy, and predatory human behavior. The ownership class is guilty of the worst crime: the brutal exploitation of the working class. Revolution is a means to counter this violence and is generally both necessary and morally justifiable. Conventional crime is caused by extreme poverty and economic disenfranchisement, products of the dehumanizing and demoralizing capitalist system.[96]

By the 1970s, such writers as Quinney, William J. Chambliss, Anthony Platt, Paul Takagi, Pepinsky, Steven Spitzer, Herman and Julia R. Schwendinger, Raymond Michalowski, and Barry Krisberg were applying the Marxist perspective to the study of criminal law and criminology.

Quinney stated that an understanding of crime in a capitalist society necessitates an understanding of the natural products and contradictions inherent in capitalism: alienation, inequality, poverty, unemployment, spiritual malaise, and economic crisis.[97] Quinney saw class as also affecting the broad categories of crime—crimes of domination and repression as well as crimes of accommodation and resistance. Crimes of domination and repression are committed by the elite class in capitalist society as well as by their agents (e.g., law enforcement agents). Crimes of accommodation and resistance are committed by the *lumpenproletariat* (a term used by Marx to indicate those cast out of the productive workforce) and by the working class, respectively. See Theory and Research 6.4 for an interview with Quinney.

POWER AND AUTHORITY RELATIONSHIPS   A second important dimension of conflict criminology is the focus on power and authority relationships. Max Weber, Dahrendorf, Austin T. Turk, and John Hagan have made contributions to this body of scholarship.

Weber's theory, like the Marxist perspective, contains a theory of social stratification that has been applied to the study of crime. Although Weber recognized the importance of the economic context in the analysis of social stratification, he did not believe that such a unidimensional approach could explain satisfactorily the phenomenon of social stratification. He added power and prestige to the Marxist emphasis on property and held these three variables responsible for the development of hierarchies in society. Weber also proposed that property differences led to the development of classes, power differences to the creation of political parties and development of classes, and prestige differences to the development of status groups.[98] Further, Weber discussed the concept of "life chances" and argued that they were differentially related to social class. From this perspective, criminality exists in all societies and is the result of the political struggle among different groups attempting to promote or enhance their own life chances.[99]

Both Dahrendorf and Turk have extended the Weberian tradition in the field of criminology by emphasizing the relationships between authorities and their subjects. Dahrendorf contended that power is the critical variable explaining crime. He argues that although Marx built his theory on only one form of power, property ownership, a more useful perspective could be constructed by incorporating broader conceptions of power.[100]

Turk, constructing his analysis from the work of both Weber and Dahrendorf, argued that the social order of society is based on the relationships of conflict and domination between authorities and subjects.[101] Focusing on power and authority

THEORY AND RESEARCH 6.4

Interview with Richard Quinney

Question: Why is social justice lacking in American society?

Quinney: Justice in a capitalist society is limited to the overall needs of a continuing capitalist system. Justice is largely limited to "criminal justice," a punitive model that does not deal with the inadequacies of the system. Social justice, on the other hand, would serve the needs of all people, including their economic well-being. The goal of social justice can be attempted in our capitalist society, but true social justice can be achieved only in a socialist society. The struggle for social justice is a struggle for the transformation of our present society in the United States.

Question: What are the chief contradictions of capitalism and how do they contribute to the extent and nature of crime in American society?

Quinney: There are many contradictions in capitalism. The basic contradiction is between the goal of progress and a better society, on the one hand, and the reality of the inability of capitalism to ever attain this goal because of the inherent class structure of capitalism. The capitalist class owns and controls the means of production and distribution and, as such, assures that a subordinate class of workers and consumers will be dominated politically and economically—to assure the continuation of the capitalist system. Classes outside of the capitalist class commit crimes out of need, frustration, and brutalization. Members of the capitalist class commit crimes out of greed and power. The rates of crime under capitalism can never be substantially reduced. Capitalism generates its own crime and rates of crime.

Question: Why is the capitalist state oppressive and coercive?

Quinney: The capitalist state exists to perpetuate capitalist economics and the social relations of capitalism. It is the policy and enforcement arm of capitalist society. Thus, the actions carried out by the branches of the state are of a control nature, including the activities associated with dispensing education, welfare, and criminal justice. The state must also provide benefits for those who suffer and fail under capitalist economics, but even these services have a control function, attempting to assure the continuation of the capitalist system.

Question: How does the early Quinney differ from the Quinney of today? Or how has your approach to the crime problem changed?

Quinney: I have moved through the various epistemologies and ontologies in the social sciences. After applying one, I have found that another is necessary for incorporating what was excluded from the former, and so on. Also, I have tried to keep my work informed by the latest developments in the philosophy of science. In addition, I have always been a part of the progressive movements of the time. My work is thus an integral part of the social and intellectual changes that are taking place in the larger society, outside of criminology and sociology. One other fact has affected my work in recent years: the search for meaning in my life and in the world.

Question: What direction do you anticipate the new criminology or the critical criminology will take in the 1980s and 1990s?

Quinney: This is the time to substantiate the critical Marxist perspective through studies of specific aspects of crime. We know generally the causes of crime. Further work is in large part a political matter—showing others through the accepted means of research. In the long run, however, our interests must go beyond the narrow confines of criminology and sociology. The theoretical, empirical, political, and spiritual issues are larger than the issue of crime.

Question: Critical or new criminology theorists have written much less about delinquency than criminality in American society. What more needs to be contributed by Marxists in this area?

Quinney: Our society emphasizes youth and the youth culture while at the same time increasingly excluding youth from gainful and meaningful employment. Youth are being relegated to the consumption sector—without the economic means for consumption. Education—including college—has traditionally provided a place for youth that are not essential to a capitalist society. But with the widening of the economic gap between classes, will education be an outlet and opportunity for the majority of adolescents and young adults? We are approaching a structural crisis (and personal crises) that will require a solution beyond what is possible in a capitalist society. Our challenge is to understand the changes that are taking place around us and to have the courage to be a part of the struggle that is necessary.

Where do you find yourself in agreement with Quinney? Where are you in disagreement? How can what he said be applied to understanding delinquency in the United States?

Richard Quinney received his Ph.D. from the University of Wisconsin, and he is presently professor of sociology at Northern

Illinois University. *The Social Reality of Crime; Criminology, Class, State, and Crime; Providence: The Reconstruction of Social and Moral Order;* and *Social Existence* are some of the books that have brought Dr. Quinney's analysis of crime and social problems to the attention of readers throughout the world. Interview conducted in February 1984, and used with permission.

relationships, this perspective of conflict theory examines the relationships between the legal authorities who create, interpret, and enforce right–wrong standards for individuals in the political collectivity and those who accept or resist but do not make such legal decisions. Turk also made the point that conflicts between authorities and subjects take place over a wide range of social and cultural norms.[102]

John Hagan and associates viewed the relationship between gender and nonserious delinquency as linked to power and control.[103] Using the data collected in Toronto, Canada, they suggested that the presence of power among fathers and the greater control of girls explain why boys more often than girls are delinquent. Unlike Hirschi's control theory, Hagan and colleagues based the measurement of class on the authority that parents have in their positions at work. Furthermore, they assumed that authority of parents at work translates into conditions of dominance in the household and in the degree of their parental control over youth.

What structures power and control within households, according to Hagan and associates, is an instrument-object relationship. Mothers and fathers are the instruments of control in the family, and sons and daughters are the objects of control. But in patriarchal households, mothers and their daughters are more likely "to be the instruments and objects of control." In these households, sons are socialized to take risks, but daughters are taught to avoid risks. This **power-control thesis** draws on the work of Bonger in assuming that the "freedom to deviate is directly related to class position, that males are freer to deviate than are females, and that males are freest to deviate in the higher classes.[104] Simon J. Singer and Murray Levine's replication of power-control theory also

According to the Marxist perspective, the very nature of capitalist society increases urban blight and contributes to the exploitation of lower-class youths.

found that a taste for risks among youths is translated into delinquent conduct.[105] Thus sons and daughters' different attitudes toward risks are manifest in their disparate involvement in delinquency, but sons are involved in offending to a greater extent than are daughters.

Hagan and colleagues contended that as mothers gain power relative to their husbands, usually by employment outside the home, daughters and sons alike are encouraged to be more open to risk taking. Parents in egalitarian families, then, redistribute their control efforts so that daughters are subjected to controls more like those imposed on sons. In contrast, daughters in patriarchal families are taught by their parents to avoid risks.[106] Hagan and colleagues concluded that "patriarchal families will be characterized by large gender differences in common delinquent behavior while egalitarian families will be characterized by smaller gender differences in delinquency."[107] Power control theory thus argues that when daughters are freed from patriarchal family relations, they also become delinquent.[108]

Robert M. Regoli and John D. Hewitt's **theory of differential oppression** is based on the assumption that authority is unjustly used against children in the United States who "find themselves living in and negotiating social arrangements that force them to adapt to adults' conceptions of what 'good children' are."[109] Children experience oppression because they exist in a social world in which adults look on them as inferior and in which they lack social power relative to adults. Accordingly, children must submit to the power and authority of adults and "when children fail to conform or when they react negatively to these pressures they begin a cycle that leads to 'delinquency.' "[110]

This microconflict theory of differential oppression employs biological ideas about behavior as well as psychological and sociological theories. It can be summarized by seven principles:

1. Parents emphasize order in the home. . . .
2. Parents' preconceptions of children establish them as inferior, subordinate, and troublemakers. . . .
3. Social control often becomes extreme to the point of oppression. . . .
4. Parents' behavior based on the preconceptions leads the children to develop a negative conception of the parent which may result in early patterns of lying and cover-ups of rule violations. . . .
5. Deviant behavior by the child leads to an escalation of parental control, possibly to the level of abuse and neglect in the form of beatings and withdrawal of affection.
6. Abuse and neglect diminishes the parent-child relationship and ultimately the child's respect for authority. . . .
7. Deviant behavior is an attempt to hurt the coercive parent and to strike out at authority and those rules it uses to maintain order. . . . [111]

Regoli and Hewitt argued that collective oppression and institutional oppression are widespread in the United States. They recognized that the oppression of children falls along a continuum and that some children are oppressed to a greater degree than others. The very basis of their theory hinges on the belief that children who are reared in highly oppressive family conditions are more likely to become delinquent than those who are not raised in such aversive environments.[112]

GROUP AND CULTURAL CONFLICT   Another dimension of conflict criminology focuses on group and **cultural conflict.** Thorsten Sellin and George B. Vold advocated this approach to the study of crime. Sellin argued that to understand the cause of crime, it is necessary to understand the concept of **conduct norms.**[113] This concept refers to the rules of a group concerning the ways its members should act under particular conditions. The violation of these rules guiding behavior arouses a group reaction.[114] Individuals are members of many groups (family group, work group, play group, political group, and religious group), and each group has its own particular conduct norms.[115] According to Sellin:

> The more complex a culture becomes, the more likely it is that the number of normative groups which affect a person will be large, the greater is the chance that the norms of these groups will fail to agree, no matter how much they may overlap as a result of a common acceptance of certain norms.[116]

Sellin noted that an individual experiences a conflict of norms "when more or less divergent rules of conduct govern the specific life situation in which a person may find himself."[117] The act of violating conduct norms is "abnormal behavior," and crime represents a particular kind of abnormal behavior distinguished by the fact that crime is a violation of the conduct norms defined by criminal law.[118] Regarding criminal law, Sellin wrote:

> The criminal law may be regarded as in part a body of rules, which prohibit specific forms of conduct and indicate punishments for violations. The character of these rules . . . - depends upon the character and interests of those groups in the population which influence legislation. In some states these groups may comprise the majority, in others a minority, but the social values which receive the protection of criminal law are ultimately those which are treasured by the dominant interest groups.[119]

Sellin also has developed a theory of "primary and secondary culture conflict." Primary culture conflict occurs when an individual or group comes into contact with an individual or group from another culture and the conduct norms of the two cultures are not compatible. Secondary culture conflict refers to the conflict arising whenever society has diverging subcultures with conduct norms.[120]

Vold, like Sellin and in the tradition of Simmel, analyzed the dimension of group conflict. He viewed society "as a congeries [an aggregation] of groups held together in a shifting, but dynamic equilibrium of opposing group interests and efforts."[121] Vold formulated a theory of group conflict and applied it to particular types of crimes, but he did not attempt to explain all types of criminal behavior. He stated that group members are constantly engaged in defending and promoting their group's status. As groups move into each other's territory or sphere of influence and begin to compete in those areas, intergroup conflict is inevitable. The outcome of a group conflict results in a winner and a loser, unless a compromise is reached—but compromises never take place when one group is decidedly weaker than the other. Like Simmel, Vold believed that group loyalty develops and intensifies during group conflict.[122]

Vold further posited that "the whole political process of law making, law breaking, and law enforcement directly reflects deep-seated and fundamental conflicts between interest groups and their more general struggles for the control of the police power of the state."[123] Vold addressed both "crime as minority group behavior" and the "political nature of much criminal behavior."[124] Crime as minority group behavior is exhibited by individuals who band together because they "are in some way at odds with organized society and with the police forces maintained by that society."[125] Vold also contended that "many kinds of criminal acts must be recognized as presenting primarily behavior in the front-line fringes of direct contact between groups struggling for the control of power in the political and cultural organization of society."[126] Crimes of a political nature are, for example, those resulting from a political protest movement, from conflict between company management and labor unions, and from attempts to overcome the caste system or racial segregation.[127]

In sum, conflict criminologists can be divided into three basic groups: those emphasizing socioeconomic class, those emphasizing power and authority relationships, and those emphasizing group and cultural conflict. Those who emphasize socioeconomic class call themselves radical, Marxist, critical, humanist, or new criminologists and do not identify with the other two groups. Some significant differences do exist between radical criminologists and the other two groups. The non-Marxist conflict criminologists emphasize a plurality of interests and power and do not put a single emphasis on capitalism

TABLE 6.1

Comparisons of Conflict Perspectives

	Legal Definitions	Legal Order	Purpose of Conflict	Capitalism
SOCIOECONOMIC CLASS (MARXIST)	Rejection	Rejection	Revolution	Rejection
POWER AND AUTHORITY RELATIONSHIPS	Acceptance	Acceptance	Reform	Acceptance
GROUP AND CULTURAL CONFLICT	Acceptance	Acceptance	Reform	Acceptance

as do the Marxist conflict criminologists. Nor do the non-Marxist conflict criminologists reject the legal order as such or the use of legal definitions of crime.[128] Table 6.1 compares the three groups of conflict criminologists.

Marxist Criminology and Explanations of Delinquent Behavior

The theoretical contributions of contemporary criminologists working within the Marxist perspective diverge from mainstream liberal assumptions, ideology, and practice. Their theoretical position is radical in the sense that the implied policy would dramatically alter the way crime is defined, criminals are treated, theories are formulated and tested and, quite possibly, even the sociopolitical-economic structure of the United States. Marxist criminologists themselves differ in their interpretation of crime, as Theory and Research 6.5 indicates.

Marxist theory about juvenile delinquency sees little to be gained by trying to understand the causes of delinquent behavior, believing that what needs to be examined are how the political economy and social structure create conditions conducive to feelings among youth of powerlessness and alienation. Marxist criminologists further contend that the dominant classes create definitions of crime to oppress the subordinate classes, that the economic system exploits lower-class youth, and that social justice is lacking for lower-class youth.

ALIENATION AND POWERLESSNESS AMONG YOUTH In *The Children of Ishmael*, Barry Krisberg and James Austin noted that youths in a capitalist society generally are seen as a group of people who are in a sense expected to remain in a holding pattern until they can take their places in the workforce.[129] They added that "young people form a subservient class, alienated, powerless, and prone to economic manipulation."[130]

Young people, according to Krisberg and Austin, also are excluded from full participation in society's political institutions. They lack organized lobbies, have limited voting power, and hold few positions of authority. Moreover, adolescents are subjected to controlling forces by the state, and, just like any other subordinate group in society, their rights, privileges, and identities are defined by the powerful arm of the state.[131]

David F. Greenberg stated, "The exclusion of young people from adult work and leisure activities forces adolescents into virtually exclusive association with one another, cutting them off from alternative sources of validation for the self."[132] Greenberg claimed that the long-term consequences of increased age segregation created by changing patterns of work and education have increased the vulnerability of youths to the expectations and evaluations of their peers.[133]

Quinney has stated that "violent gang activity may become a collective response of adolescents in slums to the problems of living in such areas of the city."[134] S. Balkan and colleagues noted that street gang activity is most frequently found in those social set-

THEORY AND RESEARCH 6.5

Variations in Marxist Criminology

Instrumental Marxists view the entire apparatus of crime control—laws, courts, police, and prisons—as the tool or instrument of the ruling class (capitalists). These authors emphasize the benefits to the elite of the crime-control structures in the society.

Structural Marxist tend to argue that the form of the legal system can work to reproduce capitalist social relations without the conscious, deliberate use of the law and criminal justice system on the part of the ruling capitalists to repress workers. The state, as part of the superstructure, is said to operate in relative autonomy from the underlying class relations of capitalist society. The criminal law takes the form it does under capitalism because it is based on capitalist notions of private property and the exchange of commodities (including labor). Because of the partial autonomy of the state and because the law as ideology must be based on claims of universal and not class interest, the legal system may not function directly in the interests of the ruling class. Indeed, it may occasionally backfire and allow the working class to make gains.

Critical theorists often combine Marxist theory with the insights of later theorists, such as Sigmund Freud and Max Weber. In particular, they pick up on Weber's concept of rationalization—that is, they are concerned with the questions of what it means to have a rational society and how to work toward that goal. They reject overly deterministic versions of Marxism (i.e., they do not see every social phenomenon as a direct expression of the class struggle). These authors tend to focus their critique on the aspects of modern culture that induce conformity and acceptance of domination, such as the ideology of mass consumption created by the advertising and entertainment industries. Critical theory is also characterized by the arguments that it is impossible to separate values from research agendas and that it is necessary to advance a progressive agenda that favors disprivileged peoples.

Some criminologists call themselves critical theorists. Based on this statement, what do you anticipate that they would emphasize in their teaching? How would they explain delinquency in the United States?

Source: B. Keith Crew contributed this discussion to this volume.

tings where poverty, unemployment, drugs, violence, and police encounters are commonplace. In such social contexts, gangs become the source of both juvenile and adult members' most meaningful social relationships and the source of protection where "life on the streets" has made survival an issue.[135]

In short, Marxist criminologists have concluded that a lengthening of the time before youths assume adult roles and are given adult responsibilities has contributed to powerlessness and alienation among youth and has been a major factor leading to delinquent behavior. Lower-class youth, especially minority ones, are the most powerless and alienated.

DEFINITIONS OF DELINQUENCY   Marxist criminologists argue that certain acts are termed *delinquent* because it is in the interest of the ruling class to so define them.[136] Marxist criminologists see the law as an oppressive force that is used to promote and stabilize existing socioeconomic relations. The law maintains order, but it is an order imposed on the powerless by the powerful.[137] Platt's *The Child Savers*, which describes the role played by wealthy "child-saving" reformers in the nineteenth century, explains how dominant classes create definitions of crime to control the subordinate classes:

> The juvenile court system was part of a general movement directed towards developing specialized labor market and industrial discipline under corporate capitalism by creating new programs of adjudication and control for "delinquent," "dependent," and "neglected" youth. This in turn was related to augmenting the family and enforcing compulsory education in order to guarantee the proper reproduction of the labor force.[138]

The contention is that because delinquents are unsocialized children who are in danger of producing not only more crime but more children like themselves, it has been necessary to find legal means to discipline them. Otherwise, they would be unprepared to supply labor for the alienating work of capitalism.[139] Definitions of delinquency, then, are enforced on the children of the "dangerous classes" as a means of forcing them to conform to alienating work roles.

ECONOMIC EXPLOITATION OF YOUTH   Marxist criminologists charge that the "haves" exploit the "have-nots," with the result that the children of the have-nots become a marginal class. Krisberg's study of twenty-two gang members in Philadelphia revealed that the harsh realities of ghetto existence fostered a psychology of survival as a functional adaptation to an uncompromising social situation or environment.[140] Indeed, the gang members perceived "survival" in Spencerian terms as they had to extend themselves in every possible way to meet their needs. One gang leader put it this way: "Survival, man, is survival of the fittest. You do unto others before they do unto you, only do it to them first."[141]

The Schwendingers also stated that capitalism produces a marginal class of people who are superfluous from an economic standpoint.[142] They went so far as to say, "the historical facts are incontrovertible: capitalism ripped apart the ancient regime and introduced criminality among youth in all stations of life."[143]

They further argued that socialization agents within the social system, such as the school, tend to reinvent within each new generation the same class system: "The children of families that *have* more *get* more, because the public educational system converts human beings into potential commodities."[144] The schools tend to be geared toward rewarding and assisting those youths who exhibit early indications of achieving the greatest potential success in institutions of higher learning and later in the job market. Yet this selection is made at the expense of those who do not exhibit such potential in their early encounters with the educational system.[145]

The Schwendingers went on to develop **instrumental theory,** which states that the most important variable in identifying delinquency potential for teenagers is their relative status position among other adolescents. Delinquency, then, is conceptualized as linked to adolescents' social networks. The three prominent social networks are "socialites," "greasers," and "intellectuals." Those youths with economically deprived backgrounds are typically identified as "greasers" and are more likely to participate in theft, burglaries, and even violence. Middle-class youths who are identified as "socialites" are more likely to become involved in such behaviors as truancy, shoplifting, and vandalism. But youths identified as "intellectuals," regardless of their class position, are least likely to become involved in illegal behaviors.[146]

Greenberg discussed juvenile theft in terms of structural obstacles to legitimate sources of funds. He pointed out that the persistent decline in teenage employment, especially among African American teenagers, has left adolescents less and less capable of financing an increasingly costly social life, the importance of which is enhanced as the age segregation of society grows. According to Greenberg, adolescent theft therefore occurs as a response to the disjunction between the desire to participate in social activities with peers and the absence of legitimate means to finance this participation.[147]

In sum, according to these studies, the structural conditions of capitalistic society lead to the exploitation of lower-class youths. This exploitation creates a marginal role for these juveniles and influences their pursuing illegitimate means to satisfy their desires.

SOCIAL INJUSTICE   Marxist and other conflict-oriented criminologists argue that social justice is lacking in American society for three reasons. First, poor and disadvantaged youth tend to be disproportionately represented in the juvenile justice system, although research indicates that actual acts of delinquent behavior are uniformly distributed throughout the social spectrum.[148] Second, female status offenders are subjected to sexist treatment in the juvenile system.[149] Third, racism is present and minorities are dealt with more harshly than are whites.[150]

Chambliss analyzed this issue of social justice in his study entitled "The Saints and the Roughnecks." He studied two groups of boys, one consisting of eight upper-middle-class boys (the Saints) and the second consisting of six lower-class boys (the Roughnecks). He found the Saints to be continually occupied with truancy, drinking, wild driving, petty theft, and vandalism. The parents of the Saints, as well as the community at large, tended to see the Saints as being essentially "good" boys who only occasionally engaged in "sowing a few wild oats." In contrast, the Roughnecks were "constantly in trouble with the police and community even though their rate of delinquency was about equal with that of the Saints."[151]

Marxist criminologists also contend that the juvenile justice system is racist, because minorities are treated more punitively than whites. At the time of arrest, minority youths are more likely to be referred to the juvenile court than are whites. Once referred to the court, they are less likely than whites to be diverted to nonjudicial agencies. Furthermore, minority youths are more likely than whites to be found delinquent during the adjudication stage of the juvenile court proceedings; and during the disposition stage, they are more likely to be sent to training school than are whites.[152]

In short, most Marxist criminologists believe that the formal juvenile justice system, as well as the informal justice system, administers different sorts of justice to the children of the "haves" than to the children of the "have-nots," to boys who commit delinquent offenses than to girls who commit "moral" offenses, and to white youths than to nonwhite youths.

A Structural and Integrated Marxist Theory of Delinquency

Mark Colvin and John Pauly, in one of the most significant articles relating the Marxist perspective to juvenile delinquency, argued that delinquency is a latent outcome of the reproduction processes of capitalism. They developed an integrated, structural theory of delinquency, the purpose of which was to provide "a comprehensive theoretical approach to understanding the social production of serious patterned delinquent behavior." Using the empirical findings of others to support their model, Colvin and Pauly contended that the power relations subjected to most lower-class workers are coercive.[153]

They argued that parents' experience of coerciveness in workplace control structures contributes to the development of coercive family control structures, which lead to alienated bonds with children. To express this in another way, the coercive social milieu in which workers exist reduces their capacity as parents to deal with their children in anything other than a repressive fashion, using physical punishments. This punitive environment, not surprisingly, hinders the bond children form with their parents.[154]

Juveniles with alienated parental bonds, according to Colvin and Pauly, are more likely to be placed in coercive school control situations, which reinforce their alienated family bonds. Their alienated bonds encourage these juveniles to become involved in association with alienated peers, who form peer group control structures. These peer group control structures create two different paths of delinquent involvement. In the first path, the experience of coerciveness in peer group control relations mutually interacts with their alienated bonds to propel them into serious, patterned, violent delinquent behavior. In the second path, the experience of reward from illegitimate sources creates an alternative utilitarian control structure that propels these juveniles into serious, patterned, instrumental delinquent behavior.[155]

Evaluation of Conflict Theory

Conflict criminology's critiques of the social order do provide two important pieces to the puzzle of why juveniles commit delinquent acts. First, the various conflict criminology perspectives call attention in a needed way to the nation's macrostructural flaws that contribute to high rates of juvenile delinquency. Second, radical humanism, also rooted in the structural inequalities of the social order, emphasizes the dignity of the person and is quick to identify the instances where children experience oppression in the United States.[156]

SUMMARY

This chapter has examined three explanations of delinquency. Social reaction has been the key concept in evaluating the labeling theories, symbolic interactionist theory of delinquency, and conflict approach to delinquency.

Social reaction takes place in a particular context that may vary from the family, to group, to school setting, to official labeling of the justice system, and even society's political decision makers. But it also takes place during the process of interaction. The process may be as varied as the formation of the self during group decision making, to the response given to labels for what is perceived as unacceptable behavior, and to the reaction to what is interpreted as the economic exploitation by the larger society. Oppression becomes a key word, especially in evaluating what takes place during the labeling process and structural exploitation of lower-class youth. For example, Marxist theorists relate delinquency to alienation and powerlessness among youth, especially lower-class youth; to the dominant class's creation of definitions of crime to control subordinate classes; to the economic exploitation of the lower class; and to the lack of social justice in American society.

KEY TERMS

capitalism, p. 171
conduct norms, p. 174
cultural conflict, p. 174
instrumental theory, p. 178
labeling perspective, p. 159

power-control thesis, p. 173
primary deviation, p. 160
process of becoming deviant, p. 160
secondary deviation, p. 160
theory of differential oppression, p. 174

CRITICAL THINKING QUESTIONS

1. What is the labeling perspective's definition of why adolescents become delinquent? Do you agree with this interpretation?
2. Were you ever labeled as a young child or juvenile? What influence did it have on your subsequent attitudes and behavior?
3. Can you identify any groups beyond young children among which official labels may be more likely to influence subsequent attitudes and behavior?
4. How is symbolic interactionist theory an extension of, but different from, labeling theory?
5. Illustrate the application of symbolic interactionist theory to decision making in youth gangs or in adolescent peer groups. How did such reference

group norms affect your decision making and behavior as an adolescent?
6. What are the various dimensions of conflict theory? How do they differ?
7. What are the explanations of delinquency according to Marxist theory? Evaluate each of these explanations.
7. Does labeling, symbolic interaction, or conflict appear to have any effect on those individuals whose stories appeared in *Voices of Delinquency*? If so, which ones?
9. As an adolescent, did you feel powerless and out of control? If so, how did you respond to these feelings?

WEB DESTINATIONS

Learn more about Labeling theory on the University of Missouri, St. Louis site.

http://www.umsl.edu/~rkeel/200/labeling.html

Read more about primary and secondary deviation on the University of Minnesota, Duluth site.

http://www.d.umn.edu/~jhamlin1/lemert.html

Check this web site for more information on symbolic interactionist theory.

www.sociology.org.uk/p2+4.htm

Learn more about Marxist Theory on the Youth for International Socialism page.

www.newyouth.com/archives/marxisttheory.asp

Read more about capitalism on the Capitalism site.

http://www.capitalism.org/

NOTES

1. Interviewed in April 1987.
2. Conversations the author and this person had over a several-year period in the late 1980s and early 1990s.
3. Lening Zhang and Steven F. Messner, "The Severity of Official Punishment for Delinquency and Change in Interpersonal Relations in Chinese Society," *Journal of Research in Crime and Delinquency* 31 (November 1994), p. 417.
4. Frederick M. Thrasher, *The Gang* (Chicago: University of Chicago Press, 1927).
5. Frank Tannenbaum, *Crime and the Community* (New York: Columbia University Press, 1938), pp. 19–20.
6. Ibid.
7. Edwin M. Lemert, *Social Pathology* (New York: McGraw-Hill, 1951).
8. Harold Finestone, *Victims of Change: Juvenile Delinquents in American Society* (Westport, Conn.: Greenwood Press, 1976), p. 198.
9. Ibid. For discussion concerning the complexity of this process of moving from primary to secondary, see Daniel L. Dotter and Julian B. Roebuck "The Labeling Approach Re-Examined: Interactionism and the Components of Deviance," *Deviant Behavior* 9 (1988), pp. 19–32.
10. Finestone, *Victims of Change*, pp. 192, 198.
11. Howard S. Becker, *Outsiders* (New York: Free Press, 1963), pp. 8–9.
12. Ibid., pp. 31–32.
13. Finestone, *Victims of Change*, p. 208.
14. Jack P. Gibbs, "Conceptions of Deviant Behavior: The Old and the New," *Pacific Sociological Review* 9 (1966), pp. 9–14; Walter R. Gove, "Labeling and Mental Illness: A Critique," in *The Labeling of Deviance: Evaluating a Perspective*, 2d ed., edited by Walter R. Gove (Beverly Hills, Calif.: Sage, 1980); John Hagan, "Extra-Legal Attitudes and Criminal Sanctioning: An Assessment and a Sociological Viewpoint," *Law and Society Review* 8 (1974), pp. 357–383; Travis Hirschi, "Labeling Theory and Juvenile Delinquency: An Assessment of the Evidence," in *The Labeling of Deviance: Evaluating a Perspective*, 2d ed., edited by Walter R. Gove (Beverly Hills, Calif.: Sage, 1980), pp. 271–293; Charles R. Tittle, "Deterrence of Labeling?" *Social Forces* 53 (1975), pp. 399–410; Charles F.

Wellford, "Labeling Theory and Criminology: An Assessment," *Social Problems* 22 (1975), pp. 332–345.
15. Zhang and Messner, "The Severity of Official Punishment for Delinquency and Change in Interpersonal Relations in Chinese Society," p. 419. See also Tittle, "Deterrence of Labeling?" and Gove, "Labeling and Mental Illness."
16. Raymond Paternoster and Leeann Iovanni, "The Labeling Perspective and Delinquency: An Elaboration of the Theory and an Assessment of the Evidence," *Justice Quarterly* 6 (1989), p. 359.
17. Zhang and Messner, "The Severity of Official Punishment for Delinquency and Change in Interpersonal Relations in Chinese Society," p. 418.
18. Ruth A. Triplett and G. Roger Jarjoura, "Theoretical and Empirical Specification of a Model of Informal Labeling," *Journal of Quantitative Criminology* 10 (1994), p. 243.
19. Raymond Paternoster and Ruth A. Triplett, "Disaggregating Self-Reported Delinquency and Its Implications for Theory," *Criminology* 26 (1988), p. 6. See also Lening Zhang, "Informal Reactions and Delinquency," *Criminal Justice and Behavior* 24 (March 1997), pp. 129–150.
20. John Braithwaite, *Crime, Shame and Reintegration* (Cambridge: Cambridge University Press, 1989). See also Toni Makkai and John Braithwaite, "Reintegrative Shaming and Compliance with Regulatory Standards," *Criminology* 32 (August 1994), pp. 361–385.
21. Triplett and Jarjoura, "Theoretical and Empirical Specification of a Model of Informal Labeling," p. 244.
22. Ruth Ann Triplett, *Labeling and Differential Association: The Effects on Delinquent Behavior*, Ph.D. dissertation, University of Maryland, 1990, pp. 74–84. For a model of informal labeling, see Triplett and Jarjoura, "Theoretical and Empirical Specialization of a Model of Informal Labeling," pp. 241–276.
23. J. D. Orcutt, "Societal Reaction and the Response to Deviation in Small Groups," *Social Forces* 52 (1973), pp. 259–267.
24. Richard A. Berk, Alec Campbell, Ruth Klap, and Bruce Western, "The Deterrent Effect of Arrest: A Baylesian Analysis of Four Field Experiences," *American Sociological Review* 57 (1992), pp. 698–708; Antony M. Pate and

Edwin E. Hamilton, "Formal and Informal Deterrents to Domestic Violence: The Dade County Spouse Assault Experiment," *American Sociological Review* 57 (1992), pp. 691–697; and Lawrence W. Sherman and Douglas A. Smith, "Crime, Punishment, and Stake in Conformity: Legal and Informal Control of Domestic Violence," *American Sociological Review* 57 (1992), pp. 680–690.

25. Zhang and Messner, "The Severity of Official Punishment for Delinquency and Change in Interpersonal Relations in Chinese Society," p. 418.

26. Francis Polymeria, Francis T. Cullen, and Joanne C. Gersten, "The Effects of Police and Mental Health Intervention on Juvenile Delinquency: Specifying Contingencies in the Impact of Formal Reaction," *Journal of Health and Social Behavior* 27 (1986), pp. 90–105.

27 Anthony Matarazzo, Peter J. Carrington, and Robert D. Hiscott, "The Effect of Prior Youth Court Dispositions on current Disposition: An Application of Societal-Reaction Theory," *Journal of Quantitative Criminology* 17 (2001), p. 169.

28. Bruce Link, Francis T. Cullen, James Frank, and John F. Wozniak, "The Social Rejection of Former Mental Patients: Understanding Why Labels Matter," *American Journal of Sociology* 92 (1987), pp. 1461–1500; Bruce Link, Francis T. Cullen, Elmer Struening, Patrick E. Shrout, and Bruce P. Dohrenwend, "A Modified Labeling Theory Approach to Mental Disorders: An Empirical Assessment," *American Sociological Review* 54 (1989), pp. 400–423.

29. Paternoster and Iovanni, "The Labeling Perspective and Delinquency," p. 387.

30. Robert J. Sampson and John H. Laub, *Crime in the Making: Pathways and Turning Points Through Life* (Cambridge: Harvard University Press, 1993).

31. Ibid., pp. 214–215, 255–256.

32. Gary F. Jensen, "Labeling and Identity," *Criminology* 18 (1980), pp. 121–129.

33. Susan Ageton and Delbert S. Elliott, "The Effect of Legal Processing on Self-Concept" (Boulder: Institute of Behavioral Sciences, University of Colorado, 1973).

34. Merry Morash, "Establishment of a Juvenile Police Record," *Criminology* 22 (February 1984), pp. 97–111.

35. Malcolm W. Klein, "Labeling Theory and Delinquency Policy," *Criminal Justice and Behavior* 13 (March 1986), pp. 47–79.

36. Melvin C. Ray and William R. Downs, "An Empirical Test of Labeling Theory Using Longitudinal Data," *Journal of Research in Crime and Delinquency* 23 (May 1986), p. 169–194.

37. Jack Foster, Simon Dinitz, and Walter C. Reckless, "Perceptions of Stigma Following Public Intervention for Delinquent Behavior," *Social Problems* 18 (1970), p. 202.

38. Stuart J. Miller, "Post-Institutional Adjustments of 443 Consecutive TICO Release," Ph.D. dissertation, Ohio State University, 1971.

39. John R. Hepburn, "The Impact of Police Intervention upon Juvenile Delinquents," *Criminology* 15 (1977), pp. 235–262.

40. Howard B. Kaplan and Robert J. Johnson, "Negative Social Sanctions and Juvenile Delinquency: Effects of Labeling in a Model of Deviant Behavior," *Social Science Quarterly* 72 (1991), pp. 98–122; Howard B. Kaplan and Hiroshi Fuku-rai, "Negative Social Sanctions, Self-Rejection, and Drug Use," *Youth and Society* 23 (1992), pp. 275–298.

41. Ross L. Matsueda, "Reflected Appraisals, Parental Labeling, and Delinquency: Specifying a Symbolic Interactional Theory," *American Journal of Sociology* 97 (1992), pp. 1577–1611.

42. Cited in Edwin M. Schur, *Labeling Deviant Behavior: Its Sociological Implications* (New York: Harper and Row, 1971), p. 35.

43. Gibbs, "Conceptions of Deviant Behavior," pp. 9–14.

44. G. Nettler, *Explaining Crime,* 3d ed. (New York: McGraw-Hill, 1984), p. 268.

45. Schur, *Labeling Deviant Behavior,* p. 14.

46. David Bordua, "On Deviance," *Annals* 312 (1969), p. 121.

47. Gibbs, "Conceptions of Deviant Behavior," pp. 9–14.

48. Donald J. Shoemaker, *Theories of Delinquency: An Examination of Explanations of Delinquency Behavior,* 3d ed. (New York: Oxford University Press, 1996), p. 203.

49. Matsueda, "Reflected Appraisals, Parental Labeling, and Delinquency," p. 1577; Karen Heimer and Ross L. Matsueda, "Role Taking, Role-Commitment, and Delinquency: A Theory of Differential Social Control," *American Sociological Review* 59 (1994), pp. 365–390; Karen Heimer, "Gender, Race, and the Pathways to Delinquency," in *Crime and Inequality,* edited by John Hagan and Ruth D. Peterson (Stanford, Calif.: Stanford University Press, 1995), p. 140–173; Karen Heimer and Ross L. Matsueda, "A Symbolic Interactionist Theory of Motivation and Deviance: Interpreting Psychological Research," in *Motivation and Delinquency,* Volume 44 of the Nebraska Symposium on Motivation, edited by D. Wayne Osgood (Lincoln and London: University of Nebraska Press, 1997), pp. 223–276; and Ross L. Matsueda and Karen Heimer, "A Symbolic Interactionist Theory of Role-Transitions, Role Commitments, and Delinquency," in *Advances in Criminological Theory,* edited by T. P. Thornberry 7 (New Brunswick, N.J.: Transaction Press, 163-213).

50. Matsueda, "Reflected Appraisals, Parental Labeling, and Delinquency," p. 1577.

51. Ibid. p. 1580.

52. Ibid.

53. Heimer, "Gender, Race, and Delinquency," p. 141.

54. Matsueda and Heimer, "A Symbolic Interactionist Theory of Role-Transitions, Role Commitments, and Delinquency," p. 234.

55. Ibid.

56. Ibid.

57. The following discussion is largely adapted from Ibid., p. 1580–1581.

58. George H. Mead, *Mind, Self and Society* (Chicago: University of Chicago Press, 1934.)

59. Matsueda, "Reflected Appraisals, Parental Labeling, and Delinquency," p. 1580. See also Mead, *Mind, Self and Society* and Herbert Blumer, *Symbolic Interactionism: Perspective and Method* (Englewood Cliffs, N.J.: Prentice-Hall, 1969).

60. Ibid., p. 1581.

61. Scott Briar and Irving Piliavin, "Delinquency, Situational Inducements, and Commitment to Conformity," *Social Problems* 13 (1965), p. 35–45.

62. James F. Short Jr. and Fred L. Strodtbeck, *Group Process and Gang Delinquency* (Chicago: University of Chicago Press, 1965).

63. Donald Gibbons, "Observations on the Study of Crime Causation," *American Journal of Sociology* 77 (1971), pp. 262–278.

64. Matsueda, "Reflected Appraisals, Parental Labeling, and Delinquency," p. 1583.

65. Charles H. Cooley, *Human Nature and the Social Order,* rev. ed. (New York: Scribners, 1922).

66. Mead, *Mind, Self, and Society.*

67. Matsueda, "Reflected Appraisals, Parental Labeling, and Delinquency," p. 1584.

68. Ibid.

69. Ibid., p. 1602.

70. Ibid.

71. Ibid., pp. 1602–1603.

72. Heimer, "Gender, Race, and Delinquency," p. 145.

73. Ibid., p. 146.

74. Ibid.

75. Karen Heimer and Ross L. Matsueda, "Role-Taking, Role Commitment, and Delinquency: A Theory of Differential Social Control," *American Sociological Review* 59 (1994), p. 365.

76. See Matsueda, "Reflected Appraisals"; Heimer and Matsueda, "Role Taking, Role Commitment, and Delinquency"; Dawn Jeglum Bartusch and Ross L. Matsueda, "Gender, Reflected Appraisals, and Labeling: A Cross-Group Test of an Interactionist Theory of Delinquency," *Social Forces* 75 (September 1996), pp. 145–177; Karen Heimer, "Gender, Interaction, and Delinquency: Testing a Theory of Differential Social Control," *Social Psychology Quarterly* 59 (March 1996), pp. 39–61.

77. Bartusch and Matsueda, "Gender, Reflected Appraisals, and Labeling," pp. 145–177; and Heimer, "Gender, Interaction, and Delinquency," pp. 39–61.

78. Heimer, "Gender, Race, and the Pathways to Delinquency," pp. 140–173.

79. Stacy De Coster and Karen Heimer, "The Relationship Between Law Violation and Depression: An Interactionist Analysis," *Criminology* 39 (November 2001), pp. 799–836.

80. Viktor Afanasyer, *Marxist Philosophy* (Moscow: Foreign Language Publishing House, n.d.), p. 14.

81. This interpretation of Hegel's "thesis–antithesis–synthesis" is frequently questioned. See Ron E. Roberts and Robert Marsh Kloss, *Social Movements: Between the Balcony and the Barricade,* 2d ed. (St. Louis: C.V. Mosby, 1979), p. 16.

82. Stephen Spitzer, "Toward a Marxian Theory of Deviance," *Social Problems* 22 (1975), p. 638.

83. Georg Simmel, *Conflict,* translated by Kurt H. Wolf (Glencoe, Ill.: Free Press, 1955), pp. 15–30.

84. Rolf Dahrendorf, "Out of Utopia: Toward a Reorientation of Sociological Analysis," in *Sociological Theory: A Book of Readings,* edited by Lewis A. Coser and Bernard Rosenberg (New York: Macmillan, 1975), p. 198.

85. David Shichor, "The New Criminology: Some Critical Issues," *The British Journal of Criminology* 20 (1980), p. 3.

86. Richard Quinney, *Critique of Legal Order: Crime Control in Capitalist Society* (Boston: Little, Brown, 1974), p. 16.

87. William Bonger, *Criminality and Economic Conditions,* abridged ed. (Bloomington: Indiana University Press, 1969), p. 24.

88. See Larry Tifft and Dennis Sullivan, *Crime, Criminology, and Anarchism: The Struggle To Be Human* (Sanday, Orkney Islands, Scotland: Cienfuegos Press, 1980); Raymond J. Michalowski, *Order, Law, and Crime: An Introduction to Criminology* (New York: Random House, 1985); and Harold E. Pepinsky, "A Sociology of Justice," *Annual Review of Sociology* 12 (1986), pp. 93–108.

89. Tifft and Sullivan, *Crime, Criminology, and Anarchism,* p. 172, and Michalowski, *Order, Law, and Crime,* pp. 406–411.

90. Pepinsky, "A Sociology of Justice," pp. 102–105.

91. Turner, Jonathan H. *The Structure of Sociological Theory* (Homewood, Ill.: Dorsey Press, 1978), p. 124.

92. Karl Marx and Frederick Engels, *The Communist Manifesto* (reprinted, New York: International Publishers, 1979), p. 9.

93. Ibid.

94. Ibid.

95. Ibid., pp. 9–21.

96. David O. Friedrichs, "Radical Criminology in the United States: An Interpretative Understanding," in *Radical Criminology,* p. 38.

97. Richard Quinney, *Criminal Justice in America: A Critical Understanding* (Boston: Little, Brown, 1974), p. 24.

98. Max Weber, "Class, Status, Party," in *Class, Status and Power,* edited by Richard Bendix and S. M. Lipset (New York: Macmillan, 1953), pp. 63–75.

99. Ibid.

100. Rolf Dahrendorf, *Class and Class Conflict in Industrial Society* (Palo Alto, Calif.: Stanford University Press, 1959).

101. A. T. Turk, "Class, Conflict, and Criminalization," *Sociological Focus* 10 (August 1977), pp. 209–220.

102. Ian Taylor, Paul Walton, and Jock Young, *The New Criminology: For a Social Theory of Deviance* (Boston: Routledge and Kegan Paul, 1973), p. 241.

103. John Hagan, A. R. Gillis, and John Simpson, "The Class Structure of Gender and Delinquency: Toward a Power-Control Theory of Common Delinquent Behavior," *American Journal of Sociology* 90 (1985) p. 1151–1178; John Hagan, John Simpson, and A. R. Gillis, "The Sexual Stratification of Social Control: A Gender-Based Perspective on Crime and Delinquency," *British Journal of Sociology* 30 (1979), pp. 25–38; John Hagan, John Simpson, and A. R. Gillis, "Class in the Household: A Power-Control Theory of Gender and Delinquency," *American Journal of Sociology* 92 (January 1987), pp. 788–816; John Hagan, A. R. Gillis, and John Simpson, "Clarifying and Extending Power-Control Theory," *American Journal of Sociology* 95 (1990), pp. 1024–1037; and John Hagan, *Structural Criminology* (New Brunswick: Rutgers University Press, 1989).

104. Hagan, Gillis, and Simpson, "The Class Structure of Gender and Delinquency," pp. 1151–1178.

105. Simon J. Singer and Murray Levine, "Power-Control Theory, Gender, and Delinquency: A Partial Replication

with Additional Evidence on the Effects of Peers," *Criminology* 26 (1988), p. 628.

106. Hagan et al., "Class in the Household," pp. 791–792.

107. Ibid., p. 793.

108. Ibid., pp. 813–814.

109. Robert M. Regoli and John D. Hewitt, "The Theory of Differential Oppression." Paper presented at the American Society of Criminology Annual Meeting, New Orleans (November 1992), p. 1.

110. Ibid.

111. Robert M. Regoli and John D. Hewitt, *Delinquency in Society: A Child-Centered Approach* (New York: McGraw-Hill, 1991), pp. 156–157.

112. Ibid., pp. 166–167.

113. In *Social Sources of Delinquency*, Ruth Rosner Kornhauser includes the discussion of Sellin under cultural deviance theory.

114. Thorsten Sellin, *Culture, Conflict, and Crime* (New York: Social Science Research Council, 1938), p. 28.

115. Ibid., p. 29.

116. Ibid.

117. Ibid.

118. Ibid., pp. 32, 57.

119. Ibid., p. 21.

120. Ibid., pp. 104–105.

121. George B. Vold, *Theoretical Criminology*, 2d ed., prepared by Thomas J. Bernard (New York: Oxford University Press, 1979), p. 283. For a more up-to-date analysis of Vold, see Thomas J. Bernard and Jeffrey B. Snipes, *Theoretical Criminology*, 4th ed. (New York: Oxford University Press, 1998), pp. 236–238.

122. Ibid.

123. Ibid., p. 288.

124. Ibid., pp. 288–296.

125. Ibid., p. 289.

126. Ibid., p. 292.

127. Ibid., pp. 293–295.

128. Friedrichs, "Radical Criminology in the United States," p. 39.

129. Barry Krisberg and James Austin, eds., *Children of Ishmael: Critical Perspectives on Juvenile Justice* (Palo Alto, Calif.: Mayfield Publishing, 1978), p. 219.

130. Ibid., p. 1.

131. Ibid., pp. 1–2.

132. David F. Greenberg, "Delinquency and the Age Structure of Society," *Contemporary Crisis* 1 (1977), p. 196.

133. Ibid.

134. Richard Quinney, *Criminology*, 2d ed. (Boston: Little, Brown, 1979), p. 227.

135. Sheila Balkan, Ronald J. Berger, and Janet Schmidt, *Crime and Deviance in America: A Critical Approach* (Belmont, Calif.: Wadsworth, 1980).

136. W. J. Chambliss, "Toward a Political Economy of Crime," *Theory and Society* 2 (Summer 1975), p. 152.

137. J. R. Hepburn, "Social Control and the Legal Order: Legitimate Repression in a Capitalist State," *Contemporary Crisis* 1 (1977), p. 77.

138. Anthony M. Platt, "The Triumph of Benevolence: The Origins of the Juvenile Justice System in the United States," in *Criminal Justice in America*, edited by Richard Quinney (Boston: Little, Brown, 1974), p. 377.

139. LaMar T. Empey, *American Delinquency: Its Meaning and Construction* (Homewood, Ill.: Dorsey Press, 1982), p. 430.

140. Barry Krisberg, "Gang Youth and Hustling: The Psychology of Survival," in Krisberg and Austin, *Children of Ishmael*, p. 244.

141. Ibid.

142. Herman Schwendinger and Julia S. Schwendinger, "Marginal Youth and Social Policy," *Social Problems* 24 (December 1976), pp. 84–91.

143. Herman Schwendinger and Julia Siegel Schwendinger, *Adolescent Subcultures and Delinquency* (New York: Praeger Publishers, 1985), p. 3.

144. Schwendinger and Schwendinger, "Marginal Youth and Social Policy," pp. 84–91.

145. Ibid.

146. Ibid.

147. David F. Greenberg, "Delinquency and the Age Structure of Society," *Contemporary Crisis* (1977), pp. 196–197.

148. Krisberg and Austin, *Children of Ishmael*, p. 53.

149. See the discussion in Chapter 7.

150. See Chapter 12 for discussions of racism in the justice system.

151. William J. Chambliss, "The Saints and the Roughnecks," *Society* 11 (1973), pp. 341–355.

152. Terence P. Thornberry, "Race, Socioeconomic Status, and Sentencing in the Juvenile Justice System," *Journal of Criminal Law and Criminology* 64 (1973), pp. 90–98; Charles W. Thomas and Anthony W. Fitch, *An Inquiry into the Association between Respondents' Personal Characteristics and Juvenile Court Dispositions* (Williamsburg, Va.: Metropolitan Criminal Justice Center, College of William and Mary, 1975); and Rosemary C. Sarri and Robert D. Vinter, "Justice for Whom? Varieties of Juvenile Correctional Approaches," in *The Juvenile Justice System*, edited by M. W. Klein (Beverly Hills, Calif.: Sage, 1976).

153. Mark Colvin and John Pauly, "A Critique of Criminology: Toward an Integrated Structural-Marxist Theory of Delinquency Production," *American Journal of Sociology* 89 (November 1983), pp. 513–551.

154. Ibid. p. 543.

155. Ibid.

156. For a review of radical humanism, see Kevin Anderson, "Humanism and Anti-Humanism in Radical Criminological Theory," in *Perspectives on Social Problems* 3 (1991), pp. 19–38; and Kevin Anderson, "Radical Criminology and the Overcoming of Alienation: Perspectives from Marxian and Gandhian Humanism," in *Criminology as Peacemaking*, edited by Harold E. Pepinsky and Richard Quinney (Bloomington: Indiana University Press, 1991), pp. 14–29.

part three

Environmental Influences on Delinquency

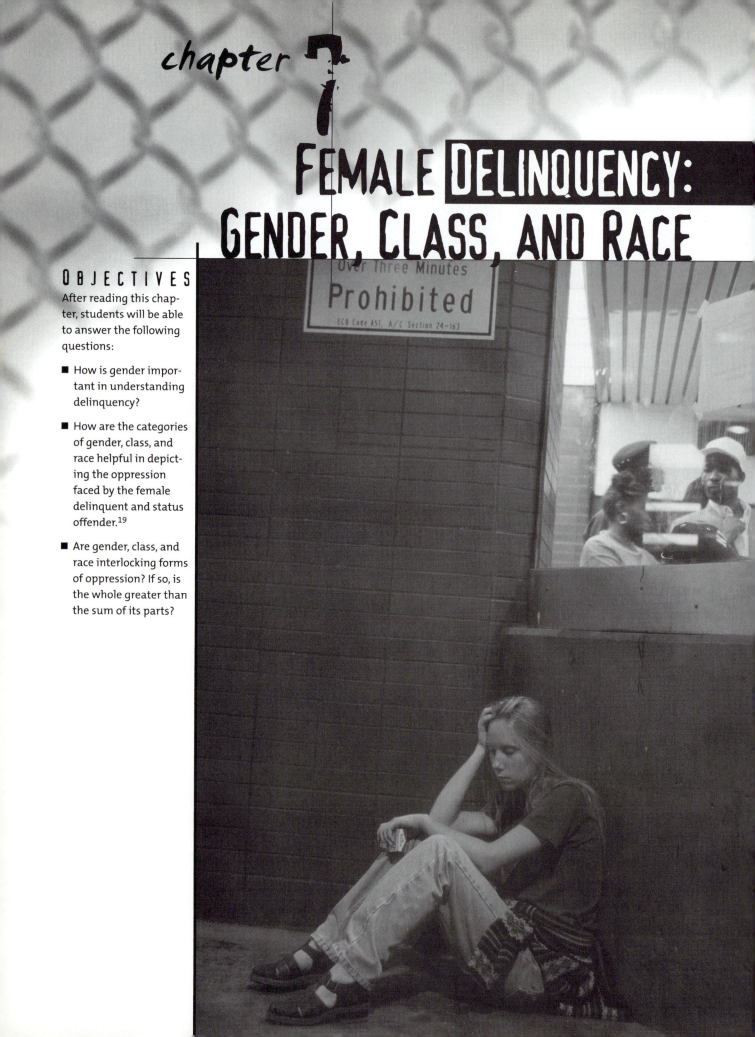

chapter 7

FEMALE DELINQUENCY: GENDER, CLASS, AND RACE

OBJECTIVES

After reading this chapter, students will be able to answer the following questions:

■ How is gender important in understanding delinquency?

■ How are the categories of gender, class, and race helpful in depicting the oppression faced by the female delinquent and status offender.[19]

■ Are gender, class, and race interlocking forms of oppression? If so, is the whole greater than the sum of its parts?

Meda Chesney-Lind, one of the most respected delinquency experts, claims that the study of delinquency is gender-biased and that delinquent theories are preoccupied with why males commit delinquent acts:

In my view, the study of crime has been an incontrovertibly male, even "macho," field. Male criminologists have studied other younger men in conflict with an admittedly unequal society and found in their behavior something repellent but also something compelling—witness a major theorist in the area calling the delinquent a "rogue male." Let's face it, male delinquency, particularly gang behavior, is a dramatic form of defiance. Perhaps for that reason, it has been thought of, at least by some criminologists, as the ultimate form of masculinity.

A quick review of the classics in the area will show that my characterization is not all that extreme and that the study of delinquency was almost always the study of male delinquency. In one early work, for example, male delinquency rates were referred to as "delinquency rates"; another 600-page book on gangs spent only one page on the female gangs found by the researcher. Girls were often not even mentioned and occasionally explicitly eliminated. Delinquency theories, then, stress male experience and male problems.[1]

What will it mean to study a field in which there has been major gender bias? How will that affect an understanding of the female delinquent and status offender?

Kathleen Daly and Chesney-Lind also stated that the study of crime and the justice process is shaped by male experiences and understanding of the social world.[2] Coramae Richey Mann charged that all of the major theorists, including Edwin H. Sutherland, Albert K. Cohen, Richard A. Cloward and Lloyd E. Ohlin, David Matza, and Travis Hirschi, lacked the development of a female perspective.[3] Dorie Klein further noted that "the criminality of women has long been a neglected subject area of criminology." She added that "female criminality has often ended up as a footnote to works on men that purport to be works on criminality in general."[4]

Carol Smart and Klein were two early criminologists to suggest that a feminist criminology should be formulated because of the neglect of the feminist perspective in classical delinquency theories.[5] Klein's 1973 article ended in a call for "a new kind of research on women and crime—one that has feminist roots and a radical orientation. . . ."[6] In a 1995 update, Klein contributed that the feminist critique of subjects such as women, crime, and justice "has exploded in volume and advanced light-years in depth, and interest. . . ."[7] Daly and Chesney-Lind defined a feminist perspective as one "in which women's experiences and ways of knowing are brought to the fore, not suppressed."[8]

Feminist criminologists are quick to agree that adolescent females have different experiences from adolescent males. They generally support that females are more controlled than males, enjoy more social support, are less disposed to crime, and have fewer opportunities for certain types of crimes.[9] They are also aware of the developmental differences between young women and young men. In addition, it is commonly accepted that "high self-esteem discourages definitions favorable to risk-taking among females but encourages these definitions among males."[10] Moreover, there is general agreement with the finding of juvenile justice research that young women's patterns of offending differ in scope and motivation from those of their male counterparts.[11]

However, feminist criminologists disagree on how the male-oriented approach to delinquency should be handled. Some feminist theorists emphasize that feminist research should be presented in textbooks "as a seamless whole rather than as a separate chapter."[12] These feminist theorists question the need for separate discussion of female delinquency, because little evidence to date suggests that separate theories are needed to account for female and male delinquency. Moreover, latent structural analysis shows that female delinquency tends to operate through the same factors as male delinquency. Empirical studies generally reveal that much more variation exists within each gender than between the sexes.[13]

In contrast, other feminist theorists argue that new theoretical efforts are needed to understand female delinquency and women's involvement in adult crime. Eileen Leonard, for example, questioned whether anomie, labeling, differential association, subculture, and Marxist theories can be used to explain the crime patterns of women. She concluded that these traditional theories do not work and that they are basically flawed.[14] Chesney-Lind's application of the male-oriented theories to female delinquency has argued that existing delinquency theories are inadequate to explain female delinquency. She suggested that there is a need for a feminist model of delinquency, because a patriarchal context has shaped the explanations and handling of female delinquents and status offenders. What this means is that adolescent females' sexual and physical victimizations at home and the relationship between these experiences and their crimes has been systematically ignored.[15]

Leonard is one of those who argued that the new theoretical efforts to understand women's crime must include an analysis of the links among gender, race, class, and culture.[16] After accusing some feminists of ignoring racial, class, ethnic, religious, and cultural differences among women, Elizabeth V. Spelman concluded that it is only through an examination of such factors that oppression against women can be more clearly grasped and understood.[17] Chesney-Lind further extended this argument when she said that adolescent females and women are victims of "multiple marginality" because their gender, class, and race have placed them at the economic periphery of society. To be labeled a delinquent takes place in a world, Chesney-Lind charged, "where gender still shapes the lives of young people in very powerful ways. Gender, then, matters in girls' lives and the way gender works varies by the community and the culture into which the girl is born."[18] For a review of the historical context of class, race, and gender, see Theory and Research 7.1.

THEORY AND RESEARCH 7.1

Historical Context of Class–Race–Gender

Two sources seem to be largely accountable for the class–race–gender analysis: experiences of African American women in the 1960s and curriculum-integration projects in higher education that were organized by women's studies faculty members.

The actual inspiration of class–race–gender analysis was the experiences of African American women in movement activities in the 1960s. From their experiences came an analysis of sexism in the civil rights and black nationalist movements and of racism in a predominately white women's feminist movement.

Their first wave of publications in the 1970s focused on black women's experiences in movement politics and on their relationships with white women. In the mid to late 1970s, their analyses became more focused on the development of black feminist thought.

The curriculum-integration projects that were largely organized by women's studies faculty members in higher education were what consolidated and popularized class–race–gender analysis. By 1985, at least eighty projects had been launched to examine how women's studies should be "redefined and reconstructed to include us all." It was not long before the class–race–gender construct was being widely articulated across the university in women's studies, African American studies, cultural or multicultural studies, sociology, anthropology, English and American studies, and history. It became a popular and widely used buzzword "to signal a way that theory and research ought to be done."

What is the importance of this sense of history to understanding the background of gender, class, and race? How would this form of analysis affect how theory and research are to be done?

Source: Kathleen Daly, "Class–Race–Gender: Sloganeering in Search of Meaning," *Social Justice* 20 (1993), pp. 56–57.

A Recent Profile in Understanding the Adolescent Female Offender

Female juvenile offenders of the 21st century continue to be similar in demographic characteristics to female juvenile offenders of the 1980s and 1990s. They are likely to have been sexually or physically abused, to be from single-parent homes, and to lack appropriate social and work-related skills. In addition, they are more likely to be under 15 and to be women of color.[20] For example, in data obtained from 29 states by the National Council on Crime and Delinquency, African American women make up almost 50 percent of all juvenile females in secure detention; Hispanic female juveniles make up 13 percent.[21]

The female adolescent, as suggested in Chapter 2, continues to be arrested for the more "female" offenses, such as prostitution, embezzlement, forgery, and counterfeiting.[22] However, some patterns of delinquent offending by adolescent females have changed since the 1980s. While adolescent females are less likely than adolescent males to become involved in serious forms of delinquency, such as violent crime, the involvement of young women with the juvenile court in recent years has increased.[23] An important implication of this increase is that state delinquency systems often underestimate the numbers and therefore are not equipped to deal effectively with female delinquents.[24]

Some of the following percentage increases remain small, but they are still an important consideration if they represent trends for the future:

- Between 1989 and 1993, the number of arrests involving female juveniles increased by 23 percent compared with an 11 percent increase in the arrests of male juveniles.
- In 1996, females represented 25 percent of all arrests of juveniles (those under 18 years of age) in the United States. This is an increase of 4 percent from 21 percent in 1983. However, this number has been rising since 1960, when females represented only 11 percent of all arrests. They represented 15 percent in 1975 and 19 percent in 1990.
- In 1996, females represented 15 percent of juvenile arrests for violent crimes.
- Between 1989 and 1993, arrests of young males for burglary, larceny–theft, and motor vehicle theft all decreased (down 6 percent, 1 percent, and 8 percent respectively), while arrests of young women for these same crimes increased (up 16 percent, 21 percent, and 28 percent respectively).
- In 1996, females represented 57 percent of the arrests for running away and 29 percent of the arrests for curfew and loitering law violations.[25]

As the numbers of female delinquents and their offenses have changed, so have their numbers in juvenile court increased. Females now make up about 20 percent of all delinquency cases handled by juvenile courts. Females are less likely than males to be formally processed with the filing of a delinquency petition. Of those petitioned cases involving females, 53 percent were adjudicated, compared to the adjudication of 59 percent of petitioned cases involving males. Of those adjudicated cases, 60 percent of the females were granted probation and 55 percent of the males were granted probation. More than 24 percent of detained adolescent females were charged with probation and parole violations, compared with 12 percent of male adolescent offenders.

Female offenders were still less likely (23 percent of adjudicated cases) than male offenders (29 percent of adjudicated cases) to be ordered to out-of-home placements following juvenile court's adjudication and disposition. Adolescent female offenders were also less likely to be placed in secure detention at some point between referral and disposition. Females were detained in 16 percent of delinquency cases, compared to 22 percent of cases involving male offenders. Females were most likely to be detained in cases involving drug offenses and public order offenses; males, in contrast, were most likely to be detained only for drug offenses. (See Table 7.1)[26]

TABLE 7.1

Processing of Male and Female Delinquents

Formal Processing	Males	Females
CASES HANDLED BY THE JUVENILE COURT	80%	20%
ADJUDICATION OF CASES FORMALLY PROCESSED	59%	53%
ADJUDICATED CASES RESULTING IN PROBATION	55%	60%
CHARGED WITH PROBATION AND PAROLE VIOLATION	12%	24%
OUT-OF-HOME PLACEMENTS	29%	23%
SECURE DETENTION	22%	16%

Source: Office of Juvenile Justice and Delinquency Prevention, *Juvenile Female Offenders: A Status of the States* (Washington, D.C.: U.S. Department of Justice, 1998).

Although every female delinquent and status offender is unique, she is likely to share the following profile with other female youthful offenders. She is now 14 to 16 years old, is poor and has grown up in a neighborhood that has a high crime rate; is likely to belong to an ethnic minority group; has a history of poor performance in school and may be a school dropout; has been a victim of physical, sexual, and/or emotional abuse; has used and abused drugs and/or alcohol; has had her medical and emotional needs ignored; sees her life as oppressive and lacks hope for the future.[27]

Thus, although sometimes called the "forgotten few," female delinquents are becoming too numerous and their problems too serious to ignore. A significant issue, then, is the importance of gender in understanding the behavior of female juvenile offenders.

How Is Gender Important in Understanding Delinquency?

Marty Beyer, a clinical psychologist who has examined adolescent males and females across the nation for the past twenty years, claims that girls develop differently from boys. Research, she adds, "has identified different vulnerabilities and protective factors in girls." Girls have a tendency to internalize, with higher rates of anxiety, depression, withdrawal, and eating disorders.[28]

Girls also are more focused on relationships than boys. This focus on connection with others "makes it difficult for them to resolve the conflict between being selfish and selfless." Girls' failure to receive sufficient nurturing and success in the family restricts the ability to feel lovable and capable and in turn hinders their identity development. Girls have more negative body images than boys during adolescence and tend to dislike themselves more than boys do. Early puberty and the simultaneous occurrence of physical development and transition to middle or high school are especially stressful for girls.[29]

Delinquent girls' problems in school and family are correlated with depression. Delinquent girls have more frequently been sexually violated than boys and thus are more likely to develop post-traumatic stress disorder in response to the violence they have experienced. Much of the behavior of delinquent girls, Beyer continues, is because of immature thinking. With much in common with delinquent boys, delinquent girls react inappropriately to perceived threat, fail to anticipate or plan, make poor choices, and minimize danger.[30]

Stephanie J. Funk's study on the need for separate risk assessment instruments for male and female delinquents found that separate risk assessments are helpful in identifying the risk for reoffending. Funk observed that the importance of social relationship for adolescent females increased their risk for delinquency in two ways. First, disruptions in family, community, and school relations affected females more negatively than males. Consequently, both potential and actual disruptions of relationships put females at risk for delinquency. Also, the importance of connection introduced a greater risk for delinquency when the others in those relationships engage in delinquent or criminal behaviors.[31]

According to Joanne Belknap and Kristi Holsinger, "The most significantly and potentially useful criminological research in recent years has been the recognition of girls and women's pathways to offending.[32] To address these pathways of offending, the National Council on Crime and Delinquency (NCCD) conducted a 1998 multidimensional study of girls in the California juvenile justice system.[33]

The first step along females' pathways into the juvenile justice system is victimization. The ages at which interviewed adolescent girls reportedly were most likely to be beaten, raped, stabbed, or shot were thirteen and fourteen.[34] A large proportion of girls first enter the juvenile justice system as runaways, who frequently are attempting to escape abuse at home.[35]

Certain abuses follow adolescent females into the juvenile justice system. Specific forms of abuse reportedly experienced by juvenile females include the consistent use of foul and demanding language by staff; the inappropriate touching, pushing and hitting by staff; the placement in isolation for trivial reasons; and the deprivation of clean clothing. Some girls were strip-searched in the presence of male officers.[36]

The majority of adolescent females' most serious charges fell into the assault category, but an examination of case files of these females revealed that most assault charges were the result of non-serious, mutual combat situations with parents. The aggression, in many cases, was initiated by the adults.[37]

The disparate treatment of minorities appeared to be an important factor in the processing of adolescent females' cases. In the NCCD study, as well as nationally, two-thirds of females in the juvenile justice system are minorities, primarily African American and Hispanic females.[38]

Another problem is that females offenders represented one of the least-serviced juvenile justice populations. There are only a few effective gender-specific programs nationally. The continuum of programs and services that are required to reduce females' entry into the juvenile justice system must be responsive both to gender and age and to developmental age.

Optimum environments for at-risk females of this age would be intensive family-based programs that are tailored to needs of adolescent females.[39] Another possibility that has merit is a community-based all-girls school setting anchoring such services as family counseling, substance-abuse prevention, specialized educational services (e.g., learning disabilities assessment), and mentoring services. A further gender-specific strategy is offering programs that provide the opportunity for the development of positive relationships between female offenders and their children.[40]

The Feminist Perspectives on Explanations of Female Delinquency

The biological, psychological, and sociological explanations of why females become involved in delinquent acts are examined in this section. Early explanations of female delinquency focused on biological and psychological factors, but more recent explanations have placed much greater emphasis on sociological factors.

This section considers the important question of whether juvenile females commit delinquent acts for reasons different from those of males. There is general agreement that the hopelessly flawed biological and psychological explanations of delinquency view troublesome adolescent females in our patriarchal society through the lens of sexism. When it comes to sociological explanations of delinquency, however, feminist criminologists come to vastly different conclusions. Some feminist criminologists challenge whether gender-specific explanations are needed, because existing theoretical constructs can account for both males' and females' delinquency.[41] Others still argue for gender-specific explanations because they claim that sociological theories of delinquent behavior fail to explain adequately the female experience in U.S. society.

Biological and Constitutional Explanations

In *The Female Offender,* initially published in 1903, Cesare Lombroso deals with crime as atavism, or the survival of "primitive" traits in female offenders.[42] First, he argued that women are more primitive, or lower on the evolutionary scale, because they are less intelligent and have fewer variations in their mental capacities than men: "Even the female criminal is monotonous and uniform compared with her male companion, just as in general women are inferior to men."[43] Second, Lombroso contended that women are unable to feel pain and, therefore, are insensitive to the pain of others and lack moral refinement.[44] He stated:

> Women have many traits in common with children; that their moral sense is deficient; that they are revengeful, jealous. . . . In ordinary cases these defects are neutralized by piety, maternity, want of passion, sexual coldness, weakness, and an undeveloped intelligence.[45]

Third, he argued, women are characterized by a passive and conservative approach to life. Although he admitted that women's traditional sex roles in the family bind them to a more home-centered life, he insisted that women's passivity can be directly traced to the "immobility of the ovule compared with the zoosperm."[46]

Lombroso contended that because most women are born with "feminine" characteristics, their innate physiological limitations protect them from crime and predispose them to live unimaginative, dull, and conforming lives. But women criminals, he argued, have inherited male characteristics, such as excessive body hair, moles, wrinkles, crow's feet, and abnormal craniums.[47] He added that the female criminal, being doubly exceptional as a woman and as a criminal, is likely to be more vicious than the male criminal.[48]

Recently, with the biosocial revival in criminology, biological or physiological explanations for delinquency have regained some popularity. In a 1968 study, Cowie and colleagues presented data on an English approved school (training school) sample that emphasize genetic factors as the major cause of delinquency.[49] These researchers even proposed that these genetic factors might be specific enough to determine the types of crimes each sex will commit.[50] T. C. N. Gibbens also reported a high rate of sex chromosomal abnormalities in delinquent girls.[51] Furthermore, Cowie and colleagues noted the above-average weight of their institutional sample and suggested that physical overdevelopment tends to draw a girl's attention to sex earlier in life, resulting in sexual promiscuity.[52] In addition, they claimed that menstruation is a distressing reminder to females that they can never be males and that this distress makes them increasingly prone to delinquent acts.[53]

In sum, the viewpoints of Lombroso and other supporters of biological explanations for female delinquency can be regarded as merely a foolish testimony to the historical chauvinism of males. Unfortunately, the study of female criminality has not yet fully recovered from the idea "that the cause of a socially generated phenomenon might be reduced to a genetically transmitted biological unit."[54]

Psychological Explanations

The claimed "innate nature" of women is the basis of much of the writing on female delinquency.[55] W. I. Thomas, Sigmund Freud, Otto Pollak, Gisela Konopka, and others addressed this "innate" female nature and its relationship to deviant behavior.

Thomas's works marked a transition from physiological explanations to more sophisticated theories embracing physiological, psychological, and social structural factors. In *Sex and Society,* he suggested that there are basic biological differences between the sexes. Maleness, according to Thomas, is "katabolic," from the animal force that involves a destructive release of energy and allows the possibility of creative work through this outward flow, but femaleness is "anabolic"—motionless, lethargic, and conservative.[56] Thomas's underlying assumptions are physiological ones, for he credits men with higher amounts of sexual energy that lead them to pursue women for sexual pleasure. In contrast, he attributes to women maternal feelings devoid of sexuality, so they exchange sex for domesticity.[57]

In his 1923 work *The Unadjusted Girl,* Thomas dealt with female delinquency as a "normal" response under certain social conditions.[58] He argued that a girl is driven by four wishes or ambitions: the desires for new experiences, for security, for response, and for recognition. He assumed that the delinquent girl's problem is not criminality but immorality, and he confined himself almost exclusively to a discussion of prostitution. According to Thomas, the major cause of prostitution rested in the girl's need for love, and a secondary factor is her wish for recognition or ambition. Thomas maintained that it is not sexual desire that motivates delinquent girls, because they are no more passionate than nondelinquent girls, but that they are using male desire for sex to achieve their own ultimate needs.[59] He added:

> The beginning of delinquency in girls is usually an impulse to get amusement, adventure, pretty clothes, favorable notice, distinction, freedom in the larger world. . . . The girls have usually become "wild" before the development of sexual desire, and their casual sex relations do usually awaken sexual feelings. Their sex is used as a condition of the realization of other wishes. It is their capital.[60]

The sad commentary on the state of theory regarding female delinquency is that until recently the psychoanalytic writings of Freud have represented the most pervasive theoretical position.[61] The structure of the personality and the psychosexual stages of development of the child are the two major concepts from which theories based on Freud's work have evolved.

The most controversial and ridiculous aspects of Freud's theory had to do with his assumption that women's sex organs make them anatomically inferior to men. Freud contended that a little girl assumes she has lost her penis as punishment and, therefore, feels traumatized and grows up envious and revengeful. A woman becomes a mother to replace the "lost penis" with a baby. The delinquent girl, in the Freudian perspective, is one who is attempting to be a man. Her drive to accomplishment is the expression of her longing for a penis.[62]

The Freudian orientation is not limited to penis envy in its explanation of female delinquency, because it suggests that at any state of psychosexual development, faulty mechanism, fixations, and other problems may occur. Freud also argued that women are inferior because they are concerned with personal matters and have little social sense. Women, according to Freud, have weaker social interests than men and less capacity for the sublimation of their interests.[63]

Peter Bols was one of the researchers who focused on the sexual aspect of Freudian psychoanalytic theory. For example, Bols directly stated that "in the girl, it seems, delinquency is an overt sexual act, or to be more correct, a sexual acting out."[64] In a later work, Bols developed three constellations of female delinquency. Those in the first constellation view delinquency as a defense against regression, a denial of the need for a nurturing mother, and an attempt to avoid homosexual surrender. The delinquent female included in the second constellation sexually acts out as a revenge against the mother, who deserves this hostility because she has degraded the girl's oedipal father. Those in the third constellation are female delinquents who attempt through sexual misconduct to restore a sense of reality to their lives. They have become emotionally alienated from their families, which have detrimentally affected their egos. Bols saw female delinquency as much more destructive and irreversible in its consequences than male delinquency.[65]

Herbert H. Herskovitz, another researcher who was influenced by the psychoanalytic tradition, stated that "the predominant expression of delinquency among females in our society is promiscuous sexual behavior."[66] The promiscuous adolescent female is psychologically maladjusted for several Freudian-based reasons: penis envy, a conscious desire for the father, and a need to be wanted and loved.[67]

Pollak's *The Criminality of Women* (1950) advanced the theory that women are more criminal than is usually believed, but that their crimes largely go unreported or are hidden. Pollak credited the nature of women themselves for the traditionally low official rates of female crime, because women are inherently deceitful and, therefore, act as instigators rather than perpetrators of criminal activity. The roles played by women are a factor in hidden crimes as well because such roles as domestics, nurses, teachers, and housewives enable them to commit undetectable crimes. The **"chivalry" factor** is further advanced as a root cause of hidden crime; that is, the police and the court forgive a girl for the same act for which they would convict a boy.[68]

Pollak also suggested two factors that influence adolescent females to become juvenile delinquents. First, he said, early physical development and sexual maturity allow a female more opportunities to engage in immoral or delinquent behavior. Second, a female's home life, especially if she has criminal parents or grows up in a broken home, may cause her to seek outside substitutes for that poor home life. She is likely to seek the company of other maladjusted females, and they will eventually become involved in a life of petty crimes.[69]

Konopka's study of delinquent females linked a poor home life with a deep sense of loneliness and low self-esteem. Konopka's conception of delinquency relied heavily on the notion of individual pathology, as she concluded that only a female who is "sick" can become delinquent.[70] Konopka identified four key factors contributing to female delinquency: (1) a uniquely dramatic biological onset of puberty, (2) a complex identification process because of a girl's competitiveness with her mother, (3) the changing cultural position of females and the resultant uncertainty and loneliness, and (4) the hostile picture that the world presents to some young females.[71]

The idea of psychological impairment, or trait, of delinquent females has received support from a number of other writers. Clyde Vedder and Dora Somerville's *The Delinquent Girl* suggested that the delinquent behavior of girls usually indicates a problem of adjustment to family and social pressure.[72] Ruth Morris, in a study conducted in Flint, Michigan, added that delinquent girls experience rational problems more frequently than do nondelinquent girls.[73] Mary Riege asserted that delinquent girls evince excessive loneliness, low self-esteem, estrangement from adults, and low capacity for friendship.[74] Emmy E. Werner and Ruth S. Smith further found in their longitudinal study that "emotional instability" and the "need for long-term mental health services in the early elementary grades" were the best predictors of delinquency in girls.[75] Finally, William Wattenberg and Frank Saunders's Detroit study found a pattern of broken or disrupted homes connected with female delinquency.[76]

Psychological causes of female delinquency have been particularly applied to explaining the behaviors of female status offenders. It has been argued that female status offenders tend to place the blame for their problems on their parents. They often feel that their need for a warm, accepting, and meaningful relationship with parental figures is not being fulfilled, so they see themselves as rejected and neglected. Female status offenders frequently reject the limits placed on their behavior both in and outside the home. A juvenile probation officer describes the difficulty of dealing with female status offenders:

> Status offenders are basically out of control and may have some emotional problems. I think they're tougher to work with than delinquents. It's easier to define what you can

do with a delinquent. If you do this, you tell the delinquent, then this is what's going to happen. But with the status offender, you have no control over them; no one really does. They have been out of control for a long time, and you're not going to get them back into control unless you take some strict measures. And the [juvenile] code is not very helpful at all.[77]

The relationship between psychological impairment and delinquency in some adolescent females has also been widely acknowledged. The female adolescent, for example, who has experienced sexual abuse at home may become involved in such destructive behavior as prostitution because of her poor self-esteem. A sixteen-year-old adolescent female who drowned two children in a bathroom while babysitting one evening was found to possess intense hostility toward her mother. A social worker in a youth shelter describes how guilt can lead to psychological impairment:

> A lot of these girls feel they've done something wrong and that it was their fault. They don't feel they are good for anything else. Some of their anger toward self is expressed in drug and alcohol abuse, mutilating self, running away, and getting themselves in situations where they will be abused again. These girls tend to be very hard toward women because their anger is toward their mother, and very soft and flirtatious with men.[78]

In sum, psychological studies of female delinquency shifted in the 1950s from the psychoanalytical to the familial-social type. Considerable research continues to perpetuate the notion that personal maladjustment characterizes the female delinquent: She has a psychological problem, is unable to perform her proper sex role adequately, or suffers from the ill effects of a bad home life.[79] This means that the legacy of sexism continues to thrive in psychological explanations as it did in biological explanations of female delinquency. This sexual ideology can be seen in the assumptions of the inherent nature of females through the works of Lombroso, Thomas, Pollak, and Freud. It can also be seen in the crime categories in which girls and women are placed. If girls and women are violent, they are defined as "masculine" and suffering from atavism, penis envy, or chromosomal deficiencies. If they conform, they are accused of manipulation, sexual maladjustment, and promiscuity.[80]

Sociological Explanations

Beginning in the late 1970s, several studies have proceeded from the assumption that sociological processes traditionally related to males could also affect the delinquent involvement of females. General agreement exists among feminists, as well as nonfeminists, that the literature that approaches female delinquency from a sociological perspective appears to offer more promise than that which includes biological or psychological causes. Researchers have focused on such sociological factors as blocked opportunity, the women's liberation movement, social bonding, masculinity, power control, and peer group influence.

BLOCKED OPPORTUNITY THEORY   The role of **blocked or limited opportunity** has received considerable attention in the sociological analysis of male delinquency. The usefulness of such variables in studying female delinquency has been largely ignored because males are seen as concerned with achieving short- and long-term status and economic success, whereas juvenile females are commonly viewed as possessing no such aspirations but instead as being satisfied to occupy a role dependent on males.[81]

Susan Datesman and colleagues found that perception of limited opportunity was more strongly related to female delinquency than it was to male delinquency. Both African American and white female delinquents regarded their opportunities less positively than did the male delinquents in their sample. Status offenders also perceived their opportunties as being less favorable than did nondelinquents.[82] Jeffery O. Segrave and Douglas N. Hastad's self-report sample of 891 male and 885 female high school students also found that perception of limited opporunties was more strongly related to delinquency among adolescent females than among adolescent males.[83] Furthermore, Stephen A. Cernkovich and Peggy C. Giordano's self-report sample of 1,335 male and female high school students showed that in general blocked opportunity was more predictive of delinquency than any other variable. The effect of perception of blocked opportunity differed according to the racial background of the juvenile. For many minority males and females, blocked opportunity had no effect whatsoever on subsequent delinquency involvement, but for white males and females, perception of limited opportunity was a strong predictor of delinquency.[84]

Paul Mazerolle reported that general strain theory (GST) offered a useful framework for assessing similarities and differences in the risks and processes leading females and males to delinquent behavior. He found that the effect of GST did not differ between males and females at significant levels of measurement. But in focusing on crime-specific effects for violent and property-related delinquency, he did find "some evidence of gender differences in the effects of negative life events and experiences on subsequent delinquency."[85]

Overall, although strain theory has been applied solely to male delinquents, the Datesman, Segrave and Hastad, and Giordano and Cernkovich studies show that the perception of blocked opportunity may be even more strongly related to female involvement in delinquency than to male involvement. Giordano and Cernkovich also suggest that the racial background of the juvenile may be more important than the gender in determining the effect of blocked opportunity.

WOMEN'S LIBERATION MOVEMENT   Freda Adler argued that the rise in crime among adult women and juvenile females is clearly linked to opportunity. Today's adolescent girl, according to Adler, faces the plight that she is instilled with almost boundless ambition, but has no opportunities for the achievement of her desired goals. The end result is that the adult and the juvenile female imitate males in both the desire for the same goals and the adoption of male roles to achieve them. Accordingly, juvenile females are abandoning the traditional three offenses—incorrigibility, running away, and promiscuity—and are becoming involved instead in more aggressive and violent acts.[86] Adler contended that the rise in official rates of female crime reflects the changes brought about by the liberation of women. The rise in female delinquency, then, is directly related to females becoming more competitive with males and more aggressive and more "masculine" in general. As Adler reported:

> "I know it's happening but I'll be damned if it still doesn't shock me when I see it," explained one exasperated sergeant who was slumped in the chair of a district precinct house in Washington, D.C. He was talking about the new problems which girls have created for police. "Last week, for instance, we got a call of a disturbance at the high school. A fight . . . after school. So we get down there and pull up and here is a hell of a crowd yelling and screaming at the kids in the center, who are fighting. I push my way through the crowd—they're going crazy like it is really a mean fight and when I get to the middle . . . I liked to fell over. Here are two husky broads, and they are fighting . . . now I don't mean any hair-pulling face-scratching kind of thing; I mean two broads squared off and duking it out. Throwing jabs and hooking in at each other and handling themselves like a couple of goddamned pro sparring partners. I mean, I got to ask myself, what the hell is going on? What in the name of God is happening to these girls anymore?"[87]

Three criticisms have been leveled against the assumption that the increase in female crime figures can be traced to the **women's liberation movement.** First, Laura Crites pointed out that female offenders most often come from minority groups. They are frequently unemployed and usually are responsible for their own support and often for that of their children. In addition, their employment potential is limited in that over half have not graduated from high school and their work experience has generally been in low-wage, low-status occupations. Crites reasons that the psychological independence and expanded economic opportunities gained through the women's rights movement are almost meaningless for this group; instead of being concerned with the ideological constructs of the women's liberation movement, the typical female offender is caught up in a struggle for economic, emotional, and physical survival.[88]

Second, Darrell J. Steffensmeier asserted that the women's liberation movement and changing sex roles have had no impact on levels of female crime, because "the changes we observed began prior to the late 1960s when the movement could be expected to have its greatest impact on levels of property crime."[89] That is, the movement can be shown to have had little impact because official female crime rates have gradually increased; they did not rise dramatically at the time when interest in the movement sharply increased.

Third, Joseph G. Weis claimed that the national arrest data and self-reports of delinquent behavior show that the new female criminal is more a social invention than an empirical reality, so the women's liberation movement cannot be held responsible for changes in female criminal delinquent behavior that data indicate simply have not happened.[90]

Giordano and Cernkovich added that Steffensmeier and Adler both tend to see liberation in terms of an individually held set of attitudes and behaviors.[91] Giordano and Cernkovich, however, found that the concept of sex roles must be understood as multidimensional, partly because important differences exist between an offender's attitudes about women in general and her attitudes about herself in particular. These researchers further challenged the causal influence of the sex-role attitudes of the women's liberation movement because no systematic differences in attitudes are present between more and less delinquent girls.[92]

In sum, Adler's view that there is a direct relationship between the women's liberation movement and the rise of female criminality attributes to female criminals and delinquents a set of motivations and attitudes that are remote from their everyday lives.[93] Giordano and Cernkovich are correct in their appraisal that female sex roles are multidimensional and require a more sophisticated analysis than one based on an individual's attitudes and behaviors.

SOCIAL CONTROL THEORY   Hirschi's social control theory states that delinquency results when a juvenile's bond to the existing social order is weakened or broken.[94] Proponents of social control theory contend that females are less involved in delinquency than males because sex-role socializations result in a greater tie to the social bond for females than for males. In addition, adolescent females may have less opportunity to engage in delinquent behavior because in general they are more closely supervised by parents. Adolescent females are also more dependent on others, whereas adolescent males are encouraged to be more independent and achievement oriented. Consequently, differences in sex-role socialization supposedly promote a greater allegiance to the social bond among females, and this allegiance insulates them from delinquency more than it does males.[95]

Bobbi Jo Anderson and colleagues found from a survey of adolescent males and females confined in the Wyoming boys' and girls' schools that there were no differences in males' and females' levels of attachment when parents and attitude toward school were controlled. Yet some gender differences were found in the effects of the various attachments on the severity of delinquency. Although attachment to parents reduced the severity of males' delinquency, attachment to peers and schools reduced the severity of females' delinquency.[96]

Furthermore, **sex-role socialization** results in greater belief in the legitimacy of social rules by girls than by boys, claim social control theorists. Austin T. Turk, analyzing the greater involvement of boys than girls in officially recorded crime, concluded that females are more likely to abide by legal norms than are males, because their patterns of activity are more restricted than those of males.[97] Gary F. Jensen and Raymond Eve, using the same data that Hirschi used in the development of control theory, found that they did provide Hirschi's social control perspective with some empirical support but that significant differences still remained between male and female delinquency.[98]

In sum, lack of commitment to the social bond appears to influence the development of delinquency in both males and females. Some evidence does suggest that socialization practices cause adolescent females to have stronger commitments to the social bond than do males, with the result that females require a greater "push" to become involved in delinquent acts. Yet much more research is needed on the relationship between social control and female delinquency.

MASCULINITY HYPOTHESIS   Several studies of female delinquents have proposed a **masculinity hypothesis.** Adler contended that as females become more male-like and acquire more "masculine" traits, they become more delinquent.[99] Francis Cullen and coworkers found that the more male and female adolescents possessed "male" personality traits, the more likely they were to become involved in delinquency, but the relationship between masculinity and delinquency was stronger for males than for females.[100] William E. Thornton and Jennifer James found a moderate degree of association between masculine self-expectations and delinquency but concluded that males were still more likely to be delinquent than were females, regardless of their degree of masculinity.[101]

Stephen Norland and Neal Shover's examination of gender roles and delinquency, however, found that "when sex . . . and degree of social support for delinquency were held constant, males and females who hold more traditionally masculine expectations for themselves were no more likely to be highly delinquent than were their counterparts who hold less traditionally masculine expectations."[102] Giordano and Cernkovich also found no strong correlations between nontraditional sex-role attitudes and female delinquency.[103]

In sum, any indicator of female delinquency appears to be more complex than the notion that as females become more like males, they become more delinquent. Perhaps if it is applied in conjunction with another sociological explanation, the masculinity hypothesis will offer a better explanation of the relationship between sex differences and delinquency.[104]

PEER GROUP INFLUENCE   The importance of **peer group influence** on male delinquency has been widely documented. Indeed, a frequently reported finding in the literature is that male delinquency is more influenced than female delinquency by delinquent peer groups or delinquent associates.[105]

Giordano and Cernkovich, pioneering the investigation of the importance of the peer group for delinquent females, argued that peer associations must be given a central role in understanding changing patterns of delinquency involvement of females. In terms of the social context in which female delinquency took place, these researchers found that a female was most likely to commit a delinquent act when she was in a mixed-sex group. The second highest number of delinquent acts were committed by a female who was alone, then with a group of females, with one other female, with a group of males, and finally with one male. Significantly, the majority of delinquent acts occurred in mixed-sex contexts with males who were regarded simply as friends.[106] Females, Giordano and Cernkovich reasoned, appear to learn delinquent modes of behavior from males, but this does not mean that a boyfriend simply uses a female as an "accomplice" or in some other passive role while he commits a crime. These researchers also noted that other females are the most important reference group of delinquent females and that African American females are more likely to commit delinquent acts with a group of females than alone.[107]

Daniel P. Mears, Matthew Ploeger, and Mark Warr, in building on Sutherland's theory of differential association and Carol Gilligan's theory of moral development, theorized that females and males are differentially affected by exposure to delinquent peers. Using data from the National Youth Survey, they found support for this hypothesis in that "moral evaluations act as a barrier to reduce or counteract the influence of delinquent peers among females, thereby producing large observed sex differences in delinquent behavior."[108]

In sum, although some evidence indicates that delinquent females learn delinquent modes of behavior from others, much more research is clearly needed. For example, in what particular ways does association with males influence delinquent behavior? What other interacting variables, along with friendship, increase the degree of delinquency involvement among females?

POWER CONTROL THEORY   John Hagan and colleagues, as discussed in the previous chapter, proposed a power-control theory to explain female delinquency.[109] Using a Marxian framework and data collected in Toronto, Canada, they contended that as mothers gain power relative to their husbands, usually by employment outside the home, daughters and sons alike are encouraged to be more open to risk taking. Parents in egalitarian families, then, redistribute their control efforts so that daughters are subjected to controls more like those imposed on sons.

In contrast, daughters in patriarchal families are taught by their parents to avoid risks.[110] Hagan and colleagues concluded that "patriarchal families will be characterized by large gender differences in common delinquent behavior while egalitarian families will be characterized by smaller gender differences in delinquency."[111] Power-control theory thus concludes that when daughters are freed from patriarchal family relations, they more frequently become delinquent.[112]

In evaluating power-control theory, Simon I. Singer and Murray Levine contended that it is unclear in what ways work relationships produce more egalitarian home environments. The balanced class categories of egalitarian households may still reflect unbalanced work situations; the husband and wife may both be managers, but the husband is likely to earn a higher income and to have more authority at work.[113] Chesney-Lind, in an even more stinging criticism, stated that power-control theory is a variation on the earlier liberation hypothesis, but now it is the mother's liberation that causes a daughter's crime.[114]

Although the surface reasons for turning to prostitution may differ for white and African American juveniles, feminist Marxist theorists contend that the underlying reason is the same: the social and economic inequities of a patriarchal, capitalist system.

LABELING AND AN INTERACTIONIST THEORY OF DELINQUENCY Dawn Jeglum Bartusch and Ross L. Matsueda, in assessing whether an interactionist model can account for the gender gap in delinquency, used data from the National Youth Survey. Based on the symbolic interactionist model of delinquency discussed in Chapter 6, they argued that "delinquency is determined in part by the self as conceived by symbolic interactionists, which in turn is determined by a process of labeling by significant others."[115] They did find some gender interactions. Parental labeling and reflecting appraisals had a larger effect on male delinquency, and parents were more likely to falsely accuse male delinquents.[116]

Karen Heimer reported that delinquency for both females and males occurred through a process of role-taking, in which youth considered the perspectives of significant others. Among both boys and girls, attitudes favoring deviance encouraged delinquency. She also found that "girls' misbehavior can be controlled by inculcating values and attitudes, whereas more direct controls may be necessary to control boys' deviance."[117]

In sum, sociological explanations appear to be far more predictive of female delinquency than are biological or psychological explanations. Strain theory, social control theory, power-control theory, and labeling and symbolic interactionist theory all have received some support. Conflict or Marxist theory may also be a promising area of inquiry concerning the relationship between sex differences and delinquency.[118]

Evaluating the Explanations of Female Delinquency

Gender is one of the strongest correlates of delinquent behavior.[119] The discussion of female delinquency readily leads to the conclusion that biological explanations are the least predictive factors. Assumptions of sexual inferiority appear to be tied more to the historical context of male chauvinism than to the reality of female delinquency. Personal maladjustment hypotheses may have some predictive ability in determining the frequency of delinquency in girls, but these variables, too, have been overemphasized in the past. Some feminists are satisfied with the conclusions of sociological studies that males and females are differentially exposed or affected by the same crimonogenic associations.[120] Other feminists, as the next two sections of this chapter will show, contend that the unique experiences of females require gender-specific theories.

How Feminist Theories Can Be Applied to Understanding Crime

There have been five expressions of feminist theory—liberal feminism, phenomenological feminism, socialist feminism, Marxist feminism, and radical feminism.[121] Some have focused more on juvenile delinquency theory than others. For example, Chesney-Lind's radical feminist theory of delinquency is one of the most exciting efforts to explain delinquent behavior in adolescent females.[122]

Liberal Feminism

Liberal feminism calls for women's equality of opportunity and freedom of choice. Liberal feminism theorists do not believe that the system is inherently unequal or that discrimination is systematic. They hold that affirmative action, the equal rights amendment, and other opportunity laws or policies provide evidence that men and women can work together to "androgynize" gender roles (blend male and female traits and characteristics) and eliminate discriminatory policies and practices.[123]

Alison M. Jaggar and Paula Rothenberg trace liberal feminism to the eighteenth- and nineteenth-century social ideals of liberty and equality.[124] Liberal feminists contend that a major reason for the discrimination against women and female adolescents is gender-role socialization. Conventional family patterns, as Hagan and other theorists in this chapter have noted, structure masculine and feminine identities.[125]

Josephina Figueira-McDonough's formulation of feminist opportunity theory contended that similar levels of strain (arising from high success aspirations and low legitimate opportunities) lead to similar delinquency patterns by both genders, provided that they are equal in their knowledge of and access to illegitimate means.[126] Adler argued in *Sisters in Crime* that both adult women and adolescent females are imitating males in the desire for the same goals and adopting male roles to achieve them. Because of this merging of gender roles, the adolescent female, as well as her older counterpart, engages in more violent crime.[127]

Phenomenological Feminism

Phenomenological feminist theory pays more attention to the regulator than the regulated. That is, phenomenological feminists examine matters such as whether adolescent females receive the benefits of chivalrous treatment, why adolescent females have received discriminatory treatment by the juvenile justice system, and how juvenile laws penalize females.

The assumption that adult female offenders are protected by the old norms of chivalry and receive more lenient treatment by the justice system is frequently accepted in adult corrections. But if this is true for adult female offenders, strong evidence exists that it is not so for adolescent females.

Although many of the writers on female delinquency in the twentieth century have claimed that adolescent females are protected more than adolescent males because they receive the benefits of chivalrous treatment, Steven Schlossman and Stephanie Wallach showed that females have been treated more harshly than males from the time of the founding of the juvenile court at the turn of the century. These researchers, using old court records and secondary sources, asserted that female juvenile delinquents often have received more severe punishment than males, although males usually have been charged with more serious crimes. They concluded that the harsh discriminatory treatment of female delinquents during the Progressive Era resulted from racial prejudice, new theories of adolescence, and Progressive Era movements to purify society.[128]

Socialist Feminism

Socialist feminists, in contrast to other feminists, give neither class nor gender the highest priority. Instead, socialist feminists view both class and gender relations as equal, as they interact with and coreproduce each other in society. To understand class, socialist feminist argue, it is necessary to recognize how class is structured by gender and to understand gender requires that one see how it is structured by class. Crime results from the interaction of these relationships, because it is the powerful who have more legitimate and illegitimate opportunities to commit crime. Low female crime rates, then, are related to women's powerless position in the United States.[129]

Marxist Feminism

Marxist feminists argue that, as private property evolved, males dominated all social institutions. Consequently, gender and class inequalities result from property relations and the capitalist mode of production.[130] Sheila Balkan, Ron Berger, and Janet Schmidt further contended that the foundation for a theory of woman's criminality rests in a capitalist mode of production. Sexism, they said, is the result of capitalist relations that structure women and juvenile power and crime. Accordingly, nonviolent female crimes such as shoplifting and prostitution reflect such conditions.[131]

Eleanor M. Miller's *Street Woman,* which is based on intensive interviews with sixty-four Milwaukee prostitutes, contended that prostitution evolves out of the profound social and economic problems confronting adolescent females, especially young women of color.[132] For African American women, constituting over half of Miller's sample, movement into prostitution occurred as a consequence of exposure to deviant street networks. Generally recruited by older African American males with long criminal records, these women organized themselves into "pseudo families" and engaged chiefly but not exclusively in prostitution. These women viewed prostitution as an alternative to boring and low-paying jobs and as a means to relieve the burdens of pregnancy and single motherhood. (The young women interviewed had a total of eighty-one children.) Although they were attracted by the excitement and money involved in prostitution, they soon learned that the life was not nearly as glamorous and remunerative as they had anticipated.[133]

For whites, Miller found, street prostitution was not so much a hustle into which one drifted as it was a survival strategy. For this group there was often a direct link between prostitution and difficulties with parents, runaway behavior, and contact with the juvenile justice system. Interviewees described family lives that were characterized by disorganization, extremely high levels of violence, and abuse. But running away from these chaotic settings resulted in their arrest and lengthy detention as status offenders.[134]

Radical Feminism

Radical feminists view masculine power and privilege as the root cause of all social relations and inequality. The most important relations in any society, according to radical feminists, are found in patriarchy, which pertains to masculine control of labor power and sexuality of women.[135] Alison M. Jaggar and Paula Rothenberg, two radical feminists, stated that women were the first oppressed group in history, that women's oppression is so widespread that it exists in virtually every known society, and that women's oppression is so deep that it is the hardest form of oppression to eradicate.[136] Radical feminists, especially, focus on sexual violence toward women.[137]

A Feminist Theory of Delinquency

The **feminist theory of delinquency**, an expression of radical feminism, contends that girls' victimization and the relationship between that experience and girls' crime have been systematically ignored. Chesney-Lind, one of the main proponents of this position, stated that it has long been understood that a major reason for girls' presence in juvenile courts is their parents' insistence on their arrest. Researchers, as well as those who work with female status offenders, are discovering today that a substantial number are victims of both physical and sexual abuse.[138]

Chesney-Lind proposed that a feminist perspective on the causes of female delinquency includes the following propositions: First, girls are frequently the victims of violence and sexual abuse (estimates are that three-quarters of sexual-abuse victims are girls), but, unlike those of boys, girls' victimization and their response to that victimization are shaped by their status as young women. Second, their victimizers (usually males) have the ability to invoke official agencies of social control to keep daughters at home and vulnerable. Third, as girls run away from abusive homes characterized by sexual abuse and parental neglect, they are forced into the life of an escaped convict. Unable to enroll in school or take a job to support themselves because they fear detection, female runaways are forced to engage in panhandling, petty theft, and occasional prostitution to survive. Finally, it is no accident that girls on the run from abusive homes or on the streets because of impoverished homes become involved in criminal activities that exploit their sexuality. Because U.S. society has defined physically "perfect" young women as desirable, girls on the streets, who have little else of value to trade, are encouraged to utilize this resource. Not surprisingly, the criminal subculture also views them from this perspective.[139] In Theory and Research 7.2, Chesney-Lind expands on this notion of the feminist theory of delinquency.

Considerable research supports the frequent victimization of adolescent females. Mimi Silbert and Ayala M. Pines found that 60 percent of the street prostitutes they interviewed had been sexually abused as juveniles.[140] R. J. Phelps and colleagues, in a survey of 192 female youths in the Wisconsin juvenile justice system, discovered that 79 percent of these youths (most of whom were in the system for petty larceny and status offenses) had been subjected to physical abuse that resulted in some form of injury.[141] Chesney-Lind and Rodriguez's investigation of the backgrounds of adult women in prison underscored the links between their victimization as children and their later criminal careers. Interviews revealed that virtually all these women were victims of physical and/or sexual abuse as youngsters; more than 60 percent had been sexually abused, and about half had been raped.[142]

THEORY AND RESEARCH 7.2

Interview with Meda Chesney-Lind

The question now is whether the theories of delinquent behavior can be used to understand female crime, delinquency, and victimization. Will the "add women and stir" approach be sufficient to rescue traditional delinquency theories? My research convinces me that it will not work. Gender stratification or the patriarchal context within which both male and female delinquency is lodged has been totally neglected by conventional delinquency theory. This omission means that a total rethinking of delinquency as a social problem is necessary.

The exclusion of girls from delinquency theory might lead one to conclude that girls are almost never delinquent and that they have far fewer problems than boys. Some might even suspect that the juvenile justice system treats the few girls who find their way into it more gently than it does the boys. Both of these assumptions are wrong.

Current work on female delinquency is uncovering the special pains that girls growing up in male-dominated society face. The price one pays for being born female is upped when it is combined with poverty and minority status, but it is always colored by gender. Consequently, sexual abuse is a major theme in girls' lives, and many girls on the run are running away from abusive and violent homes. They run to streets that are themselves sexist, and they are often forced to survive as women—to sell themselves as commodities. All of this is shaped by their gender as well as by their class and their color.

You might ask, How about the system's response to girls' delinquency? First, there has been almost no concern about girls' victimization. Instead, large numbers of girls are brought into juvenile courts across America for noncriminal status offenses—running away from home, curfew, truancy, etcetera. Traditionally, no one in the juvenile justice system asked these girls why they were in conflict with their parents; no one looked for reasons why girls might run away from home. They simply tried to force them to return home or sentenced them to training schools. The juvenile justice system, then, has neglected girls' victimization, and it has acted to enforce parental authority over girls, even when the parents were abusive. Clearly, the patterns described above require an explanation that places girls' delinquent behavior in the context of their lives as girls in a male-dominated society—a feminist model of delinquency if you will. That's what I'm working on these days.

Is it as hard for girls to grow up in male-dominated society as Chesney-Lind suggests? What do you think of her feminist theory of delinquency?

Source: Meda Chesney-Lind is professor of sociology at the University of Hawaii at Manoa. Her articles have appeared in both criminal justice journals and edited criminal justice volumes, and she is widely acknowledged as one of the top authorities on female delinquency. Interviewed in 1988.

How Gender Bias Affects the Processing of the Female Delinquent

The fundamental theme of this chapter is that adolescent females grow up in a particular social context of domination and control by males.[143] In this patriarchal society, troublesome adolescent females are quickly viewed through the lens of discrimination, exploitation, and oppression.[144] Sexism, racism, and classism, several forms of oppression they experience, are examined in this section.

Gender Relations

The oppression of gender on adolescent females can be viewed in several ways. First, adolescent females receive discriminatory treatment because of society's disapproval of sexual activity. Etta A. Anderson provided evidence that society's disapproval of sexual activity on the part of adolescent females has resulted in their discriminatory treatment by the juvenile justice system.[145] Marvin D. Krohn, James P. Curry, and Shirley Nelson-Kilger's analysis of 10,000 police contacts in a Midwestern city over a thirty-year period found that adolescent females who were suspected of status offenses were more likely than their male counterparts to be referred to juvenile court for such offenses during all three decades.[146] Christy A. Visher's examination of 785 police–suspect encounters revealed that younger females received harsher punishment than older females. She noted that "police officers adopt a more paternalistic and harsher attitude toward younger females to deter any further violation or inappropriate sex-role behavior."[147] Chesney-Lind further found that police in Honolulu, Hawaii, were likely to arrest females for sexual activity and to ignore the same behavior among males.[148]

Jean Strauss observed that juvenile court judges commonly place adolescent females in confinement for even minor offenses because they assume that these females have engaged in sexual activity and believe that they deserve punishment.[149] Yona Cohn, in her study of the disposition recommendations of juvenile probation officers, found that females constituted only one-sixth of her sample of youths in a metropolitan court, yet they constituted one-fifth of the youths sentenced to institutional care. She attributed this uneven distribution to the fact that female adolescents frequently "violate" the sexual norms of the middle-class probation officers.[150] Furthermore, Roger's study of a training school for girls in Connecticut found the treatment staff greatly concerned with residents' sexual history and habits.[151] Both Rogers and Chesney-Lind also comment on juvenile courts and detention homes' practice of forcing females to undergo pelvic examinations and submit to extensive questioning about their sexual activities, regardless of the offenses with which they are being charged.[152]

Laurie Schaffner further observed that female adolescents' sexual behavior, orientation, and histories often bring them to the attention of juvenile authorities. However, for many of these girls, rather than being the problem, much of their delinquent behavior actually is a solution to larger life dilemmas. They are taught to be sexy and frequently solve nonsexual problems, such as family and educational troubles, with sexually related romantic solutions. In examining the sexual solutions that female adolescents devise, Schaffner found from her examination of runaway shelters, psychiatric facilities, and juvenile detention facilities across the United States that much of the state's response is ultimately a criminalization of young women's survival strategies. Schaffner went on to conclude that "girls' troubles with the law often take on sexual overtones as the state participates in a gendered sexualizing and criminalizing of female attention, concerns, bodies, desires, and actions."[153]

Second, Rosemary C. Sarri concluded that juvenile law has long penalized females. She claimed that the law may not be discriminatory on its face, but the attitudes and ideologies of juvenile justice practitioners administering it may result in violations of the equal protection clause of the Fourteenth Amendment, by leading them to commit females to longer sentences than males under the guise of "protecting" the female juvenile.[154] She added that "females have a greater probability of being detained and held for longer periods than males, even though the overwhelming majority of females are charged with status offenses."[155]

Randall G. Shelden and John Horvath further found that adolescent females who were reported to court for status offenses were more likely than their male counterparts to receive formal processing or a court hearing.[156] C. R. Mann's research on runaway youths revealed that adolescent females were more likely than adolescent males to be detained and to receive harsh sentences.[157] Chesney-Lind also concluded that adolescent females are more likely than adolescent males to be held for long periods of time in detention centers.[158]

Randall R. Beger and Harry Hoffman's examination of case files of juveniles ordered into detention by an Illinois juvenile court for technical probation violations found that females are confined in detention longer than males for disobeying probation rules.[159] Probation staff interviews revealed that both personal and contextual factors accounted for the gender-based disparity in the application of detention. Five basic factors were cited as responsible for gender inequality in the application of detention: (1) probation officers perceived female offenders to be more difficult to work with than males; (2) female offenders generally had more severe family dysfunctions than males; (3) conflicts with parents was an issue because parents reacted more negatively to minor deviations by daughters; (4) inadequate community-based resources were another factor cited for gender disparity in detention length; and (5) more females than males had had multiple social service interventions before probation.[160]

Robert Terry, in a study of 9,000 youths apprehended by police in a Midwestern city, found that females were more likely to be referred to the juvenile court than males and, if referred, were more likely to receive an institutional sentence.[161] Kristine Olson Rogers found that females' average period of confinement in Connecticut was longer than that of males.[162] Clemens Bartollas and Christopher M. Sieverdes, in a study of institutionalized youths in North Carolina, found that 80 percent of the confined females had committed status offenses and that they had longer institutional stays than the males.[163]

Third, the oppressive treatment of adolescent females is hidden in a couple of ways in the juvenile justice system. Following the decriminalization of status offenders in 1979, Anne Rankin Mahoney and Carol Fenster reported that many girls appeared in court for criminal-type offenses that had previously been classified as status offenses. They suggested that juvenile justice officials may have redefined these girls to be eligible for the kinds of protectionist sanctions that have been traditionally applied.[164]

Another expression of the gender bias found in this "hidden justice" is that certain provisions of the Juvenile Justice and Delinquency Prevention Act provide that status offenders found in contempt of court for violating a valid court order may be placed in secure detention facilities. This permits juvenile judges to use their contempt power to incarcerate repeat status offenders. If a runaway girl, for example, was ordered by the court to remain at home and she chose to run away again, she might be found in contempt of court—a criminal-type offense. There is reason to believe that juvenile judges apply their contempt power differentially more often to female status offenders than to their male counterparts.[165]

Finally, the early studies, especially, found that police officers, intake personnel, and judges supported a sexual double standard. Female status offenders, as previously indicated, were more likely than their male counterparts to be petitioned to formal court proceedings, to be placed in preadjudicatory detention confinements, and to be incarcerated in juvenile institutions. But at the same time, males who committed delinquent acts frequently received harsher treatment than their female counterparts. Consistent with what is known as the "chivalry" or "paternalism" thesis, police were less likely to arrest females suspected of property or person crimes. If arrested, female delinquents were less likely than male delinquents to be formally charged with criminal offenses, and, if charged, they were less likely than males to be incarcerated for their offenses.[166]

The middle-class white youth is likely to receive a less harsh response to her offense than would a lower-class or African American youth. Female offenders are likely to get a harsher response to minor offenses that may be sexual in nature than to other types of offenses.

On balance, some evidence does exist that the discriminatory treatment of female status offenders may be declining since passage of the Juvenile Justice and Delinquency Prevention Act.[167] No longer do many states send status offenders to training school with delinquents. But the long tradition of sexism in juvenile justice will be difficult to change. Due process safeguards for female delinquents, as well as for female status offenders, must be established to ensure them greater social justice in the juvenile justice system. The intrusion of extralegal factors into the decision-making process in the juvenile court has led to discrimination against the adolescent female that must become a relic of the past.

Influence of Class

As part of the female delinquent's "multiple marginality," class oppression is another form of exploitation experienced by this young person.[168] In a number of ways, powerful and serious problems of childhood and adolescence related to poverty set the stage for the young person's entry into homelessness, unemployment, drug use, survival sex and prostitution, and, ultimately, even more serious delinquent and criminal acts. Even those adolescents coming from middle-class homes may be thrust into situations of economic survival if they choose to run away from abusive environments.

Traditional theories also fail to address the life situations of girls on the economic and political margins, because researchers typically fail to examine or talk with these girls. For example, almost all urban females identified by police as gang members have been drawn from low-income groups.[169] Lee Bowker and Malcolm Klein's examination of data on girls in gangs in Los Angeles stated the importance of classism as well as racism:

> We conclude that the overwhelming impact of racism, sexism, poverty and limited opportunity structures is likely to be so important in determining the gang membership

and juvenile delinquency of women and girls in urban ghettos that personality variables, relations with parents and problems associated with heterosexual behavior play a relatively minor role in determining gang membership and juvenile delinquency.[170]

Class becomes important in shaping the lives of adolescent females in a number of other ways. Lower-class adolescent females tend to confront higher risk levels than middle- and upper-class adolescent females. They are more likely to have unsatisfactory experiences at school, to lack educational goals beyond high school, to experience higher rates of physical and sexual abuse, to deal with pregnancy and motherhood, to be involved in drug and alcohol dependency, to confront the risk of AIDS, and to lack supportive networks at home.[171] Although not all adolescent females at risk end up in the juvenile justice system, the likelihood of such a placement is greater for lower-class girls.

Racial Discrimination

Young women of color, as well as other minority girls, often grow up in contexts much different from those of their white counterparts. Signithia Fordham's article, "Those Loud Black Girls," showed that young African American women resisted accepting the Anglo norm of femininity by being loud or asserting themselves through their voices. Yet this behavior led to negative school experiences, and it does not take long for these juvenile females to discover that it is the quiet ones who do well in school. Some of this population decided to "pass for white" or to adopt more acceptable norms of femininity in order to be successful in the school experience. Others refused to adopt this survival strategy and their tool for liberation contributed to isolating or alienating them from school success.[172]

Because racism and poverty often go hand-in-hand, these girls are forced by their minority status and poverty to deal early and on a regular basis with problems of abuse, drugs, and violence.[173] They also are likely to be attracted to gang membership.[174] Covey, Menard, and Franzese summarized the effect of ethnicity on gang membership:

> Racial differences in the frequency of gang formation such as the relative scarcity of non-Hispanic, white, ethnic gangs may be explainable in terms of the smaller proportion of the non-Hispanic European American population that live in neighborhoods characterized by high rates of poverty, welfare dependency, single-parent households, and other symptoms that characterize social disorganization.[175]

Minority girls' strategies for coping with the problems of abuse, drugs, violence, and gang membership, as Chesney-Lind has noted, "tend to place them outside the conventional expectations of white girls," and it also increases the likelihood that they will come to the attention of the juvenile justice system.[176]

There is also the belief that girls of color enjoy the benefits of chivalry much less than white girls do. Middle-class white girls, especially those who have committed minor offenses, not sexual ones, may be given greater latitude by the police, court intake officers, and juvenile court judges than their minority counterparts who have committed similar offenses. As with male minority offenders, female minority offenders are likely to be viewed as more dangerous to society and more likely to require long-term institutionalization.

The Whole Is Greater Than the Sum of Its Parts

An examination of the experience of African American women reveals that it is not as though one form of oppression is piled on another. That is, the effects of the multiple oppressions of gender, class, and race are more than mere arithmetic.[177] Diane Lewis has noted that because feminist theories of women's inequality "focused exclusively upon the effects of sexism, they have been of limited applicability to minority women subjected to the constraints of both racism and sexism."[178] Lewis further noted that "black women . . . tended to see racism as a more powerful cause of their subordinate position than sexism and to view the women's liberation movement with considerable mistrust."[179]

The Combahee River Collective's statement in 1977 about African American feminism was also an important contribution. The group stated that it is committed to challenge all forms of "racial, sexual, heterosexual, and class oppression."[180] This group's multifaceted commitments reflected that it viewed these relations as inseparable:

> We believe that sexual politics under patriarchy is as pervasive in black women's lives as are the politics of class and race. We also often find it difficult to separate race from sex oppression because in our lives they are most often experienced simultaneously. We know that there is such a thing as racial-sexual oppression which is neither solely racial nor solely sexual, e.g., the history of black women by white men as a weapon of political repression.[181]

Daly summarized this argument by saying that "unless you consider all the key relations of inequality—class, race, gender (and also age and sexuality)—you have considered none." She added that "unless you consider the inseparability of these relations in the life of one person, you do not understand what we are saying."[182] Spelman conceptualized the independence and multiple nature of gender, class, and race by saying, "how one form of oppression is experienced is influenced by and influences how another form is experienced."[183]

This suggests that gender, class, and race are interlocking forms of oppression and that the whole is greater than the parts. Thus, female delinquents, like adult women, suffer the consequences of multiple oppressions as more than some form of simple additive experience.[184]

The Continuum of Care for Female Juvenile Offenders

Adolescent females on the economic and political margins, especially those who are processed by the juvenile justice system, share many problems with their male counterparts. They are likely to be poor, to come from disrupted and violent families, and to have problems in school. But, as previously suggested, these girls also encounter problems that are unique to their sex: notably, sexual assault and abuse, dating violence, unplanned pregnancy, and adolescent motherhood. Their ability to experience the problems they share with boys, as well as those they face as girls, are conditioned by their gender, class, and race.[185]

Thus, programming for girls needs to be shaped by their unique situations and to address the special problems they have in a gendered society. Unfortunately, traditional prevention and intervention programs have been shaped largely by what boys need. Girls will sometimes benefit from these programs and sometimes the problems will be totally ignored.[186]

Social Policy 7.3 is a continuum model that was adapted from one developed by the Florida Female Initiative in 1993. It is this type of continuum of care that promises to be the most effective way of meeting adolescent females' needs and of eliminating bias from within the juvenile justice system.[187]

SUMMARY

This chapter examined the ways in which the female delinquent is expected in her culture to think, feel, and act.[188] Female delinquency, like all other social behaviors, takes place in a world where gender still shapes the lives of adolescents in powerful ways.[189]

SOCIAL POLICY 3.2

Female-Based Continuum of Care Model

BASIC PRINCIPLES

1. Whenever possible, young women should be treated in the least restrictive programming environment, considering both treatment needs and concerns for public safety.
2. Whenever possible, young women should be treated in program environments that are close to their homes. This ensures maintenance of key family relationships, including female offenders' relationships with their own children, and allows for more effective transitional services.
3. All treatment programs in the continuum should focus on treatment modalities based on or consistent with specific principles of female development. Furthermore, they should all stress the role of the relationship between staff and young women and contain elements of societal advocacy.
4. Whenever possible, treatment programs at all levels of the continuum should be prepared to address the unique needs of parenting and pregnant young women.
5. Whenever possible, programs and/or individual treatment components should be single gender or all female. When coed services are provided, an effort should be made to keep the number of young women and the number of young men equal.

PREVENTION SERVICES

Prevention services should include programs or services that provide effective prenatal care for all pregnant young women; examine the nature and structure of the family; seek to prevent domestic violence and child sexual and physical abuse; offer early childhood education, particularly for at-risk girls; offer comprehensive health and sexuality information to young women in a single-gender setting; focus on career development and life skills, particularly in nontraditional female careers; strive to create a gender-equal school environment; and address the need for effective parenting skills for both mother and father.

EARLY INTERVENTION AND DIVERSION SERVICES

Early intervention and diversion services should include programs or services that offer gender-specific counseling, especially around issues of abuse; offer remedial or tutorial education in the context of young women's specific learning styles; offer early substance abuse intervention and education; offer pregnancy assistance and prevention services specifically addressing both economic and emotional issues; confront family violence issues such as domestic violence and child sexual and physical abuse; provide for effective intake and assessment procedures that address the specific risks and needs of young women; provide for case management systems that allow, whenever possible, for specially trained individuals to handle all female caseloads and to maintain their involvement as the young woman moves throughout the juvenile justice system; offer family-based wraparound services; offer alternative family placements such as all-female group homes and foster care, where foster care parents have received specialized training in female development; offer a range of nonresidential treatment options, such as all-female day treatment programs with a family intervention component, after-school and weekend intervention and community service programs, and all-female probation groups to address issues such as substance abuse, societal pressures, relationship violence, and so forth; and offer shelter care and respite residential care for short-term crisis intervention, particularly for young women who have run away from home or who have involvement in other status offenses.

JUVENILE JUSTICE INTERVENTION SERVICES

Juvenile justice intervention services should include programs and services such as all-female group treatment homes; specialized group treatment homes for pregnant or parenting young women; all-female, staff-secure halfway houses or other small, residential models for young women adjudicated delinquent; all-female, short-term, secure residential treatment facilities for more serious offenders; all-female, longer-term, secure residential treatment facilities that offer a full range of treatment services; transitional programs and services that take into account relational and service issues; and aftercare and parole services designed to effectively reintegrate young women into the community.

In its ideal model, this continuum functions as a circle rather than as a linear process, allowing young women reentering the community from the last intervention to access services near the beginning of the continuum in order to effectively reintegrate into society.

What are the advantages of having all-female facilities? What insights did you gain from this statement?

Source: "A Female-Based Continuum of Care Model," *Juvenile Female Offenders: A Status of the States Report* (Washington, D.C.: Office of Juvenile Justice and Delinquency Prevention, 1988), pp. 1–3.

The value of feminist theory ultimately is based on accepting the assumption that juvenile females are positioned in society in ways that produce vulnerability to victimization by males, including abuse and the negative affects of poverty. This position assumes, then, that behavior is gender contextualized and that it should be examined from this perspective.[190] Patriarchal society places a moral chastity belt around the behavior of adolescent females at home, in school, and in the community. Contextual analysis is helpful in understanding adolescent females' acceptance or rejection of their expected social norms and roles.

This chapter also presented a basic agreement and several disagreements among feminists concerning female delinquency in the United States. The basic area of agreement, among feminists as well as most nonfeminists, is that delinquency theories are preoccupied with why males commit delinquent acts. A major disagreement among feminists relates to whether separate theories are needed to explain female delinquency. On the one hand are those feminists who argue that separate theories are not needed to account for female and male delinquency. On the other hand, other feminists charge that existing delinquency theories are inadequate to explain female delinquency. These theories, adds this position, represent an androcentric perspective that cannot encompass the empirical results of available research.[191]

It is concluded that both positions are essentially correct. Considerable evidence supports the finding that female delinquency operates through the same sociological factors as male delinquency and that more variation exists within each gender than between the sexes. This position also charges that proposing the need for separate theories of female crime and delinquency actually falls into a brand of reductionism by assuming that the experiences of women are universal and distinct from those of men.[192] Yet a sound argument can be made that adolescent females' sexual and physical victimization at home and the relationship between these experiences and their crimes have been ignored, and therefore new theoretical efforts are needed to deal with these experiences. The second position is also correct that new theoretical efforts are needed to examine the "multiple marginality" of adolescent females.

The problems of sexism, racism, and class and their implications have been generally ignored by criminologists. As a result, writers on female delinquency have been more concerned with the adjustment of the adolescent female to society than with the extent and consequences of oppression in their lives. An examination of how the categories of gender, class, and race are interlocked will lead to needed insight about what the female delinquent faces in U.S. society. As Dorie Klein has indicated, "[T]he road from Lombroso to the present is surprisingly straight."[193]

This chapter further examined other assumptions about female delinquency. First, female delinquents are not treated more leniently by the juvenile justice system than are male delinquents; indeed, they actually receive harsher treatment from the system. Some evidence shows that adolescent girls are treated punitively for status-type offenses, especially when sex is involved, but that they receive the benefits of chivalry when they commit delinquent offenses. The assumption that females become involved in delinquency as they become more malelike is questionable, and there is little evidence to show that female delinquents are more abnormal and pathological than their male counterparts.

The evidence also shows that sexual offenses, incorrigibility, and running away do not make up the delinquent repertoire of girls; indeed, the offenses of male and female delinquents appear to be converging and to reflect a similar pattern. Social factors are not irrelevant to an understanding of female delinquency and appear to be more influential than psychological or biological factors. The women's liberation movement has not influenced the extent and nature of female delinquency, although more research is necessary to determine what concurrent social changes may be having an impact.

Finally, the progress recently made in understanding female delinquency promises that this area of inquiry may be a fruitful one in the future. For example, much more research is needed into sociological explanations, such as blocked opportunity, the influence of peers, and the impact of labeling. In addition, although adult women and adolescent female offenders appear to have much in common, the significant differences between them need further examination. Cross-cultural comparisons that show similar patterns of female delinquency in the United States and in other cultures should be used more fully. Furthermore, little has been discovered about female delinquents' perception of their treatment by the juvenile justice system or the impact of the justice system on these youths.

KEY TERMS

blocked opportunity, p. 196
"chivalry" factor, p. 195
feminist theory of delinquency, p. 203
masculinity hypothesis, p. 199

peer group influence, p. 199
sex-role socialization, p. 198
women's liberation movement, p. 197

CRITICAL THINKING QUESTIONS

1. Why has the study of female delinquency lagged behind the study of male delinquency?
2. Why has society been so sensitive to the sexual behavior of adolescent girls?
3. How do the delinquencies of males and females compare?
4. How has the social context affected the legal context in terms of female delinquency?
5. Why is the interlocking nature of gender, class, and race so important in understanding female delinquency?

WEB DESTINATIONS

Read about Power Control and Feminist Theories on the University of Missouri, St. Louis site.
http://www.umsl.edu/~rkeel/200/powcontr.html

Many links relating to the Women's Liberation Movement can be found on the Academic Information site.
http://www.academicinfo.net/uswomenrights.html

Read about biological factors associated with blocked opportunity on the Florida State University site.
http://www.criminology.fsu.edu/crimtheory/tedeschi/criminological.htm

Learn more about liberal feminism at this site.
http://newmedia.cgu.edu/feminism/webpagesara.html

Learn more about socialist feminism at this site.
http://www.dsausa.org/archive/Fem/socfem.html

Learn more about radical feminism at this site.
http://newmedia.cgu.edu/feminism/radfem.html

Go to this New Mexico State University site to learn more about feminist criminology.
Web.nmsu.edu/~kmentor/theory/feminist.htm

Check out Meda Chesney-Lind's homepage at this site.
http://home.hawaii.rr.com/chesneylind/

NOTES

1. Interviewed in 1988.
2. Kathleen Daly and Meda Chesney-Lind, "Feminism and Criminology," *Justice Quarterly* 5 (1988), pp. 497–538.
3. Coramae Richey Mann, *Female Crime and Delinquency* (University Station: University of Alabama Press, 1984), pp. 262–263.
4. Dorie Klein, "The Etiology of Female Crime: A Review of the Literature," in *The Criminal Justice System and Women*, 2d ed., edited by Barbara Raffel Price and Natalie J. Sokoloff (New York: McGraw-Hill, 1995), p. 31.
5. Carol Smart, *Women, Crime and Criminology: A Feminist Critique* (Boston: Routledge and Kegan Paul, 1976), p. 82.
6. Klein, "Afterword: Twenty Years Ago . . . Today," in *The Criminal Justice System and Women*, p. 47.
7. Ibid., p. 48.
8. Kathleen Daly and Meda Chesney-Lind, "Feminism and Criminology," *Justice Quarterly*, p. 498.
9. Paul Mazerolle, "Gender, General Strain, and Delinquency: An Empirical Examination," *Justice Quarterly* 15 (March 1998), p. 66.
10. Karen Heimer, "Gender, Race, and the Pathways to Delinquency: An Interactionist Perspective," in *Crime and Inequality*, edited by J. Hagan and R. Peterson (Stanford, Calif.: Stanford University Press, 1994), p. 164.
11. Office of Juvenile Justice and Delinquency Prevention, "Addressing Female Development in Treatment," *Juvenile Female Offenders: A Status of the States Report* (Washington, D.C.: U.S. Department of Justice, 1998), p. 1.
12. Kathleen Daly, "Looking Back, Looking Forward: The Promise of Feminist Transformation," in *The Criminal Justice System and Women*, p. 448.
13. Josephena Figueira-McDonough and Elaine Selo, "A Reformulation of the 'Equal Opportunity' Explanation of Female Delinquency," *Crime and Delinquency* 26 (1980), pp. 333–343; John Hagan, A. R. Gillis, and John Simpson, "The Class Structure of Gender and Delinquency: Toward a Power-Control Theory of Common Delinquent Behavior," *American Journal of Sociology* 90 (1985), pp. 1151–1178; and Douglas A. Smith and Raymond Paternoster, "The Gender Gap in Theories of Deviance: Issues and Evidence," *Journal of Research in Crime and Delinquency* 24 (1987), pp. 140–172.
14. Eileen Leonard, "Theoretical Criminology and Gender," in *The Criminal Justice System and Women*, pp. 55–70.
15. Meda Chesney-Lind, "Girls, Crime and Women's Place," *Crime and Delinquency* 35 (January 1989), pp. 5–29. For an update of this article, see Chesney-Lind, "Girls, Delinquency, and Juvenile Justice: Toward a Feminist Theory of Young Women's Crime," in *The Criminal Justice System and Women*, pp. 71–88.
16. Leonard, "Theoretical Criminology and Gender," in *The Criminal Justice System and Women*, p. 67.
17. Elizabeth V. Spelman, *Inessential Woman: Problems of Exclusion in Feminist Thought* (Boston: Beacon Press, 1989), p. 14.
18. Meda Chesney-Lind, *The Female Offender: Girls, Women, and Crime* (Thousand Oaks, Calif.: Sage Publications, 1997), p. 4.
19. Spelman, *Inessential Woman*, p. 123.
20. Irene Bergsmann, "Establishing a Foundation: Just the Facts," in *1994 National Juvenile Female Offenders Conference: "A Time for Change" Monograph* (Laurel, MD.: American Correctional Association, 1994), p. 5.
21. Ibid., p. 8.
22. Eileen Poe-Yamagata and Jeffrey A. Butts, *Female Offenders in the Juvenile Justice System: Statistic Summary* (Washington, D.C.: Office of Juvenile Justice and Delinquency Prevention, 1996), p. 2.
23. Office of Juvenile Justice and Delinquency Prevention, *Juvenile Female Offenders: A Status of the States* (Washington, D.C.: Department of Justice, 1998).
24. Ibid.
25. Ibid.
26. Ibid. In another study, adolescent females in an Illinois juvenile court are detained longer than their male counterparts for technical probation infractions; see Randall R. Beger and Harry Hoffman, "The Role of Gender in Detention Dispositions of Juvenile Probation Violators," *Journal of Crime and Justice* 21 (1998), pp. 173–188.
27. Office of Juvenile Justice and Delinquency Prevention, *Guiding Principles for Promising Female Programming: An Inventory of Best Practices* (Washington, D.C.: Department of Justice, 1998).
28. Mary Beyer, "Delinquent Girls: A Development Perspective," *Kentucky Children's Rights Journal* IX (Spring 2001), p. 17.
29. Ibid., p. 18.
30. Ibid., p. 19.
31. Stephanie J. Funk, "Risk Assessment for Juveniles on Probation," *Criminal Justice and Behavior* 26 (March 1999), p. 49. For the importance of peer relationships with girls, see also Daniel P. Mears, Matthew Ploeger, and Mark Warr, "Explaining the Gender Gap in Delinquency: Peer Influence and Moral Evaluations of Behavior," *Journal of Research in Crime and Delinquency* 35 (August 1998), pp. 251–266.
32. Joanne Belknap and Karen Holsinger, "An Overview of Delinquent Girls: How Theory and Practice Failed and the Need for Innovative Changes," in *Female Offenders: Critical Perspectives and Effective Interventions*, edited by R. T. Zaplin (Gaithersburg, MD.: Aspen Publishers, 1998), p. 1.
33. Leslie Acoca and K. Dedel, *No Place to Hide: Understanding and Meeting the Needs of Girls in the California Juvenile Justice System* (San Francisco: National Council on Crime and Delinquency, 1998).
34. Ibid.
35. Acoca, "Investing in Girls: A 21st Century Strategy," *Juvenile Justice* (October 1999), p. 5.
36. Ibid., p. 6.
37. Ibid., p. 7.
38. Ibid., p. 8.

39. Ibid., p. 9.

40. Ibid., p. 10.

41. Paul Mazerolle, "Gender, General Strain, and Delinquency: An Empirical Examination," p. 66.

42. Cesare Lombroso, *The Female Offender* (New York: Appleton, 1920).

43. Ibid., p. 122.

44. Ibid., p. 151.

45. Ibid.

46. Ibid., p. 109.

47. Dorie Klein, "The Etiology of Female Crime: A Review of the Literature," *Issues in Criminology* 8 (Fall 1973), p. 9.

48. Lombroso, *The Female Offender,* pp. 150–152.

49. J. Cowie, B. Cowie, and E. Slater, *Delinquency in Girls* (London: Heinemann, 1968).

50. Ibid., p. 17.

51. T. C. N. Gibbens, "Female Offenders," *British Journal of Hospital Medicine* 6 (1971), pp. 279–286.

52. Cowie, Cowie, and Slater, *Delinquency in Girls.*

53. Ibid.

54. Anne Campbell, *Girl Delinquents* (New York: St. Martin's Press, 1981), p. 46.

55. Ibid., p. 48.

56. W. I. Thomas, *Sex and Society* (Boston: Little, Brown, 1907).

57. Ibid.

58. W. I. Thomas, *The Unadjusted Girl* (New York: Harper, 1923).

59. Campbell, *Girl Delinquents,* p. 52.

60. Thomas, *The Unadjusted Girl,* p. 109.

61. Mann, *Female Crime and Delinquency,* p. 79.

62. Sigmund Freud, *An Outline of Psychoanalysis,* translated by James Strachey (New York: Norton, 1949), p. 278.

63. Sigmund Freud, *New Introductory Lectures on Psychoanalysis* (New York: Norton, 1933), p. 183.

64. Peter Bols, "Preoedipal Factors in the Etiology of Female Delinquency," *Psychoanalytic Study of the Child* 12 (1957), p. 232.

65. Peter Bols, "Three Typical Constellations in Female Delinquency," in *Family Dynamics and Female Sexual Delinquency,* edited by Otto Pollak (Palo Alto, Calif.: Science and Behavior Books, 1969), pp. 99–110.

66. Herbert H. Herskovitz, "A Psychodynamic View of Sexual Promiscuity," in *Family Dynamics and Female Sexual Development,* p. 89.

67. Ibid.

68. Otto Pollak, *The Criminality of Women* (Philadelphia: University of Pennsylvania Press, 1950), p. 8.

69. Ibid., pp. 125–39.

70. Gisela Konopka, *The Adolescent Girl in Conflict* (Englewood Cliffs, N.J.: Prentice-Hall, 1966).

71. These key factors from Konopka's *The Adolescent Girl in Conflict* are listed in Peter C. Kratcoski and John E. Kratcoski, "Changing Patterns in the Delinquent Activities of Boys and Girls: A Self-Reported Delinquency Analysis," *Adolescence* 18 (Spring 1975), pp. 83–91.

72. Clyde Vedder and Dora Somerville, *The Delinquent Girl* (Springfield, Ill.: Charles C. Thomas, 1970).

73. Ruth Morris, "Attitudes towards Delinquency by Delinquents, Nondelinquents, and Their Friends," *British Journal of Criminology* 5 (1966), pp. 249–265.

74. Mary Gray Riege, "Parental Affection and Juvenile Delinquency in Girls," *British Journal of Criminology* (January 1972), pp. 55–73.

75. Emmy E. Werner and Ruth S. Smith, *Kauai's Children Come of Age* (Honolulu: University Press of Hawaii, 1977).

76. William Wattenberg and Frank Saunders, "Sex Differences among Juvenile Offenders," *Sociology and Social Research* 39 (1954), pp. 24–31.

77. Interviewed in May 1982.

78. Interviewed in May 1982.

79. Peggy C. Giordano and Stephen A. Cernkovich, "Changing Patterns of Female Delinquency." Research proposal submitted to the National Institute of Mental Health, February 28, 1979), p. 24.

80. Klein, "The Etiology of Female Crime: A Review of the Literature," in *The Criminal Justice System and Women,* p. 45.

81. Talcott Parsons, "Age and Sex in the Social Structure of the United States," *American Sociological Review* 7 (October 1942); James S. Coleman, *The Adolescent Society* (New York: Free Press, 1961); Ruth Rittenhouse, "A Theory and Comparison of Male and Female Delinquency" (Ph.D. dissertation, University of Michigan, Ann Arbor, 1963).

82. Susan K. Datesman, Frank R. Scarpitti, and Richard M. Stephenson, "Female Delinquency: An Application of Self and Opportunity Theories," *Journal of Research in Crime and Delinquency* 12 (1975), p. 120.

83. Jeffery O. Segrave and Douglas N. Hastad, "Evaluating Three Models of Delinquency Causation for Males and Females: Strain Theory, Subculture Theory, and Control Theory," *Sociological Focus* 18 (January 1985), p. 13.

84. Stephen A. Cernkovich and Peggy C. Giordano, "Delinquency, Opportunity, and Gender," *Journal of Criminal Law and Criminology* 70 (1979), p. 150.

85. Mazzerolle, "Gender, General Strain, and Delinquency," pp. 66, 81.

86. Freda Adler, *Sisters in Crime* (New York: McGraw-Hill, 1975), p. 106.

87. Ibid., pp. 96–97.

88. Laura Crites, "Women Offenders: Myth vs. Reality," in *The Female Offender,* edited by Laura Crites (Lexington, Mass.: Lexington Books 1976), pp. 36–39.

89. Darrell J. Steffensmeier, "Crime and the Contemporary Woman: An Analysis of Changing Levels of Property Crime," *Social Forces* 57 (1978), pp. 566–584.

90. Joseph G. Weis, "Liberation and Crime: The Invention of the New Female Criminal," *Crime and Social Justice* 6 (1976), pp. 17–27.

91. Giordano and Cernkovich, "On Complicating the Relationship between Liberation and Delinquency," p. 468.

92. Giordano and Cernkovich, "Changing Patterns of Female Delinquency," p. 25.

93. Giordano, "Girls, Guys and Gangs: The Changing Social Context of Female Delinquency," *Journal of Criminal Law and Criminology* 69 (1978), p. 127.

94. Travis Hirschi, *Causes of Delinquency* (Berkeley: University of California Press, 1969).

95. William E. Thornton, Jr., Jennifer James, and William G. Doerner, *Delinquency and Justice* (Glenview, Ill.: Scott Foresman, 1982), p. 268.

96. Bobbi Jo Anderson, Malcolm D. Holmes, and Erik Ostresh, "Male and Female Delinquents' Attachments and

the Effects of Attachments on Severity of Self-Reported Delinquency." Paper presented to the Annual Meeting of the Academy of Criminal Justice Sciences, Albuquerque, New Mexico (March 1998).

97. Austin T. Turk, *Criminality and the Legal Order* (Chicago: Rand McNally, 1969), pp. 164–165.

98. Gary F. Jensen and Raymond Eve, "Sex Differences in Delinquency: An Examination of Popular Sociological Explanations," *Criminology* 13 (February 1976), pp. 427–448.

99. Adler, *Sisters in Crime.*

100. F. T. Cullen, K. M. Golden, and J. B. Cullen, "Sex and Delinquency: A Partial Test of the Masculinity Hypothesis," *Criminology* 15 (1977), pp. 87–104.

101. William E. Thornton and Jennifer James, "Masculinity and Delinquency Revisited," *British Journal of Criminology* 19 (July 1979), pp. 225–241.

102. Stephen Norland and Neal Shover, "Gender Roles and Female Criminality: Some Critical Comments," *Criminology* 15 (1977), pp. 86–104.

103. Giordano and Cernkovich, "On Complicating the Relationship between Liberation and Delinquency," pp. 467–481.

104. Thornton and James, in "Masculinity and Delinquency Revisited," found limited support for the merger of social control theory and the masculinity hypothesis in explaining delinquency in girls, but perhaps other combinations would be more fruitful.

105. Segrave and Hastad, "Evaluating Three Models of Delinquency Causation for Males and Females"; R. E. Johnson, *Juvenile Delinquency and Its Origins: An Integrated Approach* (New York: Cambridge University Press, 1979).

106. Giordano, "Girls, Guys and Gangs," p. 132.

107. Ibid.

108. Daniel P. Mears, Matthew Ploeger, and Mark Warr, "Explaining the Gender Gap in Delinquency: Peer Influence and Moral Evaluations of Behavior," *Journal of Research in Crime and Delinquency* 35 (August 1998), pp. 251–266.

109. John Hagan, John Simpson, and A. R. Gillis, "Class in the Household: A Power-Control Theory of Gender and Delinquency," *American Journal of Sociology* 92 (January 1987), pp. 788–816; John Hagan, A. R. Gillis, and John Simpson, "The Class Structure of Gender and Delinquency: Toward a Power-Control Theory of Common Delinquent Behavior," *American Journal of Sociology* 90 (1985), pp. 1151–1178.

110. Hagan et al., "Class in the Household," pp. 791–792.

111. Ibid., p. 793.

112. Ibid., pp. 813–814.

113. Simon I. Singer and Murray Levine, "Re-Examining Class in the Household and a Power-Control Theory of Gender and Delinquency." Paper presented at the Annual Meeting of the American Society of Criminology (November 1987), pp. 23–25.

114. Meda Chesney-Lind, "Girl's Crime and Woman's Place: Toward a Feminist Model of Female Delinquency." Paper presented at the Annual Meeting of the American Society of Criminology, Montreal, Canada (November 10–14, 1987), p. 16.

115. Dawn Jegllum Bartusch and Ross L. Matsueda, "Gender, Reflected Appraisals, and Labeling: A Cross-Group Test of an Interactionist Theory of Delinquency," *Social Forces* 75 (September 1996), p. 145.

116. Ibid.

117. Karen Heimer, "Gender, Interaction, and Delinquency: Testing a Theory of Differential Social Control," *Social Psychology Quarterly* 59 (1996), p. 57.

118. Giordano and Cernkovich, "Changing Patterns of Female Delinquency," pp. 24–28.

119. Mears et al., "Explaining the Gender Gap in Delinquency: Peer Influence and Moral Evaluations of Behavior," p. 251.

120. Ibid.

121. Personal correspondence with Meda Chesney-Lind assisted in the development of this section.

122. Chesney-Lind, "Girl's Crime and Woman's Place."

123. Sally S. Simpson, "Feminist Theory, Crime, and Justice," *Criminology* 27 (November 1989), p. 607.

124. Alison M. Jaggar and Paula Rothenberg, eds., *Feminist Frameworks* (New York: McGraw-Hill, 1984), pp. 83–84.

125. Piers Beirne and James Messerschmidt, *Criminology* (San Diego: Harcourt Brace Jovanovich, 1991), p. 518.

126. Josephina Figueira-McDonough with Elaine Selo, "A Reformulation of the Equal Opportunity Explanation of Female Delinquency," *Crime and Delinquency* 26 (1980), pp. 333–343.

127. Adler, *Sisters in Crime.*

128. Steven Schlossman and Stephanie Wallach, "The Crime of Precocious Sexuality: Female Juvenile Delinquency in the Progressive Era," *Harvard Educational Review* 48 (February 1978), p. 65.

129. Kristine Olson Rogers, "For Her Own Protection . . . Conditions of Incarceration for Female Juvenile Offenders in the State of Connecticut," *Law and Society Review* 7 (1973), pp. 223–246.

130. Beirne and Messerschmidt, *Criminology.*

131. Sheila Balkan, Ronald Berger, and Janet Schmidt, *Crime and Deviance in America: A Critical Approach* (Monterey, Calif.: Wadsworth, 1980), p. 211.

132. Eleanor M. Miller, *Street Woman* (Philadelphia: Temple University Press, 1986).

133. Ibid.

134. Ibid.

135. Beirne and Messerschmidt, *Criminology,* p. 519.

136. Jaggar and Rothenberg, *Feminist Frameworks,* p. 86.

137. Beirne and Messerschmidt, *Criminology,* p. 519.

138. Chesney-Lind, "Girl's Crime and Woman's Place," p. 17.

139. Ibid., p. 20.

140. Mimi Silbert and Ayala M. Pines, "Entrance into Prostitution," *Youth and Society* 13 (1982), p. 476.

141. Cited in Chesney-Lind, "Girl's Crime and Woman's Place."

142. Ibid., p. 19.

143. Spelman, *Inessential Woman,* p. 85.

144. Ibid., p. 51.

145. Etta A. Anderson, "The 'Chivalrous' Treatment of the Female Offender in the Arms of the Criminal Justice System: A Review of the Literature," *Social Problems* 23 (1976), pp. 350–357. See also Chesney-Lind, "Judicial Enforcement of the Female Sex Role: The Family Court

and Female Delinquency," *Issues in Criminology* 8 (1973), pp. 57–59; and Kristine Olson Rogers, "For Her Own Protection, pp. 223–246.

146. Marvin D. Krohn, James P. Curry, and Shirley Nelson-Kilger, "Is Chivalry Dead?" *Criminology* 21 (1983), pp. 417–439.

147. Christy A. Visher, "Gender, Police Arrest Decisions, and Notions of Chivalry," *Criminology* 21 (1983), pp. 5–28.

148. Chesney-Lind, "Judicial Enforcement of the Female Sex Role."

149. Jean Strauss, "To Be Minor and Female: The Legal Rights of Women Under Twenty-One, *Ms.* 1 (1972), p. 84.

150. Yona Cohn, "Criteria for Probation Officers' Recommendations to Juvenile Court," *Crime and Delinquency* 1 (1963), pp. 272–275.

151. Rogers, "For Her Own Protection."

152. Chesney-Lind, "Judicial Enforcement of the Female Sex Role"; Rogers, "For Her Own Protection."

153. Laurie Schaffner, "Female Juvenile Delinquency: Sexual Solutions and Gender Bias in Juvenile Justice." Paper presented to the Annual Meeting of the American Society of Criminology in Washington, D.C. (November 1998).

154. Rosemary C. Sarri, "Juvenile Law: How It Penalizes Females," in Crites, ed., *The Female Offender*, pp. 68–69.

155. Ibid., p. 76.

156. Randall G. Shelden and John Horvath, "Processing Offenders in a Juvenile Court: A Comparison of Males and Females." Paper presented at the Annual Meeting of the Western Society of Criminology, Newport Beach, Calif. (February-March, 1986).

157. Cited in Mann, *Female Crime and Delinquency.*

158. Chesney-Lind, "Girls and Status Offenses: Is Juvenile Justice Still Sexist?" *Criminal Justice Abstracts* 20 (March 1988), p. 152.

159. Randall R. Beger and Harry Hoffman, "The Role of Gender in Detention Dispositioning of Juvenile Probation Violaters," *Journal of Crime and Justice* 21 (1998), p. 173.

160. Ibid., pp. 183–184.

161. Robert Terry, "Discrimination in the Police Handling of Juvenile Offenders by Social Control Agencies," *Journal of Research in Crime and Delinquency* 14 (1967), p. 218.

162. Rogers, "For Her Own Protection."

163. Clemens Bartollas and Christopher M. Sieverdes, "Games Juveniles Play: How They Get Their Way," mimeograph. (1985).

164. Anne Rankin Mahoney and Carol Fenster, "Family Delinquents in a Suburban Court," in *Judge, Lawyer, Victim, Thief: Woman, Gender Roles and Criminal Justice,* edited by Nicole Hahn and Elizabeth Anne Stanko (Boston: Northeastern University Press, 1982).

165. Donna M. Bishop and Charles E. Frazier, "Gender Bias in Juvenile Justice Processing: Implications of the JJDP Act," *Journal of Criminal Law and Criminology* 82 (1992), p. 1167.

166. Ibid., p. 1164.

167. Ibid., p. 1165.

168. Chesney-Lind, *The Female Offender,* p. 4.

169. Ibid., p. 44

170. Lee Bowker and Malcolm Klein, "The Etiology of Female Juvenile Delinquency and Gang Membership: A Test of Psychological and Social Structural Explanations," *Adolescence* 13 (1983), pp. 750–751.

171. For many of these findings, see Joy G. Dryfoos, *Adolescents at Risk: Prevalence and Prevention* (New York: Oxford University Press, 1990).

172. Signithia Fordham, " 'Those Loud Black Girls': (Black) Women, Silence and Gender 'Passing' in the Academy," in *Beyond Black and White: New Faces and Voices in U.S. Schools,* edited by Maxine Seller and Lois Weis (Albany: University of New York Press, 1997), pp. 81–111.

173. Chesney-Lind, *The Female Offender,* p. 23.

174. Finn-Aage Esbensen and L. Thomas Winfree, "Race and Gender Differences between Gang and Nongang Youths: Results from a Multisite Survey," *Justice Quarterly* 15 (September 1998), p. 510.

175. H. C. Covey, Scott Menard, and R. Franzese, *Juvenile Gangs,* 2d ed. (Springfield, Ill.: Charles C. Thomas, 1997), p. 240.

176. Chesney-Lind, *The Female Offender,* p. 23.

177. Spelman, *Inessential Woman,* p. 123.

178. For this discussion on African American women I am indebted to Kathleen Daly, "Class–Race–Gender: Sloganeering in Search of Meaning," *Social Justice* 20 (1993), pp. 58. For Lewis's quote, see Diane K. Lewis, "A Response to Inequality: Black Women, Racism, and Sexism," *Signs: Journal of Women in Culture and Society* 3 (1977), p. 339.

179. Lewis, "A Response to Inequality," p. 339.

180. "The Combahee River Collective Statement," in *Capitalist Patriarchy and the Case for Socialist Feminism,* edited by Zilah Eisenstein (New York: Monthly Review Press, 1979), pp. 362–372.

181. Ibid., p. 365.

182. Daly, "Class–Race–Gender," p. 58.

183. Spelman, *Inessential Woman,* p. 123.

184. Ibid.

185. Chesney-Lind, *The Female Offender,* pp. 89–90.

186. Ibid., p. 90.

187. Cited in "A Female-Based Continuum of Care Model," *Juvenile Female Offenders: A Status of the States Report,* p. 1.

188. Spelman, *Inessential Woman,* p. 14.

189. Chesney-Lind, *The Female Offender,* p. 5.

190. Donald J. Shoemaker, *Theories of Delinquency: An Examination of Delinquent Behavior,* 3d ed. (New York: Oxford University Press, 1996), p. 242.

191. G. David Curry, "Female Gang Involvement," *Journal of Research in Crime and Delinquency* 35 (February 1998), p. 115.

192. Sally S. Simpson and Lori Ellis, "Doing Gender: Sorting Out the Caste and Crime Conundrum," *Criminology* 33 (1995), p. 47.

193. Dorie Klein, "The Etiology of Female Crime: A Review of the Literature," *Crime and Social Justice: Issues in Criminology* (Fall 1973), p. 5.

chapter 8

THE FAMILY AND DELINQUENCY

OBJECTIVES

After reading this chapter, students will be able to answer the following questions:

- How do problems in the family affect adolescents?

- What are the most important factors in the family that affect the likelihood of delinquent behavior?

- What are the main forms of child abuse and neglect?

- What is the relationship of child abuse and neglect to delinquency and status offenses?

- How does the child welfare or juvenile justice system handle charges of child abuse?

A fifteen-year-old girl talks about the conflict she has with her mother:

My mom and I can't stay in the same house without jumping down each other's throat. My dad has had to pull my mom off of me a couple of times. She really scared me one time. I can't remember what we were arguing about, but I started to take off out the back door. She caught me, knocked me against the cupboard. Dad pulled her off. You get used to it after a while and learn how far you can push her. There isn't a whole lot I can do about it. She is my mom, and I've got to do what she says.[1]

If you were the social worker for the state's agency that is committed to protecting children, would you recommend that this child be taken from the home? How far could a parent go before you would take the child out of the home?

The family represents the primary agent for the socialization of children. The family is the first social group a child encounters and is the group with which most children have their most enduring relationships. The family gives a child his or her principal identity and even his or her name. The family teaches social roles, moral standards, and society's laws, and the family disciplines children who fail to comply with those norms and values. The family either provides for or neglects children's emotional, intellectual, and social needs; and as suggested in the above quote, the neglect of these basic needs can have a profound effect on the shaping of a child's attitudes and values.

This chapter discusses adolescents and family problems, the relationship between the family and delinquency, and the types and impact of child abuse and neglect.

How Adolescence and Family Problems Affect Delinquent Behavior

Divorced and single-parent families, blended families, out-of-wedlock births, homelessness, unemployment, alcohol and drug abuse, and violence are some of the family problems that affect adolescents today. Adolescents experiencing such problems are at a high risk of becoming involved in socially unacceptable behaviors.

The high divorce rate in the United States translates into an increasing number of single-parent families. Since 1970, the proportion of American households who have children living with both parents has declined significantly. In 1970, 64 percent of African American children lived with two parents, as compared with 35 percent in 1997. The comparable figures for white children are 90 percent and 74 percent, respectively.[2] Even more sobering, as many as 40 percent of white children and 75 percent of African American children will experience divorce or separation before they reach sixteen, and many of these children will experience multiple family disruptions over the process of their childhood.[3]

What needs to be addressed is the relationship between the impact of family transitions and problem behaviors, such as delinquency and drug use. An examination of the Rochester, Denver, and Pittsburgh studies reveals a consistent relationship between a greater number of family transitions and a higher level of drug use and delinquent behavior. The magnitude of the differences between juveniles with no family transitions and those with many family transitions was similar across the three cities.[4]

One problem of living in a single-parent household is the increased probability of poverty. For example, 11 percent of all American families are under the federal poverty line, but 46 percent of female-headed households with children live in poverty.[5] Economic hardship and lack of access to opportunity tend to undermine marital and parental functioning. Furthermore, adolescents who experience family transitions may have difficulty managing anger and other negative emotions that may contribute to their involvement with delinquency or drugs.

The majority of divorced parents remarry, and adolescents in these family units must learn to adjust to a new parental figure. This blended family places stress on the natural parent, the stepparent, and the children. Typically, the mother has custody of her children and the stepfather lives with his wife's children. His biological children, if any, usually visit the home on an occasional or regular basis. Few adolescents escape the experience of a blended family without feeling resentment, rejection, and confusion. Some stepparents even subject their stepchildren to emotional, physical, or sexual abuse.

Pregnancy is a life experience that many adolescents face. Pregnancy is sometimes wanted and adolescents may be married, but, more often than not, pregnancy leads to abortion or out-of-wedlock births. More than one million teen pregnancies take place each year in the United States; 52 percent bear children, about one-third abort their pregnancies, and 14 percent miscarry. Seventy-two percent of these children are born out of wedlock.[6] Typically unequipped for motherhood, teenage mothers suffer the disadvantages of reduced educational achievement, subsequent births that are close together and unplanned, low-status jobs, low incomes, and sometimes long-term welfare dependency. The children of teenage parents experience such adverse effects as lower achievement, behavioral and emotional problems, high risk of becoming teenage parents themselves, and being cast in roles that will prevent them from ever becoming successful.[7] Indeed, Rebecca A. Maynard and Eileen M. Garry found that "the sons of adolescent mothers are 2.7 times more likely to be incarcerated than the sons of mothers who delay childbearing until their early 20s."[8]

Homelessness is a phenomenon that shapes the lives of as many as 100,000 to 500,000 children a year in the United States.[9] A study of children living in temporary housing estimated that 36 percent of the middle-school-age children failed to attend school on a regular basis.[10] Homelessness, regardless of a child's age, exposes him or her to settings in which there is a high prevalence of substance abuse, promiscuous sex, pornography, prostitution, and crime.

Unemployment affects all members of the family unit in the United States. Between November 1991 and January 1994, the number of people who were officially designated as long-term unemployed—meaning that they had been out of work for six months or longer—rose from 1.3 to 1.7 million, a 31 percent increase.[11] In 1994, 6.8 percent of Americans were unemployed, idling nearly 10 million workers. Another one million were discouraged from attempting to find a job, and three million who wanted and needed full-time employment were forced to work part-time.[12] In some urban neighborhoods, 40 to 50 percent of the workforce is unemployed. Unemployment rates are typically higher for women than for men, higher for African American and other minority groups than for whites, and higher for young workers.[13]

Adolescents whose family members have substance abuse problems also have their sad stories to tell. Many of these youngsters experience neglect or abuse, and economic hardship is a common factor in these family settings. The *Uniform Crime Reports* revealed that there were 1,042,334 arrests in 2000 for drug abuse violations, 915,931 for driving under the influence, and 435,672 for liquor laws violations.[14]

Violence was a major characteristic of the family in past times, and it is no stranger to family life today. Domestic violence is rapidly becoming recognized as a pervasive problem that affects nearly one-third of the cohabiting population.[15] The National Family Violence Resurvey, based on interviews with a national probability sample of 6,002 households, found that just over 16 percent, or one of six U.S. couples, experienced a physical assault during 1985. Significantly, of the 8.7 million households where such violence occurred, 3.4 million assaults had a relatively high risk of causing injury.[16] More recent studies have found that as many as 60 percent of violent families repeat their violence in a given year.[17] Given the widespread nature of violence within the family, it is not surprising that some parents also act out their aggression on their children. In Theory and Research 8.1 Richard J. Gelles discusses some of the contributory factors in family violence.

The Relationship between the Family and Delinquency

The importance given the family as a contributing factor to delinquency has varied through the years. Karen Wilkinson has classified the attention given to the family into three periods: 1900–1932, 1933–1950, and 1950–1972. In the first period the role of the family as a contributing factor to delinquent behavior was emphasized. A broken home was considered a major cause of delinquency, and a great deal of research was done to measure its influence. In the second period the family was minimized in comparison to the school, social class standing, and influence of peers. In the third period there was re-

THEORY AND RESEARCH 8.1

Interview with Richard J. Gelles

Question: What are the most important factors contributing to family violence?

Gelles: That is a complicated question because of the emotions that child abuse and wife abuse arouse in people; people seem to want to search for simple answers. In the 1960s the simple answer was only somebody who was mentally disturbed would abuse a child or abuse a wife. In the 1970s the popular theory was that family violence (wife abuse or child abuse) was confined to poor people or black people in the community. The other popular notion was the deterministic statement that people who were abused as children grow up to be child abusers and wife abusers. There is a consistent trend toward oversimplification in the field. With that preface, I am now going to oversimplify.

I think that child abuse and wife abuse have multidimensional causes—psychological causes, social-psychological causes, social structural causes, and sociocultural causes. If I were pressed to break that multitude of causes down into simple categories, I would say that one was the cultural attitude toward violence in the United States, which accepts violence as both an instrumental act—a way of solving a problem—and as an acceptable way of expressing oneself. From our television, to corporal punishment being allowed in schools, to our lack of gun control, to our acceptance of capital punishment, to the acceptance of spanking of children in the home, to the acceptance of hitting wives under certain conditions, there is a learning environment and a moral correctness ascribed to certain forms of family violence.

The second factor would be (drawing from Merton's paradigm of goals and means) that the cultural goal of being a father, mother, husband, and wife is consistent across the country. Everyone has essentially the same goal, but few people can reach it. You have to be a perfect father, a perfect mother, a loving husband, a loving wife, and those people who are deprived of the resources to reach those goals of family sanctity and sacredness tend to be more likely to adopt the violent way of dealing with family members. If I, for instance, were under considerable stress, I might say to my wife, "Let's get a babysitter for the children and go away for the weekend." I have the economic resources to do that. Should I not have those economic resources, I think it might be different.

Theoretically, I approach family violence with an exchange/social control theory. I borrow the exchange theory from family sociology and the social control approach from Hirschi's social control perspective on juvenile delinquency. The oversimplified version of this theoretical approach is that people abuse family members because they *can*. If you were a student reading this textbook and you felt you had been treated unfairly by your professor and you were really angry, the chances are you would not take a swing at your professor because (1) your professor could have you thrown out of school, (2) the professor might hit you back and hurt you, and (3) the professor might call the police and they would come and arrest you. If you have the same anger toward a family member, none of these costs are going to be inflicted upon you. You don't get fired from a family. The police very rarely come quickly, and when they do come, they are much more interested in restoring order than in making an arrest. People don't lose social status for being violent toward family members. You do not see people intervening when children are spanked at supermarkets. So there is a general lack of cost to family members today for being violent toward family members. The attitudes of the police and the criminal justice system also reduce the costs of being violent. Thus I think that we are violent as families because there is a structural and a moral situation that allows us to hit family members which would then prohibit us from hitting people at work or citizens on the street.

What is your response to Gelles's statement? What would you add?

Source: Richard J. Gelles is professor of sociology and anthropology at the University of Rhode Island. He is the author of *The Violent Home* and *Family Violence*, and coauthor of *Behind Closed Doors: Violence in the American Family.*

vived interest in the family. Wilkinson attributes this to other variables studied as causes of delinquency that did not yield conclusive findings. Researchers in this post-1950 period also broadened their inquiry to encompass the nature of the relationship between parents and children, parental discipline and supervision, and family integration.[18]

The important role of the family in terms of understanding delinquent behavior is seen in the fact that most theories of delinquency rely heavily on the parent-child relationship and parent practices to explain delinquency.[19] The theoretical emphasis on family processes, in turn, is supported by findings that family relationships and parenting skills are directly or indirectly related to delinquent behavior.[20]

The structure versus function controversy has been one of the important and continuing debates on the relationship between family and delinquency. The structural perspective focuses on factors such as parental absence, family size, and birth order, and the functional or quality-of-life view argues for the significance of parent-child interaction, the degree of marital happiness, and the amount and type of discipline.[21]

Judith Rick Harris challenged this position with her 1995 provocative claim that parental behavior has few, if any, enduring effects on the development of children. She claims that youth's conduct, including delinquency, is predominantly influenced by peers or group socialization. The media has been struck by her central thesis that parenting does not affect children's behavior, and she has been featured in a number of lead stories about her "truly revolutionary idea." Her 1998 book, *The Nurture Assumption: Why Children Turn Out the Way They Do—Parents Matter Less than You Think and Peers Matter More,* which was written for the trade market, was widely received.[22]

The Broken Home

Some empirical evidence supports the commonly accepted notion that delinquency results from a **broken home**.[23] In 1924, George B. Mangold declared, "The broken home is probably the single most important cause of delinquency."[24] Margaret Hodgkiss's 1933 study in Cook County (Chicago) also revealed a strong difference in the incidence of broken homes among delinquents compared to nondelinquents: 66.9 percent of delinquents and 44.8 percent of nondelinquents had broken homes.[25] Glueck and Glueck's classic study, which compared 500 delinquents and 500 nondelinquents, further reported stronger evidence of the importance of broken homes: 60.4 percent of delinquents and 34.2 percent of nondelinquents came from broken homes.[26]

More recent studies, however, have questioned the relationship between broken homes and delinquency. F. I. Nye's highly respected study of the family and research by R. A. Dentler and L. J. Monroe found no significant direct relationship between delinquency and family composition.[27] Lawrence Rosen recalculated statistical relationships for eleven different studies of broken homes and male delinquency conducted between 1932 and 1968 and discovered that virtually all the studies yielded only very weak positive relationships between broken homes and delinquency.[28] Both Patricia Van Voorhis and colleagues and Margaret Farnworth found that the effects of the broken home on most forms of delinquency are negligible.[29] James Q. Wilson and R. J. Herrnstein, in reviewing the research on delinquency and single-parent homes, concluded that findings have been inconclusive, inconsistent, and ambiguous.[30]

Other researchers have shed further light on this debate. Richard S. Sterne, Jackson Toby, and T. P. Monahan reported that the factor of broken homes affects adolescent females more than males.[31] Susan K. Datesman and Frank R. Scarpitti found that the relationship for adolescent females between broken homes and delinquency depends on the type of offense involved.[32] Ross L. Matsueda and Karen Heimer's study revealed that broken homes have a larger impact on delinquency among African Americans than on other racial groups.[33] Van Voorhis and colleagues found only a moderate relationship between broken homes and status offenses.[34] Joseph F. Rankin also reported that, except for running away and truancy, the relation between broken homes and delinquency is negligible.[35] But Marvin D. Free Jr. concluded that the connection between broken homes and delinquency is more evident for status offenses, such as incorrigibility, truancy, and running away, than it is for more serious offenses.[36]

Karen Wilkinson noted that research using self-report techniques has generally not shown the single-parent home to be a major factor in the cause of delinquency, whereas studies using official statistics have.[37] Some researchers maintain that divorce is more likely to predispose a child to delinquency than the death of a parent,[38] but Steven A. Cernkovich and Peggy C. Giordano's study failed to distinguish the effects of family factors across types of parental configurations.[39] Both Travis Hirschi and Martin Gold found the greatest rate of delinquency in families with stepfathers.[40] R. J. Chilton and G. E. Markle initially found that children living in broken homes are more frequently involved in status and delinquent offenses, but when they reclassified the families on the basis of income, they found that economics appeared to have more to do with the rate of referral to the juvenile court than did family composition.[41] Finally, some research indicates that the juvenile justice system in some jurisdictions may be more likely to institute formal processing against children from broken homes.[42]

L. Edward Wells and Rankin's meta-analysis of fifty published studies dealing with broken homes and delinquency found that

1. The prevalence of delinquency in broken homes is 10–15 percent higher than in intact homes.
2. The correlation between broken homes and juvenile delinquency is stronger for minor forms of juvenile misconduct (status offenses) and weakest for serious forms of criminal behavior (such as theft and interpersonal violence).
3. The type of family break seems to affect juvenile delinquency [because] the association with delinquency is slightly stronger for families broken by divorce or separation than by death of a parent.
4. There are no consistent or appreciable differences in the impact of broken homes between girls and boys or between black youths and white youths.
5. There are no consistent effects of the child's age at breakup on the negative effects of the separated family.
6. There is no consistent evidence of the often cited negative impact of stepparents on juvenile delinquency.[43]

Birth Order

Some evidence supports the significance of **birth order** in that delinquent behavior is more likely to be exhibited by middle children than first or last children. The first child, according to this view, receives the undivided attention and affection of parents, and the last child benefits from the parents' experience in raising children as well as from the presence of other siblings, who serve as role models. The Gluecks, Nye, and William McCord, Joan McCord, and Irving Zola all reported that intermediate children were more likely to be delinquents.[44] Linda J. Waite and Lee A. Lillard found that children were initially stabilizing and later destabilizing in a marriage, because "firstborn children increase the stability of marriage through their preschool years," but "older children and children born before marriage significantly increase chances of disruption."[45]

Family Size

Research findings on **family size** generally reveal that large families have more delinquency than small families do. Hirschi explained the higher rate of delinquency with middle children as the result of family size rather than of birth position.[46] Rolf Loeber and Magda Stouthamer-Loeber suggested that a number of processes may explain why delinquency rates are greater in large families. First, parents in large families tend to have more difficulty disciplining and supervising their children than do parents with smaller families. Second, some parents with large families delegate childrearing to older siblings, who may not be equipped to execute this task. Third, large families frequently are more exposed to illegitimacy, poverty, and overcrowding.[47]

Delinquent Siblings or Criminal Parents

Some evidence indicates that siblings learn delinquency from others in the family. The Gluecks reported that a much higher proportion of delinquents than nondelinquents had **delinquent siblings** or criminal mothers and fathers.[48] Joan McCord's follow-up of the Cambridge-Somerville (Massachusetts) Youth Study revealed that the sons of fathers who had serious criminal records were likely to be raised in poor families and experience bad childrearing, which increased their risk for an early first conviction.[49] David P. Farrington also found that the delinquency of siblings is a predictor of delinquency.[50] Janet L. Lauritsen further found that delinquency is predicted equally well "by the offending of an older sibling, the offending of a younger sibling, or by the average level of offending among all adolescents in the household."[51]

Quality of Home Life

Studies have generally reported that poor quality of home life, measured by marital adjustment and harmony within the home, affects the rate of delinquent behavior among children more than whether or not the family is intact. Nye found the happiness of the marriage to be the key to whether or not children become involved in delinquent behavior.[52] The Gluecks reported good marital relationships and strong family cohesiveness in homes of more nondelinquents than delinquents.[53] William McCord and colleagues and R. C. Audry further concluded that well-integrated and cohesive families produce fewer delinquents than do less-well-adjusted families.[54] Randy L. Lagrange and Helen R. White found that parental love, especially for youths in the middle of their adolescence, functions as a "psychological anchor" to conformity.[55] Paul Howes and Howard J. Markman's longitudinal study found that the quality of the parents' relationship before marriage as well as after a child is born is related to child functioning.[56] McCord's thirty-year follow-up study found that maternal behavior directly influenced delinquency and, subsequently, adult criminality, but parental interaction with the family appeared "to have a more direct influence on the probability of adult criminal behavior."[57]

Family Rejection

Several studies have found a significant relationship between **rejection by parents** and delinquent behavior. S. Kirson Weinberg found that parents of delinquents had rejected their children.[58] McCord, McCord, and A. Howard reported that some rejecting parents often exhibited aggressive behavior as well.[59] Loeber and Stouthamer-Loeber's review of the literature found that twelve of fifteen studies reported a significant relation between rejection and delinquency.[60] Nye found that the father's rejection is more often significantly related to delinquency than the mother's rejection.[61] But a number of other studies concluded that rejection from mothers is more related to involvement with delinquency.[62]

McCord, McCord, and Zola reported that only a small percentage of delinquents had affectionate relationships with parents.[63] The Gluecks and Audry also found that parental affection is less apparent in the homes of delinquents than in those of nondelinquents.[64] W. L. Slocum and C. L. Stone further discovered that children from affectionate homes tend to be more conforming in behavior.[65] Richard E. Johnson found that young people report stronger ties to the mother, but it is the father-child bond that is more predictive of their involvement in crime, especially among the boys.[66] Rosen's longitudinal study of African American and white boys residing in Philadelphia found that lower delinquency rates were reported for African American youths who had high father-son interaction and came from small families.[67] Rankin and Roger Kern found that children who are strongly attached to both parents have a lower probability of delinquency than do those who are attached to only one parent.[68]

Discipline in the Home

Inadequate **supervision and discipline** in the home have been commonly cited to explain delinquent behavior. Hirschi found that the rate of delinquency increased with the incidence of mothers employed outside the home. He attributed this finding to unemployed mothers spending more time supervising their children's activities and behavior.[69] Nye found a slight causal relationship between the employment of the mother and delinquent behavior.[70] But the Gluecks' study failed to reveal a strong association between working mothers and delinquent behavior.[71] G. F. Jensen and R. Eve further found that the degree of supervision within the home was not a significant factor in the amount of delinquent activity of children.[72] Loeber and Stouthamer-Loeber concluded from their review of the literature that "the evidence suggests a stronger relation between lack of supervision and official delinquency than between lack of supervision and self-reported delinquency."[73]

Nye reported that strict, lax, and unfair discipline were all associated with high rates of delinquent behavior. He also found that the disciplinary role of the father was more closely related to delinquent behavior than was the disciplinary role of the mother.[74] More recently, Loeber and Stouthamer-Loeber, as well as James Snyder and Gerald Patterson, also concluded that both strict and punitive as well as lax and erratic disciplinary styles are related to delinquent behavior.[75] McCord, McCord, and Zola further found a relationship between inconsistent discipline and delinquent behavior.[76] Nye added that the disciplinary role of the father was more closely related to delinquent behavior than was the disciplinary role of the mother.[77]

John Paul Wright and Francis T. Cullen, in using data from the National Longitudinal Survey of Youth, advanced the concept of "parental efficacy" as an adaptation of Robert Sampson and colleagues' "collective efficacy" (See Chapter 4). Wright and Cullen employed "parental efficacy" because they wanted to evaluate the relationship between parental controls and supports in reducing delinquency with children. They found that support and control are intertwined and that parental efficacy exerts substantive effects on reducing children's inappropriate behaviors.[78]

Evaluation of Family Factors and Delinquency

Conflicting findings make drawing conclusions about the relationship between delinquency and the family difficult, but the following observations have received wide support:

1. Family conflict and poor marital adjustment are more likely to lead to delinquency than is the structural breakup of the family.
2. Children who are intermediate in birth order and who are part of large families appear to be involved more frequently in delinquent behavior, but this is probably related more to parents' inability to provide for the emotional and financial needs of their children than to birth position or family size.
3. Children who have delinquent siblings or criminal parents may be more prone to delinquent behavior than those who do not.
4. Rejected children are more prone to delinquent behavior than those who have not been rejected. Children who have experienced severe rejection are probably more likely to become involved in delinquent behavior than those who have experienced a lesser degree of rejection.
5. Consistency of discipline within the family seems to be important in deterring delinquent behavior.

6. As the Gluecks predicted fifty years ago, lack of mother's supervision, father's and mother's erratic/harsh discipline, parental rejection, and parental attachment appear to be the most important predictors of serious and persistent delinquency.[79] John H. Laub and Robert J. Sampson's reanalysis of the Gluecks' data found that mother's supervision, parental attachment, and parental styles of discipline are the most important predictors of serious and persistent delinquency.[80] Similarly, Loeber and Stouthamer-Loeber's meta-analysis identified parent-child involvement and supervision, child–parent rejection and discipline practices, parental criminality and deviant attitudes, and marital conflict and absence as the four dimensions of family functioning related to delinquency.[81]

7. The rate of delinquency appears to increase with the number of unfavorable factors in the home. That is, multiple handicaps within the family are associated with a higher probability of juvenile delinquency than are single handicaps.[82] (See Social Policy 8.2 Strengthening America's Families).

Child Abuse and Neglect

Child abuse and **neglect** are usually divided into three areas: neglect, physical and emotional abuse, and sexual abuse. Kathleen M. Heide has found it helpful to distinguish among three types of neglect (physical, medical, and emotional) and four types of abuse (physical, sexual, verbal, and psychological).[83] According to Heide, the types of abuse and neglect are frequently interrelated; one type of child maltreatment often leads to another. For example, children who are sexually abused by parents become victims of neglect when their parents fail to seek medical attention for sexually transmitted diseases or resulting injuries.[84] Barbara Tatem Kelley, Terence P. Thornberry, and Carolyn A. Smith have defined seven types of child maltreatment: physical abuse, sexual abuse, physical neglect, lack of supervision, emotional maltreatment, educational maltreatment, and moral-legal maltreatment.[85] For a definition of and the severity of each type, see Table 8.1.

Child abuse and neglect, like the other family problems addressed in this chapter, have a profound influence on shaping the behavior and attitudes of adolescents and adults.[86] B. F. Steele's study of 200 juvenile first-time offenders found that between 70 and 80 percent had a history of neglect and abuse.[87] Joan McCord's longitudinal study of 253 males revealed that abused, neglected, and rejected children had significantly higher rates of delinquency than did nonabused children (10 percent, 15 percent, and 29 percent versus 7 percent, respectively). Her study also found that half of the abused or neglected adolescent males as adults had been convicted of serious crimes or had become alcoholics or mentally ill.[88] José Alfaro found that 50 percent of the children reported to area hospitals as abused children later were petitioned to the juvenile court.[89]

Cathy Spatz Widom's initial study of abuse and neglect found that 29 percent of those abused and neglected as children had a nontraffic criminal record as adults, compared with 21 percent of the control group.[90] Widom and Michael G. Maxfield's updated study, which followed 1,575 cases from childhood through adolescence and into young adulthood, was able to examine the long-term consequences of abuse and neglect.[91] They found that

1. Being abused or neglected as a child increased the likelihood of arrest as a juvenile by 59 percent, as an adult by 29 percent, and for a violent crime by 30 percent;
2. Maltreated children were younger at the time of their first arrest, committed nearly twice as many offenses, and were arrested more frequently;
3. Physically abused and neglected (versus sexually abused) children were the most likely to be arrested later for a violent crime;

SOCIAL POLICY 8.2

Strengthening America's Families

To provide parents with the critical skills necessary to enhance family resilience and decrease risk factors, the Office of Juvenile Justice and Delinquency Prevention (OJJDP) launched its Strengthening America's Family Initiatives in the mid-1980s. In 1999, OJJDP joined with the Center for Substance Abuse Prevention (CSAP) and the University of Utah to continue and expand the initiative. A search for best practices found a number of effective family-focused prevention strategies that target a number of family needs and help numerous family types. These 35 identified programs vary from structured programs with standardized written curricula to open-ended support groups.

Best Practices, 1999

Program	Type	Targeted Age
EXEMPLARY I		
Functional Family Therapy	Family therapy	6–18
Helping the Noncompliant Child	Parent training	3–7
The Incredible Years: Parents, Teachers, and Children Training Series	Comprehensive	3–10
Multisystemic Therapy (MST)	Comprehensive	10–18
Preparing for the Drug Free Years	Parent training	8–14
Strengthening Families Program	Family skills training	6–10
Treatment Foster Care	Parent training	12–18
EXEMPLARY II		
Adolescent Transitions Program	Parent training	11–18
Brief Strategic Family therapy	Family therapy	0–18
Multidimensional Family Therapy	Family therapy	11–18
Parenting Wisely	Parent training	6–18
Prenatal and Early Childhood-Nurse Home Visitation Program	In-home support	0–5
Raising a Thinking Child: I Can Problem Solve Program for Families	Parent training	4–7
Strengthening Families Program: for Parents and Youth 10–14	Family skills training	10–14
MODEL		
Creating Lasting Family Connections	Parent training	9–17
DARE to Be You	Comprehensive	2–5
Effective Black Parenting Program (Center for the Improvement of Child Caring)	Parent training	2–18
Families and Schools Together	Comprehensive	3–14
Focus on Families	Parent training	3–14
Healthy and Fair Start (Family Resource Center)	In-home support	0–5
Healthy Families America	Comprehensive	0–5
Home Instruction Program for Preschool Youngsters (HIPPY)	In-home support	3–5
HOMEBUILDERS	Comprehensive	0–18
MELD	Parent training	0–5
NICASA Parent Project (Northern Illinois Council on Alcoholism and Substance Abuse)	Parent training	0–18

(continued)

Best Practices, 1999 *continued*

Program	Type	Targeted Age
Nurturing Parenting Program	Family skills training	1–18
Parents as Teachers	Parent training	0–5
Parents Who Care	Family skills training	12–16
Project SEEK (Services to Enable and Empower Kids)	Comprehensive	0–18
Strengthening Hawaii Families	Family skills training	5–12
PROMISING		
Bethesda Day Treatment	Comprehensive	10–18
Make Parenting a Pleasure	Parent training	0–8
Nurturing Program for Families in Substance Abuse Treatment and Recovery	Family skills training	0–18
Parents Anonymous®	Comprehensive	0–18
Strengthening Multi-Ethnic Families and Communities	Parent training	3–18

Note: Two-page summaries of the programs (including program training and implementation costs and direct links to individual program Web sites) can be found on the Strengthening America's Families Web site at www.strengtheningfamilies.org

Which programs appear to be most impressive to you? How do these programs enhance family resilience?

Source: Rose Alvarado and Karol Kumpfer, "Strengthening America's Families," *Juvenile Justice* 7 (December 2000), pp. 9–11.

4. Abused and neglected females were also at increased risk of arrest for violence as juveniles and adults;
5. White abused and neglected children were no more likely to be arrested for a violent crime than their nonabused and nonneglected white counterparts, but in contrast, African American abused and neglected children showed significantly increased rates of violent arrests compared with African American children who were not maltreated.[92]

Thornberry and colleagues' ongoing study of delinquency examined direct child maltreatment as well as more general exposure to family violence. The 1994 study, which interviewed 1,000 seventh and eighth grade students and their caretakers every six months for four years, found that compared with youths who were not abused or neglected, these youths had higher rates of self-reported violence (70 percent versus 56 percent).[93]

However, Matthew T. Zingraff and colleagues found from their study in Mecklenburg County, North Carolina, that although child maltreatment is an important correlate of delinquency, "the maltreatment-delinquency relationship has been exaggerated in previous research."[94] Furthermore, Zingraff and colleagues challenged the simple and

TABLE 8.1

Defining Child Maltreatment and Rating Its Severity

Subtype of Maltreatment	Brief Definition	Examples of Least and Most Severe Cases
PHYSICAL ABUSE	A caregiver inflicts a physical injury upon a child by other than accidental means.	*Least*—Spanking results in minor bruises on arm. *Most*—Injuries require hospitalization, cause permanent disfigurement, or lead to a fatality.
SEXUAL ABUSE	Any sexual contact or attempt at sexual contact that occurs between a caretaker or responsible adults and a child for the purposes of the caretakers' sexual gratification or financial benefit	*Least*—A child is exposed to pornographic materials. *Most*—A caretaker uses force to make a child engage in sexual relations or prostitution.
PHYSICAL NEGLECT	A caretaker fails to exercise a minimum degree of care in meeting a child's physical needs.	*Least*—Food is not available for regular meals, clothing is too small, child is not kept clean *Most*—A child suffers from severe malnutrition or severe dehydration due to gross inattention to his or her medical needs.
LACK OF SUPERVISION	A caretaker does not take adequate precautions (given a child's particular emotional and developmental needs) to ensure his or her safety in and out of the home.	*Least*—An 8-year-old is left alone for short periods of time (i.e., less than three hours) with no immediate source of danger in the environment. *Most*—A child is placed in a life-threatening situation without adequate supervision.
EMOTIONAL MALTREATMENT	Persistent or extreme thwarting of a child's basic emotional needs (such as the need to feel safe and accepted).	*Least*—A caretaker often belittles or ridicules a child. *Most*—A caretaker uses extremely restrictive methods to bind a child or places a child in close confinement such as a closet or trunk for two or more hours.
EDUCATIONAL MALTREATMENT	A caretaker fails to ensure that a child receives adequate education.	*Least*—A caretaker allows a child to miss school up to 15 percent of the time when he or she is not ill and there is no family emergency. *Most*—A caretaker does not enroll a child in school or provide any educational instruction.
MORAL-LEGAL MALTREATMENT	A caretaker exposes or involves a child in illegal or other activities that may foster delinquency or antisocial behavior.	*Least*—A child is permitted to be present for adult activities, such as drunken parties. *Most*—A caretaker causes a child to participate in felonies such as armed robbery.

Source: Barbara Tatem Kelley, Terence P. Thornberry, and Carolyn A. Smith, "In the Wake of Childhood Maltreatment," *Juvenile Justice Bulletin* (Washington, D.C.: U.S. Department of Justice, Office of Juvenile Justice and Delinquency Prevention, 1997), p. 4.

direct relationship between maltreatment and delinquency, which was widely used in the studies of the 1970s and 1980s, when they concluded that delinquency is only one of many possible social, social-psychological and behavioral consequences of maltreatment. Finally, Zingraff and colleagues added that status offenders appear to be affected by maltreatment more than property and violent offenders are.[95]

Extent and Nature of Child Abuse and Neglect

Child abuse has a long history. Indeed, the unsparing use of the rod and the cruelty to children in nineteenth-century America makes contemporary treatment of children seem benevolent. C. H. Kempe first exposed child abuse as a major social problem with his groundbreaking essay on the battered child syndrome.[96] Kempe's research led to an avalanche of writing on neglect, physical abuse, and sexual abuse. The passage of legislation in all fifty states in the late 1960s requiring mandatory reporting of child abuse and neglect cases also focused attention on these problems. The passage by Congress of the Child Abuse and Prevention Act and the establishment of the National Center on Child Abuse in 1974 focused further attention on these problems. In 1995 child protective service agencies received 3.1 million reports of child maltreatment.[97] See Figure 8.1 for how reports of alleged child maltreatment have increased since 1980.

A 1990 national survey of child abuse and neglect found that of those children harmed by maltreatment, 56 percent were victims of abuse. Five in ten abused children were physically abused, three in ten were emotionally abused, and ten in ten were sexually abused. Among the 46 percent who were neglected, more than half were educationally neglected, one-third were physically neglected, and one-tenth were emotionally neglected.[98]

However, according to a 1994 report by the National Council of Child Abuse and Neglect, neglect is the most common form of substantiated child maltreatment. Of

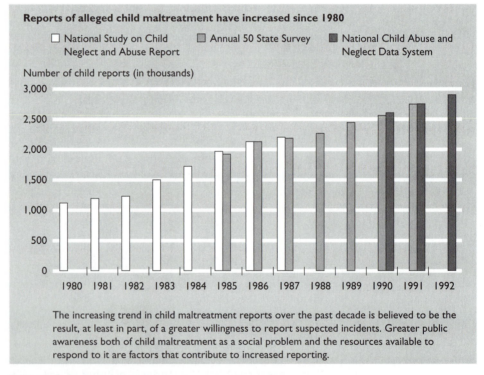

Reports of alleged child maltreatment have increased since 1980

☐ National Study on Child Neglect and Abuse Report   ▨ Annual 50 State Survey   ■ National Child Abuse and Neglect Data System

Number of child reports (in thousands)

The increasing trend in child maltreatment reports over the past decade is believed to be the result, at least in part, of a greater willingness to report suspected incidents. Greater public awareness both of child maltreatment as a social problem and the resources available to respond to it are factors that contribute to increased reporting.

FIGURE 8.1 Alleged Child Maltreatment Reports

Note: Child reports are counts of children who are the subject of reports. Counts are duplicated when an individual child is the subject of more than one report during a year.

Data Sources: NCCAN, 1994. *Child Maltreatment 1992: Reports from the States to the National Center on Child Abuse and Neglect.* NCCAN, 1993. *National Child Abuse Neglect Data System: Working Paper 2, 1991 summary data component.*

Source: H. Snyder, and M. Sickmund. 1995 (August). *Juvenile Offenders and Victims: A National Report.* Washington, D.C.: Office of Juvenile Justice and Delinquency Prevention, U.S. Department of Justice.

those substantiated incidents of maltreatment, 49 percent were neglect; 23 percent, physical abuse; 14 percent, sexual abuse; 5 percent, emotional maltreatment; 3 percent, medical neglect; and 12 percent, either other or unknown.[99] See Figure 8.2 for a 1998 report by the U.S. Department of Health and Human Services that compares the rates of maltreatment between 1990 and 1998.[100]

The maltreatment of children does emotional damage to them, but it also physically harms children. The child abuse and neglect pyramid in Figure 8.3 reveals that maltreatment sometimes results in serious injury or even death to the child.

NEGLECT   Neglect generally refers to disregarding the physical, emotional, or moral needs of children or adolescents. The Children's Division of the American Humane Association established a comprehensive definition of neglect, stating that physical, emotional, and intellectual growth and welfare are jeopardized when a child can be described in the following terms:

1. Malnourished, ill-clad, dirty, without proper shelter or sleeping arrangement;
2. Without supervision, unattended;
3. Ill and lacking essential medical care;
4. Denied normal experiences that produce feelings of being loved, wanted, secure, and worthy (emotional neglect);
5. Failing to attend school regularly;
6. Exploited, overworked;
7. Emotionally disturbed due to constant friction in the home, marital discord, mentally ill parents;
8. Exposed to unwholesome, demoralizing circumstances.[101]

Defining neglect in legal or social terms, nevertheless, does not begin to capture an accurate picture of the neglected child. Such children must be seen to realize the true hopelessness of their existence.[102] Newspapers have reported the deaths of young children due to neglect or child abuse: Jessica Cortez, Emily Hernandez, Elisa Izquierdo, Nadine Lockwood, Lisa Steinberg, and Joey Wallace. As tragic as this is, Widom noted: "But what happens to the children who survive? The babies abandoned on streets or in

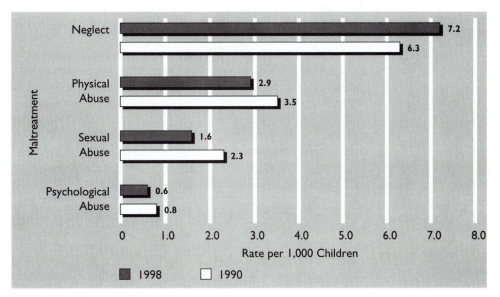

FIGURE 8.2 Rates of Maltreatment by Type, 1990 and 1998 (SDC)

Source: U.S. Department of Health and Human Services. Administration on Children, Youth and Families, *Child Maltreatment 1998: Reports from the States to the National Child Abuse and Neglect Data System* (Washington, DC: U.S. Government Printing Office, 2000), Table 4.3.

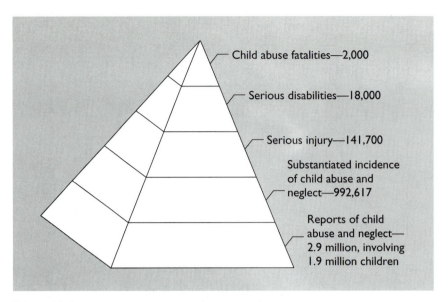

FIGURE 8.3 Child Abuse and Neglect Pyramid

Data Sources: U.S. Advisory Board on Child Abuse and Neglect; Baladerian, Verbal testimony, 1994; NCCAN, 1991, National Committee to Prevent Child Abuse.

Source: A Nation's Shame: Fatal Child Abuse and Neglect in the United States. A Report of the U.S. Advisory Board on Child Abuse and Neglect. Washington, D.C.: Administration for Children and Families, U.S. Department of Health and Human Services, 1995.

hospitals, children left unattended for days without food in filthy roach-infested apartments, or children brutally abused?"[103]

In studying the case records of 180 families that had come to the attention of authorized agencies, Leontine Young separated them into cases of severe and moderate neglect and severe and moderate abuse. She defined neglect as occurring when parents fed their children inadequately and failed to keep their children clean, to furnish adequate clothing, and to provide proper medical care. Parents who were involved in moderate neglect usually fed their children, but their children were not kept clean, nor did they have adequate clothing or proper medical care.[104]

Norman A. Polansky and colleagues' studies of neglect in Georgia and North Carolina identified five types of mothers who are frequently guilty of child neglect. The apathetic-futile mother is emotionally numb to her children and neglects both their physical and emotional needs. The impulse-ridden mother is restless and craves excitement, movement, and change. She is unable to tolerate stress or frustration and is aggressive and defiant. Typically, she neglects her children by simply taking off on an escapade with a husband or a boyfriend and letting the children fend for themselves. The mentally retarded mother has difficulty providing adequate care for her children, especially if her IQ is below 60. If emotional problems are combined with mental deficiency, then severe neglect is even more likely. The mother in a reaction depression is preoccupied with the loss of a loved one or some other traumatic event. Her persistent feelings of despair and sadness can lead to physiological illness to the degree that she is unable to cope with her own reality, much less provide for her children. Finally, the borderline or psychotic mother, lost in her fantasies, may forget to feed the children or she may even kill the children and herself in a psychotic outburst.[105]

Polansky and colleagues replicated their Appalachian study with an examination of neglect in Philadelphia. This study concluded that a general immaturity or high degree of infantilism was the strongest predictor of maternal neglect. The neglectful mother was likely to have been abused as a child, was isolated from informal helping networks, had a low rate of participation in formal organizations, had a lower IQ than the mothers used as controls, had more emotional pathology than the controls, and was "dirt" poor. The researchers also found that apathy-futility and impulse-ridden mothers were far more common in the Philadelphia study than in the Appalachian study.[106]

Polansky and colleagues, based on the data from these two research projects, developed the Childhood Level of Living Scale (CLL). Originally designed to assess families with children between the ages of four and seven, it has since been used for a wider range of ages. The CLL presents nine descriptive categories; five assess physical care and the other four asses cognitive, emotional, and psychological factors.[107] Realizing the limitations of the CLL scale, especially for issues of cultural diversity, a panel of child maltreatment experts in Ontario developed the Child Neglect Index (CNI). This scale assesses neglect in six areas: (1) supervision, (2) food and nutrition, (3) clothing and hygiene, (4) physical health care, (5) mental health care, and (6) developmental-educational care (see Figure 8.4).[108]

PHYSICAL AND EMOTIONAL ABUSE The term *physical abuse* refers to intentional behavior directed toward a child by the parents or caretaker to cause pain, injury, or death. The 1988 American Correctional Association Task Force's self-report study of female offenders found that 62 percent of the adolescent females reported that they had been physically abused; 47 percent of this survey reported eleven or more incidences of abuse. For 30 percent, this abuse began between ages five and nine.[109]

Gelles and Claire Pedrick Cornell described a case in which a parent attempted to kill her child:

> Sue was a single parent who lived in a fourth-floor walk-up apartment. Her husband had left her three years earlier, and child support payments stopped within weeks of the final divorce decree. Poverty and illness were as much a part of Sue's home as the busy activity of her 4-year-old daughter Nancy. One cold gray March afternoon, Sue took Nancy out for a walk. Together they hiked up the steep pedestal of a suspension bridge that rose up behind their apartment. At the top of the bridge, Sue hugged Nancy and then threw her off the bridge. She jumped a moment later.[110]

What was unusual about this case is that both Nancy and Sue survived. Plucked from the icy water by a fishing boat, mother and child were taken to different hospitals. When Nancy was released from the hospital six months later, she was placed out of the home. Sue's parental rights were being terminated.[111]

Murray A. Straus has been one of the strongest proponents of defining corporal punishment as physical abuse. Straus examined the extent of physical abuse using data from a number of sources, notably the 3,300 children and 6,000 couples in the National Family Violence Survey. He found that 90 percent of U.S. citizens used physical punishment to correct misbehavior. He claimed that although physical punishment may produce conformity in the immediate situation, its long-run effect is to increase the probability of delinquency in adolescence and violent crime inside and outside the family.[112]

According to Straus, the most frequent forms of corporal punishment are slapping, spanking, hitting with certain objects (e.g., hairbrush, paddle, belt), grabbing, and shoving a child roughly. Straus pointed out that nearly every child has been hit by parents, that mothers hit children more than fathers do, that no relationship exists between parents' social class and corporal punishment, and that those parents who were hit as children are more likely to hit their own children.[113] Straus identifies what he considers to be several myths of corporal punishment:

1. Spanking works better than anything else.
2. Spanking is needed when everything else fails.
3. Spanking is harmless to the child.
4. Spanking a child one or two times won't cause any damage.

20	15	5	0

CHILD'S NAME: _____   AGE: 0–2   3–5   6–12   13–16
FILE #:

WORKER'S NAME: _____   DATE: _____

SUPERVISOR

The two factors to be considered in assessing level of supervision are avoidability (i.e., extent to which a caretaker can be expected to anticipate and prevent) and severity of harm, or potential harm. CFSA identifies three specific types of harm that may result from failure to supervise:

Physical Harm	Sexual Molestation	Criminal Activity/Child Under 13
S.37(2)(a&b)	S.37(2)(c&d)	S.37(2)(k)

na	Unknown/Does Not Apply
0	1. Adequate; provisions made to ensure child's safety, caretaker knows child's whereabouts and activities, clear limits set on activities.
25	2. Inconsistent; child is occasionally exposed to situation that could cause moderate harm (e.g., young school-aged child occasionally left alone, parents do not monitor whereabouts of adolescent who occasionally comes home late in evening).
50	3. Inadequate; child is often exposed to situations that could cause moderate harm, or there is a slight possibility that child could suffer serious harm (e.g., young school-aged child often left unsupervised, or infant occasionally left alone while sleeping).
60	4. Seriously inadequate; child is often exposed to situations that could cause serious harm; (e.g., abandonment, home used as "crack house" and drugs left within reach of child, child often left to wander in dangerous neighborhood, toddler often exposed to hazardous situations).

PHYSICAL CARE

Physical harm or substantial risk of physical harm due to the caretaker's "failure to care and provide for . . . the child adequately" CFSA 37(2)(a&b).

FOOD/NUTRITION

na	Unknown/Does Not Apply
0	1. Regular and nutritional meals provided.
20	2. Meals irregular and often not prepared, but child's functioning is not impaired.
40	3. Meals irregular and often not prepared, child's functioning is impaired (e.g., child is hungry and has difficulty concentrating in class).
50	4. Inadequate food provided, there is a substantial risk that the child will suffer from malnutrition (e.g., infant given diluted formula).
60	5. Child displays clinical symptoms of malnutrition; medical attention and/or rehabilitative diet required (e.g., weight loss, anemia, dehydration, etc.).

CLOTHING AND HYGIENE

na	Unknown/Does Not Apply
0	1. Child is clean and adequately clothed.
20	2. Inadequate clothing or hygiene, but this does not appear to affect child's functioning.
40	3. Inadequate clothing or hygiene limits child's functioning (e.g., unable to go outdoors because of lack of clothing, isolated by peers because of hygiene or appearance).

FIGURE 8.4 Child Neglect Index

Note: For further information contact Nico Trocmé (416-978-5718; nico@fsw.utoronto.ca), Faculty of Social Work. University of Toronto (Version 5: Toronto, 1995).

Funding provided by the Child, Youth and Family Policy Research Centre & the Social Sciences & Humanities Research Council.

| 50 | 4. Inadequate clothing or hygiene likely to cause illness requiring medical treatment (e.g., infestation of head lice). |
| 60 | 5. Illness requiring medical treatment due to inadequate clothing or hygiene (e.g., serious infection due to poor diaper care, intestinal disorder). |

PROVISION OF HEALTH CARE

For the following three scales "not provided" means "does not provide, or refuses or is unavailable or unable to consent to . . ." (CFSA S.37(2)(e, f, g, h, & j). The extent to which harm could be avoided should be carefully considered in rating these three scales. Three factors should be examined: (a) whether a reasonable layman would recognize that a problem needs professional attention; or (b) whether a professional has recommended services or treatment; or (c) availability and/or effectiveness of treatment or services (e.g., the questionable effectiveness of services for chronic teen runners).

PHYSICAL HEALTH CARE   CFSA S.37(2)(e)

na	Unknown/Does Not Apply
0	1. Basic medical care provided.
20	2. Preventive medical care not provided (e.g., no regular checkups).
40	3. Medical care not provided for injury or illness causing avoidable distress.
50	4. Medical care not provided for injury or illness causing avoidable distress and interfering with child's functioning (e.g., chronic absence from school due to untreated illness).
60	5. Medical care not provided for injury or illness which could lead to permanent impairment or death (e.g., infant vomiting or diarrhea leading to dehydration).

MENTAL HEALTH CARE   CFSA S.37(2)(f, g, & j)

na	Unknown/Does Not Apply
0	1. Parents anticipate and respond to child's emotional needs.
25	2. Inconsistent response to emotional distress (e.g., responds only to crisis situations).
50	3. Services or treatment not provided in response to emotional distress, child at substantial risk of severe emotional or behavioral problems (anxiety, depression, withdrawal, self-destructive or aggressive behavior, child under 13 engaging in criminal activity).
60	4. Services or treatment not provided in response to emotional distress, child experiencing severe emotional or behavioral problems.

DEVELOPMENTAL AND EDUCATIONAL CARE   CFSA S.(2)(h)

na	Unknown/Does Not Apply
0	1. Child's developmental and educational needs are met.
25	2. Child's developmental and educational needs are inconsistently met (e.g., limited infant stimulation, child could benefit from remedial help in one or two subjects, child having academic difficulties due to poor school attendance).
50	3. Services or treatment are not provided in response to identified learning or developmental problems (e.g., learning disability diagnosed but caretakers refuse remedial help).
60	4. Child has suffered or will suffer serious/permanent delay due to inattention to developmental educational needs (e.g., Non-Organic Failure to Thrive identified but caretakers refuse remedial help).

For further information contact Nico Trocmé (410-978-5718; nico@fsw.utoronto.ca), Faculty of Social Work, University of Toronto (Version 5: Toronto, 1995).

Funding provided by the Child, Youth & Family Policy Research Centre & the Social Sciences & Humanities Research Council.

Reprinted with permission from Nico Trocmé, "Development and Preliminary Evaluation of the Ontario Child Neglect Index." *Child Maltreatment*, 1(2) (1996) p. 145–155. pp. 153–154.

FIGURE 8.4 Continued

5. Spanking is something that parents can't stop without training or treatment.
6. Spanking is necessary or a child will be spoiled or run wild.
7. Spanking is something that parents rarely do or do only for serious problems.
8. Spanking no longer takes place by the time a child is a teenager.
9. Spanking is necessary or parents will verbally abuse their child.
10. Spanking is an inevitable part of childrearing; indeed, it is unrealistic to expect parents never to spank.[114]

One of the reasons that Straus and others are so opposed to corporal punishment is that they claim it legitimizes violence in children. They contend that it does this by weakening the bond to parent or teacher, by undermining faith in justice, by labeling children as "bad," by providing less opportunity to learn alternatives to violence, and by lowering self-esteem.[115]

Emotional abuse is more difficult to define than physical abuse because it involves a disregard for the psychological needs of a child or adolescent. Emotional abuse encompasses a lack of expressed love and affection, as well as deliberate withholding of contact and approval. Emotional abuse may include a steady diet of putdowns, humiliation, labeling, name-calling, scapegoating, lying, demanding excessive responsibility, seductive behavior, ignoring, fear-inducing techniques, unrealistic expectations, and extreme inconsistency.[116] Randy, a sixteen-year-old boy, tells of emotional abuse he suffered:

> My father bought me a baby raccoon. I was really close to it, and it was really close to me. I could sleep with it, and it would snug up beside me. The raccoon wouldn't leave or nothing. A friend of mine got shots for it. My father got mad one night because I didn't vacuum the rug, and there were seven or eight dishes in the sink. He said "Go get me your raccoon." I said, "Dad, if you hurt my raccoon I'll hate you forever." He made me go get my raccoon, and he took a hammer and killed it. He hit it twice on the head and crushed its brains. I took it out and buried it.[117]

NATURE OF ABUSE   Some theorists argue that child abuse has five basic explanations: (1) structural factors such as lower class, large family size, or single parenting; (2) the mental illness of parents; (3) a history of abuse as a child; (4) transitory situational factors, including such "triggers" as alcohol, drug use, or unemployment; and (5) a particularly difficult, demanding, or problematic child. Stephanie Amedeo and John Gartrell's study of 218 abused children found that the characteristics of parents, including mental illness and having been abused themselves, have the greatest explanatory power of predicting abuse. Also, this study revealed that triggers or stressors, such as alcohol and drug use, perform as factors that precipitate abuse.[118]

Blair and Rita Justice contended that eight models explain the causes of abuse: (1) the psychodynamic model, (2) the character-trait or personality model, (3) the social-learning model, (4) the family-structure model, (5) the environmental-stress model, (6) the social-psychological model, (7) the mental-illness model, and (8) the psychosocial systems model.[119]

More recently, O. C. S. Tzeng and colleagues have identified nine paradigms, each of which encompasses several theories or models:

1. the Individual Determinants Paradigm, includes several theories dealing with the abnormal characteristics of the perpetrator;
2. the Sociocultural Determinants Paradigm, covers social systems theory;
3. the Individual-Environment Interaction Paradigm, involves theories considering the interaction between abusers and their environments;
4. the Offender Typology Paradigm, fits abusers into specific categories;
5. the Family Systems Paradigm, views the abusive family as a social system;
6. the Parent-Child Interaction Paradigm, includes five theories outlining parental interaction with the child;
7. the Sociobiological Paradigm, emphasizes the role played by genetic factors in human behavior;
8. the Learning Situational Paradigm, applies learning theory to abusive situations assessing that abusive-violent behavior is learned;
9. the Ecological Paradigm, brings together theories using the variables of the individual, the family, the community, and all cultural and societal factors to explain abuse.[120]

David G. Gil, in developing a classification of abusive families, found that seven situations accounted for 97.3 percent of the reported abuse cases:

1. Psychological rejection leading to repeated abuse and battering;
2. Disciplinary measures taken in uncontrolled anger;
3. Male babysitter acting out sadistic and sexual impulses in the mother's temporary absence, at times under the influence of alcohol;

4. Mentally or emotionally disturbed caretaker causing mounting environmental stress;
5. Misconduct and persistent negative behavior of a child leading to his own abuse;
6. Female babysitter abusing child during the mother's temporary absence; and
7. Quarrel between caretakers, at times when under the influence of alcohol.[121]

Research findings disagree concerning the age at which a child is most vulnerable to parental abuse. The National Incidence of Child Abuse study found that the incidence of physical abuse increased with age.[122] Gil found that half the confirmed cases of abuse involved children over six years of age and that nearly one-fifth were teenagers.[123]

Yet, while many adolescents may experience child abuse, the more serious cases still occur with infants and young children, who are more susceptible to injury. Indeed, according to some researchers, three months to three years of age is the most dangerous period in a child's life.[124] Teenagers are more physically durable, able to protect themselves better, and can leave the home if parents become too abusive.

Child abuse also seems to be more prevalent in urban areas than suburban or rural settings. Urban areas having better resources to detect child abuse does not entirely explain why so many more cases are reported to urban police. Obviously, the congested populations and poverty of the city, which lead to other social problems, partly account for abuse being predominantly an urban problem.

The abusive situation is often characterized by one parent who is aggressive and one who is passive. The passive parent commonly defends the aggressive one, denies the realities of the family situation, and clings to the intact family and to the abusive partner. The passive parent behaves as though he or she is a prisoner in the marriage relationship, condemned to a life sentence. This parent usually does not consider the option of separating from the aggressive partner because he or she is committed to the marriage, no matter how miserable the home situation may be.[125]

SEXUAL ABUSE **Sexual abuse,** or incest, here refers to any sexual activity that involves physical contact or sexual arousal between nonmarried members of a family. Oral-genital relations, fondling erogenous areas of the body, mutual masturbation, and intercourse are the main expressions of incest.[126] The National Center on Child Abuse and Neglect defines *incest* as "intrafamily sexual abuse which is perpetrated on a child by a member of that child's family group and includes not only sexual intercourse, but also any act designed to stimulate a child sexually or to use a child for sexual stimulation, either of the perpetrator or of another person."[127]

Linda Gordon's examination of incest from 1880 to 1930 found that incest appeared in 10 percent of case records of Boston child-protection agencies. Ninety-eight percent of these cases were father-daughter incest and had a common pattern: the family relations made the girl victims into second wives. That is, these victims took over many of the functions and roles of mothers, including housework, sexual relations, and child care with their father. Despite their apparent acquiescence and obedience in these incestuous families, many of these girls actively sought escape from their victimization, loitering on the streets where their low self-esteem made them easily exploitable.[128]

The seriousness of the problem of incest is becoming apparent as states pass more effective legislation on reporting of incest cases. David Finkelhor studied 796 college students in the 1970s and found that 19.2 percent of the females and 8.6 percent of the males reported that they had been sexually abused in childhood.[129] In the 1988 American Correctional Association's self-report study of the female offender, 54 percent of the juvenile respondents claimed to have been sexual victims. One-third of these respondents reported that this sexual victimization took place from three to ten times.[130] The National Center on Child Abuse and Neglect found that, in 1992, 14 percent of the 918,263 reported child maltreatment cases nationally were sexual abuse.[131] In 1993, according to the National Center on Child Abuse Prevention Research, 15 percent of the 1,016,000 cases were sexual abuse.[132]

Incest, or sexual abuse, reportedly occurs most frequently between a natural father or stepfather and a daughter, but it also may involve brother and sister, mother and son, and father and son.[133] **Father-daughter incest** usually is a devastating experience for the girl and sometimes has lifelong consequences. Stepfathers also sexually victimize stepdaughters, but natural fathers appear to be involved in more cases of sexual abuse than are stepfathers. Angela Browne and Finkelhor's review of the literature on sexual abuse revealed that abuse by fathers or stepfathers has a more negative impact than abuse by others. Experiences involving genital contact and force seem to result in more trauma for the victim.[134] The average incestuous relationship lasts about three and one-half to four years.[135] The completed act of intercourse is more likely to take place with adolescents than with younger children.

Helen, a sixteen-year-old, was sexually victimized by her father for three years. She had great difficulty getting anyone to believe that her father was committing incest. When the father was finally prosecuted, she made this statement:

> When I was thirteen, my father started coming into my room at night. He usually did it when he was drinking. He would force me to have sex with him. I told my mother. I told my teachers at school. But nobody would believe me.[136]

Some evidence exists that **brother-sister incest** takes place more frequently than father-daughter incest, but its long-term consequences are usually less damaging because it does not cross generational boundaries and often occurs as an extension of sex play.[137] But brother-sister incest can have damaging consequences for the sister if the act is discovered and she is blamed for being sexually involved with her brother. If the girl feels she has been seduced or exploited, then the damage may be even greater.

Mother-son incest is less common and only rarely reported, largely because of the strong stigmas and taboos attached to the idea of sex between boys and their mothers.[138] Mother-son incest usually begins with excessive physical contact, which eventually becomes sexually stimulating. "Don't leave me" or "don't grow up" messages are communicated to the son as the mother seeks ways to prolong physical contact with him, sleeping with him, bathing him, or dressing him.[139]

Father-son incest also is rarely reported, largely because it violates both the moral code against incest and the one against homosexuality. The stress of an incestuous relationship, as well as the threat to masculinity, often results in serious consequences for the boy when father-son incest does occur. Sons who are involved in father-son incest usually experience acute anxiety because they feel damaged, dirty, and worthless. They may cope by retreating into their own world and losing contact with reality.[140]

The National Center on Child Abuse and neglect has identified five factors that are usually present when daughter-father incest takes place: (1) the daughter's voluntary or forced assumption of the mother's role, (2) the parents' sexual incompatibility, (3) the father's reluctance to seek a partner outside the family unit, (4) the family's fear of disintegration, and (5) the unconscious sanctions by the mother.[141]

Justice and Justice have developed a classification of fathers who commit incest that is helpful in understanding their behavior.[142] They divide incestuous fathers into four groups: symbiotic personalities, psychopathic personalities, pedophilic personalities, and a small group of "others."

Symbiotic personalities, who make up 70 to 80 percent of the incestuous fathers, have strong unmet needs for warmth and for someone to whom they can be close. They hunger for a sense of belonging and intimacy. These fathers are out of touch with their needs and do not know how to meet them in healthy ways. These men, more than the others, look to the family to satisfy all their emotional needs. As relationships with their wives deteriorate, they turn to their daughters to satisfy their emotional and physical needs. They use a variety of rationalizations to justify their sexual abuse—for example, that physical intimacy is the highest form of love a father can show his daughter or that a father has exclusive property rights over the daughter and therefore can do whatever he wants. Alcohol is often used to loosen restraints on these fathers' behavior; after the sexual activity, they often blame the alcohol rather than themselves.

Psychopathic personalities seek stimulation and excitement through incestuous relationships. Sex is simply a vehicle to express the hostility they feel and to provide the excitement they have felt deprived of in the past. The psychopath feels no guilt and has little capacity to love; he simply wants immediate gratification of his needs. Fortunately, this type of incestuous father is rare.

Pedophilic personalities are attracted to young children who show no signs of physical and sexual development. These extremely immature fathers have erotic cravings for children. They want sexual activity with someone who will not reject or belittle them. Only a small amount of incest is committed by these immature and inadequate personalities.

The Justices' "other" types include psychotic fathers and those who come from a subculture that permits incest. Psychotic fathers, who make up about 3 percent of incestuous fathers, experience hallucinations and delusions, and they are most often responsible for using force in incest. In some cultural groups it is normal for the oldest daughter to assume her mother's role, both in the kitchen and in bed. The youngest daughter also is often introduced to sex by her father or brothers. This group of fathers accounts for only a small fraction of the cases of incest, because culturally sanctioned incest has lost much of the acceptance it had in the past.

Relationship of Child Abuse and Neglect to Delinquency and Status Offenses

An abused or neglected child is more likely to become involved in delinquency or status offenses. Neglect or abuse may have a negative impact on the emotional development of the child; it may lead to truancy and disruptive behavior in school, may encourage running away from home, and may generate so much pain that alcohol and drugs are sometimes viewed as a needed escape. Neglect or abuse may cause so much self-rejection, especially for victims of incest, that these youths may vent their self-destructiveness through prostitution and may even commit suicide. Neglect or abuse may also create so much anger that abused youngsters later commit aggressive acts against others.

EMOTIONAL TRAUMA OF CHILD ABUSE AND NEGLECT   Victimized children have never received the love and nurturing necessary for healthy growth and development. They often feel abandoned and lack the security of being a part of a "real" family. They struggle, sometimes all their lives, to get the nurturing and the feeling of being cared for that they have never experienced.

Victims of child abuse and neglect often have low self-esteem, considerable guilt, high anxiety, mild to serious depression, and high internal conflict.[143] Physically, they may experience disturbances in sleeping patterns, weight loss or gain, or continual illnesses. They also tend to have poor social relationships.[144] Psychotherapists report a large number of child abuse victims among their clients.[145] They also note that women who were sexually abused as children often suffer from depression.[146]

Sometimes the emotional problems of abused children are so serious that they have difficulty functioning in family, social, or institutional settings. A social worker in a Midwestern youth shelter described such youths:

> Some parents are really, really sick, but they don't see it. You can't get them to treatment. You get into some really messy situations. Their kids receive so little support that they feel so rejected and so mishandled that their only hope for survival into adulthood is to find someone in some institution or in some foster family that will make a commitment to them and will help them survive on their own. These kids need someone that will help them realize that what happened to them in their lives

Neglect is the most common form of child maltreatment, involving a lack of food, clothing, medical care, and parental supervision. Siblings are often left to care for each other as best they can.

was not their fault and that they need to develop their own strengths so that they can feel good about themselves.[147]

RUNAWAYS Teenagers who have been abused frequently run away from home.[148] One sexually abused girl explained: "I never thought about where I was running to—only what I was running from."[149] **Running away** becomes a way of coping with the pain of neglect, physical abuse, and sexual abuse. The youth often sees running away as the only way to manage an unmanageable problem. Parents sometimes tell a child to get out because they want to rid themselves of the problems that the abusive situation has created.

When abused adolescents are placed in foster homes, their running may not stop. They often choose to reject their new family rather than risk the possibility of being rejected again. Unfortunately, sometimes children are removed from abusive homes only to experience abuse all over again in a foster home.

DISRUPTIVE AND TRUANT BEHAVIOR IN SCHOOL Several studies have found that abused and neglected children have greater difficulty in school than children who are not abused.[150] According to R. S. Kempe and C. H. Kempe, "[M]any of these children become academic and social failures almost immediately upon entering school."[151] Abused and neglected school-age children tend to have deficiencies in language development,[152] are more frequently placed in special education classes,[153] are more likely to be assigned to educable mentally handicapped classes,[154] have more learning problems,[155] are more disobedient and have a greater difficulty accepting authority,[156] and have more conflict with peers.[157]

Teachers who have worked with abused and neglected children add that they have difficulty in concentrating, are aloof, have little or no confidence, frequently have emotional outbursts, have not internalized rules, and are often destructive of property.[158] Abused and neglected children are often labeled disruptive in the public school, are assigned to special learning classes, and are thus set up for failure.

DRUG AND ALCOHOL ABUSE   In an effort to blot out their pain and isolation, many abused children turn to drug and alcohol abuse.[159] Widom found that abused and neglected adolescent females were at increased risk for drug offenses.[160] S. D. Peters found an association between sexual abuse and later alcohol abuse.[161] Richard Dembo and colleagues, in an examination of a sample of youths in a detention center, reported that sexual victimization had a direct effect on drug use, whereas physical abuse had an indirect and direct effect on drug use.[162] An adolescent female from an abusive home said, "Drugs became my great escape; there wasn't nothing I wouldn't try to get high."[163] Abused children often feel they have nothing to lose by taking drugs; they are concerned only with forgetting their insecurity, anxiety, and lack of confidence. A type of love and trust relationship that they have never had with people before sometimes develops through drugs. They can finally belong, experiencing closeness and security with peers who also take drugs.

Barbara L. Myers, former director of Christopher Street, Inc., and a victim of sexual abuse as an adolescent, tells why she turned to drugs:

> I was eleven years old when I first discovered that drugs could make the terrible world around me disappear. . . . When I was on drugs, I felt high, happy, and in control of my life. When I was high, I had peers; I finally belonged somewhere—in a group with other kids who took drugs. Whatever the others were taking, I took twice as much or more. I wasn't aware like the rest of them; I got high without worrying about how much I could handle or what it would do to me. It made me feel big and powerful because I didn't care what happened to me.
>
> People said that taking too many drugs would burn out your brains. I used to think that I could become a vegetable if only I could succeed in burning out my brains. I wanted to be a vegetable. I used to picture myself as a head of lettuce. I used to look at mentally retarded people and think that they were so happy and didn't care about anything. I envied them because you could spit at them, and they would smile; they didn't seem to understand what hurt was.[164]

SEXUAL BEHAVIOR   A study of 535 young women who became pregnant as teenagers found that 66 percent had been sexually abused as children.[165] Considerable evidence shows that sexual abuse victims themselves often become involved in deviant sexual behavior. Promiscuity appears to be high among female sexual abuse victims.[166] Many female sexual abuse victims also become involved in prostitution,[167] and sexual abuse is frequently a part of the background of male prostitutes.[168]

It is not surprising that female sexual abuse victims are attracted to prostitution, because they have come to see themselves as shamed, marked, and good only for delivering sex. The self-destructive aspect of prostitution serves as another way of expressing rage for never having been loved and for having been sexually and/or physically abused. In prostitution, sexual abuse victims take control by making strangers pay for sex. Detachment has already been learned in childhood; therefore, it is relatively easy for them to disassociate themselves from brief sexual encounters.[169]

VIOLENCE AND ABUSE   The idea that violence begets violence is firmly entrenched in both the minds of professionals and those of the general public. There is considerable support for the finding that abused and neglected male victims are more likely to express their anger in ways that hurt others, whereas female victims of mistreatment are more likely to become self-destructive.[170] There is also substantial support for the finding that those who have been abused or neglected in the past are more likely to abuse or neglect their children than those who have not experienced abuse or neglect. For example, in reviewing the research on family violence, Gelles noted:

> One of the consistent conclusions of domestic violence research is that individuals who have experienced violent and abusive childhoods are more likely to grow up and become child and spouse abusers than individuals who have experienced little or no violence in their childhood.[171]

Several studies have found a positive relationship between abuse and neglect and later violent criminal acts. One study found that 85 percent of a group of teenagers who had committed murder unrelated to another crime had received severe corporal punishment as children.[172] Another investigation of crimes showed that in one-third of all homicides committed by adolescents in the state of New York, the delinquent had been either neglected or abused at home.[173] Terence P. Thornberry, using data from the Rochester Youth Development Study, found that 69 percent of youths who were maltreated as children reported later involvement in violence, compared to 57 percent of those who were not maltreated.[174] Theory and Research 8.3 presents a possible link between abuse and children who kill their parents.

Child abuse appears in the backgrounds of many famous murderers; for example, Charles Manson was severely abused as a child. In 1976, this link between homicide and abuse was legally recognized when a jury acquitted a youth who had murdered five young women, deeming him "innocent by virtue of insanity," because he had multiple personalities created by the severe abuse he had received at home.[175]

However, other studies reported that abused and nonabused delinquents did not differ in terms of violent behavior.[176] Jeffrey Fagan and colleagues found a low incidence of child abuse and parental violence among violent youthful offenders.[177] In a study of a North Carolina institutionalized population, Zingraff and Michael J. Belyea concluded that "abuse experienced as a child is neither a necessary nor sufficient condition for violent adult behavior."[178] Sara E. Gutierres and John W. Reich even reported that abused delinquents were less likely to engage in later aggressive acts.[179]

THEORY AND RESEARCH 8.3

Why Kids Kill Their Parents

Approximately three hundred parents are killed each year by their children. Kathleen M. Heide has contended that killing a parent is frequently "an act of desperation—the only way out of a family situation of abuse they can no longer endure." She claimed that there are three types of youths who kill their parents: (1) the severely abused child who is pushed beyond his or her limits, (2) the severely mentally ill child, and (3) the dangerously antisocial child. According to Heide's research, the severely abused child is the most frequently encountered type of offender.

She found that the characteristics of the severely abused child who kills one or both parents are:

- They are not violent.
- They are abused.
- Their parents are most likely substance abusers.
- They are isolated.

- They kill only when they feel there is no one to help them.
- They "block out" the murder, not revel in it.
- They see no other choice.
- They are sorry for what they did.

If you were a social worker in a male institution and a severely abused juvenile on your caseload had killed his mother, how would you help him come to grips with what he had done? What would you do first, second, third, and so forth?

Source: Kathleen M. Heide, "Why Kids Kill," *Psychology Today* 25 (September-October 1992), pp. 62–77; Kathleen M. Heide, "Parents Who Get Killed and the Children Who Kill Them," *Journal of Interpersonal Violence* 8 (December 1993), pp. 531–544.

How Child Abuse Is Handled by the Child Welfare and the Juvenile Justice System

The term "child protective services" usually refers to services that are provided by an agency authorized to act on behalf of a child when parents are unwilling or unable to do so. In all states, these agencies are required by law to conduct assessments of investigations of reports of child abuse and neglect and to offer treatment services to families where maltreatment has taken place or is likely to occur.[180]

While the primary responsibility for responding to reports of abuse and neglect rests with state and local child protective service agencies, the prevention and treatment of child maltreatment can involve professionals from many organizations and disciplines. Jurisdictions do differ in their procedures, but community responses to child maltreatment generally include the following sequences of events:

IDENTIFICATION

Individuals who are likely to identify abuse are often those in a position to observe families and children on a regular basis. These include educators, medical professionals, police officers, social service personnel, probation officers, daycare workers, and the clergy. Family members, friends, and neighbors may also be able to identify abuse.

REPORTING

Some individuals—educators, child care providers, medical and mental health professionals, social service providers, police officers, and clergy—often are required by law to report suspicions of abuse and neglect. Some states require such reporting by any person who has knowledge of abuse or neglect.

Child protective services or law enforcement agencies generally receive the initial report of alleged abuse or neglect. This initial report may include the identity of the child and information about the alleged maltreatment, the parent or other caretaker of the child, the setting in which maltreatment took place, and the person making the report.

INTAKE AND INVESTIGATION

Protective service staff are required to determine whether the report constitutes an allegation of abuse or neglect and how urgently a response is needed. The initial investigation involves gathering and analyzing information about the child and family. Protective service agencies may work with law enforcement during this intake investigation.

In some jurisdictions, a police officer always accompanies the social worker on the child-abuse or neglect investigation to protect the social worker in case the parents become assaultive, to use legal authority to take the child out of an abusive home if necessary, to gather evidence and take pictures if admissible evidence is present, and to permit the social worker to focus on the family rather than to be preoccupied with the legal investigation.

Case workers usually respond to reports of abuse and neglect within two to three days. An immediate response is required if it is determined that the child is at imminent risk of injury or impairment. If the intake worker makes the decision that the referral does not constitute an allegation of abuse or neglect, the case may be closed. If there is substantial risk of serious harm to the child or lack of supervision, state law allows the child to be removed from the home.

If the decision is to take the child out of the home, the juvenile court judge must be called for approval as soon as the social worker and police officer leave the house. If the child has been taken out of the home, a temporary removal hearing normally is held in the juvenile court within three to five days. At this hearing, the juvenile judge can decide to leave the child in the temporary placement—a foster home, youth shelter, or group home—or return the child to the parents.

Following the initial investigation, the protective service agency usually draws one of the following conclusions: (1) there is sufficient evidence to support or substantiate the allegation of maltreatment or risk of maltreatment; (2) there is insufficient evidence to support maltreatment; (3) maltreatment or the risk of maltreatment appears to be present, although there is insufficient evidence to conclude or substantiate the allegation. When sufficient evidence does not exist, additional services may be provided if it is believed that there is risk of abuse or neglect in the future.

ASSESSMENT

Protective service staff are responsible for identifying the factors that contributed to the maltreatment and for addressing the most critical treatment needs.

CASE PLANNING

Case plans are developed by protective services, other treatment providers, and the family to alter the conditions and/or behaviors that result in child abuse or neglect.

TREATMENT

Protective service and other treatment providers have the responsibility to implement a treatment plan for the family.

EVALUATION OF FAMILY PROGRESS

After implementing the treatment plan, protective services and other treatment providers evaluate and measure changes in family behavior and conditions that led to child maltreatment. They also assess changes in the risk of maltreatment and determine when services are no longer required.

CASE CLOSURE

Some cases are closed because the family resists intervention efforts and the child is regarded to be at low risk of harm. Other cases are closed when it has been determined that the risk of abuse or neglect has been eliminated or reduced to the point that the family can protect the child from maltreatment without additional intervention.

If the determination is made that the family will not protect the child, the child may be removed from the home and placed in foster care. If the decision is made that a child cannot be returned home within a reasonable time, parental rights may be terminated so that permanent alternatives can be found for the child.[181]

INVOLVEMENT OF JUVENILE OR FAMILY COURT

An adjudication (fact finding) hearing is held if a petition of abuse or neglect has been filed by the department of social services. Juvenile courts hear about 150,000 child abuse and neglect cases a year. Usually present at the adjudication hearing are the assistant district, state, or county attorney; the youth and his or her attorney; the parents and their attorney; the social worker assigned to the case; and the police officer who conducted the investigation. After the evidence has been presented, the juvenile court judge decides whether the petition charging neglect or abuse has been substantiated. If it has, a disposition hearing is set for about four weeks later.

States vary in the standard of proof needed to substantiate allegations of child abuse and neglect. Six states rely on the case worker's judgment; eighteen states, on some credible evidence; eleven states, on credible evidence; and twelve states, on the preponderance of evidence. The substantiation rate is 49 percent where the standard of evidence is the case worker's judgment; 46 percent where the standard is some credible evidence; 44 percent where the standard is credible evidence; and 43 percent where the standard is a preponderance of evidence.[182]

The concept of the **supremacy of parental rights** continues to receive widespread support among juvenile court judges and departments of social services or welfare. This concept can be defined as "a strong presumption for parental autonomy in child rearing and the philosophy that coercive intervention is appropriate only in the face of serious specifically defined harm to the child."[183] The concept of the supremacy of parental rights also has received strong support from national standards groups. The National Advisory Commission on Criminal Justice Standards and Goals and the joint Juvenile Justice Standards Project of the American Bar Association and the Institute of Judicial Administration have both proposed that coercive intervention by the state should be only a last resort.[184]

PROSECUTION OF PARENTS

The prosecution of parents in criminal court depends largely upon the seriousness of the injury to the child and upon the attitude of the district, state, or county attorney's office toward child abuse. The cases most likely to be prosecuted are those in which a child has been seriously injured or killed and those in which a father or stepfather has sexually abused a daughter or stepdaughter. The most common charges in prosecutions are simple assault, assault with intent to commit serious injury, and manslaughter or murder.

Reported cases of child abuse represent only the tip of the iceberg. Abuse and neglect cases among lower-class families are more likely to be reported than those among middle-class families. Procedures for dealing with abusive homes (and their effectiveness) vary from one state to the next. Moreover, much remains to be learned about dealing more effectively with abusive families, about creating the type of placements that will serve the best interests of the child, and about creating the kind of public policy that is necessary to reduce the amount of abuse and neglect in this nation.

SUMMARY

The social context of the U.S. family is one filled with multiple problems. Divorce and single-parent families, blended families, out-of-wedlock births, alcohol and drug abuse, poverty, and violence are problems that some families encounter. The more of these family crises that adolescents face, the more difficult it is for them to avoid problem-oriented behaviors.

Studies on the relationship between the family and delinquency have generally concluded that the quality of life within the home is more important than whether or not the home is intact, that parental rejection is associated with delinquent behavior, and that inconsistent, lax, or severe discipline is associated with increased delinquency. This research also leads to the conclusion that delinquent behavior among children increases proportionately with the accumulation of unfavorable factors within the family.

Violence toward children has been a sordid legacy throughout our history. The concept of the supremacy of parental rights has perpetuated the mistreatment of children by their parents; indeed, the state is reluctant to interfere unless severe physical injury, gross neglect, or sexual abuse has taken place. The acceptability of violence within U.S. society and the social isolation, especially of lower-class families, have contributed to the mistreatment of children. Mandatory reporting and federal funding for treatment programs for abusers and victims are calling the public's attention to the extent and nature of the abuse problem.

Research findings have consistently linked child abuse and neglect to delinquent behavior and status offenses. Children who have been neglected and abused may experience psychological problems, run away from home, become involved in truancy and disruptive behavior in school, and turn to drug and alcohol abuse. Some neglected and abused youngsters also become involved in deviant sexual behavior and in aggressive acts toward others.

To reduce the extent of child abuse and neglect in the United States, a number of strategies or interventions are needed. Widom recommends the following six principles: (1) "The earlier the intervention, the better"; (2) "Don't neglect neglected children"; (3) "One size does not fit all"—that is, "what works for one child in one context may not work for a different child in the same setting, the same child in another setting, or the same child in another period in his or her development"; (4) "Surveillance is a double-edged sword"—that is, intervention agents must be sensitive to the possibilities of differential treatment on the basis of race or ethnic background and take steps to avoid such practices; (5) "Interventions are not one-time efforts"; and (6) "Resources should be accessible."[185]

KEY TERMS

birth order, p. 223
broken home, p. 222
brother-sister incest, p. 238
child abuse, p. 226
delinquent siblings, p. 224
emotional abuse, p. 236
family size, p. 224
father-daughter incest, p. 238

father-son incest, p. 238
mother-son incest, p. 238
neglect, p. 226
rejection by parents, p. 224
running away, p. 240
sexual abuse, p. 237
supremacy of parental rights, p. 245
supervision and discipline, p. 225

CRITICAL THINKING QUESTIONS

1. What are the most serious problems of the family? What are their effects on children?
2. What conditions within the family are more likely to result in delinquent behavior by the children?
3. What is neglect? What are some examples of neglect within the home?
4. Define emotional and physical abuse. What are some examples of physical and emotional abuse within the home?
5. Define and discuss incest. What type of father is most likely to become involved in incest?
6. How are child abuse and neglect related to status offenses and delinquent behavior?

WEB DESTINATIONS

Go to this stepparent's site to learn more about blended families.
   http://www.cyberparent.com/step/

Check out this Resource Center for adolescent pregnancy prevention at this site.
   http://www.ctr.org/recapp/

The National Clearinghouse on Child Abuse and Neglect will give you additional information at this site.
   http://www.calib.com/nccanch

Read more stories about abuse and incest from the Abuse and Incest Support site.
   http://incestabuse.about.com/library/weekly/aa121997.htm

Read more about child abuse on the National Committee to Prevent Child Abuse site.
   http://www.childabuse.org

Read more about parental and children's rights from the United Nations Convention for the Rights of the Child site.
   http://www.angelfire.com/ar/jotsntitles

NOTES

1. Interviewed in September 1980.
2. Terence P. Thornberry, Carolyn A. Smith, Craig Rivera, David Huizinga, and Magda Stouthamer-Loeber, "Family Disruption and Delinquency," *Juvenile Justice Bulletin* (September 1999), p. 1.
3. Ibid.
4. Ibid., p. 4.
5. Joy Dryfoos, *Adolescents at Risk* (New York: Oxford University Press, 1990), p. 17.
6. Rebecca A. Maynard and Eileen M. Garry, *Adolescent Motherhood: Implications for the Juvenile Justice System* (Washington, D.C.: Office of Juvenile Justice and Delinquency Prevention, 1997), p. 1.
7. Dryfoos, *Adolescents at Risk*, p. 65.
8. Maynard and Garry, *Adolescent Motherhood*, p. 1.
9. Howard N. Snyder and Melissa Sickmund, *Juvenile Offenders and Victims: A National Report* (Pittsburgh, Pa.: National Center for Juvenile Justice, 1995), p. 32.
10. "Report Documents Effects of Homelessness on Education," *Education Week* (May 3, 1989), p. 10. See also John Hagan and Bill McCarthy, *Mean Streets: Youth Crime and Homelessness* (Cambridge: Cambridge University Press, 1997).
11. Staughton Lynd, "A Jobs Program for the '90s," *Social Policy* (Fall 1994), p. 23.
12. Bob Herbert, "Counting the Jobless," *New York Times,* February 23, 1994, A19.
13. See Richard B. Freeman and Harry J. Holzer, eds., *The Black Employment Crisis* (Chicago: University of Chicago Press, 1986).
14. Federal Bureau of Investigation, *Uniform Crime Reports 2000* (Washington, D.C.: U.S. Government Printing Office, 2000), p. 236.
15. Michael Hershorn and Alan Rosenbaum, "Children of Marital Violence: A Closer Look at the Unintended Victims," *American Journal of Orthopsychiatry* 55 (April 1985), p. 260. See also R. L. McNeely and Gloria Robinson-Simpson, "The Truth about Domestic Violence: A Falsely Framed Issue," *Social Work* 32 (November–December 1997), pp. 485–490.
16. Murray A. Strauss and Richard J. Gelles, "How Violent Are American Families? Estimates from the National Family Violence Resurvey and Other Studies," in *Family Abuse and Its Consequences: New Directions in Research,* edited by Gerald T. Hotaling, David Finkelhor, John T. Kirkpatrick, and Murray A. Straus (Newbury Park, Calif.: Sage, 1988), p. 17.
17. William Holmes, "Police Arrests for Domestic violence," *American Journal of Police* 12 (1993), pp. 101–125; Lawrence Sherman, *Understanding Violent Families* (New York: Free Press, 1992).
18. Karen Wilkinson, "The Broken Family and Juvenile Delinquency: Scientific Explanation of Ideology," *Social Problems* 21 (June 1974), pp. 726–739.
19. Marvin D. Krohn, Susan B. Stern, Terence P. Thornberry, and Sung Joon Jang, "The Measurement of Family Process Variables: The Effect of Adolescent and Parent Perceptions of Family Life on Delinquent Behavior," *Journal of Quantitative Criminology* 8 (1992), p. 287. For these theories of delinquency, see Travis Hirschi, *Causes of Delinquency* (Berkeley: University of California Press, 1969); Marvin Krohn, "The Web of Conformity: A Network Approach to the Explanation of Delinquent Behavior," *Social Problems* 33 (1986), pp. 81–93; Gerald Patterson, *Coercive Family Process* (Eugene, Ore.: Castilia Press, 1982); and Terence Thornberry, "Toward an Interactional Theory of Delinquency," *Criminology* 25 (1987), pp. 863–892.
20. Krohn, "The Measurement of Family Process Variables," pp. 287–288. For those studies supporting that family relationships and parenting skills are related to delinquency, see D. Elliott, D. Huizinga and S. Ageton, *Explaining Delinquency and Drug Use* (Beverly Hills, Calif.: Sage, 1985); W. B. Gove and R. Crutchfield, "The Family and Juvenile Delinquency," *Sociological Quarterly* 23 (1982), pp. 301–319; M. Krohn and J. Massey, "Social Control and Delinquent Behavior: An Examination of the Elements of the Social Bond," *Sociological Quarterly* 21 (1980), pp. 337–349; J. Laub and R. Sampson, "Unraveling Families and Delinquency: A Reanalysis of the Gluecks' Data," *Criminology* 26 (1988), pp. 355–380; R. Loeber and M. Stouthamer-Loeber, "Family Factors as Correlates and Predictors of Juvenile Conduct Problems and Delinquency." In *Crime and Justice: An Annual Review of Research,* edited by M. Tonry and N. Morris (Chicago: University of Chicago Press, 1986), pp. 29–149; W. J. McCord, J. McCord, and Irving Zola, *The Origins of Crime* (New York: Columbia University Press, 1959); F. I. Nye, *Family Relationships and Delinquency Behavior* (New York: John Wiley, 1958); G. R. Patterson and T. J. Dishion, "Contributions of Families and Peers to Delinquency," *Criminology* 23 (1985), pp. 63–79; M. D. Wiatrowski, D. B. Griswold, and M. K. Roberts, "Social Control and Delinquency," *American Sociological Review* 46 (1981), pp. 524–541.
21. Lawrence Rosen, "Family and Delinquency: Structure or Function," *Criminology* 23 (1985), p. 553.
22. John Paul Wright and Francis T. Cullen, "Parental Efficacy and Delinquent Behavior: Do Control and Support Matter? *Criminology* 39 (August 2001), p. 677. See also Judith R. Harris, "Where is the Child's Environment? A Group Socialization Theory of Development," *Psychological Review* 102 (1995), pp. 458–489; Judith R. Harris, *The Nurture Assumption: Why Children Turn Out the Way They Do. Parents Matter Less Than You Think* (New York: The Free Press, 1998).
23. W. D. Morrison, *Juvenile Offenders* (London: T. Fisher Unwin, 1896), pp. 146–147; Sophonisba P. Breckenridge and Edith Abbott, *The Delinquent Child and the Home* (New York: Russell Sage Foundation, 1912), pp. 90–91; William Healy, *The Individual Delinquent* (Boston: Little, Brown, 1915), pp. 290–291; William Healy and Augusta Bronner, *Delinquents and Criminals: Their Making and Unmaking* (New York: Macmillan, 1926), p. 123; and Ernest H. Shideler, "Family Disintegration and the

Delinquent Boy in the United States," *Journal of Criminal Law and Criminology* 8 (January 1918), pp. 709–732.

24. George B. Mangold, *Problems of Child Welfare*, rev. ed. (New York: Macmillan, 1924), p. 406.

25. Margaret Hodgkiss, "The Influence of Broken Homes and Working Mothers," *Smith College Studies in Social Work* 3 (March 1933), pp. 259–274.

26. Sheldon Glueck and Eleanor T. Glueck, *Unraveling Juvenile Delinquency* (Cambridge: Harvard University Press for the Commonwealth Fund, 1950), p. 123.

27. F. I. Nye, *Family Relationships and Delinquent Behavior;* and R. A. Dentler and L. J. Monroe, "Social Correlates of Early Adolescent Theft," *American Sociological Review* 28 (1961), pp. 733–743.

28. Lawrence Rosen, "The Broken Home and Delinquency," in *The Sociology of Crime and Delinquency,* edited by M. E. Wolfgang et al. (New York: John Wiley and Sons, 1970), pp. 489–495.

29. Patricia Van Voorhis et al, "The Impact of Family Structure and Quality on Delinquency: A Comparative Assessment of Structural and Functional Factors," *Criminology* 26 (1988), p. 248; Margaret Farnworth, "Family Structure, Family Attributes, and Delinquency in a Sample of Low-Income, Minority Males and Females," *Journal of Youth and Adolescence* 13 (1984), p. 362.

30. J. Q. Wilson and R. J. Herrnstein, *Crime and Human Nature* (New York: Simon and Schuster, 1985).

31. Richard S. Sterne, *Delinquent Conduct and Broken Homes* (New Haven, Conn.: College and University Press, 1964), p. 65; J. Toby, "The Differential Impact of Family Disorganization," *American Sociological Review* 22 (1957), pp. 505–512; T. P. Monahan, "Family Status and the Delinquent Child: A Reappraisal and Some New Findings," *Social Forces* 35 (1957), pp. 250–258; and T. P. Monahan, "Broken Homes by Age of Delinquent Children," *Journal of Social Psychology* 51 (1960), pp. 387–397.

32. Susan K. Datesman and Frank R. Scarpitti, "Female Delinquency and Broken Homes: A Re-Assessment," *Criminology* 13 (May 1975), p. 51.

33. Ross L. Matsueda and Karen Heimer, "Race, Family Structure, and Delinquency: A Test of Differential Association and Social Control Theories," *American Sociological Review* 52 (1987), p. 836.

34. Van Voorhis, "The Impact of Family Structure and Quality on Delinquency," p. 248.

35. Joseph Rankin, "The Family Context of Delinquency," *Social Problems* 30 (1977), pp. 466–479; and L. Edward Wells and Joseph Rankin, "Broken Homes and Juvenile Delinquency: An Empirical Review," *Criminal Justice Abstracts* 17 (1985), pp. 249–272.

36. Marvin D. Free, Jr., "Clarifying the Relationship between the Broken Home and Juvenile Delinquency: A Critique of the Current Literature," *Deviant Behavior* 12 (1991), pp. 109–167.

37. Karen Wilkinson, "The Broken Home and Delinquent Behavior: An Alternative Interpretation of Contradictory Findings," in *Understanding Crime: Current Theory and Research,* edited by T. Hirschi and M. Gottfredson (Beverly Hills, Calif.: Sage, 1980), pp. 21–42.

38. D. P. Farrington, *Further Analysis of a Longitudinal Survey of Crime and Delinquency* (Washington, D.C.: Final Report to the National Institute of Justice, 1983).

39. Steven A. Cernkovich and Peggy C. Giordano, "Family Relationships and Delinquency," *Criminology* 25 (1987), pp. 295–319.

40. Hirschi, *Causes of Delinquency;* and M. Gold, *Delinquent Behavior in an American City* (Monterey, Calif.: Brooks-Cole, 1970).

41. R. J. Chilton and G. E. Markle, "Family Disruption, Delinquent Conduct and the Effect of Subclassification," *American Sociological Review* 37 (February 1972), pp. 93–99.

42. R. E. Johnson, "Family Structure and Delinquency: General Patterns and Gender Differences," *Criminology* 24 (1986), pp. 65–80; H. Paguin et al., "Characteristics of Youngsters Referred to Family Court Intake and Factors Relating to their Processing," in *Juvenile Justice,* edited by H. J. Rubin (Santa Monica, Calif.: Goodyear, 1982); C. R. Fenwick, "Juvenile Court Intake Decision Making: The Importance of Family Affiliation," *Journal of Criminal Justice* 10 (1982), pp. 443–453.

43. L. Edward Wells and Joseph H. Rankin, "Families and Delinquency: A Meta-Analysis of the Impact of Broken Homes," *Social Problems* 38 (February 1991), pp. 87–88.

44. Glueck and Glueck, *Unraveling Juvenile Delinquency;* Nye, *Family Relationships and Delinquent Behavior;* and McCord, McCord, and Zola, *Origins of Crime.*

45. Linda J. Waite and Lee A. Lillard, "Children and Marriage Disruption," *American Journal of Sociology* 96 (January 1991), p. 930.

46. Hirschi, *Causes of Delinquency.*

47. Loeber and Stouthamer-Loeber, "Family Factors as Correlates and Predictors of Juvenile Conduct Problems and Delinquency," pp. 100–101.

48. Glueck and Glueck, *Unraveling Juvenile Delinquency.*

49. Joan McCord, "Crime in Moral and Social Contexts: The American Society of Criminology, 1989 Presidential Address," *Criminology* 28 (1990), p. 16.

50. David P. Farrington, "Environmental Stress, Delinquent Behavior, and Convictions," in *Stress and Anxiety,* edited by I. G. Sarason and C. D. Spielberger (Washington, D.C.: Hemisphere, 1979).

51. Janet L. Lauritsen, "Sibling Resemblance in Juvenile Delinquency: Findings from the National Youth Survey," *Criminology* 31 (August 1993), p. 387.

52. Nye, *Family Relationships and Delinquent Behavior,* pp. 47, 51.

53. Glueck and Glueck, *Unraveling Juvenile Delinquency.*

54. McCord, McCord, and Irving Zola, *Origins of Crime;* and R. C. Audry, *Delinquency and Parental Pathology* (London: Methuen, 1960).

55. Randy L. Lagrange and Helen R. White, "Age Differences in Delinquency: A Test of Theory," *Criminology* 23 (1985), pp. 19–45.

56. Paul Howes and Howard J. Markman, "Marital Quality and Child Functioning: A Longitudinal Investigation," *Child Development* 60 (1989), p. 1044.

57. Joan McCord, "Family Relationships, Juvenile Delinquency, and Adult Criminality," *Criminology* 29 (August 1991), p. 397.

58. S. Kirson Weinberg, "Sociological Processes and Factors in Juvenile Delinquency," in *Juvenile Delinquency,* edited by Joseph S. Roucek (New York: Philosophical Library, 1958), p. 108.

59. Joan McCord, William McCord, and Alan Howard, "Family Interaction as Antecedent to the Direction of Male Aggressiveness," *Journal of Abnormal Social Psychology* 66 (1963), pp. 239–242.

60. Loeber and Stouthamer-Loeber, "Family Factors as Correlates and Predictors of Juvenile Conduct Problems and Delinquency," p. 55.

61. Nye, *Family Relationships and Delinquent Behavior,* p. 75.

62. John Bowlby, *Maternal Care and Mental Health* (Geneva: World Health Organization, 1951); Hirschi, *Causes of Delinquency;* M. J. Hindelang, "Causes of Delinquency: A Partial Replication," *Social Problems* 21 (Spring 1973), pp. 471–487; R. L. Austin, "Race, Father-Absence, and Female Delinquency," *Criminology* 15 (February 1978), pp. 484–504.

63. McCord, McCord, and Zola, *Origins of Crime.*

64. Sheldon Glueck and Eleanor T. Glueck, *Unraveling Juvenile Delinquency;* and R. G. Audry, "Faulty Parental and Maternal Child Relationships, Affection, and Delinquency," *British Journal of Delinquency* 8 (1958), pp. 34–38.

65. W. L. Slocum and C. L. Stone, "Family Culture Patterns and Delinquent-Type Behavior," *Marriage and Family Living* 25 (1963), pp. 202–208.

66. Richard E. Johnson, "Attachments to Mother and Father as Distinct Factors in Female and Male Delinquent Behavior." Presented at the Annual Meeting of the American Society of Criminology Toronto, Canada (November, 1982).

67. Rosen, "Family and Delinquency," p. 569.

68. Joseph H. Rankin and Roger Kern, "Parental Attachments and Delinquency," *Criminology* 32 (November 1994), pp. 495–515.

69. Hirschi, *Causes of Delinquency.*

70. Nye, *Family Relationships and Delinquent Behavior,* p. 59.

71. Glueck and Glueck, *Unraveling Juvenile Delinquency.*

72. G. F. Jensen and Raymond Eve, "Sex Differences in Delinquency: An Examination of Popular Sociological Explanations," *Criminology* 12 (1976), pp. 427–448.

73. Loeber and Stouthamer-Loeber, "Family Factors as Correlates and Predictors of Juvenile Conduct Problems and Delinquency," p. 43.

74. Nye, *Family Relationships and Delinquent Behavior.*

75. Loeber and Stouthamer-Loeber, "Family Factors as Correlates and Predictors of Juvenile Conduct Problems and Delinquency," p. 53; James Snyder and Gerald Patterson, "Family Interaction and Delinquent Behavior," in *Handbook of Juvenile Delinquency,* edited by H. C. Quay (New York: John Wiley and Sons, 1987), pp. 216–243.

76. McCord, McCord, and Zola, *Origins of Crime;* see also W. McCord and J. McCord, *Psychopathy and Delinquency* (New York: Grune and Stratton, 1956).

77. Nye, *Family Relationships and Delinquent Behavior.*

78. Wright and Cullen, "Parental Efficacy and Delinquent Behavior: Do Control and Support Matter," p. 677.

79. Glueck and Glueck, *Unraveling Juvenile Delinquency.*

80. John H. Laub and Robert J. Sampson, "Unraveling Families and Delinquency: A Reanalysis of the Gluecks' Data," *Criminology* 26 (August 1988), pp. 355–380; and Robert J. Sampson and John H. Laub, *Crime in the Making: Pathways and Turning Points through Life* (Cambridge.: Harvard University Press, 1993).

81. Loeber and Stouthamer-Loeber, "Family Factors as Correlates and Predictors of Juvenile Conduct Problems and Delinquency."

82. See Glueck and Glueck, *Unraveling Juvenile Delinquency,* pp. 91–92.

83. Kathleen M. Heide, "Evidence of Child Maltreatment among Adolescent Parricide Offenders," *International Journal of Offender Therapy and Comparative Criminology* 38 (1994), p. 151.

84. Ibid.

85. Barbara Tatem Kelley, Terence P. Thornberry, and Carolyn A. Smith, "In the Wake of Childhood Maltreatment," *Juvenile Justice Bulletin* (Washington, D.C.: U.S. Department of Justice, Office of Juvenile Justice and Delinquency Prevention, 1997), p. 4.

86. Matthew T. Zingraff and Michael J. Belyea, "Child Abuse and Violent Crime," in *The Dilemmas of Punishment,* edited by Kenneth C. Haas and Geoffrey P. Alpert (Prospect Heights, Ill.: Waveland Press, 1986), p. 51.

87. B. F. Steele, "Child Abuse: It's Impact on Society," *Journal of the Indiana State Medical Association* 68 (1975), pp. 191–194.

88. Joan McCord, "A Forty Year Perspective on Effects of Child Abuse and Neglect," *Child Abuse and Neglect* 7 (1983), p. 265.

89. José Alfaro, "Report of the Relationship between Child Abuse and Neglect and Later Socially Deviant Behavior," *Exploring the Relationship between Child Abuse and Delinquency,* edited by R. J. Hunter and Y. E. Walker (Montclair, N.J.: Allanheld, Osmun, 1981), pp. 175–219.

90. Cathy Spatz Widom, "Child Abuse, Neglect, and Violent Criminal Behavior," *Criminology* 27 (1989), pp. 251–271. See also Cathy Spatz Widom, *The Cycle of Violence* (Washington, D.C.: National Institute of Justice, 1992), p. 3.

91. Cathy S. Widom and Michael G. Maxfield, "An Update on the 'Cycle of Violence,'" *Research in Brief* (Washington, D.C.: National Institute of Justice, 2001).

92. *Ibid.* For other support for the relationship between abuse and neglect and later violent behavior, see Carlos E. Climent and Frank R. Erwin, "Historical Data on the Evaluation of Violent Subjects: A Hypothesis-Generating Study," *American Journal of Psychiatry* 27 (1972), pp. 621–624; Dorothy O. Lewis, Shelly S. Shanok, Jonathan H. Pincus, and Gilbert H. Glaser, "Violent Juvenile Delinquents: Psychiatric, Neurological, Psychological and Abuse Factors," *Journal of the American Academy of Child Psychiatry* 18 (1979), pp. 307–319; Mark Monane, "Physical Abuse in Psychiatrically Hospitalized Children and Adolescents," *Journal of the American Academy of Child Psychiatry* 23.

93. Terence Thornberry, "Violent Families and Youth Violence," *OJJDP Fact Sheet* (Washington, D.C.: Office of Juvenile Justice and Delinquency Prevention, 1994).

94. Matthew T. Zingraff, Jeffrey Leiter, Kristen A. Myers, and Matthew C. Johnson, "Child Maltreatment and Youthful Problem Behaviors," *Criminology* 31 (1993), p. 173.

95. Ibid., pp. 194, 196.

96. C. Henry Kempe et al., "The Battered-Child Syndrome," *Journal of the American Medical Association* 181 (July 1962), pp. 17–24.

97. Kelley, Thornberry, Smith, "In the Wake of Childhood Maltreatment," p. 4.

98. See Andrea Sedlak, *Technical Amendment to the Study Findings: National Incidence and Prevalence of Child Abuse and Neglect* (Rockville, Md.: Westat, 1990).

99. National Center on Child Abuse and Neglect, *Child Maltreatment 1992: Reports from the States to the National Center on Child Abuse and Neglect* (Washington, D.C.: U.S. Department of Health and Human Services, 1994).

100. U.S. Department of Health and Human Services, Administration on Children, Youth and Families, *Child Maltreatment 1998: reports from the States to the National Child Abuse and Neglect Data System* (Washington, D.C.: U.S. Government Printing Office, 2000), Table 4.3.

101. *In the Interest of Children: A Century of Progress* (Denver: American Humane Association, Children's Division, 1966), p. 25.

102. Cynthia Crosson-Tower, *Understanding Child Abuse and Neglect* (Boston: Allyn and Bacon, 1999), p. 63.

103. Cathy Spatz Widom, "Child Victims: In Search of Opportunities for Breaking the Cycle of Violence." A speech made in the *Perspectives on Crime and Justice: 1996–1997 Lecture Series* 1 (November 1997), p. 75.

104. Leontine Young, *Wednesday's Children: A Study of Child Neglect and Abuse* (New York: McGraw-Hill, 1964).

105. Norman A. Polansky, Christine Deaix, and Shlomo A. Sharlin, *Child Neglect: Understanding and Reaching the Parent* (New York: Welfare League of America, 1972), pp. 21–52.

106. Norman A. Polansky et al., *Damaged Parents: An Anatomy of Child Neglect* (Chicago: University of Chicago Press, 1981), pp. 113–114.

107. Crosson-Tower, *Understanding Child Abuse and Neglect,* p. 64.

108. Ibid., p. 65. See also Nico Trocme, "Development and Preliminary Evaluation of the Ontario Child Neglect Index," *Child Maltreatment* 1 (1996), pp. 145–155.

109. Ilene R. Bergsmann, "The Forgotten Few: Juvenile Female Offenders," *Federal Probation* (March 1989), p. 73.

110. Richard J. Gelles and Claire Pedrick Cornell, *Intimate Violence in Families,* 2d ed. (Newbury Park, Calif.: Sage, 1985), p. 42.

111. Ibid.

112. Murray A. Straus, "Discipline and Deviance: Physical Punishment of Children and Violence and Other Crime in Adulthood," *Social Problems* 38 (May 1991), p. 133.

113. Murray A. Straus, *Beating the Devil Out of Them: Corporal Punishment in American Families* (New York: Lexington Books, 1994), pp. 5, 32, 54, 56, and 58.

114. Ibid., pp. 149–161.

115. Murray A. Straus, "Discipline and Deviance: Physical Punishment of Children and Violence and Other Crime in Adulthood," *Social Problems* 38 (May 1991), p. 148.

116. James Garbarino and Gwen Gilliam, *Understanding Abusive Families* (Lexington, Mass.: Heath, 1980), p. 68.

117. Interviewed in May 1981.

118. Stephanie Amedeo and John Gartrell, "An Empirical Examination of Five Theories of Physical Child Abuse." Paper presented at the Annual Meeting of the American Society of Criminology, Reno, Nevada (November 1989).

119. Blair Justice and Rita Justice, *The Abusive Family* (New York: Human Services Press, 1976).

120. O. C. S. Tzeng, J. W. Jackson, and H. C. Karlson, *Theories of Child Abuse and Neglect* (New York: Preaeger, 1991).

121. David G. Gil, *Violence against Children: Physical Abuse in the United States* (Cambridge: Harvard University Press, 1970), pp. 130–132.

122. *Study Findings, National Incidence and Prevalence of Child Abuse and Neglect,* pp. 1–10.

123. Gil, *Violence against Children.*

124. Kempe et al., "Battered Child Syndrome," pp. 17–24; B. Fontana, *Somewhere a Child is Crying: Maltreatment— Causes and Prevention* (New York: Macmillan, 1973); R. Galdston, "Observations of Children Who Have Been Physically Abused by Their Parents," *American Journal of Psychiatry* 122 (1965), pp. 440–443.

125. Young, *Wednesday's Children,* p. 48.

126. Justice and Justice, *The Broken Taboo: Sex in the Family* (New York: Human Sciences Press, 1979), p. 25.

127. Ibid., p. 27.

128. Linda Gordon, "Incest and Resistance Patterns of Father-Daughter Incest, 1880–1930," *Social Problems* 33 (April 1986), p. 253.

129. David Finkelhor, *Child Sexual Abuse* (New York: Free Press, 1979).

130. Bergsmann, "The Forgotten Few: Juvenile Female Offenders," p. 73.

131. U.S. Department of Health and Human Services, National Center on Child Abuse and Neglect, *Child Maltreatment 1992: Reports from the States to the National Center on Child Abuse and Neglect* (Washington, D.C.: U.S. Government Printing Office, 1994).

132. National Center on Child Abuse Prevention Research of the National Committee to Prevent Child Abuse, *Current Trend in Child Abuse Reporting and Fatalities: The Results of the 1993 Annual Fifty State Survey* (Chicago, Ill.: National Committee to Prevent Child Abuse, 1994).

133. For a more extensive discussion of the four types of incest possible within a family unit, see Crosson-Tower, *Understanding Child Abuse and Neglect,* pp. 155–162.

134. Angela Browne and David Finkelhor, "Impact of Child Abuse: A Review of the Research," *Psychological Bulletin* 99 (1986), p. 69.

135. K. C. Meiselman, *Incest: A Psychological Study of Causes and Effects with Treatment Recommendations* (San Francisco: Jossey-Bass, 1978); and Christine A. Curtois, *Adult Survivors of Child Sexual Abuse* (Milwaukee, Wisc.: Families International, 1993), p. 23.

136. Interviewed as part of a court case with which the author was involved.

137. Justice and Justice, *The Broken Taboo,* p. 192.

138. A. Nicholas Groth, "Patterns of Sexual Assault against Children and Adolescents," in *Sexual Assault of Children*

and Adolescents (Lexington, Mass.: D.C. Heath, 1978), p. 17.

139. Justice and Justice, *The Broken Taboo,* p. 194.

140. Ibid., p. 196.

141. National Center on Child Abuse and Neglect, *Child Sexual Abuse.*

142. Ibid., pp. 59–91.

143. Eli H. Newberger and Richard Bourne, "The Medicalization and Legalization of Child Abuse," *American Journal of Orthopsychiatry* 48 (October 1977), pp. 593–607; and Straus, Gelles, and Steinmetz, *Behind Closed Doors,* pp. 181–182.

144. Garbarino and Gilliam, *Understanding Abusive Families,* pp. 173–176.

145. Judith Lewis Herman and Lisa Hirschman, "Father-Daughter Incest," *Signs* 2 (1977), pp. 1–22; and C. Swift, "Sexual Victimization of Children: An Urban Mental Health Center Survey," *Victimology* 2 (1977), pp. 322–327.

146. J. Henderson, "Incest: A Synthesis of Data," *Canadian Psychiatric Association Journal* 17 (1972), pp. 299–313; B. Molnar and P. Cameron, "Incest Syndromes: Observations in a General Hospital Psychiatric Unit," *Canadian Psychiatric Association Journal* 20 (1975), pp. 1–24; P. Sloane and F. Karpinsky, "Effects of Incest on Participants," *American Journal of Orthopsychiatry* 12 (1942), pp. 666–673; and Danya Glaser and Stephen Frosh, *Child Sexual Abuse,* 2d ed. (Toronto, Canada: University of Toronto Press, 1993), p. 20.

147. Interviewed in May 1986.

148. Meda Chesney-Lind, "Girls' Crime and Women's Place: Toward a Feminist Model of Juvenile Delinquency." Paper presented at the Annual Meeting of the American Society of Criminology, Montreal, Canada (1987); M. Geller and L. Ford-Somma, *Caring for Delinquent Girls: An Examination of New Jersey's Correctional System* (Trenton, N.J.: New Jersey Law Enforcement Planning Academy, 1989).

149. "Incest: If You Think the Word Is Ugly, Take a Look at Its Effects" (Minneapolis: Christopher Street, 1979), p. 10.

150. For a review of these studies, see Diane D. Broadhurst, "The Effect of Child Abuse and Neglect in the School-Aged Child," in *The Maltreatment of the School-Aged Child,* edited by Richard Volpe, Margot Breton, and Judith Mitton (Lexington, Mass.: D.C. Heath, 1980), pp. 19–41.

151. R. S. Kempe and C. H. Kempe, *Child Abuse* (Cambridge: Harvard University Press, 1978), p. 125.

152. Florance Blager and H. P. Martin, "Speech and Language of Abused Children," in *The Abused Child: A Multidisciplinary Approach in Development Issues and Psychological Problems,* edited by H. P. Martin (Cambridge, Mass.: Ballinger, 1976), p. 85.

153. D. F. Kline and J. Christiansen, *Educational and Psychological Problems of Abused Children* (Logan: Utah State University Department of Special Education, 1975), p. 107.

154. Martin, "Neurological Status of Abused Children," p. 77.

155. Ibid.

156. M. Halperin, *Helping Maltreated Children* (St. Louis: C. V. Mosby, 1979), p. 77.

157. Kline and Christiansen, *Educational and Psychological Problems,* p. 107.

158. Comments made by teachers interviewed in 1981.

159. T. Houten and M. Golembiewski, "A Study of Runaway Youth and Their Families" (Washington, D.C.: Youth Alternatives Project, 1976); J. Streit, "A Test and Procedure to Identify Secondary School Children Who Have a High Probability of Drug Abuse," *Dissertation Abstracts International* 34 (1974), pp. 10–13; and Glaser and Frosh, *Child Sexual Abuse,* p. 20.

160. Widom, "Child Abuse, Neglect, and Violent Criminal Behavior," pp. 265–266; see also Bergsmann, "The Forgotten Few: Juvenile Female Offenders," p. 74.

161. S. D. Peters, *The Relationship between Childhood Sexual Victimization and Adult Depression among Afro-American and White Women.* Unpublished doctoral dissertation, University of California, Los Angeles, 1984.

162. Richard Dembo, Max Dertke, Lawrence La Voie, Scott Borders, Mark Washburn, and James Schmeidler, "Physical Abuse, Sexual Victimization and Illicit Drug Use: A Structural Analysis among High Risk Adolescents," *Journal of Adolescence* 10 (1987), p. 13.

163. "Incest: If You Think the Word Is Ugly," p. 11.

164. Ibid., pp. 11–12.

165. Sarah Nordgren, "Experts Find Links Between Teen Mothers, Sexual Abuse," *Waterloo Courier,* 11 September 1995, p. A1.

166. David Finkelhor, *Sexually Victimized Children* (New York: Free Press, 1979), p. 214.

167. J. James and J. Meyerding, "Easy Sexual Experiences as a Factor in Prostitution," *Archives in Sexual Behavior* 7 (1977), pp. 31–42.

168. Justice and Justice, *Broken Taboo,* p. 197.

169. See "Incest: If You Think the Word Is Ugly," p. 13.

170. Widom, "Child Abuse, Neglect, and Violent Criminal Behavior," pp. 265–266.

171. Richard J. Gelles, "Violence in the Family: A Review of Research in the Seventies," *Journal of Marriage and the Family* (November 1980), pp. 873–885.

172. E. Tanay, "Psychiatric Study of Homicide," *American Journal of Psychiatry* 120 (1963), pp. 386–387.

173. Jose D. Alfaro, *Summary Report on the Relationship between Child Abuse and Neglect and Later Socially Deviant Behavior* (New York: Select Committee on Child Abuse, 1978).

174. Terence P. Thornberry, *Violent Families and Youth Violence* (Washington, D.C.: U.S. Department of Justice, 1994), p. 1.

175. Michael S. Wald, "State Intervention on Behalf of Neglected Children: A Search for Standards for Placement of Children in Foster Care, and Termination of Parental Rights," *Stanford Law Review* 26 (1976), pp. 626–627.

176. Peter C. Kratcoski, "Child Abuse and Violence against the Family," *Child Welfare* 61 (1982), pp. 435–444.

177. Jeffrey Fagan, Karen V. Hansen, and Michael Jang, "Profiles of Chronically Violent Delinquents: Empirical Test of an Integrated Theory," in *Evaluating Juvenile Justice,* edited by James Kleugel (Beverly Hills, Calif.: Sage, 1983).

178. Zingraff and Belyea, "Child Abuse and Violent Crime," p. 59.

179. Sara E. Gutierres and John W. Reich, "A Developmental Perspective on Runaway Behavior: Its Relationship to Child Abuse," *Child Welfare* 60 (1981), pp. 89–94.

180. The first part of the following section is adapted from Howard N. Snyder and Melissa Sickmund, *Juvenile Offenders and Victims: 1999 National Report* (Washington, D.C.: Office of Juvenile Justice and Delinquency Prevention, 1999), pp. 43–44.

181. Victor E. Flango, "Can Central Registries Improve Substantiation Rates in Child Abuse and Neglect Cases," *Child Abuse and Neglect, 1991.*

182. National Advisory Commission on Criminal Justice Standards and Goals, *Juvenile Justice and Delinquency Prevention* (Washington, D.C.: U.S. Government Printing Office, 1976), p. 235.

183. Ibid., and Institute of Judicial Administration/American Bar Association Juvenile Justice Standards Project, *Standards Relating to Abuse and Neglect* (Cambridge, Mass.: Ballinger Publishing, 1977), p. 3.

184. Widom, "Child Victims," pp. 81–85.

chapter 5

THE SCHOOL AND DELINQUENCY

Columbine

OBJECTIVES

After reading this chapter, the student will be able to answer the following questions:

■ How has education evolved through the past century in the United States?

■ What relationship is there between delinquency and school failure?

■ What theoretical perspectives related to the school experience best explain delinquency?

■ What rights do students have in the school?

■ Are there promising interventions between the school and the justice system?

■ Which intervention strategies seem to be the most promising in the school setting?

HATTIESBURG, Miss.—Sobbing repeatedly *and proclaiming that he loved the girl he killed after she jilted him, Luke Woodham said Thursday that he felt like a "total reject" when he opened fire at his high school last October, killing two classmates and wounding seven.*

Woodham, 17, took the witness stand apparently against the advice of his attorneys. He described himself as an outcast and a loner who found a sense of belonging in a satanic cult that worshiped demons and cast magic spells. But he said it was a broken heart—after his girlfriend, Christina Menafee, broke up with him—that made him snap.

The breakup "destroyed me," he said, his voice breaking into heavy, racking sobs. "There's no way you people can understand what it did to me. It's just not fair. I tried to do everything I could. She didn't love me. But I loved her."

Several jurors recoiled in horror and looked into their laps as they listened to [psychologist Richard] Jepsen read an entry Woodham made in his diary last April about five months before the school shooting. In the account, Woodham said he and Boyette [the alleged leader of the satanic group] had beaten and tortured Woodham's pet dog, Sparkle, wrapping it in a sack and setting it afire, then laughing as the burning dog tried to escape.

Woodham described it as his "first kill," and after writing gruesome details, concluded, "It was true beauty."

Jepsen also read from a letter Woodham handed to a friend and alleged fellow Kroth [satanic group] member minutes before he opened fire at Pearl High School.

"All through my life I've been ridiculed," he wrote. "I was always beat on and hated. I am malicious because I am miserable." He also proclaimed, "Murder is gutsy."[1]

The October 1, 1997, shooting in Pearl, Mississippi, was another in a long line of shootings that have taken place in schoolyards in the United States. Previous shootings in the mid 1990s were in Grayson, Kentucky (two dead); Amityville, New York (one dead, one wounded); Redland, California (one dead, one wounded); Blackville, South Carolina (two dead, one wounded); Lynnville, Tennessee (two dead, one wounded); Mises Lake, Washington (three dead, one wounded); and Bethel, Alaska (two dead, two wounded). Subsequent to the Pearl, Mississippi, shooting, three students were killed and five wounded on December 1, 1997, in West Paducah, Kentucky; five students were killed and ten wounded in the March 1998 ambush in Jonesboro, Arkansas; two students were killed and twenty-four wounded on May 21, 1998, in Springfield, Oregon; and twelve students, a teacher, and two gunmen were killed and twenty-three wounded on Tuesday, April 20, 1999, in the massacre that took place in Columbine High School in Littleton, Colorado. It was the savage way in which Eric Harris and Dylan Klebold, armed with guns and bombs, laid brutal seige to Columbine High that shocked the nation.

The public in the United States wants to know what is going on in the schools of this nation. Experts are ready to render their opinions on the school killings, which range from merely an aberration, to lack of impulse control in children today, to the breakdown of the family, to the abundance of guns in the hands of young people, and to too much violence on television. What these killings certainly have done is focus attention on delinquency, especially violence, in school settings.

In the Social World of the Adolescent 9.1, Chris Geschke, a sophomore at Santana High School in Santee, California, tells what impact these school shootings have on students. Geschke was walking to his classroom in this San Diego suburb about 9:15 the morning of March 5, 2001. He passed by a bathroom, where inside a student senselessly began firing his weapon into a crowd of classmates. Before he was subdued by an off-duty police officer, the young shooter had killed two students and wounded thirteen others.

Chris saw several classmates who had been shot stagger out of the bathroom. He also saw a security guard race into the bathroom to try to subdue the crazed student. It later turned out that the security guard was wounded, but not fatally.

As Chris was running to his classroom, which was about ten feet from the bathroom, he spotted the shooter in hot pursuit of some students. The gunman shot three of Chris's classmates who were running behind Chris and fired countless rounds in Chris's general vicinity.

That Chris was able to safely make it into the classroom and close the door was a bit of a miracle. Scores of bullets whizzed past his head. Seven bullet shots were later found on the outside walls of Chris's classroom.

On March 15, 2001, Chris wrote for his English class this poignant recollection of the tragic events he was involved in at his school on March 5. Appropriately enough, his essay was entitled, "Scars on their Souls."

There is no question that an examination of delinquency in the United States must take a long look at the school experience. J. Feldhusen, J. Thurston, and J. Benning's lon-

Social World of the Adolescent 9.1

"Scars on their Souls," by Chris Geschke

"In the aftermath of the shooting at Santana High, one thing certainly rings true: bullets can do more than just physical damage.

"This is not to diminish the tragic consequences for fifteen families. Two are dead, thirteen others injured. Their blood is red, their pain cruel. Their loss cannot be measured by words, nor can their grief be consoled. The bullets surely did physical damage that can be seen with the eye. We saw arm, facial, leg, chest, and back wounds. But the invisible damage—the pain—inflicted on the heart—will never go away. In time, that invisible damage will evolve into painful or distant memories, maybe even fade unto the back of the mind. But there will always be scars on their souls.

"There is no rational reason for this irrational act. The media has tried to find a motive. Experts and Ph.D.'s have pointed to a variety of reasons and social ills in attempts to justify their own theories.

"Talk show hosts have entertained thousands of callers, each with something to say and finding a new angle to say it. Was he bullied? Did bigger students abuse him? Did drugs cause this violent reaction? Was he a victim of a broken heart? Did the school not listen? Why didn't his friends do something? Where did the system fail?

"My question is, does it matter? Will an explanation bring back Brian Zuckor or Randy Gordon [two students who were killed]? Will a reason make things all better for 1,900 students, 300 faculty members and their families? Will a rational explanation help prevent my friends' mothers and fathers from worrying now every time they walk out the front door? Will

an answer allow my mother to sleep peacefully again? Will a reason mean much to millions of other students at high schools just like Santana who watched us on TV and now worry the same thing could happen at their school?

"Their fear is real too. Again the invisible damage.

"I've learned a lot over the past couple of weeks. I've learned about my own mortality. I've learned about fate, and how easily one of those bullets could have hit me as I ran. I've retraced my steps in the past few days and felt the walls where the bullets hit. Bullets intended for me. I've learned that God was watching over me, and has an important purpose for my own life. I've learned that people hurt, inside and outside.

"But more importantly, I've learned that bullets cause invisible damage. And they leave scars on the soul."

Do you agree with Chris that the consequences of the shooting are more important to understand than the reasons why it happened? If you were a school counselor, what type of counseling would you give students who were victims of such a tragedy? What should we make of the fact that three weeks later another shooting took place at Granite Hills High School, another high school in the area?

Source: Statement by Chris Geschke and commentary by Janet Christopulos, the aunt of Chris Geschke. Used with permission.

gitudinal study found school relationships and experiences to be the third most predictive factor in delinquency, exceeded only by family and peer group relationships.[2] Delbert S. Elliott and Harwin L. Voss found that "the school is the critical social context for the generation of delinquent behavior."[3] Arthur L. Stinchcombe found that failure in school leads to rebelliousness, which leads to more failure and negative behaviors.[4] More recently, Eugene Maguin and Rolf Loeber's meta analysis found that "children with lower academic performance offended more frequently, committed more serious and violent offenses, and persisted in their offending."[5] In sum, there is considerable evidence that the school has become an arena for learning delinquent behavior.

How Education Has Evolved in the United States

The U.S. Constitution says nothing about public schools, but by 1850 nearly all the northern states had enacted free-education laws. By 1918, education was both free and compulsory in nearly every state of the union. The commitment to public education arose largely from the growing need for a uniform approach to socialization of the diverse groups immigrating to this country. Joel H. Spring, a historian, writes of this movement:

> Education during the nineteenth century has been increasingly viewed as an instrument of social control to be used to solve the social problems of crime, poverty, and Americanization of the immigrant. The activities of public schools tended to replace the social training of other institutions, such as the family and church. One reason for the extension of school activities was the concern for the education of the great numbers of immigrants arriving from eastern and southern Europe. It was feared that without some form of Americanization immigrants would cause a rapid decay of American institutions.[6]

During most of the nineteenth century, U.S. schools were chaotic and violent places where teachers unsuccessfully attempted to maintain control over unmotivated, unruly, and unmanageable children through novel and sometimes brutal disciplinary methods.[7] For example, Horace Mann reported in the 1840s that in one school with 250 pupils he saw 328 separate floggings in one week of five school days, an average of over 65 floggings a day.[8]

Widespread dissatisfaction with the schools at the turn of the twentieth century was one of the factors leading to the Progressive education movement. Its founder, John Dewey, advocated reform in classroom methods and curricula so students would become more questioning, creative, and involved in the process of their own education. Dewey was much more concerned about individualism and personal growth than rigid socialization.[9]

The 1954 U.S. Supreme Court decision that ruled racial segregation in public schools unconstitutional was a pivotal event in the history of American education; it obligated the federal government to make certain integration in schools was achieved "within a reasonable time limit."[10] The busing of children to distant schools, which arose out of the Supreme Court decision and which has resulted in the shift from neighborhood schools, remains a hotly debated issue.

During the 1960s, open classrooms, in which the teacher served as a "resource person" who offered students many activities from which to choose, were instituted as an alternative to the earlier teacher-oriented classrooms. As was the case with the Progressive education movement, the open-classroom concept was accepted more widely in private schools than in public schools.

The baby boom of the 1950s resulted in increased enrollments and more formalized student-teacher contacts in public schools in the 1960s and early 1970s. Public education also became more expensive in the 1970s because the increasing numbers of children in the classroom meant that more equipment had to be purchased (including expensive items such as computers, scientific equipment, and audiovisual aids). At the same time, teachers' unions took a firmer stance during contract talks, and many larger cities experienced teachers' strikes during this decade.

Public education used to be a source of pride for the citizens of this nation. But since at least the mid-1980s, instead of regarding education with optimism, dire warnings have been received from all sides concerning the state of education. An expert on schools put it this way in 1984:

> American schools are in trouble. In fact, the problems of schooling are of such crippling proportions that many schools may not survive. It is possible that our entire public education system is nearing collapse. We will continue to have schools, no doubt, but the basis of their support and their relationship to families, communities and states could be quite different from what we have known.[11]

What Constitutes Crime in the Schools

Crime in the schools is a serious problem now facing junior and senior high schools across the nation. This high crime rate expresses itself through vandalism, violence, and drug-trafficking gangs. Vandalism and violence are examined in this section, and Chapter 10 will explore the difficulties that youth gangs and drugs bring to the school setting.

Vandalism and Violence

There are two major reasons why so much youth crime is taking place in our schools. First, while urban schools are frequently criticized for failing to provide safe, orderly environments, the communities around these schools suffer from serious levels of crime and disorder. Unsafe schools, in other words, are lodged within unsafe neighborhoods. The level of school crime and violence is also dependent on the community context because most of the student population are members of the community. For example, if a community has a large number of adolescent drug dealers, runners, and lookouts, youth gang leaders and followers, chronically disruptive youth, and juvenile property offenders, then local schools are likely to have high rates of youth crime. Similarly, schools with little **violence** or **vandalism** are usually lodged in supportive communities with low rates of criminal or delinquent behavior.[12]

Second, schools' authoritarian atmosphere and the likelihood of failure by many students, especially those with limited learning abilities, create bored, frustrated, dissatisfied, and alienated students. In one study, students consistently rated themselves as more bored in school than in any other setting.[13] The repressive methods of education, as Martin Gold has noted, make school one of the most difficult experiences for adolescents in American society.[14] Urie Bronfenbrenner adds that "the schools have become one of the most potent breeding grounds of alienation in American society."[15]

Craig Haney and Philip G. Zimbardo drew the following comparison between public high schools and prisons: High schools, like prisons, have stark, impersonal architecture and drab interiors; give arbitrary power to teachers to punish and humiliate the pupil whose behavior is unacceptable; have regimentation and many regulations, including movement in lines and at signals from bells; restrict movement within the building; and regulate personal appearance through dress codes. The impersonality of large classes also has taught students, like inmates, to lose themselves in the crowd.[16]

The need to establish a safe learning atmosphere is a serious issue in public education today, but the added security features of many public schools make them appear even more like prisons. Uniformed police are stationed in many schools; other schools have their own security staff. Students must submit to a metal detector search to enter some schools. Electronically locked doors are appearing in more and more schools. Locker searches for drugs and weapons are everyday occurrences in many schools. Identification tags or photo ID badges for students and silent panic buttons for teachers are other means schools are using to regain control of the environment. Until it was ruled unconstitutional by the courts, a school in Boston even gave a drug test (urinalysis) to every student during the physical examination performed by the school physician at the start of each academic year.[17]

SCHOOL VIOLENCE AND THE 1970S   The pervasiveness of vandalism and violence in public schools came to public attention in the early to mid 1970s when the Senate Subcommittee to Investigate Juvenile Delinquency began an extensive examination of that phenomenon. Much of the material collected by the subcommittee appeared to show dramatic increases in overt acts of criminal violence and vandalism on the part of students. The public became alarmed, and demands were made for Congress and the executive branch of government to do something. Congress responded to the public's concern by mandating that the Department of Health, Education, and Welfare prepare a definitive report on the status of crime, violence, and vandalism in the nation's schools. That report, which was published in 1978 as *Violent Schools—Safe Schools: The Safe School Study Report to Congress,* took three years to complete and cost $2.4 million. Some of the significant findings of the Safe School Study were as follows:

1. 1.3 percent of all secondary-school pupils were attacked each month and 42 percent of those had some injury.
2. 36 percent of all assaults on twelve- to nineteen-year-olds occurred in school.
3. 2 percent of all secondary-school pupils reported theft of items valued over ten dollars in one month and about 54 percent of this theft occurred in classrooms.
4. Total crime costs equaled about $200 million per year.[18]

SCHOOL VIOLENCE AND THE 1980S   School violence became widely recognized in the 1980s as one of the critical problems of schools in the United States. A new dimension of school violence was the threat of assault, murder, or rape of teachers. In a 1980 study of 575 inner-city teachers in Los Angeles, each teacher reported that his or her environment was extremely stressful and that violence and vandalism were out of control. They reported that violence directed toward them included threats of murder, threats of rape, actual physical assault, and injury by students with and without weapons, as well as theft, arson, and other forms of vandalism of their personal property. Open-locker searches in their schools had revealed drugs, dynamite, knives, stilettos, ammunition, rifles, and handguns. Gang warfare caused a particularly volatile situation. Not surprisingly, most of these teachers had repeatedly petitioned their principals to transfer them to less violent schools.[19]

A football coach who took a job in a Los Angeles high school in the early 1980s gave a similar report about the violence of the school setting. He said: "On the first day the principal told new teachers that you don't have to worry about violence here. It didn't take me long to realize that whenever the three administrators walked on campus, they always walked in twos and had a walkie-talkie in their hands. They would never go out alone."[20]

Several 1980s surveys also documented the high rates of vandalism and violence in public schools. The National Crime Survey reported that although the school-age population has markedly declined since 1982, "the number of violent crimes in and around schools has remained high, ranging from a low of about 420,000 in 1982 and 1986, to a high of almost 465,000 in 1987."[21] This survey further revealed that nearly three million attempted or completed assaults, rapes, robberies, and thefts took place inside schools or on school property during 1987.[22]

A 1988 study on school violence that was part of the larger National Adolescent Student Health Survey (NASHS) dismissed the notion that violence in this nation's schools had gone down in the 1980s. Findings from the NASHS study, comprising surveys completed by eighth- and tenth-graders in 1987 in more than 200 public and private schools in twenty states, revealed:

1. Over one-third of the 11,000 student respondents reported that they had been threatened with harm at school.

2. Nearly one-seventh of the students reported being robbed at school, and the same percentage said that they had been assaulted either at school or while riding on the school bus.

3. Almost one-half of the adolescent male respondents and one quarter of the adolescent females had been in at least one fistfight that school year.

4. A weapon was involved in approximately one-third of the crimes against students.

5. More than one-fifth of the adolescent males surveyed admitted to carrying a knife to school at least once that year and 7 percent carried one daily.[23]

The National Crime Victimization Survey (NCVS) interviewed 10,000 youths in 1989 in public and private schools and asked only about crimes that had occurred during the six months preceding the interview. This survey revealed that an estimated 9 percent of the students, ages twelve to nineteen, were crime victims in or around their school in the previous six-month period; 2 percent reported one or more violent crimes, and 7 percent reported at least one property crime.[24]

SCHOOL VIOLENCE AND THE 1990S Two surveys in the 1990s revealed that crime and safety continued to be a problem in schools in the United States. The National School Safety Center indicated in 1992 that violent crimes committed inside schools or on school campuses had risen markedly since 1987.[25] In a 1996 national random telephone survey of more than 1,300 public high school students, nearly half reported that violence and drugs were serious problems in their schools.[26]

Surveys in the 1990s also revealed that fear concerning personal safety and violence had become a serious concern for students and their parents. A 1993 national school survey conducted by the Centers for Disease Control and Prevention (CDC) found that of the 16,000 students in grades 9–12 responding to the questionnaire, fear for their own safety compelled as many as 4.4 percent to miss a day of school each month. Twenty-two percent of the students also felt fearful enough that they carried a weapon (e.g., a knife, club, gun) during the thirty days preceding the survey.[27] A 1994 national survey of parents of seventh through twelfth graders found that 40 percent of parents of high school students were "very or somewhat worried" about the safety of their child while in school or going to and coming from school.[28] See Figure 9.1 for the percentage of students ages twelve through nineteen who reported fearing being attacked or harmed on the way to and from school, by race-ethnicity, 1989 and 1995.

Surveys in the 1990s further found that students frequently witnessed acts of intimidation, violence, and drug transactions. For example, a 1995–1996 survey that took

FIGURE 9.1 Percentage of Students Ages Twelve through Nineteen Who Reported Fearing Being Attacked or Harmed on the Way to and from School, by Race–Ethnicity: 1989 and 1995.

Note: Includes students who reported that they sometimes or most of the time feared being victimized in this way.

Source: U.S. Department of Justice, Bureau of Justice Statistics, *School Crime Supplement* to the *National Crime Victimization Survey, 1989 and 1995.* Cited in Phillip Kaufman et al., *Indicators of School Crime and Safety, 1998* (Washington, D.C.: U.S. Department of Justice; Offices of Justice Programs, 1998), p. 31.

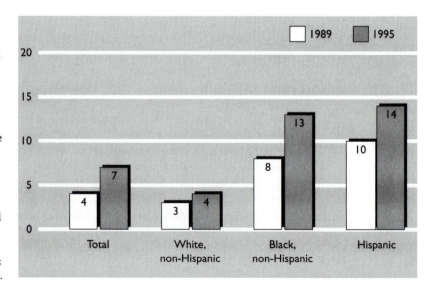

SOCIAL POLICY 9.2

Findings of Indicators of School Crime and Safety, 1999

HOMICIDES AT SCHOOL

While multiple homicide events have captured recent headlines, there still exists less than one in a million chances of suffering a school-associated violent death. For the complete school year, July 1, 1997 through June 30, 1998, there were 58 school-associated violent deaths (student and nonstudent) that resulted from 46 incidents. Forty-six of these violent deaths were homicides, 11 were suicides, and one adolescent was killed by a police officer in the course of duty.

School related homicides remain a serious problem. Since the 1992–1993 school year, there has been at least one multiple victim homicide event each year (except for 1993–1994). The number increased from two events in 1992–1993 to five events in 1997–1998.

CRIMES AWAY FROM SCHOOL

Students age 12 through 18 were more likely to be victims of serious violent crime away from school than at school. In 1997, about 24 of every 1,000 students were victims of serious violent crimes away from school (635,900). In contrast, only eight of every 1,000 students were victims of serious violent crimes at school or going to and from school (201,800).

TEACHERS VICTIMIZED AT SCHOOL

As with student crime, most crimes against teachers are theft. Teachers in urban schools are more vulnerable to crime at school than are suburban school teachers.

On average, each year from 1993 to 1997, there were 131,400 violent crimes against teachers at school and 222,800 thefts from teachers at school. This translates into a rate of 31 violent crimes for every 1,000 teachers and a rate of 53 thefts for every 1,000 teachers.

STUDENTS AND WEAPONS AND FIGHTING IN SCHOOL

Contrary to public perceptions, student weapon carrying and physical fighting have declined steadily in recent years.

Between 1993 and 1997, the percentage of high school students who carried a weapon (e.g., a club, knife, or gun) on school property, and the percentage of students in a physical fight on school property decreased significantly. These declines were similar across sex, grade, and race/ethnic subgroups, but male students, young students, and African American and Hispanic students were consistently more likely than their peers to engage in these behaviors.

For the 1997–1998 school year, the states and territories reported that they had expelled an estimated 3,930 students for bringing a firearm to school. The expulsions declined from 6,093 in 1996–1997.

If violence in the public school is declining, why do so many teachers feel unsafe in the school setting? What can be done to make public schools safer?

Source: 1999 Annual Report on School Safety (Washington, D.C.: U.S. Department of Education and the U.S. Department of Justice, 1999), pp. 3–5.

place in eleven high schools of the Los Angeles Unified School District reported a grim picture about the violence that students witnessed in the school setting. Of the 1,802 responding students, 49.1 percent had seen a weapon at school; 39.4 had experienced the intimidation of gangs, especially on the way to and from school; 38.2 percent had seen a shooting going to or coming from school; and 13.5 percent had witnessed a shooting at school.[29]

In 1998, the Department of Justice and Education published the first of what is to be an annual report on school violence. This report, *Indicators of School Crime and Safety, 1998,* provided a profile of school crime and safety and described the characteristics of the victims of these crimes. The *1999 Annual Report on School Safety* lists a number of aspects of school crime and safety (See Social Policy 9.2 for its basic findings.)

Is There a Correlation between Delinquency and School Failure?

Lack of achievement, low social status, and high dropout rate are factors most frequently cited as related to why delinquents fail in school. The 1967 report by the Task Force on Juvenile Delinquency concluded that boys who failed in school were seven times more likely to become delinquent than those who did not fail.[30] Anthony Meade showed that school failure was one of the best independent predictors of recidivism among first offenders appearing before juvenile court.[31] Albert K. Cohen was skeptical as to whether many youths can tolerate the censure and disparagement they receive at school:

> The contempt or indifference of others, particularly of those like schoolmates and teachers with whom we are constrained to associate with for long hours every day, is difficult, we suggest, to shrug off. It poses a problem with which one may conceivably attempt to cope in a variety of ways. One may make an active effort to change himself with the expectations of others; one may attempt to justify or explain his inferiority. . . . One may tell himself he really doesn't care what these people think; one may react with anger and aggression. But the most probable response is simple, uncomplicated, honest indifference.[32]

LaMar T. Empey and Steven G. Lubeck's examination of delinquents and nondelinquents in Utah and Los Angeles found that both family variables (broken homes, relations with parents, and parental harmony) and school failure (especially grades in school) were highly associated with delinquency in both settings. Yet, when the two sets of conditions were simultaneously compared, the data clearly indicated that school (as measured by dropouts) had a stronger effect on delinquency.[33] Steven A. Cernkovich and Peggy C. Giordano conclude that school factors are no less important in understanding delinquency than other variables such as parental and peer attachments.[34] Allen E. Liska and Mark D. Reed suggest that parental attachment affects delinquency, which in turn affects school performance, which then affects parental attachment.[35]

Achievement in School

Considerable evidence indicates that, whether measured by self-report or by official police data, both male and female delinquency is related to poor **academic performance** at school.[36] Studies by E. B. Palmore, by J. F. Short and F. L. Strodtbeck, and by D. J. West found that delinquents' failure to perform, or achieve, in school is caused by either a lack of aptitude or lower intelligence.[37] Studies by Sheldon and Eleanor Glueck, by G. P. Liddle, and by N. W. Silberberg and M. C. Silberberg blamed delinquents' poor performance in school on deficient reading skills.[38] Travis Hirschi claims that the causal chain shown in Figure 9.2 may eventually lead to delinquent behavior.[39]

Numerous researchers have pointed out that delinquents' lack of achievement in school is related to other factors besides academic skills. Several studies have found that

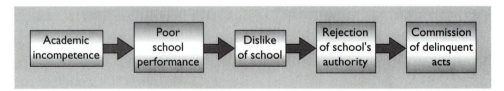

FIGURE 9.2 Hirschi's Causal Chain

Source: Travis Hirschi, *Causes of Delinquency* (Berkeley: University of California Press, 1969), pp. 131–132, 156

delinquents are more rejecting of the student role than are nondelinquents.[40] For example, William E. Schafer and Kenneth Polk asserted, "There is considerable evidence that students who violate school standards pertaining to such things as smoking, truancy, tardiness, dress, classroom demeanor, relations with peers, and respect for authority are more likely to become delinquent than those who conform to such standards."[41] F. Ferracuti and S. Dinitz, Glueck and Glueck, and Donald West also found that delinquents tend to be more careless, lazy, inattentive, and "irresponsible" in school than nondelinquents.[42]

Delinquents' performance in school may be further affected by their relationships with classmates and teachers. Several studies have concluded that the relationship between school performance and delinquency is mediated by peer influence.[43] It would appear that the more problems adolescents have in school, the more likely they will turn to peers for support and acceptance. Conversely, the more adolescents have become affiliated with a delinquent subculture, the less receptive they tend to be to the process of academic education. A number of studies also have found that delinquent or delinquency-prone youngsters tend to be less popular and have poorer relations with classmates and peers in school than nondelinquents.[44]

Several researchers relate lack of achievement to the absence of warm, supportive relations between teachers and students.[45] C. F. Cardinelli reported that schools tended to have more problems when teachers lacked genuine interest in students, and Goldman observed that good relationships among administrators, teachers, students, and even school custodians were associated with low levels of school vandalism.[46]

Maguin and Loeber did a meta-analysis of studies of academic performance and delinquency relationships and of intervention studies that were aimed at improving academic performance and reducing delinquency. As previously indicated, they found that children with lower academic performances committed more delinquent acts, committed more serious delinquent acts, and had a longer offending history than those with higher academic performances. This association was stronger for males than it was for females and for whites than it was for African Americans. Academic performance also predicted delinquent involvement independent of socioeconomic status.[47]

John Sampson and John Laub have demonstrated that high school can be a "turning point" in an individual's life course (See Chapter 2).[48] Richard Arum and Irenee R. Beattie assessed the effects of high school educational experiences on the likelihood of adult incarceration.[49] Using event history analysis and the National Longitudinal Survey of Youth data, they found that high school educational experiences have a lasting effect on an individual's risk of incarceration. This study offered specification of the high school context to identify how high school experiences can serve as a *defining moment* in an adolescent's life trajectory.[50]

In short, the evidence points to three conclusions: Lack of achievement in school is directly related to delinquent behavior, most delinquents want to succeed in school, and the explanations for poor academic achievement are more complex than lack of general aptitude or intelligence.

Social Status

Cohen's influential study of delinquent boys was one of the most comprehensive analyses ever undertaken of the role of the school in the development of delinquent subcultures. Working-class boys, as discussed in Chapter 4, feel status deprivation when they become aware that they are unable to compete with middle-class youths in the school. Although avoiding contact with middle-class youths might solve the problem, working-class boys cannot do this because they are forced to attend middle-class schools established on middle-class values. Consequently, they reject middle-class values and attitudes and form delinquent subcultures that provide them the status denied in school and elsewhere in society.[51] Jackson Toby's study based on a variation of Cohen's thesis contended that a lower-class background makes school success difficult because lower-class youths lack verbal skills and encouragement from home.[52] John C. Phillips proposed the steps by which low status in school can lead to deviant behavior; they are shown in Figure 9.3.[53]

The relationship between social class and delinquency in the school has been challenged. Cohen's argument that middle-class rewards, such as high grades, are of great importance to working-class boys has been particularly disputed. Polk and F. Lynn Richmond also found that any adolescent male who does poorly in school, regardless of class background, is more likely to become involved in delinquent behavior than one who performs well in school.[54] In another study, Polk found that controlling for social class did not alter the relationship between academic failure or success.[55] Palmore and Hammond reported a similar finding for African American and white youths.[56] Finally, George W. Nobit found that grade point average was associated with delinquency within socioeconomic classes.[57]

On balance, although the existence of a relationship between social class and delinquency in the school has mixed support, a relationship between school achievement and delinquency is much clearer.

The School Dropout

The relationship between delinquent behavior and the school dropout is a recurrent theme in the delinquency literature. An Elementary and Secondary Education Act (ESEA) Title II project in St. Paul, Minnesota, describes the student likely to become a **dropout** as follows:

> [The student likely to drop out is] one who is unable to function properly within the traditional classroom setting; who is generally recognized as an underachiever . . . who fails to establish goals regarding his future occupation; who has a record of tardiness as well as absenteeism; who lacks motivation, direction, and drive; who comes from a stressful family situation which appears to have a detrimental effect; who is hostile toward adults and authority figures; who has difficulty with community agencies and the law; who generally is not involved in any school activities; and, finally, who has had serious economic problems which threaten the completion of school.[58]

Joy Dryfoos found that poor grades and having to repeat a grade are excellent predictors of dropping out. Males are at higher risk of dropping out than females, and minority children are more likely to drop out than whites. Children whose families are on welfare have high dropout rates. Another significant antecedent of dropping out is early childbearing or marriage. Students who have been truant, have been suspended or expelled, or have been involved in other types of problem behaviors are high risks to drop out of school. Moreover, school quality affects dropout rates. Segregated schools, public vocational schools, large schools with large classes, and schools that emphasize tracking and testing have higher dropout rates.[59]

Elliott and Voss carried out the authoritative study of the school dropout. They studied 2,721 youths who entered the ninth grade in seven junior high schools in 1963 and followed them through their normal graduation year of 1967. Elliott and Voss discovered that the dropouts had much higher rates of police contact, officially recorded delinquent behavior, and self-reported delinquent behavior while in school than did those who graduated. The dropouts' delinquent behavior declined dramatically in the

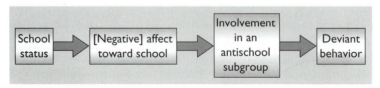

FIGURE 9.3 Phillips's Steps Leading to Deviant Behavior

period immediately after they left school and then continued to decline. In contrast, the official delinquency and self-reported delinquency of the youths who remained in school gradually increased during these years.[60] Elliott and Voss's study is clearly supportive of strain theory. They found that the act of leaving school reduced school-related frustrations and alienation and thereby lowered the motivational stimulus for delinquency.[61]

Other researchers have found similar short-term results. S. K. Mukherjee, using data from the Philadelphia birth cohort of 1945, replicated Elliott and Voss's basic finding. For high school dropouts, more than two-thirds of those who had juvenile arrest records no longer committed delinquent offenses after they dropped out.[62] Marc Le Blanc and colleagues also found that delinquency declined for dropouts after they left high school.[63]

Studies that extended the follow-up period until subjects are in their mid-twenties reported findings more consistent with a control perspective; that is, because dropping out of school represents a reduction in social control, it should result in increases in later criminal activity.[64] Polk and colleagues reported that during their early twenties dropouts consistently had higher rates of criminality than did graduates.[65] Starke R. Hathaway also followed dropouts and graduates in their mid-twenties and found that dropouts had consistently higher rates of criminal involvement.[66] Moreover, Jerald G. Bachman and Patrick M. O'Malley, in examining this relationship for a nationally representative sample of adolescents, found that through their early twenties, dropouts had higher rates of criminal activity than any other educational group.[67] Finally, Terence P. Thornberry, using a 10 percent sample of the Philadelphia cohort of 1945, discovered that "those who never graduated [the dropouts] had a considerably higher probability of becoming offenders than those who did graduate. This trend seemed particularly strong for minority subjects."[68]

G. Roger Jarjoura, in using data from the first two waves of the National Longitudinal Survey of Youth, explained some of the conflicting findings between dropping out of school and later offending behavior. He found that dropouts are not a homogeneous group. They vary by gender, race, and age; they have different reasons for dropping out of school (personal, school related, or economic); and they are dissimilar in prior misconduct (i.e., prior arrests, years sexually active, and suspensions from school). In examining these variables, adds Jarjoura, it becomes evident why dropping out enhances delinquent involvement for some, but for others it does not.[69]

Continuing research on this topic clearly reveals that the relationship between dropping out of school and delinquency is quite complex and multidimensional.[70] First, it can be examined by the short- and long-term benefits and consequences of dropping out of school and how they are related to delinquent behavior. Although there may be some short-term benefits, a number of negative long-term consequences result from dropping out of school. School dropouts have fewer job prospects, make lower salaries, are more often unemployed, are more likely to be welfare-dependent, and experience more unstable marriages. They are prone to have other problem behaviors, such as delinquency, substance abuse, and early childbearing. Society ultimately suffers the consequences of dropping out because of lost revenue from diminished taxes and increased welfare expenditures. Table 9.1 lists some consequences of school failure and dropout.[71]

The relationship between dropping out of school and delinquency can also be evaluated by whether school or nonschool reasons were involved in dropping out. Jeffrey Fagan and Edward Pabon found that nonschool reasons may have more significance for contributing to delinquent behavior than school-based factors.[72] In contrast, other studies reach the same conclusion as Elliot and Voss; that is, that school-based reasons for leaving school have the strongest connection with delinquency.[73]

Furthermore, some research has found that the relationship between dropping out of school and delinquency is affected by a variety of personal, environmental, and economic conditions.[74] Accordingly, as Donald Shoemaker suggests, school dropouts' higher or lower rates of delinquency are "not necessarily explained by the frustrating

TABLE 9.1

Consequences of School Failure and Dropout

	Consequences	
Behavior	*Short Term*	*Long Term*
Low achievement Poor grades	Nonpromotion Difficulty getting admission to college Truancy, absenteeism	Dropout Low basic skills Low employability Lack of college degree
Nonpromotion Left back	Low self-esteem Low involvement in school activities Problem behavior Alienation	Dropout
Dropout	Unemployment	No entry to labor force Welfare dependency Low-level jobs
	Low wages	Low lifetime earnings Repeated job changes
	Depression Alienation	Later regrets Poor physical health Mental health problems
	Low basic skills Delinquency	Illiteracy Criminal career, prison Marital instability Divorce
	Pregnancy Abortion	Early childbearing Social costs: lost tax revenue, welfare expenditures

Sources: Table found in Joy C. Dryfoos, *Adolescents at Risk: Prevalence and Prevention* (New York: Oxford University Press, 1990), p. 82 (Copyright © 1991 by Joy G. Dryfoos. Used by permission of Oxford University Press, Inc.); D. Kandel, V. Raveis, and P. Kandel, "Continuity in Discontinuities: Adjustment in Young Adulthood of Former School Absentees," *Youth and Society* 15 (1984), pp. 325–352; G. Berlin and A. Sum, *Toward a More Perfect Union: Basic Skills, Poor Families, and Our Economic Future* (New York: Ford Foundation, 1988), pp. 24–38. E. Ginzberg, H. Berliner, and M. Ostow, *Young People at Risk: Is Prevention Possible?* (New York: Ford Foundation, 1988), pp. 105–121.

experiences of lower-class youth in school, or by the lack of bonding with the school setting, or by any particular theoretical explanation of delinquency."[75]

Some of the Theoretical Perspectives on School and Delinquency

Most of the major theories of delinquency implicate the school as a factor contributing to delinquent behavior. Cultural deviance theorists argue that children learn deviance socially, through exposure to others and modeling of others' actions. Children may come to define delinquent behavior as acceptable because of their exposure to others whose definitions of such behavior are positive. School organizations reflect the characteristics of the community; therefore, attending school in high-crime areas may increase the likelihood of association with delinquent peers.[76]

Strain theorists contend that certain classes are denied legitimate access to culturally determined goals and opportunities and that the subsequent frustration results in the use of illegitimate means to obtain society's goals, or in rejecting them. Strain theory views the school as a middle-class institution in which lower-class children are frequently unable to perform successfully. These youths then turn to delinquency to compensate for feelings of status frustration, failure, and low self-esteem.

Social control theorists argue that delinquency varies according to the strength of a juvenile's bond to the social order. The school is acknowledged as one of the major socializing institutions, providing youths with structure, incentives, expectations, and opportunities for bonding. Accordingly, social control theorists posit that delinquency is likely to result when a strong bond to school does not develop.[77]

Labeling theorists argue that once students are defined as deviant, they adopt a deviant role in response to their lowered status. In schools, labels are attached early on the basis of achievement and behavior, and these labels may influence the subsequent treatment of youths. Therefore, students who are labeled as aggressive, difficult to manage, or slow learners at an early stage in school may be put into a slow track for the remainder of their schooling. According to labeling theorists, this differential treatment contributes to delinquent identities and behaviors.

Marxist theorists view the school as a means by which the privileged classes maintain their power over the lower classes. Subjected to the controlling forces of the state, lower-class children are exploited as they experience powerlessness and alienation. They are more likely than middle- and upper-class children to be placed in the lowest tracks, to receive poor grades, to be suspended for disciplinary reasons, and to drop out of school. According to Marxist theorists, lower-class children are being trained to accept their menial roles in the social order.

Explaining school disorder promises to be a popular area of theoretical exploration in the next few years. Wayne N. Welsh, Jack R. Greene, and Patricia H. Jenkins drew upon control theory, school climate theory, and social disorganization theory to examine the influence of individual, institutional, and community factors on misconduct in Philadelphia middle schools. One of the strong conclusions from this study is that the simplistic assumption "that 'bad' communities typically produce 'bad' children or 'bad' schools" is unwarranted.[78]

The Rights of Students

The school's authority over students comes from two principal sources: the concept of *in loco parentis* and state enabling statutes.[79] Reutter summarized *in loco parentis* as follows:

> The common law measure of the rights and duties of school authorities relative to pupils attending school is the *in loco parentis* concept. This doctrine holds that school authorities stand in the place of the parent while the child is at school. Thus, school personnel may establish rules for the educational welfare of the child and may inflict punishments for disobedience. The legal test is whether a reasonably knowledgeable and careful parent might so act. The doctrine is used not only to support rights of school authorities . . . but to establish their responsibilities concerning such matters as injuries that may befall students.[80]

State enabling statutes authorize local school boards to establish reasonable rules and regulations for operating and keeping order in schools, which do not necessarily have to be in written form.[81] A classic statement on this type of authority was made in the 1966 case of *Burnside v. Byars:*

> The establishment of an educational program requires the formulation of rules and regulations necessary for the maintenance of an orderly program of classroom learning. In formulating regulations, including those pertaining to the discipline of schoolchildren,

school officials have a wide latitude of discretion. But the school is always bound by the requirement that the rules and regulations must be reasonable. It is not for us to consider whether such rules are wise or expedient but merely whether they are a reasonable exercise of the power and discretion of the school authorities.[82]

The courts have become involved with schools in a number of important areas: procedural due process, freedom of expression, hair and dress codes, and safety.[83]

Procedural Due Process

Dixon v. Alabama State Board of Education (1961) was a major breakthrough for students' rights, because the appeals court held for the first time that due process requires a student to receive notice and some opportunity for a hearing before being expelled for misconduct.[84]

In 1969, the U.S. Supreme Court issued its far-reaching decision in *Tinker v. Des Moines Independent School District,* declaring that students do not shed their constitutional rights of freedom of speech at the schoolhouse gate. The issue that was involved in this case was whether students had the right to wear black arm bands to protest the Vietnam war. The Court ruled that school authorities did not have the right to deny free speech, even the expression of an unpopular view, unless they had reason to believe that it would interfere with the school operations.[85] In the 1986 *Bethel School District No. 403 v. Fraser* case, the Court upheld a school system's right to suspend or discipline a student who uses profane or obscene language or gestures. The Court reasoned that the use of lewd and offensive speech undermined the basic educational mission of the school.[86] In a 1988 decision, *Hazelwood School District v. Kuhlmeier,* the Court ruled that the principal could censor articles having to do with pregnancy and parental divorce in a student publication. The Court's majority justified this censorship because such publications were perceived to be part of the educational curriculum of the school.[87]

In January 1975, the U.S. Supreme Court took up the problem of due process in the schools, stating in *Goss v. Lopez* that schools may not summarily suspend students, for even one day, without following fundamentally fair and fact-finding procedures.[88] In suspensions of ten days or less, a student is entitled to oral or written notice of the charges, an explanation of the evidence, and an opportunity to be heard. The *Wood v. Strickland* ruling, issued a month after the *Goss* decision, found that school officials may be subject to suit and held financially liable for damages if they deliberately deprive a student of his or her clearly established constitutional rights.[89]

The issue of corporal punishment came before the U.S. Supreme Court in *Baker v. Owen* and *Ingraham v. Wright.*[90] Although *Baker v. Owen* merely affirmed a lower court ruling, *Ingraham v. Wright* held that reasonable corporal punishment is not cruel and unusual punishment under the Eighth Amendment to the U.S. Constitution.[91]

Freedom of Expression

Several court cases have defined students' rights to freedom of religion and expression in schools. In *West Virginia State Board of Education v. Barnette* the Supreme Court held that students could not be compelled to salute the flag if that action violated their religious rights.[92] In *Tinker* the wearing of black arm bands was declared symbolic speech and therefore within the protection of the First Amendment.[93]

Hair and Dress Codes

Court cases testing the power of school administrators to suspend students for violations of hair and dress codes were widespread in the late 1960s and early 1970s. In *Yoo v. Moynihan* a student's right to style his or her hair was held to be under the definition of the constitutional right to privacy.[94] Then, in *Richards v. Thurston,* the Court ruled that a student's right to wear long hair derived from his interest in personal liberty.[95] In

Crossen v. Fatsi a dress code prohibiting "extreme style and fashion" was ruled unconstitutionally vague, unenforceable, and an invasion of the student's right to privacy.[96] Other decisions have held that schools cannot prohibit the wearing of slacks,[97] dungarees,[98] or hair "falling loosely about the shoulders."[99]

School Searches

The use of drugs and weapons is changing the nature of police–student relations in school. In the 1990s, the police began to enforce the 1990 federal Gun-Free School Zones Act and increasingly in communities across the nation to enforce drug-free school zone laws. Drug-free zones usually include the school property along with the territory within a 1,000-foot radius of its perimeter. Alabama has the most aggressive law in this nation: territory within three miles of a school is declared drug free.[100]

The use of dogs to sniff for drugs as well as of breathalyzers and hidden video cameras, along with routine searches of students' pockets, purses, school lockers, desks, and vehicles on school grounds appear to be increasing as school officials struggle to regain control over schools. In some cases, school officials conduct their own searches, and in other cases, the police are brought in to conduct the searches.

In the *New Jersey v. T.L.O.* decision (1985), the U.S. Supreme Court examined the issue of whether Fourth Amendment rights against unreasonable searches and seizures apply to the school setting.[101] On March 7, 1980, a teacher at Piscataway High in Middlesex County, New Jersey, discovered two adolescent females smoking in a bathroom. He reported this violation of school rules to the principal's office, and the two females were summoned to meet with the assistant vice principal. When one of the females, T.L.O., claimed that she had done no wrong, the assistant principal demanded to see her purse. On examining it, he found a pack of cigarettes and cigarette rolling papers, some marijuana, a pipe, a large amount of money, a list of students who owed T.L.O. money, and letters that implicated her in marijuana dealing. T.L.O. confessed later at the police station to dealing drugs on school grounds.[102]

The juvenile court found T.L.O. delinquent and sentenced her to a year's probation, but she appealed her case to the New Jersey Supreme Court on the grounds that the search of her purse was not justified under the circumstances of the case. When the New Jersey Supreme Court upheld her appeal, the state appealed to the U.S. Supreme Court, which ruled that school personnel have the right to search lockers, desks, and students as long as they believe that either the law or school rules have been violated. The legality of a search, the Court defined, need not be based on obtaining a warrant or on having probable cause that a crime has taken place. Rather, the legality of the search depends on its reasonableness, considering the scope of the search, the student's gender and age, and the student's behavior at the time.[103]

The significance of this decision is that the Supreme Court opened the door for greater security measures because it gave school officials and the police the right to search students who are suspected of violating school rules.[104] Of eighteen cases since 1985 that were decided by state appellate decisions applying the T.L.O. decision, school officials' intervention was upheld in fifteen.[105]

In 1995, in the *Vernonia School District 47J v. Acton* decision, the U.S. Supreme Court extended schools' authority to search by legalizing a random drug-testing policy for student athletes. This decision suggests that schools may employ safe-school programs such as drug-testing procedures so long as the police satisfy the reasonableness test.[106] As drugs and guns continue to be brought onto school campuses, we can expect increased reliance on **school searches.**

Safety

As a result of limitations on the school concerning the rules under which youths can be disciplined (*Tinker*) and because of the requirements for procedural due process imposed on school administrators taking disciplinary action (*Goss, Ingraham,* and others), local school authorities have become increasingly wary of using tough methods to discipline students. Principals have become reluctant, for example, to suspend youths for acts such as acting insubordinate, wearing outlandish clothing, loitering in halls, and creating classroom disturbances, which only a few decades earlier would have drawn a quick notice of suspension. Increased judicial intervention in the academic area has contributed to (but has not caused) an increase in unruly behavior and thereby has reduced the safety of students in the public schools.[107]

In sum, judicial intervention in the school has had both positive and negative impacts. Students' rights are less likely to be abused than in the past because the courts have made it clear that students do not shed their constitutional rights at the school door. Yet school administrators who perceive themselves as handcuffed by recent court decisions have been reluctant to take firm and forceful action against disruptive students, with the result that violence and delinquency in the schools have increased.

Are There Promising Partnerships between the School and the Justice System?

There is a growing trend toward increasing partnerships between schools and various agencies of the juvenile justice system.[108] Traditionally, school partnerships with juvenile justice agencies have centered on the use of police officers as informational sources, with their efforts designed at prevention through education. Four of the well known programs initiated through earlier police-school partnerships are Drug Abuse and Education (D.A.R.E.), Police Athletic League (P.A.L.), Gang Resistance Education and Training, and Law-Related Education (all described later in this text). Police personnel who are involved with these programs use the school environment as a conduit for preventing youth crime through education and less intrusive intervention. Today, partnerships between schools and agents of the justice system are increasingly structured for student control and crime prevention, rather than education. This signals important changes in the social control mechanisms used in schools and with children.[109]

The U.S. Department of Education's report on *Violence and Discipline Problems in U.S. Public Schools 1996–1997* provides some preliminary indications on the extent of juvenile and criminal justice-public school collaboration. Taken from a national representative sample of elementary, middle, and secondary schools, this survey revealed that 97 percent of schools reported using some form of security measures. Of the surveyed schools, 84 percent reported that they had low security measures (no police officers or guards, no metal detectors, but controlled access to campus). Thirteen percent reported stringent to moderate security measures (full-time police officers or guards, metal detectors, and controlled access to campus). Of the schools with stronger security measures, 6 percent had police or other law enforcement personnel stationed for 30 hours or more at the school.[110] Despite the difficulty of gauging the extent of this collaboration, there does appear to be a growing number of schools using police officers, security personnel, or other security measures on a part-time basis (or more) to assist in maintaining school order, security, and control.[111]

The changing nature of the partnership between criminal and juvenile justice agencies and the school is as significant as the quantity of official presence. An indicator of this changing nature is the shift in language used by schools. Officers are brought into the school to "fight campus crime," "discipline," "combat victimization," and support "zero tolerance." Justice personnel in the school, formerly called resource officers and liaisons, now increasingly are called "Independent School District (ISD) Police," "security officers," "guards," and "gang intelligence officers." Yet changes in the partnership go beyond semantics. Criminal justice agencies in the school setting more frequently focus on identification and investigation, controlling campus access, drug sweeps and drug testing, strip searches, surveillance, monitoring, and crowd control.[112]

Specialized Treatment and Rehabilitation (STAR) is Texas's application of the boot camp concept within the school setting. This program brings to the school the assistance of the juvenile court, juvenile correctional authorities, the police, and parents. See Social Policy 9.3 for a description and evaluation of STAR.

SOCIAL POLICY 9.3

Specialized Treatment and Rehabilitation (STAR)

The impetus for STAR grew out of the rise of disruptive behavior on school campuses, the increasing numbers of juveniles being placed in the Texas Department of Criminal Justice Institutional Division, and an interest in the development of a boot camp program for youth. With the collaboration of the Conroe Independent School District (CISD), the Executive Director of Juvenile Services in Montgomery County, Texas, and the Montgomery County Juvenile Court, STAR began operation in November 1993. The basic goal of the STAR program was to curb disruptive and delinquent behavior in the public school system and, at the same time, to reduce student movement in and out of the schools because of discipline problems.

STAR participants are not to exceed sixteen years of age at the time of sentence. STAR levels range from I to IV. Level I is a one-day "prevention" day for youths who have broken minor rules in school. Level II is for youths who have committed more serious school violations or violations that could result in detention. Level I and Level II youths are referred to STAR by their school principal, who reports school rule violations to STAR drill instructors. Level I and II involve short-term participation for youths referred for minor violations of school rules or lesser unlawful behaviors.

Level III and Level IV require longer terms of participation and are reserved for youths whose behaviors have brought them in contact with the juvenile justice system. Level III, for example, is a twelve-week deferred adjudication program to which youths are informally sentenced by the juvenile probation department with approval and oversight of the juvenile court. Level IV, the most restrictive level of STAR, is a twenty-four-week program to which the juvenile court judge sentences the youth who has been adjudicated as a delinquent.

The daily schedule of STAR is the same for all participants. Youths arrive at 5:30 A.M. and remain there for approximately two and one-half hours. This portion of the youth's day is made up of regimented quasi-military drilling and physical activities. At 8:00 A.M. the youths are taken to their regular schools, accompanied by STAR drill instructors who remain with them throughout the school day. At the end of the school day (3:30 P.M.), STAR youths are bussed back to the STAR campus to endure an additional two hours—an hour of daily programming (e.g., reading, study time, and special presentations) and an hour of physical activities and cadence drills. The day ends at 5:45 P.M. Level III and Level IV have only Sundays away from STAR, using Saturdays to fulfill the terms of their community service sentences (e.g., cleaning buildings, picking up trash along the highways, and other needed community service.)

A twelve-months follow-up evaluation of this program was done for the ninety-four Level III and Level IV participants who completed STAR in July 1997. (The evaluation excluded Level I and Level II because data were not collected for youths not under formal supervision of the probation department.) Survey responses obtained from STAR participants, their parents, and their teachers indicated that STAR was perceived as favorable in almost every area. However, results of the recidivism analysis revealed that STAR participants offended more times for more serious offenses in a six- and twelve-month post-release follow-up when compared to Intensive Supervision Program (ISP) participants.

What is your evaluation of such a boot camp experience in a public school? Do you think that it would have much effect on youth crime if such programs were established across the nation?

Source: Chad Trulson, Ruth Triplett, and Clete Snell, "Social Control in a School Setting: Evaluating a School-Based Boot Camp," *Crime and Delinquency* 47 (October 2001), pp. 573–609.

The Most Promising Intervention Strategies in the School Setting

Schools in the United States can be improved with the increased quality of the school experience; with the greater use of alternative schools for students who cannot adapt to the traditional educational setting; with the development of a comprehensive approach that includes home, school, church/synagogue, parents, and other institutions and persons who participate in the social processes affecting students' lives; with effective school-based violence-prevention programs; and with more effective transitions from correctional contexts to the school setting.

Improving the Quality of the School Experience

A number of school-based interventions are necessary to elevate the quality of the school experience. Education must be oriented more toward the individual. Achievement should be defined in terms of a student's individual progress, not that of others in the class. This is particularly important for low achievers, who need the best facilities and the most effective teachers to allow them to realize their potentials.

Tracking systems, which classify students according to their abilities, also should be abolished.[113] Tracking systems tend to establish class systems within the school. In schools that use tracking systems, lower-track students typically receive lower grades than other students, develop a value system that elicits misbehavior rather than the academic success they feel they can never achieve, and lose self-esteem as a result of being stigmatized.[114]

Safety is one of the most important prerequisites of involvement in the educational process. Unless students feel safe, they are unlikely to involve themselves very deeply in the school experience. To ensure safety, a critical problem in large urban schools, administrators must take firm action to reduce the violence and delinquency in these settings.

Good teaching is still the first line of defense against misbehavior.[115] Good teaching can make students feel wanted and accepted and can encourage students to have more positive and successful experiences in the classroom. Gertrude Moskowitz and John L. Hayman, in a research project at three inner-city junior high schools in Philadelphia, found significant differences between effective and ineffective teachers. The best teachers expressed their feelings and enabled the students to express their emotions. The teachers combated student boredom and restlessness with timely topics, discussions, and open-ended questions. They smiled more than ineffective teachers did, and when they disciplined students, they did not raise their voices.[116]

Furthermore, students have the right to be involved in the operation of the school. Youths too frequently see themselves as immersed in an educational system that is beyond their control and unresponsive to their needs. This perception, of course, does little to increase an adolescent's desire to maintain or create positive relationships with teachers, counselors, and administrators.[117]

Finally, schools should adopt more flexible hours and schedules so that students can become oriented to the world of work. Because modern society has extended the period of adolescence, thereby isolating students from the working world, schools should incorporate work into education, particularly for those between the ages of thirteen and fifteen. Such experiences may foster the establishment of positive work role relationships at the peak age of delinquency involvement, thus reducing the negative effects of strong peer role relationships.[118]

Utilizing Alternative Schools for Disruptive Students

Disruptive behavior is a very serious problem in many of this nation's classrooms. Such behavior takes many forms: defiance of authority, manipulation of teachers, inability or unwillingness to follow rules, fights with peers, destruction of property, use of drugs in school, and physical or verbal altercations with teachers. Disruptive students require a great deal of time from teachers and counselors in order to make them accountable for their behavior and to teach them acceptable behavior. The unstructured periods of the school day—between classes, during lunch hours, and immediately after school hours—give disruptive students ample time to participate in a variety of unacceptable behaviors.

School administrators often suspend or expel students who cause trouble in the school.[119] This policy of swiftly suspending troublemakers stigmatizes them as failures and reinforces their negative behaviors. In this regard, a west coast teacher noted: "I don't think the school is dangerous through the day. Part of the reason is that they expelled 200 kids the first five or six months of the school year. Some of these students were really bad. Some of these kids were sent to an alternative school as soon as they enrolled."[120]

Alternative schools are deemed a much more satisfactory way of dealing with youths the public school cannot control or who are not doing satisfactory work in a public school setting. The National Commission on Excellence in Education's influential report, *A Nation at Risk,* states that "educationally disadvantaged students may require special curriculum materials, smaller classes, or individual tutoring to help them master the material presented."[121] The juvenile court sometimes requires disruptive students to attend an alternative school, but more frequently, students are referred by the public school.

Alternative schools, which have smaller classrooms, usually deal with "turnovers" or acting-out behaviors by taking youths out of the classroom only until they have regained control over themselves. The ultimate goal of most alternative schools is to return students to the public school setting. A student in an alternative school explains why she prefers that setting to the public school:

> The teachers here are fantastic. They're not just a teacher but here to be your friend, too. If you have a problem, you can tell them that you want to talk and they will always talk with you. In the public school, all the teachers are concerned about is your stupid work.

In an attempt to provide a safe learning environment, some schools have taken security measures that further alienate students. In fact, some researchers have compared public schools to prisons.

They give you work that you don't understand and then they pass you [on to the next grade] just to get rid of you.

It is one less student they have to worry about. Here, the classes are smaller, the teachers are younger, and there is a whole lot of them that have experienced their own problems on the streets. They have worked with students like us before, and they are qualified in what they do. They take time to make sure you understand what they teach.[122]

J. David Hawkins and John S. Wall reviewed alternative education programs and concluded that certain approaches seemed to be promising for preventing delinquent behavior.[123] Gold and David Mann's evaluation of three alternative schools revealed significant reductions in disruptive behavior in school and improved school performance for some students. But students who exhibited prior symptoms of anxiety and depression were not positively affected.[124] A national evaluation of seventeen alternative education projects indicated positive results for delinquency and behavioral problems for several of the projects.[125]

The Providence Educational Center (PEC) in north St. Louis is one of the more impressive alternative schools in the United States. Started in 1972 for serious delinquents, each class at PEC has fourteen students and two teachers. Support staff members include two social workers, two truant officers, and a physical education teacher. Individual educational goals are set for students in math, reading, and other subjects. Conventional grades are not given, and a variety of teaching techniques are used to make learning interesting. For example, one math class took a trip to a local used car lot and then to a bank to look into the financing of purchasing a car.[126]

This program has been highly praised by judges and other court officials. One St. Louis probation officer who worked with PEC commented:

I think the public school is failing a lot of kids. It is not developing a curriculum that meets the needs of inner-city youth. It takes a different breed of teacher, with patience and understanding, to do that. And I think that is what we have in Providence.[127]

The DePaul University Alternative High School in Chicago is another noteworthy alternative school. Located in the Cabrini-Green community, one of the most violent housing projects in the United States, this alternative school has a student body of more than one hundred pupils. Faculty members either have doctorates in education or have many years experience in working with disadvantaged youth. Most of the student body is made up of gang members or former gang members, who are there to graduate from high school or to be prepared to pass their GEDs. The sessions take place from 6:00 to 9:00 P.M., permitting students to work during the day. Some pupils are in their late teens or early twenties; mothers are encouraged to bring their young children to school, and day care is provided. One indicator of the seriousness of the students is that there are no signs of antisocial behavior (graffiti, drugs, weapons, or physical altercations) in the school environment.[128]

In summary, a major advantage of alternative school programs is that they deal more effectively with disruptive students than does the public school system. They also relieve the public schools of the disruptive behaviors these youths display in regular classrooms, and they tend to reduce absenteeism and dropout rates. Their success appears to be largely related to their individualized instruction, small student population, low student–adult ratio, goal-oriented classroom environment focused on work and learning, and caring, competent teachers.[129] Yet the increasingly difficult students with whom alternative school staff members must work are reducing the overall impact of these programs.

Developing More Positive School–Community Relationships

"The legendary vision of the blackboard jungle," according to Stanley Cohen, has dominated social control policy in schools. Cohen adds that the desire for a safe and secure school has contributed to a "massive investment in hardware and preventive technology: video surveillance, ultrasonic detectors, hotline to the police, redesigning buildings into clusters of manageable space." Administrators stress such problems as bomb threats, arson, violence, drug pushing, and mass disruption. Cohen concludes that the relevant literature often reads "like a blueprint for converting the school into a closed-security prison."[130]

In contrast to reducing delinquency in the school by investing in hardware and preventive technology, an alternative intervention strategy is the development of a comprehensive, or multicomponent, approach that includes home, school, and other persons and institutions that participate in the social processes affecting the students' lives. Delinquency and the quality of the public school experience, then, must be analyzed within the larger context of school–community relationships.[131]

Gary Schwartz notes the example of Parsons Park, Illinois, in which the local schools serve as "the cultural battleground of the community."[132] It was primarily through this neighborhood's educational system that ethnic traditions, family patterns, and other community standards were "woven into the fabric of local institutions." Yet the local high school in a second neighborhood in the same city was characterized as disorganized and "having little connection with the larger society's goals and values."[133] Schwartz concluded that it was no coincidence that the first area had a lower rate of juvenile delinquency and that the second had a heavy concentration of gang activity.

One way to achieve better school–community relationships is to allow representatives from various parts of the community to interact with students and to explain their roles in society. Another way is for the school to open its facilities for community events as well as to sponsor a wide range of activities designed to integrate families, the community, and students. Families and other community members also could take a larger part in the actual education of youths. For example, parents and elderly people could become volunteers or paid teacher aides. In addition, joint classes for parents and children could be conducted. Such classes, which could focus on family relations, community services, or politics, might also have an effect on parents' attitudes toward education and school.[134] Furthermore, community businesses could provide summer employment for high-risk youths who are still in school. Finally, Eugene Lang's promise to a sixth-grade East Harlem (New York City) class that he would subsidize their college study if they graduated from high school has "become one of the country's most celebrated private-sector initiatives for disadvantaged youth."[135] Twenty-two cities across the nation, as well as nine new incentive projects in New York City, have implemented similar programs.[136]

Designing Effective School-Based Violence Prevention Programs

The real or perceived threat of school violence has influenced to a large degree the way principals manage, teachers teach, and students learn. In J. H. Price and S. A. Everett's national survey of secondary school principals, one-third indicated that they had already implemented some type of violence prevention or safe school program and another third revealed that they were planning to implement such a program.[137]

Some genuine prevention efforts have been sponsored by federal and state governments. At the federal level, the Safe and Drug-Free Schools and Communities Act of 1994 has been the major initiative. This act provided $630 million in federal grants during 1995 to the states to implement violence and drug prevention programs in and around schools. State Departments of Education and local school districts are also developing guidelines and searching for effective violence prevention programs. Of the current programs being implemented, including conflict resolution curricula, peer mediation, individual counseling, locker searches and sweeps, and metal detectors, these efforts have either not been thoroughly evaluated or have been found to be ineffective.[138]

Delbert S. Elliott, Beatrix A. Hamburg, and Kirk R. Williams's *Violence in American Schools: A New Perspective* argues that "the most effective interventions [for reducing school violence] use a comprehensive, multidisciplinary approach and take into account differences in stages of individual development and involvement in overlapping social contexts, families, peer groups, schools, and neighborhoods."[139] The final chapter of this book uses the ecological, life course, and developmental approaches as a framework for organizing the previous chapters' research findings and prevention recommendations and integrates the book's various perspectives through five themes:

1. *The Interconnectedness of Family, Peer Group, School, and Neighborhood.* The interconnections among multiple social contexts result in the problems in one context being swept into another. In view of the fact that many social institutions are losing ground, this deterioration "increasingly puts pressure on schools to compensate for other institutional failures."

2. *The Dynamic Interaction between Individuals and Social Contexts in the Process of Development.* This theme relates "to the consequences of violence for schools and the functions of violence for individuals within their social settings." It is a reminder that "youth violence can have major consequences for the general climate of schools."

3. *Effective Prevention Efforts Require Collaboration.* Key in this theme is the word *collaboration.* "The prevention of violence involves building relationships among representatives of all public and private sectors that touch on the lives of youth." It is only through such collaboration that comprehensive prevention strategies can be developed "that address multiple risk factors in the overlapping social contexts relevant to the developmental stages of youth."

4. *The Need for a Public Health Approach to Violence Prevention.* This "public health strategy should be used to assess the nature and extent of youth violence and to plan and carry out violence prevention programs." These activities involve such step-by-step procedures as "public health surveillance; risk and protective factor identification, intervention design, implementation, and program monitoring as well as short- and long-term outcome assessment; and dissemination of the results to inform public policy and promote effective prevention efforts."

5. *Effective Programs and Strategies for Preventing Violence.* This theme is "organized around three intervention strategies: systemic changes for schools, programs for individual youths, and public policy positions." Some intervention efforts may be crafted for individuals, such as anger management and conflict resolution training. Others "may be designed for system reform, such as improving family relations, the quality of the school climate, the prosocial orientation of peer groups, or improving the service capacity of community agencies."[140]

In sum, Elliott and colleagues provide the developmental and contextual framework for understanding school violence. In addition, this study includes a number of policy-driven recommendations for preventing violence in U.S. schools.

Improving Transitions from Correctional Contexts to School Settings

A new priority has emerged in juvenile justice for schools to play a major role in the transition of juvenile offenders from institutional confinement to life in the community. Youthful offenders who are making the transition back to school are typically affected by social and personal influences that contributed to the conduct that placed them under the jurisdiction of the juvenile court in the first place.[141]

An example of such a venture is found in Franklin Transitional High School in Kentucky, which currently has approximately forty students. Student-to-staff ratio is about two to one because the school employs twenty staff members. Students come directly from confinement to the school. A bridge coordinator team screens returning students.

Students' length of stay at the school is based on individual needs. Although the goal is to prepare students for other educational placements, students actually can graduate from the transition school. The Institute of Families, a private agency, provides counseling services to students and their families.[142]

When an institutionalized delinquent returns to the public school setting there are potential problems. The needs of juvenile offenders, fellow students, teachers, and the community must all be considered.[143] Social Policy 9.4 outlines a strategy that is recommended for schools dealing with previously institutionalized juveniles who are enrolling in a public school.

SOCIAL POLICY 9.4

When a Delinquent Offender Returns to School

PREENROLLMENT STRATEGIES

- Contact Probation or Parole Department.
- Review juvenile records.
- Clearly communicate expectations.

WELCOMING PROCEDURES

- Review student/parent handbook.
- Develop and discuss Individual Behavior Plan.
- Create behavior contract that is signed by the student and parents.

PLACEMENT

- Use vertical counseling, i.e., assign one counselor to the student throughout the student's tenure at school.
- Carefully select classroom teachers.
- Recruit a trained adult mentor.
- Prepare classroom (e.g., ensure communication capability in the event of an emergency; remove objects that are potential weapons).

STAFF PREPARATION

- Develop and implement a crisis plan.
- Train staff in nonviolent conflict resolution.
- Share relevant information with teachers and staff members.

CLASSROOM MANAGEMENT

- Share relevant information and observations concerning the student among teachers and staff, keeping in mind that minor incidents may be significant.
- Carefully monitor the student's behavior, including relationships with others, task behavior, tardiness, and attendance.

SUPERVISION OUTSIDE THE CLASSROOM

- Provide responsible supervision in lunchroom, library, and halls.
- Assign the student a locker in a well-supervised area.
- Carefully select and monitor the student's participation in extracurricular activities.

SUPPORT SERVICES

- Make appropriate referrals to outside agencies.

INTERAGENCY COLLABORATION

- Work closely with the presiding juvenile judge and probation department.
- Provide office space on campus for the probation officer.
- Create a joint power agreement for sharing resources and juvenile records.

Remember: There are no insignificant violations of school or probation rules when it comes to students who are delinquent offenders. Any violations, threats, or assaults must be taken seriously.

Do you feel that these strategies border on overkill? That is, are previously institutionalized youths as problematic as these proposals appear to suggest?

Source: Ronald D. Stephens and June Lane Arnette, *From the Courthouse to the Schoolhouse: Making Successful Transitions: Juvenile Justice Bulletin* (Washington, D.C.: Office of Juvenile Justice and Delinquency Prevention, 2000), p. 11.

SUMMARY

The school has long been acknowledged as an important agent in the socialization of children, but public education is under sharp criticism. Public schools are accused of failing in their task of educating and socializing U.S. youth. In addition, since the 1970s, vandalism, violence, and drug trafficking have become serious problems in many schools. High rates of school crime lead to unsafe conditions and an unwholesome environment for learning. The level of achievement in school appears to be directly related to delinquent behavior, whereas learning disabilities and dropping out of school are more indirectly related. Court decisions have provided the mechanism for students to regain their rights to free speech and due process when they enter the schoolyard, but because school administrators often perceive themselves as being handcuffed by recent court decisions, they are reluctant to take firm and forceful action against disruptive students.

This chapter has again emphasized the belief that delinquent behavior can be best understood as the product of complex socialization processes operating at many different levels within the social system. For schools in the United States to improve, a number of changes involving complex socialization processes must take place. These changes include evaluating the quality of the school experience, providing more alternative schools for disruptive students, finding ways to renew urban schools, developing more positive social-community relationships, and making schools safe havens from violence.

KEY TERMS

alternative schools, p. 273
academic performance, p. 262
disruptive behavior, p. 272
dropout, p. 264
in loco parentis, p. 267

school searches, p. 269
tracking systems, p. 272
vandalism, p. 258
violence, p. 258

CRITICAL THINKING QUESTIONS

1. What is the relationship between repressive education and delinquency?
2. What are the consequences of violence and vandalism in public schools?
3. What factors are most frequently cited as contributing to the link between schools and delinquency? Rank them in importance.
4. What kind of interventions are needed to reduce the amount of delinquency in public schools?
5. Do you think a program designed to reduce bullying in school would have any effect on school violence and victimization?

WEB DESTINATIONS

Read about Dropout Prevention Resources at the National Prevention and Dropout Center and Network site.
http://www.dropoutprevention.org

Read more about alternative schools for adolescents on the National Coalition of Alternative Community School site.
http://incacs.org

Look at this timeline of school shootings with additional crime data at this site.
http://www.infoplease.com/cgi_bin/id/A0777958. html

Go to the National School Safety Center to learn more about teachers and school safety.
http://www.nsscl.org

Go to this school security page to learn more about gangs and drugs in schools.

http://www.schoolsecurity.org/faq/parents.html

NOTES

1. Carol Morello, "Sobbing Miss. School Killer Proclaims Love for Victim," *USA Today,* Friday, June 12, 1998, p. 4A.
2. John F. Feldhusen, John R. Thurston, and James J. Benning, "A Longitudinal Study of Delinquency and Other Aspects of Children's Behavior," *International Journal of Criminology and Penology* 1 (1973), pp. 341–351.
3. Delbert S. Elliott and Harwin Voss, *Delinquency and Dropout* (Lexington, Mass.: Lexington Books, 1974).
4. Arthur L. Stinchcombe, *Rebellion in a High School* (Chicago: Quadrangle Press, 1964), p. 158.
5. Eugene Maguin and Rolf Loeber, "Academic Performance and Delinquency," in *Crime and Justice: A Review of Research* 20, edited by Michael Tonry (Chicago and London: The University of Chicago Press, 1996), p 145.
6. Joel H. Spring, *Education and the Rise of the Corporate State* (Boston: Beacon Press, 1972), p. 62.
7. Joan Newman and Graeme Newman, "Crime and Punishment in the Schooling Process: A Historical Analysis," in *Violence and Crime in the Schools,* edited by Keith Baker and Robert J. Rubel (Lexington, Mass.: Lexington Books, 1980), p. 11.
8. Horace Mann and the Reverend M. H. Smith, *Sequel to the So-Called Correspondence between the Rev. M. H. Smith and Horace Mann* (Boston: W. B. Fowle, 1847).
9. John Dewey, "My Pedagogic Creed" (1897), reprinted in *Teaching in American Culture,* edited by K. Gezi and J. Meyers (New York: Holt, Rinehart, and Winston, 1968).
10. *Brown v. Board of Education of Topeka, Kansas* (1954), 347 US 483.
11. John Goodlad, *A Place Called School* (New York: McGraw-Hill, 1984), p. 1.
12. Julius Menacker, Ward Weldon, and Emanuel Hurwitz, "Community Influences on School Crime and Violence," *Urban Education* 25 (1990), pp. 68, 77.
13. Mihaly Csikszentimihalyi, Reed Larson, and Suzanne Prescott, "The Ecology of Adolescent Activities and Experience," *Journal of Youth and Adolescence* 6 (1977), pp. 281–294.
14. Martin Gold, "School Experiences, Self-Esteem, and Delinquent Behavior: A Theory for Alternative Schools," *Crime and Delinquency* 24 (1978), pp. 294–295.
15. Urie Bronfenbrenner, "The Origins of Alienation," *Scientific American* 231 (1973), pp. 41–53.
16. Craig Haney and Philip G. Zimbardo, "The Blackboard Penitentiary—It's Tough to Tell a High School from a Prison," *Psychology Today* 9 (June 1975), p. 106.
17. Kathryn A. Buckner, "School Drug Tests: A Fourth Amendment Perspective," *University of Illinois Law Review* 5 (1987), pp. 275–310.
18. U.S. Department of Health, Education and Welfare, *Violent Schools–Safe Schools: The Safe School Study Report to Congress* (Washington, D.C.: U.S. Government Printing Office, 1977), p. 177.
19. Robert J. Rubel, "Extent, Perspectives, and Consequences of Violence and Vandalism in Public Schools," in *Violence and Crime in the Schools,* edited by Keith Baker and Robert J. Rubel (Lexington, Mass.: Lexington Books, 1980), p. 19.
20. Interviewed in July 1985.
21. J. R. Wetzel, "School Crime: Annual Statistical Snapshot," *School Safety* 8 (Winter 1989), p. 8.
22. Ibid.
23. Robert M. Regoli and John D. Hewitt, *Delinquency in Society: A Child-Centered Approach* (New York: McGraw-Hill, 1991), pp. 245–246.
24. Bureau of Justice Statistics, *School Crime: A National Crime Victimization Survey Report* (Washington, D.C.: U.S. Department of Justice, 1991), p. 1.
25. National School Safety Center, *Weapons in School* (Malibu, Calif.: Pepperdine University Press, 1992).
26. Jean Johnson, Steve Farkas, and Alie Bers, *Getting By: What American Teenagers Really Think about Their Schools* (New York: Public Agenda, 1997), p. 14.
27. Laura Kann, Charles W. Warren, William A. Harris, J. L. Collins, K. A. Douglas, M. E. Collins, Barbara I. Williams, James G. Ross, and Lloyd J. Kolbe, "Youth Risk Behavior Surveillance—United States, 1993," in CDC Surveillance Summaries, *Morbidity and Mortality Weekly Report* 44 (1995), p. 6.
28. Robert Leitman, Katherine Binns, and Akhil Unni, *The Metropolitan Life Survey of the American Teacher 1994, Violence in America's Public Schools: The Family Perspective* (New York: Louis Harris, 1994), p. 5.
29. Lena M. Chao, Allan Parachini, Fernando Hernandez, Michael J. Cody, and Daniel Cochece Davis, *From Words to Weapons: The Violence Surrounding Our Schools* (Los Angeles, Calif.: ACLU Foundation of Southern California, 1997), pp. iii–iv.
30. Task Force on Juvenile Delinquency, *Juvenile Delinquency and Youth Crime* (Washington, D.C.: U.S. Government Printing Office, 1967), p. 51.
31. Anthony Meade, "Seriousness of Delinquency, the Adjudicative Decision and Recidivism: A Conceptual Configuration Analysis," *Journal of Criminal Law and Criminology* 64 (December 1973), pp. 478–485.
32. Albert K. Cohen, *Delinquent Boys: The Culture of the Gang* (New York: Free Press, 1955), pp. 123–124.
33. LaMar T. Empey and Steven G. Lubeck, *Explaining Delinquency* (Lexington, Mass.: D.C. Heath, 1971).
34. Steven A. Cernkovich and Peggy C. Giordano, "School Bonding, Race, and Delinquency," *Criminology* 30 (1992), pp. 261–291.
35. Allen E. Liska and Mark D. Reed, "Ties to Conventional Institutions and Delinquency: Estimating Reciprocal Effects," *American Sociological Review* 50 (1985), pp. 547–560.

36. LaMar T. Empey and S. G. Lubeck, *Explaining Delinquency* (Lexington, Mass.: Lexington Books, 1971); M. Gold, *Status Forces in Delinquent Boys* (Ann Arbor, Mich.: Institute for Social Research, University of Michigan, 1963); Martin Gold and D. W. Mann, "Delinquency as Defense," *American Journal of Orthopsychiatry* 42 (1972), pp. 463–479; T. Hirschi, *Causes of Delinquency* (Berkeley: University of California Press, 1969); H. B. Kaplan, "Sequel of Self-Derogation: Predicting from a General Theory of Deviant Behavior," *Youth and Society* 7 (1975), pp. 171–197; and A. L. Rhodes and A. J. Reiss Jr., "Apathy, Truancy, and Delinquency as Adaptations to School Failure," *Social Forces* 48 (1969), pp. 12–22.

37. E. B. Palmore, "Factors Associated with School Dropouts and Juvenile Delinquency among Lower-Class Children," in *Society and Education,* edited by R. J. Havighurst, B. L. Neugarten, and J. M. Falls (Boston: Allyn and Bacon, 1967); J. F. Short and F. L. Strodtbeck, *Group Process and Gang Delinquency* (Chicago: University of Chicago Press, 1965); and D. J. West, *Present Conduct and Future Delinquency* (New York: International Universities Press, 1969).

38. Sheldon Glueck and Eleanor Glueck, *Unraveling Juvenile Delinquency* (Cambridge: Harvard University Press, 1950); G. P. Liddle, "Existing and Projected Research on Reading in Relationship to Delinquency," in *Role of the School in Prevention of Juvenile Delinquency,* edited by W. R. Carriker (Washington, D.C.: U.S. Government Printing Office, 1963); and N. W. Silberberg and M. C. Silberberg, "School Achievement and Delinquency," *Review of Educational Research* 41 (1971), pp. 17–31.

39. Hirschi, *Causes of Delinquency.*

40. M. L. Erickson, M. L. Scott, and L. T. Empey, *School Experience and Delinquency* (Provo, Utah: Brigham Young University, 1964); R. J. Havighurst et al., *Growing Up in River City* (New York: John Wiley and Sons, 1962); W. Healy and A. F. Bronner, *New Light on Delinquency and Its Treatment* (New Haven: Yale University Press, 1963); and W. C. Kvaraceus, *Juvenile Delinquency and the School* (New York: World Book Company, 1945).

41. William E. Schafer and Kenneth Polk, "Delinquency and the Schools," in *Task Force Report: Juvenile Delinquency and Youth Crime* (Washington, D.C.: Government Printing Office, 1967), p. 233.

42. Franco Ferracuti and Simon Dinitz, "Cross-Cultural Aspects of Delinquent and Criminal Behavior," in *Aggression,* edited by S. H. Frazier (Baltimore: Williams and Williams, 1974); Glueck and Glueck, *Unraveling Juvenile Delinquency;* and West, *Present Conduct and Future Delinquency.*

43. J. David Hawkins and Denise M. Lishner, "Schooling and Delinquency," *Handbook on Crime and Delinquency Prevention* (Westport, Conn.: Greenwood Press, 1987), p. 181.

44. Glueck and Glueck, *Unraveling Juvenile Delinquency;* Ferracuti and Dinitz, "Cross-Cultural Aspects of Delinquent and Criminal Behavior"; Havighurst et al., *Growing Up in River City;* West, *Present Conduct and Future Delinquency.*

45. C. F. Cardinelli, "Relationship of Interaction of Selected Personality Characteristics of School Principal and Custodian with Sociological Variables to School Vandalism."

Ph.D. dissertation, Michigan State University, 1969; Ferracutti and Dinitz, "Cross-Cultural Aspects of Delinquent and Criminal Behavior"; N. Goldman, "A Socio-Psychological Study of School Vandalism," *Crime and Delinquency* 7 (1961), pp. 221–230; M. J. Hindelang, "Causes of Delinquency: A Partial Replication and Extension," *Social Problems* 20 (1973), pp. 471–487; Hirschi, *Causes of Delinquency;* C. W. Thomas, G. A. Kreps, and R. J. Cage, "An Application of Compliance Theory to the Study of Juvenile Delinquency," *Sociology and Social Research* 61 (1977), pp. 156–175; and S. Vandenberg, "Student Alienation: Orientation toward and Perceptions of Aspects of Educational Social Structure," *Urban Education* 10 (1975), pp. 262–278.

46. Cardinelli, "Interaction of Selected Personality Characteristics"; and Goldman, "A Socio-Psychological Study of School Vandalism."

47. Maguin and Loeber, "Academic Performance and Delinquency," p. 145.

48. Robert Sampson and John Laub, *Crime in the Making: Pathways and Turning Points Through Life* (Cambridge, Mass.: Harvard University Press, 1993).

49. Richard Arum and Irenee R. Beattie, "High School Experience and the Risk of Adult Incarceration," *Criminology* 37 (August 1999), p. 515.

50. *Ibid.,* p. 532.

51. Cohen, *Delinquent Boys.*

52. Jackson Toby, "Orientation to Education as a Factor in the School Maladjustment of Lower-Class Children," *Social Forces* 35 (1957), pp. 259–266.

53. John C. Phillips, "The Creation of Deviant Behavior in American High Schools," in *Violence and Crime in the Schools,* edited by Keith Baker and Robert J. Rubal (Lexington, Mass.: Lexington Books, 1980), p. 124.

54. Kenneth Polk and F. Lynn Richmond, "Those Who Fail," in *Schools and Delinquency,* p. 67.

55. Kenneth Polk, "Class, Strain, and Rebellion among Adolescents," *Social Problems* 17 (1969), pp. 214–224.

56. E. B. Palmore and P. E. Hammond, "Interacting Factors in Juvenile Delinquency," *American Sociological Review* 29 (1964), pp. 848–854.

57. George W. Nobit, "The Adolescent Experience and Delinquency: School Versus Subcultural Effects," *Youth and Society* 8 (September 1976), pp. 27–44.

58. National Advisory Council on Supplementary Centers and Services, *Dropout Prevention* (Washington, D.C.: U.S. Government Printing Office, 1975), p. 2.

59. Joy G. Dryfoos, *Adolescents at Risk: Prevalence and Prevention* (New York: Oxford University Press, 1990), p. 89.

60. Delbert S. Elliott and Harwin L. Voss, *Delinquency and Dropout* (Lexington, Mass.: Lexington Books, 1974), pp. 127–128.

61. Ibid., p. 454.

62. S. K. Mukherjee, "A Typological Study of School Status and Delinquency." Unpublished doctoral dissertation (Philadelphia: University of Pennsylvania, 1971).

63. Marc LeBlanc, Louise Biron, and Louison Pronovost, "Psycho-Social Development and Delinquency Evolution." Unpublished manuscript, University of Montreal, 1979.

64. Terence P. Thornberry, Melanie Moore, and R. L. Christensen, "The Effect of Dropping Out of High School on Subsequent Criminal Behavior," *Criminology* 23 (1985), pp. 7, 17.

65. Kenneth Polk, et al., "Becoming Adult: An Analysis of Maturational Development from Age 16 to 30 of a Cohort of Young Men." Final report of the Marion County Youth Study (Eugene: University of Oregon, 1981), pp. 300–301.

66. Starke R. Hathaway et al., "Follow-up of the Later Careers and Lives of 1,000 Boys Who Dropped Out of High School," *Journal of Consulting and Clinical Psychology* 33 (1969), pp. 370–380.

67. Jerald G. Bachman and Patrick M. O'Malley, *Youth in Transition.* Vol. VI: *Adolescence to Adulthood: Change and Stability in the Lives of Young Men* (Ann Arbor: University of Michigan Press, 1978).

68. Thornberry et al., "The Effect of Dropping Out of High School on Subsequent Criminal Behavior," pp. 10–11.

69. G. Roger Jarjoura, "Does Dropping Out of School Enhance Delinquent Involvement? Results from a Large-Scale National Probability Sample," *Criminology* 31 (May 1993), pp. 149–171. For an examination of how disciplinary procedures produce dropouts, see Christine Bowditch, "Getting Rid of Troublemakers: High School Disciplinary Procedures and the Production of Dropouts," *Social Problems* 40 (November 1993), pp. 491–509.

70. Donald J. Shoemaker, *Theories of Delinquency: An Examination of Explanations of Delinquent Behavior* (New York: Oxford University Press, 1996), p. 109.

71. Dryfoos, *Adolescents at Risk,* p. 89.

72. Jeffrey Fagan and Edward Pabon, "Contributions of Delinquency and Substance Abuse to School Dropouts among Inner-City Youth," 21 (1990), pp. 306–354.

73. Jarjoura, "Does Dropping Out of School Enhance Delinquent Involvement?" pp. 149–172.

74. Ibid.; Josefina Figueira–McDonough, "Residence, Dropping Out, and Delinquency Rates," *Deviant Behavior* 14 (1993), pp. 109–132; Timothy Hartnagel and Harvey Krahn, "High School Dropouts, Labor Market Success, and Criminal Behavior," *Youth and Society* 20 (1989), pp. 416–444; and Howard B. Kaplan and Xiaoro Liu, "A Longitudinal Analysis of Mediating Variables in the Drug Use–Dropping Out Relationship," *Criminology* 32 (1994), pp. 415–439.

75. Shoemaker, *Theories of Delinquency,* p. 110.

76. This section on theory is adapted in part from Hawkins and Lishner, "Schooling and Delinquency," pp. 190–191.

77. For research describing that African Americans are at least as bonded to the school as whites, see Stephen A. Cernkovich and Peggy C. Giordano, "School Bonding, Race, and Delinquency," *Criminology* 30 (May 1992), pp. 261–291.

78. Wayne N. Welsh, Jack R. Greene, and Patricia H. Jenkins, "School Disorder: The Influence of Individual, Institutional, and Community Factors," *Criminology* 37 (February 1999), p. 73.

79. Stephen Goldstein, "The Scope and Sources of School Board Authority to Regulate Student Conduct and Status: A Nonconstitutional Analysis," 117 *U. Pa. L. Rev.* 373, 1969.

80. E. Edmund Reutter Jr., *Legal Aspects of Control of Student Activities by Public School Authorities* (Topeka, Kans.: National Organization on Legal Problems of Education, 1970).

81. *Hanson v. Broothby,* 318 F.Supp. 1183 (D.Mass., 1970).

82. *Burnside v. Byars,* 363 F.2d 744 (5th Cir. 1966).

83. This section on the rights of students is derived in part from Robert J. Rubel and Arthur H. Goldsmith, "Reflections on the Rights of Students and the Rise of School Violence," in *Violence and Crime in the Schools,* pp. 73–77.

84. *Dixon v. Alabama State Board of Education,* 294 F.2d 150, 158 (5th Cr. 1961, cert. den., 368 U.S. 930).

85. *Tinker v. Des Moines Independent School District,* 383 U.S. 503.

86. *Bethel School District No. 403 v. Fraser,* 478 U.S. 675, 106 S.Ct. 3159, 92 L.Ed.2d 549 (1986).

87. *Hazelwood School District v. Kuhlmeier,* 488 U.S. 260, 108 S.Ct. 562, 98 L.Ed. 2d 592 (1988).

88. *Goss v. Lopez,* 419 U.S. 565.

89. *Wood v. Strickland,* 420 U.S. 308.

90. *Baker v. Owen,* 423 U.S. 907, affirming 395 F.Supp. 294 (1975); and *Ingraham v. Wright,* 430 U.S. 651 (1975).

91. 423 U.S. 907, affirming 395 F. Supp. 294 (1975).

92. *West Virginia State Board of Education v. Barnette,* 319 U.S. 624.

93. *Tinker.*

94. *Yoo v. Moynihan,* 20 Conn. supp. 375 (1969).

95. *Richards v. Thurston,* 424 F.2d 1281 (1st Cir. 1970).

96. *Crossen v. Fatsi,* 309 F.Supp. 114 (1970).

97. *Scott v. Board of Education, U.F. School District #17, Hicksville,* 61 Misc. 2d 333, 305 N.Y.S. 2d 601 (1969).

98. *Bannister v. Paradix,* 316 F. supp. 185 (1970).

99. *Richards v. Thurston.*

100. Ronald D. Stephens, "School-Based Interventions: Safety and Security," *The Gang Intervention Handbook,* edited by Arnold P. Goldstein and C. Ronald Huff (Champaign, Ill.: Research Press, 1993), p. 221.

101. *New Jersey v. T.L.O.,* 469 U.S. (1985).

102. Ibid.

103. Ibid.

104. For an extensive discussion of the relevant issues and court decisions related to the police in the schools, see Davis, *Rights of Juveniles,* Section 3–19 to 3–34.3.

105. J. M. Sanchez, "Expelling the Fourth Amendment from American Schools: Students' Rights Six Years after T.L.O.," *Law and Education Journal* 21 (1992), pp. 381–413.

106. *Vernonia School District v. Acton,* 115 S. Ct. 2394 (1995).

107. Rubel and Goldsmith, "Reflections on the Rights of Students," pp. 98–99.

108. Sheila Heavihide, *Violence and Discipline Problems in U.S. Public Schools 1996-1997* (Washington, D.C.: U.S. Department of Education, 1998).

109. Ibid.

110. Ibid.

111. Ibid.

112. Ibid.

113. For a more positive view of tracking, see Adam Gamoran and Robert D. Mare, "Secondary School Tracking and

Educational Inequality: Compensation, Reinforcement, or Neutrality?" *American Journal of Sociology* 94 (March 1989), pp. 1146–1183 and Michael D. Wiatrowski, Stephen Hansell, Charles R. Massey, and David L. Wilson, "Curriculum Tracking and Delinquency," *American Sociological Review* 47 February 1982), pp. 151–160.

114. Schafer and Polk, "Delinquency and the Schools," pp. 196–200.

115. M. Powell and J. Bergem, "An Investigation of the Differences between Tenth-, Eleventh-, and Twelfth-grade 'Conforming' and 'Nonconforming' Boys," *Journal of Educational Research* 56 (December 1962), pp. 184–190; K. H. Mueller, "Programs for Deviant Girls," in *Social Deviancy among Youth,* edited by William W. Wattenburg (Chicago: University of Chicago Press, 1966).

116. Gertrude Moskowitz and John L. Hayman, "Interaction Patterns of First-Year, Typical, and 'Best' Teachers in Inner-City Schools," *Journal of Education Research* 67 (1974), pp. 224–230.

117. Paul C. Friday and John Halsey, "Pattern of Social Relationships and Youth Crime: Social Integration and Prevention," in *Youth Crime and Juvenile Justice,* edited by P. C. Friday and V. L. Stewart (New York: Praeger, 1977), pp. 150–151.

118. Ibid.

119. See Bowditch, "Getting Rid of Troublemakers."

120. Interviewed in June 1982.

121. The National Commission on Excellence in Education, *A Nation at Risk: The Imperative for Educational Reform* (Washington, D.C.: U.S. Department of Education, 1983), p. 24.

122. Interviewed in May 1981.

123. J. David Hawkins and John S. Wall, *Alternative Education: Exploring the Delinquency Prevention Potential* (Washington, D.C.: U.S. Government Printing Office, 1981).

124. Martin Gold and David W. Mann, *Expelled to a Friendlier Place: A Study of Effective Alternative Schools* (Ann Arbor: University of Michigan Press, 1984).

125. Gary D. Gottfredson et al., *The School Action Effectiveness Study: Second Interim Report, Part I* (Baltimore: Johns Hopkins University, 1983).

126. "In St. Louis, a Program Flip-Flops," *Corrections Magazine* 2 (December 1976), pp. 29–30.

127. Ibid., p. 30.

128. The author made a site visit to this school in December 1997. He interviewed a number of students as well as the director and other faculty. This alternative school was closed in 2001 when the Cabrini–Green housing units were torn down.

129. Wall et al., *Report of the National Juvenile Justice Assessment Centers for Juvenile Delinquency Prevention: A*

Compendium of the 36 Program Models (Washington. D.C.: Government Printing Office, 1981), pp. 18–19.

130. Stanley Cohen, *Visions of Social Control: Crime, Punishment and Classification* (Cambridge, England: Polity Press, 1985), pp. 80–81.

131. Jacqueline R. Scherer, "School–Community Relations Network Strategies," in *Violence and Crime in the Schools,* p. 61.

132. Gary Schwartz, *Beyond Conformity or Rebellion* (Chicago: University of Chicago Press, 1987), p. 50.

133. Ibid., p. 22.

134. Friday and Halsey, "Patterns of Social Relationships and Youth Crime," pp. 150–151.

135. Marc Freedman, "No Simple Dream," *Public Private Ventures News* (Winter 1987), p. 2.

136. Dryfoos, *Adolescents at Risk,* p. 212.

137. J. H. Price and S. A. Everett, "A National Assessment of Secondary School Principals' Perceptions of Violence in the Schools," *Health Education and Behavior* 24 (1997), pp. 218–229.

138. Denise Gottfredson, "School-Based Crime Prevention," in *Preventing Crime: What Works, What Doesn't, What's Promising: A Report to the United States Congress,* edited by Larry Sherman and Denise Gottfredson (Washington, D.C.: U.S. Department of Justice, Office of Justice Programs, 1997), pp. 2–74; M. W. Lipset, "Juvenile Delinquency Treatment: A Meta-Analytic Inquiry into the Variability of Effects," in *Meta-Analysis for Explanation: A Casebook,* edited by T. D. Cook, H. Cooker, D. S. Cordray, H. Hartman, L. V. Hedges, R. J. Light, T. A. Louis, and F. Mosteller (New York: Russell Sage Foundation, 1992), pp. 83–127; Patrick Tolan and Nancy Guerra, *What Works in Reducing Adolescent Violence: An Empirical Review of the Field* (Boulder: University of Colorado, Center for the Study and Prevention of Violence, 1994); and D. W. Webster, "The Unconvincing Case for School-Based Conflict Resolution," *Health Affairs* 12 (1993), pp. 126–141.

139. Delbert S. Elliott, Beatrix A. Hamburg, and Kirk R. Williams, *Violence in American Schools: A New Perspective* (Cambridge: Cambridge Press, 1998), p. 1.

140. Delbert S. Elliott, Kirk R. Williams, and Beatrix Hamburg, "An Integrated Approach to Violence Prevention," in *Violence in American Schools,* pp. 379–384.

141. Ronald D. Stephens and June Lane Arnette, *From the Courthouse to the Schoolhouse: Making Successful Transitions* (Washington, D.C.: Office of Juvenile Justice and Delinquency Prevention, 2000), pp. 1–2.

142. Ibid., p. 8.

143. Ibid., p. 149.

chapter 10
GANG DELINQUENCY

OBJECTIVES

After reading this chapter, the student will be able to answer the following questions:

- What is the relationship between peer groups and gang activity?

- How have gangs evolved in the United States?

- Is there a relationship between urban-based gangs and emerging gangs in smaller cities and communities?

- How extensive is gang activity?

- How toxic is gang activity to communities?

- Why do youths join gangs?

- How can gangs be prevented and controlled?

Willie Lloyd, the legendary chief of the Almighty Unknown Vice Lords, tells how he became involved with the street gang:

I grew up on the streets of Chicago. When I was growing up, the Lords had a big impact on me. I never saw it as a gang, but a cohesive and unified principle on which a person could organize his life. Even as a kid of nine, I was intrigued by the Lords when I first saw them outside of the Central Park Theater. It was the first time I had ever witnessed so many black people moving so

*harmoniously together. They were motored by the same sense of purpose, and
they all wore similar dress and insignia. There were over a hundred guys, all
in black, with capes and umbrellas. To my young eyes, it was the most beautiful expression I had ever seen. They seemed so fearless, so proud, so much in
control of their lives. Though I didn't know one of them at the time, I fell in
love with all of them. In retrospect, I made up my mind the very first time I
saw the Vice Lords to be a Vice Lord.*[1]

**What does Lloyd mean when he says that gangs are a cohesive and unified princi-
ple on which you could organize your life? Why did Lloyd see such order in the Vice
Lords?**

Lloyd remained the leader of the Almighty Unknown Vice Lords, a Chicago-based
gang that is the second largest of the eleven divisions of the Vice Lord Nation. Whether
he was in prison, in jail, or in the community, this former chief of the Almighty Unknown Vice Lords taught his followers that it was "their obligation to extend the Nation
on the streets."

We used to have three classes a week at which I taught the brothers leadership and the
reconstruction of the Vice Lords here and throughout the state and eventually throughout the nation. I am the pioneer, and these guys are to be the engineers. The new concept will be called "the new movement."[2]

In the final two decades of the twentieth century, using Uzis, Soviet AK-47s, Ar-15s,
and other semiautomatic weapons, the Vice Lords and other urban street gangs evolved
into small criminal empires fighting for control of thriving narcotics, auto theft, prostitution, gunrunning, and extortion operations. Drugs made up the main criminal operation, particularly **crack,** or rock cocaine. The crack trade, more than anything else,
transformed these street gangs into ghetto-based drug-trafficking organizations. Juveniles remained with the gangs, but the gangs were led and controlled by adults. It was
estimated that 75 to 100 gangs were involved in cocaine distribution, and some gangs
had sales totaling up to $1 million a week.[3]

In 1988 and 1989 and through the early 1990s, an upsurge of youth gangs suddenly
occurred throughout the United States. Some of these youth gangs used names of the
national urban gangs, such as the Bloods and Crips from Los Angeles or the Gangster
Disciples, Vice Lords, or Latin Kings from Chicago. Other gangs made up their own
names, based on neighborhoods or images they wanted to depict to other peers and the
community. By the mid-1990s, nearly every city, many suburban areas, and even some
rural areas across the United States experienced the reality of youths who considered
themselves gang members.

How Peer Groups and Gangs Are Related

The increased focus on the individual in delinquency theory in the 1970s and 1980s provided a necessary balance to the previous overemphasis on group processes. But by the
late 1980s, there was some concern that most theories of delinquency had become
social-psychological rather than sociological, with the result that the group aspects of
delinquent behavior had ceased to be examined and at times were virtually ignored.[4] A
number of 1990s studies on the relationship between peers and delinquency revealed a
renewed interest in group processes.[5]

Peer Groups and Delinquent Behavior

Inquiry into group delinquency has resulted in conflicting findings. Some self-report studies have found that most delinquent behavior occurs in groups. S. P. Breckinridge and E. Abbott's study found that most delinquent acts were committed with at least one other person.[6] Research by Clifford R. Shaw and Henry D. McKay showed that 82 percent of offenders committed their offenses in groups.[7] Maynard L. Erickson and Gary F. Jensen reported that regardless of their sex or whether they are in urban settings or small towns, juveniles tend to follow herd instincts when they violate the law. These authors did find that drug offenses have the highest group frequency and that status offenses—other than drinking and smoking—have the lowest.[8] Erickson reported in another study that between 37 and 42 percent of delinquent acts are committed by one person.[9] Paul Strasburg's study of violent delinquents in New York found that 69 percent of violent crimes were committed in a group of more than one person.[10] M. M. Craig and L. A. Budd, however, using a sample of youths in New York, found that only 38 percent of offenses were committed with companions.[11] Michael J. Hindelang further indicated that group delinquency may be overestimated.[12]

Elizabeth S. Piper, using the 1958 Philadelphia cohort data, investigated the relationship between the age of the offender, the type of offense, and the number of coparticipants. Piper found that, overall, 51 percent of offenses were committed in groups. Of these, 46 percent of nonviolent offenses and 68 percent of violent offenses were committed with others. At earlier ages, most offenses were committed by lone offenders; the peak in group offending was at ages thirteen and fourteen. An increasing tendency toward lone offending occurred later in the delinquent's career. Chronic offenders with five or more offenses, especially, were likely to have a greater mix of group and lone offenses than nonchronic offenders. Another important finding of this study is a greater desistance rate among group offenders than among lone offenders, regardless of age at onset.[13]

Although there is general agreement that delinquency occurs most frequently within a group context, there is much less consensus about the nature and quality of delinquents' relationships with their friends or about the relationship between peers and delinquency. In terms of the quality of delinquents' relationships with their friends, Travis Hirschi believes that the causal significance of friendships has been overstated. In referring to these relationships as "**cold and brittle**," he argues that "since delinquents are less strongly attached to conventional adults than nondelinquents they are less likely to be attached to each other. . . . The idea that delinquents have comparatively warm, intimate social relations with each other (or with anyone) is a romantic myth."[14]

Peggy C. Giordano and S. A. Cernkovich, in examining the relationships involved in delinquent groups, found that delinquents and nondelinquents have similar **friendship patterns.** This conclusion led them to question Hirschi's "cold and brittle" assumption because Hirschi's position assumes social disability: "that is, that these kids are incapable of developing important and close friendships with each other and that they are just held together by the common quality of being losers." In contrast, these researchers believe that delinquents are able to develop good and close primary relationships.[15] Mark Warr's analysis of the National Youth Survey also found that delinquents are able to form close relationships with others. He stated that "delinquent friends tend to be 'sticky' friends (once acquired, they are not quickly lost)," but "recent rather than early friends have the greatest effect on delinquency."[16]

One of the stongest finding of criminology, according to Ross L. Matsueda and Kathleen Anderson, "is that delinquent behavior is correlated with delinquency of one's peers."[17] The process of examining this relationship between delinquency and peers has generated considerable debate. This debate has largely focused on the question of causal order. Do delinquents merely seek friends like themselves or do youths become delinquent because they associate with delinquent friends?

Robert Agnew's examination of data from the National Youth Survey found that when there is strong attachment to peers, longer periods of time spent with peers, and more extensive delinquent patterns presented, association with peers who engage in serious delinquent behavior has a strong, positive effect on delinquency.[18] Warr and Stafford's analysis of data from the National Youth Survey reveals that peer attitudes tend to affect delinquency, but this effect is small compared with that of peers' behavior. The effect of peers' behavior, according to this study, remains strong even when the adolescent's own attitude and peers' attitudes are controlled.[19] D. S. Elliot and S. Menard's compelling research found that the acquisition of delinquent peers commonly preceded the onset of delinquency, which supports the notion of peer influence as a causal factor in delinquency.[20]

Merry Morash reported that adolescent females belong to less-delinquent groups, and this is a significant factor in accounting for their lower levels of delinquency. She contends that structural and situational constraints, as well as individual-level variables, explain why females end up in the least delinquent peer groups. Structural and situational factors, she suggests, may include the tendency of males to prefer to commit crime with other males, sex-typing of females by males as inappropriate colleagues and leaders, and a crime environment that emphasizes raw physical power. Moreover, gender-related characteristics of females, such as an aversion to aggression or greater empathy, may restrain females from joining peers who are prone to violent acts.[21]

Some investigators contend that the relationship between delinquent behavior and delinquent peers is sequential or bidirectional.[22] Matsueda and Anderson found from their analysis of data from the National Youth Survey that "delinquent peer associations and delinquent behavior are reciprocally related, but the effect of delinquency on peer associations is larger than that of peer associations on delinquency."[23] Terence Thornberry and colleagues' examination of three waves of the Rochester Youth Development Study revealed that an interactional, rather than unidimensional, model better explains the relationship between peers and delinquency:

> Associating with delinquent peers leads to increase in delinquency via the reinforcing environment of the peer network. Engaging in delinquency, in turn, leads to increases in associations with delinquent peers. Finally, delinquent beliefs exert lagged effects on peers and behavior, which tend in turn to "harden" the formation of delinquent beliefs.[24]

In sum, researchers generally agree that most delinquent behavior, especially more violent forms, is committed in groups, but they disagree on the quality of relationships within delinquent groups and on the influence of groups on delinquent behavior. There seems to be some agreement that the causal path is from peers to delinquent behavior and that more than a unidimensional model is needed. It would appear that an integrated approach, combining elements of control, strain, and subculture theory, can better account for delinquent behavior in groups than can any pure model alone. This integrated approach can also provide more clarity on several theoretical questions about groups and delinquency that are still being debated. For example, how do delinquent peers influence each other? What causes the initial attraction to delinquent groups? What do delinquents receive from these friendships that results in continuing them?[25]

Different Types of Peer Groups

Walter B. Miller, in one of his analyses of youth gangs in fifteen major cities, identified eighteen types and subtypes of law-violating youth groups (see Table 10.1). Significantly, only three of these eighteen types and subtypes are designated as gangs: The others are called groups, cliques, rings, bands, networks, and crowds.[26]

Juveniles hang around in groups, and as Miller's list suggests, these groups can have many illegal functions. Two or more young people hanging around on the corner or talking on the streets, however, can have many other functions. They may be merely passing the time of day. They may have nothing else to do. They may be planning an activity or discussing athletic events.

TABLE 10.1

Types and Subtypes of Law-Violating Youth Groups

Number	Designation
1	Turf gangs
2	Regularly-associated disruptive local groups/crowds
3	Solidary disruptive local cliques
4	Casual disruptive local cliques
5	Gain-oriented gangs/extended networks
6	Looting groups/crowds
7	Established gain-oriented cliques/limited networks
7.1	Burglary rings
7.2	Robbery bands
7.3	Larceny cliques and networks
7.4	Extortion cliques
7.5	Drug-dealing cliques and networks
7.6	Fraudulent gain cliques
8	Casual gain-oriented cliques
9	Fighting gangs
10	Assaultive cliques and crowds
10.1	Assaultive affiliation cliques
10.2	Assaultive public-gathering crowds
11	Recurrently-active assaultive cliques
12	Casual assaultive cliques

Source: Adapted from Walter B. Miller, *Crime by Youth Groups and Gangs in American Cities* (Washington, D.C.: Government Printing Office), chap. 25, chart 2, 1979.

How Gangs Have Evolved in the United States

Gangs have existed in this nation since the Revolutionary War. In the War of 1812, for example, Jean Laffite led his band of pioneers and smugglers against the British in support of Andrew Jackson. The Younger and James gangs, two infamous gangs of the Wild West, have long been folk heroes.[27] Youth gangs, as we know them, also originated in the early decades of this nation's history. Some evidence indicates that youth gangs may have existed as early as the American Revolution.[28] Others suggest that they first emerged in the Southwest following the Mexican Revolution in 1813.[29] Youth gangs seemed to have spread in New England in the early 1800s, primarily because of the shift from agrarian to industrial society. Youth gangs began to flourish in Chicago and other large cities in the nineteenth century as immigration and population shifts reached peak levels. In the nineteenth century, youth gangs were primarily Irish, Jewish, and Italian.[30] In the twentieth century, youth gangs have changed rather significantly in nearly every decade.

Gangs and Play Activity: The 1920s through 1940s

Frederick Thrasher's *The Gang: A Study of 1,313 Gangs in Chicago* was a pioneering and as yet unsurpassed work on gangs.[31] Thrasher viewed gangs as a normal part of growing up in ethnic neighborhoods. Adolescents who went to school together and played together in the neighborhood naturally developed a strong sense of identity that led to their forming close-knit groups. Thrasher saw these gangs, evolving from neighborhood play groups, as bonded together without any particular purpose or goal. They were largely transitory social groupings, typically with fewer than thirty members. They were generally organized in three concentric circles: a core composed of a leader and lieutenants, the rank-and-file membership, and a few occasional members. Finally, although each gang was different, the protection of turf was universally expected gang behavior.[32]

West Side Story Era: The 1950s

From the late 1940s through the 1950s, teenage gangs became more established in urban areas, such as Boston, New York, and Philadelphia. In addition to the time they spent "hanging out," they partied together and, when necessary, they fought other gangs together. The musical *West Side Story,* later made into a movie, presented a picture of two 1950s New York youth gangs singing, dancing, and battling over turf. The Sharks, recent immigrants from Puerto Rico, defended their neighborhood while the Jets defended theirs; territorial lines were confined to neighborhood ethnic boundaries.

The 1950s gangs did not have the lethal weapons that today's gangs have, but they were very capable of violent behavior. The author was hired to work with a white gang in Newark, New Jersey, in 1960–1961. The job became available because his predecessor, who had been on the job for two weeks, had a knife held to his chest, cutting his shirt and drawing a little blood. He was warned that bad things would happen if he did not quit. He chose to resign.

Millions of dollars in federal, state, and local money were spent on projects and programs designed to prevent and control the behavior of these fighting gangs. The detached workers program, one of the most widely funded efforts, sent professional workers into the community to work with gang youths. It proved to have little or no positive effect on reducing their rates of delinquent behavior.[33]

Development of the Modern Gang: The 1960s

In the midst of a rapidly changing social and political climate in the 1960s, drugs influenced gang activity for the first time, "super-gangs" emerged in several cities, and gangs became involved in social betterment programs and political activism.

Drugs led to reduced gang activity in some urban areas. When gangs began to reduce their activities or even to disappear from some urban areas in the mid and late 1960s, some observers thought that the problem was coming to an end. New York City is one of the urban areas in which gang activity decreased significantly in the 1960s. The major reason offered for this apparent reduction of activity was the use of hard-core drugs. Lesser reasons included the civil rights movement, urban riots, growth of militant organizations, the war in Vietnam, and an exodus from the ghettos.[34]

A leader of a large Bronx gang in New York City reflected on the lack of gangs in the 1960s: "You can't keep a brother interested in clicking [gang activities] if he's high or nodding."[35] A college student who was a heroin addict for several years in Spanish Harlem in New York City during the 1960s also blamed drugs for the lack of gang activity:

> My brother was a big gang member. But we did not go for that kind of thing. Man, we were on drugs. That was cool. We were too busy trying to score to fool around with gang activity. It was everybody for himself.[36]

The 1960s was also the decade in which the major super-gangs developed. Some neighborhood gangs became larger and more powerful than other gangs in surrounding neighborhoods, and they forced these groups to become part of their gang organization. Eventually, a few gangs would control an entire city. In the 1960s, the Crips, an African American super-gang, began as a small clique in a section of south Los Angeles.[37] In Chicago the Vice Lords, Blackstone Rangers, and Gangster Disciples, all major super-gangs today, also had their beginnings during that decade. See Social World of the Delinquent 10.1 for how the Gangster Disciples (GDs) developed at this time.

Social World of the Delinquent **10.1**

The Origins of the Gangster Disciples

Larry Hoover, the chief of the Gangster Disciples, speaks:

I remember how close I came to death when I was seventeen. It was the night I was standing near the front of the Sarah Harrison Lounge drinking Wild Irish Rose, and David Barksdale, who was the sole leader of the Disciples, and his main people confronted me. I don't know how they got into my neighborhood that fast. They had me surrounded. There were only two of us, and there must have been fifty of them.

As David and I faced each other, I noticed he held a beer can in his hand. The next thing I knew, his fist was in my face. The 180 pounds of muscular raw power sternly admonished, "You are not going with Charlie Atkins. You guys are going to be Disciples." I firmly stated, "I am not going to be a Disciple." Guns were made visible. I thought, I will do anything to get out of this alive, but that is not what I said. For some reason, they didn't shoot us. That still surprises me.

My 20 soldiers and I became members of the Double 6 King Cobras, a faction of the Cobrastones led by Charles Atkins. Charlie was tough, dangerous, and very lethal. His slight build didn't discourage him from quickly losing his temper. This began a three year period from 1966 to 1969, where we were always fighting the Disciples. Out of the bloodbaths, two gangs emerged with tremendous power—the Blackstones and the Disciples.

Jeff Fort tried to make a deal with me to become a part of the Blackstone Nation. There were somewhere around 75 gang factions that made up the Nation. I did attend a few of their meetings, but he didn't offer to make me one of the Main 21. I remained bound to the Double 6 King Cobras until one night, David and his main leaders got out of their cars holding their hands in the air. This indicated there would be no shooting. They offered to form a treaty with us. We agreed to stop fighting the Disciples.

It wasn't long after that he asked me if we could merge and each have the same amount of power. We would share the power, two kings, coexisting in one land. Neither of us would be higher or more important. He would lead the Devil Disciples. I would conduct the Gangster Disciples. The merger left us 6,000 strong. It was then that I realized my sovereign power. I was a king, and I was only nineteen years old.

What characterized the early days of the development of the super-gangs? What else did you learn from these events in the life of a leader of a super-gang?

Source: Taken from *King Larry*, an unpublished biography of Larry Hoover by Linda Dippold Bartollas with the assistance of Nehemiah Russell and Samuel Dillon.

During the late 1960s, the three Chicago super-gangs became involved in social and political activism. The Vice Lords moved further than any of the other Chicago street gangs toward programs of community betterment.[38] Their social action involvement began in the summer of 1967 when the Vice Lord leaders attended meetings at Western Electric and Sears, Roebuck. Operation Bootstrap, which resulted from these meetings, formed committees for education, recreation, and law, order, and justice. A grant from the Rockefeller Foundation in February 1967 enabled the Vice Lords to found a host of economic and social ventures. The Vice Lords also worked with Jesse Jackson on Operation Breadbasket and, in the summer of 1969, joined with the Coalition for United Community Action to protest the lack of African American employees on construction sites in African American neighborhoods.

In 1968, all three street gangs worked against the reelection of Mayor Richard Daley's Democratic machine, and this political activism brought increased strain to their relationship with the Democratic Party organization.[39] The interrelationships between the legal and political contexts became apparent on the streets of Chicago as street gangs experienced what they perceived as harassment from the police. As soon as he be-

Larry Hoover, reputed leader of the Gangster Disciples street gang, is serving a life sentence in a federal penitentiary. A 1993 parole bid by Hoover was supported by several community leaders and politicians, including Chicago Mayor Eugene Sawyer, who argued that Hoover was a peacemaker who could be a Pied Piper of reform to young people in violence-wracked neighborhoods. His bid for parole was turned down, and he was later convicted in federal courts for racketeering.

gan a new term, Daley announced a crackdown on gang violence, and State's Attorney Edward Hanrahan followed by appraising the gang situation as the most serious crime problem in Chicago. The courts complied with this crackdown on gangs by increasing dramatically the number of gang members sent to prison in Illinois.[40]

Expansion, Violence, and Criminal Operations: The 1970s, 1980s, and 1990s

In the 1970s and 1980s, as their leadership was assumed by adults, street gangs became responsible for an even bigger portion of muggings, robberies, extortions, and drug-trafficking operations in the United States. One city after another reported serious problems with gangs in the early 1970s. It became apparent that the gangs of the 1970s and early 1980s were both more violent than the gangs of the 1950s and more intent on making money from crime. Furthermore, they were systematic in their efforts to extort local merchants, engage in robberies, shake down students for money, intimidate local residents, and sell stolen goods.

Some gangs became so sophisticated that the police regarded their activities as organized crime. Those gangs kept attorneys on retainer. Some even printed up business cards to further their careers in extortion, and they sold the cards to businesses for "protection" and to warn away rivals.[41]

Although the gang has been the major concept used to examine collective youth crime in urban areas for the past fifty years, little or no consensus exists as to what a gang actually is. Miller, as part of his nationwide examination of urban gangs, asked his respondents for a definition of a gang. In an analysis of 1,400 definitional elements provided by respondents, six major elements were cited most frequently: being organized, having identifiable leadership, identifying with a territory, associating continuously, having a specific purpose, and engaging in illegal activity.[42]

Through interviews, questionnaires, and visits to major cities, Miller came to the conclusion that gang members were committing as many as one-third of all violent juvenile crimes, terrorizing whole communities and keeping many urban schools in a state of siege. In Miller's study, justice system professionals reported problems with gangs in ten of the fifteen largest metropolitan areas. Respondents in Chicago, Detroit, New York, Philadelphia, Los Angeles, and San Francisco considered gang problems to be especially serious. Miller estimated that during the 1970s the number of gangs in these six cities ranged from 760 to 2,700 and included from 28,500 to 81,500 gang members.[43]

In a 1982 study, Miller expanded the original six-city survey to twenty-six localities in the United States, including twenty-four of the largest cities and two counties.

According to Miller's estimate, 2,300 youth gangs, with 100,000 members, were found in 300 cities. In addition to Boston, Chicago, Detroit, Los Angeles, New York, Philadelphia, and San Francisco, the list of cities reporting notable gang activity included Atlanta, Buffalo, Denver, Portland, and Salt Lake City. As in his earlier study, Miller concluded that law-violating youth groups accounted for a larger volume of less serious crimes, while gangs committed a smaller volume of more serious crimes. Furthermore, this study found that California's gang problems in both urban areas and smaller cities were particularly serious.[44]

Miller found that in the mid 1970s the rate of murder by firearms or other weapons was higher than ever before; the five cities that had the most serious gang problems averaged at least 175 gang-related killings a year between 1972 and 1974. Forays by small bands, armed and often motorized, seemed to have replaced the classic "rumble."

The mid 1980s were a turning point for many ghetto-based street gangs, for crack cocaine had hit the streets. These urban street gangs competed with each other for the drug trade. Several Los Angeles gangs established direct connections to major Colombian smugglers, which ensured a continuous supply of top-quality cocaine. In some Chicago neighborhoods, heavily armed teams sold drugs openly on street corners, using gang "peewees" (youngsters) as police lookouts.

The street gang traditionally has been a cultural by-product in the United States, but ganglike structures are now being reported in a number of both Eastern and Western cities. Eastern cities reporting gangs are Beijing, Hong Kong, Melbourne, Papua New Guinea, and Tokyo. Western cities include Berlin, Frankfurt, London, Madrid, Manchester, and Zurich. There have also been indications that gang activity takes place in Canada, Russia, and South America.[45]

The Nature and Extent of Gang Activity

An estimated 28,700 gangs and 780,200 gang members were active in the United States in 1998. This was a decline from an estimated 30,500 gangs and 816,000 gang members in 1997 and 31,000 gangs and 846,000 gang members in 1996. Thus, from 1996 to 1998, the estimated number of gangs and gang members in this nation decreased slightly (7 percent and 8 percent, respectively).[46] See Theory and Research 10.2 for more statistics on the number and activities of youth gangs in the United States.

Knowledge of the gang world requires an examination of the definition of gangs and the profile of gang members, and an understanding of gangs' intimidation of the school environment, of the structure and leadership of urban street gangs, of emerging gangs in small communities across the nation, of racial and ethnic backgrounds of gangs, and of female delinquent gangs.

Definitions of Gangs

Considerable disagreement about what parameters define a gang still exists. Researchers differ on questions such as

- How many youths make up a gang?
- Must gang members commit crimes as a gang to be considered a gang?
- Must gangs have some semblance of organizational structure?
- Should motorcycle gangs, skinhead groups, and white supremacist groups be considered part of the youth gang problem?[47]

Thrasher's 1927 gang study was one of the first to attempt to define a youth gang:

A **gang** is an interstitial group originally formed spontaneously and then integrated through conflict. It is characterized by the following types of behavior: meeting face to

THEORY AND RESEARCH 10.2

Recent Statistics on Gangs

The 1998 National Youth Gang Survey was administered to a representative sample of U.S. city and county jurisdictions. Key findings are as follows:

- In 1998, 48 percent of all respondents experienced gang activity, down about 3 percent from 1997 and about 5 percent from 1996, when 53 percent of all respondents reported active youth gangs.
- The largest drop from 1996 to 1998 in the number of gangs occurred in suburban counties (−24 percent), followed by rural counties (−13 percent). The largest drop in the number of gang members occurred in suburban counties (−21 percent), followed by large cities (−6 percent).
- In 1998, more respondents (42 percent) believed that the youth gang problem was "staying about the same," 28 percent believed the problem was "getting worse," and 30 percent believed it was "getting better." Compared with 1997 respondents, more 1998 respondents perceived that their gang problem was getting better.
- In 1998, respondents estimated that 60 percent of their gang members were adults (age 18 or older). This represents a significant shift from 1996 (the last time respondents were asked about gang members' demographics), when respondents estimated that exactly one-half of gang members were adults. Thus, it appears that youth gangs may be aging.
- Nationally in 1998, 46 percent of all gang members were Hispanic, 34 percent were African American, 12 percent were Caucasian, 6 percent were Asian, and 2 percent were of other race/ethnicity. From 1996 to 1998, the proportion of Hispanic and Asian gang members increased slightly, and the proportion of Caucasian and African American gang members decreased slightly.

- Respondents estimated that more than one-third (36 percent) of their youth gangs had a significant mixture of two or more racial/ethnic groups. The largest proportion of these "mixed gangs" was in small cities, where they represented 54 percent of all gangs, and the smallest proportion was in large cities (32 percent).
- Respondents were asked to estimate the proportion of youth gang members who engaged in specific types of serious and/or violent crimes. The percentage of respondents reporting involvement of "most or all" gang members was largest for drug sales (27 percent), followed by larceny/theft (17 percent), burglary/breaking and entering (13 percent), aggravated assault (12 percent), motor vehicle theft (11 percent), and robbery (3 percent).
- Respondents were asked how much their jurisdiction's youth gang problem has been affected in the past few years by the return of gang-involved adults from prison. The most common response was "somewhat." Nearly one-half (49 percent) said either "very much" or "somewhat." Suburban counties were most affected, and jurisdictions in the west reported a far greater impact of gang-involved adults returning from prison than was reported by jurisdictions in other regions.

How encouraging is it that the number of gangs and gang members is decreasing in the United States? What other factors about the gang problem are encouraging?

Source: 1998 National Youth Gang Survey (Washington, D.C.: Office of Juvenile Justice and Delinquency Prevention, 2000), pp. xiv–xvi.

---

face, milling, movement through space as a unit, conflict, and planning. The result of this collective behavior is the development of tradition, unreflective internal structure, esprit de corps, solidarity, morale, group awareness, and attachment to local territory.[48]

Miller's studies in the 1970s defined a gang more through its organizational characteristics and dynamics. A gang has "mutual interest," "identifiable leadership" and "well-developed lines of authority." Another organizational feature of the gang, according to Miller, is the desire to achieve a purpose which usually includes "the conduct of illegal activity and control over a particular territory, facility, or type of enterprise."[49]

In a 2000 publication, Finn-Aage Esbensen concluded that the following elements should be present for a group to be classified a youth gang:

- The group needs to have more than two members.
- Group members must fall within a limited age range, usually acknowledged as ages 12 to 24.
- There must be some sense of identity to the group, such as naming the gang and/or using colors or symbols to claim gang affiliation.
- Youth gangs must have some permanence, such as association with a geographical area.
- Involvement in illegal activity is a central element of youth gangs.[50]

Thrasher does not specify that a gang's definition must include illegal activity, but Miller, Esbensen, and most other gang researchers do. Thrasher's definition focuses on group interaction and Miller's observes organizational characteristics and dynamics. In contrast, Esbensen is interested in clarifying group demographics (age range, sense of identity, and permanence within a specific area). Combining all three definitions could provide a useful and comprehensive definition of a youth gang.

Profile of Gang Members

The smaller the community, the more likely it is that gang members will be juveniles. In contrast, the majority of gang members in urban communities are adults. Surveys of urban street gang samples indicate that from 14 to 30 percent of adolescents join gangs at some point.[51] Ben Shapiro of the U.S. Office of Juvenile Justice and Delinquency Prevention estimates that approximately 40 percent of urban gangs are juveniles; the remainder are adult males.[52] G. David Curry and colleagues' national survey of law enforcement agencies found that juveniles made up only 26 percent of the gang membership in established gang cities such as Chicago.[53]

Juveniles become involved as young as eight years of age, running errands and carrying weapons or messages. They are recruited as lookouts and street vendors and join an age-appropriate junior division of the gang. Gangs use younger and smaller members to deal cocaine out of cramped "rock houses" that are steel-reinforced fortresses. Gangs have long known that youngsters are invaluable because their age protects them against the harsher realities of the adult criminal justice system.[54]

Youth gang demographics include an average age of seventeen or eighteen years, and a typical age range of twelve to twenty-four. More younger members recently have joined gangs, but the greatest increases in membership have still come from the older group. Adolescent males continue to outnumber adolescent females in gangs by a wide margin. Gangs vary in size depending on whether they are traditional or specialty gangs. Large, enduring traditional (territorial) gangs average about 180 members, whereas drug trafficking gangs average only about twenty-five members. Some urban gangs (e.g., the super-gangs of Chicago) number in thousands of members.[55]

Gang members have varying commitments to the gang. J. D. Vigil[56] and Vigil and J. M. Long[57] identified four basic types of gang involvement. First, *regulars* are strongly attached to the gang and have few interests outside of the gang. The regulars are the hard core, the inner clique who make key decisions, set standards, are the key recruiters, and enforce the sanctions against violators of group norms. Second, *peripheral members* are also strongly attached to the gang but participate less often than the regulars because they have other interests besides the gang. Third, *temporary members* are marginally committed, joining the gang at a later age than the regulars and peripherals. They also tend to remain in the gang for only a short time. Fourth, *situational members* are very marginally attached and generally participate only in certain activities. They avoid the violent activities whenever possible.[58]

Ira Reiner identifies five different types of gang members based on their commitment to the gang.[59] The *at-risk* youths are not really gang members, but are pre-gang juveniles who do not belong but have expressed some interest in gang participation. *Wannabes* are recruits who are usually in their preteen years and have begun to emulate gang members' dress and values. These young members sometimes only need an opportunity to prove that they are ready for gang membership. *Associates* make up the lowest level of gang membership. They are sometimes called Fringe, Li'l Homies, or soldiers, and it is not unusual for them to be assigned undesirable tasks or dangerous activities. *Hard core* are regarded as regular members or part of the inner clique. They spend most of their time engaging in gang-related activities and are the most gang-bound in terms of life-style. This group, according to Reiner, generally constitutes no more than 10 to 15 percent of gang membership. Finally, *veteranos/O.G.s* are made up of men in their twenties or even thirties who continue to be active in gang activities. In Chicano gangs, *veteranos* are regarded as elder statesmen who may be retired but still command respect; in African American gangs, O.G.s (original gangsters) are men who have earned respect and who are often expected to teach younger members the ways of the gang.[60]

Martín Sánchez Jankowski, who spent more than ten years studying thirty-seven gangs in Los Angeles, New York, and Boston, contends that certain characteristics distinguish those who belong to gangs from those who do not. What he refers to as *defiant individualism* has seven attributes: competitiveness, mistrust or wariness, self-reliance, social isolation, survival instinct, social Darwinist world view, and a defiant air. According to Jankowski, while most members of lower-income communities display some of these traits, gang members typically display all of them. He argues that the very nature of these lower-income communities requires such traits to survive and prevail and that participation in gangs is a means or attempt to continue this spirit of defiant individualism.[61]

Gangs in School

Schools have become fertile soil for the violence of youth gangs. R. C. Huff and K. S. Trump's study of youth gangs in Cleveland, Ohio; Denver, Colorado; and south Florida found that 50 percent of their respondents reported that members of their gangs had assaulted teachers, 70 percent admitted their gang had assaulted students, more than 80 percent said gang members took guns and knives to school, and more than 60 percent claimed gang members sold drugs at school.[62]

The violence perpetrated by gangs across the nation tends to vary from one school to the next, depending on the economic and social structure of the community, the gang tradition within that school, the gang's stage of development, and the extent of drug-trafficking that is taking place. See Figure 10.1 for the percentage of students ages twelve through nineteen who reported that street gangs were present at school.

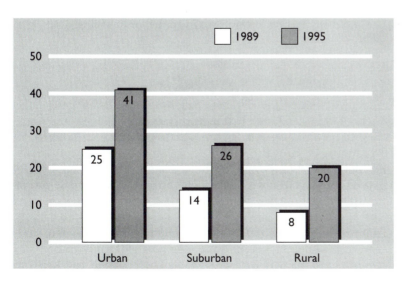

FIGURE 10.1 Percentage of Students Ages Twelve through Nineteen Who Reported that Street Gangs Were Present at School, by Urbanicity: 1989 and 1995.

Note: "At school" was not defined for the survey respondent.

Source: U.S. Department of Justice, Bureau of Justice Statistics, *School Crime Supplement* to the *National Crime Victimization Survey, 1989 and 1995.* Cited in Phillip Kaufman et al., *Indicators of School Crime and Safety, 1998* (Washington, D.C.: U.S. Department of Justice; Offices of Justice Programs, 1998), p. 35.

Gangs perpetrate school violence in a number of ways. Gang members are likely to bring concealed weapons into the school. George W. Knox, David Laske, and Edward Tromanhauser report that high school students who are gang members are significantly more likely than non-gang members to carry a firearm to school for purposes of protection.[63] Joseph F. Sheley and James D. Wright also found higher rates of ownership and carrying of firearms among gang members than non-gang members.[64] Furthermore, Charles M. Callahan and Ira Rivara found that gang members were nearly three times as likely as non-gang members to say firearm access was "easy."[65]

Gangs are also constantly recruiting new members, and non-gang members are likely to be physically assaulted if they refuse to join. An African American male who grew up in Chicago, went to college on a football scholarship, and recently graduated from law school tells how he avoided gang membership: "They were always on me to join a gang. The only way I kept from getting beaten up all the time was to run home from football practice and to run to school every morning. I kept moving all the time, but I kept out of the gangs."[66]

Moreover, because more than one gang is typically present in a high school, conflict among gangs takes place on a regular basis. This conflict may be based on competition over the drug market, or it may relate to individual gangs within that school seeking to expand their turf. Fights may erupt in the school hallways, in the cafeteria, or during dances. Warring gang youths sometimes start a mass riot; stabbings and shootings may occur during these altercations. The use of deadly weapons, of course, increases the likelihood of injuries or fatalities.

Finally, conflict among rival gangs in different schools also perpetrates violence. Fights commonly take place during athletic contests between competing schools. A drive-by shooting is the most serious violence that can erupt among rival gangs in the school setting. What usually occurs is that a gang youth is killed, and the victim's gang deems it necessary to retaliate. So before school, during lunch recess, or following school, a car speeds by, its occupants spraying bullets.[67]

A Portland, Oregon, high school head football coach tells of an incident in which a group of Crips, dressed in blue, came speeding through the school's field-house parking lot. His team was standing by him when he shouted, "Slow it down, fellas." They did slow down, pulled out a semiautomatic weapon, and pointed it at the coach and his team. The coach hit the deck and ordered his team to drop for cover. The coach said, "I thought I had bought the farm. Fortunately, they didn't pull the trigger. In my 20 years of teaching, I have never been afraid until this year."[68]

DRUGS AND GANGS   Gangs in schools today have an economic base (drug dealing), which was not true a few years ago. Drug trafficking has become an attractive option, especially with the decline of economic opportunities for minority youth. Jeffrey Fagan's study of gang drug use and drug dealing in three urban communities found that:

> Drug use is widespread and normative among gangs, regardless of the city, the extent or nature of collective violence, or their organization or social processes. Serious and violent behavior occur among the majority of the gangs.[69]

Elizabeth Huffmaster McConnell and Elizabeth Peltz's examination of gang activity in an urban high school in Dallas found that drug distribution had become so extensive that students were required to wear picture identification at all times in an attempt to control the number of "drug drops." School was an ideal setting for the distribution of drugs; mid-level distributors would come on campus, make their connections, and leave drugs with students who were street-level pushers. A single stop for the mid-level distributor resulted in contacts with multiple street-level pushers.[70]

Gangs have a number of techniques for selling drugs in schools. In some schools, gang members prop doors open with cigarette packs, then signal from windows to non-students waiting to enter the building.[71] Some gang members sell drugs in the bathrooms, in the lunch rooms, or in the parking lots. Daniel J. Monti's study of gangs and suburban schools tells how one school's lunchroom had Bloods' tables and Crips' tables.[72] Gangs also use younger children in their drug trafficking. The children first serve as lookouts. As they get older, they can become couriers (runners), who work as conduits between dealers and buyers.[73]

Urban Street Gangs

In urban settings, street gangs have become quasi-institutionalized as they compete for status and authority with schools and other social institutions. Violence in schools, as well as that of nearby neighborhoods, has encouraged students to seek protection in gang membership. Safety is ensured by wearing the proper color and style of clothes and flashing the correct gang sign. Social World of the Delinquent 10.3 lists some of these items for the Chicago area in the early 1990s. The dysfunctional nature of many families also

Social World of the Delinquent 10.3

Dress and Gang Members

IDENTIFIERS—THINGS TO REMEMBER

Please remember: If a person has one of these items, it doesn't always mean that he/she is a gang member. The best and safest thing to do is to check for some more things, such as tattoos, jewelry, et cetera.

1. **Earrings.** *Right Ear:* Disciples, Simon City Royals, and gangs affiliated with the Disciples. *Left Ear:* Vice Lords, Latin Kings, El Rukns, and gangs that are affiliated with these gangs.
2. **Hats (generally).** *Tilted to the Right:* Disciples, Simon City Royals, et cetera. *Tilted to the Left:* Vice Lords, Latin Kings, et cetera.
3. **Hats (Civil War type).** *Blue:* Disciples, Simon City Royals, et cetera *Gray:* Vice Lords, et cetera. (NOTE: Vice Lords have been known to cut off the bottom parts of the crossed rifles making a "V" out of the top parts.)
4. **Glove (one).** *Right Hand:* Disciples, Simon City Royals, et cetera. *Left Hand:* Vice Lords, Latin Kings, et cetera.
5. *The same "right" and "left" rule applies to other things such as: belt buckles, bandannas hanging from a pocket or tied to a leg, et cetera.*
6. **Stars.** *Six-Pointed:* Disciples and affiliates. *Five-Pointed:* Vice Lords and El Rukns.
7. **Crowns.** *Pointed Tips:* Latin Kings. *Rounded Tips:* Imperial Gangsters.
8. **Rabbit heads.** *Straight Ears:* Vice Lords and Latin Kings. *Bent Ear(s):* Simon City Royals.
9. **Gym shoes.** The color of the shoe versus the color of the laces or two (2) sets of laces in the shoes to represent the gang colors. Laces should be tied up the sides and not the conventional way.
10. **Graffiti.** If any graffiti is written upside-down, it shows a disrespect to that gang and was written by an opposing gang.
11. **Haircuts.** Some Vice Lords on the city's West Side have shaved the left side of their head into the shape of an arrow.
12. **Friendship beads.** Gangs have adapted this fad by having their gang's colors on the beads. These are worn on clothing, shoes, hair, even as an earring.
13. **Pockets.** The inside of the pocket has been colored the colors of the gang. This is used as a means of representing.
14. **Claddagh ring.** An Irish ring which means love, loyalty, and friendship. The Latin Kings have started wearing this ring because it has a crown on it.
15. **Roller skate laces.** *Tied up and down on the Right Side:* Disciples. *Tied up and down on the Left Side:* Vice Lords. *Tied halfway on the opposite side denotes put down to rival gang.*
16. **Pant leg cuffs.** *Rolled up on the Right Side:* Disciples. *Rolled up on the Left Side:* Vice Lords.

Are gang members as visible in their identifiers as they were ten years ago? If not, then how can we identify who is in a gang?

Source: Midwest Gang Investigators' Association, *Warning Signs for Parents* (n.d.).

raises the appeal of gangs. In contrast to the chaos of their homes, gangs appear to offer youths security, self-esteem, and status. As one gang member said, "The gang is like a family for me. I would do anything for it."[74]

Urban gangs are sometimes able to take control of schools. This control permits them to collect fees from other students for the privilege of attending school, traversing the corridors, and avoiding gang beatings. Fear and intimidation keep both students and faculty from reporting gang activities to authorities. Many urban schools have had to adopt extreme security measures to protect themselves from gang violence and drug trafficking.

TYPES OF URBAN GANGS   Richard A. Cloward and Lloyd E. Ohlin's study identified criminal, conflict, and retreatist gangs (see Chapter 4),[75] and Lewis Yablonsky's research led him to conclude that there were delinquent, violent, and social gangs.[76] Carl S. Taylor,[77] C. Ronald Huff,[78] and Fagan[79] found other types of gangs in the communities they studied.

Detroit urban gangs, according to Taylor, can be classified as scavenger, territorial, and corporate. Scavenger gangs have little sense of a common bond beyond their own impulsive behavior. Without goals, purpose, and consistent leadership, these urban survivors prey on people who cannot defend themselves. Their crime can be classified as petty, senseless, and spontaneous.[80]

A territorial gang designates as a territory something that belongs exclusively to the gang. One fundamental objective of a territorial gang is to defend its territory from outsiders. In doing so, these gangs become rulers of the streets. Today, a territorial gang defends its territory to protect its narcotic business.[81]

The organized/corporate gang has a strong leader or manager. The main focus of the organization is participation in illegal moneymaking ventures. Membership, as well as promotion, depends on a person's worth to the organization. Different divisions handle sales, distribution, marketing, and enforcement. Each member has a job to do, and part of that job is to work as a team member. Profit is the motivation to commit criminal acts. Although gang members have traditionally come from the lower class, some middle-class youths are attracted to these gangs.[82] Taylor concludes that "for the very first time in modern U.S. history, African Americans have moved into the mainstream of major crime. Corporate gangs in Detroit are part of organized crime in America."[83]

Huff's examination of gangs in Cleveland and Columbus identified three basic groups:

1. Informal hedonistic gangs, whose basic concern was to get high (usually on alcohol and/or marijuana and other drugs) and to have a good time. These gangs were involved in minor property crime more than in violent personal crime.
2. Instrumental gangs, whose focal concerns were more economic and who committed a high volume of property crimes for economic reasons. Most of these gang members used drugs, and some used crack cocaine. Some individual members of these gangs also sold drugs, but doing so was not an organized gang activity.
3. Predatory gangs committed robberies, street muggings, and other crimes of opportunity. Members of these gangs were more likely to use crack cocaine and to sell drugs to finance the purchase of more sophisticated weapons.[84]

Fagan's analysis of the crime-drug relationships in three cities identified four types of gangs. Type 1 was involved in a few delinquent activities and only alcohol and marijuana use. This type of gang, according to Fagan, had low involvement in drug sales and appeared to be a social gang. Type 2 gangs were heavily involved in several types of drug sales, primarily to support their own drug use, and in one type of delinquency: vandalism. Although this type manifested several of the subcultural and organizational features of a gang, it still seemed to be more of a party gang. Type 3 gangs, representing the most frequent gang participation, included serious delinquents who had extensive involvements with both serious and nonserious offenses. Interestingly, this type of gang had less involvement than Type 2 gangs in both drug sales and the use of serious substances (cocaine, heroin, PCP, and amphetamines). Type 4 gangs had extensive involvement in both serious drug use and serious and nonserious offenses and had higher rates of drug sales. This cohesive and organized type, predicted Fagan, "is probably at the highest risk for becoming a more formal criminal organization."[85]

A final topology is that of the *People* and *Folks,* which are the two main groups of Chicago gangs. Beginning in the Illinois prison system at the end of the 1970s, the gangs began to align themselves into the People (represented by a five-point star) and the Folks (represented by a six-point star). Thirty-one Chicago gangs now identify themselves as Folks, including the Gangster Disciples, Spanish Cobras, Imperial Gangsters, Latin Disciples, Latin Lovers, Braziers, Insane Popes, and Simon City Royals. The twenty-seven gangs identifying themselves as People include Vice Lords, El Rukns, Latin Kings, Future Stones, Gay Lords, Latin Lords, Bishops, and War Lords. There are also numerous factions within each major super-gang.[86] For example, the Latin Kings have more than thirteen and the Vice Lords have eleven different factions.[87]

ORGANIZATIONAL FEATURES OF THE URBAN GANG　Jankowski contended "that one of the reasons that society does not understand gangs or the gang phenomenon very well is that there have not been enough systematic studies undertaken as to how the gang works as an organization." He suggested that the most important organizational features of urban gangs are structure, leadership, recruitment, initiation rites, role expectations and sanctions, and migration patterns.[88] Jankowski observed three types of gang organizational structure:

1. The *vertical/hierarchical type* divides leadership hierarchically into several levels. Authority and power are related to one's position in the line of command.
2. The *horizontal/commission type* is made up of several officeholders who share about equal authority over the members. The leaders share the duties, as well as the power and authority.
3. The *influential* model assigns no written duties or titles to the leadership positions. This type of system usually has two to four members who are considered leaders of the group. The authority of the influentials is based on charisma.[89]

The most conspicuous example of the vertical/hierarchical type of leadership is found in the Chicago-based gangs. The largest of these gangs—the Gangster Disciples, the Vice Lords, the Black Disciples, and the El Rukns—have leaders who command great respect among gang members. Jeff Fort of the El Rukns (formerly Blackstone Rangers and Black P. Stone Nation), David Barksdale of the Disciples, and Larry Hoover of the Gangster Disciples are the three most legendary leaders. Social World of the Delinquent 10.4 reveals some of the power that Jeff Fort had in the 1960s with what was then called the Blackstone Rangers.

The Bloods and the Crips, the two most notorious Los Angeles gangs, are representative of the horizontal/commission type. They are not gangs at all but confederations among hundreds of subgroups or sets. Sets are formed along neighborhood lines, and most sets have twenty to thirty members.[90]

Gangs regularly go on recruiting parties, and Jankowski points out that there are three basic recruitment strategies. In the "fraternity type of recruitment," the gang presents itself as an organization that is the "in" thing to do. The "obligation type of recruitment" is one in which gang members attempt to persuade potential members that it is their duty to join. The "coercive type of recruitment" involves physical and/or psychological pressure being put on the potential member and threatening that either he or his family will be attacked if he fails to join.[91] The recruitment of younger members is generally easy because the life of a gang member looks very glamorous. With money from the sale of drugs, gang members are able to drive BMWs and Mercedes, flash big rolls of bills, and wear expensive jewelry. Recruitment begins early in the grade school years; adolescent males are most vulnerable in the junior high years.[92] But even if a

Social World of the Delinquent 10.4

Jeff Fort and the Rise of the Blackstone Rangers

A scrawny young boy by the name of Jeff Fort turned twelve years old in Woodlawn (Chicago) on the west side. He and a few friends hung around the street corners, but nobody noticed. In the beginning they stole hubcaps and groceries, dividing the proceeds among themselves. The gang became the brightest light their young minds had ever dared to believe in, flickering through the darkness of the nights poisoned by danger, degradation, and despair. They were christened the Blackstone Rangers, and the light swelled brighter from its name alone.

Jeff Fort called twenty-one leaders to him, giving them responsibility and power, understanding intuitively that sharing his power would only make him stronger. They became known as the Main 21, but the gangs were well aware that they were the Enforcers. Bull, Mad Dog, Stone, Lefty, Thunder, Tom Tucker, Leto, Hutch, Bosco, Clark, Mickey Cogwell, Porgy, A.D., Old Man, Caboo, Moose, Dog, Crazy Paul, Bop Daddy, Cool Johnnie, and Sandman handled the problems that needed to be taken care of. The code dictated behavior. Punishment was meted out for not honoring the code. Everyone understood this. They could tell you to fight Louis, and out of sheer fear you would do it in a heartbeat.

Jeff and the Main 21 held meetings in the First Presbyterian Church at 6400 South Kimbark, where a large gymnasium held thousands of Blackstones. The Main 21 were seated in a semicircle across the stage at the end of the gym. A microphone and podium were ready for the entrance of the awaited leader. He appeared out of nowhere, purposefully calm, controlled, loose, milking the crowd slowly, letting the heart rates increase steadily and build with the anticipation of what his next move would be.

He raised his fist, jerking it back hard, with power they all knew him to have. He yelled, "Blackstone," and together, as if one voice came from thousands of bodies, the thunderous roar resounded back: "Blackstone."

The spotlight circled the Main 21, then a second light appeared, dancing symmetrically with the first, increasing the rhythm, picking up a swaying motion that the bodies in the gym began to recognize and move to. A third spotlight flashed on, holding Jeff Fort in its sight, suggesting that the best was yet to come. It was.

Jeff, with his arms hanging loosely by his sides, began to feel the anticipation grow like a living thing. His breath quickening, nostrils flared, hair standing up on the back of his neck, his head slowly rotating back and forth across the crowd as if singling out each and every Stone in the audience, the piercing eyes held each one, looking directly at them.

In a deep, booming voice that sent static flying across the gym, he demanded, "Stones Run It!"

As if an electrical shock wave made its way through each nervous system, the brain registered a flight response translating to a simultaneous forward movement of thousands of bodies rising in a sea of exaltation. There were thousands of voices singing praises to their master, with right fists extended like banners hammering the wind, the thunder released its power as they claimed, "Stones Run It!"

Jeff roared back, "Stones Run It!"

"Stones Run It!" they fired back.

Strangling the microphone, tap dancing to the energy bombarding off the four walls, Jeff screamed in a hoarse, rasping voice, "Blackstones!" moving the Main 21 into action as they deliberately made their way down the stage onto the auditorium floor among the Stones, fists pounding in and out of the air above them, as if forcing it to perform with them, directing the Stones to thunder over and over and over again, "Blackstones, Blackstones, Blackstones . . . !" The reverberations echoed through each cell of each body, encoding the memory of what it meant to be a Stone for all eternity.

The Stones were literally everywhere, incorporating other gangs into the nation like a confederacy flying under one flag. Known as America's most powerful gang, they reveled in the notoriety acquired as a nation of Stones. Members were arrested for crimes ranging from reckless conduct and resisting arrest to armed robbery and murder.

Why do you think those who experienced this style of gang leadership responded with such enthusiasm? Why was Jeff Fort skillful in setting the stage for such a response?

Source: Linda Dippold Bartollas, based on her research, and assisted by Nehemiah Russell and Samuel Dillon.

youth has enough support systems at home to resist joining a gang, it is very difficult to live in a neighborhood that is controlled by a street gang and not join. A gang leader explained: "You had two choices in the neighborhood I grew up in—you could either be a gang member or a mama's boy. A mama's boy would come straight home from school, go up to his room and study, and that was it."[93]

The methods of initiation into some gangs include some or all of the following: (1) must be "jumped in" or fight the other members; (2) must participate in illegal acts; (3) must assist in trafficking drugs; and (4) must participate in "walk-up" or "drive-by" shootings. It is the drive-by shooting that has received much public attention.[94] As one article notes:

> The drive-by killing is the sometime sport and occasional initiation rite of city gangs. From the comfort of a passing car, the itinerant killer simply shoots down a member of a rival gang or an innocent bystander. Especially common among L.A.'s Bloods and Crips, the drive-by killing is the parable around which every telling of the gang story revolves. Beyond that lies a haze of images: million-dollar drug deals, ominous graffiti, and colorfully dressed marauders armed with Uzis. The sociologists tell us that gang culture is the flower on the vine of single-parent life in the ghetto, the logical result of society's indifference. It would be hard to write a morality play more likely to strike terror into the hearts of the middle class.[95]

A street gang's clothing, colors, and hand signs are held sacred by gang members. In the world of gangs, warfare can be triggered by the way someone wears his hat, folds his arms, or moves his hands. Gang identity includes following codes for dress and behavior to make certain that the gang's name and symbol are scrawled in as many places as possible. Each gang has its own secret handshakes and hand signs, known as **representing.** Rival groups sometimes display the signs upside down as a gesture of contempt and challenge.[96]

Prayers are also rituals for many gangs. They are often said before members go into battle against rival gangs or are chanted before wounded members die. One Chicago gang's prayer is, "If I should die in battle, lay two shotguns across my chest and tell all the Kings that I did my best." The Orchestra Albany (O.A.) gang's prayer is "If I die, bury me deep with O.A.s at my feet, with two shotguns at my side, and tell the boys I died with pride."[97]

Loyalty is a chief value among gangs, whether prompted by family feelings and a sense of belonging or by fear of the beatings or death that disloyalty could bring. One ex-gang member commented about the loyalty of gang members, "The gang becomes their god, and they will do anything to defend it, even die for it."[98]

Vigil, in his 1985 study of Hispanic gangs, reported that most of the time gang members make casual conversation and joke, drink beer or wine, play pickup games (baseball, basketball, football, and handball), and meet at the local barrio hangout. These gang youths speak a type of mixed Spanish-English slang; present a conservative appearance, with smartly combed-back hair; and affect a body language that is controlled, deliberate, and methodical.[99]

Fear is omnipresent in street life, Vigil added, particularly if one is unprotected, and it must be managed. The desired state is *locura,* which denotes a type of craziness or wildness. A person demonstrates this state of mind by displaying fearlessness, daring, and other unpredictable forms of destructive behavior, such as getting loco on drugs and alcohol. *Locura* also provides a sense of adventure and of the emotional support gang camaraderie enhances.[100] As one gang member expressed it:

> I was born into my barrio. It was either get your ass kicked every day or join a gang and get your ass kicked occasionally by rival gangs. Besides, it was fun and I belonged.[101]

Gang migration is another important organizational feature of urban gangs. Gang migration can take place in at least three ways: (1) the establishment of satellite gangs in another location, (2) the relocation of gang members with their families, and (3) the expansion of drug markets.

Several studies in the 1980s were unable to document the establishment of satellite gangs in other locations.[102] In addition, chiefs of two of the largest Chicago supergangs, the Vice Lords and the Gangster Disciples, informed the author in the mid 1990s that their gangs did not have the desire or the organizational capacity to form nationwide satellite gangs. These gang chiefs even questioned how much control they have over gangs in other locations that use their gang name.[103] Cheryl L. Maxson, Malcolm W. Klein, and Lea C. Cunningham, in surveying law enforcement agencies in over 1,100 cities nationwide, found that 713 reported some gang migration. The most typical pattern of this gang migration was the relocation of gang members with their families (39 percent). The next most typical pattern was the expansion of drug markets (20 percent).[104] See Figure 10.2 for a map of U.S. cities experiencing gang member migration through 1992.

In recent decades, more juveniles have remained with urban gangs into their adult years. The major reasons for this continuation of gang activity into the adult years are the changing structure of the economy, resulting in the loss of unskilled and semiskilled jobs, and the opportunities to make money from the lucrative drug markets. Those juveniles who leave their urban gangs do it for many of the same reasons as other juveniles who mature out of committing delinquent behavior. It may involve the influence of a girlfriend, a move to another neighborhood or city, or the fear of arrest and incarceration in the adult system.[105]

LAW-VIOLATING BEHAVIORS AND GANG ACTIVITIES   Despite the fluidity and diversity of gang roles and affiliation, it is commonly agreed that core members are involved in more serious delinquent acts than are situational or fringe members.[106]

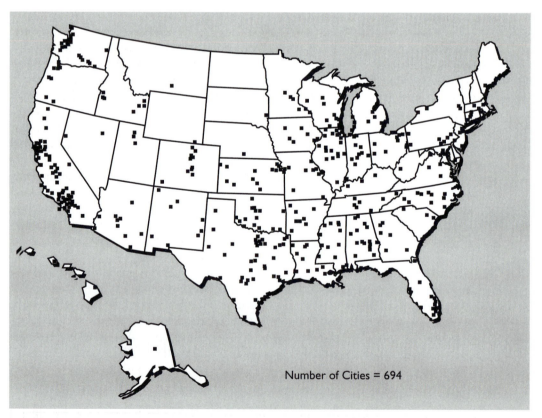

Number of Cities = 694

FIGURE 10.2 Cities Experiencing Gang Member Migration through 1992

Source: Cheryl L. Maxson, "Gang Members on the Move," *Juvenile Justice Bulletin* (Washington, D.C.: Office of Justice Programs, Office of Juvenile Justice and Delinquency Prevention, 1998), p. 6.

The follow-up of a sample of Cohort I to the age of thirty by Wolfgang and colleagues provided insights into the influence of gangs on delinquency in Philadelphia. They found that one-sixth of the whites belonged to gangs and were responsible for one-third of the offenses committed by whites; 44 percent of the nonwhites were gang members and were responsible for 60 percent of the offenses committed by nonwhites. Gang youths, who represented 29 percent of the total offender sample were responsible for 50 percent of the offenses.[107]

This study also found that boys who belonged to gangs persisted in delinquent behavior nearly three years longer than did those who never joined. But when racial aspects are examined, it became clear that the persistence of delinquent behavior was traceable primarily to the nonwhite gang members. Moreover, Wolfgang and colleagues found that 81 percent of the boys (90 percent of the nonwhites and 60 percent of the whites) became delinquent after joining a gang. Another indicator of the relationship between gang membership and delinquency is that 90 percent of the whites committed no further offenses after leaving the gang; however, for nonwhites, no clear effect of leaving the gang was evident.[108]

More recently, studies in Aurora, Colorado; Broward County, Florida; and Cleveland, Ohio, found some major differences between the behavior of gang members and at-risk youths.[109] Individual gang members in these studies reported that they had stolen more cars, that they had participated in more drive-by shootings, that they were far more likely to own guns, that they owned guns of larger caliber, and that they were more involved in selling drugs than the sample of at-risk youths.[110] Of those youths selling drugs, "gang members reported doing so more frequently, having fewer customers, making more money from the sales, and relying more on out-of-state suppliers than nongang youths who sold drugs." This study added that "both gang members and at-risk youths reported that gangs do not control drug trafficking in their communities."[111]

Studies of large urban samples found that gang members are responsible for a large proportion of violent offenses. In Rochester, gang members, who made up 30 percent of the sample, self-reported committing 68 percent of all adolescent violent offenses, which was about seven times as many serious and violent acts as nongang youths.[112] Figure 10.3 reveals the differences between gang members and nonmembers in terms of delinquent acts in the Rochester Youth Development Study. In Seattle, gang members, who made up 15 percent of the sample, self-reported committing 85 percent of adolescent robberies.[113] In Denver, gang members, who made up 14 percent of the sample, self-reported committing 89 percent of all serious violent adolescent offenses. Gang members committed about three times as many serious and violent offenses as nongang youth.[114]

A further study in Columbus, Ohio, analyzed the arrest records of eighty-three gang leaders in the years 1980–1994. During these fifteen years, the eighty-three gang leaders accumulated 834 arrests, 37 percent of which were for violent crimes (ranging from domestic violence to murder). In this project, researchers theorized that violent crimes tended to increase as the gangs began engaging in drug activity and may have been connected to the establishment of a drug market.[115]

Gang membership appears to contribute to this pattern of violent behavior. Studies in Rochester, Denver, and Seattle showed that the influence of gang membership on levels of youth violence is greater than the influence of other delinquent peers.[116] Youths commit more serious and violent acts while they belong to a gang than they do after they leave gang membership.[117] In addition, the effect of gang membership on a propensity toward violence seems to be long lasting. In all three sites, even though gang members' offense rates dropped after leaving the gang, they still remained fairly high.[118]

The overall number of youth gang homicides declined during the 1990s, but trends varied by city. The 1996, 1997, and 1998 National Youth Gang Surveys revealed that 237 cities reported both a gang problem and a gang homicide statistic in all three years. Forty-nine percent of these cities indicated a decrease in gang homicide over the three year period, 36 percent indicated an increase, and 15 percent indicated no change. The total number of gang homicides for these cities was 1,294 in 1996, 1,260 in 1997, and

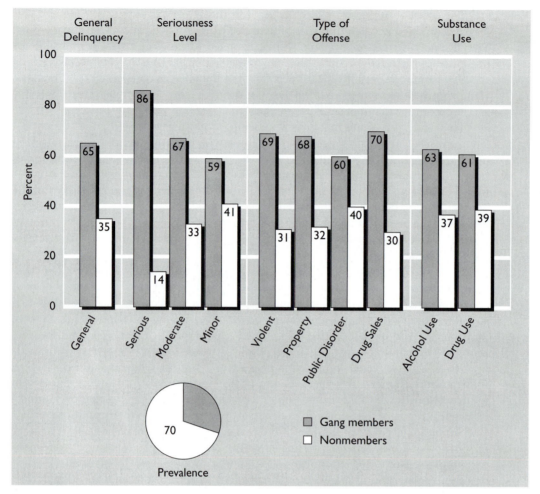

FIGURE 10.3 Percentage of Delinquent Acts Attributable to Gang Members and Prevalence of Gang Membership in Rochester

Source: Terence P. Thornberry and James H. Birch II, "Gang Members and Delinquent Behavior," *Juvenile Justice Bulletin* (Washington, D.C.: Office of Justice Programs, Office of Juvenile Justice and Delinquency Prevention, 1998), p. 3.

1,061 in 1998. Los Angeles and Chicago stand out among the cities with the highest rates of gang homicides.[119]

Gang norms seem to contribute to the elevated rates of violence in youth gangs.[120] Most gangs have norms that support the expressive use of violence to settle disputes. The gang's sanctioning of violence is also dictated by a code of honor that stresses the importance of violence in demonstrating toughness and fighting ability and in establishing status in the gang. Levels of violence, as James C. Howell summarized it, do vary "from one city to another, from one community to another, from one gang to another, and even within cliques within the same gang."[121]

S. H. Decker describes a seven-step process that accounts for the peaks and valleys in the levels of gang violence.[122] The process begins with a gang that is loosely organized:

1. loose bonds to the gang;
2. collective identification of threat from a rival gang (through rumors, symbolic shows of force, cruising, and mythic violence), reinforcing the centrality of violence that expands the number of participants and increases cohesion;
3. a mobilizing event, possibly, but not necessarily, violent;
4. escalation of activity;

5. violent event;
6. rapid de-escalation; and
7. retaliation.[123]

Juveniles' propensity for gun ownership and violence are known to be closely related. One study found that juvenile males who "own guns for protection rather than for sport are six times more likely to carry guns, eight times more likely to commit a crime with a gun, [and] four times more likely to sell drugs." This study added that these youths are "almost five times more likely to be in a gang, and three times more likely to commit serious and violent crimes than youth who do not own guns for protection."[124] In addition, gangs are more likely to recruit youths who own firearms, and gang members are more than twice as likely as those who do not belong to a gang to own a gun for protection, more likely to have peers who own guns for protection, and more likely to carry their guns outside their home.[125]

Other researchers have also discovered a "significant connection among gang involvement, gang violence, and firearms."[126] For example, one study based on the responses of 835 institutionalized male residents of six juvenile correctional facilities in four states found that "gang membership brought increases in most forms of gun-involved conduct." Indeed, 45 percent of the respondents in this study reported that gun theft is a regular gang activity, 68 percent indicated that their gang bought and sold guns on a regular basis, and 61 percent said that "driving around shooting at people you don't like" is a regular gang activity.[127]

A final dimension of law-violating behaviors of urban street gangs is an examination of the extent to which they are becoming organized crime groups. Decker, Tim Bynum, and Deborah Weisel interviewed members of African American and Hispanic gangs in San Diego and Chicago and found that only the Gangster Disciples (GDs) in Chicago are assuming the attributes of organized crime groups.[128] Several commentaries have spelled out the organizational features of the GDs, including a chairman of the board, two boards of directors (one for the streets and one for prisons), governors who control drug trafficking on the streets, regents who supply the drugs, area coordinators who collect revenues from drug-selling spots, enforcers who punish those who violate the rules, and "shorties" who staff drug-selling spots and execute drug deals.[129]

It can be argued that aspects of organized crime groups are found in such drug-trafficking gangs as the Bloods and Crips in Los Angeles, the Miami Boys of south Florida, and the Jamaican Posses of New York and Florida. Beginning in the mid 1980s, these street gangs appeared to become criminal entrepreneurs in supplying illicit drugs. In a brief period of several years, many of these street gangs developed intrastate and interstate networks for the purpose of expanding their illegal drug market sales. The Crips and Bloods of Los Angeles have been the most active in drug trafficking across the United States. A study by the U.S. Congress concluded that during the latter part of the 1980s the Crips and Bloods controlled 30 percent of the crack cocaine market across the nation.[130] The Drug Enforcement Administration claimed in a 1988 report that Los Angeles street gangs were identified with drug sales in forty-six states.[131]

Emerging Gangs in Smaller Cities and Communities

In the 1990s, nearly every city, many suburban areas, and even some rural areas across the nation experienced the reality of youths who consider themselves gang members. Thrasher's finding that no gangs he studied were alike appears to be true for these **emerging gangs** as well.[132] Curry and colleagues' 1992 national survey found that cities with emerging gangs reported that 90 percent of the gangs were made up of juveniles.[133]

Emerging gangs have been examined in Denver, Colorado; Kansas City, Missouri; Rochester, New York; and Seattle, Washington.[134] Esbensen and David Huizinga found that about 3 percent of the Denver sample of 1,527 youths belonged to a gang during their four-year study. But by the fourth year, the percentage of youths who claimed gang membership increased to nearly 7 percent. Esbensen and Huizinga further found that male gang members were involved in levels of delinquent activity that were two or three times greater than those of non-gang members. In addition to fights with other gangs, three-quarters of the gang members reported that they were involved in assaults, thefts, robberies, and drug sales.[135]

Mark S. Fleisher's street ethnography in Kansas City, Missouri, and Seattle, Washington, among teenage gang members found gang membership to be made up of "weak social ties formed among episodically homeless, socially rejected youth reared by deviant socializers."[136] Fleisher rejected the common assumption that gangs look upon the set as family. Instead, he found that "these kids kill each other over 'respect,' fight for and kill one another in combat over girls or a gram or two of cocaine, and may severely beat or even kill a gang 'brother' in a violent ritual, known in some places as the 'SOS'— 'Shoot-on-Sight' or 'Stomp-on-Sight.' "[137]

Thornberry and colleagues examined the relationship between gangs and delinquent behavior in Rochester, New York, from 1988 to 1991. They found some stability among gang members, because 21 percent were members in all three years. This research also revealed that gang members were much more heavily involved in street offenses while they were gang members than they were before or after their time with the gang.[138]

The rise of emerging gangs is being reported in many cities around the nation. Salem, Oregon, reported a 97 percent increase in the number of gang members and affiliates between October 1992 and April 1993. Davenport, Iowa, has 2,000 documented gang members and a gang-related shooting nearly each week. Des Moines, Iowa, has eighteen gangs, with a total of 1,239 members. Peoria, Illinois, decided that its gang problem was so serious that it required the intervention of Chicago-based gang consultants to negotiate a truce between two rival gangs.[139] A statement from Rochester, Minnesota, is one to which many communities across the nation can relate:

> Gangs are a new element in the greater Rochester, Minnesota, area. In 1990, there were rumors. In 1991, there was substantiated evidence of gangs. In 1992, clear indicators emerged that there were youth gangs with a stronghold in the community. In 1993, there have been regular reports of violence, fighting, and other gang related activities in the community.[140]

This nationwide expansion began in the late 1980s, and it appeared to be fueled in four different ways. First, in some communities it took place when ghetto-based drug-trafficking gangs sent ranking gang members to the community to persuade local youths to sell crack cocaine. Second, gang-related individuals operating on their own established drug-trafficking networks among community youths. Third, urban gang members whose families had moved to these communities were instrumental in developing local chapters of urban gangs. Fourth, youths in communities with little or no intervention from outsiders developed their own versions of gangs. The latter two types were less likely to become involved in drug trafficking than were the first two types.

Behind the first wave of nationwide gang expansion was urban gang leaders' knowledge that a lot of new markets were ripe for exploitation and that crack cocaine would command a high price in these new areas. To introduce the drug in these new markets, the representatives of most urban gangs promised the possibility of a gang satellite; that is, the emerging local gang would be connected by both name and organizational ties to the parent gang. However, urban gangs had neither the intent nor the resources to develop extensions of themselves in the emerging gang community. The promise of being a gang satellite was only a carrot to persuade local youths to sell crack cocaine for the urban gang. The development of drug-trafficking emerging gangs throughout the nation has seven possible stages, and the degree and seriousness of gang activity in a community depend on its stage of development.[141]

Stage 1: *Implementation.* An adult gang member, usually a high-ranking officer, comes to a city that has no gangs. On arriving, either by plane or auto, this gang member goes to a low-income, minority neighborhood where he recruits several juveniles to sell crack and be members of the new gang. The recruited juveniles are assured of a percentage of the money they make from the sale of crack. The exact percentage seems to vary from gang to gang but is typically about 10 percent.[142] The representative from the urban gang returns on a regular basis to supply drugs and pick up the money.

Stage 2: *Expansion and Conflict.* The adult who came to the community tells the recruited juveniles enough about his gang that they are able to identify with it. They start to wear the proper clothing, to learn something about gang signs, and to experience a sense of camaraderie, yet their primary motivation is still to make money from selling drugs. One Midwestern youth claimed that he was making $40,000 a month selling crack for the Unknown Vice Lords when he was arrested and institutionalized.[143] Conflict inevitably arises as drug-trafficking gangs attempt to expand their markets, usually in the same neighborhoods. Fights may break out during school functions, at athletic events and shopping centers, and in parks and other common gathering places. Weapons may be used at this time, and the number of weapons increases dramatically in the community.

Stage 3: *Organization and Consolidation.* Youths identifying with a certain gang attempt to develop a group culture during this stage. The leadership is assumed by one or more members of the core group as well as by young adult males from the community. The increased visibility of the gang attracts a sizable number of "wannabes." The gang may be larger, but it is still relatively unorganized, consisting primarily of a group of males hanging around together. Recruitment is emphasized and considerable pressure is put on young minority males to join the gang. One of these males noted, "If you are black, twelve or so, they really put pressure on you to join. It's hard not to."[144]

Stage 4: *Gang Intimidation and Community Reaction.* Several events typically take place during this stage. Some whites join the minority gangs, and other whites form gangs of their own. One youth represented the spirit of this white reaction when he said, "The blacks ain't going to push us around."[145] Minority gangs are still more likely to wear their colors and to demonstrate gang affiliation. Drugs are also increasingly sold in the school environment, and gang control becomes a serious problem in the school. A high school teacher expressed her concern: "I've never had any trouble teaching in this school. Now, with these gang kids, I'm half afraid to come to school. It's becoming a very serious situation."[146] Gangs are becoming more visible in shopping centers, and older people are beginning to experience some fear of shopping when gang youth are present. Equally disturbing, and much more serious in the long run, gangs are becoming popular among children in middle school, and some allegiance is being given to gangs among children as young as first and second grades.

Stage 5: *Expansion of Drug Markets:* Drugs are openly sold in junior and senior high schools, on street corners, and in shopping centers during the fifth stage. Crack houses are present in some minority neighborhoods. Extortion of students and victimization of both teachers and students take place frequently in the public schools. The gangs are led by adults who remain in the community, the organizational structure is more highly developed, and the number of gang members shows a significant increase. Outsiders have been present all along, but during this stage they seem to be continually coming into and going out of the community. In their mid-twenties, they roll into the community in expensive automobiles, wearing expensive clothes and jewelry and flashing impressive rolls of money.

Stage 6: *Gangs Take Over.* Communities that permit the gangs to develop to this stage discover that gangs are clearly in control in minority neighborhoods, in the school, at school events, and in shopping centers. The criminal operations of gangs also become more varied and now include robberies, burglaries, aggravated assaults, and rapes. Drive-by shootings begin to occur on a regular basis, and citizens' fear of gangs increases dramatically. The police, whose gang units usually number several officers, typically express an inability to control drug trafficking and violence.

Stage 7: *Community Deterioration.* The final stage is characterized by the deterioration of social institutions and the community itself because of gang control. Citizens move out of the city, stay away from shopping centers, and find safer schools for their children. When an emerging gang community arrives at this stage of deterioration, it is fully experiencing the gang problems of urban communities.

In sum, while a community's reaction greatly affects the seriousness of the problem, non-gang and sometimes low-crime communities across the nation in the late 1980s and early 1990s began to experience the development of gangs. These emerging gangs developed from different trajectories, but the most toxic to a community was when a ghetto-based drug-trafficking gang was able to persuade minority youths to sell crack cocaine for it and these youths, in turn, developed what they thought would be a satellite to the parent gang.

Racial and Ethnic Gangs

Hispanic, African American, Asian, white and Native American gangs constitute the basic type of racial and ethnic gangs in the United States. Hispanic and African American gangs are more numerous and have more members, but Asian gangs are rapidly increasing in the United States. African American gangs began to migrate across the nation in the late 1980s, and Asian gangs began to migrate in the 1990s.

HISPANIC GANGS Hispanic, or Latino, gangs are divided into Mexican American or Chicano, Cuban, Puerto Rican, Dominican, Jamaican, and Central American members. Hispanic gang members frequently dress distinctively, display colors, communicate through graffiti, use monikers, and bear tattoos. Chicano street gangs have unwritten codes of conduct and oral traditions that have evolved over generations and are referred to as **Movidas.**[147] These street gangs usually divide themselves into groupings called *cliques,* generally formed based on the age of the members. Some cliques may also be organized according to a specialty, such as violence. The uniform or dress readily identifies a youth or young adult as belonging to a Chicano gang. The standard dress is a white T-shirt, thin belt, khaki pants with split cuffs, and a black or blue knit beanie or a bandanna tied around the forehead. Finally, one of the most distinguishing characteristics of Chicano gangs is the loyalty they receive from gang members.

AFRICAN AMERICAN GANGS African American gangs have received more attention in this chapter than any other racial or ethnic group because most of the ghetto-based drug-trafficking gangs that have established networks across the nation are African American. For example, the Bloods and Crips from Los Angeles, the People and Folks from Chicago, and the Detroit gangs are all mostly African American. Furthermore, African American gangs usually identify themselves by adopting certain colors in addition to other identifiers, such as the hand signals shown in Figure 10.4.

ASIAN GANGS There is a variety of Asian gangs in California, including Chinese, Vietnamese, Filipino, Japanese, and Korean. The Chinese gangs, especially, have spread to other major cities in this nation, and some of the other gangs also are active outside California. Table 10.2 lists some Southeast Asian gangs in the upper Midwest. Asian gangs tend to be more organized and to have more of an identifiable leadership than is true of other street gangs. Ko-Lin Chin's examination of Chinese gangs found them to be involved in some of the nation's worst gang-related violence and heroin trafficking. Unlike other ethnic gangs, Chinese gangs are closely tied to the social and economic life of their rapidly developing and economically robust communities.[148] A study of Vietnamese youth gangs in southern California found that these youths experience multiple marginality but that they attained the American dream by robbing Vietnamese families of large amounts of cash that such families keep at home.[149]

WHITE GANGS Until the recent decades of the twentieth century, most gangs were made up of white youths. Today, according to Reiner, white youths make up about 10 percent of the gang population in the United States.[150] The 1998 National Youth Gang Survey reported that 12 percent of the gang members were white.[151] However, student surveys generally reveal a much larger representation of white adolescents among gang

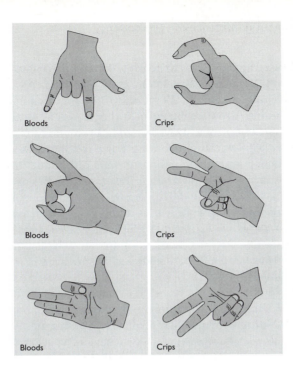

FIGURE 10.4 Gang Signs

Source: Midwest Gang Investigators' Association, *Warning Signs for Parents* (n.d.).

TABLE 10.2

Southeast Asian Gangs, Upper Midwest
(General Reference Only)

HMONG

Asian Gangster Disciples (AGD)	Appleton, WI
Asian Knights (Kings)	St. Paul, MN/Eau Claire, WI
	Wausau, WI/Stevens Point, WI
Asian Boy Crips	St. Paul, MN
Asian Mafia Crips (Clan)	St. Paul, MN
Bad Boy Crips (BBC)	Milwaukee, WI
Cobras	St. Paul, MN
Junior White Tigers	St. Paul, MN
M.O.D.	Eau Claire, WI
Tiny Man Crew (TMC)	LaCrosse, WI/Green Bay, WI
Totally Mafia Crips (TMC)	LaCrosse, WI
Totally Gangster Crips (TGC)	LaCrosse, WI
White Tigers	St. Paul, MN/Minneapolis, MN
Yellow Tigers	Milwaukee, WI
Young Cholos Lovers (YCL)	LaCrosse, WI/Minneapolis, MN

LAOTIAN

Angel Boys	Minneapolis, MN/Milwaukee, WI
Laos Boys (Lost Boys)	Minneapolis, MN
Laos Posse	Green Bay, WI/Milwaukee, WI/Elgin, IL

CAMBODIAN

Cambodian Night Creepers (CNC)	St. Paul, MN/Minneapolis, MN
Red Cambodian Bloods (RCB)	Rochester, MN/St. Paul, MN
	Minneapolis, MN

VIETNAMESE

Nasty Boys	Milwaukee, WI
M. P. L. S.	Minneapolis, MN
T. C.	Minneapolis, MN

Source: Handout of Loren A. Evenrud, Ed.D. (n.d.), police officer of the Minneapolis Police Department

members.[152] For example, a survey of nearly 6,000 eighth graders in eleven sites showed that 25 percent of the whites said they were gang members.[153]

A recent development on the West Coast is the solidifying of lower- and middle-class white youths into groups who refer to themselves as *stoners*. These groups frequently abuse drugs and alcohol and listen to heavy metal rock music. Some members of the group practice Satanism, including grave robbing, desecration of human remains, and sacrificing animals.[154] Stoner groups can be identified by their mode of dress: colored T-shirts with decals of their rock music heroes or bands, Levis, and tennis shoes. They may also wear metal-spiked wrist cuffs, collars, belts, and satanic jewelry. The recently emerging white gangs across the nation have used many of the symbols of the stoner gangs, especially the heavy metal rock music and the satanic rituals, but they are not as likely to call attention to themselves with their dress. They may refer to themselves as neo-Nazi Skinheads and are involved in a variety of hate crimes and drug trafficking.

NATIVE AMERICAN GANGS Recent interest has been given to Navajo youth gangs.[155] In 1997, the Navajo Nation estimated that about sixty youth gangs existed in Navajo country. Gang values have encouraged such risky behaviors as heavy drinking and drug use, leading frequently to mortality from injuries and alcohol. A small percentage of Navajo male youths were involved in these groups, and at most 15 percent were affiliated, peripherally, with gangs. Many gang activities involved "hanging around," drinking, and vandalism, but gang members also robbed people, bootlegged alcohol, and sold marijuana.[156]

Female Delinquent Gangs

More attention has recently been given to adolescent girls who join gangs. Traditional sociologists considered the female gang almost a contradiction in terms. Albert K. Cohen argued:

> Again the group or the gang, the vehicle of the delinquent subculture and one of its statistically most manageable earmarks, is a boy's gang. . . . If, however, female delinquents

---

WHAT WOULD YOU SAY? 10.5

Presentation to Gang Youth

You gave a two-hour presentation to the faculty of an urban school during a one-day workshop in which the faculty was examining a gang de-escalation program for that school. The next day, when school is in session, the assistant principal introduces you to one of the teachers before his class is to begin. The teacher remarks that he was impressed with your talk the day before, and he would like you to teach his class.

You are flattered by the invitation, because the teacher is reputed to be a top instructor in that school. You agree and are introduced, to find you are facing thirty male and female high school juniors and seniors, of whom 70 to 80 percent are gang members. You have had no time to prepare, but you have fifty minutes with these urban youth.

What would you say to these students? What would be your general theme and what points would you make to support your theme? Could you engage them?

Source: The author had this experience in a Chicago public school.

also have their subculture, it is a different one from that which we have described. The latter [gang] belongs to the male role."[157]

Thrasher's account of Chicago gangs also found them to be primarily male. He described the gangs that did include adolescent females as immoral rather than conflict gangs. Their chief activities included petting, illicit sex, necking, and mugging. They had names like the Lone Star Club, the Under the L gang, the Tulips, and the Night Riders. Using clandestine signals in the classroom, they arranged secret meetings in vacant lots.[158]

In 1984, Anne Campbell estimated that in New York City 10 percent of the membership of the 400 gangs was female. Female gang members ranged in age from 14 to 30. Some were married, and many had children.[159] A *CBS News* report in 1986 estimated that about 1,000 girls were involved in more than 100 female gangs in Chicago alone. These gangs, according to the report, were not sister organizations or auxiliaries to male gangs but were independent female gangs. Like their male counterparts, these female gangs staked out their own turf, adopted distinctive colors and insignia, and had physical confrontations with rival gangs.[160]

In *Sisters in Crime*, Freda Adler discussed female gangs in Philadelphia and in New York.[161] Miller and E. Ackley investigated two female gangs, the Molls and the Queens, in the inner-city district of an eastern seaport in the early 1970s. The gangs' illegal offenses included truancy, theft, drinking, property damage, sex offenses, and assault. Truancy took place about three times as frequently as the next most common offense, theft (largely shoplifting).[162] Peggy C. Giordano's 1978 examination of institutionalized adolescent females in Ohio revealed that 53.7 percent of the 108 institutionalized females had been part of a group that they called a gang, and 51.9 percent said their gang had a name. She noted that the names of these gangs (e.g., the Outlaws, the Cobras, Mojos, Loveless, Red Blood, White Knights, East Side Birds, Power) conveyed neither a particularly feminine image, nor suggested a subordinate position to a male gang.[163]

Waln K. Brown, an ex-gang member himself, carried out a more comprehensive study of female participation in youth gangs in Philadelphia in 1970.[164] He suggested that female gang participation is usually limited to sexually integrated gangs. Their functions within these integrated gangs in Philadelphia included serving as participants in gang wars or individual and small-group combat fights and acting as spies to gain information about activities being planned by other gangs. Brown noted that most females join Philadelphia gangs to be popular and to be "where the action is." But he did find one all-female African American gang. The Holy Whores were heavily involved in the subculture of violence, being accused of knifing and kicking pregnant females and of badly scarring and mutilating "cute" girls. "Getting a body" (knifing) was said to be an important part of their "rep."[165]

Lee Bowker and Klein studied a group of African American gang females in Los Angeles in 1980 and reported they never planned a gang activity: the planning was done by the males, who usually excluded the females. But the female gang members would participate in violent crimes and drug-related gang activities.[166] J. C. Quicker studied Mexican American adolescent female gangs in East Los Angeles in 1983 and drew four conclusions about them. First, he found the gangs always have a connection to a male gang; indeed, they derived their name from their male counterparts. Second, adolescent females were not coerced into the gang but had to prove their loyalty and undergo an initiation procedure. Third, these females usually operated in a democratic manner. Finally, loyalty to the gang rivaled loyalty to the family, and most friends came from within the gang. The gang, according to Quicker, offered "warmth, friends, loyalty, and socialization" as it insulated its members from the harsh environment of the barrio.[167]

M. G. Harris's study of the Cholas, a Latina gang in California's San Fernando Valley, revealed that these adolescent females are becoming more independent of male gangs. In rejecting the traditional image of the Latina as wife and mother, the gang supported a more "macha" home girl role. Gang affiliation also supported members in their

Female gang member holding revolver. Most studies have found that girl gangs serve as adjuncts to boy gangs, but that some female gang members are still involved in serious acts of delinquency.

estrangement from organized religion, as it substituted a form of familism that "provides a strong substitute for weak family and conventional school ties."[168]

Esbensen, Elizabeth Piper Deschenes, and L. Thomas Winfree Jr. found from their analysis of the Denver Youth Survey that girl gang participants committed a wide variety of offenses and at only a slightly lower frequency than boys involved in gangs. Their findings also failed to support the notion that girls involved in gangs were mere sex objects and ancillary members. This study also showed that girls aged out of gangs before boys and that girls received more emotional fulfillment from their involvement with gang activity.[169]

Campbell's 1984 examination of the relationships among adolescent females in three New York female gangs also revealed intense comaraderie and strong dependency among these gang members. But she still concluded that female gangs continued to exist as an adjunct to male gangs and that males dictated and controlled the females' activities. Campbell observed, "Girls are told how to dress, are allowed to fight, and are encouraged to be good mothers and faithful wives. Their principal source of suffering and joy is their men."[170]

Taylor found in Detroit in 1993 that women were involved in many disparate gang types, ranging from compatriots to corporate. They are frequently represented in drug-trafficking gangs.[171] Fifteen-year-old Tracie responded, "Girls is in crews, gangs, money, shooting . . . they in it all! What makes you ask that question, is you from somewhere where the girls don't count."[172] DeLores added, "Girls got guns for the same reason guys got 'em. . . . It's wild out here, you need to protect yourself. . . . It doesn't matter if it's selling crack, weed, or any kinda dope, business is business. Guns protect you and your business, right?"[173]

David Lauderback, Joy Hansen, and Daniel Waldorf studied the Potrero Hill Posse, an African American girl group in San Francisco in 1992. After sharing the common experiences of being abandoned by the fathers of their children and being abused and controlled by other men, this group of girls began hanging around together. They found that selling crack and organized "boosting" (shoplifting) were among the few resources available for supporting themselves and their children.[174]

In 1993, Beth Bjerregaard and Carolyn Smith, using data from the Rochester Youth Development Study, found that involvement in gangs for both females and males was associated with increased levels of delinquency and substance abuse. For example, female gang members reported a serious delinquency prevalence of 66.8 percent, compared to 6.6 percent for non-gang members. Although there was some similarity in the factors associated with gang membership for both males and females, lack of school success was a particularly important factor for female gang members.[175]

Joan Moore and John Hagedorn's 2001 summary of the research on female gangs reports that the majority of female gang members are involved in delinquent or criminal behaviors.[176] Delinquency rates of female gang members are lower than those of male gang members but higher than those of nongang females and males. Female gang members are likely to be involved in property crimes and status offenses, but they commit fewer violent crimes than their male counterparts. Female gang members are also heavily involved in drug dealing. For example, in Los Angeles County, drug offenses were the most frequent cause for the arrest of female gang members.[177] See Table 10.3 for Gang-Related Charges for Female Arrestees in Chicago, 1993–1996.

In sum, most studies have found that girl gangs still serve as adjuncts to boy gangs. Yet an increasing number of important studies show that female gangs provide girls with the necessary skills to survive in their harsh communities while allowing them a temporary escape from the dismal future awaiting them.[178] What these studies reveal is that girls join gangs for the same basic reasons that boys do and share with boys in their neighborhood the hopelessness and powerlessness of the urban underclass.[179]

The Theories of Gang Formation

The classical theories about the origins of juvenile gangs and gang delinquency have come from Herbert A. Bloch and Arthur Niederhoffer; Cloward and Ohlin; and Cohen, Miller, and Yablonsky.

TABLE 10.3

Gang-Related Charges for Female Arrestees in Chicago: 1993–96

Offense*	Female Arrestees with Gang-Related Charge (%)			
	1993	*1994*	*1995*	*1996*
VIOLENT (TOTAL)	46.9	40.3	34.4	38.5
Homicide	0.2	0.1	0.0	0.1
Simple battery	17.6	16.1	14.1	14.9
Mob action	9.7	5.7	3.8	4.8
All other violent offenses	19.4	18.4	16.5	18.7
DRUG (TOTAL)	36.4	37.9	44.4	37.7
Cocaine possession	14.3	9.8	8.8	2.6
Crack possession	7.0	11.6	13.9	15.6
All other drug offenses	15.1	16.5	21.7	19.5
PROSTITUTION	0.8	1.5	4.1	9.8
PROPERTY	5.1	3.4	4.4	5.1
WEAPONS	3.7	4.3	2.5	2.8
LIQUOR	5.6	10.7	7.3	3.5
OTHER	2.2	1.7	2.7	2.3

Note: Percentages may not total 100 because of rounding. Total number (n) of cases per year: 1993, *n*=2,023; 1994, *n*=2,029; 1995, *n*=2,021; 1996, *n*=2,193.

*With the exception of vice offenses (drug, prostitution, and gambling), gang-related offenses are defined by referring to the motive of the offender. Vice offenses are considered gang-related if they involve a known gang member. Almost all liquor offenses involve underage drinking.

Source: Joan Moore and John Hagedorn, "Female Gangs: A Focus on Research," *Juvenile Justice Bulletin* (Washington, D.C.: Office of Juvenile Justice and Delinquency Prevention, 2001), p. 5. These data were drawn from special tabulations provided to the authors by the Illinois Criminal Justice Information Authority (1998).

Bloch and Niederhoffer's theory was based on the idea that joining a gang is part of the experience male adolescents need to grow up to adulthood. The basic function of the gang is thus to provide a substitute for the formalized puberty rites that are found in other societies.[180] Cloward and Ohlin's theory was based on the notion that lower-class boys interact with and gain support from other alienated individuals. These youngsters pursue illegitimate means to achieve the success they cannot gain through legitimate means.[181] Cohen's theory was that gang delinquency represents a subcultural and collective solution to the problem of acquiring status that faces lower-class boys when they find themselves evaluated according to middle-class values in the schools.[182] Miller held that there is a definite lower-class culture and that gang behavior is an expression of that culture. Miller saw gang leadership as based mainly on smartness and toughness. He viewed the gang as very cohesive and with high conformity to gang norms.[183] Finally, Yablonsky suggested that violent delinquent gangs arise out of certain conditions that are found in urban slums. These conditions encourage the development of the sociopathic personality in adolescents, and such sociopathic individuals become the core leadership of these gangs.[184]

These classical theories of gangs focused on sociological variables such as strain (Cloward and Ohlin), subcultural affiliation (Miller, Cohen), and social disorganization (Yablonsky). Cohen, Cloward and Ohlin, and Miller also stressed the importance of the peer group for gang membership.[185] Each of the five theories of gang formation has received both support and criticism, but research is needed into current expressions of gang activity because the existing theories were based primarily on 1950s gangs.[186]

Other theories of gangs are associated with social disorganization theory.[187] This theory is based on the assumption that poor economic conditions cause social disorganization to the extent that there is a deficiency of social control. This lack of social control leads to gang formation and involvement because youths in low-income neighborhoods seek the social order and security that gangs offer.[188]

More recently, underclass theory has been widely used to explain the origins of gangs.[189] In the midst of big-city ghettos and barrios filled with poverty and deprivation, it is argued, gangs are a normal response to an abnormal social setting.[190] Part of the underclass's plight, according to Fagan, is that of being permanently excluded from participating in mainstream labor market occupations. Thus, members of the underclass are forced to rely on other economic alternatives, such as low-paying temporary jobs, part-time jobs, some form of welfare, or involvement in drug trafficking, prostitution, muggings, and extortions.[191] Hagedorn documented the loss of manufacturing jobs in Milwaukee during the 1980s that resulted in an increasingly segmented labor force in which minorities were consigned low-wage or even part-time work, welfare, and the illegal economy.[192] Vigil added that people who join gangs are pushed into these groups by their condition of poverty and their status as minorities. Marginal to the wider society, to their communities, and to their families, they are subject to difficulties in all areas. This multiple marginality makes them the most likely candidates for gang membership, for in a real sense, they have little else going for them. Vigil added that this "dialectic of multiple marginality [also] applies to why females now are more active in gangs."[193]

Jankowski contended that gang violence and the defiant attitude of young men are connected with the competitive struggle in poor communities. Being a product of their environment, they adopt a "Hobbesian view of life in which violence is an integral part of the state of nature."[194] The operations and survival rate of gangs vary greatly but, according to Jankowski's theory, can be accounted for by the interaction of four elements:

> (1) inequality, and individual responses to reduce inequality; (2) the ability of the gang (both leadership and rank and file) to manage the desires and behavior of people with defiant individualist characters; (3) the degree to which a collective of individuals has been capable of developing a sophisticated organization to carry out its economic activities; and (4) the extent to which it has been able to establish ties to institutions belonging to the larger society.[195]

Moreover, Scott Decker and Barrik Van Winkle state that an explanation of why youths join gangs must be seen in the larger context of pulls and pushes. Pulls relate to the attractiveness and benefits that the gang is perceived to offer a youth. Benefits frequently cited are enhanced prestige or status among friends, excitement, and making money from drugs. These personal advantages make gang involvement appear to be a rational choice. The pushes of gang membership are found in the social, economic, and cultural forces of the larger society. These forces may include needing protection from other gangs, seeking an identity to overcome feelings of marginality, being recruited or coerced into gangs, or growing up in a neighborhood in which gang membership is a tradition.[196]

Michael F. de Vries proposes that an integrated approach is needed to understand why juveniles become involved with gangs. For African American youths, strain theory is "the heart of why African Americans find gang associations worthwhile." Gangs offer deprived African American youths opportunities to obtain status and financial gain that is denied to them in the larger culture. Asian immigrants, he argues, are also experiencing such strain. Although African Americans are more "likely to engage in illicit drug distribution to counteract their inherited inferior position in society, Asians are more apt to engage in home invasions, theft, and intimidation as their way of coping with a similar strain." According to de Vries, subcultural theory appears to be helpful in explaining Hispanic gangs. Largely spared from Anglo-American culture by their own traditions, "this subcultural group places a high degree of value on an individual's prowess (machismo), territorial identity, pride, and loyalty to their own group identity." Control theory, especially for middle-class whites, helps explain why these youths become involved in gang activity. Social bonds are coming under attack as the family unit is becoming weaker.[197]

How Communities Can Prevent and Control Youth Gangs

The recent surveys of youth gangs across the nation reveal that the number of gangs and members are decreasing slightly. Yet youth gangs are still a serious social problem. Gang involvements affect the quality of life for many youngsters and in most communities across the United States.

Communities across the nation have had a tendency to deny that they have gangs even when gang youths are causing considerable problems at school and in the neighborhoods.[198] Then a dramatic incident takes place, such as the killing of an innocent victim or a shoot-out in which one or more gang youths are killed, and what began as a process of denial eventually becomes one of attempting to repress, or make gangs invisible. But despite such efforts as establishing gang units in police departments, increasing the size of these units, and harassing gang members at every opportunity, gangs begin a process of intimidation and terror that touches all aspects of community life.

Another reason that successful interventions must be found is that gangs are destructive to their members. Gangs that originated as play groups frequently become involved in dangerous, even deadly, games. Joining a gang may be a normal rite of passage for a youth, yet gangs minister poorly to such basic adolescent needs as preparation for marriage, employment, and learning to adapt to the adult world. Adolescent males who join gangs for protection are often exposed to dangers that most nongang youth are able to avoid. Adolescent females may join because they are attracted to male members but then are exploited sexually. Gang members are more likely both to commit delinquent acts and to become victims of crime than are youths who do not join gangs.[199] Finally, joining a gang may provide status and esteem in the present, but gang membership also ensures incarceration in juvenile and adult facilities.

Irving Spergel and colleagues' 1989 survey of forty-five cities with gang problems identified five strategies of intervention: (1) community organization, including community mobilization and networking; (2) social intervention, focusing on individual behavioral and value change; (3) opportunities provision, emphasizing the improvement of basic education, training, and job opportunities for youth; (4) suppression, focusing on arrest, incarceration, monitoring, and supervision of gang members; and (5) organizational development and change, or the creation of special organizational units as well as procedures.[200]

In examining the implementation of these strategies, Spergel and colleagues found that suppression (44 percent) was most frequently used, followed by social intervention (31.5 percent), organizational development (10.9 percent), community organization (8.9 percent), and opportunities provision (4.8 percent).[201] Community organization was more likely to be used with gang programs in emerging gang cities, whereas social intervention and opportunity provision tended to be primary strategies of programs in cities with chronic gang problems. But in only seventeen of the forty-five cities was there any evidence of improvement in the gang situation.[202]

Spergel and colleagues, in developing a model for predicting general effectiveness in dealing with gang problems, stated:

A final set of analyses across all cities indicate that the primary strategies of community organization and provision of opportunity along with maximum participation by key community actors is predictive of successful efforts at reducing the gang problem.[203]

Spergel and his colleagues expanded their approach to the Comprehensive Community-Wide Approach to Gang Prevention, Intervention, and Suppression Program. This model contains several program components for the design and mobilization of community efforts by school officials, employers, street outreach workers, police, judges, prosecutors, probation and parole officers, and corrections officers.[204] The Gang Violence Reduction Program, an early pilot of this model, has been implemented in Chicago. After three years of program operations, the preliminary evaluation of this project was positive among the targeted group (lower levels of gang violence, few arrests for serious gang crimes, and hastened departures of youth from gang activities).[205] The Comprehensive Community-Wide Approach to Gang Prevention, Intervention, and Suppression Program has since been implemented in five jurisdictions: Mesa, Arizona; Tucson, Arizona; Riverside, California; Bloomington, Illinois; and San Antonio, Texas.[206]

These sites initially undertook the process of community mobilization, as they identified or assessed the nature and extent of the gang problem. They then planned for program development and implementation in a problem-solving framework. It was not long thereafter that they began to implement appropriate interrelated strategies to target gang violence and its causes. At the same time, they continued to reassess the changing nature and extent of their gang problems. Their strategies consisted of a combination of community mobilization, social intervention and outreach, provision of social and economic opportunities for youth, suppression or social control, and organizational change and development.[207]

What these efforts by Spergel and colleagues demonstrate is that only an integrated, multidimensional, community-oriented effort is likely to have any long-term effect in preventing and controlling gangs in the United States. This gang prevention and control model must have several components: (1) the community must take responsibility for developing and implementing the model; (2) it is a structural model that takes very seriously the hopelessness arising from the unmet needs of underclass children; (3) prevention programs, especially in the first six years of school, must be emphasized; (4) supporters of this model must coordinate all the gang intervention efforts taking place in a community; and (5) sufficient financial resources must be available to implement the model.

SUMMARY

Youngsters derive meaning and have their needs met or ignored in their social contacts with family members, peers, teachers, and leaders and participants in churches, community organizations, and school activities. Some youngsters find little reason to become involved in law-violating activities. But others, with needs frustrated and nowhere else to find hope, become attracted to street gangs. These gangs become quasi-families and offer acceptance, status, and esteem.

Youth gangs are proliferating across the United States. Even small towns and rural areas are contending with the rise of youth gangs. Much is the same and much is new about youth gangs. It is not new that gangs are violent, but the wide use of gun violence—especially involving automatic and semiautomatic handguns—is new. Drug trafficking has been connected with gangs in the past, but not to the extent that it is in the present. Drug gangs are also more predominant now than in the past. Youth gangs have further become street gangs, particularly in urban areas. This means that juveniles have stayed with the gang, but more and more control is assumed by adults. In some urban gangs, juveniles are now a minority of gang membership.

Gangs have thrived because of the poverty and underclass conditions in many urban neighborhoods. The hopelessness of these environments makes drug trafficking attractive and gang membership desirable even with the high possibility of being injured, killed, or imprisoned. Police gang units seem to be helpless to defuse gangs' violence or prevent their spread. Grassroots community groups have had some success with gang members, but gang reduction ultimately depends on providing children of the underclass with more positive options than they have today.

KEY TERMS

"cold and brittle," p. 286
crack, p. 285
emerging gangs, p. 305
friendship patterns, p. 286

gang, p. 292
locura, p. 301
Movidas, p. 308
representing, p. 301

CRITICAL THINKING QUESTIONS

1. Why are gangs so popular among young people?
2. How have street gangs changed through the years?
3. Discuss the seven possible stages of development that an emergent gang may go through. How does the gang's stage of development relate to the degree and seriousness of gang activity in the community?
4. Discuss the development of gangs in recent years in your community. At what stage are they? What gang activities are evident? If gangs have not yet developed in your community, analyze why this is so.
5. You have an opportunity to work with eight gang members who are between fourteen and sixteen-years-of-age. You have decided to design the twenty sessions around the theme of hopelessness. What would you do in these sessions to help instill more hope in the lives of these young men?

6. In your community or nearby communities, what activities are females involved in with male youth gangs? Are there any separate female gangs?
7. Why have adults taken over so many youth gangs? With adults in leadership roles, what roles are reserved for youths?
8. Why is denial such a favorite strategy of police chiefs, school superintendents, and public officials for dealing with gangs? How much has this strategy been used in the community where you live or in a situation you know of?
9. What do you think is the most effective means to break up street gangs?
10. Are there any ways in which gangs could have a positive impact on adolescents?

11. A particularly heinous crime has been committed by gang youths in your community. The community, which has been in a state of denial, is now alarmed. They invite you to speak to a group of concerned and leading citizens to develop a community-based plan to deal with gangs. What will you tell this group? What are the main steps in your plan?

WEB DESTINATIONS

Find many links on gang and peer influence at the Florida State University site.
http://www.criminology.fsu.edu/jjclearinghouse/jj13.html

Visit the National Youth Gang Center website.
http://www.iir.com/nygc

Learn more about street gangs from the Streetgangs website.
http://www.streetgangs.com/

Visit Larry Hoover's homepage to learn more about the Gangster Disciples.
http://members.aol.com/JCAC6/gd.html

Go to this Chicago Gang site to learn more about the Vice Lords.
http://sobs.org/chilocal/gangs/gnghome.html

Learn more about racial and ethnic gangs at this National Criminal Justic Reference Service.
http://www.ncjrs.org/txtfiles/fs-9412.txt

Go to this site to learn more about females in gangs at this site.
http://www.faculty.smsu.edu/m/mkc09bf/nogangs/Girls/girls%20and%20gangs.htm

NOTES

1. Interviewed in 1982 at the Iowa State Penitentiary at Fort Madison.
2. Ibid.
3. "The Drug Gangs," *Newsweek,* 28 March 1988, p. 27.
4. Robert J. Bursik, Jr., "Social Disorganization and Theories of Crime and Delinquency: Problems and Prospects," *Criminology* 26 (November 1988), p. 523.
5. See Mark Warr and Mark Stafford, "The Influence of Delinquent Peers: What They Think or What They Do," *Criminology* 29 (November 1991), pp. 851–866; Robert Agnew, "The Interactive Effects of Peer Variables on Delinquency," *Criminology* 29 (February 1991), pp. 47–72; Mark Warr, "Age, Peers, and Delinquency," *Criminology* 31 (February 1993), pp. 17–40; and Terence P. Thornberry, Alan J. Lizotte, Marvin D. Krohn, Margaret Farnworth, and Sung Joon Jang, "Delinquent Peers, Beliefs, and Delinquent Behavior: A Longitudinal Test of Interactional Theory," *Criminology* 32 (February 1994), pp. 47–83.
6. S. P. Breckinridge and Edith Abbott, *The Delinquent Child and the Home* (New York: Russell Sage Foundation, 1917).
7. Clifford R. Shaw and Henry D. McKay, "The Juvenile Delinquent" in *Illinois Crime Survey* (Illinois Associations for Criminal Justice, 1931).
8. Maynard L. Erickson and Gary F. Jensen, "Delinquency Is Still Group Behavior: Toward Revitalizing the Group Premise in the Sociology of Deviance," *Journal of Criminal Law and Criminology* 68 (1977), pp. 388–395.
9. Maynard Erickson, "The Group Context of Delinquent Behavior," *Social Problems* 19 (1971), pp. 115–129.
10. Paul Strasburg, *Violent Delinquents* (New York: Monarch Press, 1978).
11. M. M. Craig and L. A. Budd, "The Juvenile Offender: Recidivism and Companions," *Crime and Delinquency* 13 (1967), pp. 344–351.
12. Michael J. Hindelang, "With a Little Help from Their Friends: Group Participation in Reported Delinquent Behavior," *British Journal of Criminology* 16 (1976), pp. 109–125.
13. Elizabeth S. Piper, "Violent Offenders: Lone Wolf or Wolfpack?" Paper presented at the Annual Meeting of the American Society of Criminology, San Diego, California (November 1985).
14. Hirschi, *Causes of Delinquency,* p. 141.
15. Interview with Peggy Giordano conducted in 1984 and contained in Clemens Bartollas, *Juvenile Delinquency* (New York: John Wiley, 1985), pp. 352–354.
16. Warr, "Age, Peers, and Delinquency," pp. 17, 25.
17. Ross L. Matsueda and Kathleen Anderson, "The Dynamics of Delinquent Peers and Delinquent Behavior," *Criminology* 36 (1998), p. 270.
18. Agnew, "The Interactive Effects of Peer Variables on Delinquency," p. 47.
19. Warr and Stafford, "The Influence of Delinquent Peers," p. 851.
20. Delbert S. Elliott and Scott Menard, "Delinquent Friends and Delinquent Behavior: Temporal and Developmental Patterns," in *Delinquency and Crime: Current Theories,* edited by J. David Hawkins (Cambridge: Cambridge University Press, 1996).
21. Merry Morash, "Gender, Peer Group Experiences, and Seriousness of Delinquency," *Journal of Research in Crime and Delinquency* 25 (1986), pp. 43, 61.
22. Mark Warr, "Life-Course Transitions and Desistance from Crime," *Criminology* 36 (May 1998), p. 185.

23. Matsueda and Anderson, "The Dynamics of Delinquent Behavior and Delinquent Theory," p. 269.

24. Thornberry et al., "Delinquent Peers, Beliefs, and Delinquent Behavior," p. 47. For another study consistent with interactional theory, see Scott Menard and Delbert S. Elliott, "Delinquent Bonding, Moral Beliefs, and Illegal Behavior: A Three-Wave Panel Model," *Justice Quarterly* 11 (June 1994), pp. 174–188.

25. Giordano's interview in Bartollas, *Juvenile Delinquency,* p. 354.

26. Walter B. Miller, *Crime by Youth Groups and Gangs in American Cities* (Washington, D.C.: U.S. Government Printing Office, Chapter 25, chart 2, 1979).

27. Carl S. Taylor, *Dangerous Society* (East Lansing, Mich.: Michigan State University Press, 1990), pp. 2–3.

28. Luc Sante, *Low Life: Lures and Snares of Old New York* (New York: Vintage Books, 1991).

29. Robert Redfield, *Folk Culture of Yucatán* (Chicago: University of Chicago Press, 1941).

30. James C. Howell, *Youth Gangs: An Overview* (Washington, D.C.: Office of Justice Programs, Office of Juvenile Justice and Delinquency Prevention, 1998), p. 2; and Sante, *Low Life: Lures and Snares of Old New York.*

31. Frederick Thrasher, *The Gang: A Study of 1,313 Gangs in Chicago* (Chicago: University of Chicago Press, 1927).

32. Ibid., p. 45.

33. See Walter B. Miller, "The Impact of a Total Community Delinquency Control Project," *Social Problems* 10 (Fall 1962), pp. 168–191.

34. Craig Collins, "Youth Gangs of the 70s," *Police Chief* 42 (September 1975), p. 50.

35. Ibid.

36. Interviewed in March 1974.

37. John C. Quicker and Akil S. Batani-Khalfani, "Clique Succession among South Los Angeles Street Gangs, the Case of the Crips." Paper presented to the Annual Meeting of the American Society of Criminology, Reno, Nevada (November 1989).

38. See David Dawley, *A Nation of Lords: The Autobiography of the Vice Lords* (Garden City, N.Y.: Anchor Books, 1973).

39. James Jacobs, *Stateville: The Penitentiary in Mass Society* (Chicago: University of Chicago Press, 1977).

40. Ibid.

41. Paul Weingarten, "Mean Streets," *Chicago Tribune Magazine* 19 (September 1982), p. 12.

42. Walter B. Miller, "Gangs, Groups, and Serious Youth Crime," in *Critical Issues in Juvenile Delinquency,* pp. 120–121.

43. Walter B. Miller, *Violence by Youth Gangs and Youth Groups as a Crime Problem in Major American Cities* (Washington, D.C.: U.S. Government Printing Office, 1975). Much of the following material is derived from Chapter 15 of Miller's study.

44. Walter B. Miller, *Crime by Youth Gangs and Groups in the United States.* A report prepared for the National Institute of Juvenile Justice and Delinquency Prevention of the United States Department of Justice, February 1982.

45. Malcolm K. Klein, *Studies on Crime and Crime Prevention* (Stockholm, Sweden: Scandinavian University Press, 1993), p. 88.

46. National Youth Gang Center, *1998 National Youth Gang Survey* (Washington, D.C.: Office of Juvenile Justice and Delinquency Prevention, 2000), p. xiv.

47. Finn-Aage Esbensen, *Preventing Adolescent Gang Involvement: Juvenile Justice Bulletin* (Washington, D.C.: Office of Juvenile Justice and Delinquency Prevention, 2000), p. 2.

48. Thrasher, *The Gang,* p. 57.

49. Miller, "Gangs, Groups, and Serious Youth Crime," p. 121.

50. Esbensen, *Preventing Adolescent Gang Involvement,* pp. 2–3.

51. James C. Howell, *OJJDP Fact Sheet* (Washington, D.C.: The Office of Juvenile Justice and Delinquency Prevention, 1997), p. 1.

52. Elaine S. Knapp, *Embattled Youth: Kids, Gangs and Drugs* (Chicago: The Council of State Governments, 1988), p. 13.

53. G. David Curry, Robert J. Fox, Richard A. Ball, and Darryl Stone, "National Assessment of Law Enforcement Anti-Gang Information Resources," Report to the U.S. Department of Justice, National Institute of Justice, 1993).

54. Ibid., pp. 11–12.

55. Howell, "Youth Gangs: An Overview," p. 2. See also Scott H. Decker and B. Van Winkle, *Life in the Gang: Family, Friends, and Violence* (New York: Cambridge University Press, 1996).

56. J. D. Vigil, "Cholos and Gangs: Culture Change and Street Youths in Los Angeles," in *Gangs in America,* edited by C. Ronald Huff (Newbury Park, Calif.: Sage, 1990).

57. J. D. Vigil and J. M. Long, "Emic and Etic Perspectives on Gang Culture: The Chicano Case," in *Gangs in America.*

58. Discussion of Vigil and Long's topology is adapted from Randall G. Shelden, Sharon K. Tracy, and William B. Brown, *Youth Gangs in American Society* (Belmont, Calif.: Wadsworth, 1997), pp. 69–70.

59. Ira Reiner, *Gangs, Crime and Violence in Los Angeles: Findings and Proposals from the District Attorney's Office* (Arlington, Va.: National Youth Gang Information Center, 1992), pp. 40–44.

60. Adapted from Shelden, Tracy, and Brown, *Youth Gangs in American Society,* pp. 70–71.

61. Martín Sánchez Jankowski, *Islands in the Street: Gangs and American Urban Society* (Berkeley: University of California Press, 1991).

62. C. Ronald Huff and K. S. Trump, "Youth Violence and Gangs: School Safety Initiatives in Urban and Suburban School Districts," *Education and Urban Safety* 28 (1996), pp. 4492–4503. For the violence of youth gangs in schools, see also George G. Knox, *An Introduction to Gangs* (Berrien Springs, Mich.: Vande Vere Publishing, 1993); I. A. Spergel, G. D. Curry, R. A. Ross, and R. Chance, *Survey of Youth Gang Problems and Programs in 45 Cities and 6 Sites* (Chicago: University of Chicago, School of Social Service Administration, 1989); and C. Ronald Huff, "Youth Gangs and Public Policy," *Crime and Delinquency* 35 (1989), pp. 524–537.

63. George W. Knox, David Laske, and Edward Tromanhauser, "Chicago Schools Revisited," *Bulletin of the*

Illinois Public Education Association 16 (Spring 1992). For the relationship between gangs and weapons, see also Edward Tromanhauser, "The Relationship between Street Gang Membership and the Possession and Use of Firearms." Paper presented at the Annual Meeting of the American Society of Criminology, Boston, Massachusetts (November 1994).

64. Joseph F. Sheley and James D. Wright, "Gun Acquisition and Possession in Selected Juvenile Samples," *Research in Brief* (Washington, D.C.: National Institute of Justice, 1993).

65. C. Callahan and I. Rivara, "Urban High School Youth and Handguns: A School-Based Survey." *Journal of the American Medical Association* (June 1992).

66. Comment made in 1985 to the author.

67. For more information on drive-by shootings, see William B. Sanders, *Gangbangs and Drive-Bys: Grounded Culture and Juvenile Gang Violence* (New York: Aldine de Gruyter, 1994).

68. Ronald D. Stephens, "School-Based Interventions: Safety and Security," in *The Gang Intervention Handbook*, edited by Arnold P. Goldstein and C. Ronald Huff (Champaign, Ill.: Research Press, 1993), pp. 222–223.

69. Jeffrey Fagan, "The Social Organization of Drug Use and Drug Dealing among Urban Gangs," *Criminology* 27 (1989), pp. 633–664.

70. Elizabeth Huffmaster McConnell and Elizabeth Peltz, "An Examination of Youth Gang Problems at Alpha High School." An unpublished paper.

71. See "Dope Fiend Teaches Algebra at Austin High," *Austin Voice* 9 (March 1 and March 8, 1994), p. 1.

72. Daniel J. Monti, *Wannabe: Gangs in Suburbs and Schools* (Cambridge, England: Blackwell, 1994), p. 92.

73. Patricia Wen, "Boston Gangs: A Hard World," *Boston Globe*, Tuesday, May 10, 1988, p. 31. For a description of the various roles within gang drug trafficking, see Felix M. Padilla, *The Gang as an American Enterprise* (New Brunswick, N.J.: Rutgers University Press, 1992).

74. Interviewed in 1991.

75. Richard A. Cloward and Lloyd E. Ohlin, *Delinquency and Opportunity: A Theory of Delinquent Gangs* (New York: Free Press, 1960).

76. Lewis Yablonsky, *The Violent Gang* (New York: Macmillan, 1962).

77. Taylor, *Dangerous Society.*

78. C. Ronald Huff, "Youth Gangs and Public Policy," *Crime and Delinquency* 35 (October 1989), pp. 524–537.

79. Jeffrey Fagan, "The Social Organization of Drug Use and Drug Dealing among Urban Gangs," *Criminology* 27 (1989), pp. 633–664.

80. Taylor, *Dangerous Society,* p. 4.

81. Ibid., p. 6.

82. Ibid, p. 7.

83. Carl S. Taylor, "Gang Imperialism," in *Gangs in America*, edited by C. Ronald Huff (Newbury Park, Calif.: Sage, 1990), p. 113.

84. Huff, "Youth Gangs and Public Policy," pp. 528–529.

85. Fagan, "Drug Use and Drug Dealing among Gangs," pp. 649–651.

86. See L. J. Bobrowski, *Collecting, Organizing and Reporting Street Crime* (Chicago: Chicago Police Department, Special Function Group, 1988).

87. In a 1998 conversation, Willie Johnson, the leader of the Vice Lord Nation, reported that there are now eleven divisions of the Vice Lord Nation.

88. For an expanded list of the organizational characteristics of urban gangs, see George W. Knox, *An Introduction to Gangs* (Berrien Springs, MI: Vande Vere Publishing, 1991), pp. 16–27.

89. Ibid., pp. 64–66.

90. Joan Moore, Diego Vigil, and Robert Garcia, "Residence and Territoriality in Chicano Gangs," *Social Problems* 31 (December 1985), pp. 182–194.

91. Jankowski, *Islands in the Street,* pp. 49–50.

92. Knapp, "Embattled Youth," p. 13.

93. Interview conducted in 1985.

94. For more information about the drive-by shooting, see William B. Sanders, *Gangbangs and Drive-Bys: Grounded Culture and Juvenile Gang Violence* (New York: Aldine De Gruyter, 1994).

95. "When You're a Crip (Or a Blood)," *Harper's Magazine,* March 1989, p. 51.

96. William Recktenwald, "Street Gangs Live—and Often Kill—by Their Sacred Symbols," *Chicago Tribune,* 9 January 1984.

97. Ibid.

98. Ibid.

99. James Diego Vigil, "The Gang Subculture and Locura: Variations in Acts and Actors." Paper presented at the Annual Meeting of the American Society of Criminology, San Diego, California (November 1985), pp. 5, 10.

100. Ibid., p. 13.

101. Quoted in Ibid., p. 6.

102. John M. Hagedorn, *People and Folks: Gangs, Crime and the Underclass in a Rustbelt City,* 2d ed. (Chicago: Lake View Press, 1988); Ronald C. Huff, "Youth Gangs and Public Policy," *Crime and Delinquency* 35 (1989), pp. 524–537; and Dennis P. Rosenbaum and Jane A. Grant, "Gangs and Youth Problems in Evanston" (Chicago: Northwestern University, Center for Urban Affairs, 1983).

103. These conversations took place in 1994 and 1995 on prison visits to these gang leaders.

104. Cheryl Maxson, Malcolm W. Klein, and Lea C. Cunningham, "Street Gangs and Drug Sales." Report to the National Institute of Justice, 1993. See also Cheryl L. Maxson, "Gang Members on the Move," *Juvenile Justice Bulletin* (Washington, D.C.: Office of Justice Programs, Office of Juvenile Justice and Delinquency Prevention, 1998).

105. See Reiner, *Gangs, Crime and Violence in Los Angeles.*

106. Jeffrey Fagan, "Social Processes of Delinquency and Drug Use among Urban Gangs," in *Gangs in America,* pp. 199–200. See also Jeffrey Fagan, "The Social Organization of Drug Use and Drug Dealing among Urban Gangs, *Criminology* 27 (1989), pp. 633–669.

107. Marvin E. Wolfgang, Terence P. Thornberry, and Robert M. Figlio, *From Boy to Man: From Delinquency to Crime* (Chicago: University of Chicago Press, 1987), pp. 155–156.

108. Ibid., pp. 156–158.

109. See C. Ronald Huff, *Criminal Behavior of Gang Members and At-Risk Youths: Research Preview* (Washington, D.C.: National Institute of Research, 1998), p. 1.

110. Ibid., pp. 1–2.

111. C. Ronald Huff, *Comparing the Criminal Behavior of Youth Gangs and At-Risk Youths: Research in Brief* (Washington, D.C.: Office of Justice Programs, 1998), p. 1. See also Scott H. Decker and Barrik Van Winkle, " 'Slinging Dope': The Role of Gangs and Gang Members in Drug Sales," *Justice Quarterly* 11 (December 1994), pp. 583–603.

112. Terence P. Thornberry, "Membership in Youth Gangs and Involvement in Serious and Violent Offending," in *Serious and Violent Juvenile Offenders: Risk Factors and Successful Interventions,* edited by R. Loeber and D. P. Farrington (Thousand Oaks, Calif.: Sage Publications, 1998), pp. 147–166.

113. Sara R. Battin-Pearson, Terence P. Thornberry, J. David Hawkins, and Marvin D. Krohn, "Gang Membership, Delinquent Peers, and Delinquent Behavior," *Juvenile Justice Bulletin* (Washington, D.C.: Office of Justice Programs, Office of Juvenile Justice and Delinquency Prevention, 1998); and Sara R. Battin, Karl G. Hill, Robert D. Abbott, Richard F. Catalano, and J. David Hawkins, "The Contribution of Gang Membership to Delinquency beyond Delinquent Friends," *Criminology* 36 (February 1998), pp. 93–115.

114. David Huizinga, "Gangs and the Volume of Crime." Paper presented at the Annual Meeting of the Western Society of Criminology, Honolulu, Hawaii, 1997.

115. Huff, *Criminal Behavior of Gang Members and At-Risk Youths,* p. 2.

116. Battin, et al., "The Contribution of Gang Membership to Delinquency beyond Delinquent Friends," pp. 93–115; Huizinga, "The Volume of Crime by Gang and Nongang Members"; and Thornberry, "Membership in Youth Gangs and Involvement in Serious and Violent Offending," pp. 147–166.

117. Finn-Aage Esbensen and D. Huizinga, "Gangs, Drugs, and Delinquency in a Survey of Urban Youth," *Criminology* 31 (1993), pp. 565–589.

118. Howell, "Youth Gangs: An Overview," p. 9.

119. G. David Curry, Cheryl L. Maxson, and James C. Howell, "Youth Gang Homicides in the 1990s," *OJJDP Fact Sheet* (Washington, D.C.: Office of Juvenile Justice and Delinquency Prevention, 2001), p. 1. See also James C. Howell, "Youth Gang Homicides: A Literature Review," *Crime and Delinquency* 45 (April 1999), p. 208–241.

120. Howell, "Youth Gangs: An Overview."

121. Ibid.

122. Scott H. Decker, "Collective and Normative Features of Gang Violence," *Justice Quarterly* 13 (1996), p. 262.

123. Ibid.

124. Howell, "Youth Gangs: An Overview," p. 10. See Beth Bjerregaard and Alan J. Lizotte, "Gun Ownership and Gang Membership," *Journal of Criminal Law and Criminology* 86 (1995), pp. 37–53.

125. Bjerregaard and Lizotte, "Gun Ownership and Gang Membership," pp. 37–53.

126. Coordinating Council on Juvenile Justice and Delinquency Prevention, *Combating Violence and Delinquency: The National Juvenile Justice Action Plan* (Washington, D.C.: Juvenile Justice and Delinquency Prevention, 1996), p. 35.

127. Joseph F. Sheley and James D. Wright, *Youth, Guns, and Violence in Urban America.* Paper presented at the National Conference on Prosecution Strategies against Armed Criminals and Gang Violence: Federal, State, and Local Coordination, San Diego, California (Washington, D.C.: National Institute of Justice, 1992).

128. Scott H. Decker, Tim Bynum, and Deborah Weisel, "A Tale of Two Cities: Gangs as Organized Crime Reports," *Justice Quarterly* 15 (September 1998), pp. 395–425.

129. James McCormick, "The 'Disciples' of Drugs—and Death," *Newsweek* (February 5, 1996), pp. 56–57; and I. A. Spergel, *The Youth Gang Problem* (New York: Oxford University Press, 1995).

130. General Accounting Office, *Nontraditional Organized Crime* (Washington, D.C.: U.S. Government Printing Office, 1989).

131. Drug Enforcement Administration, *Crack Availability and Trafficking in the United States* (Washington, D.C.: U.S. Department of Justice, 1988).

132. Thrasher, *The Gang.*

133. Curry et al., "National Assessment of Law Enforcement Anti-Gang Information Resources."

134. For a review of recent gang research, including that of emergent gangs, see James C. Howell, "Recent Gang Research: Program and Policy Implications," *Crime and Delinquency* 40 (October 1994), pp. 495–515.

135. Finn-Aage Esbensen and David Huizinga, "Gangs, Drugs, and Delinquency in a Survey of Urban Youth," *Criminology* 31 (1993), pp. 565–589.

136. Mark S. Fleisher, "Youth Gangs and Social Networks: Observations from a Long-Term Ethnographic Study." Paper presented to the Annual Meeting of the American Society of Criminology, Miami, Florida (November 1994), p. 1.

137. Ibid., p. 4.

138. Terence P. Thornberry, Marvin D. Krohn, Alan J. Lizotte, and Deborah Chard-Wierschem, "The Role of Juvenile Gangs in Facilitating Delinquent Behavior," *Journal of Research in Crime and Delinquency* 30 (1993), pp. 55–87.

139. "Youth Violence: Gangs on Main Street, USA," *Issues in Brief* (Winter 1993), pp. 3, 5.

140. Ibid., p. 3.

141. This seven-stage development scheme was developed from conversations with a variety of individuals across the nation, ranging from gang leaders and gang members to police administrators, school officials, and newspaper reporters.

142. Gang youth were very reluctant to talk about the percentage.

143. Interviewed in August 1990.

144. Interviewed in February 1991.

145. Interviewed in October 1989.

146. Comment made to the author following a gang seminar he presented in March 1990.

147. For an examination of Chicano gangs, see James Diego Vigil, *Barrio Gangs: Street Life and Identity in Southern California* (Austin: University of Texas Press, 1988); and Joan Moore, *Home Boys: Gangs, Drugs, and Prison in the Barrios of Los Angeles* (Philadelphia: Temple University Press, 1978).

148. See Ko-Lin Chin, "Chinese Gangs and Extortion," in *Gangs in America,* pp. 129–145.

149. James Diego Vigil and Steve Chong Yun, "Vietnamese Youth Gangs in Southern California," in *Gangs in America,* pp. 146–162.

150. Reiner, *Gangs, Crime and Violence in Los Angeles: Findings and Proposals from the District Attorney's Office*, p. 114.

151. National Youth Gang Center, *1998 National Youth Gang Survey*, p. xiv.

152. Howell, "Youth Gangs: An Overview," p. 2.

153. Finn-Aage Esbensen and D. W. Osgood, *National Evaluation of G.R.E.A.T.: Research in Brief* (Washington, D.C.: Office of Justice Programs, National Institute of Justice, 1997).

154. For an examination of the seriousness of the problem of Satanism among American youth, see Philip Jenkins and Daniel Maier-Katkin, "Satanism: Myth and Reality in a Contemporary Moral Panic." Revised paper presented at the American Society of Criminology, Baltimore, Maryland (November 1990).

155. See Eric Henderson, Stephen J. Kunitz, and Jerrold E. Levy, "The Origins of Navajo Youth Gangs," *American Indian Culture and Research Journal* 23 (1999), pp. 243–264.

156. Ibid.

157. Albert K. Cohen, *Delinquent Boys: The Culture of the Gang* (Glencoe, Ill.: Free Press, 1955), pp. 46–48.

158. Thrasher, *The Gang*.

159. Anne Campbell, *The Girls in the Gang: A Report from New York City* (New York: Basic Blackwell, 1984), p. 5.

160. Found in Jack E. Bynum and William E. Thompson, *Juvenile Delinquency: A Sociological Approach* (Boston: Allyn and Bacon, 1989), p. 295.

161. Freda Adler, *Sisters in Crime: The Rise of the New Female Criminal* (McGraw-Hill, 1975).

162. The Molls are discussed in W. B. Miller, "The Molls," *Society* 11 (1973), pp. 32–35, and the Queens in E. Ackley and B. Fliegel, "A Social Work Approach to Street Corner Girls," *Social Work* 5 (1960), pp. 29–31.

163. Peggy C. Giordano, "Girls, Guys and Gangs: The Changing Social Context of Female Delinquency," *Journal of Criminal Law and Criminology* 69 (1978), p. 130.

164. Waln K. Brown, "Black Female Gangs in Philadelphia," *International Journal of Offender Therapy and Comparative Criminology* 21 (1970), pp. 221–229.

165. Ibid., pp. 223–227.

166. Lee Bowker and M. W. Klein, "Female Participation in Delinquent Gang Motivation," *Adolescence* 15 (1980).

167. J. C. Quicker, *Home Girls: Characterizing Chicano Gangs* (San Pedro, Calif.: International University Press, 1983).

168. M. G. Harris, *Cholas: Latino Girls and Gangs* (New York: AMS Press, 1988), p. 172.

169. Finn-Aage Esbensen, Elizabeth Piper Deschenes, and L. Thomas Winfree, Jr., "Differences between Gang Girls and Gang Boys: Results from a Multi-Site Survey." Paper presented to the 1998 Annual Meeting of the Academy of Criminal Justice Sciences in Albuquerque, New Mexico, pp. 20–21.

170. Campbell, *The Girls in the Gangs*; see also Anne Campbell, "Female Participation in Gangs," in *Gangs in America*, pp. 163–182.

171. Carl S. Taylor, *Girls, Gangs, Women and Drugs* (East Lansing: Michigan State University Press, 1993), p. 48.

172. Ibid., p. 95.

173. Ibid., pp. 102–103. For a study of female gang members in Fort Wayne, Indiana and their trafficking crack cocaine, see D. B. Kitchen, *Sisters in the Hood*. Ph.D. dissertation, Western Michigan University, 1995.

174. David Lauderback, Joy Hansen, and Daniel Waldorf, "Sisters Are Doin' It for Themselves: A Black Female Gang in San Francisco," *Gang Journal* 1 (1992), pp. 57–72.

175. Beth Bjerregaard and Carolyn Smith, "Gender Differences in Gang Participation, Delinquency, and Substance Abuse," *Journal of Quantitative Criminology* 9 (1993), pp. 347–348.

176. Joan Moore and John Hagedorn, "Female Gangs: A Focus on Research," *Juvenile Justice Bulletin* (Washington, D.C.: Office of Juvenile Justice and Delinquency Prevention, 2001).

177. Ibid.

178. Karen Joe and Meda Chesney-Lind, "Just Every Mother's Angel: An Analysis of Gender and Ethnic Variations in Youth Gang Membership." Paper presented at the Annual Meeting of the American Society of Criminology, Phoenix, Arizona (November 1993), p. 9.

179. Ibid.

180. H. A. Bloch and A. Niederhoffer, *The Gang: A Study in Adolescent Behavior* (New York: Philosophical Library, 1958).

181. Richard A. Cloward and Lloyd E. Ohlin, *Delinquency and Opportunity: A Theory of Delinquent Gangs* (Glencoe, Ill.: Free Press, 1960).

182. Cohen, *Delinquent Boys: The Culture of the Gang*.

183. Walter B. Miller, "Lower-Class Culture as a Generating Milieu of Gang Delinquency," *Journal of Social Issues* 14 (1958), pp. 5–19.

184. Lewis Yablonsky, *The Violent Gang* (New York: Macmillan, 1962).

185. Bjerregaard and Smith, "Gender Differences in Gang Participation, Delinquency, and Substance Use," p. 333.

186. See Patrick G. Jackson, "Theories and Findings about Youth Gangs," *Criminal Justice Abstracts* (June 1989), pp. 322–323.

187. See Gerald D. Suttles, *The Social Order of the Slum: Ethnicity and Territory in the Inner City* (Chicago: University of Chicago Press, 1968); and Thrasher, *The Gang*.

188. Jankowski, *Islands in the Street*, p. 22.

189. See William Julius Wilson, *The Truly Disadvantaged: The Inner City, the Underclass, and Public Policy* (Chicago: University of Chicago Press, 1987).

190. G. David Curry and Irving A. Spergel, "Gang Homicide, Delinquency, and Community," *Criminology* (1988), pp. 381–405.

191. J. E. Fagan, "Gangs, Drugs, and Neighborhood Change," in *Gangs in America*, 2d ed., edited by C. R. Huff (Thousand Oaks, Calif.: Sage Publications, 1996), pp. 39–74.

192. Hageborn, *People Folks*.

193. J. D. Vigil, *Barrio Gangs: Street Life and Identity in Southern California* (Austin: University of Texas Press, 1988), p. 101.

194. Jankowski, *Islands in the Street*, p. 139.

195. Ibid.

196. Decker and Van Winkle, *Life in the Gang*, pp. 64–66.

197. Correspondence from Michael F. de Vries. See also R. E. Johnson, A. C. Marcos, and S. J. Bahr, "The Role of Peers in the Complex Etiology of Adolescent Drug Use," *Criminology* 25 (1987), pp. 323–340.

198. See Huff, "Youth Gangs and Public Policy."

199. Short, "Gangs, Neighborhood, and Youth Crime," p. 3.

200. I. A. Spergel, G. D. Curry, R. A. Ross, and R. Chance, *Survey of Youth Gang Problems and Programs in 45 Cities and 6 Sites.* Tech. Report No. 2, National Youth Gang Suppression and Intervention Project (Chicago: University of Chicago, School of Social Service Administration, 1989), p. 211.

201. Ibid., p. 212.

202. Ibid., p. 216.

203. Ibid., p. 218.

204. Spergel et al.

205. Howell, "Youth Gangs: An Overview," p. 13.

206. Ibid., p. 14.

207. Terence P. Thornberry and James H. Burch II, "Gang Members and Delinquent Behavior," *Juvenile Justice Bulletin* (Washington, D.C.: Office of Justice Programs, Office of Juvenile Justice and Delinquency Prevention, 1997), p. 4.

  **11**

DRUGS AND DELINQUENCY

After reading this chapter, the student will be able to answer the following questions:

- How are social attitudes related to drug use?

- How much drug use is there among adolescents in American society?

- What are the main types of drugs used by adolescents?

- What is the relationship between drug abuse and delinquency?

- What theoretical explanation best explains the onset of drug use?

- What can be done to prevent and control drug use among U.S. adolescents?

I started using drugs when I was eight years old. It makes you feel like you can beat anything that comes along. I thought, "Wow, this is great!" When I was nine, someone asked me if I wanted to take some acid. I figured, sure, why not? This was really great because I could sit around and watch the walls melt. My English teacher deteriorated in her chair one time at school. As the years went by, I started to peddle a lot of speed and acid. Pretty soon, I was drug dependent. I needed speed in the morning, and I had to take speed in school to make it through the day. It got to the point that I couldn't handle speed anymore. I was too juiced up. Now I regret doing so many drugs because I can't remember simple things that I should remember, like talking with someone over the phone the night before. I became spacey; in fact, people have called me spacey for two years now.[1]

Drug and alcohol use and juvenile delinquency have been identified as the most serious problem behaviors of adolescents.[2] As the adolescent female realized in the opening quotation, drug use can have toxic consequences. The good news is that substance abuse among adolescents has dropped dramatically since the late 1970s. The bad news is that drug use has significantly increased among high-risk youths and is becoming commonly linked to juvenile lawbreaking. More juveniles are also selling drugs than ever before in the history of the United States. Furthermore, the spread of AIDS within populations of drug users and their sex partners promises to make the problem of substance abuse even more difficult to control.[3]

Young people usually prefer substances that are not too costly. Beer and marijuana meet this criterion better than hard drugs do. Availability and potency are also important in drug use, for the substances are generally used as a means to other ends, such as achieving excitement. For example, marijuana and alcohol are used at rock concerts, parties, dances, football games, and outings to add to the excitement that is already present in such activities and to produce excitement when it seems to be lacking. In addition to excitement, experience-enhancing substances serve the purpose of exploring new social spheres, sexual relationships, and unfamiliar places. Narcotic substances also are ingested to escape to or retreat from the external world into a private inner self.

There is a difference between drug use and drug abuse. Drug use can be viewed as a continuum that begins with nonuse and includes experimental use, culturally endorsed use, recreational use, and compulsive use (See Figure 11.1).[4] As an example of culturally endorsed use, peyote has been used sacramentally in the Native American church for centuries. Twenty-three states exempt this sacramental use of peyote from criminal penalties.[5]

Adolescent drug use only becomes abuse when the user becomes dysfunctional (e.g., is unable to attend or perform in school or to maintain social and family relationships; exhibits dangerous, reckless, or aggressive behavior; or endangers the adolescent's health). The drug-dependent compulsive user's life usually revolves around obtaining, maintaining, and using a supply of drugs.[6] One youth's experience with the abuse of drugs that led to delinquent behavior is described in Social World of the Delinquent 11.1 Becoming a Dope Fiend.

How Social Attitudes Are Related to Drug Use

The beginnings of most social phenomena are typically easy to trace. For example, American jazz began over a century ago in the city of New Orleans. It fused the existing musical art forms of African Americans—spirituals, work songs, and blues—with white folk music, rhythms of Hispanic America and the Caribbean, melodies of French dances, and marching band instrumentation. The environmental movement of the late 1960s and early 1970s grew out of the writings of biologist Rachel Carson, along with a better understanding of the effects of pollution on ecosystems. Similarly, the roots of today's get-tough campaign against drunk driving are easily identified. In 1980, a thirteen-year-old California youth was struck down and killed by a hit-and-run driver. The child's mother was stunned that the operator of the automobile was not only drunk at the time but was out on bail for his third drunk-driving offense. It further appeared unlikely that he would be punished for the killing. Accordingly, this mother launched Mothers Against Drunk Drivers (MADD) and initiated a nationwide campaign against drunk driving.[7]

The roots of drug abuse are more difficult to uncover. Certainly, the use of opium dates back to the ancient Greeks, and references to marijuana appear in early Arab, Greek, Hindu, and Chinese writings. In addition, when Spanish explorer Francisco

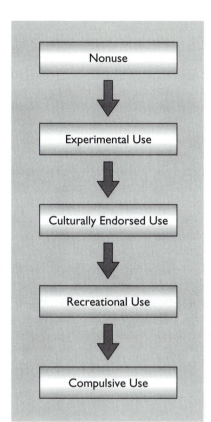

FIGURE 11.1 The Drug Use Continuum

Source: Howard Abadinsky, *Drugs: An Introduction,* 4th ed. (Belmont, CA.: Wadsworth/Thompson Learning, 2001), p. 5.

Social World of the Delinquent 11.1

Becoming a Dope Fiend

When I was fourteen years old, my uncle used to put me on a bus in Chicago to deliver packages. But I didn't know what was in those packages. A woman got wind of it, and on my birthday she offered to turn on five of us with sex and heroin. I went last to see if anything was going to happen to them. They were all high and sick. I was really reluctant to go on with it. I was sitting there wanting to do it and yet not wanting to do it. She coaxed me into it by saying "If you do it, I'll give you some ass." She gave me the dope, and I was too sick to have sex with her.

I didn't shoot any more dope for three months until I saw her again. I told her, "Don't you owe me something?" She said, "No, I paid you. When you go on another trip for your uncle, let me know and I will really make it worth your while." She conned me through sex into bringing the dope to her. I still didn't know what was in the packages. Later, I found out that she

was taking half an ounce from the package and filling it with whatever kind of mix she had. Then she would send me on my way. She did that three times, but I finally figured out what was in the package. That one shot of dope made my mind more aware of street life. That first high, even though you are sick, makes a dope addict go back. And before I knew it, I was shooting dope with her all the time.

What did this interviewee mean when he said "that one shot of dope made me more aware of street life?" What did he mean when he said: "That first high, even though you are sick, makes a dope addict go back?" Do you agree with him?

Source: Interview conducted in November 1980.

Pizarro stumbled upon the Inca empire in the sixteenth century, the chewing of coca had been taking place for centuries. Even in the brief history of the United States the onset of drug taking as a social phenomenon remains a mystery.

It can be argued that it all began with Thomas Dover, who in 1709 developed a form of medicinal opium known as Dover's Powder. This patent medicine, which began a trend of introducing patent medicines containing opium, became widely used because of its euphoric and anesthetic properties. Patent medicines were soon sold in pharmacies, in grocery and general stores, at traveling medicine stores, and through the mail. Marketed under such labels as Ayer's Cherry Pectoral, Gofrey's Cordial, McMunn's Elixir, Mrs. Winslow's Soothing Syrup, and Dover's Powder, they were seductively advertised as "consumption cures," "cough mixtures," "painkillers," "soothing syrups," and "women's friends."

In the nineteenth century, morphine was introduced as a pain reliever. The hypodermic syringe was then invented, and the use of morphine by injection became both legitimate and familiar to physicians and the public. By the 1890s, morphine by needle had become so common that syringes were produced inexpensively for mass consumption. For example, the 1897 edition of the Sears, Roebuck catalog contained hypodermic kits for as little as $1.50, with extra needles available at 25 cents each or $2.75 per dozen.[8]

The rise of the "counterculture" in the 1960s is often linked to a drug revolution in U.S. life. Indeed, the more these college-aged youth were alienated from government and disagreed with the U.S. policy in Vietnam, the more likely they were to use illicit drugs.[9] This drug revolution also took place among middle-class adolescents and young adults in both urban and rural America. Increasing numbers of youths chose to embrace or be "turned on" to drugs, because they were "turned off" by society. Commentators began to conclude that this society was an "addicted society" and that drugs were contributing in a significant way to the unraveling of U.S. life.

During the past four decades new drugs have been introduced into U.S. life, drug use has gone down with all but high-risk users, a crack epidemic took place in urban areas in the 1980s, and a war on drugs was declared and, in large measure, has been lost.

In the mid 1990s there seemed to be an increase in the use of illicit drugs by U.S. adolescents. According to research conducted by the Rand Corporation, this increase was directly related to the feeling of complacency in local communities and, on the federal level, to the seriousness of the drug problem.[10] Lana Harrison and Andrea Kopstein explained that at the same time, and perhaps affected by this complacency, teenagers' "perceived dangers and disapproval of nearly all illicit drugs declined in 1993." They added that "fewer students saw any level of marijuana use, even regular use, as dangerous" and that "the perceived risks associated with cocaine use declined."[11]

Prevalence and Incidence of Drug Use Among Adolescents

Society may be concerned about youths' use of harder drugs, but alcohol remains the drug of choice for most adolescents. Drug use among adolescents was extremely high during the late 1960s and into the 1970s, reaching epidemic proportions. Overall rates of illicit drug use appeared to peak sometime around 1979 and decreased during the 1980s and through the 1990s.[12] Even with the leveling off that took place, rates of illicit drug use among youth remain high.[13]

This downward trend was evident for marijuana until its use began to increase dramatically in the early 1990s. A similar downward trend took place with cocaine, except that previous year prevalence rates plateaued between 1979 and 1985 before starting to decrease. Although cigarette use peaked in 1974, it did not decline significantly until about 1979. Cigarette use has generally been stalled since the late 1970s, with the hint of a decrease in the 1990s. Finally, the highest past year prevalence rates of inhalants were recorded in 1985, with slight reductions since that time.[14] This downward trend is clearly indicated in the University of Michigan's annual survey of teens, Monitoring the Future, which examined the trends in past use among high school seniors from 1975 through 1997. Figure 11.2 illustrates the trends for several substances.

A National Household Survey on Drug Abuse, conducted by the Substance Abuse and Mental Health Services Administration and containing a nationally representative sample of 24,505 people twelve and older, revealed that in 1997, alcohol was the most widely used drug for adolescents, cigarettes were second, marijuana was third, and cocaine and inhalants were a distant fourth and fifth. According to this national survey on drug abuse, 11.4 percent of juveniles ages twelve to seventeen reported using illicit drugs in the thirty days prior to the time they were interviewed. Between 1995 and 1996, the percent of juveniles using illicit drugs declined from 10.9 percent to 9.0 percent. The highest rate for illicit drug use was in 1979 (16.3 percent) and the lowest was 5.3 percent in 1992.[15]

Three important issues relate to the prevalence and incidence of drug use among adolescents. The first is that drinking alcohol remains a serious problem with too many U.S. adolescents. In 1997, according to the National Household Survey of Drug Abuse, 11 million current drinkers were ages twelve to twenty and had used alcohol during the thirty days prior to the interview. Of this group, 4.8 million, or more than 40 percent, engaged in binge drinking, meaning that they drank five or more drinks on one occasion in the past month. Two million of this group were heavy drinkers, meaning that they had five or more drinks on one occasion on five or more days in the past month. Among twelve- to seventeen-year-old youths, the rate of current alcohol use was about 50 percent in 1979, fell to about 21 percent in 1992, and has remained fairly stable since then.[16]

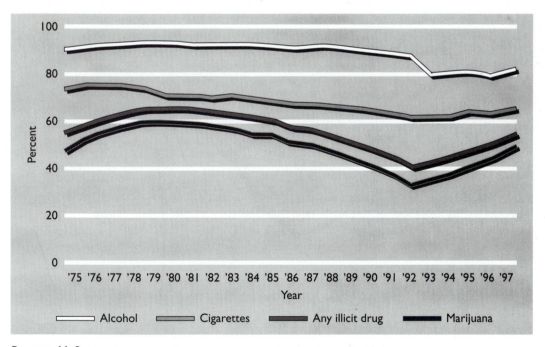

FIGURE 11.2 Lifetime Prevalence of Drug Use by Twelfth Graders: Monitoring the Future Study

Source: University of Michigan, *Monitoring the Future Study* (Washington, D.C.: National Institute on Drug Abuse, 1997).

The second issue, according to Richard Dembo, "is that there are no indications that drug use is declining among 'high-risk' youths, including juvenile arrestees. The relationship between drug use and crime among adolescents entering or involved with the juvenile justice system remains strong and positive."[17] The problem is not only the fact that high-risk youths have far higher rates of alcohol and other drug use (particularly marijuana and cocaine) than other adolescents, but also that large proportions of juvenile detainees report experiencing negative psychological and behavioral effects related to their substance abuse.[18]

The third issue is a new development that shows that teenagers have increased their use of marijuana. According to the Household Survey on Drug Abuse, nearly one in ten twelve- to seventeen-year-old youths in 1997 were current users of marijuana. Marijuana smoking among young people age twelve to seventeen had more than doubled from 1992 to 1997, and continued its significant increase between 1996 and 1997, from 7.1 percent to 9.4 percent. This increase is far below the peak reached in 1979 (14.2 percent), but it still indicates a reversal of the downward pattern of marijuana use that began in the early 1980s and continued to drop sharply until 1992.[19] See Figure 11.3 for the increase use of marijuana among juveniles in recent years.

The rate of past-month illicit drug use among teenagers was higher among those who were currently using cigarettes and alcohol, compared with teenagers not using cigarettes and alcohol. The increase in illicit drug use between 1996 and 1997 also occurred only among youths who were using cigarettes and alcohol. In 1996, 3.8 percent of youth nonsmokers used illicit drugs, and in 1997, 3.6 percent of nonsmokers used illicit drugs. But among youth who were smokers, the rates of past-month illicit drug use were 32.5 percent in 1996 and 42.8 percent in 1997.[20]

Recent studies have shown a marked decrease in sex differences among drug users. Female high school students are slightly more likely than high school males to smoke

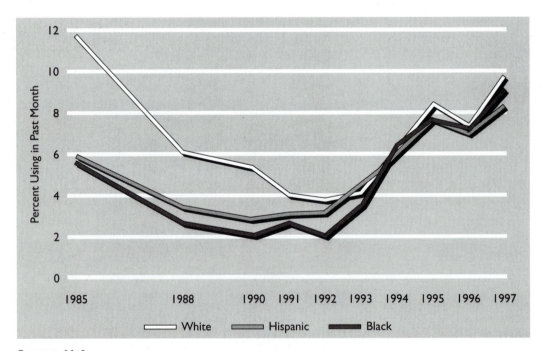

FIGURE 11.3 Past Month Marijuana Use among Youth, Age 12–17: 1985–1997

Source: Substance Abuse Health Service Administration, *Preliminary Estimates from the 1997 National Household Survey on Drug Abuse* (Rockville, Md.: Department of Health and Human Services, 1998), p. 16.

cigarettes and to use some illicit drugs, including amphetamines; surprisingly, they use alcohol and marijuana at about the same rates as male high school seniors. Nevertheless, male adolescents are much more likely to be involved in heavy drinking and drunk driving than female adolescents.[21]

The rates of illicit drug use in 1997 were about the same for white, African American, and Hispanic youths. For white youths, the rates for illicit drug use increased significantly from 9.2 percent in 1996 to 11.8 percent in 1997, but for African American and Hispanic youths, the rates for illicit drug use remained the same between 1996 and 1997.[22]

Moreover, a survey by Jeffrey Fagan and colleagues of 665 inner-city high school seniors in four cities found that marijuana was the most frequently used drug among both male and female adolescents. Adolescent females, who were rarely involved in serious drug use, frequently took part in drug sales, especially the sale of marijuana. These researchers surmised that a pattern of reciprocity may be taking place, whereby selling marijuana provides these females with the money to obtain it for personal use.[23]

Adolescents vary, of course, in terms of how frequently they use drugs and the type of drugs they use. The variables of age, gender, urban or rural setting, social class, and availability strongly affect the types of drugs used and have some effect on the frequency of drug use. Some drug users take drugs only at parties and on special occasions, some reserve them for weekends, and some use drugs every day. In Social World of the Adolescent 11.2, a twenty-five-year-old from an upper-class background talks about his adolescent drug use.

Studies indicate that while fewer adolescents appear to be experimenting with drugs, those who use them tend to do so more frequently. Heavy users tend to be males, whites, and youths who do not plan to attend college. Substance abuse is more common on the East and West coasts and less common in the South. Low achievers in school abuse drugs more than do high achievers.[24]

Social World of the Delinquent 11.2

"Cocaine Is Just Evil, in Every Way"

I first tried pot when I was in eighth grade. It was peer pressure that drove me to start it. I wanted to be popular. Everybody else was drinking beer and smoking pot; I wanted to do it, too.

I first did coke [cocaine] when I was about sixteen or seventeen. I really got into it when I moved to Arizona right after high school. I did it every day in every form. It's the most addicting thing I ever tried. It's better than sex; you crave it more than food; you'll do anything to get it, anything.

I quit doing cocaine because I got tired of being sick. Coming down was horrible, worse for me than for anyone else I knew. I would just lie there and wish I was dead. Now, I will not associate with people who do hard drugs.

I guess I don't have as much of a problem with pot as I do with other drugs. I still do it once in a while, but not because I have to or need to. It's like some people go to the bar after work to have a relaxing beer. I don't drink, but I go home and have a joint after work to relax. For some people, I don't think there is anything wrong with that. Other people can't even handle the smallest amount of pot without getting crazy.

But there is really no comparison physically, mentally, and emotionally between pot and coke and what they do to you. Cocaine is just evil, in every way. It takes over your mind and your body and your money. I would never do it again!

Do you agree with the interviewee that pot is relatively harmless? How is it possible to persuade more high-risk young people that cocaine is evil in every way?

Source: Interviewed in August 1995.

In sum, although drug use among adolescents peaked during the late 1970s, rates of illicit drug use in this nation remain high, especially among high-risk youth. The use of the licit drugs, alcohol and tobacco, are also at extremely high levels, and little progress has been made in reducing their use since the crest of the drug epidemic. Binge drinking, according to a 1997 national household survey, was taking place at extraordinarily high levels. This national survey further reported increases in the prevalence of illicit drug use between 1996 and 1997.[25]

The Main Types of Drugs

The licit and illicit drugs used by adolescents, in decreasing frequency, are alcohol, tobacco, marijuana, cocaine, inhalants and stimulants (amphetamines and hallucinogens), and heroin. The licit drugs are those that are permitted by those who are of age (eighteen and older for tobacco and twenty-one and older for alcohol). The illicit drugs are those that are forbidden by law. Exceptions would be drugs that are prescribed by a physician or marijuana in those jurisdictions that permit the use of this drug. A number of illicit drugs take control of adolescents' lives when they become addicted. Addiction, according to James A. Inciardi, "is a craving for a particular drug, accompanied by physical dependence, which motivates continuing usage, resulting in tolerance to the drug's effects and a complex of identifiable symptoms appearing when it is suddenly withdrawn."[26]

Alcohol and Tobacco

The reaction to Prohibition fostered the view of alcohol use as acceptable behavior that should be free from legal controls. The public did not perceive alcohol as a dangerous drug then nor does it now. What makes **alcohol** so dangerous is that it relaxes inhibitions, and adolescents participate in risky behavior while under its influence. Adolescents' alcohol use is also linked to property destruction, fights, academic failure, occupation problems, and conflict with law enforcement officials.[27] Youths who are under the influence of alcohol may commit delinquent acts that they otherwise would not:

> Drugs and alcohol, that's the main reason why I'm here. All the times I broke the law I was drunk or high. I mainly stole cars. I just liked to hot-wire cars and joyride when I was wasted. I could have never done it if I was straight; it's easy when you're drunk. I guess drugs and alcohol will be my biggest obstacle when I get out of here, that and my attitude.[28]

The increased number of adolescents who abuse alcohol is becoming a matter of grave public concern. Television programs portraying adolescent alcoholics, television commercials with adolescents saying that "it is not cool" to drink, and talk shows on adolescents and drinking all are expressions of this growing concern.

Tobacco use is often neglected in a discussion of drugs, because it is not considered a mind-altering drug. Yet there is considerable evidence that tobacco users suffer severe health consequences from prolonged use and subject others to the same consequences. A 1993 analysis quantified the major factors contributing to death in the United States and found that tobacco contributed to 400,000 deaths annually, whereas alcohol contributed to 100,000 deaths and all illicit drugs combined contributed to 20,000 deaths.[29]

Marijuana

Marijuana is the most frequently used illicit drug. An interesting indicator of the popularity of marijuana is the number of street terms that have been used to designate the substance. The many names given to it include *A-bomb, Acapulco Gold, African black, aunt mary, baby, ashes, bammy, birdwood, California red, Colombian gold, dope, giggleweed, golden leaf, hay, Mexican brown, Mexican green, Panama gold, pot, reefer, reefer* *weed, shit, seaweed, stinkweed, Texas tea,* and *weed.*[30] One youth describes the effect of smoking marijuana:

> When I smoke pot I feel silly all over like I'm being tickled, but I can't see who is doing it. Then I start getting the "munchies," and I like want to eat everything in sight. I can't help myself. I just eat and eat and don't get full. Then, I just sit there staring at the wall and "veg out" until it wears off. Unless I have some more grass, 'cause then I smoke some more.[31]

Heated debates about the hazards of using marijuana have been waged for some time. Recent research has documented more ill effects of long-term marijuana use than were suggested in the past. For example, several studies have concluded that marijuana smoking is a practice that combines the hazardous features of alcohol and tobacco as well as a number of pitfalls of its own. Disturbing questions also remain about marijuana's effect on vital systems of the body, on immunity and resistance, on the brain and mind, and on sex and reproduction.[32]

Cocaine

Cocaine, the powder derivative of the South American coca plant, is replacing other illegal drugs in popularity. Cocaine is known to users as *coke, lady snow, nose candy, toot,* and *Super Fly.* The major source of cocaine is Colombia, and its distribution has become a major diplomatic issue in many Central and South American countries.

Cocaine is so expensive ($40 to $125 a gram on the streets) that it is generally used in very sparing quantities. Until recently, it was believed to be less addicting than other illegal hard drugs. Users crave the extreme mood elevation, elation, and grandiose feelings and heightened physical prowess that cocaine induces, and when these begin to wane, a corresponding deep depression is experienced. Users are strongly motivated to use the drug again to restore the euphoria.

Snorting (inhaling) is the most common method of using cocaine. Freebasing became popular in the 1980s. Freebase cocaine is derived from a chemical process in which the purified cocaine is crystallized. The crystals are crushed and smoked in a special heated glass pipe. Smoking freebase cocaine provides a more potent and a quicker rush and a more powerful high than regular cocaine gives. The intravenous use of cocaine has also been taking place more frequently in recent years. This means of administration produces a powerful high, usually within fifteen to twenty seconds. A related method is the intravenous use of cocaine along with another drug, which is known as *speedballing.* Speedballing intensifies the euphoric effect but can be quite dangerous. It was speedballing that killed actor-comedian John Belushi in 1982.[33]

In 1996, there were an estimated 675,000 new cocaine users, which is much less than the 1.2 to 1.3 million cocaine initiates per year from 1980 to 1986. However, the rate of new use among twelve- to seventeen-year-old youths increased from 4.0 in 1991 to 11.3 in 1996. Although the bad news is that the first use of cocaine among this age group was at its highest level in thirty years, the good news is that the 1997 level of new use of cocaine for this age group was about equal to the 1994 and 1995 levels (see Figure 11.4).[34]

A less expensive, more potent version of cocaine has achieved great popularity in the past two decades. Called crack, this dangerous substance has generated great concern among law enforcement and health professionals. Crack apparently arrived in inner-city neighborhoods in Los Angeles, Miami, and New York between 1981 and 1983.[35] Since then, it has spread through the nation. It is known by users as *hard white, white,* or *flavor.* There are also *bricks, boulders, eight-ball* (large rocks), *doo-wap* (two rocks), and *crumbs.* Crack is most typically smoked in special glass pipes or makeshift smoking devices. It is also smoked with marijuana in cigarettes, which are called *geek joints, pin joints,* or *lace joints.* A *shotgun,* which is secondary smoke exhaled from one crack user into the mouth of another, also provides the desired high.[36] Crack is frequently smoked in crack houses, which may be abandoned buildings or the homes of crack dealers or users. See Social World of the Delinquent 11.3 for why interviewed crack users regard crack as so attractive.

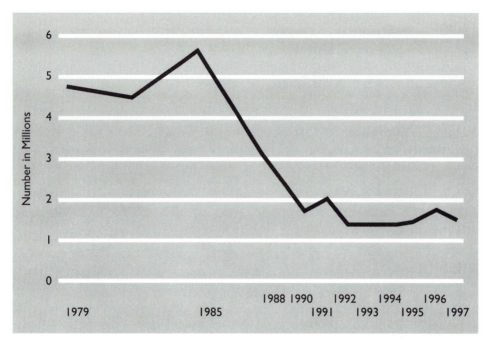

FIGURE 11.4 Number of Persons Age Twelve and Older Using Cocaine in the Past Month, 1979–1997

Source: Substance Abuse Health Service Administration, *Preliminary Estimates from the 1997 National Household Survey on Drug Abuse* (Rockville, Md.: Department of Health and Human Services, 1998), p. 17.

Social World of the Delinquent 11.3

The Rush and the High

Although none of our respondents reported instant addiction, most did say that they found crack powerfully attractive, at least for some period in their lives. To learn why, we asked them about the allure of cocaine smoking, what exactly they liked about it. One young man spoke for most others when he exclaimed, "I've never felt nothin' like that!" Other answers ranged from the description of the euphoric boost of self-confidence one gets from directly ingesting such a strong central nervous system stimulant ("the feeling that you're on top of things") to statements about how smoking cocaine makes one feel "hyper" and "smarter, faster and better, you know, sorta' like the $6 million man." Another respondent exclaimed that, after a hit on the pipe, "You don't care about nothin' else." This point was echoed by a number of others, including one who noted that, after a couple of hits, "the rest of the world is gone." Thus, in addition to explosive euphoria and heightened self-confidence, respondents often described a carefree, nirvana-like state. Another reported, "It just puts you in a frame of mind that separates you from everybody else. It puts your head on a different level. It's a thousand things. It's a way of coping and it's a way of escape."

What other means of coping could these crack users pursue that would provide deep satisfaction to them? Will sufficient punishment deter them from using crack when they are no longer in confinement?

Source: Craig Reinarman, Dan Waldorf, Sheila B. Murphy, and Harry G. Levine, "The Contingent Call of the Pipe: Bingeing and Addiction among Heavy Cocaine Smokers," in *Crack in America: Demon Drugs and Social Justice*, edited by Craig Reinarman and Harry G. Levine (Berkeley: University of California Press, 1997), p. 82.

In addition to high rates of prostitution, other consequences of the addiction of adolescent girls and adult women to crack are widespread child abuse and child neglect and the toxic effects of crack during pregnancy.[37] The use of crack during pregnancy contributes to the premature separation of the placenta from the uterus, which results in stillbirths and premature infants. Infants who survive cocaine use in utero suffer withdrawal symptoms at birth and are at greater risk of stroke and respiratory ailments.[38] There is also a greater risk of sudden infant death syndrome (SIDS) among cocaine-exposed infants. Such infants have a 17 percent incidence of SIDS, compared with 1.6 in the general population.[39] Furthermore, cocaine-exposed infants are more likely to experience emotional disorders, learning disabilities, and sensorimotor problems.[40]

Inhalants

Many types of **inhalants** are used by adolescents, but what they have in common is that youths have to inhale the vapors to receive the high that they seek. One frequently used inhalant is butyl nitrite, commonly called *RUSH*. RUSH is packaged in small bottles and can often be found in adult bookstores, as well as on the street. Other inhalants that are easier for young drug users to obtain are chlorohydrocarbons and hydrocarbons—which can be inhaled directly from gasoline, paint thinner, glue, or aerosol cans.

The use of these drugs brings about a feeling of excitement that is often followed by a disorientation accompanied by slurred speech and a feeling of sleepiness. The use of inhalants can also be followed by mild to severe headaches as well as nosebleeds. Chronic use of some inhalants is associated with neurological damage and injury to the liver and kidneys.[41]

Sedatives

Like inhalants, many different forms of **sedatives,** or barbiturates, are used by youth. The common factor among all barbiturates is that they are taken orally and that they affect the user by depressing the nervous system and inducing a drowsy condition. On the street, barbituates are known by the color of their capsule. Seconal pills are known as *reds;* Amytals are called *blue devils;* and Tuinals are known as *rainbows.* Another popular sedative is methaqualone, which is known as *Quaaludes* or *Ludes* on the street.

Adolescents often abuse prescription drugs. Benzodiazepines (minor tranquilizers or sedatives) are among the most widely prescribed of all drugs. Valium, Librium, and Equanil are most commonly prescribed for anxiety or sleep disorders, and to obtain them, adolescents simply raid their parents' medicine cabinets. When these prescription drugs are used in combination with other controlled substances, they produce effects that are similar those of alcohol and barbiturates.[42]

Amphetamines

Amphetamines were first made in Germany in the 1880s, but it was not until the Second World War that they were first used by Americans. All the military branches issued Benzedrine, Dexedrine, and other types of amphetamines to relieve fatigue and anxiety, especially in battle conditions. Amphetamines became more readily available after the war and were widely used by students studying for examinations, by truck drivers who had to stay alert for extended periods of time, by people attempting to lose weight, and by people seeking relief from nasal congestion. The amphetamines that were ingested at the time included *bennies, black beauties, King Kong pills, pinks,* and *purple hearts.*[43]

In the late 1980s and early 1990s, Ecstasy (MDMA), Crank (methamphetamine), and Ice (methamphetamine), three new drugs, arrived on the U.S. drug scene. MDMA, which was used by psychiatrists and other therapists because of its therapeutic benefits, had become a Schedule I drug by 1986, which meant that its manufacture, distribution, and sale violated federal law. It still maintained some popularity among undergraduate populations across the nation. In the 1990s, **Ecstasy,** the common name for MDMA, became popular on college campuses and with adolescents and was widely used at parties, sometimes

Teens buying drugs from an adult male to sell to other kids. Drug-trafficking juveniles are not always involved in gangs because some juveniles sell drugs independently of any gang affiliation.

called "raves" in the United States but more frequently referred to by this term in the United Kingdom. Ecstasy is usually ingested orally in tablet or capsule form, is sometimes snorted, and occasionally smoked. MDMA is reported to produce profound pleasurable effects, such as acute euphoria and positive changes in attitude and self-confidence.[44]

In 1988 and 1989, crank, a powerful stimulant that has an adrenaline-like effect on the body, gained popularity. Crank was produced in illegal laboratories in California, trafficked by Hell's Angels and other biker gangs, and sold to members of the white working class.[45] Crank was one of the drugs most frequently used by those who wrote stories for *Voices of Delinquency*.

Ice, a crystalline form of methamphetamine with the appearance of rock salt, was predicted to set off a new drug epidemic of the 1990s and beyond.[46] This plague, contrary to media hype, never materialized and appears to be a problem only in Hawaii.[47]

Hallucinogens

A parade of hallucinogens has become readily available to adolescents who are interested in embracing mind-expanding experiences. Leading the parade in the 1960s was D-lysergic acid diethylamide, more popularly known as LSD. Public hysteria arose in the late 1960s against LSD and other psychedelic substances, and its use dramatically declined in the 1970s.

PCP, or phencyclidine, a nervous system excitant that has analgesic, anesthetic, and hallucinogenic properties, was introduced in the late 1960s and became popular during the 1970s. First marketed as the **PeaCe Pill**, PCP was also known as *angel dust, animal tank, aurora borealis, buzz, devil dust, DOA, dummy dust, elephant, elephant juice, goon, THC*, and *rocket fuel*. The hysteria over PCP mounted during the 1970s, as it became apparent how dangerous the drug was.[48]

Use of PCP declined during the 1980s. For example, the national samples of high school seniors who had used PCP at least once dropped from 13 percent in 1979 to less than 3 percent by 1990.[49] Yet the drug's dangers are demonstrated by the number of users who visit hospital emergency rooms because of acute reactions to PCP; in 1987, emergency rooms reported 8,000 incidents involving PCP, sometimes in combination with other drugs.[50]

The National Household Survey on Drug Abuse found that in 1996, there were an estimated 1.1 million new hallucinogen users, approximately twice the annual average observed during the 1980s. The rate of initiation among twelve- to seventeen-year-old youths increased between 1991 and 1996 from 11.7 to 25.8 per thousand potential new users.[51]

Heroin

Opium, which is derived from certain species of poppy, is the source of heroin, morphine, paregoric, and codeine, some of which are still used medically. **Heroin,** a refined form of morphine, was introduced about the turn of the twentieth century. Heroin has been called *horse, shit, smack, H, harry, henry, boy, brown,* and *black tar.*[52]

Heroin is highly addicting and seemed to be experiencing a return to popularity in the late 1990s, especially among adults. The National Household Survey on Drug Abuse estimated that there were 325,000 heroin users in 1997. In 1996, according to this survey, an estimated 171,000 individuals used heroin for the first time. The estimated number of new users and the rate of initiation for juveniles were at the highest levels in thirty years.[53]

Chronic heroin use, unlike the use of most other drugs, appears to produce relatively minor direct or permanent physiological damage. Nevertheless, street heroin users typically neglect themselves and, as a result, report such disorders as heart and lung abnormalities, scarred veins, weight loss, malnutrition, endocarditis (a disease of the heart valves), stroke, gynecological problems, hepatitis, local skin infections, and abscesses.[54] The danger of heroin overdose has for several decades marked heroin as a very dangerous drug. For example, the Drug Abuse Warning Network has found that more than 20,000 heroin overdoses result in emergency room treatment each year, and 3,000 result in a stop at the morgue.[55]

Table 11.1 provides a summary of the short- and long-term consequences of using alcohol and other drugs. Although individuals differ in their reactions to drugs, especially people who have sensitivities and allergies to small amounts of substances, it is obvious that the more drugs are used and the greater the frequency of use, the more serious the damage will be.[56]

The Relationship between Drug Use and Delinquency

An issue currently under debate is whether drugs cause delinquency or delinquency leads to drug use, or whether some other factors precede both delinquency and the onset of drug use.[57] Considerable research has found that delinquency tends to precede the use of drugs.[58] Other research suggests that a casual association is a product of shared antecedents.[59] It is possible that a common factor, or syndrome, exists that underlies both delinquent behavior and drug use; this common factor may explain the frequency and type of drug use.[60]

A number of researchers, as previously discussed, found that substance abuse is just one of an interrelated and overlapping group of adolescent problem behaviors, including delinquency, teen pregnancy, school failure, and dropping out of school.[61] Substance abuse, then, is one of the problem behaviors developed by adolescents during their early life course. John M. Wallace Jr. and Jerald G. Bachman summarized what is involved in Richard and Shirley L. Jessors' "problem behavior" model:

> The basic theoretical structure of much present research can be subsumed under the "problem behavior" model posited by the Jessors. The Jessors' model is a comprehensive framework comprised of antecedent background variables and three systems of social-psychological and behavioral variables—the personality system, the perceived environment system, and the behavior system. The variables in the three primary systems interrelate to produce within the individual a greater or lesser proneness to become involved in problem behaviors. More specifically, the theory hypothesizes that young people who are less invested in traditional versus deviant behaviors, who are more strongly tied to peers than to parents, who are alienated from society, who have low self-esteem, and who hold unconventional beliefs, values, and attitudes are prone to become involved in problem behavior. The Jessors and their colleagues used their

TABLE 11.1

Consequences of Substance Abuse during Adolescence

	Consequences	
Substance	Short Term	Long Term
CIGARETTES[a]		
Occasional use	Vulnerability to other drugs	Unknown
Frequent use	Bad breath	Excess morbidity, mortality
	Respiratory problems	
ALCOHOL		
Occasional use	None	None
Frequent use	Drunk driving, leading to accidents, arrests, mortality	Alcoholism
		Cirrhosis of liver
	Impaired functioning in school	Stomach cancer
	Family problems	
	Depression	
	Accidental death (e.g., by drowning)	
MARIJUANA[b]		
Occasional use	Vulnerability to other drugs	Inconclusive
Frequent, high	Impaired psychological functioning	Respiratory problems
	Impaired driving ability	Possible adverse reproductive effects
	Loss of short-term memory	Decrease in motivation
ILLICIT DRUG USE		
Cocaine[a,c]	Physical symptoms, such as dry mouth, sweats, headache, nosebleeds, and nasal passage irritation	Drug dependence
		Rhinitis, ulcerated nasal septum
	Loss of sleep	Hepatitis
	Chronic fatigue	Psychological effects: depression, anxiety
	Feelings of depression	
	Suicidal ideation	Convulsions
		Social and financial problems
MULTIPLE SUBSTANCE USE[a]	Dysfunction	Drug dependence
	Drop out of school	Chronic depression, fatigue
	Suspension from school	Truncated education
	Motor vehicle accidents	Reduced job stability
	Illegal activities	Marital instability
		Crime

[a]M. Newcomb and P. Bentler, *Consequences of Adolescent Drug Use: Impact on the Lives of Young Adults* (Newbury Park, Calif.: Sage, 1988), pp. 219–222.

[b]R. Peterson, "Marijuana Overview," in *Correlation and Consequences of Marijuana Use* (National Institute on Drug Abuse, *Research Issues* 34, 1984), pp. 1–19.

[c]Based on findings from a study reported by D. Chitwood, "Patterns and Consequences of Cocaine Use," in *Cocaine Use in America: Epidemiologic and Clinical Perspectives,* edited by N. Koxel and E. Adams (National Institute on Drug Abuse, USDHHS, NIDA Research Monograph, 61, 1985), pp. 111–129.

Source: Joy G. Dryfoos, *Adolescents at Risk: Prevalence and Prevention* (New York: Oxford University Press, 1990), p. 48. Copyright © 1991 by Joy G. Dryfoos. Used by permission of Oxford University Press, Inc.

longitudinal dataset to test the theoretical model and found it to be quite successful in explaining adolescent problems—particularly drug use.[62]

Recent longitudinal studies of high-risk youths in Denver, Pittsburgh, and Rochester have also provided evidence of the overlap of substance abuse with other problem behaviors.[63] These three longitudinal studies found that substance abuse was significantly related to delinquency in youth, regardless of race. Delinquent girls were at higher risk for drug use than were delinquent boys. Delinquency was further related to early sexual activity or pregnancy.[64] These studies concluded that "targeting delinquency and substance abuse simultaneously in intervention and prevention programs will more likely enhance the effectiveness of such programs in each problem area than will programs that focus uniquely on either substance abuse or delinquency."[65]

Previous research has indicated large racial/ethnic differences in adolescent drug use, with the highest use among Native Americans, somewhat lower use among white and Hispanic youth, and lowest use among African American and Asian youth.[66] In contrast, Delbert S. Elliott, David Huizinga, and Scott Menard's analysis of the National Youth Survey found no association between social class, race, and substance abuse. Although lower-class youths and African Americans did have higher prevalence rates of serious delinquent behavior, whites had higher prevalence rates of minor delinquent acts and of alcohol, marijuana, and polydrug use. Urban residents had higher rates of marijuana and polydrug use and were also more at risk of becoming sellers.[67] Wallace and Bachman also found that controlling for background and life-style reduced or eliminated many of the racial-ethnic differences in drug use. Their data further revealed that several life-style factors, including time spent in peer-oriented activities, educational values and behaviors, and religious commitment, were strongly related to drug use and helped to explain the subgroup differences.[68]

In the past decade, consensus has been increasing on the findings that explain the onset and continuing use of illicit drugs. First, there is widespread agreement that there is a sequential pattern of involvement in drug use during adolescence.[69] Denise B. Kandel and colleagues, using cross-sectional research and longitudinal data, proposed a developmental model for drug-use involvement. According to this model, alcohol use follows a pattern of minor delinquency and exposure to friends and parents who drink. The use of marijuana follows participation in minor delinquency and adoption of beliefs and values that are consistent with those held by peers but opposed to parental standards. Finally, use proceeds to other illicit drugs if relationships with parents are poor and there is increased exposure to peers who use a variety of illegal drugs.[70]

Second, in examining drug use, it is important to identify in which of three major groups users belong. Some youths or adults experiment once or twice and then discontinue drug use. Others continue drug use into young adulthood, but drug use does not interfere with their lives in any major ways. Those in a third group become addicted or dependent on drugs, and their entire lifestyle is likely to be designed around acquiring drugs daily. Members of this third group also frequently commit crimes to maintain their drug supply.

Third, a number of risk factors appear to be related to delinquency and drug use. Pre-perinatal risk factors consist of perinatal difficulties, minor physical abnormalities, and brain damage. Early developmental risk factors are found in the family environment, including a family history of alcoholism, poor family management practices, and family conflict. Other risk factors are early antisocial behavior and academic failure. Community risk factors involve living in economically deprived areas and disorganized neighborhoods. According to J. David Hawkins, Richard F. Catalano, and Devon D. Brewer, the more of these risk factors a child has, the more likely it is that he or she will become involved in drug abuse.[71]

There is little debate that youths who use hard-core drugs are more likely to engage in chronic delinquent behavior.[72] Elliott and Huizinga found that nearly 50 percent of serious juvenile offenders were also multiple drug users. Eighty-two percent of these offenders reported use, beyond experimentation, of at least one illicit drug. Incident rates of alcohol use among serious offenders were four to nine times those of nonoffenders, and rates of marijuana use among serious offenders were fourteen times those of nonoffenders.[73] Jeffrey Fagan and colleagues' survey of inner-city youths also found that heavy substance use was more prevalent and frequent among serious delinquents, but the type of substance used was more strongly associated with delinquency than was the frequency of drug use.[74]

David M. Altschuler and Paul J. Brounstein's examination of drug use and drug trafficking among inner-city adolescent males in Washington, D.C., found that the use and sales of drugs affected the frequency and seriousness of delinquent behavior. The heaviest users were significantly more likely than nonusers to commit property offenses; those who trafficked in drugs were significantly more likely to commit crimes against the person than youths who did not sell drugs, and adolescents who both used and sold drugs were the most likely to commit offenses against property and persons.[75]

An official in the South Carolina criminal justice system had this to say about how the involvement of drugs led to violence among adolescent females in South Carolina gangs:

> There are very few South Carolina towns that don't have any gang activity in them. Most of the larger towns, such as Greenville and Charleston, have national gangs. Even some smaller towns, like Lake City in Florence County, have national gangs. All of the gangs, whether they are national or not, are male dominated.
>
> Females are termed as "associates" and carry no decision-making powers. They are primarily used as fronts for the drug trade. The female's home is used to deal drugs out of because she is less likely to be suspected of wrong-doing.
>
> A dramatic example of how these girls are used by the male gangs in South Carolina happened only recently. Police officials had pulled over some gang members. Since the gang members knew that they would be searched, one of the males gave the weapon he was carrying to the female who was with them. While the police officer was searching the gang members, the female drew the gun and killed him.[76]

Is There a Correlation between Chronic Offending and Drug Use?

Youths who sell drugs, whether they are users or not, are chronic offenders. Adolescent girls involved in prostitution are chronic offenders and are also at high risk to be drug users. An examination of drug use through the life course is typically involved in determining whether chronic offenders and substance abusers continue their chronic offending and drug use into adulthood.

Drug-Trafficking Juveniles

There is some evidence, as stated in the preceding chapter, that independents sell drugs as frequently as, or perhaps more than, drug-trafficking gangs do. For example, Malcolm W. Klein, Cheryl L. Maxson, and Lea C. Cunningham found that "crack distribution, while including many individual gang members, was not primarily a street gang phenomenon."[77]

Some juveniles also sell drugs independently of any gang affiliation, especially in suburban settings and schools. But in urban settings, drug trafficking is typically controlled by adults. A student on academic scholarship in college told about his role in the gang's drug-trafficking operation:

> I must have been ten or eleven, and I was told to show up on this street corner. When I got there, they gave me a gun and told me to keep watch. If anyone came around, they told me to shoot them. They were taking care of business inside the crack house. Fortunately, nobody came around because I would have shot them. It surely would have changed my life.[78]

A teenage boy dealing drugs outdoors. Illicit drug use among juveniles crosses race, class, and gender boundaries and begins as early as elementary school. Many schools are responding to the problem by declaring school property a "Drug Free Zone" and encouraging students to join groups such as DARE.

Our understanding of juveniles and drug trafficking is heightened by Felix M. Padilla's *The Gang as an American Enterprise*[79] and Daniel J. Monti's book, *Wannabe Gangs in Suburbs and Schools.*[80] Padilla studied a Hispanic drug-dealing gang in Chicago. He found that this drug enterprise had an occupational hierarchy, in which the cocaine and marijuana suppliers or distributors were on top, followed by "older guys," chiefs, and "mainheads." The street-level dealers, or mainheads, were juveniles who barely made a survival income and who usually had to supplement their drug income through stealing. Yet they never quite got ahead because they would inevitably be arrested, and the distributor would have his attorney bail them out. It would then take them months to repay the distributor.

Monti's examination of gangs in suburbs and schools focused on juveniles' selling drugs. He found that the gangs, especially the Gangster Disciples, had real control in the suburban schools he studied. The Crips and Bloods were also represented in these schools. The drugs that were sold included marijuana, different types of pills, and some crack cocaine. The girls' involvement in drug trafficking typically consisted of holding drugs for boys, usually their boyfriends, when the boys thought they might be searched by the police or school officials. According to Monti, the youths who sold drugs kept the profits for themselves and did not pool the money with the gang. He also depicted drug dealing as a lucrative and exciting trade.[81] One interviewed youth commented:

> A third teenager from yet another gang was more deeply involved in drug dealing and gave no indication of leaving the trade. "It's an everyday thing now," he said. [In one week] I made twenty-five hundred. At the first of the month you can make like ten thousand, because everybody gets their [welfare] checks then. They come to you and spend their whole check on it."[82]

Drug Use and Prostitution

Adolescent girls who become drug users, especially of crack cocaine, often become prostitutes. Their involvement in prostitution, intravenous drug use, and sex-for-crack exchanges puts them at high risk for HIV infection.

Inciardi and colleagues, in interviews conducted with 100 serious female delinquents, found that eighty-six reported a median of 200 acts of prostitution. Their initial alcohol and marijuana involvement typically took place between the ages of eight and ten, and by age twelve, they were experimenting with cocaine and heroin. At the time of the interview, the frequent prostitutes used alcohol regularly, marijuana and cocaine (usually crack) daily, pills at least once or twice a week, and sometimes heroin. For 42 percent of these prostitutes, heroin use included intravenous use.[83]

A number of other studies have found a positive relationship between drug addiction and prostitution. Jennifer James interviewed 100 women who were addicts, prostitutes, or addict-prostitutes and concluded that addiction often leads to prostitution and prostitution can lead to drug addiction.[84] Marsha Rosenbaum's *Women on Heroin*[85] and Eleanor Miller's *Street Women* further suggested that addiction and prostitution frequently cannot be disentangled.[86] In Social World of the Delinquent 11.4, a teenage prostitute from the Midwest describes her world.

Inciardi and colleagues stated that "women who trade sex for drugs, or money to buy drugs, drift in and out of both drug use and prostitution. Due to the instability of their lifestyles, it is impossible to group them by either their drug use or their sexual practices."[87] But "in the crack house," they add, "a barter system exists in which sex and crack are the currency."[88]

Drug-addicted prostitutes face another threat to their personal well-being: AIDS (acquired immunodeficiency syndrome). Intravenous drug use and unprotected sexual intercourse make these high-risk adolescents vulnerable to this disease, for which no

Social World of the Delinquent 11.4

Interview with a Teenage Prostitute

Question: Why does a teenage girl become a prostitute?

Answer: If you're working for yourself, the money is pretty good. If you are working regular, you make $1,000 or more a week if you work every night. You can either work in a massage parlor or on the streets.

Question: How old are teenage prostitutes, and how do they learn what to do?

Answer: They are usually fifteen and up. Older women have a lot of influence and power over younger ones. Most street prostitutes have pimps, who have a lot of control over their girls.

Question: What are the advantages of having a pimp?

Answer: Some girls feel that pimps help you as much as you can help them. They feel that their pimps care about them. When you are new to a territory, it is nice to have a man who knows the territory and will take care of you. They furnish a roof over your head, provide all the necessities that you need, and make certain you eat well. The pimp is there to bail you out when you go to jail. He makes certain that none of the other pimps hassle or rob you.

As far as I'm concerned, there ain't no advantages in having a pimp. They would like you to believe they will take care of you, but after they get you, you might see clothes but that's about it. Some will give you a little spending money, but the majority take it all. If you need something, they will either take you out to buy it or give you money to buy it. A lot of prostitutes are into drugs, and as long as they are getting their drugs, they're happy. Coke, heroin, and weed are the drugs most widely used. . . .

Prostitutes just turn their feelings off. They take it as their job and just look at the money. They go in and try to get the job done as fast as they can. It is necessary to turn your feelings back on when you are with your man [pimp].

What does this teenage prostitute imply is the relationship between drugs and prostitution? Why would drug dependency make it difficult to walk away from prostitution?

Source: Interviewed by Linda Dippold Bartollas in June 1981 in a Midwestern city.

known cure exists. This disease has a long incubation period (close to eight years from contact with HIV, the human immunodeficiency virus, to clinical manifestation), which means that infected prostitutes can spread the disease to hundreds of sexual contacts.

Drug Use through the Life Course

Two basic pathways are possible for substance-abusing youths. They may only be substance abusers who are not involved in other delinquent activities. These offenders may desist from substance abuse during their adolescent years, or they may continue to use drugs as adults. Alternatively, substance-abusing youths may also participate in other delinquent activities. These youths, too, may desist from one or both types of activity during adolescent or continue to be involved in one or both as adults.

There is some evidence that about two-thirds of substance-abusing youths continue to use drugs after reaching adulthood, but about half desist from other forms of criminality. Those who persist in both crime and substance abuse as adults typically came from poor families, did poorly in school, used multiple types of drugs, were chronic offenders, and had an early onset of both drug use and delinquent behavior.[89]

Drug addicts, like those with a history of delinquency and criminality, sometimes have a turning point, or change, when they walk away from drug use. Those who were deeply entrenched in the drug world as adolescents and continue this activity in their adult years find it particularly difficult to give up drugs. Those who are able to stay with the straight life typically have had a religious experience or have had an extremely positive experience in a therapeutic community for drug addicts.[90]

Kandel and colleagues reported that significant status changes, including marriage and parenthood, were correlated with the cessation of marijuana smoking among those in their mid to late twenties.[91] L. A. Goodman and W. H. Kruskal found that reasons for cessation involved the imposition of internal control with controls imposed externally.[92] L. Thomas Winfree Jr., Christine S. Sellers, and Dennis L. Clason examined the reasons for adolescents' cessation of and abstention from substance use and found that social learning variables clearly distinguished abstainers from current users, but they were less able to distinguish former users from current users or former users from abstainers.[93]

One reason many drug addicts relapse is that they do not find the straight life sufficiently exciting, fulfilling, or satisfying. A former adolescent drug addict had given speeches in the community about how close she had been to being sentenced to the penitentiary, about the numerous burglaries she had committed, and about the damage that chemicals had done to her body, to her relationship with her parents, and to her reputation. Yet she returned to chemicals, and she gave the following explanation of why she failed:

> I found that living without drugs wasn't that good. All my friends do drugs; you have no social life without drugs. My boyfriend even went back to drugs. The night I saw him shoot up coke, I was devastated. I had to do something. I went to a friend's house and smoked some grass. I decided then that I was going to smoke pot, but I wasn't going back to chemicals. But it wasn't long before I went back to chemicals. It is really a good high, but I'm hooked on them now. I couldn't wait all day yesterday until we broke some crystal [took speed] last night.[94]

Some of the Theoretical Explanations for the Onset of Drug Use

A number of theories have been proposed for the onset and escalation of adolescents' drug use. It is claimed that a bleak economic situation has created a generation of youths and young adults in urban inner cities who experience doubt, hopelessness, and uncertainty on an everyday basis. The poor's hopelessness, according to this position, has encouraged them to find ways to seek solace and relief from their pain. Drug and alcohol abuse is an immediate fix for their hopelessness but, in the long run, creates other problems.

Drug use by peers is consistently found to be the strongest predictor of an individual's involvement in drug use. In fact, the argument can be made that drug use begins and continues primarily because juveniles or adults have contact with peers who use drugs and who provide role models, as well as social support, for drug using. Peer influence, not surprisingly, is especially important during adolescence. Peers appear to influence beginning marijuana use but seem to be less important for starting the use of alcohol or hard-core drugs. Once peers persuade a person to begin using drugs, then a pattern of use is established that may eventually lead to addiction and continued use.[95]

Another explanation for the onset and continued use of drugs relates to the contention that addicts have an addiction-prone personality and suffer from deep-rooted personality disorders. Isidor Chein and colleagues' celebrated study, *The Road to H,* contended that youthful heroin addicts suffered from such personality disorders as "weak ego functioning," "defective superego," and "inadequate masculine identification." This addiction-prone personality, according to these authors, was unable "to enter into prolonged, close, friendly relations with either peers or adults," had "difficulties in assuming a masculine role," was "frequently overcome by a sense of futility, expectation of failure, and general depression," was "easily frustrated and made anxious," and found "frustrations and anxiety intolerable."[96]

A further explanation of the appeal of substance abuse, especially in the inner city, is that it represents such a high or peak experience. Anthropologist Philippe Bourgois put it this way: "Substance abuse in general, and crack in particular, offers the equivalent of a born-again metamorphosis. Instantaneously," he says, "the user is transformed from an unemployed, depressed high school dropout, despised by the world—and secretly convinced that his failure is due to his own inherent stupidity and disorganization." Bourgois explained why it is such a sensate experience: "There is a rush of heart-palpitating pleasure, followed by a jaw-gnashing crash and wide-eyed alertness that provides his life with concrete purpose: Get more crack—fast!"[97]

The attempt to explain a social phenomenon by a single theory has a long history in sociology, but, like delinquency theory, substance abuse theory owes its origins to several theoretical explanations. For some individuals, drugs are an escape from the dreariness and crushing toxicity of their home environment. For others, substance abuse is an attempt to escape from emotionally crippling problems. For still others, substance abuse arises as part of normal peer influence. Integrated or interactional models combining the effects of strain, control, and social learning theories appear to make most sense in explaining why people use or abuse alcohol and drugs.[98]

How Drug Use Can Be Prevented and Treated

Prevention and treatment are the most effective means to control drug use among adolescents in U.S. society. There is abundant evidence that deterrent tactics, such as the federal "war on drugs," have been ineffective with both juveniles and adults. An unfortunate consequence with juveniles of this war on drugs is that increasing numbers of minority youths who were involved in using or selling crack have been brought into the justice system for extensive periods of time. It can also be argued that this war on drugs has been a factor contributing to the spread of youth gangs across the nation.[99]

Prevention

N. Tobler did a meta-analysis of data from 143 adolescent drug prevention programs that is helpful in evaluating their effectiveness. She found that the programs could be divided into the following groups:

1. *Knowledge-oriented only.* Based on the assumption that drug education will change attitudes that will, in turn, decrease use. Strategy makes use of information on long-term effects, which is presented by instructors, limited group participation, and "scare" tactics.
2. *Affective strategies only.* Based on the assumption that psychological factors place certain children at risk of abuse. Strategy is aimed at social growth, self-esteem building, and values clarification. No mention is made of drugs.
3. *Social influence and life skills.* Based on a combination of approaches that assumes that peer pressure is the major factor in abuse.
   a. *Refusal skills.* Based on the assumption that specific behaviors can be taught to deal with social influences. Strategy teaches interpersonal resistance skills; deals with social pressures; utilizes "say no" training; and employs peer role models.
   b. *Social and life skills.* Based on the assumption that generic social skills are needed for problem solving and decision making about substance use. Strategy promotes personal sense of competency, teaches communication skills, uses feedback, introduces values clarification, and teaches coping skills.
4. *Knowledge plus affective strategies.* Based on the assumption that both attitudes and values must be altered to change behavior. Strategy provides information and decision-making skills.
5. *Alternative strategies.* Based on the assumption that changes have to be made in correlates (predictors) of drug use, such as school failure and delinquency.
   a. *Introduce activities.* Replace negative behaviors with positive activities, such as jobs and volunteerism.
   b. *Teach competence in high-risk youth.* Make up for individual deficits using basic skills training, programs such as Outward Bound, and individual attention.[100]

Tobler concluded from her research that social influence and peer interventions were found to have the most lasting effect on all outcome measures. The alternative strategies were second in effectiveness, but their effect was only half that of the social influence and peer programs. Significantly, she found that informational programs had practically no effect.[101]

These programs need to be implemented during early childhood and family interventions, during school-based interventions, and during comprehensive and communitywide efforts. The important dimensions of drug-prevention interventions, as is continually emphasized throughout this text, is a multidimensional approach centering on the family, school, and community.

Treatment Intervention

Treatment for drug abusers takes place in psychiatric and hospital settings for youngsters whose parents can afford it or who have third-party insurance benefits. Other youngsters, especially those substance abusers who have committed minor forms of delinquency, receive the benefits of treatment in privately administered placements, which vary tremendously in the quality of program design and implementation. Substance abusers who are involved in serious forms of delinquency will likely be placed in county or state facilities whose basic organizational goal is custodial and security-oriented. These youths generally receive some exposure to substance abuse counseling, especially in group contexts.

Substance-abusing youths with typical multiple problems may be more malleable than adult offenders, but there is little evidence that the majority of substance abuse programs are any more successful than those for adult substance abusers. Élan in Maine; Rocky Mountain in Colorado; Provo Canyon in Utah; and Cascade, Cedu, and Hilltop in California are privately administered therapeutic schools or emotional growth programs that appear to be several notches above the average substance abuse program for juveniles.[102]

Élan, a therapeutic community for juveniles in Poland Springs, Maine, is a treatment program for substance abusers and predelinquent children between the ages of twelve and twenty. Joe Ricci, a former drug addict and one of the success stories of Daytop (a therapeutic community for drug addicts) in New York City and Dr. Gerald Davidson, a psychiatrist, started Élan in 1971.[103]

The program involves intense peer pressure, self-responsibility, hard physical and emotional work, and self-disclosure. Élan has grown into a finely tuned million-dollar operation with twenty-five therapeutic staff members, seventeen educational staff members, forty support staff members, five houses, a school, and 140 residents. This two-year program costs $38,765 a year (twelve months). Among the population in September 1995, sixty were funded by parents or third-party insurance, fifty-five by school districts, and the remaining twenty-five by state agencies. About 60 to 70 percent of those individuals who are admitted to this program graduate or receive "diplomas." Of this number, according to an in-house evaluation, about 80 percent have stayed out of trouble. Supporters think that Élan is an exemplary therapeutic experience for youths; foes regard it as coercive and brutal.[104]

The philosophy of Élan, like that of similar therapeutic experiences for juveniles, is perhaps correct—that substance abusers need a confrontational environment with intense pressure from peers and staff to change. It may well be that the 60 to 70 percent who stay at Élan to complete the two-year program are ready to change or to desist from drugs and negative behaviors, and this explains their high success rate. But privately administered programs such as Élan do not have enough places available for the juveniles who need such a therapeutic experience.

SUMMARY

This chapter has examined the abuse of drugs and alcohol among U.S. adolescents. Drug and alcohol abuse is one form of problem behavior, and its onset, duration, and offset are determined by the dynamics of the interchange between the environment and the youth, which vary over developmental periods. An understanding, then, of the severity, onset, and duration of any problem behavior, including drug and alcohol abuse, must rely heavily on a study of both macro- and microsocial environments.

The good news is that the trend of drug use appears to have declined significantly from the late 1970s, with perhaps slight increases since the early 1990s. The bad news is that high-risk children are becoming increasingly involved in substance abuse. Although the use of crack cocaine may be declining across the nation, it remains the drug of choice for disadvantaged youth. It is disconcerting that teenagers have increased their use of marijuana; indeed, there is some evidence that marijuana use among young people age twelve to seventeen has nearly doubled since 1992.

Early prevention efforts in school, as well as in other social contexts, appear to be making headway with low-risk children. At the same time, prevention, treatment, or punishment do not appear to be reducing in any noteworthy way the amount or seriousness of substance abuse with high-risk children in this nation. The fact that substance abuse is usually one of several problems for high-risk youth makes it more difficult to achieve any degree of success with therapeutic intervention. It is apparent that those most involved in frequent and serious forms of delinquent behaviors are also likely to use and sell hard drugs, to become involved in prostitution, and to continue drug abuse and criminality into their adult years.

KEY TERMS

alcohol, p. 332
amphetamines, p. 335
cocaine, p. 333
heroin, p. 336

inhalants, p. 335
marijuana, p. 332
sedatives, p. 335
Ecstasy, p. 335

CRITICAL THINKING QUESTIONS

1. Why is drug use so popular in American society?
2. Explain why the typical drug user will use drugs up to a certain point and will go no further? At the same time, why do other youths who seem to be as committed to this stopping point continue using drugs?
3. Is there something going on in society that would influence the use of marijuana to rise in the mid 1990s?

4. Why would a youth pursue only the drug pathway rather than the delinquency/drug pathway?
5. Why do college students drink as much as they do? How is their drinking related to the subject matter of this chapter?

WEB DESTINATIONS

Read more about marijuana from the National Institute on Drug Abuse site.
http://alcoholism.about.com/library/blnida07.htm?iam=dpile&terms=%2Bmarijuana

Read more about zero tolerance at the Zero Tolerance to Crime site.
http://www.geocites.com/Pentagon/Barracks/3952

Visit this cocaine fact sheet.
http://www.lec.org/DrugSearch/Documents/cocaine.html

Learn more about drug-trafficking juveniles on this National Criminal Justice Reference Service site.
http://www.ncjrs.org/txtfiles/fs-9412.txt

NOTES

1. Interviewed in June 1981.
2. Matthew G. Muters and Christina Bethke were extremely helpful in doing the literature review and in drafting materials for this chapter.
3. Rand Drug Policy Research Center, *Newsletter,* June 1995, p. 1.
4. Howard Abadinsky, *Drugs: An Introduction,* 4th ed. (Belmont, CA.: Wadsworth/Thompson Learning, 2001), p. 4.
5. In 1990, the U.S. Supreme Court ruled 6–3 in an Oregon case that states can prohibit the use of peyote by members of the Native American church. But Congress enacted a statute providing a defense for those who use the substance "with good faith practice of a religious belief."
6. Abadinsky, *Drugs: An Introduction,* p. 4.
7. The following section on social attitudes and drug use is adapted from James A. Inciardi, *The War on Drugs II* (Mountain View, Calif.: Mayfield, 1992), pp. 1–3.

8. *1897 Sears, Roebuck Catalogue* (1897; reprint, New York: Chelsea House, 1968), p. 32 of insert on drugs.
9. See Lana Harrison and Andrea Kopstein, "A Twenty-Plus Year Perspective on Adolescent Drug Use." This paper was presented at the Annual Meeting of the American Society of Criminology, Miami, Florida (November 1994), p. 5.
10. Rand Drug Policy Research Center, *Newsletter,* pp. 1, 7.
11. Harrison and Kopstein, "A Twenty-Plus Year Perspective on Adolescent Drug Use," p. 13.
12. See J. G. Bachman, L. D. Johnston, and P. M. O'Malley, "Explaining the Recent Decline in Cocaine Use among Young Adults: Further Evidence That Perceived Risks and Disapproval Lead to Reduced Drug Use," *Journal of Health and Social Behavior* 31 (1990), pp. 173–184; J. G. Bachman, L. D. Johnston, P. M. O'Malley, and R. H. Humphrey, "Explaining the Recent Decline in Marijuana

Use: Differentiating the Effects of Perceived Risks, Disapproval and General Lifestyle Factors," *Journal of Health and Social Behavior* 29 (1988), pp. 91–112; National Institute of Drug Abuse, *NIDA: Capsules: Overview of the 1988 National Survey on Drug Abuse* (Rockville, Md.: Government Printing Office, 1989); National Institute of Drug Abuse, *NIDA Notes* (Rockville, Md.: Government Printing Office, 1991).

13. Ann H. Crowe, *Drug Identification and Testing in the Juvenile Justice System: Summary* (Washington, D.C.: Office of Juvenile Justice and Delinquency Prevention, 1988), p. 3.

14. Harrison and Kopstein, "A Twenty-Plus Year Perspective on Adolescent Drug Use," p. 9.

15. Substance Abuse Mental Health Service Administration (SAMHSA), *Preliminary Estimates from the 1997 National Household Survey on Drug Abuse* (Washington, D.C.: U.S. Department of Health and Human Services, 1998), pp. 1–2.

16. Ibid., p. 1.

17. Richard Dembo, Linda Williams, Jeffrey Fagan, and James Schmeidler, "Development and Assessment of a Classification of High Risk Youths," *Journal of Drug Issues* 24 (1994), p. 26.

18. R. L. Dembo, L. Williams, E. Berry, A. Getreu, M. Washburn, E. D. Wish, and J. Kern, "A Longitudinal Study of the Relationships among Alcohol Use, Marijuana/Hashish Use, Cocaine Use and Emotional/Psychological Functioning Problems in a Cohort of High Risk Youths," *International Journal of Addictions* 25 (1990), pp. 1341–1382.

19. Substance Abuse Mental Health Service Administration, *Preliminary Estimates from the 1997 National Household Survey on Drug Abuse,* p. 1.

20. Rand Drug Policy Research Center, *Newsletter,* p. 1.

21. Substance Abuse Health Service Administration, *Preliminary Estimates from the 1997 National Household Survey on Drug Abuse,* p. 13.

22. Ibid., pp. 13–14.

23. Jeffrey Fagan, Joseph G. Weis, and Yu-Tech Cheng, "Delinquency and Substandard Use among Inner-City Students," *Journal of Drug Issues* (Summer 1990), p. 351.

24. Joy G. Dryfoos, *Adolescents at Risk: Prevalence and Prevention* (New York: Oxford University Press, 1990), p. 54.

25. Substance Abuse Mental Health Service Association, *Preliminary Estimates from the 1997 National Household Survey on Drug Abuse,* p. 1.

26. Inciardi, *The War on Drugs II,* p. 62.

27. Public Health Service, *Healthy People 2000: National Health Promotion and Disease Prevention Objectives—Full Report with Commentary* (Washington, D.C.: DHHS Publication, 1991).

28. Interview of this institutionalized youth conducted in 1981.

29. J. M. McGinnis and W. H. Foege, "Actual Causes of Death in the United States," *JAMA* 270 (November 10, 1993), pp. 2207–2212.

30. For many other names, see Inciardi, *The War on Drugs II,* p. 44.

31. Interviewed in September 1995.

32. For an examination of these studies, see Helen C. Jones and Paul W. Lovinger, *The Marijuana Question* (New York: Dodd, Mead, 1985).

33. Inciardi, *The War on Drugs II,* p. 94.

34. Substance Abuse Health Service Administration, *Preliminary Estimates from the 1997 National Household Survey on Drug Abuse,* p. 3.

35. Gordon Witkin, "The Men Who Created Crack," *U.S. News and World Report,* August 29, 1991, pp. 44–53. See also Malcolm W. Klein, Cheryl L. Maxson, and Lea C. Cunningham, " 'Crack,' Street Gangs, and Violence," *Criminology* 29 (November 1991), pp. 623–650.

36. Inciardi, *The War on Drugs II,* p. 116.

37. Ibid.

38. Ibid., p. 93.

39. "Cocaine Abuse," *NIDA Capsules,* November 1989, p. 2.

40. James N. Hall, "Impact of Mother's Cocaine Use," *Street Pharmacologist* 11 (October 1987), p. 1.

41. T. M. McSherry, "Program Experiences with the Solvent Abuser in Philadelphia," In *Epidemiology of Inhalant Abuse: An Update,* edited by R. A. Crider and B. A. Rouse (Washington, D.C.: National Institute on Drug Abuse Research Monograph 85, 1989), pp. 106–120.

42. Abadinsky, *Drugs: An Introduction,* p. 82.

43. Inciardi, *The War on Drugs II,* p. 39.

44. Abadinsky, *Drugs: An Introduction,* p. 143–144.

45. *Substance Abuse Report,* October 1, 1988, pp. 1–3.

46. *Time,* September 18, 1989, p. 28; *Drug Enforcement Report,* October 24, 1989, p. 8.

47. *Drug Enforcement Report,* 3 January 1990, p. 7.

48. Ibid., p. 49.

49. University of Michigan News and Information Services, January 24, 1991.

50. National Institute on Drug Abuse, Division of Epidemiology and Statistical Analysis, *Annual Data, Data from the Drug Abuse Warning Network* (Rockville, Md.: National Institute on Drug Abuse, 1990), pp. 200–210.

51. Substance Abuse Health Service Administration, *Preliminary Estimates from the 1997 National Household Survey on Drug Abuse,* p. 3.

52. Inciardi, *The War on Drugs II,* p. 63.

53. Substance Abuse Health Service Administration, *Preliminary Estimates from the 1997 National Household Survey on Drug Abuse,* p. 2.

54. For an overview of medical complications associated with heroin addiction, see Jerome J. Platt, *Heroin Addiction: Theory, Research, and Treatment* (Malabar, Fla.: Robert E. Krieger, 1986), pp. 80–102.

55. National Institute on Drug Abuse, *Annual Data, Data From the Drug Abuse Warning Network, Annual Trend Data.*

56. Dryfoos, *Adolescents at Risk,* pp. 48–49.

57. David M. Altschuler and Paul J. Brounstein, "Patterns of Drug Use, Drug Trafficking, and Other Delinquency among Inner-City Adolescent Males in Washington, D.C.," *Criminology* 29 (1991), p. 590.

58. Lloyd D. Johnson et al., "Drugs and Delinquency: A Search for Causal Connections," in *Longitudinal Research on Drug Use: Empirical Finds and Methodological*

Issues, edited by Denise B. Kandel et al. (Washington, D.C.: Hemisphere, 1978), pp. 137–156; J. C. Friedman and A. S. Friedman, "Drug Use and Delinquency among Lower Class, Court Adjudicated Adolescent Boys," in *Drug Use in America* 1 (Washington, D.C.: National Commission on Marijuana and Drug Abuse: Government Printing Office, 1973); J. A. Inciardi, "Heroin Use and Street Crime," *Crime and Delinquency* 25 (1979), pp. 335–346; L. N. Robins and G. E. Murphy, "Drug Use in a Normal Population of Young Negro Men," *American Journal of Public Health* 57 (1967), pp. 1580–1596.

59. Altschuler and Brounstein, "Patterns of Drug Use, Drug Trafficking, and Other Delinquency Among Inner-City Adolescent Males in Washington, D.C.," p. 590; R. Jessor and S. L. Jessor, *Problem Behavior and Psychosocial Development: A Longitudinal Study of Youth* (New York: Academic Press, 1977); R. L. Akers, "Delinquent Behavior, Drugs and Alcohol: What is the Relationship?" *Today's Delinquent* 3 (1984), pp. 19–47; D. S. Elliott and D. Huizinga, *The Relationship between Delinquent Behavior and ADM Problems* (Boulder, Colo.: Behavior Research Institute, 1985); D. S. Elliott, D. Huizinga, and S. Menard, *Multiple Problem Youth: Delinquency, Substance Use, and Mental Health Problems* (New York: Springer-Verlag, 1989).

60. See Marc Le Blanc and Nathalie Kaspy, "Trajectories of Delinquency and Problem Behavior: Comparison of Social and Personal Control Characteristics of Adjudicated Boys on Synchronous and Nonsynchronous Paths," *Journal of Quantitative Criminology* 14 (1998), pp. 181–214; and Helene Raskin White, "Marijuana Use and Delinquency: A Test of the 'Independent Cause' Hypothesis," *Journal of Drug Issues* (1991), pp. 231–256.

61. Richard Jessor and Shirley L. Jessor, *Problem Behavior and Psychosocial Development: A Longitudinal Study of Youth* (New York: Academic Press, 1977); Denise B. Kandel, "Epidemiological and Psychosocial Perspectives on Adolescent Drug Use," *Journal of American Academic Clinical Psychiatry* 21 (1982), pp. 328–347; and Lee N. Robins and Kathryn S. Ratcliff, "Risk Factors in the Continuation of Childhood Antisocial Behavior into Adulthood," *Internal Journal of Mental Health* 7 (1979), pp. 96–116.

62. John M. Wallace Jr. and Jerald G. Bachman, "Explaining Racial/Ethnic Differences in Adolescent Drug Use: The Impact of Background and Lifestyle," *Social Problems* 38 (August 1991), p. 334. See also Richard Jessor and Shirley Jessor, *Problem Behavior and Psychosocial Development*; and Richard Jessor, "Problem Behavior Theory, Psychosocial Development, and Adolescent Problem Drinking," *British Journal of Addiction* 82 (1987), pp. 331–342.

63. David Huizinga, Rolf Loeber, and Terence Thornberry, *Urban Delinquency and Substance Abuse Initial Findings: Research Summary* (Washington, D.C.: U.S. Department of Justice; Office of Juvenile Justice and Delinquency Prevention, 1994).

64. Peter W. Greenwood, "Substance Abuse Problems Among High-Risk Youth and Potential Interventions," *Crime and Delinquency* 38 (October 1992), p. 447.

65. Quoted in Ibid.

66. Wallace and Bachman, "Explaining Racial/Ethnic Differences in Adolescent Drug Use," p. 333.

67. Delbert S. Elliott, David Huizinga, and Scott Menard, *Multiple Problem Youth: Delinquency, Substance Use, and Mental Health Problems* (New York: Springer-Verlag, 1989).

68. Wallace and Bachman, "Explaining Racial/Ethnic Differences in Adolescent Drug Use," p. 333.

69. Bureau of Justice Statistics, *Drugs, Crime, and the Justice System* (Washington, D.C.: Government Printing Office, 1993), p. 23.

70. Denise B. Kandel, Ronald C. Kessler, and Rebecca Z. Margulies, *Longitudinal Research on Drug Use: Empirical Findings and Methodological Issues* (Washington, D.C.: Hemisphere, 1978).

71. J. David Hawkins, Richard F. Catalano, and Devon D. Brewer, "Preventing Serious, Violent, and Chronic Juvenile Offending," in *A Sourcebook: Serious, Violent and Chronic Juvenile Offenders,* edited by James C. Howell, Barry Krisberg, J. David Hawkins, and John L. Wilson (Thousand Oaks, Calif.: Sage, 1995), pp. 48–49.

72. Delbert S. Elliott, David Huizinga, and Suzanne S. Ageton, *Explaining Delinqueny and Drug Use* (Beverly Hills, Calif.: Sage, 1985).

73. D. S. Elliott and D. Huizinga, "The Relationship between Delinquent Behavior and ADM Problem Behaviors." Paper prepared for the ADAMHA/OJJDP State of the Art Research Conference on Juvenile Offenders with Serious Drug/Alcohol and Mental Health Problems, Bethesda, Maryland (April 17–18, 1984).

74. Fagan, Weis, Cheng, "Delinquency and Substance Use among Inner-City Students," p. 351.

75. Altschuler and Brounstein, "Patterns of Drug Use, Drug Trafficking and Other Delinquency among Inner-City Adolescent Males in Washington, D.C.," p. 587.

76. Interviewed in April 1995.

77. Klein, Maxson, and Cunningham, " 'Crack,' Street Gangs, and Violence," p. 623.

78. Interviewed in April 1995.

79. Felix M. Padilla, *The Gang as an American Enterprise* (New Brunswick, N.J.: Rutgers University Press, 1992).

80. Daniel J. Monti, *Wannabe Gangs in Suburbs and Schools* (Cambridge, England: Blackwell, 1994).

81. Ibid., pp. 76, 90.

82. Ibid., p. 55.

83. James A. Inciardi, Anne E. Pottieger, Mary Ann Forney, Dale D. Chitwood, and Duane C. McBride, "Prostitution, IV Drug Use, and Sex-for-Crack Exchanges among Serious Delinquents: Risks for HIV Infection," *Criminology* 29 (May 1991), p. 226.

84. Jennifer James, "Prostitution and Addiction: An Interdisciplinary Approach," *Addictive Diseases: An International Journal* 2 (1976), pp. 601–618.

85. Marsha Rosenbaum, *Women on Heroin* (New Brunswick, N.J.: Rutgers University Press, 1981).

86. Eleanor Miller, *Street Women* (Philadelphia: Temple University Press, 1986).

87. James A. Inciardi, Dorothy Lockwood, and Anne E. Pottieger, *Women and Crack-Cocaine* (New York: Macmillan, 1993), p. 67.

88. Ibid., p. 68.

89. Marcia Chaiken and Bruce Johnson, *Characteristics of Different Types of Drug-Involved Youth* (Washington, D.C.: National Institute of Justice, 1988), p. 14.

90. The author has interviewed a number of adult former drug addicts and staff of therapeutic communities, and these explanations were typically given for why a drug addict went straight and stayed clean.

91. See D. B. Kandel and J. A. Logan, "Patterns of Drug Use from Adolescence to Young Adulthood: Periods of Risk for Initiation, Continued Use, and Discontinuation," *American Public Health* 74 (1984), pp. 660–666.

92. L. A. Goodman and W. H. Kruskal, *Measures of Association for Cross Classification* (New York: Springer-Verlag, 1979).

93. L. Thomas Winfree Jr., Christine S. Sellers, and Dennis L. Clason, "Social Learning and Adolescent Deviance Abstention: Toward Understanding the Reasons for Initiating, Quitting, and Abiding Drugs," *Journal of Quantitative Criminology* 9 (1993), p. 101.

94. Interviewed in July 1983.

95. For the positive relationship between peers and drug use, see T. J. Dishion and R. Loeber, "Adolescent Marijuana and Alcohol Use: The Role of Parents and Peers Revisited," *American Journal of Drug and Alcohol Abuse* 11 (1985), pp. 11–25; D. S. Elliott, D. Huizinga, and S. S. Ageton, *Explaining Delinquency and Drug Use;* Terence P. Thornberry, Margaret Farnworth, Marvin D. Krohn, and Alan J. Lizotte, "Peer Influence and Initiation to Drug Use," Working Paper No. 2 (National Department of Justice, n.d.); and D. B. Kandel, "Adolescent Marijuana Use: Role of Parents and Peers," *Science* 181 (1973), pp. 1067–1081.

96. Isidor Chein, Donald L. Gerard, Robert S. Lee, and Eva Rosenfeld, *The Road to H: Narcotics, Juvenile Delinquency, and Social Policy* (New York: Basic Books, 1964), p. 14.

97. Philippe Bourgois, "Just Another Night on Crack Street," *New York Times,* 12 November 1989, pp. 52–53, 60–65, 94.

98. Greenwood, "Substance Abuse Problems among High-Risk Youth and Potential Interventions," p. 449.

99. Thomas J. Dishion, Deborah Capaldi, Kathleen M. Spracklen, and Fuzhong Li, "Peer Ecology of Male Adolescent Drug Use," *Development and Psychopathology* 7 (1995), p. 803.

100. N. Tobler, "Meta-Analysis of 143 Adolescent Drug Prevention Programs: Quantitative Outcome Results of Program Participants Compared to a Control or Comparison Group," *Journal of Drug Issues* 16 (1986), pp. 537–567.

101. Ibid.

102. Deanna Atkinson, an administrator in the Élan program, suggested this list of noteworthy programs in a September 1995 telephone conversation.

103. For the early history of Élan, see Philip B. Taft, Jr., "Élan: Does Its Bizarre Regimen Transform Troubled Youth or Abuse Them?" *Corrections Magazine* 5 (March 1979), pp. 18–28.

104. Information on Élan provided by Deanna Atkinson in a September 1995 telephone conversation.

PREVENTION, DIVERSION, AND TREATMENT

chapter 12

PREVENTION, DIVERSION, AND CORRECTION

OBJECTIVES

After reading this chapter, the student will be able to answer the following questions:

- What types of prevention programs are likely to work with high-risk youngsters?

- What are the advantages and disadvantages of diversionary programs?

- What treatment modalities are most widely used with juvenile delinquents?

- What are the ingredients of effective programs?

CHAPTER 12 OUTLINE

A thirty-year-old therapist talks about the influence a foster parent had on him as a youngster:

Does treatment work? It *worked for me. I was heading in one direction and that direction included training school, drugs, and gangs. Then, Mr. Jones came along, and he totally turned my life around. He [former foster*

*parent] taught me how to love. He wouldn't give up on me, and his love
turned me around. I don't know where I would be today if it weren't for him,
probably the penitentiary.*[1]

> How important are such subjects as prevention and treatment in the study of juvenile delinquency? With what type of youthful offender is treatment likely to be effective? With what type of offender is treatment likely to be ineffective?

Saul Alinsky, a community organizer, used to tell a parable about social change. In this parable, a man is walking by the riverside when he notices a body floating down stream. A fisherman also notices the body, leaps into the stream, pulls the body ashore, gives mouth-to-mouth resuscitation, saving the person's life. The same thing happens a few minutes later, and then again and again. When yet another body floats by, the fisherman this time completely ignores the drowning man and starts running upstream along the bank. The observer asks the fisherman why he is not trying to rescue the drowning body. "This time," replies the fisherman, "I'm going upstream to find out who the hell is pushing those poor folks into the water."[2]

This parable has an important message for students of delinquency: As long as we do nothing about original causes, we will just be pulling out bodies, mopping up the casualties. But Alinsky gave a twist to his story. While the fisherman was busy running up the bank to find the ultimate source of the problem, Alinsky asked, who was going to help those who continued to float down the river?

The study of delinquency, then, includes not only finding the broad answers to the problem of youth crime, but also helping youth in trouble who continue to flounder in their lives. Accordingly, in addition to examining the broad questions about youth crime, this chapter discusses the prevention and treatment of delinquency.

Voices of Delinquency contains stories in which prevention and treatment had positive impact on youngsters' lives. In several stories, a strong parent figure intervened. One youth tells of the influence of a coach who would not quit on him. Several stories describe the positive impact of institutional staff. One youth describes how he experienced a turning point when his brother, the hero of his life, was convicted of murder and sent to prison.

The Justice Policy Institute of the Center on Juvenile and Criminal Justice of Northwestern University of Law profiled twenty-five individuals who were petitioned into juvenile court as hard-core delinquents when they were young, and who turned their lives around. The book, *Second Chances—100 Years of the Children's Court: Giving Kids a Chance to Make a Better Choice*, profiles these twenty-five. Derrick Thomas's story is in Social World of the Delinquent, 12.1.

Delinquency Prevention

The prevention of youth crime is certainly a desirable goal. An emphasis on prevention was written into federal law in the Juvenile Delinquency Prevention Act of 1972, the Juvenile Justice and Delinquency Prevention Act of 1974, and the Juvenile Justice Amendments of 1977 and 1980.[3] In the midst of this federal emphasis, prevention has still been largely ignored in the study of delinquency. Yet there is evidence that the declining but still disturbing levels of teenage violent behavior and use of firearms, the continuing problems with drugs and alcohol, and the emerging of nationwide gangs are creating renewed interest in the development and evaluation of delinquency prevention programs.

Three different levels of delinquency prevention have been identified. **Primary prevention** is focused on modifying conditions in the physical and social environment that

Social World of the Delinquent 12.1
The Derrick Thomas Story

Tears streamed down his face as his mother cradled 14-year-old Derrick Thomas, already over six feet tall, in her arms. After years of beating the system, of committing crimes and not getting caught, of conning adults with his engaging smile and winning personality, Thomas's number had finally come up. He was going to juvenile jail.

Placed on home confinement while awaiting trial on a burglary charge, his first juvenile court referral, Thomas repeatedly left the house. His pre-trial services officer had reached her breaking point. She pulled Thomas out of class and summoned him and his mother to her office to break the bad news. For the next 30 days, Thomas would be locked up.

At the time, "getting locked up seemed like the worst thing that could happen to me," says Thomas, who went on to become a ten-time All-Pro linebacker for the Kansas City Chiefs and one of the National Football League's all-time sack leaders. But getting involved in the juvenile justice system actually turned out to be "one of the most important breaks I ever got." Through the court, Thomas would meet several people who helped him turn his life around. His juvenile court experiences led him to set up his own foundation for troubled inner-city youths and inspired him to use his life to make a difference on behalf of other troubled youths.

In public speaking engagements, Thomas told audiences the same thing he said in testimony before the United States Congress and the Missouri General Assembly, words that are a fitting epilogue to this profile: "I come to you today to say you can make a difference and to tell you that there are any number of success stories in the juvenile justice system, just like mine," he said.

Derrick Thomas died on February 8, 2000, from complications following an automobile accident. Was he right in his belief that we can make a difference in the lives of troubled youngsters? Why are some individuals so much more effective than others in making a difference in the lives of others?

Source: Office of Juvenile Justice and Delinquency Prevention, "Second Chances: Giving Kids a Chance to Make a Better Choice," in *Juvenile Justice Bulletin* (Washington, D.C.: U.S. Department of Justice, 2000), pp. 21–23. For a copy of the book *Second Chances*, see the Children and Family Justice Center (CFJC) at www.cjcj.org or write to CJCJ, c/o *Second Chances*, 1622 Folsom Street, San Francisco, CA 94103.

lead to delinquency. **Secondary prevention** refers to intervention in the lives of juveniles or groups identified as being in circumstances that dispose them toward delinquency. Secondary prevention also takes place in diversionary programs, in which youngsters in trouble are diverted from formal juvenile justice programs. **Tertiary prevention** is directed at the prevention of recidivism.[4] Tertiary prevention takes place in traditional rehabilitation programs.

A History of Well-Meant Interventions

Delinquency prevention has a sad history. The highway of delinquency prevention is paved with punctured panaceas.[5] A member of the Subcommittee on Human Resources of the Committee on Education and Labor put it this way: The public is looking for an inexpensive panacea. . . . [T]hese periodic panaceas for delinquents come along every 2 to 3 years in my experience. The harm they do is to divert the attention of the public from any long-term comprehensive program of helping youth, working to strengthen school systems, communities, job opportunities, housing and recreational programs.[6]

One reason for society's seeking of **panaceas** stems from the tendency to seek easy answers to complex problems.[7] Another reason is the frustration and sense of futility in

A police officer with a police dog in the classroom. He is involved in a delinquency prevention program for teens.

a continuous, losing battle with juvenile crime that makes policymakers eager to discover a solution. Furthermore, the receptivity toward panaceas is found in the belief society has in prevention—as exemplified by the expression "An ounce of prevention is worth a pound of cure."

Prevention panaceas have ranged from biological and psychological interventions to group therapy, gang intervention, recreational activities, job training and employment, community organization, and even structured reorganization of the entire society. The most widely known models of delinquency prevention are the Cambridge-Somerville Youth Study in Massachusetts; the New York City Youth Board; Mobilization for Youth in New York City; Boston's Midcity Project; Walter C. Reckless and Simon Dinitz's self-concept studies in Columbus, Ohio; the Chicago Area Projects; and La Playa de Ponce in Puerto, Rico.

A number of studies have examined the effectiveness of delinquency prevention programs. Michael C. Dixon and William W. Wright concluded from their examination of these programs that "few studies show significant results."[8] Richard J. Lundman, Paul T. McFarlane, and Frank Scarpitti drew the same pessimistic conclusion: "[I]t appears unlikely that any of these [delinquency prevention] projects prevented delinquent behavior."[9] Lundman and Scarpitti collaborated on a later study of delinquency prevention and, adding fifteen projects to the twenty-five previously studied, concluded: "A review of forty past or continuing attempts at the prevention of juvenile delinquency leads to the nearly inescapable conclusion that none of these projects has successfully prevented delinquency."[10] These researchers even went on to say that given the poor history of past attempts at delinquency prevention, there is little reason to expect any greater success with any efforts.[11]

Prevention programs have received a number of other criticisms besides those dealing with their ineffectiveness. They are accused of widening the nets of social control over children because they have resulted in sweeping more children to some program, agency, or system. Critics also charge that prevention programs are far too expensive. As part of its national evaluation of delinquency prevention, the U.S. Justice Department spent more than $20 million to provide intervention and services to 20,000 juveniles in sixty-eight cities. Providing piecemeal solutions to the profound problems that lead to juvenile crime is a further criticism directed at prevention programs. Finally, the rights of children, critics say, are sometimes compromised in prevention interventions.[12]

In the 1990s, the Office of Juvenile Justice and Delinquency Prevention began to target the prevention of serious and violent juvenile offending. It was recognized that these serious and violent juvenile (OVJ) offenders are responsible for a disproportionate number of crimes and that reducing chronic juvenile delinquency is a critical challenge of today's society.[13] A multifaceted, coordinated approach toward these youths was identified, with prevention as a critical first step.[14] Pilot programs were established in a number of sites across the United States in the final few years of the twentieth century. The promise and problems of this new focus on prevention will be evaluated later in this chapter.

Comprehensive Strategy for Delinquency Prevention

A comprehensive framework, or strategy, for delinquency prevention was developed in the 1980s in the United States. This comprehensive framework is made up of a typology of cause-focused strategies and of an awareness of the common components of the programs that work. Advocates are hopeful that this strategy will bring more effectiveness and greater emphasis on delinquency prevention in this society.

TYPOLOGY OF CAUSE-FOCUSED STRATEGIES   At the National Center for the Assessment of Delinquent Behavior and Its Prevention, J. David Hawkins, Joseph G. Weis, and colleagues have conducted extensive research to identify promising approaches to delinquency prevention. Their work suggests three general principles for delinquency prevention:

1. Prevention approaches should focus on the causes of delinquency if they are to be effective.
2. There are multiple correlates and causes of delinquency. They operate within the institutional domains of family, school, peers, and community. Effective prevention should address these multiple causes in all of these settings.
3. Delinquency results from experiences during the process of social development. Different causal elements are more salient at different stages in the developmental process. Therefore, different prevention techniques are required at different stages in the socialization of youths.[15]

The National Juvenile Justice Assessment Centers have developed a typology for conceptualizing and organizing approaches to delinquency prevention according to the causes of delinquency they address. Included within this typology is a framework for systematically planning and evaluating delinquency prevention efforts.[16] This typology promises to provide a solid basis for developing an effective technology of delinquency prevention. The twelve strategies of this typology are listed in Theory and Research 12.2.

Each of these twelve strategies is based on an assumption regarding a cause of delinquency and aims at modifying or eliminating that cause.[17] Because the strategies are ideal types, prevention programs may utilize combinations of several of these strategies or in some cases may not address any presumed causes of delinquency.[18]

Programs That Work

Perry Preschool, School Development Program, Program Development Evaluation, Parent Training, Family First, and Raising a Thinking Child are promising prevention programs that have been established in recent years. What these programs have in common are a cause-based orientation, extensive evaluation, and positive findings on their effectiveness.

PERRY PRESCHOOL   The Perry Preschool's early childhood demonstration program, operated by the High/Scope Foundation in Ypsilanti, Michigan, has received national

Strategies of Delinquency Prevention

1. Biological/psychological strategies assume that delinquent behavior derives from underlying physiological, biological, or biopsychiatric conditions. These strategies seek to remove, diminish, or control these conditions.

2. Psychological/mental health strategies assume that delinquency originates in internal psychological states viewed as inherently maladaptive or pathological. They seek to directly alter such states and/or the environmental conditions thought to generate them.

3. Social network development strategies assume that delinquency results from weak attachments between youth and conforming members of society. They seek to increase interaction, attachments, and/or involvement between youth and nondeviant others (peers, parents, other adults) as well as the influence that nondeviant others have on potentially delinquent youth.

4. Criminal influence reduction strategies assume that delinquency stems from the influence of others who directly or indirectly encourage youth to commit delinquent acts. They seek to reduce the influence of norms toward delinquency and those who hold such norms.

5. Power enhancement strategies assume that delinquency stems from a lack of power or control over impinging environmental factors. They seek to increase the ability or power of youths to influence or control their environments either directly or indirectly (by increasing the power or influence over communities and institutions in which youths participate). Efforts to increase community or institutional influence or power over youth are not power enhancement.

6. Role development/role enhancement strategies assume that delinquency stems from a lack of opportunity to be involved in legitimate roles or activities which youth perceive as personally gratifying. They attempt to create such opportunities. To meet the conditions of role development, roles developed or provided must be perceived by youth as worthwhile (i.e., sufficiently valuable or important to justify expenditure of time and effort).

7. Activities/recreation strategies assume that delinquency results when youths' time is not filled by nondelinquent activities. They seek to provide nondelinquent activities as alternatives to delinquent activities.

8. Education/skill development strategies assume that delinquency stems from a lack of knowledge or skills necessary to live in society without violating its laws. Education strategies provide youth with personal skills that prepare them to find patterns of behavior free from delinquent activities, or provide skills or assistance to others to enable them to help youth develop requisite skills.

9. Clear and consistent social expectations strategies assume that delinquency results from competing or conflicting demands and expectations placed on youth by legitimate organizations and institutions such as media, families, schools, and communities that impinge on the lives of youth. Inconsistent expectations or norms place youth in situations where conformity to a given set of norms or expectations results in an infraction of another set of norms or expectations.

10. Economic resource strategies assume that delinquency results when people do not have adequate economic resources. They seek to provide basic resources to preclude the need for delinquency.

11. Deterrence strategies assume that delinquency results because there is a low degree of risk or difficulty associate with committing delinquent acts. They seek to change the cost-benefit ratio of participation in crime. They seek to increase the cost and decrease the benefit of criminal acts through restructuring opportunities and minimizing incentives to engage in crime.

12. Abandonment of legal control/social tolerance strategies assumes that delinquency results from social responses that define youths' behaviors as delinquent. . . . [S]uch responses—whether in the general form of rules or in the more specific form of an instance of legal processing—may cause youths whose behaviors are so treated to perceive themselves as "outsiders" and, consequently, to engage in delinquent acts.

Do you think such strategies will make delinquency prevention more effective? What are the advantages of such strategies?

Source: J. David Hawkins et al., Report of the National Juvenile Justice Assessment Centers: A Typology of Cause-Focused Strategies of Delinquency Prevention (Washington, D.C.: U.S. Government Printing Office, 1980), pp. vii–ix.

recognition for its impact on pregnancy, education, and delinquency.[19] Directed by David Weikart, the program involved a small random sample of disadvantaged African American children who attended a high-quality, two-year preschool program and received weekly home visits from program personnel. Compared to controls at age twenty-seven, according to official police records and an excellent research design, the children who had attended this enrichment program had half as many arrests as members of the control group and were less likely to be chronic offenders. Self-reported behavior at age twenty-seven, consistent with police and court data, revealed that preschool attendees reported less fighting and involvement with the police than did nonattendees.

Analysis of data from this early childhood program revealed that the arrest data were influenced by two variables: educational attainment and rating of social behavior by teachers through elementary school. This study demonstrates the well-established link between childhood experience and later social behavior. Both power enhancement and education and skill development strategies were at work here; those with preschool intervention improved in later classroom behavior and intellectual performance throughout elementary grades. This, in turn, ultimately affected the amount of schooling that students completed and indirectly reduced delinquency rates.[20]

One of the consistent findings of delinquency research is that the earlier the onset of any kind of problem behavior, the greater are the consequences and lasting effect. Although no other preschool or Head Start program has been identified as being designed to prevent later delinquency, the Perry Preschool demonstration program showed that early positive intervention can have later positive results.[21]

SCHOOL DEVELOPMENT PROGRAM   Developed by James Comer and colleagues at the Yale Child Study Center, the School Development Program has been implemented in more than 100 elementary and middle schools in the United States. This model uses three team components to improve school and community integration: a planning and management team (made up of the principal, teachers, parents, counselors, and support staff); a mental health team (composed of a psychologist, the principal, teachers, a nurse, social workers, and counselors); and a parents' group (e.g., the PTA).[22]

The School Development model requires extensive parent outreach and involvement. Parents are involved in the management team and the PTA. They participate in workshops designed to improve their children's skills. They are also encouraged to participate in whatever activities support their children's academic and social development. In this program that emphasizes problem solving, collaboration, and consensus, teachers and school administrators arrange their schedules to accommodate those of working parents.[23]

In the midst of the enthusiasm engendered by this power enhancement and education and skill development strategy, critics have observed that implementation of this program is costly; depends heavily on the principal's support, understanding, and commitment to the process; and requires the engagement of a considerable number of participants to facilitate the process.[24] This School Development model requires several years to implement and is now in the process of nationwide evaluation.

PROGRAM DEVELOPMENT EVALUATION   In connection with the Center for Social Organization of Schools at Johns Hopkins University, Gary Gottfredson and Denise Gottfredson developed a prevention model that is designed to improve youths' attachment to school, to increase the school's responsiveness to the range of student needs, and to improve the school's relationships with its community.[25]

Program Development Evaluation (PDE) has been implemented in all grade levels and throughout the school districts in California, Illinois, Maryland, Michigan, New York, and South Carolina.[26] The PDE model is a school management strategy that is designed to identify school problems and to develop a program for managing them. A School Improvement Team—made up of teachers, parents, school administrators, and district-level staff—follows predetermined steps to determine school problems, to establish goals and objectives, to develop programs, and to monitor the implementation process. Guided by a trained coordinator, the PDE process is continually evaluated and adjusted to changing needs.[27]

Extensive evaluations of this education and skill development strategy have consistently revealed positive results. A study of its implementation in Baltimore schools revealed significant improvement in teacher morale and innovation as well as a decrease in negative attitudes and rebellious behaviors among students. An evaluation of PDE in Charleston, South Carolina found that this prevention strategy resulted in improved classroom organization and clarity of rules.[28]

PARENT TRAINING Another highly respected prevention program is the training that the Oregon Social Learning Center gives parents in techniques that are designed to monitor and change their children's behavior. G. R. Patterson and his colleagues at this learning center discovered that the parents of socially aggressive children did not identify with the role of parent and were not attached to their children. They then designed a therapy program that focused on teaching parents how to interact with, and change their behavior toward, their children.[29]

Parents begin this family intervention program by reading a programmed text, *Living with Children,* and then select a specific behavior of their child that they want to work on with trained therapists. The purpose of the process is to teach parents to record their child's behavior and to administer punishments and rewards in a consistent and appropriate way. Staff members frequently contact families through telephone calls and home visits, and parents are encouraged to participate in structured parent-training groups.[30]

The most frequent criticism of this program relates to its applicability to high-risk populations. Patterson's research is derived from Eugene, Oregon, a university community that is not typical of high-crime areas. Attempts to apply it to high-risk populations have found that it is ineffective with dysfunctional families, with disinterested or apathetic parents, and with parents who are unable to master the educational materials.[31]

J. David Hawkins and colleagues have also developed a parent-training program as part of their larger emphasis on the social development approach to preventing delinquent behavior. (See the next section for a discussion of the social development model.) This program is operating in the Seattle elementary schools and provides seven sessions for parents of first- and second-graders. Entitled "Catch 'Em Being Good," these sessions have the goal of teaching parents what to expect from their children and how to establish a reward and punishment system. In later grades, parents are offered four sessions entitled "How to Help Your Child Succeed in School," which focus on parent-child communication and homework help.[32]

Preliminary evaluations have shown that participating parents reported improved parenting skills and reduced rates of aggressiveness among their children. A special effort has been made to involve the parents of high-risk children, but, like the Oregon parent-training program, this Seattle-based training program has had the same lack of participation from parents of high-risk children, especially high-risk minority children.[33]

FAMILIES FIRST The Edna McConnell Clark foundation has provided the funding for the development of a family preservation program that has been implemented in ten states. This model—called "Families First" or "Homebuilders"—is designed for families who are at imminent risk of losing a child to out-of-home-placement. The basic goals of this program are to keep children safe, to keep families together, and to improve the family's capacity to function.[34]

What is different about this model from traditional service-provision programs is that it establishes a short-term intensive case management relationship with involved families. On the assumption that the families who are most likely to need services are unlikely to seek them out, counselors visit families in their homes. Counselors, who work with only two to four families at a time, are available twenty-four hours a day for up to six weeks. Services focus on problem solving, with the intent to connect families with their communities by integrating them into the social service system and teaching them life management skills. Although the evaluation findings have been mixed, with the major debate centering on the accuracy with which at-risk families are selected, there is still strong support for the finding that "families served are significantly more likely to avoid out-of-home placements for their children for up to one year.[35]

RAISING A THINKING CHILD   This is a culture-free primary prevention program for parents and their children, ages 4 to 7. Derived from a curriculum that was developed for use in schools and originally called "Interpersonal Cognitive Problem Solving" (ICPS), the curriculum is now called "I Can Problem Solve." The purpose of this prevention program is to help children think about ways to solve interpersonal problems when they are young so that they will be able to make good decisions when they reach adolescence and adulthood.[36] In 1997, Raising a Thinking Child was recognized as an exemplary juvenile delinquency prevention program by the Strengthening America's Family Project and in this same year it was recognized as among the six top violence prevention programs in a five-state area by the Mid-Atlantic Region of the U.S. Department of Health and Human Services.[37]

Common Components of the Programs That Work

Joy Dryfoos's analysis of the 100 most successful delinquency prevention programs identified the following common program components:

- High-risk children are attached to a responsible adult who is responsive to that child's needs. Techniques that are typically used include individual counseling and small group meetings, individual tutoring and mentoring, and case management.
- A number of different kinds of programs and services are in place in a communitywide, multiagency, collaborative approach. Partners in the communitywide network include schools, businesses, community health and social agencies, church groups, police and courts, and universities.
- In these programs, an emphasis is placed on early identification and intervention, in which children and families are reached in the early stages of development of problem behaviors. As demonstrated in data on pregnancy, school achievement, substance abuse, and delinquency prevention, early identification and intervention has both short- and long-term benefits.
- The more successful programs located outside the school generally provide controversial services, such as family planning, and overnight shelter for homeless and runaway youth. These programs appeal to those youngsters "turned off" by the school system. These programs also have the advantage that they can offer weekend and summer programs.
- Many successful programs feature professional or nonprofessional staff who require training to implement the program. For example, such programs as Life Skills training, school-based management, cooperative learning, and team teaching require extensive inservice training and ongoing supervision.
- Personal and social skills training are also found in many of these programs. This approach involves teaching youths about their own risky behavior, providing them with coping skills, and helping them make healthy decisions about the future.
- Several of the successful approaches use older peers to influence or help younger peers, either in social skills training or as tutors. The training and supervision by the peer mentors appear to be important aspects of this component.[38]

In sum, providing individual attention to high-risk youngsters and realizing the necessity of developing broad community-wide interventions are the two program components that appear to have the widest application.

The Violent Juvenile and Delinquency Prevention

Another prevention strategy emerged in the 1990s. Spearheaded and funded by the Office of Juvenile Justice and Delinquency Prevention, the belief emerged that the most effective strategy for juvenile corrections is to place the thrust of the prevention and diversion emphases on high-risk juveniles who commit violent behaviors. These juveniles, the ones that officials are quick to dump into the adult system, commit the more serious and most frequent delinquent acts. At the same time that the seriousness of their behaviors has affected changes in juvenile codes across the nation, research is beginning to find that these high-risk youths can be impacted by well-equipped and well-implemented prevention and treatment programs.[39]

These programs are based on the assumption that the juvenile justice system does not see most serious offenders until it is too late to intervene effectively.[40] This strategy also presumes that if we want to reduce the overall violence in American society, it is necessary to successfully intervene in the lives of high-risk youthful offenders, who commit about 75 percent of all violent juvenile offenses.[41]

The general characteristics of these programs is that they address key areas of risk in youths' lives, that they seek to strengthen the personal and institutional factors contributing to healthy adolescent development, that they provide adequate support and supervision, and that they offer youths a long-term stake in the community.[42] It is emphasized that these prevention programs for high-risk youths must be integrated with local police, child welfare, social service, school, and family preservation programs. Comprehensive approaches to delinquency prevention and intervention require strong collaborative efforts between the juvenile justice system and other service provision systems, including health, mental health, child welfare, and education. An important component of a community's comprehensive plan is to develop mechanisms that effectively link these service providers at the program level.[43]

The comprehensive or multi-systemic aspects of these programs are designed to deal simultaneously with many aspects of youths' lives. The intent is that they are intensive, often involving multiple contacts weekly, or even daily, with at-risk youth. They build on youths' strengths, rather than focusing on their deficiencies. These programs operate mostly, though not exclusively, outside the formal justice system, under a variety of public, nonprofit, or university auspices. Finally, they combine accountability and sanctions with increasingly intensive rehabilitation and treatment services. This is achieved through a system of graduated sanctions, in which an integrated approach is used to stop the penetration of youthful offenders into the system.[44] See Figure 12.1 for an overview of this comprehensive prevention strategy.

In 1996, three communities—Lee and Duval Counties in Florida, and San Diego County in California—collaborated with the Office of Juvenile Justice and Delinquency Prevention to apply the processes and principles that were set forth in the *Comprehensive Strategy*. Initial evaluations of the three pilot projects reported that each of the sites has benefitted significantly from the Comprehensive planning process. Although it was deemed premature to assess the long-term impact on juvenile delinquency, there are several short-term indicators of success.[45] The following are among the pilot sites' accomplishments:

- Enhanced communitywide understanding of prevention services and sanctions options for juveniles.
- expanded networking capacity and better coordination among agencies and service providers.
- Institution of performance measurement systems.
- Hiring of staff to spearhead the ongoing Comprehensive Strategy planning and implementation efforts.
- Development of comprehensive 5-year strategic action plans.[46]

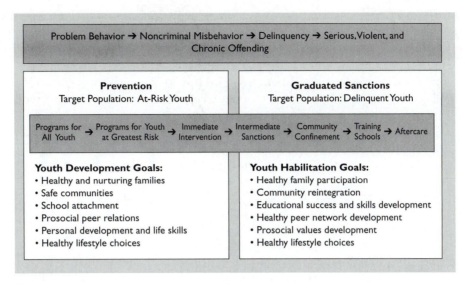

FIGURE 12.1 Overview of Comprehensive Strategy

Source: Mark A. Matese and John A. Tuell, *Update on the Comprehensive Strategy for Serious, Violent, and Chronic Juvenile Offenders* (Washington, D.C.: Office of Justice Programs; Office of Juvenile Justice and Delinquency Prevention, 1998), p. 1.

How Diversion Works

The emphasis on **diversion programs** began in 1967 when the President's Commission on Law Enforcement and Administration of Justice recommended the establishment of alternatives to the juvenile justice system.[47] This recommendation was based on the labeling perspective and Edwin Sutherland's differential association theory. The National Strategy for Youth Development and Delinquency Prevention tied labeling theory to diversion in identifying three processes that block juveniles from satisfactory maturation and weaken their ties to societal norms: the entrapment of negative labeling; the limited access to acceptable social norms; and the resulting process of reflection, alienation, and estrangement.[48] Sutherland's differential association theory provided another justification for diversion, because it holds that individuals learn delinquent behavior from "significant others." Policymakers began to be concerned about placing status offenders and minor offenders with serious offenders because the former would learn delinquent motives, techniques, and rationalization from the latter.[49]

Traditional Forms of Diversion

Early proponents of diversion programs also claimed that these interventions offered numerous other advantages that would lead to a more effective and humane justice process. These included the reduction of caseloads, a more efficient administration of the juvenile justice system, and provision of therapeutic environments in which children and parents could resolve family conflicts.[50]

Diversion can come either from the police and the courts or from agencies outside the juvenile justice system, such as drop-in centers, alternative schools, social and mental health clinics, and youth service bureaus. With diversion initiated by the courts or police, the justice subsystems retain control over youthful offenders. But even with diversion outside the formal jurisdiction of the justice system, youthful offenders are usually referred back to the juvenile court if they do not participate in these programs. See Treatment Intervention 12.3 for a discussion of **Youth Service Bureaus,** one of the

TREATMENT INTERVENTION   12.3

Youth Service Bureaus

The first youth service bureaus were established in Chicago and in Pontiac, Michigan, in 1958. Several more were organized in the early 1960s, but the major impetus to these community agencies came in 1967, when the President's Commission on Law Enforcement and Administration of Justice recommended the establishment of youth service bureaus (YSBs) to work with youthful offenders outside the justice system. They were organized under a variety of names, such as youth resource bureau, youth assistance program, Listening Post, and Focus on Youth, but the youth service bureau was the name most often used.

Sherwood Norman's analysis of youth service bureaus has been influential in shaping the conception of YSBs objectives and functions. He identified three possible functions of this diversionary agency: service brokerage, resource development, and system modification. The service brokerage function means that the YSB acts as an advocate for youths to ensure that they receive the services they need. The YSB is also responsible for working with citizens in developing new resources that are presently unavailable. Finally, when the attitudes and practices of established institutions are found to be contributing to antisocial behavior in juveniles, system modification becomes an important function of the YSB.

Youth service bureaus across the country, especially in the 1970s, offered a variety of programs. Drop-in centers were established where youths could find recreational and social activity. YSB hotlines, where volunteers counseled troubled youths over the phone, were quite common. For a typical announcement of a YSB hotline, see Figure 12.2. YSB truancy programs received referrals from school, worked with juveniles concerning school problems, and provided tutoring, counseling, and other needed services. Some YSBs made arrangements for temporary care for runaways and other adolescents who needed temporary homes. A twenty-four-hour crisis intervention program was sometimes available to distraught young people. Programs for pregnant teenagers provided counseling and referral to local agencies, prenatal instruction and care, family planning informa-

Y.S.B.
Hotline·········
● ●

WOULD YOU LIKE TO HELP THE YOUTH OF THIS COMMUNITY?

WOULD YOU LIKE TO WORK WITH A SOCIAL SERVICE AGENCY?

DO YOU HAVE TIME TO SPEND AS A VOLUNTEER?

THE YOUTH SERVICE BUREAU IS IN NEED OF HOTLINE VOLUNTEERS. THE Y.S.B. IS A NON-PROFIT ORGANIZATION FOUNDED TO DIVERT YOUNG PEOPLE FROM THE JUVENILE JUSTICE SYSTEM. THE Y.S.B. HANDLES ALL TYPES OF PROBLEMS THAT ARE CONCERNED WITH YOUTH, INCLUDING SCHOOL, DRUGS, SEX, POLICE, FAMILY, AND MANY OTHER DEVELOPMENTAL AND SITUATIONAL PROBLEMS. VOLUNTEERS ARE NEEDED TO WORK ON THE HOTLINE EVENINGS EVERY DAY OF THE WEEK. FOR MORE INFORMATION CALL THE HOTLINE NUMBER OR COME BY THE OFFICE. ASK FOR RON OR STEVE.

● ●

FIGURE 12.2 Y. S. B. Hotline

Source: Youth Service Bureau, Springfield, Illinois.

tion, and whatever else was needed to help the youth and her family deal with the pregnancy.

The drying up of federal funding at the end of the 1970s made survival increasingly difficult for these diversionary agencies, and they quickly began to disappear in the 1980s. By the end of the 1980s, this highly regarded diversionary program existed only in the memories of those who had worked and been served by this agency.

Would this type of diversionary agency have a function in the community in which you live? What other agencies currently provide such services?

Source: Sherwood Norman, *Youth Service Bureau: A Key to Prevention* (Paramus, N.J.: National Council on Crime and Delinquency, 1972), pp. 12–13; *Phase I Assessment of Youth Service Bureaus, Summary Report of Youth Service Bureau Research Group for LEAA* (Boston: Boston Unversity, 1975).

most widely used diversionary programs of the 1960s and 1970s before they began to be closed for lack of funding in the 1980s.

The most positive characteristic of traditional diversionary programs is that they minimize the penetration of youthful offenders into the justice system.[51] Yet empirical studies of diversion generally have not demonstrated that doing something (treatment or services) is necessarily better than doing nothing. Researchers warn that the overlooked, negative consequences of diversion challenge the viability of this concept.[52] Some of these negative effects include widening the net of juvenile justice by increasing the number of youths under the control of the system, increasing the size of the system (budget and staff), creating new legal entities, altering traditional programs, ignoring clients' due process rights or constitutional safeguards, and labeling minor offenders.[53]

In sum, excited by the original vision of diversion, reformers promised that it would bring far-reaching, positive changes in juvenile justice. But the problem does not rest with the original vision: It is in the business of implementation that things have gone wrong—goals are displaced, and vested interests operate. Administrators of these programs too often made the wrong decisions about the wrong young people at the wrong time.[54]

New Forms of Diversion

In the 1990s, a new form of diversion developed in the United States. Expressions of this new form included community courts, alternative dispute resolution, gun courts, teen courts, and drug courts. Community courts offer a less bureaucratic and more timely response to offenses against the community. An offend in community court typically will be required to complete a restorative contract, including restitution payments. Alternative dispute resolution, such as family group conferences and restorative justice conferences, involve carefully structured meetings among offenders, victims, their families, and other members of the community. Gun courts provide intensive behavioral and attitudinal intervention that are designed to affect juveniles' orientation to weapons and increase their awareness of the reality of weapon injuries. Teen courts, which are also known as peer juries or youth courts, already number between 400 and 500 programs. They represent voluntary, nonjudicial alternatives for juveniles charged with minor law violations. Finally, drug courts offer such legal incentives as deferred prosecution for drug defendants willing to participate in drug treatment.[55] Teen courts, drug courts, and juvenile mediation programs are described in greater detail.

TEEN COURTS   Teen courts, also known as youth courts, have become a widely used intervention for young and usually first-time offenders. In 1998, an evaluation of teen courts was done; a total of 335 teen court programs responded, which was more than 70 percent of the programs contacted.[56] See Figure 12.3 for a graph of the rise of teen courts across the nation.

More than two-thirds of the court programs surveyed indicated that they had existed for less than five years; 20 percent had been operating for less than one year. Most teen courts have relatively small caseloads: 48 percent of the programs revealed that they received fewer than 100 referrals per year. Survey findings also indicated that teen courts in the United States handled about 65,000 cases in 1998.[57]

Four possible case-processing models can be used by teen courts:

- **Adult Judge.** An adult serves as judge and rules on legal terminology and courtroom procedure. Youth serve as attorneys, jurors, clerks, bailiffs, and so forth.
- **Youth Judge.** This is similar to the adult judge model, but a youth serves as judge.
- **Tribunal.** Youth attorneys present the case to a panel of three youth judges, who decide the appropriate disposition for the defendant. A jury is not used.
- **Peer Jury.** This model does not use youth attorneys: the case is presented to a youth jury by a youth or adult. The youth jury then questions the defendant directly.[58]

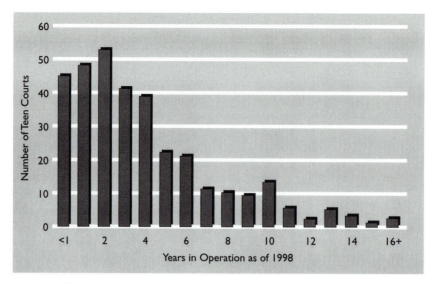

FIGURE 12.3 Most Teen Courts Are Less than Five Years Old.

Source: Jeffrey Butts, Dean Hoffman, and Janeen Buck "Teen Courts in the United States: A Profile of Current Programs," *OJJDP Fact Sheet* (Washington, D.C.: Office of Juvenile Justice and Delinquency Prevention, 1999), p. 1.

Most teen courts surveyed indicated that they used only one case-processing model: 47 percent used the adult judge model, 12 used the peer jury model, 10 percent used the tribunal model, and 9 percent used the youth judge model. The remaining 22 percent used more than one case-processing model. (See Table 12.1.)[59]

Teen courts usually handle first-time offenders who are charged with such offenses as theft, misdemeanor assault, disorderly conduct, and possession of alcohol. The majority (87 percent) of teen courts reported that they rarely or never accept juveniles with prior arrest records. Community service was most frequently used as a disposition in teen court cases. Other dispositions that were used included victim apology letters (86 percent), apology essays (79 percent), teen court jury duty (75 percent), drug/alcohol classes (59 percent), and monetary restitution (34 percent).[60]

THE JUVENILE DRUG COURT MOVEMENT   Currently, more than 244 drug court programs are underway or being planned, with 25 of these programs dedicated to juveniles. The **juvenile drug court movement** is part of the adult drug court movement that has been stimulated by Title V of the Violent Crime Control and Law Enforcement Act of 1994. This Act authorizes the Attorney General to make grants to states, state and local courts, units of local government and Indian tribal governments to establish drug courts.[61]

TABLE 12.1

The most popular teen court model is an adult judge with youth attorneys.

	Percent of U.S. Teen Courts Using Each Model		
Teen Court Model	*Used Exclusively*	*Used in Some Cases*	*Total*
Adult Judge	47%	17%	64%
Youth Judge	9	5	14
Tribunal	10	2	12
Peer Jury	12	14	26

Source: Jeffrey Butts, Dean Hoffman, and Janeen Buck, "Teen Courts in the United States: A Profile of Current Programs," *OJJDP Fact Sheet* (Washington, D.C.: Office of Juvenile Justice and Delinquency Prevention, 1999), p. 2.

A number of strategies are common to **juvenile drug courts** compared with traditional juvenile courts:

- Much earlier and much more comprehensive intake assessments;
- Much greater focus on the functioning of the juvenile and the family throughout the juvenile court system;
- Much closer integration of the information obtained during the assessment process as it relates to the juvenile and the family;
- Much greater coordination among the court, the treatment community, the school system, and other community agencies in responding to the needs of the juvenile and the court;
- Much more active and continuous judicial supervision of the juvenile's case and treatment process;
- Increased use of immediate sanctions for noncompliance and incentives for progress for both the juvenile and the family.[62]

Currently, six states operate juvenile drug courts, with the greatest activity in California (two programs) and Florida (four programs). For example, the Escambia County Juvenile Drug Court (Pensacola, Florida) began operations in April, 1996. It is a twelve-month, three-phase approach to treating substance use and abuse. Phase I lasts about two months, Phase II lasts four months, and Phase III lasts six months. The drug court judge supervises treatment of up to forty offenders by reviewing reports from treatment personnel to determine the need for either positive or negative incentives to encourage participation and involvement.[63]

JUVENILE MEDIATION PROGRAM   The purpose of a juvenile mediation program is for all involved parties to join together to resolve differences without court involvement. The Juvenile Mediation Program, which serves Brooke, Hancock, Marshall, Ohio, Tyler, and Wetzel counties in West Virginia works with school-age children and adolescents who are ages 6 to 18 and their families and/or guardians. First established in 1997 in Brooke County, it has since spread to the other five counties.[64]

Status and nonviolent offenders from the six counties are eligible to participate in the program. The mediator's responsibilities include determining the sincerity of the accused juvenile's remorse, deciding a fair and just penalty for his or her wrongdoing, and concluding whether any services are necessary. The mediation hearing does not proceed until the juvenile has admitted guilt of a crime. A waiver of rights must also be signed for the process to proceed. The waiver relinquishes the rights of having witnesses or lawyers present.[65]

The program is designed to last for no more than 90 days and is terminated under one of the following conditions: (1) Successful: juveniles completed the required contractual agreement in 90 days; (2) Unsuccessful: juveniles failed to meet the required agreement and are referred to the probation department for formal proceedings; and (3) Dismissal: the mediator recommended dismissal prior to disposition. As of September 30, 2000, the rate of successful contract resolutions was 93 percent, or 625 of the first 670 participants. As of July 1, 2001, all 625 juveniles have remained free of delinquent and status offenses.[66]

The Treatment Debate

Correctional treatment came under increased criticism in the late 1960s and early 1970s. In 1966, reporting on the results of 100 empirical evaluations of treatment, Walter C. Bailey concluded that there seemed to be little evidence that correctional treatment is effective.[67] In 1971, James Robison and Gerald Smith added that "there is no evidence to support any program's claim to superior rehabilitative strategy."[68] In 1974, the late Robert Martinson startled both correctional personnel and the public with the pronouncement "with few and isolated exceptions, the rehabilitative efforts that have been reported so far have had no appreciable effect on recidivism."[69] The media quickly simplified Martinson's statement into the idea that "nothing works" in correctional treatment. In 1975, Douglas Lipton, Martinson, and Judith Wilks published the *Effectiveness of Correctional Treatment,* which critically evaluated the effectiveness of correctional treatment programs.[70] In that same year, Martinson announced on *60 Minutes* that "there is no evidence that correctional rehabilitation reduces recidivism."[71] A spirited debate on the "nothing works" thesis has continued to rage since the late 1970s.

Ted Palmer, a correctional researcher in California, challenged Lipton and his colleagues' research by tabulating 82 studies mentioned in the book and showing that 39 of them, or 48 percent, had positive or partly positive results on recidivism.[72] Palmer used Martinson's own words to reject the "nothing works" thesis:

> These programs seem to work best when they are new, when their subjects are amenable to treatment in the first place, and when the counselors are not only trained people, but "good people" as well.[73]

Paul Gendreau and Robert R. Ross reviewed the literature published between 1973 and 1978 and found that 86 percent of the 95 intervention programs studied reported success.[74] According to Gendreau and Ross, this success rate was "convincing evidence that some treatment programs, when they are applied with integrity by competent practitioners in appropriate target populations, can be effective in preventing crime or reducing recidivism."[75] In the late 1970s, Martinson conceded that "contrary to [his] previous position, some treatment programs *do* have an appreciable effect on recidivism. Some programs are indeed beneficial."[76] But, despite Martinson's recantation of his "nothing works" thesis and Palmer's and Gendreau and Ross's defense of correctional treatment, the general mood regarding offender rehabilitation in the late 1970s and early 1980s was one of pessimism and discouragement.

In the late 1980s Gendreau and Ross reviewed the offender rehabilitation literature for the period between 1981 and 1987 and again found that the number and variety of successful reported attempts at reducing delinquent behavior dismiss the "nothing works" hypothesis.[77] Moreover, the rehabilitative evidence in the 1980s grew at a much greater rate than it did during the 1970s and developed several strategies for developing more effective programs.[78]

Several meta-analyses evaluating the effectiveness of correctional treatment have been done. The statistical tool of meta-analysis has been developed to enable reviewers to combine findings from different experiments. In meta-analysis, the "aggregation and side-by-side analysis of large numbers of experimental studies" is undertaken.[79] One of the advantages of meta-analysis is that it can "incorporate adjustments for the fact that studies vary considerably in the degree of rigour of their experimental design."[80] Theory and Research 12.4 summarizes the findings of the most widely cited studies of meta-analyses of correctional treatment.

The Most Frequently Used Treatment Modalities

Various treatment modalities are used widely in community-based corrections and have been established in nearly every training school in the United States. Psychotherapy, transactional analysis, reality therapy, behavior modification, family therapy, guided group interaction, and positive peer culture are the traditional treatment modalities most commonly used in juvenile justice. Drug and alcohol abuse interventions and rational emotive therapy also are used increasingly.

Psychotherapy

Various adaptations of Freudian **psychotherapy** have been used by psychiatrists, clinical psychologists, and psychiatric social workers since the early twentieth century. In ei-

THEORY AND RESEARCH 12.4

Meta-analyses of Correctional Treatment

- Garrett (1985) surveyed 111 papers and found a significant overall effect of treatment on a variety of outcomes including reoffending.
- Gottschalk and colleagues (1987) examined community-based interventions and found a weaker effect.
- Lab and Whitehead (1989) and Lab and Whitehead (1988) reported predominantly negative findings in their meta-analysis as they described only a few promising results.
- Izzo and Ross (1990), in comparing programs that contained a cognitive component with those that did not, found a marked superiority in terms of reduced recidivism following the former.
- Andrews and colleagues (1990) incorporated findings from 150 research reports and included studies undertaken with adult offenders. They found overall positive effects of correctional treatment.
- Lipsey examined 397 outcome studies based on work with offenders aged between twelve and

twenty-one and accounting for a sample in excess of 40,000 clients. A principal finding of this survey was that a total of 64.5 percent of the experiments showed positive effects of treatment in reducing recidivism.

Thus, in taking all of these meta-analyses together, the net effect of treatment is, on an average, a reduction in recidivism rates of between 10 percent and 12 percent.

Are these meta-analyses encouraging or discouraging about correctional treatment? Why do you think the meta-analyses had findings that were contradictory?

Source: James McGuire and Philip Priestley, "Reviewing 'What Works': Past, Present, and Future," in *What Works: Reducing Reoffending—Guidelines from Research and Practice*, edited by J. McGuire (New York: John Wiley and Sons, 1995), pp. 8–9.

ther a one-to-one relationship with a therapist or in a group context, juvenile offenders are encouraged to talk about past conflicts that cause them to express emotional problems through aggressive or antisocial behavior. The insight that offenders gain from this individual or group psychotherapy supposedly helps them resolve the conflicts and unconscious needs that drive them to crime. As a final step of psychotherapy, youthful offenders become responsible for their own behavior.

Within the community, psychotherapy has been used recently much more with middle- and upper-class youthful offenders than with lower-class youngsters. Middle- and upper-class youths who abuse drugs or alcohol or who have conflicts at home are likely to be referred for psychotherapy. Other than in a few private settings, little psychotherapy takes place in institutional contexts. The few psychiatrists and clinical psychologists available in these settings spend most of their time doing intake evaluations for classification purposes and crisis intervention with acting-out youths. Crisis intervention generally consists of one interview in which the therapist recommends a treatment plan for the resident's cottage; psychiatrists may also prescribe medication to calm a youth.

Transactional Analysis

Transactional analysis (TA) focuses on interpreting and evaluating interpersonal relationships. This treatment modality tries to teach youthful lawbreakers to relate to others in an adult, mature way.[81]

In applying this modality, the TA leader usually first does a script analysis, which is an attempt to understand how the "tapes" of the past are influencing the behavior of the juvenile in the present. This concept of script analysis is based on the premise that human memory acts as a three-track tape that records the events individuals experienced during their first years of life, the meaning attached to those events, and the emotions they experienced when these events occurred. Each person replays his or her tape when similar situations are encountered later in life. The consequence of negative script replay is that many individuals become "losers," failing to attain their goals and becoming involved in self-defeating behavior. The TA leader seeks to discover the youth's script by diagnosing his or her voice, vocabulary, demeanor, gestures, and answers to questions. TA is based on the belief that persons can change their scripts, and the function of the TA leader is to help individuals make this change. For example, if a mother has told her daughter that she will never succeed at anything and if this has become a self-fulfilling prophecy, the therapist tries to communicate to the daughter that she can succeed in achieving her goals.[82]

One of the hopeful outcomes of the life-script interview is that offenders are willing to negotiate a treatment contract; that is, the youths will state how they wish to change. This treatment contract normally has both short- and long-range goals, project group goals, academic goals, and social behavior goals. Once goals are set, the youth is considered to be in treatment. Throughout the treatment period these goals and progress toward them are constantly reviewed by staff. Social World of the Delinquent 12.5 relates the success of TA with one youthful offender.

Reality Therapy

Reality therapy, a very popular treatment modality, was developed by two Los Angeles psychiatrists, William Glasser and G. L. Harrington. This modality assumes that irresponsible behavior arises when persons are unable to fulfill their basic needs. Accord-

---

Social World of the Delinquent 12.5

A TA Success Story

Bill, a 16-year old African American youth, had spent several years in juvenile institutions before he arrived at the training school. Although his home was intact, he felt a great deal of rejection from his mother. His offenses involved incorrigibility at home and in school and two charges of assault and battery toward peers (fighting in school). His average to above-average intelligence was not apparent from his school performance. Psychiatric reports diagnosed him as withdrawn and as having schizoid tendencies.

His first adjustment report stated: "The prognosis is poor. Extremely depressed about his home life, especially his relationship with mother, Bill is experiencing conflict with peers and staff alike. Bill is resistant to his placement and refuses to become involved in any institutional program."

Then Bill was persuaded by a TA leader to join a group. TA fascinated Bill, who took an active part in the group and never missed a meeting; he also read all he could find on this therapy. More important, he used the concepts of TA to change his behavior and his perception of himself. He frequently informed staff, "I changed from the Child to the Adult state on that one, didn't I?" Bill decided he would finish his last three years of high school, which he did at the institutional high school in the next year and a half. He was granted a home visit to resolve his conflict with his mother, but when she blatantly rejected him on the visit, he used TA to work through the pain of rejection. He applied to Ohio State University, was accepted, and on his release from the training school, became a college student. Four years later, the youth given such a poor prognosis received his college diploma.

Why do you think TA worked with this youth? With what type of youthful offenders is it likely to work? Unlikely to work?

Source: Case study of a youth with whom the author worked.

ing to this approach, the basic human needs are relatedness and respect, and one satisfies these needs by doing what is realistic, responsible, and right.[83]

The three Rs of reality therapy are reality, responsibility, and right-and-wrong. In using this approach with older delinquent girls at the Ventura School in California, Glasser always made each adolescent face the reality of her behavior in the present; he refused to accept any reason for irresponsible behavior; and he expected the girls to maintain a satisfactory standard of behavior.[84]

There are several advantages in using this modality with juveniles. The first is that paraprofessionals can play a major role in working with clients because the basic tenets are easily learned. Second, paraprofessionals are much more attracted to the basic assumptions of reality therapy than to other treatment modalities. For example, they like its emphasis on responsibility, its negation of extenuating circumstances, and its focus on the present. Third, it seems to be easier to achieve consistent treatment with this modality.

Behavior Modification

Behavior modification refers to the application of instrumental learning theory to problems of human behavior. It is based on the assumption that all behavior is under the control of its consequences in the external environment. If a behavior is reinforced immediately and systematically in a positive way, the frequency and rate of that behavior should increase, but if a behavior does not receive a positive reinforcement, the frequency should decrease. Attention, praise, money, food, and privileges are positive reinforcers; threats, confinement, punishment, and ridicule are negative reinforcers. Positive reinforcers produce the more effective and enduring behavior changes. A wide variety of techniques reinforce positive and extinguish negative behavior. They include systematic desensitization, extinction of undesirable responses, training in assertiveness, counterconditioning, conditioning against avoidance responses, and the use of tokens. Behavior modification uses environmental contingencies to alter the offender's response.[85]

One of the great strengths of behavior modification therapy is that it appears to have a greater impact on the sociopathic offender than other treatment modalities. A major reason for this is that behavior modification techniques can immediately reinforce target behaviors. Behavior modification also appears to have a greater impact on the manipulator than more traditional therapies. Furthermore, behavior modification is specific and is often effective in short-term intervention. Finally, behavior modification is one of the more flexible of the treatment modalities.[86]

Critics of behavior modification have leveled several major criticisms against it. One of the most frequent attacks states that treating only the offender's overt symptoms is too superficial to be effective. Many critics also charge that this treatment method is not lasting. Humanists believe that the human being is too unique and complicated to be treated only according to his or her overt behavior. Another criticism states that the principles of behavior modification require considerable consistency and continuity, if not sophistication, which is atypical of correctional treatment. Finally, critics feel that it is very difficult to apply behavior modification to youths who do not manifest overt behavioral problems.

Guided Group Interaction

Guided group interaction (GGI) has probably been used more than any other treatment modality. It has been used in at least eleven states: Florida, Georgia, Illinois, Kentucky, Maryland, Michigan, Minnesota, New Hampshire, New Jersey, South Dakota, and West Virginia. Since the 1950s, when this modality was first used, it has been based on the assumption that peers could confront other peers and force them to face the reality of their behavior more effectively than could staff.

The GGI approach is characterized by giving residents responsibility for decision making. The adult leader constantly refers the decision making back to the group. When informed that a fellow group member planned to run away, for example, one staff member retorted: "So what do you want me to do? He's your buddy; he's part of your group. You can talk to him if you have to; but it's up to all of you to help one another."[87]

Youthful offenders usually go through several stages in becoming involved in guided group interaction. Youths initially are guarded in their responses, but as their defenses begin to weaken, they learn to give up their games and defenses because of the encouragement received from peers and the group leader. In the second stage, the residents' interpersonal problems are brought into the open. They are encouraged to talk about themselves and to have their values scrutinized and challenged by the group. In the third stage, the offenders begin to examine the difficulties they have had with their environment. The group members, who begin to develop real trust among themselves, probe the problems of institutional and street living. The fourth stage is that in which the offenders feel secure and accept reeducation. When they see that their problems are not unique and that dealing with them is possible, they feel less antagonistic toward the group and become more receptive to what is said. In the final stage, the residents set up an outline of a plan for change. Using his or her own self-evaluation, as well as that of the group, each youth makes a conscious decision about the way he or she wants to behave in the future.[88]

A strength of GGI is its determination to circumvent the values of the delinquent-peer subculture. This modality, in urging residents to be honest and open with each other, attempts to move group participants to a more positive, pro-social stance. Another advantage is that it represents a comprehensive strategy for dealing with troubled youth. It is, in effect, a total system for mitigating the impact of a delinquent subculture. A third advantage is that GGI seems to have gained acceptance on the state level. Also important is the fact that GGI can be led by line staff, thereby increasing staff involvement in the treatment process. A final advantage is that responsibility is given to offenders; thus, in interacting with peers, offenders become aware of their problems and are directed toward their resolution.

Positive Peer Culture

The concept of **positive peer culture** (PPC) has generated considerable excitement in juvenile corrections, especially in the 1970s. Developed by Harry Vorrath and associates as an outgrowth of guided group interaction, PPC has been implemented in all of the juvenile state institutions in West Virginia, Michigan, and Missouri.[89]

Vorrath believes that PPC "is a total system for building positive youth subcultures."[90] The main philosophy of PPC is to "turn around" the negative peer culture and to mobilize the power of the peer group in a positive way. PPC does this by teaching group members to care for one another: Caring is defined as wanting what is best for a person. Vorrath believes that once caring becomes "fashionable" and is accepted by the group, "hurting goes out of style."[91]

PPC involves the same stages as GGI, but it places more emphasis on positive behavior. Group members learn to speak of positive behaviors as "great," "intelligent," "independent," "improving," and "winning." In contrast, negative behavior is described as "childish," "unintelligent," "helpless," "destructive," "copping out," and "losing."

Rational Emotive Therapy

From their research with the criminally insane at St. Elizabeth Hospital in Washington, D.C., Samuel Yochelson and Stanton E. Samenow concluded that there is a criminal personality that incorporates some 52 errors in thinking.[92] The basic rationale of **rational**

emotive therapy is to identify the errors characteristic of a youthful offender's thinking. These errors include the blaming of others, the attempt to control or manipulate, the inability to empathize, the desire to play a victim role, the failure to accept obligations, and the attempt to lie or confuse.[93]

The therapist attempts to determine the sequence of thoughts, feelings, events, and other factors that make up the "offense syndrome" and then to get the offender to "own" his or her behaviors. Once the offender owns the behaviors, he or she is taught how to intervene in the illegal behavior when it first starts, to bring it under control. After a prolonged period of treatment, the offender is moved into residential aftercare, joins a support group, and is given continued access to treatment.[94]

This is a cognitive restructuring strategy that is specifically targeted at the dysfunctional cognitive patterns of offenders. These dysfunctional cognitive patterns, or thinking errors, support, excuse, and even reinforce criminal behavior. This approach presumes that the use of such errors releases inhibitions toward committing a crime, which "frees one" to behave in a criminal or delinquent manner. The job of the counselor is to correct these thinking errors, and the task of the facility is to provide an environment in which such errors can be corrected by treatment and custody staff and also by residents in group sessions or day-to-day institutional living.[95]

In the 1980s, this notion that offenders have certain personality characteristics leading to basic errors in thinking became popular as society's need to control and reform serious habitual offenders increased. During the 1980s, the Ohio Department used this approach in some of its institutions and Paint Creek Youth Center also incorporated Yochelson and Samenow's principles into the facility token economy or point system. During the 1990s, rational emotive therapy was widely adopted throughout the nation.

Drug and Alcohol Abuse Interventions

Drug and alcohol abuse by juveniles, as well as their drug trafficking in the community, constitutes a serious social problem today. A director of guidance in a training school acknowledged the seriousness of the problem when he said, "Rarely do we get a boy who doesn't have some history of drug or alcohol abuse in his background."[96]

Drug and alcohol abuse interventions are increasingly being developed in community-based and institutional settings to assist those who need help with these problems. Training schools are conducting these groups in several ways. Institutionalized juveniles assessed to have a problem with alcohol and/or drugs are placed in a separate cottage or in a chemical-abuse group. Specialized staff are hired to work in these cottages or lead these groups. Also, in some training schools, the social worker or another cottage staff member conducts on-going drug and alcohol abuse groups. Furthermore, outside groups, such as Alcoholics Anonymous (AA) or Narcotics Anonymous (NA) come into the institution and hold groups for interested residents.

In considering the extensiveness of the problem of drug use and trafficking among juvenile offenders, too few programs still are being offered in juvenile placements. The programs that are offered tend to be relatively unsophisticated, lacking adequate theoretical design, treatment integrity, and evaluation follow-up. Unquestionably, effective alcohol and drug abuse programs represent one of the most important challenges of juvenile justice today.

What Works for Whom and in What Context

The overall quality of treatment in juvenile justice is not impressive. Enforced offender rehabilitation has sometimes resulted in making delinquents worse rather than better through treatment. The frequent criticism that offender rehabilitation is defective in theory and a disaster in practice has been true on too many occasions. Program designs often have given little consideration to what a particular program can realistically accomplish with a particular group of offenders and frequently have relied on a single cure for a variety of complex problems. In addition, programs generally have lacked integrity, because they have not delivered the services they claimed with sufficient strength to accomplish the goals of treatment. Furthermore, the research on offender rehabilitation generally has been inadequate, with many projects and reports on rehabilitation almost totally lacking in well-developed research designs.[97]

Still, enough progress has been made that the various meta-analyses and literature reviews from the 1980s indicated that treatment programs had somewhat more positive findings in reducing recidivism than earlier studies had revealed.[98] The emerging picture receiving increased support in the 1990s is that " 'something' apparently works, though no generic method or approach, as distinct from individual programs, especially shines." Or to state this differently, several methods appear promising but none usually has produced major reductions in recidivism.[99]

Correctional treatment must discover what works for which offenders in what context. In other words, correctional treatment could be more effective if amenable offenders were offered appropriate treatments by matched workers in environments conducive to producing positive effects.[100]

To match up individual offenders with the treatments most likely to benefit them will be no easy task. Only through well-planned and soundly executed research will the necessary information be gained. The Panel of Rehabilitative Techniques recommends the use of the "template-matching technique."[101] This technique creates a set of descriptors, or a "template," of the kinds of people who are most likely to benefit from a particular treatment according to the theory or basic assumptions underlying it.[102] Because of the scarcity of treatment resources, matching programs to those offenders most likely to profit from them is only sensible.

SUMMARY

The most desirable strategy is to prevent delinquent behavior before it can occur, but delinquency prevention programs have generally fallen short of controlling youth crime. Of the various delinquency prevention programs developed in the twentieth century, grass-roots community groups appear to offer the most promising approach. It is too early to determine whether the recent effort to prevent delinquency in high-risk youths will have any effect. But for delinquency prevention programs to have a real impact on youth crime in America, it will be necessary to modify the social, economic, and political conditions of American society that lead to crime. Until that happens, primary and secondary delinquency prevention programs are chipping at the tip of the iceberg rather than dealing with the base of the problem.

Diversion, in its broad sense, comes from programs sponsored by the police, the juvenile court and probation officers, and agencies outside the justice system. Although in the 1960s and 1970s diversionary programs often were looked upon as a panacea for youth crime, mounting evidence now challenges the efficacy of diversionary programs. The most serious criticism is that they result in more youths getting caught in the net of the juvenile justice system. Drug and teen courts are newly developed forms of diversion, and it is too early to determine what their long-term impact will be.

As indicated in this chapter, we might have expected too much from correctional treatment. Violent and inhumane training schools are among the least promising places for treatment to take place. But even in community-based programs, the lack of resources for overworked staff, clients' histories of failure, and drug and alcohol addictions result in far more failures than successes. The danger, however, is to expect too little from correctional treatment. Some delinquents do profit from treatment in community-based and institutional settings. The programs simply may make their present confinement more bearable, or they may provide a sense of mission or purpose for offenders so that they can go on to live crime-free lives. In sum, some programs are effective, and some treatment agents do have positive impacts on delinquents.

KEY WORDS

behavior modification, p. 371
diversion programs, p. 363
drug and alcohol abuse interventions, p. 373
guided group interaction (GGI), p. 371
juvenile drug courts, p. 366
panaceas, p. 355
positive peer culture (PPC), p. 372
primary prevention, p. 354

psychotherapy, p. 368
secondary prevention, p. 355
rational emotive therapy, p. 372
reality therapy, p. 370
teen courts, p. 365
tertiary prevention, p. 355
transactional analysis (TA), p. 369
youth service bureaus, p. 363

CRITICAL THINKING QUESTIONS

1. Why have delinquency prevention programs been so popular in the United States?
2. Do you believe that prevention programs will have any effect on high-risk offenders? If they were to prove effective, how would that change youth crime in this nation?
3. Why are diversionary programs sometimes seen as being coercive?
4. Which treatment modality is the most promising for use in correctional institutions? Why?
5. Why has treatment traditionally had so little effect on reducing recidivism? What will have an impact on reducing the likelihood of future youthful offenders becoming involved in crime?

WEB DESTINATIONS

For links on various prevention programs, go to the Florida State University site.
http://www.criminology.fsu.edu/jjclearinghouse/jj19.html

Go to the Office of Juvenile Justice and Delinquency Prevention to learn more about delinquency prevention. Use the site's search box to access information.
http://ojjdp.ncjrs.org/

Learn more about youth service bureaus at the Governor's Prevention Initiative for youth at this site.
http://www.dmhas.state.ct.us/sig/

NOTES

1. Interviewed in May 1988.
2. Stanley Cohen, *Visions of Social Control: Crime, Punishment and Classification* (Cambridge, England: Policy Press, 1985), p. 236.
3. J. David Hawkins et al., *Reports of the National Juvenile Justice Assessment Centers: A Typology of Cause-*
Focused Strategies of Delinquency Prevention (Washington, D.C.: U.S. Government Printing Office, 1980), p. 1.
4. For development of these levels of prevention, see Steven P. Lab, *Crime Prevention: Approaches, Practices and Evaluations* (Cincinnati: Anderson, 2000), pp. 19–22.

5. James O. Finckenauer, *Scared Straight! and the Panacea Phenomenon* (Englewood Cliffs, N.J.: Prentice-Hall, 1982), p. 4.

6. U.S. Congress, House, Subcommittee on Human Resources of the Committee on Education and Labor, *Hearings, Oversight on Scared Straight!*, 96th Cong., 1st Sess., 4 June 1979, p. 305.

7. Finckenauer, *Scared Straight!*, p. 4.

8. Cited in Ibid., p. 35.

9. Richard J. Lundman, Paul T. McFarlane, and Frank R. Scarpitti, "Delinquency Prevention: A Description and Assessment of Projects Reported in the Professional Literature," *Crime and Delinquency* 22 (July 1976), p. 307.

10. Richard J. Lundman and Frank R. Scarpitti, "Delinquency Prevention: Recommendations for Future Projects," *Crime and Delinquency* 24 (April 1978), p. 207.

11. Ibid.

12. Richard J. Lundman, *Prevention and Control of Juvenile Delinquency*, 3rd ed. (New York: Oxford University Press, 2001).

13. Gail Wasserman, Laurie S. Miller, and Lynn Cothern, "Prevention of Serious and Violent Juvenile Offending," *Juvenile Justice Bulletin* (April 2000), p. 1.

14. Office of Juvenile Justice and Delinquency Prevention, *Guide for Implementing the Comprehensive Strategy for Serious, Violent, and Chronic Juvenile Offenders* (Washington, D.C.: U.S. Department of Justice, 1995), p. 17.

15. J. David Hawkins and Joseph G. Weis, "The Social Development Model: An Integrated Approach to Delinquency Prevention," *Journal of Primary Prevention* 6 (Winter 1985), pp. 77–78.

16. Hawkins et al., *Typology of Cause-Focused Strategies.*

17. See Hawkins et al., *Typology of Cause-Focused Strategies*, for the development of this typology and the goals of each strategy, pp. 11–25.

18. See Jerry P. Walker, Albert P. Cardarelli, and Dennis Billingsley, *The Theory and Practice of Delinquency Prevention in the United States: Review, Synthesis, and Assessment* (Columbus: National Institute of Law Enforcement and Criminal Justice, Ohio State University, 1976), p. 147.

19. Greg Parks, "The High/Scope Perry Preschool Project," *Juvenile Justice Bulletin* (Washington, D.C.: Office of Juvenile Justice and Delinquency Prevention, 2000), pp. 1–2.

20. Ibid.

21. Ibid.

22. Catherine H. Conly, *Street Gangs: Current Knowledge and Strategies* (Washington, D.C.: U.S. Department of Justice, 1993), pp. 37–38.

23. Ibid., p. 60.

24. Susan Hlesciak Hall and Anne Henderson, "The Comer Process: Bonding to Family and School," *Community Education Journal* (Fall 1990), p. 22.

25. Conly, *Street Gangs*, p. 37.

26. Ibid., p. 38.

27. See Gary D. Gottfredson, *A Workbook for Your School Improvement Program* (Baltimore: Johns Hopkins University Press, 1988).

28. Results reported in "School Development and Management," Chapter 5, *Communities that Care: Action for Drug Abuse Prevention, A Guide for Community Leaders*, (March 5, 1991), p. 101.

29. G. R. Patterson, "Children Who Steal," in *Understanding Crime: Current Theory and Research*, edited by Travis Hirschi and Michael Gottfredson (Beverly Hills, Calif.: Sage, 1980), p. 114.

30. Dryfoos, *Adolescents at Risk: Prevalence and Prevention* (1990), p. 133.

31. Ibid., p. 133.

32. D. Hawkins, R. Catalano, G. Jones, and D. Fine, "Delinquency Prevention through Parent Training: Results and Issues from Work in Progress," in *Children to Citizens: Families, Schools, and Delinquency Prevention*, Vol. 3, edited by J. Wilson and G. Loury (New York: Springer-Verlag, 1987), pp. 186–204.

33. Ibid.

34. Conly, *Street Gangs*, p. 41.

35. Ibid.

36. Myrna B. Sahure, "Preventing Violence the Problem-Solving Way," *Juvenile Justice Bulletin* (Washington, D.C.: Juvenile Justice and Delinquency Prevention, 1999). p. 1.

37. Ibid., p. 2.

38. Dryfoos, *Adolescents at Risk*, pp. 228–233.

39. James C. Howell, ed., *Guide for Implementing the Comprehensive Strategy for Serious, Violent, and Chronic Juvenile Offenders* (Washington, D.C.: Office of Juvenile Justice and Delinquency Prevention, 1995), p. 10.

40. Ibid., p. 3.

41. Ibid., p. 5.

42. Ibid.

43. Ibid., pp. 9–10.

44. Ibid., p. 11.

45. Kathleen Coolbaugh and Cynthia J. Hansel, "The Comprehensive Strategy: Lessons learned From the Pilot Sites," *Juvenile Justice Bulletin* 2000). p. 1.

46. Ibid., p. 10.

47. President's Commission on Law Enforcement and Administration of Justice, *Task Force Report on Juvenile Delinquency and Youth Crime* (Washington, D.C.: U.S. Government Printing Office, 1967), p. 2.

48. Youth Development and Delinquency Prevention Administration, *The Challenge of Youth Service Bureaus* (Washington, D.C.: U.S. Government Printing Office, 1973).

49. Edwin H. Sutherland and Donald R. Cressey, *Criminology*, 9th ed. (Philadelphia: J.B. Lippincott, 1974).

50. Andrew Rutherford and Robert McDermott, *National Evaluation Program Phase I Report: Juvenile Diversion* (Washington, D.C.: U.S. Government Printing Office, 1976), pp. 2–3.

51. Arnold Binder and Gilbert Geis, "Ad Populum Argumentation in Criminology: Juvenile Diversion as Rhetoric," *Crime and Delinquency* 30 (1984), pp. 309–333.

52. Rutherford and McDermott, *Juvenile Diversion*, p. 5; see also Lloyd E. Ohlin, "The Future of Juvenile Justice Policy and Research," *Crime and Delinquency* (July 1983), pp. 463–472; Thomas Blomberg, "Diversion and Accelerated Social Control," *Journal of Criminal Law*

and Criminology 68 (1977), pp. 274–282; Charles E. Frazier, "Official Intervention, Diversion from the Juvenile Justice System, and Dynamics of Human Services Work: Effects of a Reform Goal Based on Labeling Theory," *Crime and Delinquency* 32 (April 1986), pp. 157–186.

53. Rutherford and McDermott, *Juvenile Diversion*; Dennis B. Anderson and Donald F. Schoen, "Diversion Programs: Effects of Stigmatization on Juvenile/Status Offenders," *Juvenile and Family Court Journal* 36 (Summer 1985), pp. 13–25.

54. Stanley Cohen, *Visions of Social Control*, p. 93.

55. Jeffrey A. Butts and Adele V. Harrell, *Delinquents or Criminals: Policy Options for Young Offenders* (Washington, D.C.: Urban Institute, 1988), p. 9.

56. Survey results are found in Jeffrey Butts, Dean Hoffman, and Jancen Buck "Teen Courts in the United States: A Profile of Current Programs," *OJJDP Fact Sheet* (Washington, D.C.: Office of Juvenile Justice and Delinquency Prevention, 1999).

57. Ibid., p. 1.

58. T. M. Godwin, *Peer Justice and Youth Empowerment: an Implementation Guide for Teen Court Programs* (Lexington, KY: American Probation and Parole Association, 1998).

59. Butts, Hoffman, and Buck, "Teen Courts in the United States," p. 1.

60. Ibid., p. 2.

61. Marilyn Roberts, Jennifer Brophy, and Caroline Cooper, *The Juvenile Drug Court Movement* (Washington, D.C.: Office of Juvenile Justice and Delinquency Prevention, 1997), p. 1.

62. Ibid., pp. 1–2.

63. Ibid., p. 2.

64. Robert R. Smith and Victor S. Lombardo, "Evaluation Report of the Juvenile Mediation Program," *Corrections Compendium* (Laurel, Maryland: American Correctional Association, 2001), p. 1.

65. Ibid., p. 2.

66. Ibid., p. 21.

67. Walter C. Bailey, "Correctional Outcome: An Evaluation of 100 Reports," *Journal of Criminal Law, Criminology, and Police Science* 57 (June 1957), pp. 153–160.

68. J. Robison and G. Smith, "The Effectiveness of Correctional Programs," *Crime and Delinquency* 17 (1971), pp. 67–70.

69. Robert Martinson, "What Works?—Questions and Answers about Prison Reform," *Public Interest* 35 (Spring 1974), pp. 22–54.

70. Douglas Lipton, Robert Martinson, and Judith Wilks, *The Effectiveness of Correctional Treatment* (New York: Praeger, 1975).

71. CBS Television Network. Excerpted from *60 Minutes* segment, "It Doesn't Work" (August 24, 1975).

72. Ted Palmer, "Martinson Revisited," *Journal of Research in Crime and Delinquency* 12 (July 1975), pp. 133–152.

73. Ibid., p. 137.

74. Paul Gendreau and Robert Ross, "Effective Correctional Treatment: Bibliotherapy for Cynics," *Crime and Delinquency* 27 (October 1979), pp. 463–489.

75. Robert R. Ross and Paul Gendreau, eds., *Effective Correctional Treatment* (Toronto: Butterworth, 1980), p. viii.

76. Robert Martinson, "New Findings, New Views: A Note of Caution Regarding Sentencing Reform," *Hofstra Law Review* 7 (Winter 1979), 244.

77. Paul Gendreau and Robert R. Ross, "Revivification of Rehabilitative Evidence," *Justice Quarterly* 4 (September 1987), pp. 349–407.

78. Ibid. For a review of the meta-analyses of correctional treatment in the 1980s, see Ted Palmer, *The Re-Emergence of Correctional Intervention* (Newbury Park, Calif.: Sage Publications, 1992), pp. 50–76.

79. James McGuire and Philip Priestley, "Reviewing 'What Works': Past, Present, and Future," in *What Works: Reducing Reoffending—Guidelines from Research and Practice,* edited by James McGuire (New York: John Wiley & Sons, 1995), pp. 7–8.

80. Ibid.

81. Eric Berne, *Transactional Analysis in Psychotherapy* (New York: Grove Press), p. 355.

82. Thomas A. Harris, *I'm OK—You're OK* (New York: Harper and Row, 1967), pp. 37–53.

83. William Glasser, *Reality Therapy* (New York: Harper and Row, 1965), p. xii.

84. Ibid., excerpts from pp. 44–45.

85. J. L. Bernard and Russell Eisenman, "Verbal Conditioning in Sociopaths with Spiral and Monetary Reinforcement," *Journal of Personality and Social Psychology* 6 (1976), p. 203–206.

86. Ralph Schwitzgebel and David A. Kolb, "Inducing Behavior Change in Adolescent Delinquents," *Behaviour Research and Therapy* 1 (1964), pp. 297–304.

87. See Dennis A. Romig, *Justice for Our Children: An Examination of Juvenile Delinquent Rehabilitation Programs* (Lexington, Mass.: D. C. Heath, 1978), pp. 20–21.

88. Ibid., p. 87.

89. Ibid., pp. 92–93.

90. Interview with Harry Vorrath quoted in Oliver J. Keller Jr. and Benedict S. Alper, *Halfway Houses: Community Centered Correction and Treatment* (Lexington, Mass.: D. C. Heath, 1970), p. 55.

91. Robert J. Wicks, *Correctional Psychology: Themes and Problems in Correcting the Offender* (San Francisco: Canfield Press, 1974), pp. 50–51.

92. Samuel Yochelson and Stanton E. Samenow, *The Criminal Personality*, 2 vols. (New York: J. Aronson, 1976, 1977).

93. David Berenson, *Ohio Department of Youth Services Sex Offender Project: Preliminary Report on a Treatment Program for Adolescent Sex Offenders* (Columbus: Department of Youth Services, 1989).

94. Ibid., pp. 6–8.

95. David Lester and Patricia Van Voorhis, "Cognitive Therapies," in *Correctional Counseling and Rehabilitation,* 3rd. ed., edited by Patricia Van Voorhis, Michael Braswell, and David Lester (Cincinnati: Anderson Publishing, 1997), p. 172.

96. Interviewed in August 1996.

97. Lee Sechrest, Susan O. White, and Elizabeth D. Brown, eds., *The Rehabilitation of Criminal Offenders* (Wash-

ington, D.C.: National Academy of Sciences, 1979); and Susan Martin, Lee Sechrest, and Robin Redner, eds., *Rehabilitation of Criminal Offenders: Directions for Research* (Washington, D.C.: National Academy of Sciences, 1981).

98. For an examination of the various meta-analyses, see Palmer, *Re-Emergence of Intervention,* pp. 50–76. See also Izzo and Ross, "Meta-Analyses of Rehabilitation Programs for Juvenile Delinquents," pp. 134–142.

99. Ibid., p. 48.

100. Sechrest, White, and Brown, eds., *The Rehabilitation of Criminal Offenders,* pp. 35–37.

101. Ibid.

102. Ibid.

part five

SOCIAL CONTROL OF DELINQUENCY

AN OVERVIEW OF THE JUVENILE JUSTICE PROCESS

OBJECTIVES

After reading this chapter, the student will be able to answer the following questions:

- How is the juvenile justice process a system?

- In what ways are the juvenile and adult justice systems the same?

- In what ways are they different?

- What are the stages in the juvenile justice system?

- Why is the violent juvenile the key to effective interventions with juvenile offenders?

- How do graduated sanctions work?

- Why is minority over-representation such a serious issue for the juvenile justice system?

- What will the juvenile justice system look like in the 21st century?

Stephen J. Morse, a professor of law at the University of Pennsylvania, introduces his article on immaturity and irresponsibility with these words:

Our image of teenage offenders vacillates. We see them as *wayward youths, as kids gone wrong, but who are nonetheless not "bad." This image is of the teen as a victim. They are misguided, immature, insufficiently socialized, but not evil. What they need is a therapeutic response that will permit natural maturation and socialization and set them on the right path. In contrast, we also see teen offenders as hostile predators, the products of unfortunate environments and perhaps heredity, who have little or no human sympathy or regard. This image is of the teen as a full-fledged criminal. Because they are evil and fully responsible, they must be punished to satisfy just desserts and to protect the public. At the extreme, they deserve to be executed. In the anecdotal reports that fill the media and that often drive public policy, it is not hard to find either image.*[1]

> **Which position do you believe is receiving more media coverage now? If a juvenile commits a serious crime, how difficult do you think it would be for a defense attorney to convince the court that the juvenile needs a treatment response?**

Morse goes on to say in a carefully reasoned argument that the moral and legal responsibility of mid- to late-adolescents is open to question. He claims that although there appear to be significant differences between adolescents and adults on variables bearing on the theory of responsibility, the question still remains whether these differences are substantial enough to warrant differential moral and legal treatment.[2] Elizabeth S. Scott, a professor of law, and Thomas Grisso, a professor of psychiatry, use a developmental lens to support "a presumption of youthful diminished responsibility for younger and mid-adolescents."[3] Marty Beyer, a child psychotherapist who has done extensive work with violent youthful offenders, argues even more forcefully that juveniles developmentally have less maturity, culpability, and competency than adults (see Juvenile Law, 13.1).[4]

However, in support of the "get-tough with juveniles" position, the argument is frequently made that society has some fifteen-, sixteen-, and seventeen-year-old youthful offenders who function on adult levels. Traditional treatment, this position adds, does not know how to deal with these kids. Ernest van den Haag charges that the only thing that seems to have an impact on these kids is to take them off the streets and put them in jail or training school (see the interview in Chapter 3). He claims that we are too soft on juvenile crime. He wants us to make the crime irrational for the juvenile. It is difficult to argue with van den Haag concerning the ineffectiveness of society's means of preventing, correcting, and controlling juvenile crime.

The juvenile justice system is responsible for controlling and correcting the behavior of law-violating juveniles. The system's inability to accomplish its basic mission has resulted in massive criticism from all sides. Indeed, both liberals and conservatives want to reduce the scope of the juvenile court's responsibilities. Conservatives want to refer serious youthful offenders to the adult court, while some liberals recommend divesting the juvenile court of its jurisdiction over status offenders.

Another position that is building momentum is to abolish the juvenile court. Barry C. Feld, a widely published law professor in juvenile law and procedures, argues that it makes no sense to maintain a separate court because there are no practical or operational differences between the juvenile and adult courts. "Is there any reason," he questions, "to maintain a separates court whose only distinctions are procedures under which no adult would agree to be tried?"[5] He charges that, regardless of the constitutional and legislative reforms of the past two decades, "the juvenile court remains essentially unreformed."[6] He suggests that the adult court "could provide children with all the procedural guarantees already available to adult defendants and additional enhanced protections because of the children's vulnerability and immaturity."[7]

Juvenile Law 13.1

Interview with Marty Beyer

"The offense is often the primary basis for determining intention and competency of children under 18 in adult or juvenile court. But the capacity of juveniles to plan or to stop an action is affected by how far they have progressed developmentally. They need a developmental assessment to examine the unique interweaving of immaturity, disabilities, and trauma (and the different developmental pressures on girls) in order to understand the delinquent act, the young person's capacity to waive rights or cooperate with counsel, and his or her amenability to treatment.

The fact is that adolescents think differently from adults. Even late in their teens young people can have immature thought processes, including:

- First, not anticipating: adolescents often do not plan or do not follow their plan and get caught up in an unanticipated event.
- Second, fear interferes with the adolescent's ability to make choices, particularly if they have been mistreated in the past.

- Third, minimizing danger: risk-taking typical of adolescents reduces their use of mature cognitive strategies because they seldom consider the worst possible outcomes of their actions.
- Fourth, having only one choice: in situations where adults see several choices, adolescents may believe they have only one option.

Do you agree with Dr. Beyer that adolescents typically lack the cognitive development of adults? Does society then need a juvenile system separate from the adult system to treat juveniles? How about juveniles who commit a violent crime?

Source: Statement that Marty Beyer sent the author in January of 2002.

How the Structures and Functions of the Juvenile Justice System Work

Like most systems, private or public, the juvenile justice system is concerned first with maintaining its equilibrium and surviving. The system is able to survive by maintaining internal harmony while simultaneously managing environmental inputs. The police and the juvenile court, juvenile probation, residential and day treatment programs, detention facilities, long-term juvenile institutions, and aftercare are all closely interrelated, so changes in one organization have definite consequences elsewhere within the system.

Structures and Functions

The juvenile justice system is made up of three basic subsystems. These subsystems—the police, the juvenile court, and corrections—consist of between 10,000 and 20,000 public and private agencies, with annual budgets totaling hundreds of millions of dollars. Many of the 40,000 police departments across the nation have juvenile divisions, and over 3,000 juvenile courts and about 1,000 juvenile correctional facilities exist in the United States.[8] Of the 50,000 employees in the juvenile justice system, more than 30,000 are employed in juvenile correctional facilities, 6,500 are juvenile probation officers, and the remainder are aftercare, or parole, officers and staff who work in residential programs. In addition, several thousand more employees work in diversion programs and private juvenile correctional systems.[9]

A juvenile judge lecturing white male juvenile, with his guardian present.

The functions of the three subsystems differ somewhat. The basic work of the police is law enforcement and maintaining order. The function of maintaining order, which occupies most of police officers' time, involves such responsibilities as settling family disputes, providing emergency ambulance service, directing traffic, furnishing information to citizens, preventing suicides, giving shelter to drunks, and checking the homes of families on vacation. The law-enforcement function requires that the police deter crime, make arrests, obtain confessions, collect evidence for strong cases that can result in convictions, and increase crime clearance rates. The police must also deal with juvenile lawbreaking and provide services juveniles need.

The juvenile courts are responsible for disposing of cases referred to them by **intake divisions** of probation departments, supervising juvenile probation, making detention decisions, dealing with cases of child neglect and dependency cases, and monitoring the performance of youths who have been adjudicated delinquent or status offenders. The *parens patriae* philosophy of the juvenile court charges the court with treating rather than punishing youngsters appearing before juvenile judges. But the treatment arm of the juvenile court goes only so far, and youths who commit serious crimes or persist in juvenile lawbreaking may be sent to training schools or transferred to the adult court.

The corrections system is charged with the care of youthful offenders sentenced by the courts. Juvenile probation, the most widely used judicial disposition, supervises offenders released to probation by the courts, ensuring that they comply with the conditions of probation imposed by the courts and desist from delinquent behavior in the community. Day treatment and **residential programs** are charged with preparing youths for their return to the community, with preventing unlawful behavior in the program or in the community, and with providing humane care for youths directed to the programs. Long-term juvenile correctional institutions have similar responsibilities, but the officials of these programs also are charged with deciding when each youth is ready to be released to the community. Officials of long-term institutions must also ensure that residents receive their constitutional and due process rights. Aftercare, or parole, officers, the final group in the juvenile justice system, have the responsibility of supervising youths released from long-term juvenile correctional institutions. Like probation officers, aftercare officers are expected to make certain that youthful offenders fulfill the terms of their aftercare agreements and avoid delinquent behavior.

Stages in the Juvenile Justice Process

The means by which juvenile offenders are processed by juvenile justice agencies are examined throughout this text. The variations in the juvenile justice systems across the nation make it difficult to describe this process, but Figure 13.1 is a flowchart of the juvenile justice system and the criminal justice system that shows what these systems have in common. The process begins when the youth is referred to the juvenile court. Some jurisdictions permit a variety of agents to refer the juvenile, whereas in others the police alone are charged with this responsibility. The more common procedure is that the youth whose alleged offense has already been investigated is taken into custody by the police who have made the decision to refer the juvenile to the juvenile court.

The intake officer, usually a **probation officer,** must decide whether the juvenile should remain in the community or be placed in a shelter or detention facility. As indicated in Figure 13.1, the intake officer has a variety of options in determining what to do with the youth, but in more serious cases, the juvenile generally receives a petition to appear before the juvenile court.

The juvenile court judge, or the referee in many jurisdictions, hears the cases of juveniles referred to the court. If the juvenile is to be **transferred to the adult court,** this must be done before any juvenile proceedings take place. Otherwise, an adjudicatory hearing, whose primary purpose is to determine whether the juvenile is guilty of the delinquent acts alleged in the petition, takes place. The court hears evidence on these allegations. *In re Gault* (see Chapter 15) usually is interpreted to guarantee to juveniles the right to representation by counsel, freedom from self-incrimination, the right to confrontation, and the right to cross-examine witnesses. Some states also give juveniles the right to a jury trial.

A disposition hearing takes place when a juvenile has been found delinquent in the adjudicatory stage. Most juvenile court codes now require that the adjudicatory and disposition hearings be held at different times. The number of dispositions juvenile judges have available to them varies from one jurisdiction to the next. In addition to the standard disposition of warning and release, placement on juvenile probation, or adjudication to the department of youth services or corrections, some judges can place juveniles in a publicly or privately administered day treatment or residential program. Some jurisdictions even grant juvenile judges the authority to send a juvenile to a particular correctional facility.

The juvenile adjudicated to a training school is generally treated somewhat differently in small states than in large states. In small states with one training school for males and (usually) one for females, a youth adjudicated to a training school usually is sent directly to the appropriate school. But large states that have several facilities for males and perhaps more than one for females may send the youth to a classification, or diagnostic, center to determine the proper institutional placement. Training school residents currently are not confined as long as they were in the past and are frequently released within a year. Institutional release takes place in a variety of ways, but the juvenile released from the training school is generally placed on aftercare status. To be released from this supervision, the juvenile must fulfill the rules of aftercare and must avoid unlawful behavior.

Recidivism in the Juvenile Justice System

The early cohort studies certainly did not present a favorable picture of the effect of the juvenile justice process on juvenile delinquents. The Philadelphia cohort studies found that the probability of becoming an adult offender increased dramatically for individuals with a record of juvenile delinquency. Both cohort studies found that stricter punishments by the juvenile justice system were likely to encourage rather than to eliminate further delinquent behavior.[10] The Racine cohort studies found that an increase in frequency and seriousness of misbehavior typically occurred in the periods following the administration of sanctions by the justice system and that those who had police contacts as juveniles were

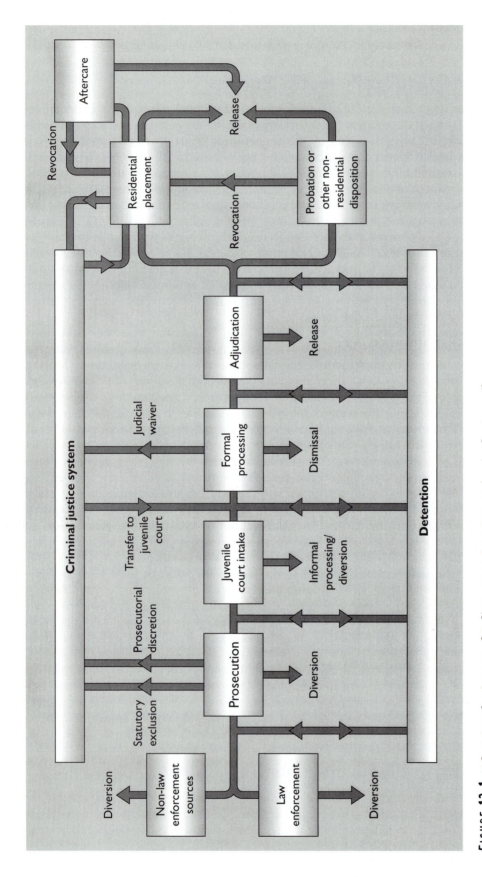

FIGURE 13.1 What Are the Stages of Delinquency Case Processing in the Juvenile Justice System?

Note: This chart gives a simplified view of caseflow through the juvenile justice system. Procedures vary among jurisdictions.

Source: Howard N. Snyder and Melissa Sickmund, *Juvenile Offenders and Victims: 1999 National Report* (Washington, D.C.: Office of Juvenile Justice and Delinquency Prevention, 1999), p. 98.

more likely to have police contacts as adults.[11] The Columbus cohort study further found that the impact of institutional treatment was basically negative. In fact, after institutionalization, the length of time between arrests decreased dramatically.[12] What these studies found was that the probability of continuing with juvenile crime and of going on with adult crime increased for individuals who were brought to the attention of the juvenile justice system. See Social World Of the Delinquent 13.2 for an example of how juveniles sometimes get worse rather than better with the intervention of the justice system.

A recent cohort study conducted in Maricopa County Juvenile Court (Phoenix, Arizona) found a somewhat more favorable picture of youths' contact with the juvenile justice system. Records captured the complete juvenile court careers of more than 150,000 youths who were born between 1962 and 1977. It was found that 54 percent of males and 73 percent of females who entered the juvenile justice system never returned on a new referral. Recidivism was much higher for males than females: 19 percent of males accrued four or more referrals, compared with 5 percent of females. Because there was a standing policy in this county that all youths arrested be referred to the juvenile court for screening, this study provides a complete history of local youths' official contact with the juvenile justice system.[13]

Fragmentation of the Juvenile Justice System

The lack of cooperation and communication among some practitioners exists on a large scale within the juvenile justice subsystems. Ideally, as previously stated, juvenile justice agencies are so interrelated that the flow of justice moves in the following sequence: law violation, police contact, judicial process, disposition, and rehabilitation. Figure 13.1 illustrates this flow of justice.

In reality, cooperation and communication are typically so lacking among the subsystems that the entire system becomes disjointed and fragmented. In fact, the

Social World of the Delinquent 13.2

Progression toward a Criminal Career

Juvenile homes are where you formed most of your friendships. You had to play it tough. I wasn't a tough kid, but I learned to play tough in juvenile halls in order to survive. If you weren't tough you were picked on. You had to talk your shit, hoping you would scare everyone else off. But sooner or later, you had to prove how tough you were.

I started going in and out of juvenile halls around the age of ten. I was busted at the age of twelve for burglary and was sent to training school for the first time. Your regular program was two years there. I came out when I was fourteen and got busted again; I was only out for a short while. Then I went to a different training school and did a year there. I came out when I was fifteen, and before you know it, I was sent to Preston [California]. I did two years there. Came out when I was seventeen. On my next bust, they put me in Tracy. One step before the prison or "Big House." Tracy is where you learned to kill people. They were

going to keep me there until I was twenty-one. They let me out when I was nineteen.

Doing a crime didn't scare you because you would go to detention and all the people you knew were there. They taught you to be tough and survive. You learned the discipline of the place. When you got out and got busted, you went to the next step up according to your age, and you would see all the people you knew from the other places. You got tougher as you went. You picked up a lot of violence going through the system. The juvenile facilities put you through the training so you would make it in prison.

Is this a typical statement of a juvenile delinquent? Does juvenile processing become as much a school of crime as this former delinquent suggests?

Source: Interviewed in June 1988.

fragmentation is so great that both the juvenile and adult justice systems frequently are referred to as nonsystems.

Juvenile justice actually is more fragmented than adult corrections because juvenile offenders are dealt with in quite different ways in different communities. An offender may be referred to social worker agencies in one jurisdiction, processed as an adult in another, and be dealt with by the juvenile court in still another. In some jurisdictions, offenses are ignored in favor of dealing with the youths' emotional problems; other jurisdictions use all available community resources before committing youths to juvenile institutions; others are quick to commit offenders to juvenile institutions for even minor offenses; and others place juveniles in adult facilities.

This fragmentation is caused by several factors. The first is the lack of a common goal among the segments of the juvenile justice system. Each subsystem selects its own goals, which vary, unfortunately, with each new police chief, juvenile judge, chief probation officer, or institutional superintendent. A second cause of fragmentation is that local governments control their own affairs and set standards that are often reflections of local biases rather than of professional competence. Local bias becomes quite apparent when the goals standards of such commissions as the National Advisory Commission for Criminal Justice Standards and Goals of the American Correctional Association's accreditation process are compared with the actual practices in juvenile justice. Another cause of fragmentation is the extensive proliferation of agencies responsible for juvenile justice in the United States.

The consequences of fragmentation are manifested in duplicated and soaring costs. The establishment of identical recreation programs for the same adolescents and treatment of a family with multiple problems by several different agencies at the same time are examples of such duplication. The usual outcome is agencies working at cross-purposes.

Negative impact on juvenile offenders is another possible consequence of fragmentation. Youths who are guilty only of minor crimes still are placed in training schools with youths who have committed serious crimes. Such offenders may not be able to protect themselves against more antisocial delinquents and, even if they are able to protect themselves, their institutional stay can result in their learning even more about a criminal way of life. In addition, more sophisticated offenders are able to play off agencies against one another as they avoid attempts to change their behavior. This disjointed system results in some adolescent males and females being sentenced to inappropriate institutions or in their being denied needed services.

Fragmentation also creates tension among professionals working with juvenile offenders. Conflict particularly arises between the juvenile judge and the police when the police may want to see the "one-person crime wave" put away and the judge disagrees and places the youth on probation. Prosecuting attorneys are unhappy with judges who fail to waive a youth who has committed a serious offense to the adult court. Probation officers become unhappy when judges neither read their reports nor follow their recommendations. Institutional social workers and aftercare specialists often disagree over the decision of when a youth should be released and to whom. The aftercare specialist may challenge the placement recommendation of the institutional social worker because he or she believes the youth has not had sufficient confinement.

Juvenile justice clearly can function effectively only to the degree that each segment of the system takes into account its subparts. The efficiency, accountability, and fairness of the system depend greatly on the coordination and communication among the subsystems. As long as many jurisdictions continue to go their own ways, the juvenile justice system will remain disjointed and fragmented.

Comparison of the Juvenile and Adult Justice Systems

There is much similarity between the juvenile and adult justice systems. Both are made up of three basic subsystems and interrelated agencies. The flow of justice in both is supposed to progress from law violation to police apprehension, judicial process, judicial disposition, and rehabilitation in correctional agencies. The basic vocabulary is the same in the juvenile and adult systems, and even when the vocabulary differs, the intent remains the same.

> **Adjudicatory hearing** is a trial.
> **Aftercare** is parole.
> **Commitment** is a sentence to confinement.
> **Detention** is the same as holding in jail.
> **Dispositional hearing** is the same as a sentencing hearing.
> **Juvenile court officer** is a probation officer.
> **Petition** is an indictment.
> **Taking into custody** is the same as being arrested.
> A **petitioner** is a prosecutor.
> A **respondent** is a defense attorney.
> A **minor** is a defendant.

Both the juvenile and adult systems are under fire to get tough on crime, especially on offenders who commit violent crimes. Both must deal with case overloads and institutional overcrowding, must operate on fiscal shoestrings, and face the ongoing problems of staff recruitment, training, and burnout. Theory and Research 13.3 further describes the common ground and differences between the juvenile and adult justice systems.

The Relationship between Treatment and Punishment in the Juvenile Justice System

To correct the behavior of the juvenile delinquent, there have been four basic correctional models: (1) the Rehabilitation Model, which has three variations; (2) the Justice Model; (3) the Balanced and Restorative Justice Model, and (4) the Crime Control Model. Here, the similarities and differences among these models are identified, following which an emerging model in juvenile justice, one based more on a balanced approach between treatment and punishment, receives attention. This balanced approach is much more focused on punishment and accountability than has been the case in juvenile justice in the past.

Traditional Models in Juvenile Justice

The goal of **rehabilitative philosophy** is to change an offender's character, attitudes, or behavior patterns to diminish his or her propensities for youth crime.[14] The medical model, the adjustment model, and the reintegration model are all expressions of rehabilitative philosophy.

The **medical model,** the first treatment model to be developed from the rehabilitative philosophy, contends that delinquency is caused by factors that can be identified, isolated, treated, and cured. Its proponents believe that delinquents should be treated as though they had a disease. Punishment should be avoided because it does nothing to solve delinquents' problems and only reinforces the negative self-image these youths in trouble have.

The **adjustment model** was developed in the late 1960s and 1970s when some proponents of rehabilitation became dissatisfied with the medical model. According to the adjustment model, delinquents need treatment to help them deal with the problems that lead them to crime. The emphasis is placed upon delinquents' responsibility at the present time. Youthful offenders cannot change the facts of their emotional and social deprivations of the past, but they can demonstrate responsible behavior in the present and can avoid using past problems as an excuse for delinquent behavior. Various therapies are used. These therapies are not based on punishment, because punishment is seen as only increasing delinquents' alienation and behavior problems.

Generalizations about the Juvenile and Criminal Justice Systems

Although the juvenile and criminal justice systems are more alike in some jurisdictions than in others, generalizations can be made about the distinctions between the two system and about their common ground.

Juvenile Justice System	Common Ground	Criminal Justice System
	Operating Assumptions	
■ Youth behavior is malleable. ■ Rehabilitation is usually a viable goal. ■ Youths are in families and not independent.	■ Community protection is a primary goal. ■ Law violators must be held accountable. ■ Constitutional rights apply.	■ Sanctions should be proportional to the offense. ■ General deterrence works. ■ Rehabilitation is not a primary goal.
	Prevention	
■ Many specific delinquency prevention activities (e.g., school, church, recreation) are used. ■ Prevention is intended to change individual behavior and is often focused on reducing risk factors and increasing protective factors in the individual, family, and community.	■ Educational approaches to specific behaviors (drunk driving, drug use).	■ Prevention activites are generalized and are aimed at deterrence (e.g., Crime Watch).
	Law Enforcement	
■ Specialized "juvenile" units are used. ■ Some additional behaviors are prohibited (truancy, running away, curfew violations). ■ Some limitations are placed on public access to information. ■ A significant number of youth are diverted away from the juvenile justice system, often into alternative programs.	■ Jurisdiction involves full range of criminal behavior. ■ Constitutional and procedural safeguards exist. ■ Both reactive and proactive approaches (targeted at offense types, neighbor-hoods, etc.) are used. ■ Community policing strategies are employed.	■ Open public access to all information is required. ■ Law enforcement exercises discretion to divert offenders out of the criminal justice system.
	Intake—Prosecution	
■ In many instances, juvenile court intake, not the prosecutor, decides what cases to file. ■ The decision to file a petition for court action is based on both social and legal factors. ■ A significant portion of cases are diverted from formal case processing. ■ Intake or the prosecutor diverts cases from formal processing to services operated by the juvenile court, prosecutor's office, or outside agencies.	■ Probable cause must be established. ■ The prosecutor acts on behalf of the State.	■ Plea bargaining is common. ■ The prosecution decision is based largely on legal facts. ■ Prosecution is valuable in building history for subsequent offenses. ■ Prosecution exercises discretion to withhold charges or divert offenders out of the criminal justice system.

Juvenile Justice System	Common Ground	Criminal Justice System
	Detention—Jail/Lockup	
■ Juveniles may be detained for their own protection or the community's protection. ■ Juveniles may not be confined with adults unless there is "sight and sound separation."	■ Accused offenders may be held in custody to ensure their appearance in court. ■ Detention alternatives of home or electronic detention are used.	■ Accused individuals have the right to apply for bond/bail release.
	Adjudication—Conviction	
■ Juvenile court proceedings are "quasi-civil" (not criminal) and may be confidential. ■ If guilt is established, the youth is adjudicated delinquent regardless of offense. ■ Right to jury trial is not afforded in all states.	■ Standard of "proof beyond a resonable doubt" is required. ■ Rights to be represented by an attorney, to confront witnesses, and to remain silent are afforded. ■ Appeals to a higher court are allowed. ■ Experimentation with specialied courts (i.e., drug courts, gun courts) is underway.	■ Defendants have a constitutional right to a jury trial. ■ Guilt must be established on individual offenses charged for conviction. ■ All proceedings are open.
	Disposition—Sentencing	
■ Disposition decisions are based on individual and social factors, offense severity, and youths' offense history. ■ Dispositional philosophy includes a significant rehabilitation component. ■ Many dispositional alternatives are operated by the juvenile court. ■ Dispositions cover a wide range of community-based and residential services. ■ Disposition orders may be directed to people other than the offender (e.g., parents). ■ Disposition may be indeterminate, based on progress demonstrated by the youth.	■ Decisions are influenced by current offense, offending history, and social factors. ■ Decisions hold offenders accountable. ■ Decisions may give consideration to victims (e.g., restitution and "no contact" orders). ■ Decisions may not be cruel or unusual.	■ Sentencing decisions are bound primarily by the severity of the current offense and the offender's criminal history. ■ Sentencing philosophy is based largely on proportionality and punishment. ■ Sentence is often determinate, based on offense.
	Aftercare—Parole	
■ Function combines surveillance and reintegration activities (e.g., family, school, work).	■ The behavior of individuals released from correctional settings is monitored. ■ Violation of conditions can result in reincarceration.	■ Function is primarily surveillance and reporting to monitor illicit behavior.

(continued)

Do these generalizations make the juvenile justice seem more or less like the adult justice system?

Source: Howard N. Snyder and Melissa Sickmund, *Juvenile Offenders and Victims: 1999 National Report* (Washington, D.C.: Office of Juvenile Justice and Delinquency Prevention, 1999), pp. 94–96.

A basic assumption of the **reintegration model** is that delinquents' problems must be solved in the community where they began. This model also assumes that society has a responsibility for helping law violators reintegrate themselves back into community life. The reintegration model recommends community-based corrections for all but hard-core offenders, offers those hard-core offenders who must be institutionalized a wide variety of reentry programs, and provides the necessary services so that delinquents can restore family ties and obtain employment and education.[15] Supporters of the reintegration model established a wide variety of community-based programs in the 1970s, including diversion programs, residential and day treatment programs, and programs to treat drug abusers.

The **justice model** holds to the belief that punishment should be the basic purpose of the juvenile justice system. Among the variants of the justice model for youth crime are those proposed by David Fogel, the Report of the Committee for the Study of Incarceration, and the Report of the Twentieth Century Fund.[16]

The concept of "just desserts" is the pivotal philosophical basis of the justice model. Fogel believes that offenders are volitional and responsible human beings, and therefore they deserve to be punished if they violate the law. The punishment shows that the delinquent is blameworthy for his or her conduct. The decisions concerning delinquents should be based not on their needs but on the penalties that they deserve for their acts.[17] Punishment is not intended to achieve social benefits or advantages, such as deterrence or rehabilitation; rather, the only reason to punish an offender is because he or she deserves it. However, the punishment given an offender must be proportionate to the seriousness of the crime.

Building on more than a decade of research and practical experience, **the balanced and restorative model** is an integrated model that seeks to reconcile the interests of victims, offenders, and the community through programs and supervision practices. (For the background and philosophy of this model, see Social Policy 13.4. Restorative Philosophy). In these programs, competency development activities are intended to reinforce community protection and accountability objectives, as shown in Figure 13.2.[18] The balanced and restorative model uses many of the same principles as the justice model to develop model systems for community supervision of juvenile offenders based on the balanced approach and the restorative justice philosophy.[19]

The public has become increasingly intolerant of serious youth crime and is more and more receptive to the **crime control model,** which emphasizes punishment as the remedy for juvenile misbehavior. The crime control model is grounded on the conviction that the first priority of justice should be the protection of the life and property of the innocent. Supporters of the crime control model, which is based on the classical school of criminology (examined in Chapter 3) charge that punishment is the preferred correctional model because it both protects society and deters crime. Youthful offenders are taught not to commit further crimes, while noncriminal youths receive a demonstration of what happens to a person who breaks the law.[20]

Comparison of the Four Models

The rehabilitation model is more concerned that juvenile delinquents receive therapy than that they be institutionalized. The crime control model, on the other hand, is a

SOCIAL POLICY 13.4

Restorative Philosophy

A restorative approach has been a major development in criminological thinking, being grounded in traditions of justice from the ancient Arab, Greek, and Roman civilizations. The purpose of restorative justice is to restore victims, to restore offenders, and to restore communities as a result of their participation in a plurality of stake holders. Restorative justice is seen as an alternative in juvenile justice to either rehabilitation or retribution. Its appeal to liberals is a less punitive juvenile justice system. Its appeal to conservatives is an emphasis on victim empowerment, on empowering families, and on fiscal savings because of the parsimonious use of punishment.

In adult justice, restorative justice is found in victim-offender mediation, victim notification, victim input in sentencing, victim input in plea bargaining, family group conferences, healing circles, restorative probation, reparation boards on the Vermont model, and Chinese Bang Jiao programs.

Restorative justice is increasingly found in juvenile justice in terms of restorative probation, anti-bullying programs in school, conflict resolution in school, teen courts, drug courts, healing circles, victim mediation, victim notification, and victim input in juvenile court dispositional matters.

In what type of case is restorative justice more likely to be used? In what cases would it be rarely used?

Source: John Braithwaite, "Restorative Justice: Assessing Optimistic and Pessimistic Accounts," in *Crime and Justice: A Review of Research* 25, edited by Michael Tonry (Chicago and London: The University of Chicago Press, 1999), pp. 1, 4.

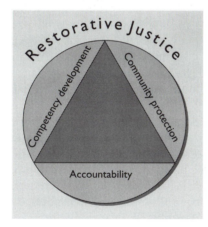

FIGURE 13.2 The Balanced and Restorative Justice Model

Source: Gordon Bazemore and Mark S. Umbreit, *Balanced and Restorative Justice* (Washington, D.C.: Office of Juvenile Justice and Delinquency Prevention, 1994), p. 1.

punishment model which contends juveniles must pay for their crimes. Those who back the crime control model also claim that punishment has social value for both offenders (deterrence) and society (protection). The justice model strongly advocates that procedural safeguards and fairness be granted to juveniles who have broken the law. Yet proponents of this model also firmly hold that juveniles should be punished according to the severity of their crimes. The balanced and restorative model is an accountability model that is focused on recognizing the needs of victims, on giving proper attention to the protection of society, and on providing competency development for juveniles entering the system. Table 13.1 compares the four models.

Emerging Approach to Handling Youthful Offenders

There is no question that there is wide support for using the crime control model on the "serious and violent juvenile" (SIJ) offender. For example, from 1992 through 1997,

TABLE 13.1

Comparison of the Rehabilitation, Justice, Crime Control, and Balanced and Restorative Models

Policy	Rehabilitation	Justice	Crime Control	Balanced and Restorative
Approach to the offender	Behavior is caused or determined; based on Positivism	Free will; based on the Classical School	Free will; based on the Classical School	Free will; based on the Classical School
Purpose of sentencing	Change behavior or attitude	Doing justice	Restore law and order	Community protection
Type of sentencing advocated	Indeterminate	Determinate	Determinate	Determinate
Role of treatment	Goal of correctional process	Voluntary but necessary in a humane system	Ineffective and it actually coddles offenders	Voluntary but necessary in a humane system
Crime control strategy	Use therapeutic intervention to eliminate factors causing crime	Justice as fairness for victims, for offenders, and for practitioners in the system	Declare war on youth crime by instituting get tough policies	Make juvenile offenders accountable for their behavior

Source: Adapted from Clemens Bartollas, *Correctional Treatment: Theory and Practice,* © 1985, p. 75.

legislatures in forty-seven states and the District of Columbia enacted laws that made their juvenile justice systems more punitive.[21] See Table 13.2. Many states have added to the purpose clauses of their juvenile codes phrases such as "provide effective deterrents"; "hold youths accountable for criminal behavior"; "balance attention to youthful offenders, victims, and the community"; and "impose punishments consistent with the seriousness of the crime."[22]

Yet, in Table 13.3, it can be seen that in 1997 about as many states were emphasizing prevention/diversion/treatment philosophical goals as were advocating punishment philosophical goals. Nearly twice as many states placed importance on both in their juvenile codes. The trend toward a balanced and restorative approach is also seen in the late 1990s. At the end of the 1997 legislative session in seventeen states, the language of the balanced and restorative justice philosophy was incorporated, emphasizing offender accountability, public safety, and competency development.[23]

How the Juvenile Justice and Delinquency Prevention Act of 1974 Has Affected Juvenile Corrections

In the Juvenile Delinquency Prevention and Control Act of 1968, Congress recommended that children charged with status offenses be handled outside the juvenile court system. In 1974, Congress passed the **Juvenile Justice and Delinquency Prevention Act** of 1974 (JJDPA), that required the deinstitutionalization of status offenders and non-offenders and the separation of juvenile delinquents from adult offenders as a condition for state participation in the Formula Grant Programs. In 1980, an amendment to the 1974 Act required that juveniles be removed from adult jail and lockup facilities. The 1992 amendment to the Act required that states determine the existence and extent of "disproportionate confinement of minority youth." Where it is a problem, the state must

TABLE 13.2

Juvenile Justice System Becoming More Punitive
From 1992 through 1997, legislatures in 47 States and the District of Columbia enacted laws that made their juvenile justice systems more punitive.

State	Changes in law or court Rule*			State	Changes in law or court Rule*		
Alabama	T		C	Montana	T	S	C
Alaska	T		C	Nebraska			
Arizona	T	S	C	Nevada	T		C
Arkansas	T	S	C	New Hampshire	T	S	C
California	T		C	New Jersey		S	C
Colorado	T	S	C	New Mexico	T	S	C
Connecticut	T	S	C	New York			
Delaware	T	S	C	North Carolina	T		C
D. of Columbia	T	S		North Dakota	T		C
Florida	T	S	C	Ohio	T	S	C
Georgia	T	S	C	Oklahoma	T	S	C
Hawaii	T		C	Oregon	T	S	C
Idaho	T	S	C	Pennsylvania	T		C
Illinois	T	S	C	Rhode Island	T	S	C
Indiana	T	S	C	South Carolina	T		C
Iowa	T	S	C	South Dakota	T		
Kansas	T	S	C	Tennessee	T	S	C
Kentucky	T	S	C	Texas	T	S	C
Louisiana	T	S	C	Utah	T		C
Maine			C	Vermont			
Maryland	T		C	Virginia	T	S	C
Massachusetts	T	S	C	Washington	T		C
Michigan		S	C	West Virginia	T		C
Minnesota	T	S	C	Wisconsin	T	S	C
Mississippi	T		C	Wyoming	T		C
Missouri	T	S	C				

*T = Transfer provisions, S = Sentencing authority, C = Confidentiality

Source: Howard N. Snyder and Melissa Sickmund, *Juvenile Offenders and Victims: 1999 National Report* (Washington, D.C.: Office of Juvenile Justice and Delinquency Prevention, 1999), p. 89. *From:* authors' adaptation of Torbet et al.'s *State responses to serious and violent juvenile crime* and Szymanski's *State legislative responses to violent juvenile crime: 1996–97 update.*

demonstrate efforts to reduce it. The Act was further modified in 1996, especially in terms of contacts of juveniles with adults in correctional facilities.[24] See Social Policy 13.5.

Deinstitutionalization of Status Offenders

Before the 1974 Act was implemented, one of the critical issues of juvenile corrections was the difficulty that status offenders and noncriminal youths had when they were placed in institutions with juvenile delinquents. Status offenders and noncriminal youths frequently stayed longer in these institutions because they often had more difficulty complying with rules and limits than most delinquent youth.[25] A more disturbing issue was that status offenders and noncriminal youths frequently were victimized by delinquent youth in institutional contexts. Bartollas, Miller, and Dinitz document the plight of these youths in attempting to survive with aggressive delinquents. On too many occasions, they became the cottage's scapegoats and were victimized in every conceivable way. As one institutionalized status offender put it to Bartollas one day, "I don't belong here. These guys are animals."[26]

TABLE 13.3

Some Juvenile Codes Emphasize Prevention and Treatment Goals, Some Stress Punishment, and Others Seek a Balanced Approach

Philosophical goals stated in juvenile code purpose clauses, 1997

Prevention/diversion/ treatment	Punishment	Both prevention/diversion/treatment and punishment	
Arizona*	Arkansas	Alabama	Nevada
Dist. of Columbia	Georgia	Alaska	New Hampshire
Kentucky	Hawaii	California	New Jersey
Massachusetts	Illinois	Colorado	New Mexico
North Carolina	Iowa	Connecticut	New York
Ohio	Louisiana	Delaware	North Dakota
South Carolina	Michigan	Florida	Oklahoma
Vermont	Missouri	Idaho	Oregon
West Virginia	Rhode Island	Indiana	Pennsylvania
		Kansas	Tennessee
		Maryland	Texas
		Maine	Utah
		Minnesota	Virginia
		Mississippi	Washington
		Montana	Wisconsin
		Nebraska	Wyoming

■ Most States seek to protect the interests of the child, the family, the community, or some combination of the three.

■ In 17 States, the purpose clause incorporates the language of the balanced and restorative justice philosophy, emphasizing offender accountability, public safety, and competency development.

■ Purpose clauses also address court issues such as fairness, speedy trials, and even coordination of services. In nearly all States, the code also includes protections of the child's constitutional and statutory rights.

*Arizona's statutes and court rules did not contain a purpose clause; however, the issue is addressed in case law.

Source: Author's adaptation of Torbet and Szymanski's *State legislative responses to violent juvenile crime: 1996–97 update* [unpublished background research]. Office of Juvenile Justice and Delinquency Prevention, "1999 National Report Series," *Juvenile Justice Bulletin* (Washington, D.C.: U.S. Department of Justice, 1999), p. 3.

It can be argued that status offenders still are placed in private training schools with delinquents, yet few are placed in public correctional facilities (see Chapter 17). There is also the attempt to keep status offenders separate from juvenile delinquents in community residential programs. For example, status offenders are typically placed in youth shelters, but delinquents are confined in juvenile detention centers.

Jail and Lockup Removal of Juveniles

Another way that the JJDPA has affected juvenile corrections is that few juveniles are confined presently in jails with adults. Before the JJDPA was enacted in 1974, between 500,000 and one million youths were confined in jails each year.[27] In 1996, the average daily population of juveniles in jail was 8,100.[28]

The reason so many youths remain confined in county jails and police lockups is that many juvenile court jurisdictions in the United States simply have no alternatives available. For example, juveniles who are transferred to adult court to await criminal trial make up an increasingly large category of juveniles confined in adult jails.

Total jail removal remains a distant goal; at least forty states continue to resist full compliance with the jail-removal mandate. Two arguments have been made to explain this failure to comply with the JJDPA mandate. Some claim that the resistance is attributable to the failure of federal officials to push harder for compliance. Others argue that states lack the necessary resources and alternatives to implement the jail-removal mandate.[29]

Some states, however, have taken a strong stand against the jailing of juveniles. In Utah, legislation was passed that makes jailing a juvenile a misdemeanor.[30] In 1986, California adopted the strongest law in the nation prohibiting the confinement of children in jails and lockups for adults. What is so encouraging about SB 1637, which became effective on January 1, 1987, is that California had been jailing about 20 percent of United States' incarcerated juveniles.[31] Also, since 1984, Illinois, Missouri, North Carolina, Tennessee, and Virginia have enacted legislation prohibiting the jailing of juveniles or restricting the number of admissions.[32]

Focusing Attention on Disproportionate Minority Confinement

One of the most serious indictments of the juvenile justice system is the mounting evidence of unfair treatment of African American and Hispanic males by the juvenile justice system. It is argued that African American and Hispanic youths are overrepresented in arrest, conviction, and incarceration with respect to their population base because of a pattern of racist decision making.

Carl E. Pope and William H. Feyerherm's highly regarded assessment of the issue of discrimination against minorities reveals that two-thirds of the studies found "both direct and indirect race effects or a mixed pattern (being present at some stages and not at others)."[33] They add that selection bias can take place at any stage and that small racial differences may accumulate and become more pronounced as minority youth are processed into the juvenile justice system.[34]

The Coalition for Juvenile Justice (then the National Coalition of State Juvenile Justice Advisory Groups) brought national attention to the problem of disproportionate minority confinement in their 1988 Annual report to Congress. In that same year, Congress responded to evidence of disproportionate confinement of minority juveniles in secure facilities by amending the Juvenile Justice and Delinquency Prevention (JJDP) Act of 1974 to provide that states must determine whether the proportion of minorities in confinement exceeds their proportion in the population of the state. If there is overrepresentation, states must demonstrate efforts to reduce it.[35] Figure 13.3 graphs how African Americans are overrepresented at all stages of the juvenile justice process.

During the 1992 reauthorization of the JJDP act, Congress substantially strengthened the effort to address disproportionate confinement of minority youth in secure facilities. Eliminating DMC (disproportionate minority confinement) was elevated to the status of a "core requirement" alongside deinstitutionalization of status offenders, removal of juveniles from adult jails and lockups, and separation of youthful offenders from adults in secure institutions. See Table 13.4 for a summary of state compliance with DMC core requirements, as of December 1997.

Do Graduated Sanctions Represent a New Day in Juvenile Justice?

In adult corrections, increased attention has been given to a system of intermediate sanctions. In recent decades, the system of intermediate sanctions has included a sys-

---

SOCIAL POLICY 13.5

Core Requirements of the Juvenile Justice and Delinquency Prevention Act (JJDPA)

The core requirements of the Juvenile Justice and Delinquency Prevention Act primarily address custody issues.

The Juvenile Justice and Delinquency Prevention Act of 1974, as amended, (the Act) establishes four custody-related requirements:

- The "deinstitutionalization of status offenders and nonoffenders" requirement (1974) specifies that juveniles not charged with acts that would be crimes for adults "shall not be placed in secure detention facilities or secure correctional facilities."
- The "sight and sound separation" requirement (1974) specifies that "juveniles alleged to be or found to be delinquent and [status offenders and nonoffenders] shall not be detained or confined in any institution in which they have contact with adult persons incarcerated because they have been convicted of a crime or are awaiting trial on criminal charges." This requires that juvenile and adult inmates cannot see each other and no conversation between them is possible.
- The "jail and lockup removal" requirement (1980) states that juveniles shall not be detained or confined in adult jails or lockups. There are, however, several exceptions to the jail and lockup removal requirement. Regulations implementing the Act exempt a juvenile held in secure adult facilities if the juvenile is being tried as a criminal for a felony or has been convicted as a criminal felon. In addition, there is a 6-hour grace period that allows adult jails and lockups to hold delinquents temporarily until other arrangements can be made. Jails and lockups in rural areas may hold delinquents up to 24 hours under certain conditions. Some jurisdictions have obtained approval for separate juvenile detention centers that are collocated with an adult jail or lockup facility.
- The "disproportionate confinement of minority youth" requirement (1992) specifies that states determine the existence and extent of the prob-

lem in their state and demonstrate efforts to reduce it where it exists.

Regulations effective December 10, 1996, modify the Act's requirements in several ways:

- Clarify the sight and sound separation requirement—in nonresidential areas brief, accidental contact is not a reportable violation.
- Permit time-phased use of nonresidential areas for both juveniles and adults in collocated facilities.
- Expand the 6-hour grace period to include 6 hours both before and after court appearances.
- Allow adjudicated delinquents to be transferred to adult institutions once they have reached the state's age of full criminal responsibility, where such transfer is expressly authorized by state law.

The revised regulations offer flexibility to states in carrying out the Act's requirements. States must agree to comply with each requirement to receive Formula Grants funds under the Act's provisions. States must submit plans outlining their strategy for meeting the requirements and other statutory plan requirements. Noncompliance with core requirements results in the loss of 25% of the state's annual Formula Grants Program allocation.

As of 1998, 55 of 57 eligible states and territories are participating in the Formula Grants Program. Annual state monitoring reports show that the vast majority are in compliance with the requirements, either reporting no violations or meeting *de minimis* or other compliance criteria.

Does the JJDPA support a liberal or conservative agency? What do you think explains its support among policymakers?

Source: Howard N. Snyder and Melissa Sickmund, *Juvenile Offenders and Victims: 1999 National Report* (Washington, D.C.: Office of Juvenile Justice and Delinquency Prevention, 1999), p. 88.

---

tem of graduated sanctions, ranging from fines, day reporting centers, drug courts, and intensive probation, to residential placements.

This same movement is beginning to gain momentum in juvenile justice, but in juvenile justice this system of graduated sanctions is focused on serious, violent, and

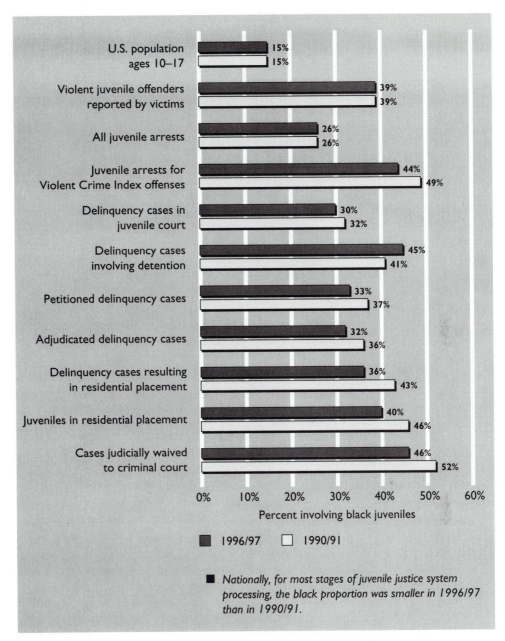

FIGURE 13.3 Overrepresentation of African American Youths at All Stages of the Juvenile Justice System, Compared with Their Proportion in the Population

Source: Howard N. Snyder and Melissa Sickmund, *Juvenile Offenders and Victims: 1999 National Report* (Washington, D.C.: Office of Juvenile Justice and Delinquency Prevention, 1999), p. 192. From: authors' analysis of Bureau of the Census' *Estimates of the population of States by age, sex, race, and Hispanic origin: 1990–1997* [machine-readable data files] for 1991 and 1997, Bureau of Justice Statistics' *National Crime Victimization Survey* [machine-readable data files] for 1991 and 1996, FBI's *Crime in the United States* reports for 1991 and 1997, OJJDP's *Juvenile court statistics* reports for 1991 and 1996, OJJDP's *Children in Custody Census of public and private juvenile detention, correctional, and shelter facilities 1990/91* [machine-readable data file], and OJJDP's *Census of Juveniles in Residential Placement 1997* [machine-readable data file].

chronic juvenile offenders. These offenders are moved along a continuum through a well-structured system that addresses both their needs and the safety of the community. At each level, juvenile offenders are subject to more severe sanctions if they continue in their delinquency offenses.[36]

TABLE 13.4

**Summary of State Compliance with DMC Core Requirement[1]
(as of December 1997)**

- States that have completed the identification and assessment phases and are implementing the intervention phase:

Alaska	Kansas	North Dakota
Arizona	Maryland	Ohio
Arkansas	Massachusetts	Oklahoma
California	Michigan	Oregon
Colorado	Minnesota	Pennsylvania
Connecticut	Mississippi	Rhode Island
Florida	Missouri	South Carolina
Georgia	Montana	Tennessee
Hawaii	Nevada	Texas
Idaho	New Jersey	Virginia
Illinois	New Mexico	Washington
Indiana	New York	Wisconsin
Iowa	North Carolina	Utah

- States that have completed the identification and assessment phases and are formulating a time-limited plan of action for completing the intervention phase.

Alabama	South Dakota	West Virginia

- States (and the District of Columbia) that have completed the identification phase, submitted a time-limited plan of action for the assessment phase, and agreed to submit a time-limited plan for addressing the intervention phase:

Delaware	Louisiana
District of Columbia	Nebraska

- Territories that have completed the identification phase (it has been determined that minority juveniles are not disproportionately arrested or detained in the following territories):

American Samoa	Republic of Palau
Guam	Virgin Islands
Northern Mariana Islands	

- States that have completed the identification phase and are exempt from the DMC requirement because the minority juvenile population in the states does not exceed 1 percent of the total juvenile population:

Maine	Vermont

- State that has now reached 1 percent minority population (statewide) and will begin conducting the identification phase:

New Hampshire

- Territory that is exempt from complying with the DMC requirement (as it has been exempted by the U.S. Census Bureau from reporting racial statistics due to the homogeneity of the population):

Puerto Rico

- States that were not participating in the Formula Grants Program in FY 1997:

Kentucky	Wyoming

[1]Pursuant to Section 31.303(j) of the OJJDP Formula Grants Regulation (28 C.F.R. Part 31)

Source: Heida M. Hsia and Donna Hamparian, *Disproportionate Minority Confinement: 1997 Update* (Washington, D.C.: Office of Juvenile Justice and Delinquency Prevention, 1998), p. 4.

Core Principles of a System of Graduated Sanctions

According to Wilson and Howell, a model graduated system combines the treatment and rehabilitation of youth with fair, humane, reasonable, and appropriate sanctions. It offers a continuum of care that consists of diverse programs. Included in this continuum are immediate sanctions within the community for both first-time nonviolent offenders and for most serious offenders, secure care programs for most violent offenders, and aftercare programs that provide high levels of both social control and treatment services.[37]

Each of the graduated sanctions is intended to consist of gradations, or sublevels, that together with appropriate services constitute an integrated approach. This approach is designed to stop the youthful offender's further penetration into the juvenile system by inducing law-abiding behavior as early as possible through the combination of treatment sanctions and appropriate interventions. The family must be involved at each level in the continuum. Aftercare must be actively involved in supporting the family and in reintegrating the youth into the community. Programs will need to use the Risk and Needs Assessments to determine the placement that is appropriate for the offender. The effectiveness of interventions depends on their being swift, certain, consistent, and incorporating increased sanctions, including the possible loss of freedom. As the severity of sanctions are increased, so must the intensity of treatment be increased. These sanctions could ultimately mean confinement in a secure setting, ranging from a secure community-based facility to a public or private training school, camp, or ranch. The programs that are most effective for hard-to-handle youths address key areas of risk in their lives, provide adequate support and supervision, and offer youths a long-term stake in the community.[38]

Trends for the Twenty-First Century

The present problems with youth violence, as well as a growing cohort of older juveniles in the future, will surely place pressure on the juvenile justice system and its policymakers to resolve several pressing issues facing the system. How these issues are resolved will greatly determine how the juvenile justice system will function in the twenty-first century.

- *Issue:* There is increased dissatisfaction with the juvenile justice system. There is even a question as to whether the juvenile justice system will survive.

    First Trend: It likely that the adult justice system will be involved more with older juveniles than it currently is and that the structure of the juvenile justice system will change in rather significant ways. But it is very unlikely that this nation will give up anytime in the near future on its century-long experiment with a separate system for juveniles.

- *Issue:* There is concern about the increased numbers of juveniles being transferred to the adult court and sent to adult prison, sometimes receiving long prison terms.

    Second Trend: There is no reason to believe that in the next couple of decades, fewer juveniles will be transferred to the adult court and sentenced in that court.

- *Issue:* State legislatures are increasingly becoming involved in passing laws related to the social control of juveniles.

    Third Trend: Legislatures are likely to become more involved, rather than less involved, in juvenile court law. One of the purposes of this increased involvement will be to raise penalties against gang members and those who try to recruit children into gangs. This trend signals a shift toward punishing juveniles and adults on the basis of who they are rather than what they have done.

■ *Issue:* Some argue that the death penalty would be a deterrent to the juvenile who might otherwise kill, especially if it were more widely used. Others are horrified that the state is even considering executing youthful offenders.

Fourth Trend: The execution of juveniles will probably take place less frequently in the future than it has in the immediate past. Indeed, many juvenile death penalty sentences were reversed in the 1990s.

■ *Issue:* In U.S. society, too many juveniles have guns and, unquestionably, the increased number of teenagers with firearms has contributed to the high rates of juvenile violence. The debate focuses on the key issue of how to get guns out of the hands of juveniles. To express this in another way, what kinds of gun control measures, if any, will prove successful for youthful violent offenders?

Fifth Trend: The issue of gun control may be the most serious problem facing juvenile justice in the early decades of the twenty-first century. The real progress, especially in urban areas, that was made in the 1990s in reducing the availability of guns to juveniles will probably continue in this century.

■ *Issue:* There is a concentrated effort at the present time to focus prevention and treatment interventions on serious, violent, and chronic offenders.

Sixth Trend: It is unlikely that the Juvenile Justice and Delinquency Prevention Office and the national programs that are founded by this office will have any short- or long-term effects on reducing chronic and violent behaviors among a certain subset of high-risk juveniles.

■ *Issue:* There is evidence that the juvenile justice system is becoming increasingly discriminatory when it comes to the processing of minorities.

Seventh Trend: Remembering that the growth in the juvenile population will come largely from poor youngsters, many of whom are members of minorities, there is a good chance that the system will demonstrate less, rather than more, fairness in handling minorities in the future.

■ *Issue:* After a number of years of expansion, the growth of youth gangs stalled in the final years of the twentieth century. Youth gangs were still considered extremely problematic at the end of the century.

Eighth Trend: Youth gangs will continue to persist as a serious problem in the twenty-first century. They provide too much of a support system for those who lack such support systems in other social settings.

■ *Issue:* It is widely agreed that there are more troubled teenagers now than in the past. The rise in the 1990s in some categories of drug use among adolescents may be perceived as a signal that drug use has not bottomed out with mid- and low-risk youths and that these youths need treatment intervention.

Ninth Trend: It is likely that there will be an increased return to the medicalization of delinquents in the near future, which will mark a return to the 1960s and will place a different spin on diversion. Consistent with the past, those who receive such treatment in private hospitals and treatment centers will be children of the haves rather than the have nots.

SUMMARY

This chapter has examined the organizational context of correcting and controlling crime in the United States. The juvenile justice system has improved during the past twenty years, but the improvements hardly seem to have scratched the surface of the problem of designing a justice system that will effectively deal with youth crime in the United States. The serious problem of juvenile delinquency in the United States challenges the juvenile justice system to mobilize a coordinated and unified approach. But conflicting philosophies and strategies for dealing with youth crime and a fragmented system that varies from one jurisdiction to another make it nearly impossible for the juvenile justice process to handle delinquency effectively. The recent efforts to coordinate a continuum of sanctions towards violent and chronic youthful offenders are certainly hopeful and represent positive directions for the juvenile justice system. The next four chapters will examine more clearly how the system works and what can be done to make it more effective.

KEY TERMS

aftercare, p. 389

adjudicatory hearing, p. 389

adjustment model, p. 389

balanced and restorative model, p. 392

commitment, p. 389

crime control model, p. 392

detention, p. 389

dispositional hearing, p. 389

intake division, p. 384

juvenile court officer, p. 389

Juvenile Justice and Delinquency Prevention Act, p. 394

justice model, p. 392

medical model, p. 389

minor, p. 389

petition, p. 389

petitioner, p. 389

probation officer, p. 385

reintegration model, p. 392

rehabilitative philosophy, p. 389

residential programs, p. 384

respondent, p. 389

taking into custody, p. 389

CRITICAL THINKING QUESTIONS

1. The juvenile justice system has devised four ways to deal with delinquency: the rehabilitative model, the justice model, the balanced and restorative model, and the crime control model. Which do you think works best? Why? Why is the balanced and restorative model gaining such popularity nationwide?

2. After reading this chapter, do you feel encouraged or discouraged about the ability of society to deal effectively with delinquency? Why?

3. Evaluate the recent thrusts to work with violent and chronic juvenile offenders. Is this likely to have much of an impact? Justify your answer.

4. Does society really need a juvenile system? Be able to debate your explanation.

WEB DESTINATIONS

Learn more about the balanced and restorative model at the Office of Juvenile Justice and Delinquency Prevention at this site.
http://ojjdp.ncjrs.org/pubs/implementing/rolechanges.html

Learn more about the crime control model and delinquency at the Justice Center web site University of Alaska Anchorage.
http://www.uaa.alaska.edu/just/research/8906dfys.html

Use the search box on the Office of Juvenile Justice and Delinquency Prevention site to find out more about disproportionate minority confinement of juveniles.
http://ojjdp.ncjrs.org/

Read more about the 1974 Juvenile Justice and Delinquency Prevention Act at the National Criminal Justice Reference Service site.
http://www.ncjrs.org/txtfiles/ojjdpact.txt

NOTES

1. Stephen J. Morse, "Immaturity and Irresponsibility," *The Journal of Criminal Law & Criminology* 88 (1998), p. 15.
2. *Ibid.*, p. 66.
3. Elizabeth S. Scott and Thomas Grisso, "The Evolution of Adolescence: A Developmental Perspective on Juvenile Justice Reform," *The Journal of Criminal Law & Criminology* 88 (1988), p. 88.
4. Marty Beyer, "Immaturity, Culpability & Competency in Juveniles: A Study of 17 Cases," *Criminal Justice* (summer 2000), pp. 26–35.
5. Barry C. Feld, "The Transformation of the Juvenile Court," *Minnesota Law Review* 75 (February 1991), p. 578.
6. *Ibid.*, p. 723.
7. *Ibid.*, pp. 723–724.
8. For specific numbers of staff in juvenile corrections, see Timothy J. Flanagan and Kathleen Maguire, *Sourcebook of Criminal Justice Statistics-1999* (Washington, D.C.: U.S. Government Printing Office, 2000).
9. Ibid.
10. Marvin E. Wolfgang, Robert M. Figlio, and Thorsten Sellin, *Delinquency in a Birth Cohort* (Chicago: University of Chicago Press, 1972), pp. 91, 131.
11. Lyle W. Shannon, *Assessing the Relationships of Adult Criminal Careers to Juvenile Careers: A Summary*, pp. 14–15.
12. Donna Martin Hamparian, et. al., *The Violent Few: A Study of Dangerous Juvenile Offenders* (Lexington, Mass.: Lexington Books, 1980), p. xvii.
13. Howard N. Snyder and Melissa Sickmund, *Juvenile Offenders and Victims: 1999 National Report* (Washington, D.C.: Office of Juvenile Justice and Delinquency Prevention, 1999), p. 80.
14. Andrew von Hirsch, *Doing Justice: The Choice of Punishments* (New York: Hill & Wang, 1976), p. 12.
15. President's Commission on Law Enforcement and Administration of Justice, *Task Force Report: Corrections* (Washington, D.C.: U. S. Government Printing Office, 1967).
16. David Fogel, " . . . *We Are the Living Proof: The Justice Model for Corrections* (Cincinnati: Anderson Publishing Company, 1975); Andrew von Hirsch, *Doing Justice: The Choice of Punishments* (New York: Hill & Wang, 1976; Twentieth Century Fund Task Force on Sentencing Policy Toward Young Offenders, *Confronting Youth Crime* (New York: Holmes and Meier, 1978).
17. Fogel, "We Are the Living Proof."
18. D. W. Ness, "Restorative Justice," in *Criminal Justice, Restitution, and Reconciliation*, ed. Burt Galaway and Joe Hudson (Monsey, N.J.: Willow Tree Press, 1990; H. Zehr, *Retributive Justice, Restorative Justice* (Akron, Penn: Mennonite Central Committee, 1985); H. Zehr, *Changing Lenses* (Scottsdale, Penn: Herald Press, 1990).
19. Dennis Mahoney, Dennis Romig, and Troy Armstrong, "Juvenile Probation: The Balanced Approach," *Juvenile and Family Court Journal* 39 (1988); and G. Bazemore, "On Mission Statements and Reform in Juvenile Justice:
The Case for the Balanced Approach, *Federal Probation* 56 (1992).
20. See James Q. Wilson, *Thinking About Crime*, revised edition (New York: Basic Books, 1983); and Ernest van den Haag, *Punishing Criminals: Concerning a Very Old and Painful Question* (New York: Hill and Wang, 1976).
21. Snyder and Sickmund, *Juvenile Offenders and Victims*, p. 89.
22. Ibid.
23. Ibid.
24. Howard N. Snyder and Melissa Sickmund, *Juvenile Offenders and Victims: 1999 National Report* (Washington, D.C.: National Center for Juvenile Justice, 1999), pp. 87–88.
25. Paul Lerman, "Child Convicts," *Transaction* 8 (July/August, 1971, pp. 35–42; Clemens Bartollas, Stuart J. Miller, and Simon Dinitz, *Juvenile Victimization: The Institutional Paradox* (New York: Halsted Press, 1976), pp. 151–168.
26. Ibid.
27. The estimated number of youths confined in jails during the 1970s ranged from 900,000 (Children's Defense Fund) to 100,000 (National Council on Crime and Delinquency). See also Rosemary C. Sari, "Gender Issues in Juvenile Justice," *Crime and Delinquency* 29 (1983), p. 390.
28. Bureau of Justice Statistics, *Prison and Jail Inmates at Midyear 1996* (Washington, D.C.: U.S. Department of Justice, 1997), pp. 6–7.
29. Charles E. Frazier and Donna M. Bishop, "Jailing Juveniles in Florida: the Dynamics of Compliance to a Sluggish Federal Referral Initiative." Paper presented to the Annual Meeting of the American Society of Criminology, Baltimore, Maryland (November 1990), pp. 1–2.
30. Ira M. Schwartz, Linda Harris, and Laurie Levi, "The Jailing of Juveniles in Minnesota: A Case Study," *Crime and Delinquency* 34 (April 1988), p. 146.
31. David Steinhart, "California's Legislature Ends the Jailing of Children: The Story of a Policy Reversal," *Crime and Delinquency* 34 (1988), pp. 169–170.
32. David Steinhart and Barry Krisberg, "Children in Jail," *State Legislatures* 13 (1987), pp. 12–16.
33. Carl E. Pope and William Feyerherm, *Minorities and the Juvenile Justice System* (Washington, D.C.: Office of Juvenile Justice and Delinquency Prevention, 1995), pp. 2–3.
34. Ibid. See Donna M. Bishop and Charles E. Frazier, *A Study of Race and Juvenile Processing in Florida.* A report submitted to the Florida Supreme Court Racial and Ethnic Bias Study Commission, 1990.
35. Snyder and Sickmund, *Juvenile Offenders and Victims: 1999 National Report*, p. 192.
36. Krisberg, et al., *Guide for Implementing the Comprehensive Strategy for Serious, Violent, and Chronic Juvenile Offenders*, p. 133.
37. Ibid.
38. Ibid., pp. 12–13.

chapter 14

THE POLICE AND THE JUVENILE

OBJECTIVES

After reading this chapter, the student will be able to answer the following questions:

- What has been the history of police-juvenile relations?

- How have juvenile attitudes toward the police changed?

- How are juvenile offenders processed?

- What are the legal rights of juveniles?

- How does the prevention and deterrence of juvenile offenders take place?

- What is the extent of police deviance with juveniles?

A director of a youth service bureau describes what he feels is an exemplary juvenile police officer:

Darrell Dirks, a juvenile officer, *is beautiful. He talks like a kid. He walks down the halls of school. Kids will punch him in the shoulder. He'll smile and punch them in the shoulder. He solves many crimes simply because he talks with the kids and hangs out with them. They'll tell him who is doing what. The kids have more respect for him than I've ever seen in a juvenile police officer. When I was down there a couple of days ago, two kids came in his office just to talk with him. One was a runaway and didn't know what to do, but she went to the police to talk with Darrell because she knew he would help.*[1]

What are some of the qualities that make Darrell Dirks special with juveniles? How is it possible for someone working in the juvenile or criminal justice system to become a Darrell Dirks in relating to juveniles?

Darrell Dirkses are found in many police departments in the United States. These officers are a real credit to police work, and they do their best to make a difference in the lives of young people. Yet there are several reasons why most police officers prefer to avoid juveniles committing delinquent acts. Juvenile crime represents one of the most demanding and frustrating areas of police work. A common complaint of police officers is that arrested juvenile offenders are back on the streets before the officers have had a chance to complete the necessary paperwork. Also, with the rise of youth gangs and with the increased numbers of juveniles carrying weapons, policing juveniles is much more dangerous than it used to be. Finally, police departments give little status to those dealing with youth crime because they regard the juveniles as a poor "bust."

In the United States, policing takes place in a free and democratic society. It is a government that values human rights and the freedom of the individual. What this means is that democratic systems of government build a delicate balance between individual rights and collective needs. The balance, based on a long history of constitutional government, is weighted on the side of individual rights.

But in the midst of valuing human freedom and the restraint of government, crime has become a serious concern in the United States. In this context, "get tough" strategies for dealing with crime have become increasingly popular. This has led to the conviction that intensified law enforcement is the only remedy for the crime crisis facing this nation.

Policing juveniles is similar in some ways to policing adults, and in other ways it is quite different. It is similar in that both juveniles and adults have constitutional protections. It is similar in that juveniles can be as hostile to the police as adults can be, and armed juveniles, of course, are as dangerous as armed adults. It is similar in that both juveniles and adults are involved in gangs, some of which traffic drugs. It is similar in that alcohol and drugs affect the functioning of both juveniles and adults. A major difference between policing juveniles and adults is that adult offenders have an increased opportunity for wrongdoing because of the widespread availability of drugs. Large supplies of drugs and cash provide both temptation and opportunity, and the police corruption scandals that have taken place in so many cities are reminders of corrupt officers ("rotten apples") and corrupt structures, or subcultures, within departments ("rotten barrels"). Another major difference is the belief that juveniles are more salvageable than adults. Few would argue with the widely held tenet that juveniles are more likely than adults to experience a turning point where they walk away from crime.

Accordingly, the importance of police-juvenile relations cannot be minimized. The police are usually the first contact a youth has with the juvenile justice system. As the doorway into the system, the police officer can use his or her broad discretion to either detour youths or involve them in the system. In a real sense, the police officer becomes an on-the-spot prosecutor, judge, and correctional system when dealing with a juvenile offender.

The History of Police-Juvenile Relations

In the seventeenth and eighteenth centuries, the American colonists and immigrants installed in the small colonial towns such informal methods of control as the "mutual pledge," the "watch and ward," and the constable system. These informal methods of control by the family, the church, and the community were sufficient until the expansion of towns in the late eighteenth and nineteenth centuries resulted in increased disorder and crime. To deal with their crime problem, New York, Boston, and

Philadelphia created police forces in the 1830s and 1840s, and by the 1870s, all major cities had full-time police forces. At that time, however, the police were drawn from the least educated segments of society, were ill-treated, and were poorly paid. Furthermore, they often became instruments of political corruption, used for personal gain and political advantage.

In the late nineteenth century, law-violating juveniles received various kinds of treatment from officers walking the beat. Juveniles might receive the same treatment as adult offenders, or they might be treated as erring children and receive only slaps on the wrist. Juvenile offenders were sometimes taken to the parish priest for admonition and spiritual instruction.

In the first third of the twentieth century, the New York City, Portland, Oregon, and Washington, D.C. police departments began to address the problem of juvenile crime. The New York City Police Department began a program in 1914 that, with prevention as its goal, helped juveniles develop relationships with local police. This idea of prevention became so popular that 90 percent of the nation's cities had instituted some type of juvenile program by 1924.[2] The Police Athletic League (PAL) was launched in the 1920s, and by the 1930s, most large departments had either assigned welfare officers to difficult districts, initiated employment bureaus for youthful males, assigned officers to juvenile courts, or set up special squads to deal with juvenile crime.[3]

In the 1930s, August Vollmer introduced the concept of a youth bureau in the Berkeley, California, police department, emphasizing the importance of crime prevention by the police. Youth bureaus were soon established in other urban departments as the need arose for police specialists in juvenile law enforcement. These specialized units were variously called *crime prevention bureaus, juvenile bureaus, youth aid bureaus, juvenile control bureaus,* and *juvenile divisions.*

The role of the **juvenile officer** developed further after World War II, and it was formalized when a group of juvenile officers organized the Central States Juvenile Officers Association in 1955 and the International Juvenile Officers Association in 1957. Through their participation in these regional, national, and international associations, juvenile officers expended considerable effort in developing the duties, standards, procedures, and training necessary for dealing with juvenile lawbreakers. As defined by the officers themselves, the basic responsibility of the juvenile officer was to be helpful, rather than punitive, in handling youthful offenders.

In the 1960s, a number of police programs designed to improve relations with juveniles and to reduce delinquency were developed throughout the United States. Police officers came into the public schools to interact with grade school and high school students and to discuss some aspects of the law with them. The Police Athletic League programs were expanded to cover leadership training, full- and part-time employment opportunities, and moral training, as well as extensive recreational programs (See Treatment Intervention 14.1). To prevent and control delinquency, the police also became involved in truancy prevention programs, drug abuse rehabilitation, and the actual supervision of youthful offenders.

The degree of involvement in juvenile work varied among different police departments during the 1970s. Although some departments became even more actively involved in juvenile work, the trend in the late 1970s and early 1980s was for police departments to move away from deep involvement in juvenile work. Budgetary constraints, as well as the administrative problems caused by specialization, caused many police departments to drop their juvenile divisions or to limit their jurisdiction to dependent, neglected, and abused children. Detective divisions in these departments generally assumed responsibility for juvenile and adult criminal investigations.

In the 1980s and 1990s, the proliferation of substance abuse among young people resulted in the movement of the police back into the schools. This trend in juvenile-police relations was more concerned with preventing the use of drugs than with diverting drug users from the juvenile justice system. The widely used Drug Abuse Resistance Education (DARE) program, which will be evaluated later in this chapter, demonstrated this trend in police-juvenile work.

TREATMENT INTERVENTION 14.1

Police Athletic League (PAL)

PAL started with a bang—a rock through a window.

A gang of New York toughs, harassing storekeepers and generally making life miserable in their neighborhood, threw the rock that eventually pioneered this new approach to the problem of juvenile delinquency.

Lieutenant Ed W. Flynn of the Police Department Crime Prevention Bureau was on duty that fateful day. To him it was another day of kids getting in trouble. But it was more than that.

Lieutenant Flynn liked kids. He wondered at the uselessness of always punishing them. He wondered why they couldn't be reached before they were in trouble.

That day, he made it a point to search out the gang's ringleader. They talked, Flynn looking for the reasons behind the kids' antisocial behavior, the ringleader pouring out the frustrations of the ghetto, telling the cop, "Man, we ain't got no place to play . . . nothin' to do. The cops are always hasslin' us. We can't even play baseball."

Flynn thought about that. A staunch baseball fan himself, he began to wonder: "Why should the police chase kids for doing what was normal? Why not help those kids form a team? Give them a place to play under police supervision. Be a friend instead of an enemy."

Flynn found a playground where the group could play under the eyes of friendly policemen.

The team was an instant success. Before the year was out, there were close to a dozen such teams in the city. In 1937, PAL dedicated its first indoor youth center and in 1941, it became incorporated under the laws of the state of New York.

That was the birth of PAL.

Presently, PAL in New York City provides programming for 65,000 children, including:

- Seventeen full-time youth centers and seventy-one part-time centers operating from October through May,
- summer day camps,
- educational programs (computer training, illustrated art and poetry contests, homework help and remedial reading, and many others),
- employment training and placement,
- sports and precinct programs (17,000 teams in basketball, baseball, flag football, and soccer) and
- child care (five Headstart centers and four day care centers).

PAL has become the largest juvenile crime prevention program in the United States, with over three million youth members. The National PAL encompasses more than 500 cities, townships, and counties.

Why have the police in so many jurisdictions responded so enthusiastically to PAL? Why don't we hear more about PAL? Is it as good and as positive to juveniles as it appears to be?

Source: New Mexico Police Athletic League, http://www.nmpal.com. and New York City Police Athletic League, http://www.palnyc.org.

In addition to the drug prevention programs of the 1980s, the police in the 1990s were called upon to provide security and safety in the school, to enforce drug-free school zone laws and the Gun-Free School Zones Act, and to conduct various school attendance programs. Needless to say, the explosion of drug-trafficking gangs across the nation and the greater accessibility of firearms among adolescents have made it much more difficult to provide safety for students and personnel and to ensure the enforcement of the law.

Juveniles' Attitudes toward the Police

The subject of juveniles' attitudes toward the police received considerable attention in the 1970s but has received little empirical examination in recent years. Robert Portune's 1971 study of almost 1,000 junior high students in Cincinnati found that whites had more favorable attitudes toward the police than African Americans, that girls had more favorable attitudes than boys, and that students from middle- and upper-class families had better attitudes than those from lower-class families. He also found that hostility toward the law and police increased progressively during grades seven through nine.[4]

Several studies have reported that juveniles who have had contact with the police have more negative attitudes toward police than do those who have not had contact. L. Thomas Winfree Jr. and Curt T. Griffiths's 1977 study of students in seventeen high schools found that to a considerable degree, juveniles' attitudes toward the police are shaped by contacts with police officers. Negative contacts, according to Winfree and Griffiths, influence juvenile attitudes more than do the factors of sex, race, residence, or socioeconomic status and appear to be twice as important as positive ones in determining juvenile attitudes toward police officers.[5]

William T. Rusinko et. al., in examining about 1,200 ninth grade students in three junior high schools in Lansing, Michigan in 1978, explored the importance of police contact in formulating juveniles' attitudes toward the police. They found that positive police contacts by the white youths in their study clearly neutralized their encounters with police that had negative connotations. But these researchers found that positive police contact did not reduce the tendency for African American youths to be less positive in their opinions of police. The findings agree with several other studies that show the development of a culturally accepted view of police among African Americans independent of their arrest experience.[6]

Scott H. Decker, in a 1981 review of the literature on attitudes toward the police, concluded that youths had more negative attitudes toward the police than did older citizens and that race, the quality of police services, and previous experiences with the police also affected citizens' attitudes.[7] In 1990, James R. Davis found in a very small sample of New Yorkers younger than 20 years of age, however, that attitudes toward the police were not statistically related to age.[8]

Respect for and deference to police officers may result in leniency. Youths who are disrespectful, hostile, or in any way abusive toward police officers are more likely to end up in juvenile court.

Komanduri S. Murty, Julian B. Roebuck, and Joann D. Smith found in a 1990 Atlanta study that "older, married, white-collar educated, and employed respondents reported a more positive image of the police than their counterparts—younger, single, blue-collar, low-educated, unemployed/underemployed respondents."[9] Murty and colleagues offered support for previous findings that younger African American males are particularly hostile toward the police. These researchers demonstrated that the chances that respondents will have negative attitudes toward the police also vary, in descending order, with residence in high-crime tracts, single marital status, negative contacts with the police, and blue-collar occupations.[10]

Michael J. Leiber, Mahesh K. Nalla, and Margaret Farnworth's 1998 study challenges the traditional argument that juveniles' interactions with the police are the primary or sole determinant of youths' attitudes toward the police. Instead, according to these authors, juveniles' "attitudes toward authority and agents of social control develop in a larger sociocultural context, and global attitudes toward police affect youths' assessment of specific police contacts." Using a sample of Iowa youth who were accused of delinquency or adjudicated as delinquent, they found that social background variables (particularly minority status) and subcultural preferences (particularly commitment to delinquent norms) affected youths' attitudes toward the police both directly and indirectly (through police-juvenile interactions).[11]

The Monitoring the Future survey of high school seniors revealed that the percentage of respondents who feel that the police are doing a "good" or "very good" job has continued to decline since the 1980s. For example, in 1984, 36.9 percent of the 3,287 seniors responded "good" or "very good" in evaluating the performance of the police; yet, in 1996, only 26.6 percent of the 2,455 seniors responding were willing to give the police this same high rating. Little variation existed in the ratings among male seniors (28.6 percent) and female seniors (26.5 percent), but as anticipated from previous studies, there was a disturbing difference between white seniors (30.7 percent) and African American seniors (14.6 percent). This appears to be particularly significant when it is compared to the 31.7 percent of the 1984 African American seniors who perceived the police's performance in positive terms.[12]

We can draw several conclusions from these studies. Juveniles' attitudes toward the police are formed in a larger sociocultural context. It is within this sociocultural context that youths' attitudes toward authority and police are shaped. Most youths appear to have positive attitudes toward the police. Younger juveniles have more positive attitudes than older ones. Whites are usually more positive toward the police than African Americans, and girls are more positive than boys. Middle- and upper-class youngsters tend to be more positive than lower-class ones. The more deeply committed a juvenile is to crime, the more hostile he or she is toward the police. But the findings about the influence of contacts with the police are mixed. Some researchers have found that the more contacts a juvenile has with the police, the more negative he or she feels about the police. Others have concluded that for white youths, positive contacts tend to neutralize the effect of negative contacts. Finally, a survey of high school seniors reveals that the attitudes of juveniles toward the police seem to be on a sharp decline during the past two decades.

How Juvenile Offenders Are Processed

In responding to juvenile lawbreakers, police are influenced by a variety of individual, sociocultural, and organizational factors. They can choose a more or less restrictive response to an individual offender. In What Would You Do? 14.2, Ann Miller, a police detective with the Cedar Falls Police Department explains some of her reasoning in terms of how juvenile offenders should be handled.

WHAT WOULD YOU DO?   14.2

Detective Ann Miller Responds

"Let us take an incident: A juvenile male is involved in some form of criminal mischief. He causes a little damage to a house (for example, egging, spray-painting, etc.) and his basic intention was not to do any major damage, but primarily as a prank.

How I would handle this depends on several factors. How much damage was done, what kind of damage, the juvenile's intent, and how the victim feels. If the damage is minor and the victim does not want to press charges but still wants some type of restitution, the juvenile may be asked to come back and clean up the damage and/or pay for the damage himself. Along with that is the juvenile's intent and attitude. Was it just a prank and the juvenile is apologetic for it or does he have the attitude that he won't go back and clean it up and does not feel remorseful for the damage? Finally, how much support does the juve-

nile have at home? Are the parents supportive of the police and victim and will they hold the juvenile accountable for his actions or is there no support at home. If the attitude of the juvenile is poor and if the juvenile is not going to be held accountable for the damage by his parents then I would most likely have to handle it in a more formal way with charges."

Do you feel that Detective Miller's statement is a reasonable one? What do some of the stories in *Voices of Delinquency* suggest is a real advantage of not being arrested and processed through the juvenile system?

Source: Interviewed in September 2001.

Factors That Influence Police Discretion

Police **discretion** can be defined as "the choice between two or more possible means of handling a situation confronting the police officer."[13] Discretion is important, for the police actually act as a court of first instance in initially categorizing a juvenile. The police officer thus becomes a legal and social traffic director who can use his or her wide discretion to detour juveniles from the juvenile justice system or involve them in it.

Police discretion has come under attack because many believe the police abuse their broad discretion. But most police contact with juveniles is impersonal and nonofficial and consists simply of orders to "Get off the corner," "Break it up," or "Go home." Studies generally estimate that only 10 to 20 percent of police-juvenile encounters become official contacts.[14] For example, Bordua's study of the Detroit police found only 5,282 official contacts out of 106,000 encounters.[15]

The point can also be made that the juvenile justice system could not function without police discretion. Urban courts, especially, are overloaded. Probation officers' caseloads are entirely too high. Many juvenile correctional institutions are jammed to capacity. If police were to increase by two to three times the number of youths they referred to the system, the resulting backlog of cases would be unmanageable.

The police officer's disposition of the juvenile offender is mainly determined by nine factors: (1) nature of the offense, (2) citizen complainants, (3) gender, (4) race, (5) socioeconomic status, (6) other individual characteristics of the juvenile, (7) nature of the interaction between the police officer and the juvenile, (8) departmental policy, and (9) external pressures in the community (See Table 14.1).

NATURE OF THE OFFENSE   The most important factor determining the disposition of the misbehaving juvenile is the seriousness of the offense. Donald J. Black and Albert J. Reiss Jr. point out that the great bulk of police encounters with juveniles pertain to matters of minor legal significance, but the probability of arrest increases with the legal seriousness of the alleged offense.[16]

TABLE 14.1

Factors That Influence the Disposition of Juvenile Offenders

INDIVIDUAL FACTORS
Personality characteristics of the juvenile
Personality characteristics of the police officer
Interaction between the police officer and the juvenile

SOCIOCULTURAL FACTORS
Citizen complaints
Gender of the juvenile
Race/ethnicity of the juvenile
Socioeconomic status of the juvenile
The influence of cultural norms in the community and values of the wider society on both juveniles and police officers
External pressures in the community to arrest certain types of juvenile offenders

ORGANIZATIONAL FACTORS
Nature of the offense
Departmental policy

CITIZEN COMPLAINANTS   A number of studies have found that the presence of a citizen or the complaint of a citizen is an important determining factor in the disposition of an incident involving a juvenile.[17] If a citizen initiates a complaint, remains present, and wishes the arrest of a juvenile, the chances are that the juvenile will be arrested and processed.[18] If the potential arrest situation results from police patrol, the chances are much greater that the youth will be warned and released.

SEX OF THE OFFENDER   Traditionally, girls have been less likely than boys to be arrested and referred to the juvenile court for criminal offenses, but there is some evidence of the erosion of police "chivalry" in the face of youthful female criminality.[19] Yet, as Chapter 7 noted, girls are far more likely to be referred to the court if they violate traditional role expectations for girls, such as running away from home, failing to obey parents, or being sexually promiscuous.[20] In short, the police tend to reflect the views of complaining parents, for example, that girls should be chaste and should be protected from immoral behavior.

RACE OF THE OFFENDER   Studies differ on the importance of race in determining juvenile disposition. On the one hand, several studies (after results were corrected to account for offense seriousness and prior record) have found that the police are more inclined to arrest minority juveniles.[21] The strongest evidence showing race as a determining factor is found in the Philadelphia cohort study. Marvin Wolfgang et al. concluded "that the most significant factor related to a boy not being remediated by the police, but being processed to the full extent of the juvenile justice system, is his being nonwhite."[22] However, several other studies failed to find much evidence of racial bias. Although it is difficult to appraise the importance of race in the disposition of cases involving juveniles because African Americans and members of other minority groups appear to be involved in serious crimes more often than whites, it does seem that racial bias makes minority juveniles the special targets of the police.[23]

SOCIOECONOMIC STATUS   Substantiating the effect of class on the disposition of cases involving juveniles is difficult because most studies examine race and socioeconomic status together. But lower-class youngsters, according to many critics of the juvenile justice system, receive different "justice" than middle- or upper-class ones. What they mean by this is that lower-class youths are dragged into the net of the system for the same offenses for which white middle- and upper-class juveniles often are sent home. Patrol and juvenile police officers generally agree that there is more concern about "saving" middle- and upper-class juveniles than lower-class ones, but they justify this use of discretion by saying that the problematic behavior of middle- and upper-class children is more likely to be corrected because their parents can afford psychotherapy and other such resources.

INDIVIDUAL FACTORS OF THE OFFENDER   Such individual factors as prior arrest record, previous offenses, age, peer relationships, family situation, and conduct of parents also have a bearing on how the police officer handles each juvenile.[24] A juvenile who is older and has committed several previous offenses is likely to be referred to the juvenile court. Merry Morash found that fitting the common image of a delinquent and dangerous person increases a youth's chances of arrest.[25] The family of the juvenile is also an important variable. An assistant police chief who had spent several years working as a juvenile officer put it this way:

> Most juvenile problems derive from the parents. You've got to get the parents involved to be successful. You've some parents who are concerned, and you can tell they'll take things by the handle when they're dealing with the problem. Other parents simply don't care. If you want to make any headway in this work, it is necessary to stay on top of the family.[26]

NATURE OF POLICE-JUVENILE INTERACTION   Three studies found that a juvenile's deference to a police officer is influential in determining disposition. In 1964, Irving Piliavin and Scott Briar discovered that if a youth is polite and respectful, the chances for informal disposition are greatly increased. But if the juvenile is hostile, police will probably judge him or her to be in need of the juvenile court.[27] Carl Werthman and Piliavin found in 1967 that the hostility and scorn that African American gang members display toward the police resulted in a high rate of court referral.[28] Richard J. Lundman, Richard E. Sykes, and John P. Clark's 1980 replication of Black and Reiss' study concluded that in encounters in which no evidence links a juvenile to an offense, the demeanor of the juvenile is the most important determinant of whether or not formal action is taken.[29]

More recently, the relationship between demeanor and arrest of adult offenders has stirred up considerable controversy among criminologists. David A. Klinger's 1994 and 1996 studies of police behavior in Dade County, Florida, spearheaded this debate in challenging the long-standing belief that police officers are more likely to arrest citizens who do not show them an acceptable level of deference. His basic argument is that demeanor has been measured improperly and has not been controlled adequately for other important variables.[30] Robert E. Worden and Robin L. Shepard's 1996 reanalysis of data collected for the Police Services Study found that the original finding of the importance of disrespectful or hostile demeanor toward the police in influencing the likelihood of arrest holds.[31]

The police officer's personality also shapes the nature of police-juvenile interaction. An officer who "just plain doesn't like kids" is more prone to hassle juveniles than one who is concerned; and when a juvenile reacts with profanity or aggressive behavior to this harassment, the officer may decide an official contact is necessary. An officer who loses his or her "cool" may likewise become involved in a confrontation requiring an official contact.

DEPARTMENTAL POLICY   Departments vary in their policies on handling misbehaving juveniles. In his 1970 study of forty-six police departments in southern California, Malcolm Klein found that some departments referred four out of five to the juvenile court, whereas others warned and released virtually all juvenile contacts.[32] Nathan Goldman's 1969 study of four Pennsylvania communities reported that the proportion of juvenile arrests varied from 9 percent in one community to a high of 71 percent in another.[33] James Q. Wilson found in 1968 that the more professional police departments had higher numbers of juveniles referred to the juvenile court, because they used discretion less than the departments that were not as professional.[34]

EXTERNAL PRESSURES IN THE COMMUNITY   The attitudes of the press and the public, the status of the complainant or victim, and the philosophy and available resources of referral agencies usually influence the disposition of juvenile lawbreakers. The press can do much to encourage a get-tough policy with youthful offenders; for example, a series of newspaper articles on violent youth crime or gang activity can alarm the public and put pressure on police departments to get youthful thugs off the streets. In addition, the higher the socioeconomic status of the complainant or victim, the more likely that a juvenile will be arrested and processed for a crime. On the other hand, when police officers believe that the juvenile court is too permissive to juvenile crime, this "wrist-slapping" may discourage them from arresting youthful offenders.[35] Finally, the police officer who has available such community resources as a youth services bureau frequently responds to juvenile encounters differently from the officer who has no available community resources.

In sum, sufficient studies have been done to provide an outline of an empirical portrait of the policing of juveniles. Of the nine factors influencing police officers' dispositions of juveniles, the seriousness of the offense and complaints by citizens appear to be more important than the other seven factors. Yet individual characteristics of the juvenile, as well as departmental policy and external pressures in the community, also are highly influential in determining how police-juvenile encounters are handled.

Informal and Formal Dispositions of Juvenile Offenders

A patrol officer or juvenile officer has at least five options when investigating a complaint against a juvenile or arriving at the scene of law-violating behavior: warning and releasing the juvenile to the community; making a station adjustment; referring the juvenile to a diversionary agency; issuing a citation and referring him or her to the juvenile court; and taking him or her to a detention facility (See Figure 14.1).

WARNING AND RELEASING TO THE COMMUNITY   The least severe sanction is applied when the patrol officer decides merely to question and release the youth. Commonly, this occurs when a juvenile is caught committing a minor offense. The patrol officer usually gives an informal reprimand to the youth on the street or takes the

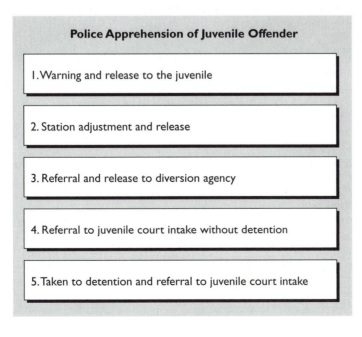

FIGURE 14.1 Police–Juvenile Dispositional Alternatives

Police Apprehension of Juvenile Offender

1. Warning and release to the juvenile

2. Station adjustment and release

3. Referral and release to diversion agency

4. Referral to juvenile court intake without detention

5. Taken to detention and referral to juvenile court intake

juvenile in for a longer interview at the police station. In 1997, about 25 percent of juveniles were handled informally within the department and released.[36]

Until the 1970s, a patrol officer often warned a juvenile, "This better not happen again, or I'll beat your ass the next time I catch you." It was not unheard of for a patrol officer to bring out a paddle and to give the erring juvenile two or three whacks. Now it would be very unwise for a patrol officer to strike a juvenile under any circumstances because of the potential liability that he or she might face if the juvenile's parents decided to sue.

MAKING A STATION ADJUSTMENT   The juvenile can be taken to the station, have the contact recorded, be given an official reprimand, and then be released to the parents. In this situation, the first thing that is done when the juvenile is brought to the station is to contact the parents. In some police departments, juveniles can be placed under police supervision, to remain under supervision until released from probation.

REFERRING TO A DIVERSION AGENCY   The juvenile can be released and referred to a diversion agency. In some jurisdictions, the police operate their own diversion program, but, more typically, juveniles are referred to agencies such as Big Brothers or Big Sisters, a runaway center, or a mental health agency. In 1997, about 1 percent were referred to diversion programs.[37]

ISSUING A CITATION AND REFERRING TO THE JUVENILE COURT   The police officer can issue a **citation** and refer the youth to the juvenile court. The intake counselor of the juvenile court, who is usually a probation officer, then decides whether or not a formal petition should be filed and the youth should appear before the juvenile judge. The juvenile is returned to the family with this disposition.

In 1997, more than two-thirds of the juveniles arrested by the police were referred to court intake. About 91 percent of these juveniles were referred to court intake, but the other 9 percent were referred to criminal courts for prosecution as adults.[38] Law enforcement agencies referred less than half of the formally processed status offenses in 1996, but they referred 86 percent of the delinquency cases to the juvenile court.[39] Table 14.2 gives the percent of delinquency cases referred to juvenile court by police agencies in 1996:

TABLE 14.2

Percent of Delinquency Cases Referred to Juvenile Court by Law Enforcement Agencies in 1996

Total Delinquency	86%
Murder	96
Burglary	95
Robbery	95
Motor Vehicle Theft	94
Drugs	93
Shoplifting	92
Aggravated Assault	91
Weapons	91
Vandalism	90
Forcible Rape	90
Disroderly Conduct	87
Simple Assault	83
Escape	67
Obstruction of Justice	36
Probation Violation	13

Source: Howard N. Snyder and Melissa Sickmund, *Juvenile Offenders and Victims: 1999 National Report* (Washington, D.C.: National Center for Juvenile Justice, 1999), p. 143.

TAKING TO THE DETENTION CENTER   Finally, the police officer can issue a citation, refer the youth to the juvenile court, and take him or her to a detention center. An intake worker at the detention center then decides whether the child should be returned to the parents or left at the detention center. A juvenile is left in detention when he or she is thought to be dangerous to self or others in the community or has no care in the home. A few communities have shelter care facilities that are available for status offenders. In communities that lack detention facilities, juveniles must be taken to the county jail or the police lockup, both of which are inappropriate places for juveniles. Taking youths out of their own homes and placing them in detention facilities clearly must be a last resort.

Police Attitudes Toward Youth Crime

The police overall have more positive attitudes today toward youthful offenders than in the past, but three occupational determinants of the police work against even more positive attitudes toward youth crime.[40] First, the police see themselves as skilled in their ability to apprehend criminals, but the leniency of juvenile court codes makes them believe that nothing will happen to apprehended youths unless the offense is serious.[41] The police, in large cities especially, think that youth crime is out of control because of the permissiveness of the juvenile justice system. In 1977, Edward M. Davis, who was then chief of police for Los Angeles, predicted some grim consequences of this permissiveness:

> As the juvenile justice system continues to operate under present constraints, we know that it is building an army of criminals who will prey on our communities. The benign neglect that we have shown has made children with special problems into adult monsters that will be with us forever. If improvements to this system don't come, it will ensure a generation of criminals who will make the current batch look like kids on a Sunday school picnic.[42]

The dangers in their jobs also require the police to be alert to assailants who indicate trouble or danger; therefore, experienced police officers know that they must be guarded in a police-juvenile encounter because juveniles' unpredictability and resistance make their arrests difficult.[43] The hardcore offender represents the greatest danger to the police officer. Violent gang members, for example, have few qualms about killing police officers.[44] This is especially true for adult street gang members, but it is increasingly true for juveniles who are members of street and youth gangs. See the interview with Loren A. Evenrud in Social Policy 14.3 for more details on the increased dangers in juvenile work today for the police officer.

Furthermore, the police must always defend the authority of their position, which requires them to quash any verbal or physical abuse from either teenagers or adults.[45] Juveniles offenders, especially those who have had prior contact with the system, are likely to challenge the authority of the police officer. They usually know how far they can push the officer, and they are quite cognizant of their rights. Juveniles are even more likely to challenge the authority of the police officer when they are with peers; therefore, new officers are advised to avoid talking with a youthful offender in front of his or her peers.[46]

Patrol officers are particularly reluctant to engage in a police-juvenile encounter; their first reaction is to call out juvenile police officers or detectives who work with juveniles to get this "mess" off their hands. But juvenile officers and detectives who work with juveniles on a day-to-day basis are more service-oriented than patrol officers. The police officers who run such programs as DARE and SPEDA in the public schools, who are involved in the Police Athletic League, and who interact with juveniles in other prevention programs usually feel quite positive about police-juvenile interactions. As previously stated, the positive attitudes that some juvenile officers and detectives have toward youthful offenders enable them sometimes to develop remarkable rapport with these offenders.

The Legal Rights of Juveniles

The rights of juveniles in custody have changed dramatically since the days when the "third degree" was given at the station. Although some departments have lagged behind others in granting due process rights to juveniles under arrest, the majority of them now comply with court decisions concerning the rights of juveniles. Yet because few juvenile cases are appealed, police practices by which juveniles are denied their due process rights are usually known only at the local level.[47]

Search and Seizure

The Fourth Amendment to the Constitution of the United States protects citizens from unauthorized **search and seizure.** In 1961, the Supreme Court decision in *Mapp v. Ohio* affirmed Fourth Amendment rights for adults. This decision stated that evidence gathered in an unreasonable search and seizure—that is, evidence seized without probable cause and without a proper search warrant—was inadmissible in court.[48] In *State v. Lowry* (1967), the Supreme Court applied the Fourth Amendment ban against unreasonable searches and seizures to juveniles:

> Is it not more outrageous for the police to treat children more harshly than adult offenders, especially when such is violative of due process and fair treatment? Can a court countenance a system, where, as here, an adult may suppress evidence with the usual effect of having the charges dropped for lack of proof, and, on the other hand, a juvenile can be institutionalized—lose the most sacred possession a human being has, his freedom—for "rehabilitative" purposes because the Fourth Amendment right is unavailable to him?[49]

Juveniles thus must be presented with a valid search warrant unless they have either waived that right, have consented to have their person or property searched, or have been apprehended in the act. When these conditions have not been met, courts have overturned rulings against juveniles. For example, a 1966 District of Columbia ruling suppressed evidence seized when the police entered a juvenile's apartment without a warrant at 5:00 A.M. to arrest him. The court held that "the Fourth Amendment to the United States Constitution is a protection designed to secure the homes and persons of young and old alike against unauthorized police searches and seizures."[50]

In another case, a Houston police officer stopped a car being driven without lights and issued the driver, a youth, a traffic ticket for that offense as well as for driving without a driver's license. The youth was taken to a police station because the officer had some questions about the automobile's ownership. Five hours after the initial contact, another police officer searched the youth without his consent and without a search warrant and discovered fifty milligrams of marijuana. For this possession of marijuana the youth was committed to the Texas Youth Council. An appellate court released the youth from training school, finding that a search some five hours after the original arrest for driving without lights "can hardly be justified as incidental to the arrest for a traffic offense."[51]

Interrogation Practices

The Fourteenth Amendment of the Constitution affirms that standards of fairness and due process must be used in obtaining confessions. Current standards also require that the totality of circumstances in extracting confessions must be taken into consideration in determining the appropriateness of a confession.

The Supreme Court decision *Haley v. Ohio* is an early example of **police interrogation** excesses. In the *Haley* case, a fifteen-year-old youth was arrested at his home five days after a store robbery in which the owner was shot. Five or six police officers questioned the boy for about five hours; he then confessed after being shown what were alleged to be the confessions of two other youths. No parent or attorney was present during the questioning. The Supreme Court invalidated the confession, stating:

> The age of the petitioner, the hours when he was grilled, the duration of his quizzing, the fact that he had no friend or counsel to advise him, the callous attitude of the police toward his rights combine to convince us that this confession was wrung from a child by means which the law should not sanction. Neither man nor child can be allowed to stand condemned by methods which flout constitutional requirements of due process of law."[52]

The Supreme Court also ruled in *Brown v. Mississippi* that force may not be used to obtain confessions.[53] In this case, police used physical force to extract a confession. Other confessions have been ruled invalid because the accused was too tired, was questioned too long, and was not permitted to talk with spouse, friends, or lawyer either while being interrogated or until he or she confessed.[54]

Juveniles taken into custody are entitled to the rights stated in the 1966 **Miranda v. Arizona** decision. This Supreme Court decision prohibits the use of a confession in court unless the individual was advised of his or her rights before interrogation, especially of the right to remain silent, the right to have an attorney present during questioning, and the right to be assigned an attorney by the state if he or she could not afford one.[55] *In re Gault* (see Chapter 13) made the right against self-incrimination and the right to counsel applicable to juveniles.[56] But the *Gault* decision failed to clarify whether or not a juvenile could waive the protection of the *Miranda* rules; it also failed to specify what is necessary for a juvenile to waive his *Miranda* rights intelligently and knowingly. For example, is a juvenile's ability to waive his rights impaired if he is under the influence of drugs or alcohol or in a state of shock?

The 1979 *Fare v. Michael C.* decision applied the "totality of the circumstances" approach to the interrogation of juveniles. The circumstances behind this case are that Michael C. was implicated in a murder that took place during a robbery. The police arrested the sixteen-year-old youth and brought him to the station. After he was advised of his *Miranda* rights, he requested to see his probation officer. When this request was denied, he proceeded to talk to the police officer, implicating himself in the murder. The Supreme Court ruled in this case that Michael appeared to understand his rights, and when his request to talk with his probation officer was denied, he expressed his willingness to waive his rights and continue the interrogation.[57]

Thomas Grisso found that virtually all the juveniles interrogated by the St. Louis police in 1981 had waived their *Miranda* rights. He then questioned whether juveniles were even "capable of providing a meaningful waiver of the rights to avoid self-incrimination and to obtain legal counsel."[58] After surveying a sample of juveniles, Grisso found that almost everyone younger than fourteen and that half the juveniles in the fifteen- to sixteen-year-old age bracket had less than adequate understanding of what their *Miranda* rights entailed.

Several court cases have held that the minority status of a juvenile is not an absolute bar to a valid confession. A California case upheld the confession of two juveniles from Spanish-speaking families. Although both had been arrested before, one had an I.Q. of sixty-five to seventy-one, with a mental age of ten years and two months.[59] Similarly, a North Carolina court of appeals approved the confession of a twelve-year-old youth who was charged with shooting out a window in a camper truck.[60] Moreover, a Maryland appellate court approved the confession of a sixteen-year-old youth who was a school dropout and had an eighth grade education. He was charged with firebombing and burning a store and a school during a racial confrontation.[61]

To protect juveniles against police interrogation excesses, many jurisdictions have a statutory requirement that a parent, someone acting *in loco parentis* for the child, or counsel for the child must be present at police interrogation in order for a confession to be admissible. In *Commonwealth v. Guyton* (1989), the Massachusetts court held that no other minor, not even a relative, can act as an interested adult.[62] Other courts have ruled that the interested adult may be a child's relative.[63] Some states attempt to protect the juvenile by requiring that the youth be taken to the juvenile detention center or to the juvenile court if not returned immediately to the parents' custody. They obviously prefer that police interrogation take place within juvenile facilities rather than at a police station.

Fingerprinting

Fingerprinting, along with pretrial identification practices, has traditionally been highly controversial procedures in juvenile corrections. Some juvenile court statutes require that a judge approve the taking of fingerprints of juveniles, control access to fingerprint records, and provide for fingerprint destruction under certain circumstances.[64] In many other jurisdictions, the police department determines policy; some police departments routinely fingerprint all juveniles taken into custody and suspected of serious wrongdoing. The Juvenile Justice and Delinquency Prevention Act of 1974 recommended that fingerprints be taken only with the consent of the judge, that juvenile fingerprints not be recorded in the criminal section of the fingerprint registry, and that they be destroyed after their purpose has been served.

A 1969 Supreme Court decision that reversed a Mississippi ruling is the most important case dealing with juvenile fingerprints. In this case, a rape victim had described her assailant only as an African American youth. The only leads at the outset of the police investigation were finger and palm prints found on the sill and borders of the window of the victim's home. Without warrants the police took at least twenty-four African American youths to police headquarters, where they were questioned, fingerprinted, and then released without charge. A fourteen-year-old youth who had performed yard work for the victim was brought to headquarters the day after the offense, questioned, fingerprinted, and released. He was interrogated on several additional occasions over the next four days; several times he was shown to the victim in her hospital room, but she did not identify the youth as her assailant. The police then drove the youth ninety miles to another city, where he was confined overnight in jail. The next day the youth signed a confession statement and was returned to the jail in his community. He was fingerprinted a second time and his fingerprints, along with those of twenty-three other African American youths, were sent to the FBI for comparison with the latent prints taken from the window. The FBI reported that the youth's prints matched those taken from the window. The Supreme Court found that the fingerprint evidence used at the trial was the second set and rejected this evidence because the police had not complied with procedures required in the Fourth Amendment:

> The detention at police headquarters of petitioner and the other young Negroes was not authorized by a judicial officer; petitioner was unnecessarily required to undergo two fingerprinting sessions; and petitioner was not merely fingerprinted during the [first] detention but also subjected to interrogation.[65]

Yet, during the late 1980s and 1990s, fingerprinting of juvenile offenders took place frequently across the United States. At the end of 1997, 46 states and the District of Columbia allowed law enforcement agencies to fingerprint juveniles who had been arrested for felonies or had reached a certain age.[66]

Pretrial Identification Practices

Both photographing and placing juveniles in lineups are highly controversial. Another recent practice is to notify the school district regarding juveniles who have been convicted of serious or violent crimes. The Juvenile Justice and Delinquency Prevention Act recommended that a photograph not be taken without the written consent of the juvenile judge and that the name or picture of any juvenile offender not be made public by the media.

An important case in terms of these **pretrial identification practices** took place in California. A rape victim was shown pictures of a young male taken by the police in another matter. She could not make positive identification, but a few days later she was asked to come to the probation office at a time when this young male was present. This time she did identify him as her assailant. She was also certain of his identification as her assailant at the detention hearing some six weeks later. But the California appellate court held the one-on-one identification attempts to be constitutionally defective: "The practice of showing suspects singly to persons for the purpose of identification has been widely condemned." The judgment was upheld, however, on the basis that the victim's identification of the young male at trial was based on her observation of him during the rape, rather than during the three identification attempts.[67]

Another important case was *United States v. Wade* (1967), in which the Supreme Court ruled that the accused has a right to have counsel present at postindictment lineup procedures.[68] In *Kirby v. Illinois* (1972), the Court went on to add that the defendant's right of counsel at postindictment lineup procedures goes into effect as soon as the complaint or the indictment has been issued.[69] In the *in re Holley* decision (1970), a juvenile accused of rape had his conviction reversed by the appellate court because of the lack of counsel during the lineup identification procedure.[70]

At the end of 1997, forty-five states and the District of Columbia had statutes permitting photographing of juveniles under certain circumstances for criminal history record purposes. Juvenile codes in forty-two states allowed names, and sometimes even pictures and court records, of juveniles who were involved in delinquency proceedings to be released to the media.[71]

How Does the Prevention and Deterrence of Juvenile Offenders Take Place?

Juvenile delinquency poses a difficult problem for the police. Police officers must deal with the range of behaviors from drug-trafficking street gangs to status and runaway offenses. That more juveniles own handguns and are exhibiting violent behavior are two of the major challenges facing the police today. The interview with Sergeant Loren A. Evenrud of the Minneapolis Park Police, Minneapolis, Minnesota, describes these and other challenges facing the police (Social Policy 14.3).

Community-based, school-based, and gang-based interventions are three ways police departments are attempting to implement community-based policing in the prevention and deterrence of youth crime.

Police-juvenile relations take place in the larger context of community policing. In a February 1992 department publication, former New York City Police Commissioner Lee P. Brown defines community policing "as a partnership with the public aimed at reducing crime, arresting offenders, reducing the fear of crime, and improving the quality of life in every neighborhood in the City of New York."[72]

Community-oriented policing (COP), according to Vincent J. Webb and Nanette Graham, is "contemporary American policy."[73] A 1992 survey of the twenty-five largest police departments in the nation revealed that 78 percent reported practicing community policing, 13 percent planned to adopt a community policing program for the near future, and only 9 percent had no plans for a community policing program.[74] It is no wonder that the 1994 crime bill provided nearly nine billion dollars in federal support over the next twelve years to support community policing and related initiatives.

Community-oriented policing appears to be useful in juvenile justice for a number of reasons. It moves police officers from anonymity in the patrol car to *direct* engagement with a community that gives them more immediate information about neighborhood problems and insights into their solutions. COP frees officers from an emergency response system and permits them to engage more directly in *proactive crime prevention*. In addition, COP makes police operations more visible to the public, which *increases police accountability to the public; decentralizes* operations, which allows officers

SOCIAL POLICY 14.3

Interview With Loren A. Evenrud

Question: How has policing with juveniles changed in the past ten years?

Answer: The most obvious change is the dramatic increase in violence among the juvenile population. The availability of firearms has increased manyfold, therefore police can no longer confront juvenile violators in traditional ways. Front-line law enforcement professionals have been forced to apply the highest level of the "use of force continuum" in daily street contacts. For example, officers are often forced to make a "felony stop" on juveniles reported to be in possession of a firearm. This means in the real world that the juvenile will be placed in a prone position in the street or in a park until police can neutralize the situation. This recent phenomenon has placed considerable stress on citizens, not to mention individual police officers who are trying to bring the rule of law to the community.

Question: What has been the impact of street gangs on policing in the community?

Answer: It is abundantly clear that gangs today have collectively learned how to manipulate the community as well as the criminal justice system. It is also well-known that gang members transport negative, anti-social behaviors from the prison culture to our local communities. Gang-connected males today are tougher and are prone to use threats and intimidation to achieve status and property. With no legitimate means of support, these adult males have effectively learned to manipulate females and children. As a result, gangs have become stronger and more entrenched, with more adult males assuming leadership roles without ever meeting even the most basic educational, ethical, and social standards. The gang phenomenon is really about men running kids, and little will change until the issue of the negative adult male role model is addressed. Fundamentally, gangs today are philosophically opposed to the rule of law, which is clearly essential in a healthy society.

Gangs have also changed. Unlike gangs in the early 1900s, when a young person hung out for a time with a local street gang for protection, the typical gang member today is a career criminal who survives by victimizing others. The reality is that gang youth are not growing out of gangs as in the past. Gangs today feature adult leaders who, in essence, call all the shots. The gang organizational structure has been proven to work; therefore, few gang-connected youth have chosen to follow a legitimate career path. Obviously, this decision is also impacted by other economic and societal factors.

Police are now faced with criminal street gangs that span the ethnic and social spectrum. Along with African American, Asian American, Anglo American, Hispanic American, Native American, and even Somalian American gangs, communities in the upper Midwest have been faced with clusters of Neo-Nazi youth who have adopted the philosophies and practices of white supremacist/extremist groups who base their ideology on hate. Occasionally, these hate groups mobilize white youth to challenge openly persons of color in public and private settings. It is appropriate to view any group that threatens the social order in the community as a threat group. Gang organizations or "nations" of any type victimize and polarize communities across the nation.

From a police perspective, it is critical that all helping professionals share in the monitoring of threat groups. It is no secret that the code of silence is very difficult to penetrate and crime victims must have support from all agency professionals. In essence, there must be a melding of aggressive law enforcement with effective gang prevention programs.

Why is the police role with gangs so difficult? What insights does Sergeant Evenrud provide about gangs?

Source: Loren A. Evenrud received his Ph.D. in Educational Policy and Administration from the University of Minnesota in 1987 and is a widely acknowledged expert on street gangs. He has also published numerous articles on gangs in local, state, and national publications. Interviewed in August 1995.

greater familiarity with the workings and needs of various neighborhoods; encourages officers to view *citizens as partners,* which improves relations between the public and the police; and moves decision making and discretion to those who best know the community's problems and expectations.[75]

Community-Based Interventions

Community relations is a major focus of police officers who work with juveniles. They must cultivate good relations with school administrators and teachers, with the staffs of community agencies, with the staffs of local youth organizations and youth shelters, with the juvenile court, and with merchants and employees at popular juvenile hangouts. Of course, the juvenile police officer also must develop good relations with parents of youthful offenders as well as with the offenders themselves. The officer who has earned the respect of the youths of the community will be aware of what is happening in the community and will be called upon for assistance by youths in trouble. Detective Ann Miller gives an example of good community relations with the following comments:

> The most challenging task of working with juveniles is to get them to realize the importance of the decisions they make. Lots of juveniles have an attitude, in which they think they are untouchable and nothing will happen to them.
>
> I don't think juveniles respond to me differently than they would to a male police officer. The bottom line is the type of rapport you build with juveniles. If you are a jerk, juveniles will respond in negative ways. But if you treat juveniles with decency and respect, the chances are that they will respond to you in the same way.
>
> What I find exciting about working with juveniles is that you can have a positive effect on kids. Kids want to learn. The challenge is to be there and to encourage kids to make something positive happen even though they have had trouble in the past. There are some kids I've arrested three or four times before they are able to get some positive things going in their lives.[76]

The police are called on to intercede in a variety of juvenile problems. They have been charged to enforce the curfew ordinances that more and more communities across the nation are passing. Juvenile arrests for curfew law violations increased very dramatically from 1993 to 1996. Although it is unlikely that more youths were violating curfew in 1996 than in 1993, communities apparently decided that keeping juveniles off the streets would reduce juvenile violence.[77]

Juvenile drug abuse arrest rates almost doubled between 1992 and 1996. Self-report studies, as previously reported, do not reflect a large change in drug use among adolescents at this period. In view of the fact that the increase in drug abuse arrests was attributable to arrests for marijuana possession, what seems to have taken place is that

A police officer interacting with a group of kids. Establishing good community relations is crucial for police officers who work with juveniles.

communities have become more concerned about marijuana use among youth and that the police have responded to this concern by arresting more youth for this offense.[78]

Communities have further turned to the police to prevent hate crimes committed by teenagers toward minority groups—Jews and other ethnic groups, and homosexuals. Most hate crimes appear to be committed by offenders under the age of twenty. This is not surprising when it is remembered that films, music, and humor often target young people as the primary audience for a culture of hate.[79]

Police agencies across the nation have further devised special programs aimed at intensive concentration on chronic youthful offenders. The most popular and controversial of these programs is Serious Habitual Offender Drug Involved (S.H.O.D.I.), initiated by the Office of Juvenile Justice and Delinquency Prevention in Ventura, California; Colorado Springs, Colorado; and Jacksonville, Florida.[80] S.H.O.D.I. concentrates on monitoring the behavior of known juvenile offenders. A key to these programs is giving police access to full data on delinquents' arrest records that can be checked by computer any time a youth is stopped for questioning. Once a delinquent is identified—based on guidelines such as four arrests for four serious crimes within a year—police officers keep a closer watch on this youth. "When the kids aren't where they're supposed to be, we go out looking for them," says Gary Higgins of the Jacksonville, Florida, Sheriff Department.[81] Social workers called *trackers* are assigned to these offenders to monitor their behavior up to twenty-four hours a day. When targeted youth are arrested, they are typically held without bond pending a court appearance, are likely to be transferred to the adult court, and are likely to be sentenced to long-term institutional care. Although the youths' attorneys frequently complain that the program leads to police harassment and unfair labeling of their clients, police officials are convinced that it is an effective way to deal with hard-core juvenile offenders.[82]

The control of gun-related violence in the youth population is one of the most serious problems facing the police in deterring youth crime. Indeed, about 80 percent of the homicides of persons fifteen to nineteen years old are committed with guns.[83]

Some communities have pursued a number of strategies to get the guns out of the hands of juveniles. The Kansas City (MO) Gun Experiment is one of the more innovative efforts. A working group made up of the Department of Justice (DOJ), the U.S. Attorney's Office, and the Kansas City Police Department decided to focus police efforts in high-crime neighborhoods by routinely stopping traffic violators and curfew violators. During these stops, police looked for any infraction that would give them the legal authority to search a car or pedestrian for illegal guns. Special gun-intercept teams proved to be ten times more cost effective than regular police patrols.[84]

Programs adopted by other communities include seizing firearms from juvenile offenders in school and ensuring that firearms information is submitted to the federal Alcohol, Tobacco, and Firearms agency for tracing; developing appropriate intervention programs for youth who bring guns to school; developing a broad-based, multidisciplinary strategy to inform juveniles about the dangers of using firearms; preventing them from illegally possessing firearms; rigorously enforcing firearms laws as they relate to juveniles; and reviewing existing state firearms statutes in light of the Youth Handgun Safety Act and Department of Justice's Model Code and making appropriate revisions to eliminate illegal handgun possession and use by juveniles.[85]

In many larger cities, police departments form juvenile units to handle youth crime. A 1997 survey of law enforcement agencies (those with 100 or more sworn officers) reported that a large proportion of these agencies had special units targeting juvenile justice concerns (See Table 14.3).[86]

In the midst of this positive portrait of policing, some mention needs to be made of police corruption and the improper or excessive use of force, which constitute two of the most widely cited criticisms of policing in the United States. Indeed, the two are not separate because police corruption is frequently linked with brutality. Herman Goldstein defines "police corruption" as "the misuse of authority by the police officer in a manner designed to provide personal gain for the officer or for others."[87]

TABLE 14.3

Special Units Targeting Juvenile Justice Concerns

Special units	Type of agency	
	Local police	Sheriff
Drug education in schools	95%	79%
Juvenile crime	66	49
Gangs	55	50
Child abuse	48	53
Domestic violence	46	37
Missing children	33	28
Youth outreach	32	24

Source: Office of Juvenile Justice and Delinquency Prevention, *Juvenile Offenders and Victims: 1999 National Report (Washington, D.C.: U.S. Government Printing Office, 2000), p. 139.*

However, juveniles are much less involved than adults with police officers who are corrupt. They are not usually key players in major drug operations in which corrupt police might be involved. Organized crime figures do not generally involve juveniles when deals are made with corrupt police. Yet what is interesting is that juvenile offenders from urban areas, especially street gang members, are often aware when there is police corruption in their neighborhoods. (See the story by Walter, who grew up in Cleveland, Ohio).[88]

Juvenile offenders may not be involved in police corruption nearly to the degree that adult offenders are, but they often feel that they experience police harassment on a regular basis and police brutality at least occasionally. The juvenile offenders who are minority males and known for previous offenses are those most critical of police practices. Juveniles charge that police "run them off" the streets without justification, that police stop and arrest them without probable cause, and that police are quick to put their hands on them.

School-Based Interventions

Developing effective delinquency prevention programs in the school is one of the most important challenges facing the police at the present time. Community predelinquent programs have included courses in high school, junior high, and elementary school settings about school safety, community relations, drug and alcohol abuse, city government, court procedures, bicycle safety, and juvenile delinquency. The Officer Friendly Program and McGruff "Take a Bite Out of Crime," were established throughout the nation to develop better relations with younger children.

More recently, popular prevention programs included GREAT (Gang Resistance Education and Training) and Law-Related Education (LRE). As of June 1997, more than 2,400 officers from forty-seven states and the District of Columbia had completed GREAT training. In at least forty-two school jurisdictions police officers teach the nine-week curriculum to middle school students.[89] A 1995 evaluation, based on a cross-sectional survey of 5,935 eighth graders from forty-two schools where GREAT is taught, found "that students who completed the GREAT lessons reported more prosocial behaviors and attitudes than their peers who did not finish the program or failed to participate in the first place."[90]

Law-Related Education (LRE) is designed to teach students the fundamental principles and skills needed to become responsible citizens in a constitutional democracy.[91] A 1985 national curriculum survey reported that LRE has been added to the curriculum in more than half of the forty-six states involved in the study.[92] One of the few studies evaluating LRE programs found that, when properly conducted, these programs can reduce tendencies toward delinquent behavior and improve a range of attitudes related to responsible citizenship. Successful students, this study found, were also less likely to associate with delinquent peers and to use violence as a means of resolving conflict.[93]

As if the role of the police with juveniles is not difficult enough, the police have recently received more responsibilities. They have been charged to enforce the curfew ordinances that more and more communities across the nation are passing. Communities have turned to the police to prevent hate crimes committed by teenagers toward minority groups, Jews and other ethnic groups, and homosexuals.

The police have been further charged to do something about the rising juvenile involvement in satanic practices and rituals and about the spread of graffiti from inner-city to downtown and suburban areas.

Today, the need for substance abuse prevention programs demands creativity and involvement on the part of the police. The DARE program, discussed in Social Policy 14.4, is a widely replicated effort by the police to prevent substance abuse. New York City's Project SPECDA (School Program to Educate and Control Drug Abuse), which is a collaborative project of the city's police department and board of education, is an-

SOCIAL POLICY 14.4

Project DARE

Project DARE is designed to equip elementary school children with skills for resisting peer pressure to experiment with tobacco, drugs, and alcohol. Developed in 1983 as a cooperative effort by the Los Angeles Police Department and the Los Angeles Unified School District, this program uses uniformed law enforcement officers to teach a formal curriculum to students in the classroom. Using a core curriculum consisting of seventeen hour-long weekly lessons, DARE gives special attention to fifth- and sixth-graders to prepare them for entry into junior high and high school, where they are most likely to encounter pressure to use drugs. Since it was founded, DARE has expanded to encompass programs for middle and high school students, gang prevention, conflict resolution, parent education, and after-school recreation and learning. As the most popular school-based drug education program in the United States, it is administered in about 70 percent of this nation's school districts, reaching 25 million students in 1996. It has also been adopted in forty-four other countries.

Several evaluations done in the 1980s and early 1990s were positive about the effectiveness of the DARE program. However, DARE began to be more critically evaluated in the mid 1990s, and the reservations about its effectiveness appear to be gathering momentum. A 1994 meta-analysis of DARE programs by the Research Triangle Institute in North Carolina raised questions about the effectiveness of DARE and other substance abuse programs. It found that these programs were most effective in increasing students' knowledge about substance abuse and enhancing their social skills, but the effect of these programs was more modest on attitudes toward drugs and the police and on improving self-esteem. This evaluation further found that its short-term effects on substance abuse by fifth- and sixth-graders were small. Dennis P. Rosenbaum and Gordon S. Hanson's 1994 longitudinal evaluation was also critical of DARE's effectiveness. In this randomized experiment conducted with 1,584 students in the year following exposure to the program, Rosenbaum and Hanson found that "D.A.R.E. had no statistically significant main effects on drug use behaviors and had few effects on attitudes or beliefs about drugs."

Why do you believe that the program evaluations of DARE were not more positive? If DARE is not effective in preventing drug and alcohol abuse, what do you think would be effective with middle school and junior high youths?

Source: National Institute of Justice, *The D.A.R.E. Program: A Review of Prevalence, User Satisfaction, and Effectiveness* (Washington, D.C.: U.S. Department of Justice, 1994), p. 1; Dennis P. Rosenbaum and Gordon S. Hanson, "Assessing the Effects of School-Based Education: A Six-Year Multilevel Analysis of Project D.A.R.E.," *Journal of Research in Crime and Delinquency* 35 (November 1998), pp. 381–412.

other highly praised drug prevention program. In this project, a sixteen-session curriculum, with the units split evenly between fifth and six grades, imparts basic information about the risks and effects of drug use, makes students aware of the social pressures that cause drug use, and teaches acceptable methods of resisting peer pressure to experiment with drugs.[94]

In addition to drug prevention programs, the police respond to incidents ranging from student fights and assaults to drug and weapon possession. Officers also regularly drive by schools during night and weekend patrol to prevent vandalism and burglary to school property. In addition, the police are responsible for providing security and safety to the school. In some schools, this requires conducting searches of students as they come into the school, monitoring the halls, doing conflict mediation when necessary, and protecting students as they come to and go home from school. The police are frequently called upon to assist the school in searching for weapons and drugs on school property and are charged to enforce drug-free school zone laws and the federal Gun-Free School Zones Act. The police are expected to enforce school attendance programs in a few school districts across the nation.

Some school administrators have chosen to employ police officers full time during school hours. The specific duties and responsibilities of these police-school liaison officers are generally agreed upon by the police department and the school system as well because both the police and the school share the cost. These liaison officers, or student resource officers, typically patrol school grounds, hallways, parking lots, stairways, and bathrooms; handle trespassers, class cutters, and truants; check student identification; handle disruptive students; investigate criminal complaints; and prevent disturbances at after-school activities.[95]

Gang-Based Interventions

The number of street gangs, as previously discussed, has increased dramatically across the nation since the late 1980s. The characteristics of these gangs vary widely from one city to another. Some of the gangs are simply groups of adolescents who hang around together and who seldom get into any serious trouble. Other gangs engage in extensive drug activity, and some have become involved in violent drive-by shootings in which innocent citizens have been killed.

The 1996 National Youth Gang Survey queried police and sheriffs' departments across the nation. Of the 2,629 agencies responding to the survey, approximately 53 percent reported activity among gangs in their jurisdiction in 1996. The highest level of gang activity was in large cities (74 percent), followed by suburban counties (57 percent), small cities (34 percent), and rural counties (25 percent). Significantly, nearly 75 percent of cities surveyed with populations greater than 25,000 reported youth gangs in 1996.[96]

Drugs, as well as violence, have made gangs a problem to the police. Indeed, police officers caught a group of Los Angeles Crips conducting a drug sales seminar in St. Louis, Missouri.[97] Once a community becomes aware of the seriousness of the gang problem, usually after a violent gang incident has taken place, then pressure is typically put on the police to solve the problem. Police departments have frequently responded to this pressure by pursuing one of three intervention strategies (units) to work with gangs.[98]

The Youth Service Program is one such strategy. This departmental unit is formed to deal with a specific gang problem and is not a permanent unit within the police department. Officers continue to perform their regular duties and are not exclusively concerned with gang problems. The gang detail is a second type of unit. The officers in these units generally are pulled from detective units or juvenile units. The gang detail differs from the Youth Service Bureau in that its officers are assigned solely to gang problems and do not routinely work on other assignments. The **gang unit** is the third type of unit. The members of these permanent units see themselves as specialists who are working on gang problems. For example, many gang units will develop extensive intelligence networks with gang members in the community.[99]

In 1966, the Dallas Police Department began an anti-gang initiative grant from the Office of Community Oriented Policing Services to combat violent gang activity. The grant period lasted from June 1, 1996 through May 31, 1997. The study focused on the effect of three suppression tactics: saturation patrol, aggressive curfew, and truancy enforcement. The findings indicated that aggressive curfew and truancy enforcement led to significant reductions in gang violence, whereas simple saturation patrol had little effect on gang violence.[100]

SUMMARY

In the late nineteenth century and early twentieth century, policing juveniles began to be viewed differently from policing adults. This movement, which coincided with other reforms in community-based and institutional care of delinquents, emphasized the prevention of juvenile delinquency and the development of specialized units to work with juveniles. Police involvement in delinquency prevention programs and police diversionary programs for juveniles declined in the late 1970s and early 1980s. Budgetary constraints, as well as administrative problems caused by specialization, encouraged departments to move away from such deep involvement in police-juvenile relations. However, in the late 1980s and 1990s, the rise of juvenile violence and drug use and the proliferation of youth gangs encouraged the police to resume their emphasis on prevention, especially in teaching courses to elementary and middle-grade students.

Today, the most important social factor in understanding police-juvenile relations is the public's expectation that the police will both clean up the juvenile crime problem and prevent youth crime in rich and poor communities alike. Significant organizational factors include the commitment of the police to community-oriented policing (COP) and the increased responsibilities toward the juvenile, which place a heavy burden on police resources.

The importance of police-juvenile relations cannot be overstated because the police are usually the first contact a juvenile has with the justice system. Police-juvenile relations have come a long way in the past two centuries—or for that matter, in the past two decades. Juveniles overall now have better attitudes toward the police than in the past. Even juvenile offenders often look upon the police as having a job to do: the job of the police is to catch juvenile lawbreakers, and the job of the juvenile offenders is to avoid being caught. The police have wide discretion toward juvenile lawbreaking, but, as several studies have found, 80 to 90 percent of the police-juvenile encounters result in diversion from the juvenile justice system. The most important factor influencing the police disposition of the juvenile is the crime committed. Juveniles, like adults, have been granted increased due process rights at the time of arrest.

The police also must deal with the serious problem of violent youth crime. What makes this task difficult today is that too many juveniles possess handguns, too many communities have gangs, too many juveniles desire drugs, and too many juveniles are venting their frustrations in hate-crimes toward others. The police in recent years have experienced some success with police-juvenile relations. Their role in reducing the availability of handguns with juveniles is credited with playing a major role in reducing juvenile homicides in urban settings.

KEY TERMS

citation, p. 416
discretion, p. 412
fingerprinting, p. 420
gang unit, p. 427

juvenile officer, p. 408
Miranda v. Arizona, p. 419
New Jersey v. T. L. O., p. 418
police interrogation, p. 418

CRITICAL THINKING QUESTIONS

1. Why do the attitudes of minority and white youths vary so much? Why would youthful offenders feel differently toward the police than nonoffenders? Have your experiences with the police made a difference in how you feel about the police?

2. Summarize the rights of a juvenile taken into custody.

3. Evaluate the S.H.O.D.I. program. Do you believe that it should be extended more widely across the nation?

4. What is your evaluation of DARE? For those of you who have been exposed to a DARE program, did it make a difference in your using or not using drugs?

5. Why is the role of the police with juveniles more difficult than it was in the past?

WEB DESTINATIONS

To get more information on the Police Athletic League in New York.
http://www.palnyc.org/

Learn more about school searches at this site.
http://eric-web.tc.columbia.edu/monographs/ uds107/school_school.html

Learn more about community policing at the community policing consortium site.
http://www.communitypolicing.org/

Read more about the *Miranda v. Arizona* case at this site.
http://library.thinkquest.org/2760/miranda.htm? tqskip=1

Read more about police interrogation at the FindLaw site.
http://caselaw.lp.findlaw.com/data/ constitution/amendment05/09.html

Find out more about search and seizure at the Florida State University site.
http://www.fsu.edu/~crimdo/fagan.html

NOTES

1. From an interview in October 1982.

2. Robert M. Fogelson, *Big-City Police* (Cambridge, Mass.: Harvard University Press, 1977), pp. 86–87.

3. Ibid.

4. Robert Portune, *Changing Adolescent Attitudes toward Police* (Cincinnati: W. H. Anderson Company, 1971).

5. L. Thomas Winfree, Jr., and Curt T. Griffiths, "Adolescents' Attitudes toward the Police: A Survey of High School Students," in *Juvenile Delinquency: Little Brother Grows Up* (Beverly Hills, Calif.: Sage Publications, 1977), pp. 79-99.

6. William T. Risinko, W. Johnson Knowlton, and Carlton A. Hornung, "The Importance of Police Contact in the Formulation of Youths' Attitudes Toward Police," *Journal of Criminal Justice* 6 (1978), p. 65. J. P. Clark and E. P. Wenninger, "The Attitudes of Juveniles toward the Legal Institution," *Journal of Criminal Law, Criminology and Police Science* 55 (1964), pp. 482-489; D. C. Gibbons, *Delinquent Behavior* (Englewood Cliffs, N.J.: Prentice-Hall, 1976); V. I. Cizanckas and C. W. Purviance, "Changing Attitudes of Black Youths," *Police Chief* 40 (1973), p. 42.

7. Scott H. Decker, "Citizen Attitudes Toward the Police: A Review of Past Findings and Suggestions for Future Policy," *Journal of Police Science and Administration* 9 (1981), pp. 80–87.

8. James R. Davis, "A Comparison of Attitudes Toward the New York City Police," *Journal of Police Science and Administration* 17 (1990), pp. 233–242.

9. Komanduri S. Murty, Julian B. Roebuck, and Joann D. Smith, "The Image of Police in Black Atlanta Communities," *Journal of Police Science and Administration* 17 (1990), pp. 250–257.

10. Ibid., p. 256.

11. Michael J. Leiber, Mahesh K. Nalla, and Margaret Farnworth, "Explaining Juveniles' Attitudes toward the Police," *Justice Quarterly* 15 (March 1998), pp. 151–174.

12. Kathleen Maguire and Ann L. Pastore, eds., *Bureau of Justice Statistics SOURCEBOOK of Criminal Justice Statistics-1996* (Washington, D.C.: U.S. Department of Justice, 1997), p. 184.

13. Richard W. Kobetz and Betty B. Bosarge, *Juvenile Justice Administration* (Gaithersburg, Md.: International Association of Chiefs of Police, 1973).

14. James Q. Wilson, "Dilemmas of Police Administration," *Public Administration Review* 28 (September-October 1968).

15. David J. Bordua, "Recent Trends: Deviant Behavior and Social Control," *Annals* 359 (January 1967), pp. 149–163.

16. Donald J. Black and Albert J. Reiss Jr., "Police Control of Juveniles," *American Sociological Review* 35 (February 1979), pp. 63–77.

17. Robert M. Terry, "Discrimination in the Handling of Juvenile Offenders by Social Control Agencies," *Journal of Research in Crime and Delinquency* 4 (July 1967), pp. 218–230; Nathan Goldman, *The Differential Selection of Juvenile Offenders for Court Appearance* (New York: National Council on Crime and Delinquency 1963), pp. 35–47; Black and Reiss, "Police Control of Juveniles," pp. 63–77; Irving Piliavin and Scott Briar, "Police Encounters with Juveniles," *American Journal of Sociology* 70 (September 1964), pp. 206–214.

18. Terry, "Handling of Juvenile Offenders;" Black and Weiss, "Police Control of Juveniles"; and Robert M. Emerson, *Judging Delinquents: Context and Process in Juvenile Court* (Chicago: Aldine Publishing Company, 1969), p. 42.

19. Gail Armstrong, "Females under the Law–Protected But Unequal," *Crime and Delinquency* 23 (April 1977), pp. 109–120; and Meda Chesney-Lind, "Judicial Paternalism and the Female Status Offender," *Crime and Delinquency* 23 (April 1977), pp. 121–130; Meda Chesney-Lind, "Girls and Status Offenses: is Juvenile Justice Still Sexist?" *Criminal Justice Abstracts,* (March 1988), p. 144–165.

20. Meda Chesney-Lind, "Juvenile Delinquency: The Sexualization of Female Crime," *Psychology Today* 8 (July 1974), pp. 43–46; and I. Richard Perleman, "Antisocial Behavior of the Minor in the United States," in *Society, Delinquency, and Delinquent Behavior,* edited by Harwin L. Voss (Boston: Little, Brown & Company, 1970).

21. Theodore N. Ferdinand and Elmer C. Luchterhand, "Inner-City Youths, the Police, the Juvenile Court, and Justice," *Social Problems* 17 (Spring 1970), pp. 510–527; *Goldman, Differential Selection for Juvenile Offenders;* Piliavin and Briar, "Police Encounters with Juveniles."

22. Marvin E. Wolfgang, Robert M. Figlio, and Thorsten Sellin, *Delinquency in a Birth Cohort* (Chicago: University of Chicago Press, 1972), p. 252.

23. Philip W. Harris, "Race and Juvenile Justice: Examining the Impact of Structural and Policy Changes on Racial Disproportionality," (Presented at the 39th Annual Meeting of The American Society of Criminology, Montreal, Quebec, Canada, November 13, 1987).

24. James T. Carey et al., *The Handling of Juveniles from Offense to Disposition* (Washington, D.C.: U.S. Government Printing Office, 1976), p. 419; A. W. McEachern and Riva Bauzer, "Factors Related to Disposition in Juvenile-Police Contacts," in *Juvenile Gangs in Context,* edited by Malcom W. Klein (Englewood Cliffs, N.J.: Prentice-Hall, 1967), pp. 148–160; Thorsten Sellin and Marvin E. Wolfgang, *The Measurement of Delinquency* (New York: John Wiley & Sons, 1964), pp. 95–105; Ferdinand and Luchterhand, "Inner-City Youths," pp. 510–527.

25. Merry Morash, "Establishment of Juvenile Police Record," *Criminology* 22 (February 1984), pp. 97–111.

26. Interviewed in August 1980.

27. Piliavin and Briar, "Police Encounters with Juveniles," pp. 206–214.

28. Werthman and Piliavin, "Gang Members and Police," pp. 56–98.

29. Richard J. Lundman, Richard E. Sykes, and John P. Clark, "Police Control of Juveniles: A Replication," in *Police Behavior: A Sociological Perspective,* edited by Richard J. Lundman (New York: Oxford Press, 1980), pp. 147–148.

30. David A. Klinger, "Demeanor or Crime? Why 'Hostile' Citizens Are More Likely To Be Arrested," *Criminology* 32 (1994), pp. 475–493; David A. Klinger, "More on Demeanor and Arrest in Dade County," *Criminology* 34 (1996), pp. 61–82.

31. Robert E. Worden and Robin L. Shepard, "Demeanor, Crime, and Police Behavior: A Reexamination of the Police Services Study Data," *Criminology* 34 (1996), pp. 83–105.

32. Malcolm W. Klein, "Police Processing of Juvenile Offenders: Toward the Development of Juvenile System Rates," in Los Angeles County Sub-Regional Board, California Council on Juvenile Justice, Part III.

33. Nathan Goldman, "The Differential Selection of Juvenile Offenders for Court Appearance," in *Crime and the Legal Process,* edited by William Chambliss (New York: McGraw-Hill Book Company, 1969).

34. Wilson, "Dilemmas of Police Administration," p. 19.

35. Donald J. Black, "Production of Crime Rates," *American Sociological Review* 35 (August 1970), pp. 733–748; Joseph W. Eaton and Kenneth Polk, *Measuring Delinquency* (Pittsburgh: University of Pittsburgh Press, 1961); Lyle W. Shannon, "Types and Patterns of Delinquency Referral in a Middle-Sized City," *British Journal of Criminology* 10 (July 1963), pp. 206–214; and Norman L. Weiner and Charles V. Willie "Decisions by Juvenile Officers," *American Journal of Sociology* 76 (September 1971), pp 199–210.

36. Howard N. Snyder and Melissa Sickmund, *Juvenile Offenders and Victims: 1999 National Report* (Washington, D.C.: National Center for Juvenile Justice, 1999), p. 139.

37. Ibid.

38. Ibid.

39. Ibid.

40. Jerome Skolnick, *Justice Without Trial,* 3rd ed (New York: Macmillan, 1994).

41. Ibid.

42. Edward M. Davis, "Juvenile Justice Since the Gault Decision," *Police Chief* 44 (1977), p. 8.

43. Skolnick, *Justice Without Trial.*

44. Interviewed homicide detectives are quick to say that juveniles who murder are more hard and less feeling than they were in the past.

45. Skolnick, *Justice Without Trial.*

46. This advice that the police officer hears in the academy and from his or her training officer applies to everyone who works with gang youth.

47. The following section is adapted from H. Ted Rubin, *Juvenile Justice: Police Practice and Law* (Santa Monica, Calif.: Goodyear Publishing Company, 1979, pp. 75–82.

48. *Mapp v. Ohio,* 367 U.S. 643 (1961).

49. *State v. Lowry* 230 A.2d 907 (1967).

50. In *re Two Brothers and a Case of Liquor,* Juvenile Court of the District of Columbia, 1966, reported in *Washington Law Reporter* 95 (1967), p. 113.

51. Ronald D. Stephens, "School-Based Interventions: Safety and Security," *The Gang Intervention Handbook,* edited by Arnold P. Goldstein and C. Ronald Huff (Champaign, Ill.: Research Press, 1993), p. 221.

52. *Haley v. Ohio,* 332 U.S. 596, 1948.

53. *Brown v. Mississippi,* 399 F. 2d 467 (5th Circ. 1968).

54. Davis, *Rights of Juveniles,* Section 3-45.

55. *Miranda v. Arizona,* 384 U.S. 436 (1966).

56. *In re Gault,* 387 U.S. (1967).

57. *Fare v. Michael C.,* 442 U.S. 23, 99S.Ct. 2560 (1979).

58. T. Grisso, *Juveniles' Waiver of Rights: Legal and Psychological Competence.* New York: Plenum Press, 1981.

59. *People v. Lara,* 62 Cal. Reporter, 586 (1967), cert. denied 392 U.S. 945 (1968).

60. *In re Mellot,*217 S.E. 2d 745 (C.A.N. Ca. 1975).

61. *In re Dennis P. Fletcher,* 248 A 2d. 364 (Md. 1968), cert. denied 396 U.S. 852 (1969).

62. *Commonwealth v. Guyton,* 405 Mass. 497 (1989).

63. *Commonwealth v. McNeil,* 399 Mass. 71 (1987).

64. Elyce Z. Ferster and Thomas F. Courtless, "The Beginning of Juvenile Justice, Police Practices, and the Juvenile Offender," *Vanderbilt Law Review* 22 (April 1969), pp. 598–601.

65. *Davis v. Mississippi,* 394 U.S. 721 (1969).

66. Snyder and Sickmund, *Juvenile Offenders and Victims: 1999 National Report,* p. 101.

67. *In re Carl T.,* 81 Cal. Reporter 655 (2nd. C.A. 1969).

68. *United States v. Wade,* 388 U.S. 218, 87 S.Ct. 1926 (1967).

69. *Kirby v. Illinois,* 406 U.S. 682, 92 S.Ct. 1877 (1972).

70. *In re Holley,* 107 R.I. 615, 268 A.2d 723 (1970).

71. Snyder and Sickmund, *Juvenile Offenders and Victims: 1999 National Report,* p. 101.

72. Cited in Peter C. Kratcoski and Duane Dukes, *Issues in Community Policing* (Cincinatti, OH.: Anderson Publishing Co., 1994), p. 36.

73. Vincent J. Webb and Nanette Graham, "Citizen Ratings of the Importance of Selected Police Duties." Paper presented at the Annual Meeting of the American Society of Criminology (November 7–12, 1994), p. 7.

74. Kratcoski and Dukes, *Issues In Community Policing,* p. 38.

75. U.S. Department of Justice, "Community Policing," *National Institute of Justice Journal,* 225 (1992), pp. 1–32.

76. Interviewed in September 2001.

77. Snyder and Sickmund, *Juvenile Offenders and Victims: 1999 National Report,* p. 132.

78. Ibid.

79. See Mark S. Hamm, *American Skinheads: the Criminology and Control of Hate Crime* (Westport, CT.: Praeger Publishers, 1993), pp. 63–64.

80. See Wolfgang Pindur and Donna K. Wells, "Chronic Serious Juvenile Offenders," *Juvenile and Family Court Journal,* 37 (1986), pp. 27–30.

81. "Kids, Crime and Punishment," NBC-TV News Special, 26 July 1987.

82. Ibid.

83. Lois A. Fingerhut, *Firearm Mortality among Children, Youth, and Young Adults 1–34 Years of Age, Trends and Current Status: United States, 1985–1990* (Hyattsville, Md.: National Center for Health Statistics, 1993).

84. L. W. Sherman, J. W. Shaw, and D. P. Rogan, *The Kansas City Gun Experiment: Research in Brief* (Washington, D.C.: National Institute of Justice, U.S. Department of Justice, 1995).

85. Coordinating Council on Juvenile Justice and Delinquency Prevention, *Combating Violence and Delinquency,* p. 46.

86. Snyder and Sickmund, *Juvenile Offenders and Victims: 1999 National Report,* p. 139.

87. Herman Goldstein, *Policing a Free Society* (Cambridge: Ballinger, 1977), pp. 93–94.

88. A number of juveniles who have grown up in urban neighborhoods have made comments indicating that they were cognizant when police were involved in wrongdoings.

89. Finn-Aage Esbensen and D. Wayne Osgood, *National Evaluation of G.R.E.A.T.* (Washington, D.C.: National Institute of Justice, Office of Justice Programs, 1997), p. 1.

90. Ibid.

91. Norman D. Wright, "From Risk to Resiliency: The Role of Law-Related Education." Publication printed in an Institute on Law and Civil Education pamphlet (Des Moines, Iowa), June 20–21, 1995.

92. Carole L. Hahn, "The Status of the Social Studies in Public School in the United States: Another Look," *Social Education* 49 (1985), pp. 220–223.

93. Judith Warrent Little and Frances Haley, *Implementing Effective LRE Programs* (Boulder, Colo.: Social Science Education Consortium, 1982).

94. William DeJong, *Arresting the Demand for Drugs: Police and School Partnership to Prevent Drug Abuse* (November 1987), p. 5.

95. See Richard Lawrence, "The Role of Police-School Liaison Officers in School Crime Prevention." Paper presented at the Annual Meeting of the Academy of Criminal Justice Sciences, Albuquerque, March 11, 1998.

96. John P. Moore and Craig P. Terrett, *Highlights of the 1996 National Youth Gang Survey* (Washington, D.C.: Office of Juvenile Justice and Delinquency Prevention, 1998), p. 1–2.

97. Ronald D. Stephens, "School-Based Interventions: Safety and Security," *The Gang Intervention Handbook,* Arnold P. Goldstein and C. Ronald Huff, eds. (Champaign, Ill.: Research Press, 1993), p. 219.

98. Jerome A. Needle and William Vaughn Stapelton, "Police Handling of Youth Gangs," *Reports of the National Juvenile Justice Assessment Centers* (Washington, D.C.: U.S. Department of Justice, 1983).

99. Ibid.

100. Eric J. Fritsch, Tory J. Caeti, and Robert W. Taylor, "Gang Suppression Through Saturation Patrol, Aggressive Curfew, and Truancy Enforcement: A Quasi-Experimental Test of the Dallas Anti-Gang Initiative," *Crime and Delinquency* 45 (January 1999), pp. 122–139.

chapter 15

THE JUVENILE COURT

OBJECTIVES

After reading this chapter, the student will be able to answer the following questions:

- How did the juvenile court begin?

- What pretrial procedures are involved in juvenile court proceedings?

- How is a trial conducted in the juvenile court?

- What are various forms of sentencing?

- What can be done to improve the juvenile court?

CHAPTER 15 OUTLINE

Gustav L. Schramm, a long-term juvenile judge in Pittsburgh, describes the monumental responsibility of a juvenile judge:

Neither umpire nor arbiter, *[the juvenile judge] is the one person who represents his community as parens patriae, who may act with the parents, or when necessary even in place of them, to bring about behavior more desirable. As a judge in a juvenile court he does not administer criminal law. The child before him is not a defendant. There is no conviction, no sentence. There is no life-long stigma of a criminal record. In a juvenile court the judge administers equity; and the child, still immature and unable to take his place as an adult before the law, is the recipient of consideration, of guidance and of correction. The stake is no less than the saving of a human being at a time more favorable than any in an uncertain future.*

—Gustav L. Schramm[1]

> Do you believe that the reality of what happens in juvenile court is close to what Judge Schramm says takes place? Do you think that most juveniles who appear before the juvenile court regard the juvenile judge as a parental figure?

Schramm claims, as do other advocates of the juvenile court, that the informal setting of this court and the parental demeanor of the judge enable wayward youths to be saved or rescued from their lives of crime. Indeed, during the first half of the twentieth century the juvenile court, a unique contribution to the world of jurisprudence, was widely praised for its attempt to redeem the wayward youths of the United States.[2]

Critics eventually challenged these idealistic views of the juvenile court. They claimed that the juvenile court had not succeeded in rehabilitating youthful offenders, in bringing justice and compassion to them, or even in providing them with their due process rights.[3] Some investigators even accused the juvenile court of doing great harm to the juveniles who appeared before it.[4]

Today, three different positions have emerged concerning the role of the juvenile court. One position continues to support the *parens patriae* philosophy, or the state as parent, and to hold to "the best interest of the child" standard for decision making. According to Judge Leonard P. Edwards, implicit in this position is that "children are different from adults, that they have developmental needs which they cannot satisfy without assistance and that care and supervision are critical to their upbringing."[5] Edwards then made this telling statement, "If children were no different from adults, the juvenile court would be unnecessary."[6] This position contends that the juvenile court is superior to the criminal court because the juvenile court offers the rehabilitation of offenders, the protection of children, and the flexibility to provide the needed individualized justice for children in their formative years.[7] The concept of individualized justice is actually the hallmark of the juvenile court:

> Individualized justice for children is the legitimate goal of the juvenile justice system. The court must, within the bounds of state and constitutional law, tailor its response to the peculiar needs of the child and family, with goals of (1) rehabilitating the child; (2) reuniting the family; and (3) protecting the public safety.[8]

A second position proposes that the justice model replace the *parens patriae* philosophy as the basis of juvenile court procedures. Such increasingly popular proposed procedural changes as decriminalization of status offenders, determinate sentencing, mandatory sentencing, and opening up juvenile proceedings and records strike at the very heart and core of traditional juvenile court proceedings.[9] The wide acceptance of these recommendations, as Barry C. Feld notes, is seen in the fact that "about one-third of the states now use the present offense and prior record [in the juvenile court] to regulate at least some sentencing decisions through determinate or mandatory minimum sentencing statutes or correctional administrative guidelines."[10] The proposed Model Juvenile Justice Code, which has attracted considerable attention, is also based on the principles of the justice model.[11] The 1994 revisions in Minnesota's juvenile code show how a state has been influenced by the justice model in the remodeling of its juvenile code.[12]

A third position is building momentum to abolish the juvenile court.[13] For example, Proposition 102 amended the Arizona Constitution in 1996 so that juvenile courts no longer have "exclusive" or "original" jurisdiction for offenders under eighteen years of age.[14] Feld, as previously suggested, is one of the most articulate spokespeople for this position. Feld argues that an integrated criminal court with a youth discount would provide youthful offenders with greater protections and justice than they currently receive in the juvenile justice system and more proportional and humane consequences than judges currently inflict on them as adults in the criminal justice system.[15] He contends that "a statutory sentencing policy that integrates youthfulness and limited opportunities to learn self-control with principles of proportionality and reduced culpability would provide" youthful offenders with categorical fractional reductions of sentences given to adults.[16] This categorical approach is what Feld means by an explicit "youth discount" at sentencing. For example, a fourteen-year-old delinquent might receive 25 to 33 percent of the adult penalty; a sixteen-year-old, 50 to 66 percent; and an eighteen-year-old adult, the full penalty.[17] In a recent article, "Abolish the Juvenile Justice Court," Feld makes his point even stronger (see Juvenile Law, 15.1). Although the juvenile court would likely survive the implementation of the justice model, perhaps in a much altered form, this movement is sounding the death knell of the juvenile court.[18]

Juvenile Law 15.1

Abolish the Juvenile Court

Within the past decades, judicial decisions, legislative amendments, and administrative changes have transformed the juvenile court from a nominally rehabilitative social welfare agency into a scaled-down, second-class criminal court for young people. The reforms have converted the historical ideal of the juvenile court as a social welfare institution into a penal system that provides young offenders with neither therapy nor justice. The substantive and procedural convergence between juvenile and criminal courts eliminates virtually all the conceptual and operational differences in strategies of criminal social control for youths and adults. No compelling reasons exist to maintain, separate from an adult criminal court, a punitive juvenile court whose only remaining distinctions are its persisting procedural deficiencies. Rather, states should abolish juvenile courts' delinquency jurisdictions and formally recognize youth-fulness as a mitigating factor in the sentencing of younger criminal offenders. Such a policy would provide younger offenders with substantive protections comparable to those afforded by juvenile courts, assure greater procedural regularity in the determination of guilt, and avoid the disjunctions in social control caused by maintaining two duplicative and inconsistent criminal justice systems.

How do you feel about abolishing the juvenile court? What would be the disadvantages of such a move across the United States?

Source: Barry C. Feld, "Abolish the Juvenile Court: Youthfulness, Criminal Responsibility, and Sentencing Policy," *Journal of Criminal Law and Criminology* 88 (Fall 1997), p. 68.

In sum, significant changes are clearly sweeping through the 100-year old corridors of the juvenile court. As we enter the first decade of the twentieth-first century, what is actually taking place is that all three positions are represented. For minor offenses, as well as status offenders in most states, the "best interest of the child" position is the guiding standard of juvenile court decision making. For offenders who commit more serious delinquent acts, the principles of the justice model in the adjudicatory and disposition hearings are increasingly used. Repetitive or violent youthful offenders are commonly transferred quickly to the adult court and handled as adults. Perhaps the question is not whether the traditional juvenile court will change but whether the court will survive.

How the Juvenile Court Originated

During the final decades of the nineteenth century, the Progressive Reformers viewed childhood as a period of dependency and exclusion from the adult world. To institutionalize childhood, they enacted a number of "child-saving" laws, including compulsory school attendance and child labor laws. The creation of the juvenile court was another means to achieve unparalleled age segregation of children. There were a number of contextual factors that influenced the creation of the juvenile court.[19]

Legal Context

The juvenile court was founded in Cook County (Chicago), Illinois, in 1899, when the Illinois legislature passed the Juvenile Court Act. The *parens patriae* doctrine provided a legal catalyst for the creation of the juvenile court, furnishing a rationale for the use of informal procedures for dealing with juveniles and for expanding state power over children. The *parens patriae* doctrine was also used to justify the juvenile court's activities to determine the causes of delinquent behavior and to make decisions on the disposition of cases. The kindly parent, the state, could thus justify relying on psychological and medical examinations rather than on trial by evidence. Once the *parens patriae* rationale was applied to juvenile proceedings, the institution of the juvenile court followed.

Political Context

In *The Child Savers,* Anthony Platt discussed the political context of the origin of the juvenile court. He claimed that the juvenile court was established in Chicago and later elsewhere because it satisfied several middle-class interest groups. He saw the juvenile court as an expression of middle-class values and of the philosophy of conservative political groups. In denying that the juvenile court was revolutionary, Platt charged:

> The child-saving movement was not so much a break with the past as an affirmation of faith in traditional institutions. Parental authority, education at home, and the virtues of rural life were emphasized because they were in decline at this time. The child-saving movement was, in part, a crusade which, through emphasizing the dependence of the social order on the proper socialization of children, implicitly elevated the nuclear family and, more especially, the role of women as stalwarts of the family. The child savers were prohibitionists, in a general sense, who believed that social progress depended on efficient law enforcement, strict supervision of children's leisure and recreation, and the regulation of illicit pleasures. What seemingly began as a movement to humanize the lives of adolescents soon developed into a program of moral absolutism through which youths were to be saved from movies, pornography, cigarettes, alcohol, and anything else which might possibly rob them of their innocence.[20]

Economic Context

Platt contended that the behaviors that the **child savers** selected to be penalized—such as engaging in sex, roaming the streets, drinking, fighting, frequenting dance halls, and staying out late at night—were found primarily among lower-class children. Therefore, juvenile justice from its inception, he argued, reflected class favoritism that resulted in the frequent processing of poor children through the system while middle- and upper-class children were more likely to be excused.[21]

The children of the poor were a particular problem to the child savers because the juvenile court emerged in the wake of unprecedented industrial and urban development in the United States. This process was closely connected with large-scale immigration to urban centers of people who had different backgrounds from the indigenous population. These immigrants brought new social problems to Chicago and other urban centers, and the child savers were determined to "rescue" the immigrant children and to protect them from their families.[22]

Sociocultural Context

Three social conditions that characterized the last thirty years of the nineteenth century led to the founding of the juvenile court. First, many citizens were incensed by the treatment of children during this period, especially the procedure of jailing children with adults. The jails were (and still are by many) considered highly injurious to youthful offenders because of the deleterious effects of their association with adult criminals. Disenchantment of urban dwellers also became widespread. The population of Chicago tripled between 1880 and 1890, mostly by immigration, creating such problems as filth and corruption, poverty, the rise of crime, and corruption in city government. Furthermore, the higher status given middle-class women made them interested in exerting their newfound influence to improve the lives of children. In fact, child saving became an avocation for some middle-class women who wanted to do something outside the home.[23]

These pressures for social change took place in the midst of a wave of optimism that swept through U.S. society during the Progressive Era, the period from 1890 to 1920. The emerging social sciences assured reformers that their problems with delinquents could be solved through positivism. According to positivism, youths were not responsible for their behavior and needed treatment rather than punishment. For example, the judge and scientific experts could work together in a separate court to discover a child's problem and to provide the cure.

Middle-class religious humanitarianism was another societal pressure for change. Such writers as Charles Dickens and Mary Carpenter challenged Christians to rescue children from degrading slums. The importance of religious humanitarianism is evident in the fact that many of the well-known child savers were ministers and most of the child-saving institutions were private charities, supported, at least in part, by mainline religious denominations.

How the Norms of the Juvenile Court Have Changed

The concept of the juvenile court was rapidly accepted across the nation because the same cultural, political, and economic conditions existed elsewhere. Thirty-one states had instituted juvenile courts by 1905, and by 1928, only two states did not have a juvenile court statute. In Cook County, the amendments that followed the original act brought the neglected, the dependent, and the delinquent together under one roof. The "delinquent" category comprised both status offenders and actual violators of criminal law.

Juvenile courts throughout the nation were patterned on the Chicago court. Children in trouble were offered informal and noncriminal hearings. Their records generally were kept confidential, and the hearings were not open to the public. Children were detained separately from adults. Reformers then proposed that the noncriminal aspects of the proceedings be echoed in the physical surroundings of the court:

> The courtroom should be not a courtroom at all; just a room, with a table and two chairs, where the judge and the child, the probation officer and the parents, as occasion arises, come into close contact, and where in a more or less informal way the whole matter may be talked over.[24]

Reformers further advocated that the juvenile judge sit at a desk rather than on a bench and that he occasionally "put his arm around his shoulder and draw the lad to him."[25] But the sympathetic judge was instructed not to lose any of his judicial dignity. The goals of the court were defined as investigation, diagnosis, and the prescription of treatment. Lawyers were deemed unnecessary because these civil proceedings were not adversary trials but informal hearings in which the best interests of the children were the chief concern.

In short, the juvenile court was founded on several admirable directives: that the court should function as a social clinic designed to serve the best interests of children in trouble; that children who were brought before the court should be given the same care, supervision, and discipline as would be provided by a good parent; that the aim of the court is to help, to restore, to guide, and to forget; that children should not be treated as criminals; and that the rights to shelter, protection, and proper guardianship are the only rights of children.[26]

Changes in Legal Norms

The group known as the **constitutionalists,** one of the most formidable foes of the juvenile court, contended that the juvenile court was unconstitutional because under its system the principles of a fair trial and individual rights were denied. The constitutionalists were particularly concerned that the children appearing before the court have procedural rights as well as the rights to shelter, protection, and guardianship. The constitutionalists also believed that dependent and neglected children are different from children who break the law and therefore must be dealt with through separate judicial proceedings, that diagnostic and treatment technologies are not sufficiently developed to ensure that the delinquent can be treated and cured of his or her misbehavior, and that the state must justify interference with a youth's life when his or her freedom is at stake.[27] The constitutionalists recommended that the procedures of the juvenile court be modified by the adoption of separate procedures for dealing with dependent and neglected children and those who are accused of criminal behavior; by the use of informal adjustments to avoid official court actions as frequently as possible; and by the provision of rigorous procedural safeguards and rights for children appearing before the court at the adjudicatory stage.[28]

A series of decisions by the U.S. Supreme Court in the 1960s and 1970s demonstrated the influence of the constitutionalists on juvenile justice. The five most important cases were: **Kent v. United States** (1966), **In re Gault** (1967), **In re Winship** (1970), **McKeiver v. Pennsylvania** (1971), and **Breed v. Jones** (1975).

KENT V. UNITED STATES (1966)　　The *Kent* decision, the first in which the U.S. Supreme Court dealt with a juvenile court case, concerned the matter of **transfer.** Juvenile Law 15.2 presents the facts of this case. The juvenile judge did not rule on the motions of Kent's counsel. He held no hearings, nor did he confer with Kent, Kent's mother, or Kent's counsel. The judge instead entered an order saying that after full investigation he was transferring jurisdiction to the criminal court. He made no findings and entered no reasons for the waiver.

Juvenile Law 15.2

Kent v. United States

Morris A. Kent, Jr., a sixteen-year-old youth living in Washington, D.C., was on juvenile probation and was charged with three counts each of housebreaking and robbery and two counts of rape. His mother retained an attorney who had Kent examined by two psychiatrists and a psychologist. The attorney then filed a motion for a hearing on the question of waiver, together with a psychiatrist's affidavit that certified that Kent was "a victim of severe psychopathology," and recommended hospitalization for psychiatric observation. Counsel contended that psychiatric treatment would make Kent a suitable subject for juvenile court rehabilitation. His counsel also moved for access to juvenile court probation records.

What did Supreme Court Justice Fortas mean when he said "that there may be grounds for concern that the child receives the worst of both worlds?" Do you agree with his criticism of the juvenile court?

Source: Kent v United States, 383 U.S. 541, 86 S.Ct. 1045, 16 LEd. 2d 84 (1966).

On appeal, the U.S. Supreme Court held that the juvenile court proceedings were defective. The Court held that during a transfer hearing, Kent should have been afforded an evidential hearing; that Kent should have been present when the court decided to waive jurisdiction; that the attorney should have been permitted to examine the social worker's investigation of the youth, which the court used in deciding to waive jurisdiction; and that the judge should have recorded a statement of reasons for the transfer. Justice Fortas, in the decision, stated:

> There is evidence, in fact, that there may be grounds for concern that the child receives the worst of both worlds; that he gets neither the protection accorded to adults nor the solicitous care and regenerative treatment postulated for children.[29]

The Court decided that withholding Kent's record essentially meant a denial of counsel. The Court also held that a juvenile has a right to be represented by counsel, that a youth charged with a felony has a right to a hearing, and that this hearing must "measure up to the essentials of due process and fair treatment." Finally, a juvenile's attorney must have access to his or her social or probation records.[30]

IN RE GAULT (1967) In May 1967 the U.S. Supreme Court reversed the conviction of a minor in *In re Gault*. This influential and far-reaching decision represented a new dawn in juvenile court history because, in effect, it brought the light of constitutional procedure into juvenile courts. No longer could due process and procedural safeguards be kept out of the adjudication proceedings. Juvenile Law 15.3 gives the facts of this case.

The U.S. Supreme Court in this case overruled the Arizona Supreme Court for its dismissal of a writ of habeas corpus. This writ had sought Gault's release from the training school.[31] Justice Fortas, for the Court majority, ruled on four of the six issues raised in the appeal:

1. Notice, to comply with due process requirements, must be given sufficiently in advance of scheduled court proceedings so that reasonable opportunity to prepare will be afforded, and it must "set forth the alleged misconduct with particularity."
2. The due process clause of the Fourteenth Amendment requires that in respect of proceedings to determine delinquency which may result in commitment to an institution in which the juvenile's freedom is curtailed, the child and his parent must be notified of the child's right to be represented by counsel retained by

Juvenile Law 15.3

In re Gault

Gerald Gault, a fifteen-year-old Arizona boy, and a friend, Ronald Lewis, were taken into custody on June 8, 1964, on a verbal complaint made by a neighbor. The neighbor had accused the boys of making lewd and indecent remarks to her over the phone. Gault's parents were not notified that he had been taken into custody; he was not advised of his right to counsel; he was not advised that he could remain silent; and no notice of charges was made either to Gerald or his parents. Additionally, the complainant was not present at either of the hearings. In spite of considerable confusion about whether or not Gerald had made the alleged phone call, what he had said over the phone,

and what he had said to the judge during the course of the two hearings, Judge McGhee committed him to the State Industrial School "for the period of his minority (that is, until twenty-one) unless sooner discharged by due process of law."

What due process rights did this case grant juveniles? What due process rights did juveniles still lack after this decision?

Source: *In re Gault,* 387 U.S. 1, 18 L. Ed. 2d 527, 87 S. Ct. 1428 (1967).

them, or if they are unable to afford counsel, that counsel will be appointed to represent the child.

3. The constitutional privilege against self-incrimination is applicable in the case of juveniles as it is with respect to adults.

4. No reason is suggested or appears for a different role in respect of sworn testimony in juvenile courts than in adult tribunals. Absent a valid confession adequate to support the determination of the Juvenile Court, confrontation and sworn testimony by witnesses available for cross-examination are essential for a finding of "delinquency" and an order committing Gerald to a state institution for a maximum of six years.[32]

Justice Fortas, in delivering the Court's opinion, recalled other cases that had provided juveniles with due process of law. In both *Haley v. Ohio* (1948) and *Gallegos v. Colorado* (1962), the Supreme Court had prohibited the use of confessions coerced from juveniles, and in *Kent* the Court had given the juvenile the right to be represented by counsel.[33] Justice Fortas concluded his review of legal precedent with the sweeping statement that juveniles have those fundamental rights that are incorporated in the due process clause of the Fourteenth Amendment to the U.S. Constitution.

The *In re Gault* decision affirmed that a juvenile has the right to due process safeguards in proceedings in which a finding of delinquency can lead to institutional confinement. The decision also established that a juvenile has the right to notice of the charges, right to counsel, right to confrontation and cross-examination, and privilege against self-incrimination. But the Court did not rule that juveniles have the right to a transcript of the proceedings or the right to appellate review.

In choosing not to rule on these two latter rights, the Court clearly did not want to turn the informal juvenile hearing into an adversary trial. The cautiousness of this decision was underlined by a footnote stating that the decision did not apply to preadjudication or postadjudication treatment of juveniles.

IN RE WINSHIP (1970) In *Winship* the Supreme Court decided that juveniles are entitled to proof beyond a reasonable doubt during the adjudication proceedings.[34] Juvenile Justice 15.4 presents the facts of this case. In ruling that the "preponderance of evidence" is not a sufficient basis for a decision when youths are charged with acts that would be criminal if committed by adults, the *Winship* decision not only expanded the

Juvenile Law 15.4

In re Winship

The Winship case involved a New York boy who was sent to a state training school at the age of twelve for taking $112 from a woman's purse. The commitment was based on a New York statute that permitted juvenile court decisions on the basis of a "preponderance of evidence," a standard that is much less strict than "beyond a reasonable doubt."

What is the actual difference between "preponderance of evidence" and proof beyond a reasonable doubt? What was the importance of this difference in this case?

Source: In re Winship, 397 U.S. 358, 90 S. Ct. 1968, 25 L. Ed. 2d 368 (1970).

In re Gault ruling, but also reflected other concerns of the U.S. Supreme Court. The Court desired both to protect juveniles at adjudicatory hearings and to maintain the confidentiality, informality, flexibility, and speed of the juvenile process in the prejudicial and postadjudicative states. The court obviously did not want to bring too much rigidity and impersonality to the juvenile hearing.

MCKEIVER V. PENNSYLVANIA (1971)   The Supreme Court heard three cases together (*McKeiver v. Pennsylvania, In re Terry,* and *In re Barbara Burrus*) concerning whether the due process clause of the Fourteenth Amendment guaranteeing the right to a jury trial applies to the adjudication of a juvenile court delinquency case.[35] The decision, which was issued in *McKeiver v. Pennsylvania,* denied the right of juveniles to have jury trials. Juvenile Justice 15.5 summarizes the facts of these three cases.

Juvenile Law 15.5

The Right of a Jury Trial for Juveniles

McKeiver v. Pennsylvania

Joseph McKeiver, age sixteen, was charged with robbery, larceny, and receiving stolen goods, all of which were felonies under Pennsylvania law. This youth was found delinquent at an adjudication hearing and was placed on probation after his request for a jury trial was denied.

In Re Terry

Edward Terry, age fifteen, was charged with assault and battery on a police officer, misdemeanors under Pennsylvania law. His counsel request for a jury trial was denied, and he was adjudicated a delinquent on the charges.

In Re Barbara Burrus

Barbara Burrus and approximately forty-five other youths, ranging in ages from eleven to fifteen years, were the subjects of juvenile court summonses in Hyde County, North Carolina. The charges arose out of a series of demonstrations in the county in late 1968 by African American adults and children protesting school assignments and a school consolidation plan. These youths were charged with willfully impeding traffic. The several cases were consolidated into groups for hearing before the district judge, sitting as a juvenile court. A request for a jury trial in each case was denied. Each juvenile was found delinquent and placed on probation.

Some states now permit jury trial for juveniles. How can they grant a jury trial with this Supreme Court decision?

Source: McKeiver v. Pennsylvania, 403 U.S. 528, 535 (1971); In re Terry, 215 Pa. SUPER 762 (1970); and In re Barbara Burrus, 275 N.C. 517, 169 S.E.2d 879 (1969).

The Supreme Court, in ruling that juveniles do not have the right to a jury trial, gave the following reasons:

1. Not all rights that are constitutionally assured for the adult are to be given to the juvenile.
2. The jury trial, if required for juveniles, may make the juvenile proceedings into a fully adversary process and will put an end to what has been the idealistic prospect of an intimate, informal protecting proceeding.
3. A jury trial is not a necessary part even of every criminal process that is fair and equitable.
4. The jury trial, if injected into the juvenile court system, could bring with it the traditional delay, the formality, and the clamor of the adversary system.
5. There is nothing to prevent an individual juvenile judge from using an advisory jury when he or she feels the need. For that matter, there is nothing to prevent individual states from adopting jury trials.[36]

A number of states do permit jury trials for juveniles, but most adhere to the constitutional standard set by the Supreme Court. Surveys of states report that juveniles choose jury trials in only about 1 to 3 percent of cases.[37] The significance of the *McKeiver* decision is that the Court indicated an unwillingness to apply further procedural safeguards to juvenile proceedings, especially during the preadjudicatory and postadjudicatory treatment of juveniles.

BREED V. JONES (1975)   The question of transfer to an adult court, first considered in the *Kent* case, was taken up again in the *Breed v. Jones* decision.[38] This case questioned whether a juvenile could be prosecuted as an adult after an adjudicatory hearing in the juvenile court. The increased use of transfers, or the binding over of juveniles to the adult court, makes this decision particularly significant (see Juvenile Law 15.6).

The U.S. Supreme Court ruled that Breed's case did constitute double jeopardy; a juvenile court cannot adjudicate a case and then transfer the case over to the criminal court for adult processing on the same offense. The significance of *Breed* is that prosecutors must determine which youthful offenders they want to transfer to the adult court before juvenile court adjudication; otherwise, the opportunity to transfer, or certify, those youths is lost.[39]

Juvenile Law 15.6

Breed v. Jones

In 1971 the juvenile court in California filed a petition against Jones, who was then seventeen, alleging that he had committed an offense that, if committed by an adult, would have constituted robbery. Jones was detained pending a hearing. At the hearing, the juvenile judge took testimony, found that the allegations were true, and sustained the petition. At the dispositional hearing, Jones was found unfit for treatment in the juvenile court, and it was ordered that he be prosecuted as an adult offender. At a subsequent preliminary hearing, Jones was held for criminal trial. An in-

formation hearing was held against him for robbery, and he was tried and found guilty. Counsel objected that Jones was being subjected to double jeopardy, but the defendant was committed to the California Youth Authority.

What is double jeopardy? Why is it important for juveniles and adults in the legal process?

Source: Breed v. Jones, 421 U.S. 519, 95 S.Ct. 1779 (1975).

Today, as is indicated in more detail later in this chapter, nearly every state has defined the specific requirements for transfer proceedings in its juvenile code. At present, when a transfer hearing is conducted in the juvenile court, due process law usually requires: (1) a legitimate transfer hearing, (2) a sufficient notice to the juvenile's family and defense attorney, (3) the right to counsel, and (4) a statement of the court order regarding transfer.

The Role Expectations of Juvenile Court Actors

Judges, referees, prosecutors (or petitioners), and defense attorneys (or respondents) are the main participants in the juvenile court process, and their roles have changed significantly in recent years.

Judges

The juvenile court judge, the ultimate decision maker, is the most important person in the juvenile court. The most traditional role of the juvenile court judge is to decide the legal issues in the cases that appear before the court. The judge must make a determination, according to Edwards, "whether certain facts are true, whether a child should be removed from a parent, what types of services should be offered to the family and whether the child should be returned to the family and the community or placed permanently in another setting."[40]

The juvenile court judge also has the following role responsibilities:

1. To set standards within the community and the criminal and juvenile justice system related to juvenile justice.
2. To make certain that juveniles appearing before the court receive the legal and constitutional rights to which they are entitled.
3. To ensure that the systems that detect, investigate, resolve, and bring cases to court are working fairly and efficiently.
4. To make certain that adequate numbers of attorneys of satisfactory quality are available to represent juveniles in court.
5. To know how cases that do not reach the juvenile court are being resolved.
6. To monitor the progress of the child, the family, and the supervising agency to make certain that each complies with the terms of the court's orders.
7. To be an advocate within the community on behalf of children and their families.
8. In some communities the juvenile court judge is the administrator of the juvenile probation department and court staff.[41]

More specifically, juvenile judges rule on various pretrial motions such as arrest, search and seizure, interrogation, and lineup identification; make decisions about the continued use of or the need for detention of youths before juvenile court hearings; make decisions about plea-bargaining agreements; settle questions of evidence and procedure and guide the questioning of witnesses; hold dispositional hearings or approve the contract presented and decide on the necessary treatment; handle waiver, or transfer, proceedings; and handle appeals where allowed by statute.[42]

Significant changes, however, are occurring in the funding process and in the administration of the juvenile court. In some jurisdictions, separately organized juvenile courts are being recast as juvenile divisions of a multijurisdictional trial court. The central responsibility for budget preparation and presentation then is shared by the trial court administrator and the presiding judge of the trial court. State legislatures also are assuming more responsibility for funding trial courts; this trend will probably continue because it is seen as leading to a more uniform system of justice. Furthermore, some state legislatures are transferring the responsibility for administering juvenile probation and detention services from the judiciary to the state executive branch. Finally, more judges are taking the bench through appointment rather than through a victory in a public election; they have very different relationships with local funding authorities than elected judges have.

Juvenile court judges not only have important and difficult jobs but also wield considerable power. Power, of course, sometimes corrupts, and occasionally a judge becomes a despot or dictator in the court. David Matza, addressing the abuse of power in the juvenile court, refers to the justice of some judges as **kadi justice.**[43] The *kadi* is a Moslem judge who sits in the marketplace and makes decisions without any apparent reference to rules or norms; he or she seems to make a completely free evaluation of the merits of each case. The "justice" of these judges has caused considerable criticism of the juvenile court.

Yet the majority of juvenile judges rise to the challenge and do extremely competent jobs. Procedural safeguards and due process rights for juveniles are scrupulously observed in their courts. These judges are always seeking better means of detention and reserve the use of correctional institutions as a last resort. They are very committed, work long hours, and sometimes pass up promotions to more highly paid judgeships with greater prestige. These judges usually improve the quality of juvenile justice in their jurisdictions.

Referees

Many juvenile courts employ the services of a **referee,** who has been called the *arm of the court.* A referee is called a *commissioner* in the State of Washington and a *master* in Maryland. California has both referees and commissioners. A number of states, such as Florida and Iowa, use only judges in the juvenile court; in other states, referees, masters, and commissioners are the primary hearing officers. Referees may or may not be members of the bar, but their basic responsibility is to assist judges in processing youths through the courts. They hear cases at the fact-finding stage and sometimes in detention hearings, but if a judicial disposition is necessary, it is usually left to a juvenile judge.

Prosecutors

The prosecutor, or petitioner, is expected to protect society and at the same time to ensure that children who would harm society are provided their basic constitutional rights. Almost two-thirds of prosecutors' offices handling juvenile cases transferred at least one juvenile case to criminal court in 1994.[44]

In larger courts, prosecutors are typically involved at every stage of the proceedings, from intake and detention through disposition and review. The prosecutor is particularly involved before the adjudication stage because witnesses must be interviewed, police investigations must be checked out, and court rules and case decisions must be researched. The prosecutor also plays a role in detention decisions and represents the local or state government in all pretrial motions, probable cause hearings, and consent decrees. The prosecutor further represents the state or county at transfer hearings, at the adjudication hearing, and at the disposition of the case. In some urban courts, the prosecutor may frequently be involved in plea bargaining with the defense counsel. Prosecutors in some states are even permitted to initiate appeals for the limited purpose of clarifying a given law or procedure. Furthermore, the prosecutor represents the state or county on appeals and in habeas corpus proceedings. Some critics argue that the prosecutor in the juvenile court has come to dominate juvenile court proceedings.[45]

Defense Attorneys

The number of juveniles represented by counsel, or respondents, has been gradually increasing since the early 1960s. Juveniles in more serious cases are especially likely to be represented by counsel.[46] Yet Feld found that nearly half the juveniles who appeared before the juvenile courts for delinquency and status-offense referrals in Minnesota, Nebraska, and North Dakota were not represented by counsel. Equally serious, he found that many of the juveniles who were placed out of their homes in these states did not have counsel.[47]

Feld added in a 1999 publication that "waiver of counsel is the most common explanation why so many youths appear without counsel."[48] Even though more juveniles now are being represented by counsel, considerable confusion still exists among defense attorneys concerning their proper role in the courtroom, and many questions have been raised about their effectiveness in court. Defense counsels have at least three roles to choose from: (1) assist the court with its responsibilities to children, (2) serve as a legal advocate for the child, and (3) be a guardian or parent surrogate to the child.[49]

Public defenders frequently do a better job of representing youth than do private and court-appointed attorneys, particularly when the same public defender must appear in juvenile court day after day. Court-appointed private counsel, particularly those who need the work to supplement slim private practices, can be more easily swayed to the court's wishes.[50]

Some evidence exists that children who have counsel may get more severe dispositions than those without counsel.[51] For example, it has been found that juveniles with counsel were more likely to receive an institutional disposition than those without counsel.[52] When it exists, there are two possible explanations for this positive relationship between counsel and punitive dispositions: First, the juvenile judge is punishing youths who choose to be represented by counsel. Second, the youths who have committed the more serious crimes are the ones requesting counsel, and they are the ones most likely to be adjudicated to training school or transferred to the adult court. Although the former may have been true in the past, the latter is typically true today.

The Pretrial Procedures

The types of cases that are under the jurisdiction of the juvenile court vary widely among and even within states, but they generally include those involving delinquency, neglect, and dependency. Figures 15.1 and 15.2 diagram the juvenile court's processing of status offense and delinquent cases in 1996. Juvenile courts also may deal with cases concerning adoption, termination of parental rights, appointment of guardians for minors, custody, contributing to delinquency or neglect, and nonsupport. The detention hearing, the intake procedure, and the transfer procedure all take place before the adjudication stage of juvenile court proceedings.

The Detention Hearing

Legislative acts that govern the juvenile court normally require that the police either take a child to an intake officer of the court or a detention facility or release the child to his or her parents. The criteria for detention are based on the need to protect the child and to ensure public safety. The decision to detain must be made within a short period of time, usually forty-eight to seventy-two hours, excluding weekends and holidays. Urban courts, which have intake units on duty twenty-four hours a day for detention hearings, frequently act within a few hours.[53]

In some states, intake officers of the juvenile court, rather than juvenile judges, conduct **detention hearings.** Such a procedure represents a progressive move, because having the same judge preside over both the detention hearing and the adjudication hearing is a poor practice. Some states still require that the juvenile judge be responsible for the policies and operations of the detention facility. Juvenile judges also are usually required to decide, to preclude inappropriate or overly long detention, whether a child who was admitted to detention a few days earlier must remain locked up.

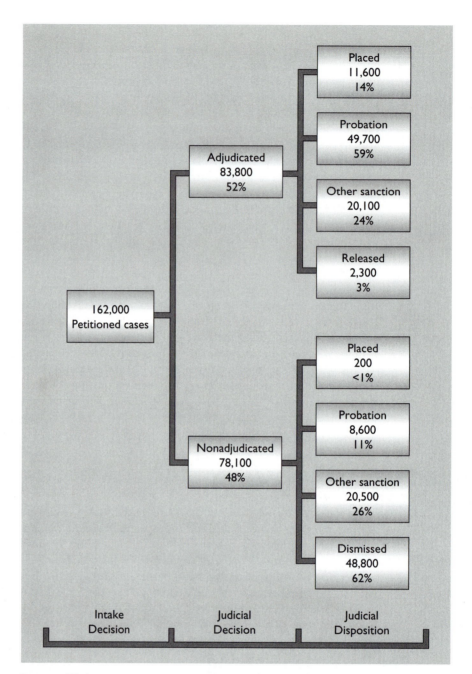

FIGURE 15.1 Juvenile Court Processing of Petitioned Status Offense Cases, 1996

Note: Detail may not add to totals because of rounding.

Source: Anne L. Stahl, "Offenders in Juvenile Court, 1996," *Juvenile Justice Bulletin* (Washington, D.C.: Office of Juvenile Justice and Delinquency Prevention, 1999), p. 9.

In 1995, detention was used in 22 percent of drug law violations, 22 percent of person offense cases, 22 percent of public order cases, and 15 percent of property offense cases.[54] Juveniles who are held in detention may be assigned to one of four different types of placements. The detention hall or detention home physically restricts the youth for a short period. Shelter care is physically nonrestrictive and is available for those who have no homes or who require juvenile court intervention. The third type of placement is the jail or police lockup. The fourth is in-home detention. In-home detention restricts

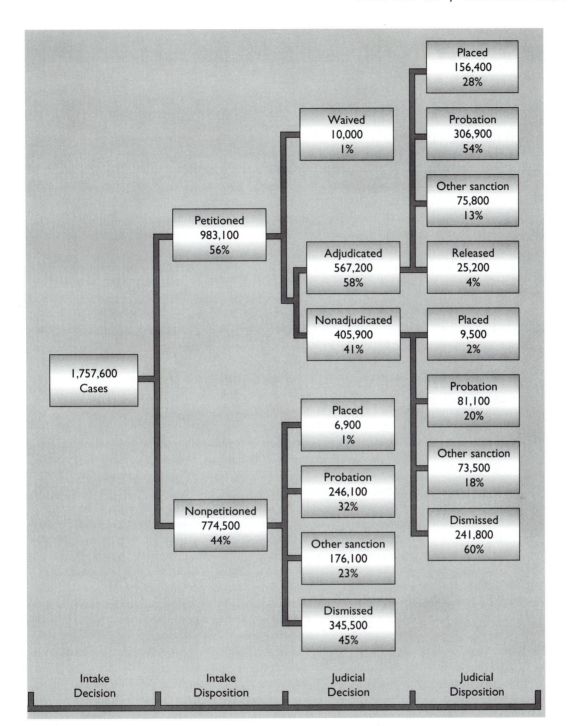

FIGURE 15.2 Juvenile Court Processing of Delinquency Cases, 1996

Note: Detail may not add to totals because of rounding.

Source: Anne L. Stahl, "Offenders in Juvenile Court, 1996," *Juvenile Justice Bulletin* (Washington, D.C.: Office of Juvenile Justice and Delinquency Prevention, 1999), p. 6.

a juvenile to his or her home and is supervised, normally by a paraprofessional staff member. See Juvenile Law 15.7 for structure, programming, and recommendations for detention facilities in the United States.

Five states have legislated a hearing on probable cause for detained youths, and appellate cases in other states have moved in the direction of mandating a probable cause

Juvenile *Law* 15.7

Detention Facilities

Detention centers are administered by state agencies, city or county government, welfare departments, juvenile courts, or private vendors, but the majority of detention facilities are administered by the county. In 1997, according to a survey conducted by the National Council on Crime and Delinquency, 73 percent of the forty-four responding states operated detention facilities at the county level; 36 percent operated detention facilities at the state level; 30 percent operated detention facilities under multiple jurisdictions; 16 percent had court-administered or -operated detention facilities; and 11 percent contracted with private vendors to provide detention services.

The states of Connecticut, Vermont, and Delaware as well as Puerto Rico have complete responsibility for administering juvenile detention centers. Georgia, Massachusetts, New Hampshire, Rhode Island, and Maryland operate regional detention facilities; Utah and Virginia also encourage the establishment of regional detention centers by reimbursing counties for their construction.

The traditional model of detention for youths was woefully inadequate. A grim-looking detention facility usually was attached to the building that housed the administrative offices and hearing rooms of the juvenile court. Locked outer doors and high fences or walls prevented escapes. The lack of programming made it clear that these facilities were intended merely to be holding centers. A former resident, interviewed in May 1981, described her experience in a traditional detention home:

> It [the facility] sucks. It was the worst place I've ever been in. They're [the staff] cruel. They used to give work details for punishment. For an entire hour, I scrubbed the kitchen floor with a toothbrush. They can get away with this, and it is not against the law. The place is falling apart. They are just not very caring people. They didn't do much for me except scare me.

Fortunately, the nationwide movement to develop standards for detention as well as more innovative detention programs resulted in marked improvement in the overall quality of detention facilities and programs during the past two decades. The bureau of detention standards, in those states that have such overseeing units, usually inspects detention centers once a year; this inspection ensures better-quality detention practices.

Attention homes, which were initiated in Boulder, Colorado by the juvenile court to improve the detention process for children, have spread to other jurisdictions. The stated purpose of the attention homes program is to give youths *attention* rather than *detention*. Problem resolution is the focus of the program, and professional services are provided to residents on a contractual basis. These nonsecured facilities have no fences, locked doors, or other physical restraints. They also are characterized by more extensive programming and by more intensive involvement between residents and staff than is typical in other facilities.

Home detention, a nonresidential approach to detention, was first used in St. Louis, Newport News, Norfolk, and Washington, D.C., and now is used throughout the United States. The in-home detention program is commonly within the organizational structure of the juvenile court and is administered by the community services unit of the probation department. An in-home detention coordinator typically meets with the intake officer, a field probation officer, and sometimes a juvenile officer before the detention hearing to decide whether a youth is an appropriate candidate for in-home detention. Some jurisdictions use a release risk evaluation to decide whether in-home detention for a particular youth should be recommended to the juvenile judge. Youths who are placed on in-home detention are required to remain at home twenty-four hours a day; the in-home detention worker visits the youth and family seven days a week and also makes random phone calls throughout the day to make certain that the juvenile is at home. As mentioned in Chapter 16, electronic monitoring is starting to be used as part of home-detention programs.

What are the detention facilities like in your jurisdiction? Does anyone in the class know of Attention Homes or Home Detention programs?

Source: Kelly Dedel, "National Profile of the Organization of State Juvenile Correctional Systems," *Crime and Delinquency* 44 (October 1998), p. 514.

hearing to justify further detention. Courts in Georgia and Alaska have ruled that a child is entitled to counsel at a detention hearing and to free counsel if the child is indigent. The supreme courts of California and Alaska and an appellate court in Pennsylvania all have overturned cases in which no reason or inadequate reason was stated for continuing detention. Finally, courts in the District of Columbia, Baltimore, and Nevada have ruled that a juvenile who is in detention is entitled to humane care. The appeals court in the District of Columbia stated that there is a statutory obligation to provide a juvenile with care "as nearly as possible equivalent to that which should have been given him by his parents."[55]

Steven Schlossman's detailed account of the history of Milwaukee's juvenile court found that judges and probation officers frequently relied on detention to make juveniles cooperative.[56] Although Charles E. Frazier and Donna M. Bishop's study of detention found no evidence that detention status greatly affected the severity of judicial dispositions, it did find that juveniles who were male, white, and older were more disadvantaged by detention than were those who were female, nonwhite, and younger.[57]

Court decisions have differed concerning **bail** for a juvenile. Decisions have found that juveniles have a constitutional right to bail; that juvenile act procedures, when applied in a manner consistent with due process, provide an adequate substitute for bail; or that juveniles do not have a constitutional right to bail. Nine states (Arkansas, Colorado, Connecticut, Georgia, Massachusetts, Nebraska, Oklahoma, South Dakota, and West Virginia) have enacted laws granting juveniles the right to bail. On the other hand, Hawaii, Kentucky, Oregon, and Utah deny juveniles the right to bail.

Alida V. Merlo and William D. Bennett's examination of bail in Massachusetts revealed that bail was a factor in 72 percent of the cases statewide in 1988. The trend in Massachusetts for higher bail is reflected in the detention admissions receiving from $101 to $500 bail (up 16 percent), $501 to $1,000 bail (up 70 percent), and over $1,000 bail (up 48 percent). These statewide developments, they concluded, suggest that juvenile judges may be starting to use bail as a means of ensuring the youth's detention and that judges, without actually using the term, may be engaging in the practice of preventive detention.[58]

The U.S. Supreme Court decision in the *Schall v. Martin* (1984) case represents an example of a fundamental change that seems to be occurring in detention practices.[59] The plaintiffs originally filed a lawsuit in federal district court claiming that the New York Family Court Act was unconstitutional because it allowed for the preventive detention of juveniles:

> The District Court struck down the statute as permitting detention without due process and ordered the release of all class members. The Court of Appeals affirmed, holding . . . the statute is administered not for preventive purposes, but to impose punishment for unadjudicated criminal acts, and that therefore the statute is unconstitutional.[60]

The Supreme Court, however, reversed the decision of the appeals court. Justice Rehnquist, in writing the opinion for the majority, declared that the "preventive detention under the statute serves the legitimate state objective held in common with every State, of protecting both the juvenile and the society from the hazards of pretrial crime."[61] The ultimate impact of this decision has yet to be felt, but some experts believe that the Court's ruling may encourage a significant expansion of preventive, or secure, detention for juveniles.

The constitutionality of preventive detention may have been confirmed by the Supreme Court in *Schall v. Martin,* but this policy still raises several controversial issues. First, there is the technical difficulty of accurately predicting which offenders should be detained to prevent their commission of further offenses before trial. Second, the detainee experiences preventive detention as punitive confinement, regardless of the stated purpose of the practice. Finally, there are issues of the propriety of incarceration before the determination of guilt and of the procedural safeguards that must accompany such a practice. Indeed, evaluations of the detention process indicate that the majority of juveniles who are preventively detained are not charged with serious offenses.[62]

The Intake Process

Intake essentially is a preliminary screening process to determine whether a court should take action and, if so, what action, or whether the matter should be referred elsewhere. Larger courts usually handle this function through a specialized intake unit. Probation officers or other officers of the court screen incoming cases in smaller courts.[63]

In 1995, 21 percent of all delinquency cases were dismissed at intake, usually for lack of legal sufficiency. Another 24 percent were processed informally, with the juvenile agreeing to a voluntary disposition, but more than half (55 percent) were processed formally and involved either an adjudicatory hearing or a hearing to consider waiving jurisdiction to the adult or criminal court.[64]

Intake procedures follow complaints to authorities against children. Juvenile law varies from state to state regarding who is permitted to sign such a complaint. Typically, most complaints are filed by the police, although they may be initiated and signed by a victim or by the youth's parents. In some states, parents, victims, probation staff, social service staff, neighbors, or anyone else may go directly to the court to file a complaint. Complaints also may be brought by school officials and truant officers.

After the intake officer receives the complaint, he or she must first decide whether the court has statutory jurisdiction. If the statutory guides are unclear, the intake officer should seek the advice of the prosecuting attorney. Once legal jurisdiction is established, the second step is to conduct a preliminary interview and investigation to determine whether the case should be adjudicated nonjudicially or petitioned to the court. This evaluation procedure varies from jurisdiction to jurisdiction, principally because so many juvenile courts have failed to provide written guidelines. Therefore the intake officer usually has broad and largely unregulated discretion in making the intake decision.

OPTIONS FOR THE DISPOSAL OF CASES The intake unit, especially in larger urban courts, may have up to five options for the disposal of cases: (1) outright dismissal of the complaint, (2) informal adjustment (chiefly diversion to a nonjudicial agency), (3) informal probation, (4) consent decree, and (5) filing of a petition.

Outright dismissal of the complaint takes place when legal jurisdiction does not exist or when the case is so weak that the intake officer questions the feasibility of petitioning the youth to the juvenile court. **Informal adjustment** means that the intake officer requires restitution from the youth, warns him or her, and then dismisses the case or diverts the youth to a social agency, such as a youth service bureau. The diversion agency supervises such referrals and generally reports to the intake unit on the youth's progress; status offenders and juveniles charged with minor offenses typically are dealt with under this option.

Informal probation, which has been under increased criticism since the 1970s, involves the casual supervision of a youth by a volunteer or probation officer, who reserves judgment on the need for filing a petition until the intake officer (or other designated person) sees how the youth fares during the informal probation period. See Juvenile Law 15.8 for more information on informal sanctions.

A **consent decree** is a formal agreement between the child and the court in which the child is placed under the court's supervision without a formal finding of delinquency. Consent decrees provide an intermediate step between informal handling and probation. The consent decree is used less often than the other options that are currently open to the intake officer. The consent decree, it should be noted, comes after the petition but before the adjudication hearing.

If none of these options is satisfactory, the intake officer can choose to file a petition. Unfortunately, the broad discretionary power given intake workers has often been abused. For example, Duran Bell, Jr. and Kevin Lang's study of intake in Los Angeles County revealed the importance of extralegal factors, especially cooperative behavior, in reducing the length of detention and the effect of age in increasing the length of detention.[65]

Research is needed to determine which approach to intake will result in the greatest services to youth and the least misuse of discretion. But until a systematic examina-

Juvenile Law 15.8

Informal Sanctions

Informal processing is considered when decision makers (police, intake workers, probation officers, prosecutors, or other screening officers) believe that accountability and rehabilitation can be achieved without the use of formal court intervention.

Informal sanctions are voluntary and, consequently, the court cannot force a juvenile to comply with an informal disposition. If the court decides to handle the matter informally (in lieu of formal prosecution), a youthful offender agrees to comply with one or more sanctions such as voluntary probation supervision, community service, and victim restitution. In some jurisdictions, before juveniles are offered informal sanctions, they must agree that they committed the alleged act.

When informally handled, the case is usually held open pending the successful completion of the informal disposition. Upon successful completion of these arrangements, the charges against the offender are dismissed. But if the offender does not fulfill the court's conditions for informal handling, the case is likely to be reopened and formally prosecuted.

Informal handling is less common than in the past but is still used in a large number of cases. According to *Juvenile Court Statistics 1996,* 44 percent of delinquency cases disposed in 1996 were handled informally, compared with more than half in 1987.

What is your evaluation of informal sanctions? What do you see as their strengths and weaknesses?

Source: Howard N. Snyder, and Melissa Sickmund, *Juvenile Offenders and Victims: 1999 National Report* (Washington, D.C.: National Center for Juvenile Justice, 1999), p. 159.

---

tion of the intake process is done, the principles of doing the least harm possible to the youth and of fairness should guide the intake screening process.

The Transfer Procedure

For the past two decades, juvenile offenders have been increasingly transferred to adult court. This has been accomplished in some states by lowering the age of judicial waiver, in some states by excluding certain offenses from juvenile court jurisdiction, and in other states by passing legislation aimed at transfer of serious juvenile offenders.[66] As shown in Figure 15.3, many states have a combination of transfer provisions.

A recent move in several states grants prosecutors, rather than juvenile court judges, the nonreviewable discretionary power to determine the court before which juveniles would be required to appear. For example, the state of Florida has recently expanded the discretionary power of prosecutors in dealing with juveniles who are sixteen or older.[67] Table 15.1 indicates which states allow prosecutors to try juveniles in either juvenile or criminal court.

Every state currently has some provision for transferring juvenile offenders to adult criminal courts. Vermont (age 10), Montana (age 12), and Georgia, Illinois, and Mississippi (age 13) transfer children at very young ages; more states transfer children at fourteen than at any other age; and seven states transfer children at either fifteen or sixteen years of age.

Fifteen states exclude murder from juvenile court jurisdiction. Ten states exclude rape, eight exclude armed robbery or robbery, six exclude kidnapping, and three exclude burglary. Eleven states use a combination of offense categories.[68]

Judicial waiver and **legislative waiver** are the two basic mechanisms (also called *remand, certification,* and *waiver of jurisdiction*) for transferring juvenile offenders to the adult criminal justice system. Judicial waiver, the most common, takes place after a judicial hearing on a juvenile's amenability to treatment or his or her threat to public safety.[69]

	Judicial waiver			Concurrent jurisdiction	Statutory exclusion	Reverse waiver	Once an adult/ always an adult
	Discretionary	Presumptive	Mandatory				
Total number of states	46	15	14	15	28	23	31
Alabama	■				■		■
Alaska	■	■			■		
Arizona	■	■		■	■	■	■
Arkansas	■			■		■	
California	■	■					■
Colorado	■	■		■		■	
Connecticut			■			■	
Delaware	■		■		■	■	■
Dist. of Columbia	■	■		■			■
Florida	■			■	■		■
Georgia	■		■			■	
Hawaii	■						■
Idaho	■				■		
Illinois	■	■	■		■		
Indiana			■		■		
Iowa	■				■	■	■
Kansas	■	■					
Kentucky	■		■			■	
Louisiana	■		■	■	■		
Maine	■						■
Maryland	■				■	■	
Massachusetts				■	■		
Michigan	■			■			■
Minnesota	■	■			■		■
Mississippi	■				■	■	■
Missouri	■						■
Montana	■			■	■		
Nebraska				■		■	
Nevada	■	■			■	■	■
New Hampshire	■	■					■
New Jersey	■	■					
New Mexico					■		
New York					■	■	
North Carolina	■		■				
North Dakota	■	■	■				■
Ohio	■		■				■
Oklahoma	■			■	■	■	■
Oregon	■				■	■	
Pennsylvania	■	■			■	■	■
Rhode Island	■	■	■		■		■
South Carolina	■		■		■	■	
South Dakota	■				■	■	■
Tennessee	■					■	■
Texas	■						■
Utah	■	■			■		■
Vermont	■			■	■	■	
Virginia	■		■	■		■	■
Washington	■				■		■
West Virginia	■		■				
Wisconsin	■				■	■	■
Wyoming	■			■		■	

FIGURE 15.3 Most States Have a Combination of Transfer Provisions

In states with a combination of transfer mechanisms, the exclusion, mandatory waiver, or concurrent jurisdiction provisions generally target the oldest juveniles and/or those charged with the most serious offenses, while those charged with relatively less serious offenses and/or younger juveniles may be eligible for discretionary waiver.

Source: Office of Juvenile Justice and Delinquency Prevention *1999 National Report Series* (Washington, D.C.: U.S. Department Justice, 1999), p. 13. Author's adaptation of Torbet and Szymanski's *State legislative responses to violent juvenile crime: 1996–97 update.*

TABLE 15.1

In States with Concurrent Jurisdiction, the Prosecutor Has Discretion to File Certain Cases, Generally Involving Juveniles Charged with Serious Offenses, in Either Criminal Court or Juvenile Court

State	Minimum age for concurrent jurisdiction	Concurrent jurisdiction offense and minimum age criteria, 1997							
		Any criminal offense	Certain felonies	Capital crimes	Murder	Certain person offenses	Certain property offenses	Certain drug offenses	Certain weapon offenses
Arizona	14		14						
Arkansas	14		14	14	14	14			14
Colorado	14		14		14	14	14		14
Dist. of Columbia	16				16	16	16		
Florida	NS	16[a]	16	NS[b]	14	14	14		14
Georgia	NS			NS					
Louisiana	15				15	15	15	15	
Massachusetts	14		14			14			14
Michigan	14		14		14	14	14	14	
Montana	12				12	12	16	16	16
Nebraska	NS	16[c]	NS						
Oklahoma	15				15	15	15	16	15
Vermont	16	16							
Virginia	14				14	14			
Wyoming	14	17	14						

Examples: In Arizona, prosecutors have discretion to file directly in criminal court those cases involving juveniles age 14 or older charged with certain felonies (defined in State statutes). In Florida, prosecutors may "direct file" cases involving juveniles age 16 or older charged with a misdemeanor (if they have a prior adjudication) or a felony offense, as well as those age 14 or older charged with murder or certain person, property, or weapon offenses; no minimum age is specified for cases in which a grand jury indicts a juvenile for a capital offense.

Note: Ages in minimum age column may not apply to all offense restrictions, but represent the youngest possible age at which a juvenile may be filed directly in criminal court. "NS" indicates that in at least one of the offense restrictions indicated, no minimum age is specified.

[a]Applies to misdemeanors and requires prior adjudication(s), which may be required to have been for the same or a more serious offense type.

[b]Requires grand jury indictment.

[c]Applies to misdemeanors.

Source: Office of Juvenile Justice and Delinquency Prevention, *1999 National Report Series* (Washington, D.C.: U.S. Department of Justice, 1999), p. 16. Author's adaption of Griffin et al.'s *Trying Juveniles as Adults in Criminal Court: An Analysis of State Transfer Provisions*.

Judicial waiver, as previously discussed in regard to the *Kent v. United States* and *Breed v. Jones* decisions, contains certain procedural safeguards for youthful offenders. The criteria that are used to determine the transfer decision typically include the age and maturity of the child; the seriousness of the referral incident; the child's past record; the child's relationship with parents, school, and community; whether the child is considered dangerous; and whether court officials believe that the child may be helped by juvenile court services. Most juvenile court judges appear to be influenced primarily by prior record and the seriousness of the present offense.

Legislative waiver is accomplished in five ways. The first occurs when legislatures simply exclude certain offenses from juvenile court jurisdiction. Any juvenile, then, who commits a specified offense automatically goes before the adult court. The second lowers the age over which the juvenile court has jurisdiction. For example, if a state's age of juvenile court jurisdiction is eighteen, the legislature may lower the age to sixteen. The third form of legislative waiver specifies that juveniles of specific ages who commit specific crimes are to be tried by adult court. This method of legislative waiver focuses as much on the offense as it does on the age of the offender. The fourth method of legislative waiver involves statutes that simply state that anyone who commits a specific crime may be tried in adult court. This approach is attractive to those who believe that any youth who violates the law should receive an appropriate punishment. The fifth method is for state legislatures to give both the juvenile and the adult courts concurrent jurisdiction over all children who are under the jurisdictional age of the juvenile court.

Statutes mandating that the decision to prosecute a juvenile as an adult be made on the basis of the seriousness of the offense charged are inconsistent with the rehabilitative philosophy of the juvenile court. Legislative waiver also is problematic because it usually has a rationale of incapacitation of chronic offenders through longer sentences than those provided by the juvenile process.[70]

In the midst of a great deal of confusion, three conclusions can be drawn about judicial and legislative waiver. First, more juveniles are being transferred to the adult court. In 1996, 10,000 were judicially waived, and this number is considerably larger than in 1987 when 6,888 were judicially waived (See Table 15.2 for the number of cases transferred to criminal court by judicial waiver from 1987 to 1996).[71]

Second, juveniles who are waived to adult court are not always the most serious or intractable. Of the cases waived in 1995, 47 percent involved a person offense as the most serious charge, 34 percent involved a property offense, and 13 percent involved a drug law violation.[72] M. A. Bortner, in an examination of 214 remanded juveniles and

TABLE 15.2

The Characteristics of Waived Cases Changed between 1987 and 1996

	1987	1992	1996
TOTAL CASES WAIVED	**6,800**	**10,300**	**10,000**
MOST SERIOUS OFFENSE			
Person	28%	39%	43%
Property	55	41	37
Drugs	9	11	14
Public order	7	8	6
GENDER			
Male	95%	96%	95%
Female	5	4	5
AGE AT TIME OF REFERRAL			
Under 16 years	7%	12%	15%
16 or older	93	87	85
RACE/ETHNICITY			
White	57%	47%	51%
Black	41	50	46
Other	2	3	3
PREDISPOSITION DETENTION			
Detained	58%	53%	51%
Not detained	42	47	49

Note: Detail may not add to 100% due to rounding.

Source: Anne L. Stahl, "Delinquency Cases Waived to Criminal Court, 1987–1996," *OJJDP Fact Sheet* (Washington, D.C.: Office of Juvenile Justice and Delinquency Prevention, 1999), p. 1.

interviews with key decision makers, found that remanded juveniles were not typically dangerous or intractable, nor was there evidence to suggest that their remand enhanced public safety. Bortner added that organizational and political factors accounted for the high rate of remand.[73] Leona Lee's examination of waiver in the Maricopa County Juvenile Court revealed that the most important factor influencing the waiver decision was previous waiver: Those juveniles who had been previously waived were most likely to be waived again in future referrals.[74]

Third, although some transferred youths receive severe penalties in adult court, including the death penalty, waivers in general are not resulting in more severe penalties for juvenile offenders. Adult criminal courts tend to treat less seriously those cases certified to them by the juvenile court.[75] Yet in a study of transferred juveniles convicted of felonies in the seventy-five largest counties, most were sent to prison. Also, in this same study, those juvenile transfers convicted of murder received longer sentences than their adult counterparts. The maximum prison sentence imposed on transferred juveniles convicted of murder in 1994 was twenty-three years and five months; this was 2 years and 5 months longer than the average maximum prison sentence for adults eighteen or older.[76] Furthermore, an examination by Carl Rudman and colleagues of 177 violent youths who were considered for transfer in four urban areas found that transferred youths who were convicted in criminal court received severe sanctions, in both nature and length.[77]

In sum, the number of juveniles who are waived to adult court is likely to increase in the future because of pressures on the court to crack down on juvenile crime. The potential effect of this situation on judicial decision making makes this one of the most critical areas for ongoing research in juvenile justice.

What Happens during a Juvenile Trial

The trial stage of juvenile court proceedings is divided into the adjudicatory hearing, the disposition hearing, and judicial alternatives.

The Adjudicatory Hearing

The **adjudicatory hearing,** or fact-finding stage of the court's proceedings, usually includes the following steps: the child's plea, the presentation of evidence by the prosecution and by the defense, cross-examination of witnesses, and the judge's finding. In 1997, juveniles were adjudicated delinquent in more than half (57 percent) of the 996,000 cases referred to the court.[78] See Table 15.3 for the delinquency cases formally processed and adjudicated in 1997.

These steps serve as protections to ensure that youths are entitled to proof beyond a reasonable doubt when they are charged with an act that would constitute a crime if it had been committed by an adult and that the judge follows the rules of evidence and dismisses hearsay from the proceedings. Hearsay is dismissed because it can be unreliable or unfair, inasmuch as it cannot be held up for cross-examination. The evidence must be relevant and must contribute to the belief or disbelief of the act in question.

Prosecutors in most juvenile courts begin these proceedings by presenting the state's case. The arresting officer and witnesses at the scene of the crime testify, and any other evidence that has been legally obtained is introduced. The defense attorney then cross-examines the witnesses. Defense counsel also has the opportunity at this time to introduce evidence that is favorable to his or her client, and the youth may testify in his or her own behalf. The prosecutor then cross-examines the defense witnesses. The prosecution and the defense present summaries of the case to the judge, who reaches a finding or a verdict.

TABLE 15.3

In 1997, Juvenile Courts Formally Processed 996,000 Delinquency Cases—Most of These Petitioned Cases Were Adjudicated Delinquent, and, Once Adjudicated, Most Were Ordered to Residential Placement or Formal Probation

Most serious offense	Delinquency cases formally processed in 1997 Number	Percentage of total	Percentage of petitioned cases Adjudicated	Waived	All other cases	Percentage of adjudicated cases Residential placement	Formal probation
TOTAL DELINQUENCY	996,000	57%	57%	1%	42%	29%	55%
PERSON OFFENSES	228,200	58%	54%	1%	45%	30%	56%
Criminal homicide	1,700	86	38	31	31	63	29
Forcible rape	5,100	79	58	3	39	43	42
Robbery	29,300	87	61	4	36	44	45
Aggravated assault	48,900	72	57	2	41	31	55
Simple assault	121,000	49	51	0	49	25	60
Other violent sex offense	7,900	78	57	1	42	28	58
Other person offense	14,300	65	52	1	47	28	61
PROPERTY OFFENSES	445,600	53%	58%	1%	41%	27%	57%
Burglary	104,300	77	64	1	35	33	56
Larceny-theft	166,200	41	56	0	44	24	57
Motor vehicle theft	36,200	74	65	1	33	41	50
Arson	5,400	58	60	1	39	26	62
Vandalism	58,200	51	54	0	46	19	61
Trespassing	27,800	43	49	0	51	22	55
Stolen property offense	24,200	72	59	1	40	30	49
Other property offense	23,200	71	57	0	42	17	64
DRUG LAW VIOLATIONS	114,500	63%	58%	1%	41%	25%	55%
PUBLIC ORDER OFFENSES	207,600	61%	58%	0%	41%	34%	49%
Obstruction of justice	103,200	78	65	0	35	43	44
Disorderly conduct	36,500	40	47	0	53	15	58
Weapons offense	24,600	64	62	1	37	28	58
Liquor law violations	5,200	47	55	0	45	14	58
Nonviolent sex offense	6,100	56	63	1	36	40	52
Other public order	31,900	59	50	0	50	18	44
VIOLENT CRIME INDEX*	85,000	77%	58%	3%	39%	37%	50%
PROPERTY CRIME INDEX**	312,100	52%	60%	1%	40%	29%	56%

■ As a general rule, the more serious the offense, the more likely the case was to be brought before a judge for formal (court-ordered) sanctioning. For example, juvenile courts formally processed 41% of all larceny-theft cases in 1997, compared with 77% of all burglary cases.

■ Cases involving youth adjudicated for serious person offenses, such as homicide, rape, or robbery, were most likely to result in residential placement. Cases involving youth adjudicated for minor offenses, such as vandalism or disorderly conduct, were least likely to result in residential placement.

■ The relatively high residential placement rate for public order offense cases stems from the inclusion in that category of certain obstruction of justice offenses that have a high likelihood of placement (e.g., escapes from confinement and probation and parole violations).

*Includes criminal homicide, forcible rape, robbery, and aggravated assault.
**Includes burglary, larceny-theft, motor vehicle theft, and arson.
Note: Detail may not add to totals because of rounding.

Source: Melissa Sickmund, "Offenders in Juvenile Court," *Juvenile Justice Bulletin* (Washington, D.C.: Office of Juvenile Justice and Delinquency Prevention, 2000), p. 9.

James Parker, 16 is led out of court by Sheriff Kim Cronk, left, and Mayor Jay Davis, right, Tuesday, February 20, 2001, in New Castle, Indiana, following an extradition hearing to send him back to New Hampshire where he and Robert Tulloch, 17, face murder charges. Parker and Tulloch are wanted in connection with the stabbing deaths of two Dartmouth professors, January 27. Parker refused extradition and will return to court next week.

Ten states provide for a **jury trial** for juveniles, but jury trials are seldom demanded. Statutory provisions often close juvenile hearings to the general public, but this decision varies from one jurisdiction to the next. The right to a speedy trial has been provided by state court decisions and by statutes that limit the amount of time that can elapse between the filing of a complaint and the actual hearing.[79]

Unfortunately, the typical hearing sometimes falls short of achieving the desired objectives. Cases in large urban courts are sometimes heard so rapidly that they constitute what Lemert refers to as "the three-minute children's hour."[80] Representation by counsel can also be little more than a charade. Judges, in the way they phrase their question about legal representation or even by tone of voice, can persuade parents to waive the right of counsel.

In sum, the typical adjudication hearing has come a long way since the *In re Gault* decision. Although some judges and defense attorneys are exemplary in the support they give to the due process protection of juveniles during this stage of the court's proceedings, other judges and defense attorneys fall short in living up to either the spirit or the letter of post-*Gault* juvenile law. Significantly, the prosecutor has become a prominent figure at these proceedings.

The Disposition Hearing

Once a child has been found delinquent at the adjudicatory stage, some juvenile court codes still permit judges to proceed immediately to the disposition hearing. But the present trend is to hold **bifurcated hearings,** or split adjudicatory and disposition hearings, because a split hearing gives the probation officer appointed to the case an opportunity to prepare a social study investigation of the youth.

The disposition stage of the court's proceedings normally is quite different from the fact-finding stage, especially when it is held at a different time. The traditional purpose has been to administer individualized justice and to set in motion the rehabilitation of the delinquent; therefore the judge is not limited as much by constitutional safeguards as he or she was at the adjudication hearing. Rules of evidence are relaxed, parties and witnesses are not always sworn in, and hearsay testimony may be considered.[81] The starting point of the disposition hearing is usually the written social study of the child prepared by the probation officer. This report examines such factors as school attendance and grades, family structure and support, degree of maturity and sense of responsibility, relationships with peers, participation in community activities, and attitudes toward authority figures. In this final stage of the proceedings, juveniles are permitted to have legal counsel, and the *Kent* decision ensures the right of counsel to challenge the facts of the social study.

In 1997, 55 percent of the adjudicated youth were placed on formal probation during the disposition hearing. In 29 percent of the cases, the juvenile was placed in a residential facility or another out-of-the-home placement.[82]

The factors that influence judicial decision making at the dispositional stage can be separated into formal and informal factors. The three most important formal factors are (1) the recommendation of the probation officer and the information contained in the social study investigation, (2) the seriousness of the delinquent behavior and previous contacts with the court, and (3) the options available. The recommendation of the probation officer in the social study report is usually followed by the juvenile judge. The seriousness of the delinquent behavior and the previous contacts with the court probably have the greatest impact on judicial decision making at this stage. Terence Thornberry confirmed that seriousness of the current offense and the number of previous offenses have the greatest impact.[83] Bortner's examination of disposition decision making in a large Midwestern county revealed that age, prior refer-

Lionel Tate, 13, left, looks at his mother, Kathleen Grossett-Tate, prior to opening statements in his murder trial in Fort Lauderdale, Florida, Tuesday, January 16, 2001. Lionel Tate is being tried as an adult, and faces a mandatory life sentence with no possibility of parole for 25 years if convicted for first-degree murder in the death of 6-year-old Tiffany Eunick. Tate says he accidentally killed Eunick while imitating pro wrestlers.

rals, and the detention decision surfaced as the most important influences.[84] Studies of the juvenile courts in Colorado, Pennsylvania, and Tennessee revealed that prior decisions by juvenile court personnel are related more strongly to disposition than any other factor.[85] Finally, the juvenile judge is influenced by the options that are available. The most desirable placement might not be available in that jurisdiction, or the desired placement might have no space for the youth. Judge Forest Eastman reflected on this when he said:

> It is frustrating for a juvenile judge not to have the treatment or treatment programs that are absolutely necessary. You may at times know or think you know what needs to be done, but you can't find anyone who provides that kind of service for this type of kid.[86]

The informal factors that sometimes influence judicial decision making at the disposition stage are the values and philosophy of the judge; the social and racial background of the youth, as well as his or her demeanor; the presence or absence of a defense counsel; and potential political repercussions of the delinquent acts. In terms of the values and philosophy of the judge, some judges work from a legal model, some from an educational model, and some from a medical model. The model that a particular judge emphasizes will of course affect his or her handling of juvenile delinquents.[87]

Ruth D. Peterson found that racial, ethnic, gender, and age factors affected the disposition of older adolescents in New York state courts. Race and ethnicity did not significantly influence disposition decisions in New York City, but minority youths tended to become targets of stereotypes and to receive harsh treatment outside the city.[88] Barry Krisberg and colleagues were even more critical of the disposition decisions for minority youths, especially disproportionate incarceration of these youths in juvenile facilities. They warned:

> In a society committed to pluralism and social justice the growing numbers of incarcerated minority youth is a harbinger of future social turmoil. This problem must be placed at the top of our national agenda to reform the juvenile justice system.[89]

In sum, the process of judicial decision making at the disposition stage is influenced by a variety of formal and informal factors. The more informal factors intrude on the decision-making process, the more problematic the decisions are likely to be.

Judicial Alternatives

The alternatives that are available to different juvenile courts vary significantly. Large urban courts have all or most of the following alternatives at their disposal, but rural courts may have only a few.

1. *Dismissal* is certainly the most desired disposition. The fact-finding stage may have shown the youth to be guilty, but the judge can decide, for a variety of reasons, to dismiss the case.
2. *Restitution* also is usually very desirable. Youths may be required to work off their debt with a few hours each week, but their lives are not seriously interrupted.
3. *Psychiatric therapy* as an outpatient, whether in the court clinic, the community mental health clinic, or with a private therapist, is a treatment-oriented decision and is often reserved for middle-class youths to keep them from being sent to "unfitting" placements.
4. *Probation,* the most widely used disposition, seems to be a popular decision with delinquents as well as a good treatment alternative for the court. Probation is sometimes set for a specific length of time, usually a maximum of two years. The judge

can direct the probation officer to involve the youth in special programs, such as alternative schools, speech therapy, or learning disability programs.

5. *Foster home placements* are more restrictive, inasmuch as youths are removed from their natural homes. These placements are used most frequently for status offenders and dependent, neglected children.

6. *Day treatment programs* are a popular alternative with juveniles because the youths who are assigned to these programs return home in the evening. But these programs are few in number and are available in only a few states.

7. The option of *community-based residential programs,* such as group homes and halfway houses, is available to many judges. These residential facilities may be located in the community or in a nearby community, but they are not as desirable as community-based day programs, because youths are taken from their homes to live in these facilities.

8. *Institutionalization in a mental hospital* may be seen as appropriate for a child's needs. This placement requires a psychiatric evaluation, after which a recommendation may be made to initiate proceedings for commitment to a mental hospital.

9. *County or city institutions* are available to a few judges across the nation. Placement in these facilities may be deemed appropriate for a youth who needs more security than probation offers but does not require long-term placement in the state training school.

10. *State or private training schools* are usually reserved for those youths who have committed serious crimes or for whom everything else has failed. In some states, state training schools include minimum- (forestry camps, farms, and ranches), medium- and maximum-security institutions.

11. *Adult facilities* or *youthful offender facilities* are used as alternatives in a few states if the youth has committed a serious offense and is seen as too hard-core for juvenile correctional institutions.

The Right to Appeal

Juveniles do not yet have a constitutional right to appeal. Nevertheless, practically all states grant them the right to appeal by statute. The states are following the lead of the U.S. Supreme Court, which pointed out in *Gault* that juveniles should have the same absolute right to appeal as do adults under the equal protection clause of the Constitution. Since that ruling, most state legislatures have passed laws granting juveniles the right to appeal. State courts have also ruled that state statutes granting the right to appeal for juveniles must be applied uniformly to all juveniles. This decision effectively undermines the past practice in which some courts gave judges the discretion to determine which juvenile cases could be appealed. The common practice today is to give juveniles the same rights to appeal that adults have.[90]

The right to appeal is limited for the most part to juveniles and their parents. States may appeal in some circumstances, but this right is seldom exercised and few cases have come before the courts. Another issue of appeal concerns the type of orders that may be appealed. Although states generally permit the appeal of final orders, what is "final" varies from state to state. Most state statues call for the case to be appealed to an appellate court, but a few states call for a completely new trial. Other common statutory rights of juveniles at appeal are the right to a transcript of the case and the right to counsel.[91]

Organizational factors limit the use of appellate review of juvenile court decisions. Many juveniles lack counsel at trial who can make a record and obtain a transcript. Even fewer juveniles have access to appellate counsel. In addition, juvenile public defenders' caseloads frequently preclude the luxury of filing appeals. Many public defender neither authorize their attorneys to file appeals nor advise their clients of the possibility of an appeal. The only study that compared rates of appeals by criminal defendants and juvenile delinquents found that convicted adults appealed more than ten times as much as did juveniles.[92]

The Juvenile Sentencing Structures

Determinate sentencing is a new form of sentencing in juvenile justice and is replacing in some jurisdictions the traditional form, indeterminate sentencing. In addition, increasing numbers of juvenile courts are using a blended form of sentencing. Finally, the death penalty for juveniles, the most severe form of sentencing used by the state, is examined in this section.

Criticism of the decision making of the juvenile court has increased in the past twenty years. Early on, the criticism focused on the arbitrary nature of the decision making that violated the due process rights of juveniles; more recently, this criticism has been based on the belief that the juvenile court is too "soft" on crime. This latter criticism, especially, has led to a number of attempts to change sentencing and other juvenile procedures.

One of the first efforts at reform was the Juvenile Justice Standards Project, jointly sponsored by the Institute of Judicial Administration and the American Bar Association. Officially launched in 1971 by a national planning committee under the chairmanship of Judge Irvin R. Kaufman, comprehensive guidelines for juvenile offenders were designed that would base sentences on the seriousness of the crime rather than on the needs of the youth. The proposed guidelines represented radical philosophical changes and still are used by proponents to attempt to standardize the handling of juvenile lawbreakers.

The belief that disparity in juvenile sentencing must end was one of the fundamental thrusts of the recommended standards. To accomplish this goal, the commission attempted to limit the discretion of juvenile judges and to make them accountable for their decisions, which would then be subject to judicial review. Also important in the standards was the provision that certain court procedures would be open to the public, although the names of juveniles still would remain confidential (See Figure 15.4 for the changes that have taken place with juvenile court proceedings).

At the beginning of the twenty-first century, juvenile court judges remain quite concerned about these proposed standards. Their basic concern is that these standards attack the underlying philosophy and structure of the juvenile court. Judges also are concerned about how these standards would limit their authority. They see the influence of the hardliners behind this movement toward standardization and feel that the needs of children will be neglected in the long run. They also challenge the idea that it is possible, much less feasible, to treat all children alike.

Nevertheless, the adoption of the standards has been taking place across the nation. New York State was the first to act on them through the Juvenile Justice Reform Act of 1976, which went into effect on February l, 1977. The act orders a determinate sentence of five years for Class A felonies, which include murder, first-degree kidnapping, and first-degree arson. The initial term can be extended by at least one year. The juvenile, according to the act, should be placed in a residential facility after the first year. Then, if approved by the director of the division, the confined youth can be placed in a nonresidential program for the remainder of the five-year term. But the youth must remain under intensive supervision for the entire five-year term.

In 1977, the state of Washington also created a determinate sentencing system for juveniles in line with the recommendations of the Juvenile Justice Standards Project. Moreover, in the 1980s, a number of states stiffened juvenile court penalties for serious juvenile offenders, either by mandating minimum terms of incarceration (Colorado, Kentucky, and Idaho) or by enacting a comprehensive system of sentencing guidelines (Arizona, Georgia, and Minnesota.[93]

In 1995, the Texas Legislature introduced such "get tough" changes in the juvenile justice system as lowering the age at which waiver could occur to fourteen years old for capital, first degree and aggravated controlled substance felony offenses and greatly expanding the determinate sentence statute that was first enacted in 1987. Under determinate sentences, any juvenile, regardless of age, can be sentenced for up to

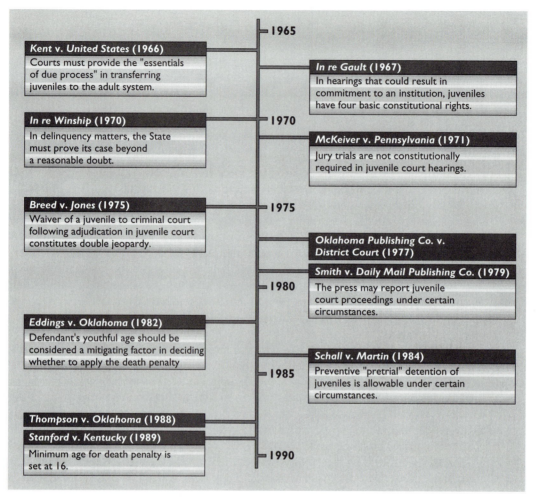

FIGURE 15.4   Time Line of Juvenile Justice Decisions   A series of U.S. Supreme Court decisions made juvenile courts more like criminal courts but maintained some important differences.

Source: Office of Juvenile Justice and Delinquency Prevention, *1999 National Report Series* (Washington, D.C.: Department of Justice, 1999), p. 7.

forty years in the Texas Youth Commission, with possible transfer to the Texas Department of Corrections. Finally, prosecutors can choose to pursue determinate sentence proceedings rather than delinquency proceedings, but they first must obtain grand jury approval.[94]

Daniel P. Mears and Samuel F. Field's examination of the determinate sentencing statute for Texas found the increased proceduralization and criminalization of juvenile courts did not eliminate consideration of age, gender, or race/ethnicity in sentencing decisions.[95]

In the 1990s, nearly every state enacted mandatory sentences for violent and repetitive juvenile offenders. The development of graduated, or accountability-based, sanctions was another means in the 1990s that states used to ensure that juveniles who are adjudicated delinquent receive an appropriate disposition by the juvenile court. Several states have created a "blended" sentencing structure for cases involving repeat and serious juvenile offenders. Blended sentences are a mechanism for holding those juveniles accountable for their offenses. This expanded sentencing authority allows criminal and juvenile courts to impose either juvenile or adult sentences, or at times both, in cases involving juveniles.[96] See Figure 15.5 for blended sentencing options.

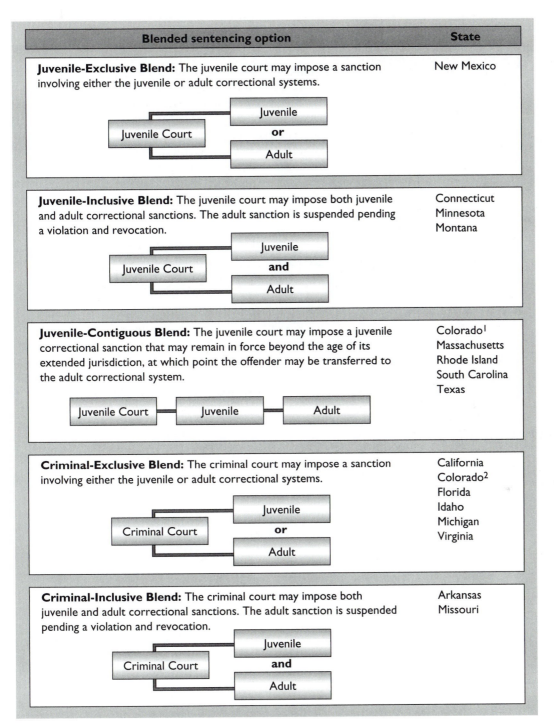

Blended sentencing option	State
Juvenile-Exclusive Blend: The juvenile court may impose a sanction involving either the juvenile or adult correctional systems.	New Mexico
Juvenile-Inclusive Blend: The juvenile court may impose both juvenile and adult correctional sanctions. The adult sanction is suspended pending a violation and revocation.	Connecticut Minnesota Montana
Juvenile-Contiguous Blend: The juvenile court may impose a juvenile correctional sanction that may remain in force beyond the age of its extended jurisdiction, at which point the offender may be transferred to the adult correctional system.	Colorado[1] Massachusetts Rhode Island South Carolina Texas
Criminal-Exclusive Blend: The criminal court may impose a sanction involving either the juvenile or adult correctional systems.	California Colorado[2] Florida Idaho Michigan Virginia
Criminal-Inclusive Blend: The criminal court may impose both juvenile and adult correctional sanctions. The adult sanction is suspended pending a violation and revocation.	Arkansas Missouri

FIGURE 15.5 Blended Sentencing Options Create a "Middle Ground" between Traditional Juvenile and Adult Sanctions

Note: Blends apply to a subset of juveniles specified by state statute.

[1]Applies to those designated as "aggravated juvenile offenders."

[2]Applies to those designated as "youthful offenders."

Source: Office of Juvenile Justice and Delinquency Prevention, *1999 National Report Series* (Washington, D.C.: U.S. Department of Justice, 1999), p. 19. Author's adaptation of Patricia Torbet's *State Responses to Serious and Violent Juvenile Crime.*

Death Penalty for Juveniles

Another disadvantage of being waived to adult court is that juveniles can be executed for their crimes.[97] According to Victor Streib, a professor of law at Cleveland State University, the United States has put approximately 350 juveniles to death since the seventeenth century. These juveniles account for 1.8 percent of the total 19,000 executions in the United States that have been carried out since that date.[98] The first juvenile execution occurred in 1642 in Plymouth Colony, Massachusetts, when sixteen-year-old Thomas Graunger was put to death for sodomizing a horse and a cow.[99]

Fourteen states have never executed juveniles, but Georgia leads all states with forty-one juvenile executions, followed by North Carolina and Ohio, with nineteen each. Table 15.4 lists the executions of juvenile offenders from January 1, 1973, through January 1, 2000).

Of the thirty-eight states that permit capital punishment, twenty-five allow it for those who were under the age of eighteen when they committed the crime (see Table 15.5). In 1982, in the case of *Eddings v. Oklahoma,* the Supreme Court was able to avoid directly addressing the constitutionality of the juvenile death penalty by ruling that "the chronological age of a minor is itself a relevant mitigating factor of great weight."[100] Monty Lee Eddings was sixteen when he shot and killed an Oklahoma State Highway Patrol officer, but his execution sentence was reversed in 1982 because of his age."[101] In 1988, the Court heard the case of *Thompson v. Oklahoma.*[102] Wayne Thompson was fifteen when he was arrested along with his half brother—then age twenty-seven—and two other older men, for the shooting and stabbing death of Charles Keene, Thompson's former brother-in-law. The Court ruled by a five-to-three vote that "the Eighth and Fourteenth Amendments prohibit the execution of a person who was under sixteen years of age at the time of his or her offense."[103]

TABLE 15.4

Executions of Juvenile Offenders, January 1, 1973 through January 1, 2000.

Name	Date of Execution	Place of Execution	Race	Age at Crime	Age at Execution
Charles Rumbaugh	9/11/85	Texas	White	17	28
J. Terry Roach	1/10/86	South Carolina	White	17	25
Jay Pinkerton	5/15/86	Texas	White	17	24
Dalton Prejean	5/18/90	Louisiana	Black	17	30
Johnny Garrett	2/11/92	Texas	White	17	28
Curtis Harris	7/1/93	Texas	Black	17	31
Frederick Lashley	7/28/93	Missouri	Black	17	29
Ruben Cantu	8/24/93	Texas	Latino	17	26
Chris Burger	12/7/93	Georgia	White	17	33
Joseph Cannon	4/22/98	Texas	White	17	38
Robert Carter	5/18/98	Texas	Black	17	34
Dwayne Allen Wright	10/14/98	Virginia	Black	17	24
Sean Sellers	2/4/99	Oklahoma	White	16	29
Douglas Christopher Thomas	1/10/00	Virginia	White	17	26
Steven Roach	1/13/00	Virginia	White	17	23
Glen McGinnis	1/25/00	Texas	Black	17	27

Source: Victor L. Streib, "Moratorium on the Death Penalty for Juveniles," *Law and Contemporary Problems* 61 (1998), p. 63. Updated March 2000 from Death Penalty Information Center at Victor+Streib&oq=&url=http.

TABLE 15.5

Minimum Death Penalty Ages in United States by Jurisdiction

Age 18	Age 17	Age 16
California	Georgia	Alabama
Colorado	New Hampshire	Arizona[a]
Connecticut	North Carolina	Arkansas[a]
Illinois	Texas	Delaware[a]
Kansas		Florida[a]
Maryland	4 states	Idaho[a]
Nebraska		Indiana
New Jersey		Kentucky
New Mexico		Louisiana
New York		Mississippi[a]
Ohio		Missouri
Oregon		Montana[a]
Tennessee		Nevada
Washington		Oklahoma
Federal		Pennsylvania[a]
		South Carolina[a]
14 states and		South Dakota[a]
federal		Utah[a]
		Virginia[a]
		Wyoming
		20 states

Note: Unless otherwise noted, minimum age is expressly stated in statute. Thirteen jurisdictions do not allow death penalty: Alaska, District of Columbia, Hawaii, Iowa, Maine, Massachusetts, Michigan, Minnesota, North Dakota, Rhode Island, Vermont, West Virginia, and Wisconsin.

a. Minimum age is required by U.S. Constitution per U.S. Supreme Court in *Thompson v. Oklahoma,* 487 U.S. 815 (1988).

b. Minimum age is required by Florida Constitution per Florida Supreme Court in *Allen v. State,* 636 So. 2d 494 (Fla. 1994).

Source: Victor L. Streib, "Moratorium on the Death Penalty for Juveniles," *Law and Contemporary Problems* 61 (1998), p. 63.

The Court finally upheld the constitutionality of the death penalty with juveniles in two 1989 cases. In the case of *Stanford v. Kentucky,* Kevin Stanford, a seventeen-year-old African American youth repeatedly raped and sodomized his victim during a robbery. He then drove her to a secluded area, where he shot her point-blank in the face and the back of the head. A jury convicted Stanford of first-degree murder, first-degree sodomy, first-degree robbery, and receiving stolen property. Stanford was sentenced to death on September 28, 1998 and was transferred to death row, where he awaits execution.[104] In *Wilkins v. Missouri,* sixteen-year-old Heath A. Wilkins of Missouri stabbed Nancy Allen Moore to death as she worked behind the counter of a convenience store on July 27, 1985. The jury in the Wilkins' trial found that he was guilty of first-degree murder, armed criminal action, and carrying a concealed weapon. During the sentencing hearing, both the prosecution and Wilkins himself urged the court to apply the death penalty. The aggravating circumstances within the case led the court to the decision that the death penalty was in fact appropriate and sentenced Wilkins to die. The Missouri Supreme Court later upheld this decision.[105] Yet, in 1995, in keeping with the pattern of most juvenile death decisions, the Wilkins' decision was reversed.[106]

As of June 30, 1996, forty-seven individuals were on death row for crimes committed while they were juveniles. Although all were seventeen or younger at the time of their offenses, their ages at that time ranged from eighteen to thirty-six. Under death sentences in twelve states, they had been on death row from a few weeks to more than sixteen years. Texas held seventeen, or 40 percent, of the forty-seven on death row. All were male and two-thirds were minority offenders.[107] According to Streib, the typical "case of the juvenile offender on death row is that of the seventeen-year-old African-American or Hispanic male whose victim is a white adult.[108]

Streib is the strongest, most vocal opponent of the juvenile death penalty.[109] The human rights organization, Amnesty International, and the United Nations General Assembly also have expressed their disapproval of the juvenile death penalty. Suzanne D. Strater makes a telling argument in this regard, when she states:

> In addition to traditional arguments against the juvenile death penalty, the conflict between a state's duty as *parens patriae* to protect children on the one hand, and its role in executing children on the other, provides another reason why there should be no capital punishment of children.[110]

SUMMARY

Three conclusions can be drawn from the examination of the juvenile court and its procedures in this chapter. First, too much has clearly been expected from a court that lacks sufficient resources and community support to fulfill its mission. The court's lack of sufficient supervision throughout its history has also frequently resulted in discretionary abuses.

Second, U.S. Supreme Court and other court decisions from the 1960s and early 1970s have given juveniles more due process rights during court proceedings. Indeed, the typical juvenile court hearing today has many of the trappings of an adult trial. The actors of justice are present, witnesses are cross-examined, and proof beyond a reasonable doubt must be established. However, certain U.S. Supreme Court decisions in the 1970s show that the Court appears to be unwilling to transform the activities of the juvenile court completely into the adversarial proceedings of the adult court.

Third, the future of the juvenile court is currently being debated because critical evaluation during recent years has forced policymakers to rethink the proper role and responsibility of the court. The resolution of this debate will have long-term repercussions on juvenile justice in this nation. The juvenile court clearly will be restructured, a process that is already taking place in many states. Few want to keep the juvenile court as it is, but increasing numbers wish to eliminate it. It is amazing how adult criminal courts, which until now have had absolutely no advocates in terms of their expediency, fairness, or effectiveness, suddenly have become a new panacea. The hope, of course, is that the juvenile court will survive. The eternal optimism found in this nation that we can make a difference in the lives of children must remain in juvenile justice.

KEY TERMS

adjudicatory hearing, p. 455
attention homes, p. 448
bail, p. 449
bifurcated hearing, p. 457
child savers, p. 437
consent decree, p. 450
constitutionalists, p. 438
detention center, p. 448

detention hearing, p. 445
home detention, p. 448
informal adjustment, p. 450
informal probation, p. 450
intake, p. 450
judicial waiver, p. 451
jury trial, p. 455
kadi justice, p. 444

CRITICAL THINKING QUESTIONS

1. Define the main types of waiver to the adult court.
2. Why is waiver such a controversial matter in juvenile justice?
3. Do you believe that plea bargaining should be more widely used in the juvenile court?
4. Do you think the structure of the juvenile court should be changed? Why or why not?
5. What can be done to handle the variation in juvenile court procedures from jurisdiction to jurisdiction?
6. How should the juvenile justice system handle the status offender?
7. How should juveniles who commit serious crimes be handled?

WEB DESTINATIONS

Find more information and links on the juvenile court process and related subjects at the Western Illinois University site.
http://www.wiu.edu/library/govpubs/guides/ p&cjuven.htm

To find general information as well as an overview of the juvenile court go to the Supreme Court of Arizona in Maricopa County.
http://www.superiorcourt.maricopa.gov/ juvenile/Juvenile.html

Learn more about jury trials and juveniles at this site.
http://www.ideal.net.au/~robertsj/justice.html

Learn more about juvenile sentencing at this site.
http://www.sentencingproject.org/pubs/juvenile. pdf

Learn more about juveniles and the death penalty at this site.
http://dailynews.yahoo.com/fc/us/Death_Penalty/

To learn more about juvenile sentencing guidelines go to the Utah government site.
http://www.sentencing.state.ut.us/Juvenile Guidelines

Find out general juvenile information on the Juvenile Info Network site.
http://www.juvenilenet.org

Find out more about juvenile disposition at these two sites.
http://www.collegecourse.com/sou/crim/crim361/ mod15
http://www.sgc.wa.gov/JUVSTD.htm

NOTES

1. Gustav L. Schramm, "The Judge Meets the Boy and His Family," *National Probation Association 1945 Yearbook,* pp. 182–194.
2. G. Larry Mays, "Transferring Juveniles to Adult Courts: Legal Guidelines and Constraints." Paper presented to the Annual Meeting of the American Society of Criminology, Reno, Nevada (November 1989), p. 1.
3. Barry Krisberg, *The Juvenile Court: Reclaiming the Vision* (San Francisco: National Council on Crime and Delinquency, 1988); Arnold Binder, "The Juvenile Court: The U.S. Constitution, and When the Twain Shall Meet," *Journal of Criminal Justice* 12 (1982), pp. 355–366; and Charles E. Springer, *Justice for Children* (Washington, D.C.: U.S. Department of Justice, 1986).
4. Lisa Aversa Richette, *The Throwaway Children* (New York: J.B. Lippincott, 1969); Patrick Murphy, *Our Kindly Parent—The State* (New York: Viking Press, 1974); and Howard James, *Children in Trouble: A National Scandal* (New York: Pocket Books, 1971); William Ayers, *A Kind and Just Parent* (Boston: Beacon Press, 1997).
5. Leonard P. Edwards, "The Juvenile Court and the Role of the Juvenile Court Judge," *National Council of Juvenile and Family Court Judges* 43 (1992), p. 4.
6. Ibid.
7. Ibid.
8. Cited in Ibid.
9. Dean J. Champion, "Teenage Felons and Waiver Hearings: Some Recent Trends, 1980–1988," *Crime and Delinquency* 35 (October 1985), p. 578.
10. Barry C. Feld, "The Transformation of the Juvenile Court," *Minnesota Law Review* 75 (February 1991), p. 711.

11. Drafted by the American Legislative Exchange Council and Rose Institute of State and Local Government at Clarement McKenna College.

12. For an extensive discussion of these sweeping changes in Minnesota's juvenile code, see Barry C. Feld, "Violent Youth and Public Policy: A Case Study of Juvenile Justice Law Reform," *Minnesota Law Review* 79 (May 1995), pp. 965–1128.

13. See Barry Feld, "The Transformation of the Juvenile Court," pp. 691–725; Feld, "Criminalizing Juvenile Justice: Rules of Procedure for Juvenile Court," *Minnesota Law Review* 69 (1984), pp. 141–164; Janet E. Ainsworth, "Re-Imagining Childhood and Reconstructing the Legal Order: The Case for Abolishing the Juvenile Court," in *Child, Parent, and State,* edited by S. Randall Humm, Beate Anna Ort, Martin Mazen Anbari, Wendy S. Lader, and William Scott Biel (Philadelphia: Temple University Press, 1994), pp. 561–595.

14. Jeffrey A. Butts and Adele V. Harrell, *Delinquents or Criminals: Policy Options for Young Offenders* (Washington, D.C.: The Urban Institute, 1998), p. 1.

15. Barry C. Feld, *Bad Kids: Race and the Transformation of Juvenile Court* (New York: Oxford University Press, 1999), p. 324.

16. Ibid., p. 317.

17. Ibid.

18. For a biting criticism of this proposal to abolish the juvenile court, see Mark I. Soler, "Re-Imagining the Juvenile Court," in *Child, Parent, and State,* pp. 596–624.

19. Feld, *Bad Kids,* p. 44.

20. Anthony M. Platt, *The Child Savers,* 2d ed. (Chicago: University of Chicago Press, 1977).

21. Ibid. See also Sanford J. Fox, "Juvenile Justice Reform: An Historic Perspective," *Stanford Law Review* 22 (1970), p. 1187; and Douglas Rendleman, "*Parens Patriae:* From Chancery to the Juvenile Court," *South Carolina Law Review* 28 (1971), p. 205, for interpretations similar to Platt's.

22. David Shichor, "Historical and Current Trends in American Juvenile Justice," *Juvenile and Family Court Journal* 34 (August 1983), p. 61.

23. Frederic L. Faust and Paul J. Brantingham, eds., *Juvenile Justice Philosophy* (St. Paul, Minn.: West Publishing, 1974), pp. 569–575.

24. Platt, *The Child Savers,* p. 144.

25. Ibid.

26. Faust and Brantingham, eds., *Juvenile Justice Philosophy,* pp. 568–569.

27. Ibid., pp. 574–575.

28. Ibid.

29. *Kent v. United States,* 383 U.S. 541, 86 S.Ct. 1045, 16 L.Ed. 2d 84 (1966).

30. Ibid.

31. *In re Gault,* 387 U.S. 1, 18 L.Ed. 2d 527, 87 S.Ct. 1428 (1967).

32. Ibid.

33. *Haley v. Ohio,* 332, U.S. 596 (1948); and *Gallegos v. Colorado,* 370 U.S. 49, 82 S.Ct. 1209 (1962).

34. *In re Winship,* 397 U.S. 358, 90 S.Ct. 1968, 25 L.Ed. 2d 368 (1970).

35. *McKeiver v. Pennsylvania,* 403 U.S. 528, 535 (1971); *In re Barbara Burrus,* 275 N.C. 517, 169 S.E. 2d 879 (1969).

36. Ibid.

37. Barry Feld, "Violent Youth and Public Policy: A Case Study of Juvenile Justice Law Reform," *Minnesota Law Review* 79 (1995), pp. 965–1128.

38. *Breed v. Jones,* 421 U.S. 519, 95 S.Ct. 1779 (1975).

39. H. Ted Rubin, *Juvenile Justice: Policy, Practice, and Law* (Santa Monica, Calif.: Goodyear Publishing, 1979), p. 177.

40. Edwards, "The Juvenile Court and the Role of the Juvenile Court Judge," p. 25.

41. Ibid., pp. 25–28. For a more expansive list of the juvenile judge's role responsibilities, see Rule 24 of the California Judicial Council.

42. Forest Eastman, "Procedures and Due Process," *Juvenile and Family Court Journal* 35 (1983). For a more extensive examination of the juvenile judge's role, see Ted H. Rubin, *Behind the Black Robes: Judges and the Court* (Beverly Hills, Calif.: Sage, 1985).

43. David Matza, *Delinquency and Drift* (New York: John Wiley and Sons, 1964), p. 118.

44. Carol J. DeFrances, *Juveniles Prosecuted in State Criminal Courts: National Survey of Prosecutors, 1994* (Washington, D.C.: Office of Juvenile Justice and Delinquency Prevention, 1997), p. 1.

45. For other examinations of the prosecutor's role in the juvenile court, see John H. Laub and Bruce K. MacMurray, "Increasing the Prosecutor's Role in Juvenile Court: Expectation and Realities," *Justice System Journal* 12 (1987), pp. 196–209; and Charles W. Thomas and Shay Bilchik, "Prosecuting Juveniles in Criminal Courts: A Legal and Empirical Analysis," *Journal of Criminal Law and Criminology* 76 (Northwestern University, School of Law, 1985), pp. 439–479.

46. See Floyd Feeney, "Defense Counsel for Delinquents: Does Quality Matter?" Paper presented at the Annual Meeting of the American Society of Criminology, Montreal, Canada (November 1987).

47. Barry C. Feld, "Criminalizing Juvenile Justice: Rules of Procedure for the Juvenile Court," *Minnesota Law Review* 69 (1984), pp. 191, 199.

48. Feld, *Bad Kids,* p. 128

49. H. Ted Rubin, *Juvenile Justice: Policy, Practice, and Law,* p. 177.

50. Ibid.

51. See Charles Thomas and Ineke Marshall, "The Effect of Legal Representation on Juvenile Court Disposition." Paper presented at the Southern Sociological Society (1981); and S. H. Clarke and G. G. Koch, "Juvenile Court: Therapy or Crime Control and Do Lawyers Make a Difference?" *Law and Society Review* 14 (1980), pp. 263–308.

52. Ibid.

53. Brenda R. McCarthy, "An Analysis of Detention," *Juvenile and Family Court Journal* 36 (1985), pp. 49–50. For other discussions of detention, see Lydia Rosner, "Juvenile Secure Detention," *Journal of Offender Counseling, Services, and Rehabilitation* 12 (1988), pp. 77–93; and Charles E. Frazier and Donna M. Bishop, "The Pretrial Detention of Juveniles and Its Impact on Case Disposi-

tion," *Journal of Criminal Law and Criminology* 76 (1985), pp. 1132–1152.

54. Anne L. Stahl, *Delinquency Cases in Juvenile Court, 1995* (Washington, D.C.: Office of Juvenile Justice and Delinquency Prevention, 1998), p. 1.

55. *Creek v. Stone*, 379 F.2d 106 (D.C. Cir. 1967).

56. Steven L. Schlossman, *Love and the American Delinquent: The Theory and Practice of "Progressive" Juvenile Justice, 1825–1920* (Chicago: University of Chicago Press, 1977).

57. Charles E. Frazier and Donna M. Bishop, "The Pretrial Detention of Juveniles and Its Impact on Case Dispositions," *Journal of Criminal Law and Criminology* 76 (Northwestern University, School of Law, 1985), p. 1151.

58. Alida V. Merlo and William D. Bennett, "Criteria for Juvenile Detention: Who Gets Detained?" Paper presented to the Annual Meeting of the American Society of Criminology, Reno, Nevada (November 1989), p. 8.

59. *Schall v. Martin* (1984), *United States Law Review* 52 (47), pp. 4681–4696.

60. Ibid., p. 4681.

61. Ibid.

62. Barry C. Feld, "Criminalizing Juvenile Justice: Rules of Procedure for the Juvenile Court," *Minnesota Law Review* 69 (Minnesota Law Review Foundation, December 1984), pp. 191, 199.

63. Duran Bell Jr. and Kevin Lang, "The Intake Dispositions of Juvenile Offenders," *Journal of Research on Crime and Delinquency* 22 (1985), pp. 309–328. See also Randall G. Sheldon and John A. Horvath, "Intake Processing in a Juvenile Court: A Comparison of Legal and Nonlegal Variables," *Juvenile and Family Court Journal* 38 (1987), pp. 13–19.

64. Stahl, *Delinquency Cases in Juvenile Court, 1995*, pp. 1–2.

65. Bell and Lang, "The Intake Dispositions of Juvenile Offenders," p. 324.

66. Barry Krisberg et al., "The Watershed of Juvenile Justice Reform," *Crime and Delinquency* 32 (January 1986), p. 9; Barry C. Feld, "Legislative Policies toward the Serious Juvenile Offender," *Crime and Delinquency* 27 (October 1981), p. 500.

67. Charles W. Thomas and Shay Bilchik, "Prosecuting Juveniles in Criminal Courts," pp. 439–479.

68. Barry C. Feld, "The Juvenile Court Meets the Principle of the Offense: Legislative Changes in Juvenile Waiver Statutes," *Journal of Criminal Law and Criminology* 78 (1987), pp. 512–514.

69. Feld, "Legislative Policies toward the Serious Juvenile Offender," p. 500.

70. Ibid., pp. 501–502.

71. Stahl, *Delinquency Cases Waived to Criminal Court, 1987–1996* (Washington, D.C.: Office of Juvenile Justice and Delinquency Prevention, 1999), p. 1.

72. Stahl, *Delinquency Cases in Juvenile Court, 1995*, p. 2.

73. M. A. Bortner, "Traditional Rhetoric, Organizational Realities: Remand of Juveniles to Adult Court," *Crime and Delinquency* 32 (January 1986), pp. 53–73.

74. Leona Lee, "Factors Determining Waiver in a Juvenile Court," *Journal of Juvenile Justice* 22 (1994), p. 329.

75. Dean J. Champion, "Teenage Felons and Waiver Hearings: Some Recent Trends, 1980–1988," *Crime and Delinquency* 35 (October 1989), p. 584.

76. Snyder and Sickmund, *Juvenile Offenders and Victims, 1999*, p. 175.

77. Carl Rudman, et al., "Violent Youth in Adult Court: Process and Punishment," *Crime and Delinquency* 32 (January 1986), pp. 75–96.

78. Melissa Sickmund, "Offenders in Juvenile Court, 1997," *Juvenile Justice Bulletin* (Washington, D.C.: Office of Juvenile Justice and Delinquency Prevention, 2000), p. 9.

79. For example, in the Laws of Pennsylvania, Act No. 333 (Section 18a) requires a hearing date within ten days after the filing of a petition.

80. Edwin M. Lemert, "The Juvenile Court—and Realities," in *Juvenile Delinquency and Youth Crime*, President's Task Force Report (Washington, D.C.: U.S. Government Printing Office, 1967), p. 94.

81. Rubin, *Juvenile Justice*, p. 137.

82. Sickmund, "Offenders in Juvenile Court," p. 9.

83. Terence P. Thornberry, "Sentencing Disparities in the Juvenile Justice System," *Journal of Criminal Law and Criminology* 70 (Summer 1979), pp. 164–171.

84. M. A. Bortner, *Inside a Juvenile Court: The Tarnished Idea of Individualized Justice* (New York: New York University Press, 1982).

85. Lawrence Cohen, "Delinquency Dispositions: An Empirical Analysis of Processing Decisions in Three Juvenile Courts," *Analytic Report* 9 (Washington, D.C.: U.S. Government Printing Office, 1975), p. 51.

86. Interviewed in 1981.

87. Rubin, *Juvenile Justice*, pp. 139–140. See also Joseph B. Sanborn, "Factors Perceived to Affect Delinquent Dispositions in Juvenile Court: Putting the Sentencing Decision into Context," *Crime and Delinquency* 42 (January 1996), pp. 99–113.

88. Ruth D. Peterson, "Youthful Offender Designations and Sentencing in the New York Criminal Courts," *Social Problems* 35 (April 1988), pp. 125–126. See also Christina De Jong and Kenneth C. Jackson, "Putting Race into Context: Race, Juvenile Justice Processing, and Urbanization, *Justice Quarterly* 15 (September 1998), pp. 487–504; and Barry C. Feld, "Social Structure, Race, and the Transformation of the Juvenile Court." Paper presented to the Annual Meeting of the American Society of Criminology, Washington, D.C. (November 1998).

89. Barry Krisberg, et al. *The Incarceration of Minority Youth* (Minneapolis, Minn.: University of Minnesota, Hubert H. Humphrey Institute of Public Affairs, 1986).

90. Samuel M. Davis, *Rights of Juveniles: The Juvenile Justice System*, 2d ed. (New York: Clark Boardman, 1986).

91. Ibid., pp. 634–637.

92. Feld, *Bad Kids*, p. 136.

93. Martin L. Forst, Bruce A. Fisher, and Robert B. Coates, "Indeterminate and Determinate Sentencing of Juvenile Delinquents: A National Survey of Approaches to Commitment and Release Decision-Making," *Juvenile and Family Court Journal* 36 (Summer 1985), p. 1.

94. Daniel P. Mears and Samuel H. Field, "Theorizing Sanctioning in a Criminalized Juvenile Court," *Criminology* 38 (November 2000), pp. 985–986.

95. Ibid., p. 983.

96. Barry C. Feld, "Violent Youth and Public Policy: Minnesota Juvenile Justice Task Force and 1994 Legislative Reform." Paper presented at the annual meeting of the American Society of Criminology, Miami (1994), p. 4. See also Feld, "Violent Youth and Public Policy: A Case Study of Juvenile Justice Law Reform," *Minnesota Law Review* 79 (May 1995), pp. 965–1128.

97. Christina Bethke and Matthew G. Muters did the research and prepared a draft of this section on the death penalty.

98. Victor L. Streib, "The Juvenile Death Penalty Today: Present Death Row Inmates Under Juvenile Death Sentences and Death Sentences and Executions for Juvenile Crimes, January 1, 1973, to June 30, 1995." Unpublished, 1995, p. 3.

99. Victor Streib, *The Death Penalty and Juveniles* (Bloomington, Indiana: Indiana University Press, 1988).

100. *Eddings v. Oklahoma,* 102 S.Ct. (1982).

101. Ibid.

102. *Thompson v. Oklahoma,* 102 S.Ct. (1988).

103. Ibid.

104. *Stanford v. Kentucky,* 492 U.S. 361 (1989).

105. *Stanford v. Kentucky.*

106. "Capital Punishment for Minors," *Journal of Juvenile Law* (1994), pp. 150–167.

107. Streib, "The Juvenile Death Penalty Today," p. 14.

108. Ibid., p. 9.

109. See Streib, *The Death Penalty and Juveniles,* and Victor L. Streib, "Perspectives on the Juvenile Death Penalty in the 1990s," in *Child, Parent, and State: Law and Policy Reader,* eds. S. R. Humm, et al. (Philadephia: Temple University Press, 1994), pp. 646–665.

110. Susanne D. Strater, "The Juvenile Death Penalty: In the Best Interests of the Child?" *Loyola University Chicago Law Review* 26 (1995), p. 160.

chapter 16
COMMUNITY-BASED CORRECTIONS

OBJECTIVES

After reading this chapter, the student will be able to answer the following questions:

■ What are the most important functions of juvenile probation?

■ How has juvenile probation changed?

■ Which residential and nonresidential programs in the community seem to be the most effective?

■ How does juvenile aftercare work?

■ How effective are community-based corrections?

A female counselor in a runaway house says about a former resident:

I had a girl come in who was abused at home and whose mother wanted her to come in. I sat down and talked to her, and she was like living death. She wouldn't communicate or talk with me. That night, her best friend did acid and then stood in front of a train. She opened herself up, stayed here ten days, and straightened herself up.[1]

What does it mean that she was like "living death"? Why would the death of her friend have such an effect on this resident?

Community-based programs, as this anecdote aptly illustrates, can sometimes have a significant positive impact on a youngster's life. Probation, day treatment and residential programs, and aftercare are the basic forms of community-based corrections. These services are alternatives to institutional placements and keep juvenile delinquents out of training schools, jails, and adult prisons. Community-based programs captured the support of the public in the late 1960s and early 1970s because they were regarded as more humane, more economical, and more effective in rehabilitating offenders than training schools. Proponents of community-based corrections argued that they should be used for all but hard-core offenders. A few supporters even advocated closing all the state training schools.

How Community-Based Corrections Have Evolved

Probation and parole developed in the nineteenth century in the United States, but they were more directly applied to juveniles in the twentieth century. During the twentieth century, all of the major forms of community-based corrections for juveniles evolved. These forms had their periods of expansion, especially in the 1960s and 1970s, but the closing years of the twentieth century were also a time of retrenchment and "get tough" policies on youthful offenders. The early years of the twenty-first century have been a time of developing a new mission, including intensive programs for high-risk probationers, and intermediate sanctions.

Nineteenth-Century Developments

The first community-based corrections for juveniles grew out of juvenile aftercare, or parole, used to supervise juveniles after their institutionalization. Such programs are nearly as old as juvenile correctional institutions. By the 1820s, superintendents of houses of refuge had the authority to release juveniles when they saw fit. Some juveniles were returned directly to their families, and others were placed in the community as indentured servants and apprentices who could reenter the community as free citizens once they finished their terms of service. This system became formalized only in the 1840s, when states set up inspection procedures to monitor the supervision of those with whom youths were placed.

Juvenile aftercare was then influenced by the development of adult parole in the late 1870s. Zebulon Brockway, the first superintendent of Elmira Reformatory in New York State, permitted parole for carefully selected prisoners. When they left the institution, parolees were instructed to report to a guardian on arrival, to write immediately to the superintendent, and to report to the guardian on the first of each month.

Juvenile aftercare programs spread throughout the United States in the early decades of the twentieth century and took on many of the features of adult parole. Juveniles were supervised in the community by aftercare officers, whose jobs were similar to those of parole officers in the adult system. The parole board did not become a part of juvenile corrections, for in more than two-thirds of the states, institutional staffs continued to decide when youths would return to the community.

Probation as an alternative to institutional placements for juveniles arose from the effort of John Augustus, a Boston cobbler, in the 1840s and 1850s. Augustus, who is called *the father of probation,* spent considerable time in the courtroom and in 1841 persuaded a judge to permit him to supervise an offender in the community rather than sentence the offender to an institution. Over the next two decades, Augustus worked with nearly two thousand individuals, including both adult and juvenile offenders. As the first probation officer, Augustus initiated several services still used in probation today: investigation and screening, supervision, educational and employment services, and the provision of aid and assistance.[2] See Treatment Intervention 16.1, John Augustus: Planting the Seeds of Juvenile Probation.

The Commonwealth of Massachusetts built on Augustus's work with the establishment in 1869 of a visiting probation agent system. This system released on probation contrite youthful offenders, who were permitted to return to their parents and to stay with them as long as they obeyed the law.[3] Probation had become statewide in Massachusetts by 1890, although the authority then rested with the courts rather than with municipal authorities. Illinois, Minnesota, Missouri, New Jersey, Rhode Island, and Vermont later adopted probation statutes.

Expansion and Retrenchment in the Twentieth Century

In the twentieth century, probation services changed as they became more widespread. Probation services spread to every state and were administered by both state and local authorities. The use of volunteer probation workers had disappeared by the turn of the century, only to return in the 1950s. Probation became more treatment oriented: Early in the century the medical treatment model was used and later, in the 1960s and 1970s, probation officers became brokers who delivered services to clients. The upgrading of standards and training also was emphasized in the 1960s and 1970s.

Residential programs, the third type of community-based juvenile corrections to appear, had their origins in the Highfields Project, a short-term guided-group-interaction program. Known officially as the New Jersey Experimental Project for the Treatment of Youthful Offenders, this project was established in 1950 on the former estate of Colonel and Mrs. Charles Lindbergh. The Highfields Project housed adjudicated youths who worked during the day at the nearby New Jersey Neuro-Psychiatric Institute and met in two guided-group-interaction units five evenings a week at the Highfields facility. Similar programs were initiated in the 1960s at South Fields in Louisville, Kentucky; Essexfields in Newark, New Jersey; Pinehills in Provo, Utah; the New Jersey centers at Oxford and

TREATMENT INTERVENTION 16.1

John Augustus: Planting the Seeds of Juvenile Probation

I bailed nineteen boys, from 7 to 15 years of age, and in bailing them it was understood, and agreed by the court, that their cases should be continued from term to term for several months, as a season of probation; thus each month at the calling of the docket, I would appear in court, make my report, and thus the cases would pass on for five or six months. At the expiration of this term, twelve of the boys were brought into court at one time, and the scene formed a striking and highly pleasing contrast with their appearance when first arraigned. The judge expressed much pleasure as well as surprise at their appearance, and remarked that the object of law had been accomplished and expressed his cordial approval of my plan to save and reform.

Why do you believe that John Augustus was so committed to keeping juveniles and adults out of the formal justice system? Does he represent an example of how much difference one person can make?

Source: John Augustus's remarks are found in Howard N. Snyder and Melissa Sickmund, *Juvenile Offenders and Victims: 1999 National Report* (Washington, D.C.: Office of Juvenile Justice and Delinquency Prevention, 1999), p. 86.

Farmingdale for boys and at Turrell for girls; and the START centers established by the New York City Division for Youth.

The most dramatic advance in the rise of community-based corrections took place when the state of Massachusetts closed all its training schools in the early 1970s. Jerome Miller, commissioner of the department of youth services, was able to accomplish this correctional reform because he had the support of Governor Francis Sargent and the media. Except for a few girls remaining at Shirley Training School and a few youths sent to private training schools in other states, Massachusetts placed all its adjudicated juvenile delinquents in community-based corrections.

This correctional reform in Massachusetts, along with the reform spirit of the times and the availability of federal funding, caused community-based corrections to be widely discussed in juvenile justice circles. The idea of deinstitutionalization, or using alternatives to juvenile institutions, became popular in numerous states, and commitments to training schools declined in nearly every state. Soon, Kansas, Minnesota, North Dakota, Oregon, South Dakota, and Utah were placing nearly as many juveniles in residential and day treatment programs as they were assigning to institutions.

In the late 1980s and early 1990s, retrenchment became apparent in community-based corrections. The decline in federal funding, along with the get tough mood of society, meant the closing of some residential and day treatment programs. Although probation remained the most widely used judicial disposition, both probation and aftercare services were charged to enforce a more hard-line policy with juvenile offenders. Probation officers themselves admitted that probation was too "soft" or permissive. A probation supervisor at the time noted:

> I'm sure a lot of kids feel probation is a joke. Some kids feel that short of locking them up, anything is a joke. There are some aspects of the juvenile court system that tends [sic] to lend itself [sic] to that criticism. The training school has been running at full capacity for years, which means that when someone goes in the front door, someone else has to go out the back door. The average stay is only four or five months. If you're a kid who has done multiple felonies, it's a joke.[4]

Looking toward the Future

In the twentieth-first century, a new mission in community-based corrections is being defined, based upon expansion rather than retrenchment. The new mission has a number of themes. Intensive supervision is proposed as the means by which high-risk juvenile offenders could be left in the community without jeopardizing the protection of society. More attention is also being given to substance abusers, primarily because so many offenders have histories of substance abuse. More emphasis has been placed on community restitution programs and work orders. Indeed, in some court systems, restitution is almost an inevitable condition of probation status. Furthermore, a system of intermediate sanctions is being discussed and implemented in some jurisdictions. In addition, bureaucratic efficiency and accountability are demanded of community-based programs. Finally, there appears to be a trend of returning responsibility to the counties while, at the same time, permitting privately operated programs to play a major role in administering community-based programs. See Table 16.1 for a time line of the most important events in the evolution of community-based corrections for juveniles.

Probation

Probation permits juvenile offenders to remain in the community under the supervision of a probation officer, subject to certain conditions imposed by the court. Probation, which many consider to be the brightest hope of corrections, has several different

TABLE 16.1

Time Line of Community-Based Corrections for Juveniles in the United States

Date	Event
1820s	Superintendents of Houses of Refuge had the power to release juveniles from the institution
1840s	States set up inspection procedures to monitor the supervision of those with whom juveniles were placed
1841	John Augustus began to supervise juvenile and adult offenders in Boston
1869	Commonwealth of Massachusetts established a visiting probation agent system which supervised youthful offenders
1890	Probation was established statewide in Massachusetts
1950	Highfields Project was established
2000	New mission in community-based corrections was being defined

connotations in the juvenile justice system. Probation is a legal system in which an adjudicated delinquent can be placed. Probation is also an alternative to institutionalization. Moreover, probation is a subsystem of the juvenile justice system. Finally, probation includes the activities, functions, and services that characterize this subsystem's transactions with the juvenile court, the delinquent, and the community.[5]

In 1998, the juvenile court ordered probation in 58 percent of the more than one million cases that received a juvenile court sanction. Probation was ordered in 58 percent of the cases involving person offenses, 59 percent involving property offenses, 59 percent of the cases involving drug law violations, and 54 percent involving public order offenses.[6] See Table 16.2 for the percent change in adjudicated delinquency cases that resulted in formal probation between 1989 and 1998.

The Administration of Probation

Probation departments are administered by the local juvenile court or by the state administrative office of courts in 23 states and the District of Columbia. In fourteen states, probation is administered by a combination of structures, usually with services provided by the juvenile court in urban counties and by a state executive system of probation in smaller counties. In ten states, probation administration takes place statewide

TABLE 16.2

Across offenses, the likelihood of probation for cases in which the juvenile was adjudicated delinquent increased since 1994.

Most Serious Offense	1989	1994	1998
TOTAL	55%	53%	58%
PERSON	54%	53%	58%
PROPERTY	57%	55%	59%
DRUGS	54%	51%	59%
PUBLIC ORDER	50%	50%	54%

Note: Detail may not add to 100% because of rounding.

Source: Meghan C. Black, *Juvenile Delinquent Probation Caseload, 1989–1998* (Washington, D.C.: Office of Juvenile Justice and Delinquency Prevention, 2001, p. 2.

through an executive branch department. In three states, the county executive administers probation services (See Table 16.3). While juvenile probation continues to be predominantly organized under the judiciary, there has been a recent movement to transfer these services to a state court judicial department.[7]

Providing **probation subsidies** to local systems complying with state standards can benefit both state and local government agencies. The state thereby ensures uniformity of probation services and practices throughout the state, and the costs of probation services are reduced for local units of government, which are usually operating on a fiscal shoestring.

Procedures vary from state to state. Michigan assigns state-paid probation officers to work with local probation officers. In New York State, local communities that are willing to meet state staffing patterns for probation services are reimbursed for up to 50 percent

TABLE 16.3

Probation supervision tends to be administered by local juvenile courts or by a state executive branch agency.

State Administration		Local Administration	
Judicial Branch	*Executive Branch*	*Judicial Branch*	*Executive Branch*
Connecticut	Alaska	Alabama	**California**
Hawaii	**Arkansas**	Arizona	**Idaho**
Iowa	Delaware	**Arkansas**	**Minnesota**
Kentucky	Florida	**California**	**Mississippi**
Nebraska	**Georgia**	Colorado	New York
North Carolina	**Idaho**	District of	Oregon
North Dakota	**Kentucky**	Columbia	**Washington**
South Dakota	**Louisiana**	**Georgia**	**Wisconsin**
Utah	Maine	Illinois	
West Virginia	Maryland	Indiana	
	Minnesota	Kansas	
	Mississippi	**Kentucky**	
	New Hampshire	**Louisiana**	
	New Mexico	Massachusetts	
	North Dakota	Michigan	
	Oklahoma	**Minnesota**	
	Rhode Island	Missouri	
	South Carolina	Montana	
	Tennessee	Nevada	
	Vermont	New Jersey	
	Virginia	Ohio	
	West Virginia	**Oklahoma**	
	Wyoming	Pennsylvania	
		Tennessee	
		Texas	
		Virginia	
		Washington	
		Wisconsin	
		Wyoming	

Note: Bolded states indicate that probation is provided by a combination of agencies. Often larger, urban counties operate local probation departments, while the state administers probation in smaller counties.

Source: Hunter Hurst IV and Patricia M. Torbet, (1993). *Organization and Administration of Juvenile Services: Probation, Aftercare, and State Institutions for Delinquent Youth.* In Howard N. Snyder and Melissa Sickmund (1995). *Juvenile Offenders and Victims: A National Report,* NCJ 153569.

of their operating costs. California, Nevada, Oregon, and Washington have developed probation subsidy programs that encourage decreased commitments of juvenile delinquents to state training schools by counties. The California Probation Subsidy Statute, until it was phased out in 1978, authorized the state to pay each county up to $4,000 for every juvenile delinquent not committed to a state correctional institution. Counties were required to improve probation services by employing additional probation officers and reducing caseloads.[8] Washington's juvenile probation subsidy is modeled after the one in California. Ninety percent of Washington's thirty-nine counties participate in the program,[9] which has been instrumental in reducing commitment rates to juvenile institutions and in improving the quality of probation services.

The Operation of Probation Services

Intake, investigation, and supervision, the basic functions of probation services, take place in an increasingly "get tough" approach to juvenile crime. In intake, the initial decision is made about what to do with the law-violating juvenile. The preparation of the social history report, which is provided for the assistance of the juvenile judge at the disposition stage of the juvenile court proceedings, is the most important process during investigation. The supervisory function is divided into managing a caseload, providing treatment services, and maintaining surveillance.

INTAKE   The intake officer is usually a probation officer, although larger probation departments may have separate intake units in which intake officers are not probation officers. Regardless of the organizational structure of the intake unit, the intake officer is the chief decision maker for juveniles prior to the juvenile court proceedings. The intake officer has two important decisions to make: what to do with the case and whether to detain the youth until a detention hearing can be scheduled.

The intake officer commonly is faced with one of the following situations: parents bring a child in on their own, parents bring a child in because of a letter requesting their presence, or a police officer brings in a child who has been apprehended on suspicion of committing an unlawful act. Parents who walk in with their child typically complain, "My kid won't obey," "My kid won't do the chores," "My kid won't come home at night," or "My kid is running around with the wrong crowd." They want someone in authority to say, "You're going to get punished unless you clean up your act." After interviewing both youth and parents, sometimes separately, the intake officer might make a contract with the child and parents, by which each agrees to an acceptable compromise solution, or the intake officer might decide to refer the youth to a diversion agency.[10]

Parents whose child has been apprehended by the police for a criminal act are commonly instructed by letter to bring their child to the intake unit at a particular time. The intake officer must conduct a preliminary investigation at this time and, on the basis of the findings, make a decision on what to do about the petition. Ordinarily, the child is not retained in a detention facility but is released to the parents.

Police officers also frequently bring juveniles who have been apprehended committing an unlawful act to the intake unit. As part of the preliminary investigation, the intake officer must get in touch with the parents and make an immediate decision about the need for detention. The child is detained if judged dangerous to self or others or lacks supervision in the home.

INVESTIGATION   Investigation requires that probation officers prepare a **social history report** on a youth ruled delinquent to aid the judge in making the correct disposition. If a juvenile court uses a bifurcated hearing (separate adjudicatory and disposition stages), the judge orders a social history when a juvenile is found delinquent at the adjudicatory or fact-finding stage. But if the court combines the adjudicatory and disposition stages, the social history must be completed before a juvenile appears in front of the judge, who waits until the youth has been found delinquent to read the report.

The probation officer usually has thirty to sixty days to write this report. In writing this report, the probation officer reviews the youth's arrest record, reports of the current offense, any available psychiatric or psychological evaluations, and any information from social agencies. Furthermore, the probation officer interviews the youth and the parents, usually at least once in the home. It may also be necessary for the probation officer to interview the arresting officer, school administrators or teachers, neighborhood religious leaders, and peers who know of or were involved in the alleged offense. Peers often volunteer information, saying to the probation officer, "I hear you're Fred's PO. I want you to know that he's a real crazy and did the crime," or "John is a real loser. Let me tell you some of the other shit he's done."

SUPERVISION   When a juvenile judge sentences a youth to probation, the probation officer generally takes the youth aside and explains the meaning of probation. The probationer is informed of how frequently he or she will report to the probation officer and of the importance of complying with the conditions of probation. See Juvenile Law 16.2 for some of the probation rules for one juvenile probation office.

The length of time a youth must spend on probation varies from state to state. In some states, the maximum length is until the juvenile reaches the age of majority, normally sixteen or eighteen but sometimes twenty-one years of age. Other states limit the length of time a juvenile or adult can spend on probation: in Illinois it is limited to five years; in New York, to two years; in Washington, D.C., to one year; and in California, to six months.[11]

The supervisory function is divided into casework management, treatment, and surveillance. Effective casework management requires that a probation officer keep an up-to-date casework file, carry out periodic reviews, decide how each client is to be handled, and divide probationers into several categories—depending upon their needs and the risk they present to the community. Those with more serious needs and who present a greater risk to the community are required to report to their probation officer more frequently.

Surveillance requires that the probation officer make certain that probationers comply with the conditions of probation and that they do not break the law. The probation officer has a number of opportunities to observe the behavior of probationers in the office, at home, and perhaps at school. The probation officer also visits their parents. If a probationer's behavior is unacceptable, the probation officer is likely to receive reports from school or from law enforcement agencies.

The importance of surveillance was underscored in the mid-1970s when, with the emphasis on law and order, probation services were accused of failing to protect society. If a youth does not comply with the conditions of probation or commits another delinquent act, the probation officer must inform the judge by filing a notice of violation. If the violation is serious enough, the probation officer must recommend that probation be revoked. Thus the probation officer has a law enforcement role as well as a treatment role. In What Would You Do? 16.3, probation officers reveal the questions that they consider in making decisions. The answers to these questions clearly place the probation officer in an enforcement role.

Risk Control and Crime Reduction

The current emphasis in juvenile probation, as in adult probation, is on risk control and crime reduction approaches, such as restitution and community service, intensive supervision, house arrest, and electronic monitoring.

RESTITUTION AND COMMUNITY SERVICE   Financial **restitution** and community service orders have become widely used conditions of juvenile probation in recent years. Indeed, a 1977 survey of juvenile courts identified fewer than 15 formal restitution programs, but by 1985, formal programs were known to exist in more than 400 jurisdictions,

Juvenile Law 16.2

Probation Rules

1. Obey all federal, state, and local laws.
2. Must contact Juvenile Court Officer if taken into custody for questioning on a new law violation(s), by the next working day.
3. No possession or usage of alcohol or drugs, unless prescribed by a doctor.
4. Obey parent(s) rules, including assigned household chores.
5. Attend all scheduled appointments with Juvenile Court Officer, assigned Tracker, and/or Volunteer Juvenile Court Officer.
6. Continued involvement in a school program, includes supervision and monitoring by Juvenile Court School Liaison.
7. Obey the following curfew regulations.
8. Participate in family therapy until successfully discharged, if deemed appropriate.
9. Juvenile to participate in individual counseling until successfully discharged, if deemed appropriate.
10. Make reasonable restitution as agreed upon in the Restitution Contract.
11. Complete _____ hours of Community Service Work Project.
12. Participate in tutoring, if appropriate.
13. Letter of apology to the victim(s) for your actions.
14. No use of verbal/physical violence nor intimidation.
15. To participate in outpatient substance evaluation and cooperate with recommended counseling. To pay service fee to insure completion of evaluation.
16. To attend AA/NA meetings weekly.
17. May not frequent establishments nor residences where controlled substances/alcohol are served, nor associate with individuals involved.
18. May not leave Black Hawk County without permission from Juvenile Court Officer.
19. May not use or possess weapons of any kind.
20. To actively seek and maintain employment.

Failure to comply with the above rules will result in one, or a combination, of the following consequences/ recommendations to the Court:

1. Grounding.
2. Tightening of curfew hours.
3. Assignment of Community Service Work Project hours.
4. Tracking and Monitoring.
5. Supervision by Juvenile Court School Liaison/ participation/ completion in School Violence Program.
6. Day Treatment Program.
7. Additional appointments with Juvenile Court Officer.
8. Assignment of two hours of Community Service Work Project for each hour, or part of an hour, of unauthorized school absence.
9. Forty-eight hour detention hold.
10. Return to Court for modification of last Court Order.

As a juvenile, would you have found the above rules restrictive? Are they too restrictive? What would you add or omit?

Source: Materials provided by Juvenile Court Services of Blackhawk County (Waterloo, Iowa) in October of 2001.

and more than 35 states now have statutory authority to order monetary or community service restitution.[12] Part of the reason for the skyrocketing growth of restitution programs is that the Office of Juvenile Justice and Delinquency Prevention has spent $30 million promoting the use of restitution in 85 juvenile courts throughout the nation.[13] See Figure 16.1 for the dramatic growth of restitution programs.

Another survey of restitution programs found that most jurisdictions (75 percent) provided for both financial restitution and community service within the same program. Many programs also engaged in activities related to developing or implementing restitution orders. More than half of the programs provided victims or job information services or sponsored work crews. About one-third used victim-offender mediation, provided transportation to jobs, and arranged for job slots in the private sector. Finally,

Decisions Probation Officers Face

To make the decision of whether to revoke probation, modify the conditions of probation, or place a juvenile outside the home, probation officers consider such questions as:

1. Is the juvenile a danger to self or others?
2. Is the juvenile exceeding the limits in the home, community, and school?
3. Is the family amenable to services?
4. How can the scarce resources be used wisely with this juvenile?
5. What are other consequences that can be imposed without court intervention (e.g., community service)?

To make the decision on what to do with a juvenile on Informal Adjustment Agreement who is not following home rules, violating curfew, dropping dirty U. A.s [urine analysis], or failing to attend the Second Change Program, probation officers consider such questions as:

1. Does the juvenile show any remorse for his or her actions?
2. Does the juvenile want to change or make an adjustment to the Contract?

3. Have all other options been utilized?
4. Is the charge worth sending to the Court to get compliance? (Is Simple Misdemeanor worthy of the expense of Court action?)

To answer the question of what to do with a juvenile who is already adjudicated delinquent with the charge of Possession with Intent to Deliver a Controlled Substance and who continues to use/drop dirty U. A., probation officers consider such questions as:

1. Does use of evaluation/treatment help?
2. Does a 48-hour lock-up work? (take away freedom)
3. Have we tried all other services and consequences?
4. Would it be fair to modify the Court Order with a *mittimus* withheld to placement or commitment to Training School in Eldora?

What questions do you think would have the most influence on probation officers in these three scenarios? Why?

Source: Materials provided by Juvenile Court Services of Blackhawk County (Waterloo, Iowa) in October 2001.

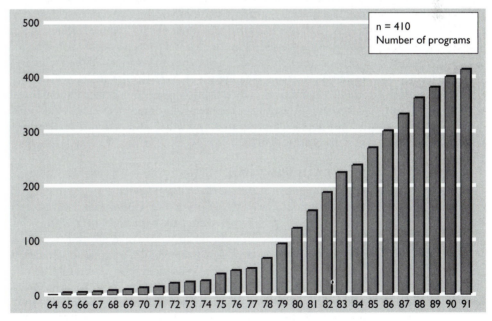

FIGURE 16.1 Dramatic Rise of Restitution Programs (Average)

Source: Peter R. Schneider and Matthew C. Finkelstein, *New Trends in Restitution Programming: Results from the 1991 RESTITTA Survey,* 1996 (Washington, D.C.: Office of Juvenile Justice and Delinquency Prevention, 2000), p. 15.

one in four programs provided subsidized employment for some probationers assigned restitution.[14]

The goals most commonly mentioned by restitution programs are:

- Holding juveniles accountable
- Providing reparation to victims
- Treating and rehabilitating juveniles
- Punishing juveniles[15]

To help with repayment, some juvenile courts have instituted job-skill preparation classes to train juveniles with ordered restitution to find jobs and hold them. Some programs have courted the private and public sectors for jobs in which juveniles required to make restitution can work, earn money, and compensate victims. Juveniles who have completed all other probation conditions except their restitution payments may have their probation term extended.[16]

With community work restitution, juveniles are generally ordered to perform a certain number of work hours at a private nonprofit or government agency. Some large probation departments have established up to 100 sites where this service may be performed. Sites typically include public libraries, parks, nursing homes, animal shelters, community centers, day-care centers, youth agencies, YMCAs and YWCAs, and the local streets. Some restitution programs involve supervised work crews; in these situations, juveniles go to a site and work under the supervision of an adult.[17]

Youthful offenders in Hennepin County, Minnesota (Minneapolis), find themselves very quickly dispatched by the juvenile judge to the Saturday work squads for a specified amount of community service. A first-time property offender will usually be given a sentence of forty hours. Each Saturday morning, youths who are assigned to the work squad are required to be at the downtown meeting place at 8:00. The coordinator of the program, who is on the staff of the probation department, then assigns each to a specific work detail; these include recycling bottles and cans, visiting with patients at a nursing home, doing janitorial work, cleaning bus stops, planting trees or removing barbed wire fences at a city park, and working at a park reserve. This program sends out five trucks each Saturday with ten youths and two staff members in each truck.[18]

A 1991 survey found that most of the juveniles referred to programs strictly for juveniles are diverted from the formal justice system. Some restitution programs accept both juveniles and adults. This survey also revealed the racial breakdown of participants in these programs (see Figure 16.2).[19] Community service programs are more widely used than are financial restitution programs because many juveniles lack the means to pay financial restitution. Some probation offices have a full-time restitution officer who administers such programs, and other offices divide restitution into formal and informal programs.

INTENSIVE SUPERVISION   In the 1980s and 1990s, as probation continued to be criticized as a lenient measure that allowed offenders to escape punishment, intensive supervision programs (ISP) became more widely used in juvenile probation. Georgia, New Jersey, Oregon, and Pennsylvania are experimenting with or have such statewide programs for juveniles.[20] But more and more juvenile judges, especially in metropolitan juvenile courts, are placing high-risk juveniles on small caseloads and assigning them more frequent contact with a probation officer than would be true of traditional probation.

The Juvenile Court Judges' Commission in the Commonwealth of Pennsylvania developed an intensive probation project because of its concern with increased commitments to training schools. In addition to investing $1,868,014 to support intensive probation and aftercare programs, the Commission also provides program guidelines and monitoring to each county that is willing to set up an intensive probation program. By the end of 1989, thirty-two counties had established intensive probation programs using such standards as providing a caseload size of no more than fifteen high-risk

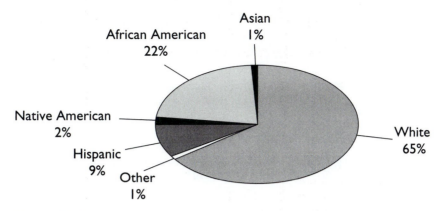

FIGURE 16.2 Racial Breakdown of Restitution Programs (Average)

Source: Peter R. Schneider and Matthew C. Finkelstein, *New Trends in Restitution Programming: Results from the 1991 RESTITTA Survey,* 1996 (Washington, D.C.: Office of Juvenile Justice and Delinquency Prevention, 2000), p. 13.

delinquents for each intensive probation officer, requiring a minimum of three face-to-face contacts per week with each of these youths and a minimum of one contact per week with the family and/or guardian, and establishing intensive probation services for a minimum of six months and a maximum of twelve months.[21]

Intensive supervision programs are widely used in adult corrections and have received considerable praise for their effectiveness in keeping high-risk offenders out of long-term confinement.[22] However, two national reviews of intensive supervision programs in juvenile probation have discovered that "neither the possible effectiveness nor the possible ineffectiveness of these programs had been carefully examined. As a result, their status in this regard, including their impact on recidivism, was essentially unknown."[23]

There has been a recent concern to develop an Integrated Social Control (ISC) model of intensive supervision addressing the major causal factors identified in delinquency theory and research. This proposed model integrates the central components of strain, control, and social learning theories. It contends that the combined forces of inadequate socialization, strains between educational and occupational aspirations and expectations, as well as social disorganization in the neighborhood lead to weak bonding to conventional values and activities in the family, community, and school. Weak bonding, in turn, can lead youths to delinquent behavior through negative peer influence. Figure 16.3 shows a diagram of this model.

ELECTRONIC MONITORING AND HOUSE ARREST House arrest is a sentence imposed by the court whereby youths are ordered to remain confined in their own homes for the length of their sentence. They may be allowed to leave their homes for medical reasons, school, employment, and approved religious services. They may also be required to perform community service. Electronic monitoring equipment may or may not be used to monitor juveniles' presence in a residence where they are required to remain.[25]

Electronic monitoring was inspired by a New Mexico district court judge's reading of a comic strip in which the character Spiderman was tracked by a transmitter affixed to his wrist. The judge approached an engineer, who designed an electronic bracelet to emit a signal picked up by a receiver placed in a home telephone. The bracelet was designed so that if the offender moved more than 150 feet from the home telephone, the transmission signal would be broken, alerting the authorities that the offender had fled his or her home.[26]

Electronic monitoring equipment receives information about monitored offenders and transmits the information over telephone lines to a computer at the monitoring agency. Two basic types are used: continuously signaling devices that constantly monitor

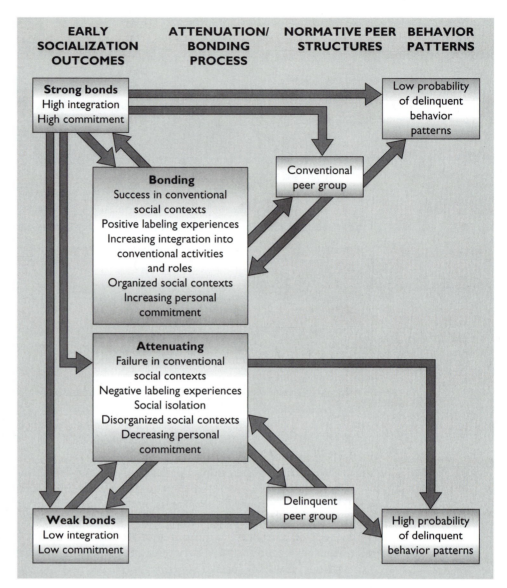

FIGURE 16.3 Integrated Strain-Control Paradigm

Source: Barry Krisberg et al., *Juvenile Intensive Supervision: Planning Guide* (Washington, D.C.: Office Of Juvenile Justice and Delinquency Prevention, 1994), p. 7.

the offender's presence at a particular location and programmed contact devices that contact the offender periodically to verify his or her presence.[27]

According to a National Institute of Justice survey, officials in 33 states were using electronic monitoring devices to supervise nearly 2,300 adult offenders in 1988.[28] In contrast to the wide popularity in adult corrections, a November 1988 survey identified only eleven juvenile programs that used it.[29] The juvenile programs frequently used private contractors for the equipment and sometimes adapted the programs from the ones being used in adult probation in that jurisdiction. These programs in juvenile justice included the following goals:

- To increase the number of juveniles safely released into existing home confinement programs
- To reduce the number of juveniles returned to juvenile detention for violating home confinement restrictions
- To reduce the number of field contracts required of home confinement officers

- To provide a reasonably safe alternative to confinement for lower-risk offenders
- To provide for early reunification with the child's family
- To allow the juvenile to return to school.[30]

The Community Volunteer

As stated earlier, probation began with volunteers, with professional staff appearing by the turn of the twentieth century. But in the 1950s, Judge Keith J. Leenhouts initiated a court-sponsored **volunteer program** in Royal Oak, Michigan, that sparked the rebirth of the volunteer movement. Today, over two thousand court-sponsored **volunteer programs** are in operation, using volunteers to assist probation officers in a variety of ways. The use of volunteers has become one of the most valuable ways to help offenders adjust to community life.

The National Information Center on Volunteers in Court has identified several areas in which volunteers can work effectively with juvenile offenders. A volunteer can provide a one-to-one support relationship for the youth with a trustworthy adult; can function as a child advocate with teachers, employers, and the police; can be a good role model; can set limits and teach prosocial values; can teach skills or academic subjects; and can help the youth to develop a realistic response to the environment.

In addition to these areas of direct contact, volunteers can assist in administrative work. They can help recruit, train, and supervise other volunteers; serve as consultants to the regular staff; become advisers to the court, especially in the policymaking area; develop good public relations with the community; and contribute money, materials, or facilities.

Volunteers can improve the morale of the regular probation staff, because they are usually positive and enthusiastic about the services they are providing. Since many volunteers are professionals (physicians, psychiatrists, psychologists, and dentists), they can provide services that the probation department may not have the financial resources to obtain. Finally, their contributions can reduce the caseload of the regular staff.

Several criticisms have been leveled at volunteer programs. They often create more work than they return in service. Volunteers cannot handle serious problems and sometimes can harm their clients. Parents may resist the volunteer as an untrained worker. But proper screening, training, and supervision can do much to ensure a high quality of probation services from volunteers.

The Role Residential and Day Treatment Programs Play

Residential and day treatment programs are usually reserved for juvenile probationers who are having difficulty dealing with the looseness of probation supervision. In day treatment programs, juveniles attend the program in the morning and afternoon and return home in the evening. In residential programs, which are usually group homes or foster care placements, delinquents are taken away from the supervision of parents and are assigned twenty-four hours a day to their new placement. Some group homes are like the halfway houses used in adult corrections and serve as a placement for juveniles on aftercare status who have nowhere else to go.

Administration of Residential and Day Treatment Programs

Community-based residential and day treatment programs are either state-sponsored, locally operated or privately operated. Twenty-six states sponsor residential and day treatment programs under **community corrections acts.**

The Minnesota Community Corrections Act, which has become a model for other community corrections acts, provides a state subsidy to any county or group of counties that chooses to develop its own community corrections system. Juvenile delinquents who are adjudicated to a training school are "charged back" to the county and the costs are subtracted from the county's subsidy. Counties in Minnesota have been understandably reluctant to commit youths to training school because of the prohibitive cost and therefore have both established and encouraged a wide variety of residential and day treatment programs.

The deinstitutionalization movement in Massachusetts has resulted in the development of a wide network of residential and day treatment programs for youths. The Department of Youth Services administers some of these programs, but more often the department contracts bids for these youths from private vendors in the community. The department also monitors the services provided by these programs.

California's Probation Subsidy Act, which was replaced by the County Subvention Program in 1978, also led to the development of a network of residential and day treatment programs for youth. At one point, the forty-seven participating California counties were receiving $22 million a year for community-based programs. This major state commitment permitted the establishment of the largest number of residential and day treatment programs in the nation. However, the 1978 County Subvention Program, along with the passage of Proposition 13, severely curtailed the funding of such community programs.

Privately run programs usually are administered by a board of directors, who appoint the staff to operate their programs. In addition to the contract funds these programs receive from state and local governments, they also depend on such sources as federal, state, and local bodies and foundations. These programs provide either "halfway-in" facilities for probationers sentenced by the juvenile court or placements for juveniles on aftercare status. Private agencies usually must maintain minimum statewide or court standards.

The Types of Residential and Day Treatment Programs

Group homes, day treatment programs, and wilderness programs are the main types of community-based programs. Group homes are a residential placement in which juveniles are adjudicated, either while they are on probation or when they are released from a training school. Day treatment programs are nonresidential programs which juveniles attend during the day, returning home in the evening. Wilderness programs, sometimes called "survival programs," take place in such settings as the mountains, the woods, the sea, and the desert. The intent of these survival programs is to improve youths' self-confidence and sense of self-reliance.

GROUP HOMES   Such terms as group residence, halfway house, group home, and attention home are used in various parts of the United States to identify a small facility serving about thirteen to twenty-five youths. **Group homes** fulfill several purposes: they provide an alternative to institutionalization; they serve as a short-term community placement, wherein probation and aftercare officers can deal with youths' community problems; and they serve as a "halfway-in" setting for youths having difficulty adjusting to probation and as a "halfway-out" placement for delinquents who are returning to the community but lack an adequate home placement.

Intake criteria, treatment goals, length of stay, target population services, services offered, physical facilities, location in reference to the rest of the city, and house rules of group homes throughout the United States are extremely diverse. Some homes are treatment-oriented, using a modality such as guided group interaction (GGI) to generate a supportive environment among residents and staff. In guided group interaction, residents are expected to support, confront, and be honest with one another so that they can help each other deal with their problems. In contrast, other group homes deliberately avoid establishing a comfort climate, and staff members may even try to arouse anxiety.[31]

The Silverlake Experiment, which was patterned on the Highfields Project discussed earlier in this chapter, was set up in Los Angeles County in the mid 1960s. This program, which was in a large family residence in a middle-class neighborhood, provided group living for male youths between the ages of fifteen and eighteen. As was the case at Highfields, only twenty residents at a time lived in the group home, and all participated in daily group meetings.[32]

A well-developed **group home model** is the **teaching-family group model,** which was developed in 1967 with the establishment of the Achievement Place group home in Lawerence, Kansas. The teaching-family group model is currently used in more than forty homes in twelve states.[33] The Criswell House in Florida, established in 1958, houses twenty-five youths on probation and parole and uses guided group interaction. In the 1970s, Florida developed a network of nine group homes modeled on Criswell House.[34] The Dare Program in Massachusetts is another widely used model. Established in 1964, this program has ten specialized programs and thirteen community residences, including nine group homes, four foster home programs, two residential schools, shelter care programs, and an intensive care high-security facility.[35]

The House of Umoja in Philadelphia, Pennsylvania, is recognized as one of the most impressive group homes in the nation. Each of the group homes serves fifteen youths in a program that creates intensive family feelings within a framework of African-inspired consciousness. Headed by Sister Falaska Fattah, the House of Umoja deals almost entirely with gang delinquents. It had its beginnings when Sister Falaska's husband, Daoud, who had been a gang member himself, returned to the streets to study the gangs. Sister Falaska saw possible solutions to the violence of gangs in "the strength of the family, tribal concepts, and African value systems." She and her husband then created an African-style extended family in which members of the gangs could find alternative values to those of their street-life culture. Since the House of Umoja was established in the early 1970s, it has sheltered more than 300 boys who have belonged to seventy-three different street gangs.[36]

Unfortunately, such exciting programs as the House of Umoja or the Achievement Place are not typical of group homes across the nation. In too many group homes, beds (vacancies) are hard to find and group homes may even have long waiting lists. Residents also typically have longer stays than they would have in training schools, and this raises real questions about whether group homes are a less punitive placement than juvenile institutions.

DAY TREATMENT PROGRAMS   Nonresidential **day treatment programs** multiplied nationwide during the early 1970s. Their popularity can be traced to the advantages they offer community-based corrections: they are more economical because they do not provide living and sleeping quarters; they make parental participation easier; they require fewer staff members; and they are less coercive and punishment-oriented than residential placements are.

Nonresidential programs usually serve male juveniles, although California operates two such programs for girls as well as several coeducational programs. These nonresidential programs have been used widely by the California Community Treatment Project. The New York Division for Youth has also established several nonresidential programs, called STAY. The STAY programs also expose youths to a guided-groups-interaction experience.

Another nonresidential program is conducted by the Associated Marine Institutes (AMI). Twenty-five of their forty schools and institutes are nonresidential. Funded by state and private donations, this privately operated program tailors its institutes to the geographical strengths of each community, using the ocean, wilderness, rivers, and lakes to stimulate productive behavior in juvenile delinquents. In the nonresidential programs, which include both males and females, the fourteen- to eighteen-year-old trainees live at home or in foster homes. Youths are referred to this program either by the courts or by the Division of Youth Services (see Treatment Intervention 16.4).[37]

TREATMENT INTERVENTION 16.4

Programs of the Associated Marine Institutes

Since 1969, the Associated Marine Institutes have been working with juvenile delinquents. Over the years, new institutes were started throughout the United States and in the Cayman Islands.

AMI's main objective is to develop attitudes in the youths it serves which will help them meet their responsibilities, develop employable skills, increase self-confidence, and encourage further education. After attending the program, each youth is placed in a school, a job, or the armed forces. Aftercare coordinators monitor youths for three years after they graduate to offer assistance.

In September of 1993, Attorney General Janet Reno and President Bill Clinton visited the Pinellas Marine Institute in St. Petersurg, Florida, one of the forty schools of AMI. In a nationally televised program where he announced his crime bill, the president said, "These programs are giving young people a chance to take their future back, a chance to understand that there is good inside them."

One of the ingredients of AMI's programs is a strong commitment to meaningful work. It looks upon work as one of the most beneficial forms of therapy and teaches that nothing worthwhile is achieved without hard work.

Academic success is also emphasized. The intent of the AMI programs is to motivate students and to give them the right tools and opportunities so that they can succeed in school. Indeed, the goal of the AMI teaching staff is to prepare youths to take their GED exam and then attend vocational school, community college, or a four-year college.

A further important ingredient of this program is modeling. AMI staff support the belief that what they do is more important than what they say. Their philosophy on modeling is: Tell me, I'll forget. Show me, I may remember. Involve me, I'll be committed.

Source: "The Programs of the Associated Marine Institute." Mimeograph, n.d.

For the Marine Institutes, which constitute most of the schools, the contract that the youth signs on entering the program sets individual goals for the training period in a dozen categories, including diving, ship-handling skills, ocean science, lifesaving, first aid, and such electives as photography and marine maintenance. The major incentive for youths is the opportunity to earn official certification as scuba divers. Other incentives that are designed to maintain enthusiasm include sew-on patches; certificates awarded for short-term achievement in first aid, ship-handling skills, and diving; trophies for trainee of the month; and field trips, such as a cruise to the Bahamas or the Florida Keys.[38]

Project New Pride is a day treatment program that offers services to juveniles in Denver, Colorado, who have committed serious offenses. Most of the youngsters involved in the project are African Americans or Mexican Americans. This program offers intensive services for youths during the first three months and then continues with treatment geared to the juveniles' needs and interests for a nine-month follow-up period. Academic education, counseling, employment, and cultural education are the four main areas of service. For academic education, youths are assigned to either the New Pride Alternative School or the Learning Disabilities Center. The purpose of the counseling is to enhance self-image and to help the youth cope with the environment. Job preparation is emphasized in this program through a job-skills workshop and on-the-job training. The purpose of cultural education is to expose participants to a range of experiences and activities in the Denver area.[39]

Project New Pride has established four primary goals in working with its difficult clientele: (1) reduction of recidivism, (2) job placement, (3) school reintegration, and (4) re-mediation of academic and learning disabilities. The project has had some success

At the Associated Marine Institutes, youths are given the oppurtunity to learn valuable social skills as well as concrete technical skills such as diving, marine photography, and ship handling. The positive approach such programs take has proven more effective in turning juvenile delinquents around than have punitive measures.

in achieving the first three of these goals, but less success in educational re-mediation. The popularity of this project has been demonstrated by its replication in Boston; Chicago; Fresno, California; Haddonfield, New Jersey; Kansas City, Missouri; Los Angeles; Pensacola, Florida; Providence, Rhode Island; San Francisco; and Washington, D.C.[40]

The better known programs, such as AMI and Project New Pride, continue to thrive, but with the decline of federal funding sources in the late 1970s and early 1980s, many day treatment programs have had to close their doors. There is no question that these programs play a much smaller role in community-based corrections than they did a couple of decades ago.

WILDERNESS PROGRAMS   **Outward Bound** is the most widely used wilderness program. The main goal of Outward Bound is to use the "overcoming of a seemingly impossible task" to gain self-reliance, to prove one's worth, and to define one's personhood. An Outward Bound program usually includes rock climbing, rappelling, mountain walking, backpacking, high-altitude camping, and survival alone. The wilderness experience generally lasts three to four weeks and has four phases: training in basic skills, a long expedition, a solo trek, and a final testing period. The locations of these programs include forests, high mountains, canoe country, the sea, and the desert.

The first Outward Bound program in the United States was established at the Colorado Outward Bound School in 1962. The other original Outward Bound Schools were in Minnesota, Hurricane Island, Northwest, North Carolina, Southwest, and Dartmouth College. Variations of the standard Outward Bound course were established throughout the United States during the 1970s.[41] There are still at least seven Outward Bound programs in the United States.[42]

Arthur Conquest, a former delinquent who is now an Outward Bound instructor, tells why he thinks this learning experience works for delinquents:

> . . . But I think in the end, and I don't just mean the end of the course, but when the kids have to deal with life—they'll have whatever it takes to go to the wall. That's what an Outward Bound course for these kids is for—when things get tough, you've got to

At a summer rehabilitation camp, teenage delinquents practice calisthenics and learn wilderness survival skills.

really believe in yourself, persevere, go to that wall, and do all the things you're capable of doing.[43]

VisionQuest, another survival program, was started by Robert Ledger Burton in 1973 in Tucson, Arizona. This controversial program currently has 250 staff members and 250 youngsters enrolled from ten states. Its wide variety of programs includes wilderness training, a mule-and-horse train, an alternative school, nine group homes, and a home-based counseling program. This rigorous twelve-to eighteen-month program requires that youth complete two "high impact" experiences, such as wilderness training, a sea survival experience, or the mule-and-horse wagon train. The wagon train, which travels from one coast to the other, has been the subject of a CBS television documentary, a *Life* magazine pictorial article, and innumerable newspaper articles.[44]

How Juvenile Aftercare Works

Parole, or **juvenile aftercare,** as it is usually called, is concerned with the release of a youth from an institution when he or she can best benefit from release and can make an optimal adjustment to community living. In 1994, thirty-six state agencies reported that 57,359 juveniles were released from institutional care. The average length of stay for juveniles released was 9.8 months. The recidivism rates for eighteen agencies averaged 36.5 percent (the follow-up periods used to estimate recidivism for eighteen of these nineteen agencies averaged 3.7 years).[45]

Once a youth is adjudicated to a state training school, the state normally retains jurisdiction until his or her release. The authority to make the decision about when to release a youth from training school is usually given to institutional staff, although a number of states give other agencies and boards the authority to parole juveniles. Often the cottage staff will review the progress of each youth at designated intervals, and, when the staff recommends release, the recommendation is reviewed by a board made up of staff from throughout the institution. If this board concurs, the recommendation must be approved by an institutional coordinator at the youth authority or youth commission.

Cottage staffs usually consider several factors in recommending a youth for release. The juvenile's overall institutional adjustment—including performance in school, participation in recreation, and relationships with peers in the cottage—is reviewed. The youth's attitude is also evaluated; personality conflicts with staff, especially those in the cottage, will usually be interpreted as the result of a poor attitude. The probability of community success is considered: A youth's willingness and ability to set realistic goals are frequently seen as evidence of readiness to return to the community. Finally, reports on the juvenile's performance on the cottage work detail and on personal hygiene generally must be positive before the staff will recommend release.

The Administration and Operation of Aftercare Services

Aftercare is the responsibility of the state and is administered by the executive branch in forty-four states. In four states, aftercare is under the organization of the probation department and is administered by probation officers. In three states, other means of organizing and administering aftercare are used.[46]

Early release from training school because of overcrowded conditions has complicated the decision-making process for institutional release. In six states, a parole board appointed by the governor considers early release for institutionalized juveniles.[47] Michael D. Norman's study of the Utah Youth Parole Authority found that the early-release criteria were primarily related to institutional behavior, rather than prospects for successful reintegration into the community.[48]

The Nokomis Challenge Program was launched by the Michigan Department of Social Services in 1989. It combines three months of residential and wilderness experience in a remote wilderness camp with nine months of intensive community-based aftercare. It is designed for low- and medium-risk youths convicted of a felony offense who would otherwise be given a fourteen- to sixteen-month placement in a residential facility. The basic focus of the Nokomis program is on relapse prevention. A 1996 evaluation found that only about 40 percent of the youth in this study successfully completed the twelve-month program. This evaluation also revealed "that the Nokomis youth failed at a faster rate than graduates of regular residential programs, in spite of the fact that they were receiving intensive aftercare following their release." The evaluation went on to indicate that "the main weakness of the experimental group in Nokomis was related to the community phase of the program."[49]

Another aftercare program that perhaps has been more successful is at the Florida Environmental Institute (FEI). This program, which is also known as "The Last Chance Ranch," targets the state's most serious and violent juvenile offenders. Located in a remote area of Florida's Everglades, FEI offers a residential phase as well as a nonresidential aftercare program. Its strong emphasis on education, hard work, social bonding, and aftercare has resulted in positive results among participants. The 30 percent recidivism rates of youths who have gone through the program are substantially less than the 50 to 70 percent rates of traditional training school programs.[50]

An **interstate compact** is sometimes initiated when a youth has no acceptable home placement within his or her own state. The institutional social worker usually contacts the appropriate agency in another state where the youth has a possible placement and submits an interstate compact for the transfer of the youth to that state after release from training school. The state of original jurisdiction retains authority over the youth and is kept advised of the juvenile's status.

The aftercare or probation officer (probation officers in many jurisdictions have aftercare youth as part of their caseloads) who is responsible for the case sometimes corresponds with or may even visit the institutionalized youth in training school. In many states, a youth cannot be released until the aftercare officer approves the home placement plan submitted by the institutional home worker. This usually involves a visit to the home by the officer to make certain that the home is a good placement. At other times, the aftercare officer must locate an alternate placement, such as a foster or group home. In Social Policy 16.5, Beth Peters, a juvenile parole officer for Hennepin County, tells how aftercare has changed and why it is not more effective than it is.

As Ms. Peters reminds us, part of the problem in juvenile aftercare is that youthful offenders usually are sent back to the same communities (and same families) and exposed again to the same problems they could not handle earlier. Most of their friends

SOCIAL POLICY 16.5

Interview with Beth Peters, a Juvenile Patrol Officer

These kids who get out need the same type of supportive environment they had in the institution. What we are doing is taking a kid in a dysfunctional environment and putting them in a structured environment in the institution. Then, once paroled, we are returning them back to their same environment at home. They are usually going back to the same peers, often gangs, and we are telling them to take the positive peer culture they learned in the institution and integrate it into their lives. This strategy doesn't breed a high rate of success. As a system we need to provide transitional programming in the community.

Kids on aftercare have also changed. Ten years ago I had kids who had car theft or damage to property offenses. Now, I'm working with kids who are carrying weapons, adjudicated for drive-by shootings, assaults with weapons, and even murder. What used to be solved with fists is now being solved by hurting or killing each other. The population is a whole lot harder.

Before, you could go tell a kid to get a job at McDonald's. Now, you may tell a kid to go get a job for minimum wage, but they look at you like you're crazy. "Hey," they tell you, "I can make $500 a day selling crack. Why should I work for minimum wage?"

Source: Interviewed in August 1995.

are still around, and it is not long before a friend suggests that they commit another crime. If the returnee is determined, the youth might be able to say, "Hey, get out of my face; I don't want to hear that business." But if the young person cannot find a job—and jobs are scarce for delinquent youths who frequently are school dropouts—or feels under financial pressure, it becomes harder and harder not to return to crime.

Most youths on aftercare status are placed on supervision in the community for a year or more after release. The aftercare officer, who is expected to monitor the behavior of youths under supervision, provides each youth with a list of rules. These rules usually resemble those given to adult parolees and pertain to such matters as obeying parents, maintaining a satisfactory adjustment at school or at work, being at home a certain time every night, avoiding contact with other delinquents, avoiding the use or possession of any narcotic, and reporting to the aftercare officer as requested.

Risk Control and Crime Reduction

The current emphasis in aftercare is on short-term behavior control. The Office of Juvenile Justice and Delinquency Prevention has developed an intensive aftercare program that incorporates the principles of preparing youths for release to the community, of facilitating youth-community interaction and involvement, and of monitoring youths' reintegration into the community.[51]

Similar to juvenile probation, intensive supervision programs are being increasingly used. As of 1992, there were over eighty aftercare intensive supervision programs in the United States.[52] The intensive program in thirty counties in Pennsylvania and the Violent Juvenile Offender Research and Development Programs in Boston, Detroit, Memphis, and Newark have been particularly noteworthy. New York has also developed an intensive supervision program for juveniles on parole.

In 1988, the Juvenile Court Judges' Commission of Pennsylvania implemented pilot Intensive Aftercare programs in Philadelphia and Allegheny Counties for youths who would be classified as habitually serious and violent offenders.[53] The sample in Philadelphia consisted of ninety juveniles who were released from the Bensalem Youth Development Center between December 1988 and January 1990. Placed in a caseload of no more than twelve and supervised by probation officers, about 50 percent of the juveniles assigned to intensive aftercare were rearrested, compared to 64 percent of the control subjects, with equal seriousness of new offenses for both groups.[54] By the end of 1989, thirty counties in Pennsylvania had established intensive aftercare programs.[55]

Lifeskills '95 is an intensive aftercare treatment program in California that is designed to assist high-risk and chronic juvenile offenders who are released from secure confinement.[56] The basic paradigm of this intensive aftercare program uses a series of lifestyle and life skill treatment modalities in an integrated educational approach to healthy decision making.[57] Don A. Josi and Dale K. Sechrest's 1995 study of this treatment intervention compared the parole performances of a control group and an experimental group of California Youth Authority offenders. They found that in the first ninety days those in the control group were about twice as likely as the experimental group to be unemployed, to lack the resources to gain or maintain employment, and to have been arrested.[58]

There has also been a concern to develop an integrated theoretical framework for guiding intensive supervision of chronic juvenile offenders. Made up largely of combinations of social control, strain, and social learning theories, this Intensive Aftercare Program (IAP) model focuses on the reintegrative process.[59] Figure 16.4 shows the program elements of this model. Underlying assumptions of this model are that chronic and serious delinquency is related to weak controls produced by social disorganization, inadequate socialization, and strain; that strain is produced by social disorganization independent of weak controls; and that peer group influences intervene as a social force between youths with weak bonds and/or strain on the one hand and delinquent behaviors on the other.[60]

This Intensive Aftercare Program (IAP) was initially implemented in Clark County (Las Vegas, Nevada); Denver, Arapaho, Douglas, and Jefferson Counties, and metropolitan Denver, Colorado; Essex, Newark, and Camden Counties, New Jersey; and City of Norfolk, Virginia. The participation of the New Jersey counties ended in 1997, but the other three programs carried through on preparing high-risk offenders for progressively

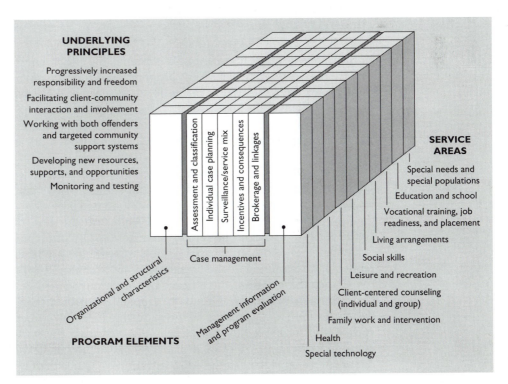

FIGURE 16.4 Intervention Model for Juvenile Intensive Aftercare

Source: David M. Altschuler and Troy L. Armstrong, *Intensive Aftercare for High-Risk Juveniles: Policies and Procedures* (Washington, D.C.: Office of Juvenile Justice and Delinquency Prevention, 1994), p. 3.

increased responsibility and freedom in the community. The well-developed transition components that began shortly after a youth was adjudicated to an institution and continued through the early months of community adjustment are particularly striking about these programs (See Table 16.4 for these transition components. The results of the first five years of implementation (1995–2000) reveal a dramatically improved level of communication and coordination between institutional and aftercare staff as well as the ability to involve parolees in community services almost immediately after institutional release.[61]

Yet in-house detention and electronic monitoring programs still have not received the attention that they deserve in juvenile aftercare.[62] Juvenile aftercare also emphasizes drug and alcohol urinalyses (sometimes called "drug drops") and is turning to "boot camp" programs as a means of releasing juveniles early from training schools.

If the rules are violated or a law is broken, in both traditional and intensive aftercare, a youth may be returned to a training school. Although guidelines for the revocation of parole for juveniles have not been formulated by court decisions, revocation of a youth's aftercare status is no longer based solely on the testimony of the aftercare officer, who could be influenced by personality clashes or prejudice toward the client. Today, most jurisdictions have formal procedures for the **revocation of aftercare.** The aftercare officer may initially investigate the charge and, if the finding is that the youth did commit the offense, will report the violation to the supervisor. The supervisor may review the case and make the decision, or a revocation committee may examine the violation. The aftercare officer may be required to submit a written recommendation for revocation, but is not allowed to testify, and the youth is permitted to speak in self-defense.

The Effectiveness of Community-Based Corrections

In the minds of many juvenile justice students, the effectiveness of community-based corrections is beyond debate. Some proponents of community-based corrections go so far as to look upon the juvenile institution as irredeemably evil and the community programs as unequivocally good.[63] They appear to regard the juvenile delinquent as an underdog who is a nearly helpless victim of society's labeling process and to see flexible and adaptive community care as protecting delinquents from nasty and destructive institutional care.[64]

A more widely held view is that whatever the weaknesses of community-based programs, they do keep delinquents out of inhumane and costly long-term training schools. These more moderate advocates of community-based programs also argue that the further a youth is allowed to penetrate the juvenile justice system, the more difficult it becomes for him or her to be reintegrated successfully into community life. It is also contended that community-based services improve the probability of successful client reintegration because staff and clients are closer to community resources.[65]

Critics still question the efficacy of community-based corrections. They claim that community programs tend to supplement rather than replace institutions, thereby leading to a widening of the net of the juvenile correctional system. That is, youths who formerly would have been diverted from the system now are placed in community programs. Critics also charge that such variables as race, class, and gender are more important in the administration of justice than offense or law-oriented variables.

Hard-line critics also challenge the capability of community-based corrections to ensure community safety because of the laxity of supervision on probation and because of the excessive number of runaways from residential programs. Critics point to

TABLE 16.4

Transition Components of IAP Programming

Transition Component	IAP site		
	Colorado	*Nevada*	*Virginia*
EARLY PAROLE PLANNING	Initial plan complete at 30 days after institutional placement: final plan complete at 60 days prior to release.	Initial plan complete at 30 days after institutional placement; final plan complete 30 days prior to furlough.	Initial plan complete 30 days after institutional placement; final plan complete 30 days prior to release.
MULTIPLE PERSPECTIVES INCORPORATED IN PLAN	Case manager, institutional staff, youth, parents and community providers all routinely involved.	Parole officer; institutional community liaison, institutional staff, and youth; parent participation limited.	Parole officer, institutional case manager, youth, interagency "Community Assessment Team," and parent.
PAROLE OFFICER VISITS TO INSTITUTION	One to two times per week; routine.	Once per month; routine since spring 1997.	One to two times per month; routine.
TREATMENT BEGUN IN INSTITUTION AND CONTINUED IN COMMUNITY	Via community providers. Includes multifamily counseling, life skills training, individual counseling, and vocational skills training; done routinely.	Via an institutional-community liaison and parole officers. Includes life skills and drug/alcohol curriculums; done routinely until liaison vacancy.	Via one provider at Hanover only. Drug/alcohol treatment; sporadic use; State policy discourages contract services by community providers for institutionalized youth.
YOUTH PRERELEASE VISITS TO COMMUNITY	Supervised day trips to community programs, beginning 60 days prior to release.	Not allowed.	Not allowed.
PREPAROLE FURLOUGH	Overnight/weekend home passes, beginning 30 days prior to release.	Thirty-day conditional release to community, prior to official parole.	Not allowed.
TRANSITIONAL RESIDENCE	Not part of the design, but occurs for some youth.	Not part of the design.	Two group homes in Norfolk; 30- to 60-day length of stay; used for most youth.
TRANSITIONAL DAY PROGRAMMING	Two day-treatment programs in Denver; used for almost all youth during the first few months after release.	One day-supervision/treatment program; used for most youth.	Day treatment used for youth who do not go to group homes.
PHASED SUPERVISION LEVELS ON PAROLE	Informal system: contact once per week during the first few months, down to once per month later.	Four-phase system: contact four times per week during furlough; three times per week next 90 days; two times per week next 60–90 days; once per week next 30–60 days.	Four-phase system: group home; contact five to seven times per week next 60 days; three to five times per week next 60 days; three times per week last 30 days.

Source: Richard G. Wiebush, Betsie McNulty, and Thalo Le, *Implementation of the Intensive Community-Based Aftercare Program* (Washington, D.C.: Office of Juvenile Justice and Delinquency Prevention, 2000), p. 2.

the permissive tendency of many juvenile judges to keep youths on probation regardless of the number or types of crimes they commit. Finally, critics question the ability of community-based programs to correct or rehabilitate delinquents.

Empirical studies on probation tend to demonstrate its effectiveness,[66] but the findings on residential programs are more mixed than those on probation.[67] Studies on Outward Bound found initial lower recidivism rates than control groups, but the differences totally disappeared after five years.[68] Evaluations of restitution also revealed mixed findings.[69] Intensive supervision projects, in both probation and parole, are being established across the nation, but these newly implemented programs are still in the process of evaluation.

The conflicting evidence (as well as the flaws in the research) certainly makes it difficult to conclude that community-based programs result in lower rates of recidivism than institutional programs. Nevertheless, a convincing case can be made that community-based programs are at least as successful as training schools, with less trauma to youths and less cost to the state.

SUMMARY

Community-based corrections is made up of probation, residential and day treatment programs, and aftercare. The development of community-based corrections profited from the spirit of reform that existed at the turn of the twentieth century and later during the 1960s. Support of community programs declined in the 1970s because the hard-liners persuaded the public of the great extent and danger of youth crime. Instead of being able to consider closing all state training schools, as Massachusetts had done in the early 1970s, proponents of community-based corrections found themselves in a position of defense or withdrawal. The "get tough" mood with serious youth crime remained in place in the 1990s, as the public became even more concerned about the threat to public safety of gun carrying, drug-using, and gang-involved juveniles. The fact still remains that more delinquents are treated in the community than are adjudicated to training schools because juvenile judges continue to support the least-restrictive, or soft-line, approach for minor offenders.

The early years of the twenty-first century should be a time of expansion for community-based corrections. The prohibitive expense of long-term institutions should mean increased use of alternatives. Perhaps the amount of decarceration of juveniles desired by reformers in the 1970s will never be attained, but the economics of placing juveniles in long-term institutions will probably mean that these end-of-the-line facilities will come to be reserved for hard-core and violent offenders.

KEY TERMS

community corrections acts, p. 485
day treatment programs, p. 487
electronic monitoring, p. 483
group home, p. 486
group home model, p. 487
interstate compact, p. 491
juvenile aftercare, p. 490
Outward Bound, p. 489
probation, p. 473

probation subsidies, p. 477
residential programs, p. 474
restitution, p. 479
revocation of aftercare, p. 494
social history report, p. 478
surveillance, p. 479
teaching-family group home model, p. 487
volunteer programs, p. 485

CRITICAL THINKING QUESTIONS

1. What are the job responsibilities of a probation officer?
2. What are the differences between probation and aftercare services?
3. What are the main types of residential and nonresidential programs for juvenile delinquents?
4. Of the programs discussed in this chapter, which do you believe is the most effective for helping offenders reintegrate into the community?

5. What specific strategies can departments of juvenile corrections pursue to enlist greater support from the community for community programs?
6. How effective are community-based corrections? What is the essential link in increasing the effectiveness of community-based corrections?

WEB DESTINATIONS

Learn more about John Augustus at the American Probation and Parole Association site.
http://www.appa-net.org/the_early_years.htm

Learn more about the Outward Bound Program by visiting the Outward Bound home page.
http://www.outwardbound.org/

NOTES

1. Interviewed in May 1981.
2. *John Augustus, First Probation Officer* (Montclair, N.J.: Patterson-Smith Company, 1972), pp. 4–5.
3. Board of State Charities of Massachusetts, *Sixth Annual Report* (1869), p.269.
4. Interviewed in June 1988.
5. National Advisory Commission on Criminal Justice Standards and Goals, *Corrections* (Washington D.C.: U.S. Government Printing Office, 1973), p. 312.
6. Meghan C. Scahill, *Juvenile Delinquency Probation Caseload, 1988–1997* (Washington, D.C.: Office of Juvenile Justice and Delinquency Prevention, 2000), p. 1.
7. Patricia McFall Torbet, *Juvenile Probation: The Workhorse of the Juvenile Justice System* (Washington, D.C.: Office of Juvenile Justice and Delinquency Prevention, 1996), p. 2.
8. See Edwin M. Lemert and Forrest Dill, *Offenders in the Community* (Lexington, Mass.: D. C. Heath and Company, 1978), for more information on and evaluation of the probation act in California.
9. *Juvenile Probation Subsidy Program: An Evaluation* (Olympia, Wash.: Community Services Division, Department of Social and Health Services, 1975), p. 3.
10. Larry Grubb, a juvenile probation officer in Sangamon County, Illinois, was extremely helpful in shaping this section on the functions of probation.
11. Clifford Simonsen and Marshall S. Gordon III, *Juvenile Justice in America* (Encino, Calif.: Glencoe Publishing Co., 1979), p. 203.
12. Anne L. Schneider, "Restitution and Recidivism Rates of Juvenile Offenders: Results from Four Experimental Studies," *Criminology* 24 (1986), p. 533.
13. William G. Staples, "Restitution as a Sanction in Juvenile Court," *Crime and Delinquency* 32 (April 1986), p. 177.

14. Office of Juvenile Justice and Delinquency Prevention, *National Trends in Juvenile Restitution Programming* (Washington, D.C.: Government Printing Office, 1989), p. 3.
15. Anne L. Schneider, *Guide to Juvenile Restitution* (Washington, D.C.: U.S. Department of Justice, 1985), p. 1.
16. Ibid.
17. Albert R. Roberts, *Juvenile Justice: Policies, Programs, and Services* (Chicago: Dorsey, 1989) p. 134.
18. Information gained during an on-site visit and updated in a phone call to a staff member in September, 2001.
19. The results of a 1991 survey found in Peter R. Schneider and Matthew C. Finkelstein, *New Trends in Restitution Programming: Results from the 1991 RESTTA Survey* (Washington, D.C.: Office of Juvenile Justice and Delinquency Prevention, 1996).
20. See James Byrne, ed. *Federal Probation* 50 (1986) and Emily Walker, "The Community Intensive Treatment for Youth Program: A Specialized Community-Based Program for High-Risk Youth in Alabama," *Law and Psychology Review* 13 (1989), pp. 175–199.
21. Cecil Marshall and Keith Snyder, "Intensive and Aftercare Probation Services in Pennsylvania." Paper presented to the Annual Meeting of the American Society of Criminology, Baltimore, Maryland (November 7, 1990), p. 3.
22. For a review of these programs, see Clemens Bartollas and John P. Conrad, *Introduction to Corrections*, 2nd. ed. (New York: HarperCollins, 1992).
23. Ted Palmer, *The Re-Emergence of Correctional Intervention* (Newbury Park, Calif.: Sage, 1992), p. 82.
24. Barry Krisberg, *et al.*, *Juvenile Intensive Supervision Planning Guide* (Washington, D.C.: Office of Juvenile Justice and Delinquency Prevention, 1994), p. 7.

25. Joan Petersilia, *Expanding Options for Criminal Sentencing* (Santa Monica, Calif.: Rand, 1987), p. 32.

26. Richard A. Ball, Ronald Huff, and J. Robert Lilly, *House Arrest and Correctional Policy: Doing Time at Home* (Newbury Park, Calif.: Sage, 1988), pp. 35–36.

27. Annesley K. Schmidt, "Electronic Monitoring of Offenders Increases," in *Research in Action* (Washington, D.C.: U.S. Department of Justice, 1989), p. 3.

28. Ibid., p. 3.

29. Joseph B. Vaughn, "A Survey of Juvenile Electronic Monitoring and Home Confinement Programs," *Juvenile and Family Court Journal* 40 (1989), pp. 4, 22. For a description of another program, see Michael T. Charles, "The Development of a Juvenile Electronic Monitoring Program," *Federal Probation* 53 (1989), pp. 3–12.

30. Vaughn, "A Survey of Juvenile Electronic Monitoring and Home Confinement Program."

31. Oliver J. Keller, Jr. and Benedict S. Alper, *Halfway Houses: Community-Centered Correction and Treatment* (Lexington, Mass.: D. C. Heath, 1970).

32. LaMar T. Empey and Stephen Lubeck, *The Silverlake Experiment: Testing Delinquency Theory and Community Intervention.* (Chicago: Aldine, 1971).

33. D. L. Fixsen, E. L. Philllips, and M. M. Wolf, "The Teaching Family Model of Group Home Treatment," in *Closing Correctional Institutions,* edited by Yitzak Bakal (Lexington, Mass.: D. C. Heath, 1973).

34. Ronald H. Bailey, "Florida," *Corrections Magazine* 1 (September 1974), p. 66.

35. Information from Dynamic Action Resistance Enterprise (DARE), Jamaica Plain, Mass.

36. Refer to Robert L. Woodson, *A Summons to Life: Mediating Structure and the Prevention of Youth Crime* (Cambridge, Mass.: Ballinger, 1981), for the most up-to-date statement on the House of Umoja.

37. Information on Associated Marine Institute supplied in a phone conversation with Ms. Magie Valdès in 1996.

38. Ibid. See also Ronald H. Bailey, "Can Delinquents Be Saved by the Sea?" *Corrections Magazine* 1 (September 1974), pp. 77–84.

39. S. E. Laurence and B. R. West, *National Evaluation of the New Pride Replication Program: Final Report,* Vol. 1 (Lafayette, Calif.: Pacific Institute for Research and Evaluation, 1985).

40. Ibid.

41. Refer to Joshua L. Miner and Joe Boldt, *Outward Bound USA: Learning Through Experience* (New York: William Morrow, 1981). For recent examination of Outward Bound type programs, see Steven Flagg Scott, "Outward Bound: An Adjunct to the Treatment of Juvenile Delinquents: Florida's STEP Program," *New England Journal on Criminal and Civil Confinement* 11 (1985), pp. 420–436; and Thomas C. Castellano and Irina R. Soderstrom, "Wilderness Challenges and Recidivism: A Program Evaluation." Paper presented to the Annual Meeting of the American Society of Criminology, Baltimore, Maryland (November 1990).

42. Anthony W. Salerno, "Boot Camps: A Critique and a Proposed Alternative." *Journal of Offender Rehabilitation* 20 (1994), p. 148.

43. Quoted in Joshua L. Miner and Joe Boldt, *Outward Bound USA: Learning through Experience* (New York: William Morrow, 1981), pp. 327–328.

44. Paul Sweeney, "VisionQuest's Rite of Passage," *Corrections Magazine* 8 (February 1982), pp. 22–32. For a more critical evaluation of VisionQuest, see Peter W. Greenwood and Susan Turner, *The VisionQuest Program: An Evaluation* (Santa Monica, Calif.: Rand, 1987).

45. George M. Camp and Camille Graham Camp, *The Corrections Yearbook,* 1995 (South Salem, N.Y.: Criminal Justice Institute, 1995), p. 16.

46. Patricia McFall Torbet, *Organization and Administration of Juvenile Services: Probation, Aftercare, and State Delinquent Institutions* (Pittsburgh: National Center for Juvenile Justice, 1988), p. 23.

47. Dean J. Champion, *The Juvenile Justice System: Delinquency, Processing, and the Law* (New York: Macmillan, 1992), p. 446.

48. Michael D. Norman, "Discretionary Justice: Decision-Making in a State Juvenile Parole Board," *Juvenile and Family Court Journal* 37 (1986), pp. 19–25.

49. Elizabeth Piper Deschenes, Peter W. Greenwood, and Grant Marshall, *The Nokomis Challenge Program Evaluation* (Santa Monica, Calif.: Rand, 1996).

50. J. D. Howell, et al., eds., *Sourcebook on Serious, Violent, and Chronic Juvenile Offenders* (Thousand Oaks, Calif.: Sage Publications, 1995).

51. D. M. Altschuler and T. L. Armstrong, *Intensive Aftercare for High-Risk Juveniles: A Community Care Model* (Washington, D.C.: Office of Juvenile Justice and Delinquency Prevention, 1994).

52. Palmer, *The Re-Emergence of Correctional Intervention,* p. 86.

53. Henry Sontheimer, Lynne Goodstein, and Michael Kovacevic, *Philadelphia Intensive Aftercare Probation Evaluation Project* (Pittsburgh: Center for Juvenile Justice Training and Research, 1990), p. 3. See also Lynne Goodstein and Henry Sontheimer, "The Implementation of an Intensive Aftercare Program for Serious Juvenile Offenders: A Case Study," *Criminal Justice and Behavior* 24 (September 1997), pp. 332–359.

54. Ibid., p. x.

55. Marshall and Snyder, "Intensive and Aftercare Probation Services in Pennsylvania," p. 4. For a description of two other programs, see Peter W. Greenwood, Elizabeth Piper Deschenes, and Helen Giglio, "Research Design and Program Description for the Skillman Intensive Aftercare Experiment" (Santa Monica, Calif.: Rand Corp., 1989).

56. Don A. Josi and Dale K. Sechrest, "A Pragmatic Approach to Parole Aftercare Evaluation of a Community Reintegration Program for High-Risk Youthful Offenders," *Justice Quarterly* 16 (March 1999), p. 66.

57. William Degnan, *Lifeskills Post-Parole Treatment Program* Sanger, CA.: Operation, New Hope, 1994).

58. Josi and Sechrest, "A Pragmatic Approach to Parole Aftercare Evaluation of a Community Reintegration Program for High-Risk Youthful Offenders," p. 66.

59. David M. Altschuler and Troy L. Armstrong, *Intensive Aftercare for High-Risk Juveniles: Policies and Procedures*

(Washington, D.C.: Office of Juvenile Justice and Delinquency Prevention, 1994), p. 3.

60. For more extensive examination of these intensive aftercare programs, see Betsie McNulty, Rick Wiebush, and Thao Le, "Intensive Aftercare Programs for Serious Juvenile Offenders: Preliminary Results of Process and Outcome Evaluation." Paper presented to the Annual Meeting of the American Society of Criminology, Washington, D.C. (November 1998).

61. Richard G. Wiebush, Betsie McNulty, and Thao Le, *Implementation of the Intensive Community-Based Aftercare Program* (Washington, D.C.: Office of Juvenile Justice and Delinquency Prevention, 2000), p. 17.

62. For an example of a house detention component of an aftercare program, see W. H. Barton and Jeffrey A. Butts, "Visible Options: Intensive Supervision Program for Juvenile Delinquents," *Crime and Delinquency* (1990), pp. 238–256.

63. Andrew T. Seull, *Decarceration: Community Treatment and the Deviant—A Radical View* (Edgewood Cliffs, N.J.: Prentice-Hall, 1977), p. 43.

64. Ibid.

65. For a recent study that examined the effects of the closing of the Montrose training school in Maryland and found that "the noninstitutionalized group's recidivism was significantly higher than that of the institutionalized groups both during and after the period of institutionalization," see Denise C. Gottfredson and William H. Barton, "Deinstitutionalization of Juvenile Offenders," *Criminology* 31 (November 1993), pp. 591–66.

66. Frank F. Scarpitti and Richard M. Stephenson, "A Study of Probation Effectiveness," *Journal of Criminal Law, Criminology, and Police Science* 59 (1968), pp. 361–369.

67. For one of the more positive studies, see Barry Krisberg, James Austin, and Patricia A. Steele, *Unlocking Juvenile Corrections: Evaluating the Massachusetts Department of Youth Services* (San Francisco, Calif.: The National Council on Crime and Delinquency, 1989), p. 41.

68. Joseph Nold and Mary Wilpers, "Wilderness Training as an Alternative to Incarceration," in *A Nation without Prisons,* ed. Calvert R. Dodge (Lexington, Mass.: Heath, 1975), pp. 157–158.

69. For a more positive assessment, see Anne L. Schneider, "Restitution and Recidivism Rates of Juvenile Offenders: Results from Four Experimental Studies," *Criminology* 24 (1986), p. 533. For a critical assessment, see Eugene Doleschal, "The Dangers of Criminal Justice Reform," *Criminal Justice Abstracts* 14 (MArch 1982), p. 135.

chapter 17

INSTITUTIONS FOR JUVENILES

OBJECTIVES

After reading this chapter, the students will be able to answer the following questions:

- What types of experience do juveniles have in various institutional placements?

- Do some juveniles receive more benefit or harm from institutionalization than others? How effective are these institutions in correcting juvenile crime?

- What are juveniles' rights during institutional confinement?

- What can be done to improve juvenile correctional institutions in the United States?

*I*n 1910, Hastings Hart, a social reformer, declared that juvenile institutions are no substitute for the home:

However good an institution may be, however kindly in spirit, however genial its atmosphere, however homelike its cottages, however fatherly and motherly its officers, however admirable its training, it is now generally . . . agreed that institution life is at its best artificial and unnatural, and that the child ought to be returned at the earliest practicable moment to the more natural environment of the family.[1]

What is your evaluation of Hastings Hart's statement about the value of juvenile institutionalization? When is juvenile institutionalization necessary for a youth? What type of experience needs to be present for a juvenile correctional institution to be constructive or helpful?

Some observers feel that institutional placement does irreparable harm to juveniles and should no longer be used. Others look on institutionalization as a measure of last resort that should be used only when everything else has failed. Still others encourage the increased use of juvenile institutions because of their supposed deterrent effect on youth crime.

This chapter focuses on long-term juvenile institutional placements. They include reception or diagnostic centers, ranches and forestry camps, boot camps, and training schools. Juveniles can also be sent to adult prisons. See Figure 17.1 for these various long-term institutional placements for juveniles.

How Juvenile Institutions Have Evolved in the United States

Before the end of the eighteenth century, the family was commonly believed to be the source or cause of deviancy, and, therefore, the idea emerged that perhaps the well-adjusted family could provide the model for a correctional institution for children. The house of refuge, the first juvenile institution, reflected the family model wholeheartedly; it was designed to bring the order, discipline, and care of the family into institutional life. The institution was to become the home, the peers, the siblings, and the staff the parents.[2]

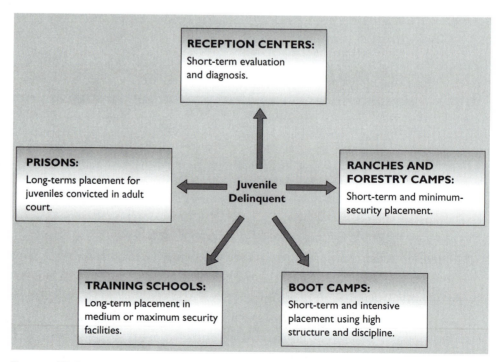

FIGURE 17.1 Long-Term Institutional Placements for Juveniles

The New York House of Refuge, which opened on January 1, 1825, with six girls and three boys, is usually acknowledged as the first house of refuge. Several similar institutions already existed in England and Europe.[3] Over the next decade or so, Boston, Philadelphia, Bangor, Richmond, Mobile, Cincinnati, and Chicago followed suit in establishing houses of refuge for males. Twenty-three schools were chartered in the 1830s and another thirty in the 1840s. Some houses of refuge were established by private philanthropists, some by the state government or legislature, and some jointly by public authorities and private organizations. The vast majority of the houses of refuge were for males. The average capacity was 210; the capacity ranged from 90 at Lancaster, Massachusetts, to 1000 at the New York House of Refuge for Boys.[4]

Although based on different correctional philosophies, these houses of refuge resembled existing state prisons and county jails. Some were surrounded by walls to maintain security. The buildings were usually four stories high; the five-by-eight-foot rooms were windowless and had iron-lattice slabs for doors. On entering the institution, youths were dressed in identical clothing and given identical haircuts. Troublemakers were punished by a diet of bread and water, solitary confinement, whipping with a cat-o'-nine-tails, or being manacled to a ball and chain.[5]

The development of the **cottage system** and the construction of these juvenile institutions outside cities were two reforms of the mid-nineteenth century. The cottage system was introduced in 1854 and quickly spread throughout the nation. This new system housed smaller groups of youths in separate buildings, usually no more than twenty to forty youths per cottage. Early cottages were log cabins; later cottages were built from brick or stone. Now called **training schools** or industrial schools, these juvenile facilities were usually constructed outside cities so that youths would be reformed through exposure to the simpler rural way of life. It was presumed that residents would learn responsibility and new skills as they worked the fields and took care of the livestock. Their work would enable the institution, in turn, to provide its own food and perhaps even realize a profit.

Barbara M. Brenzel's study of the State Industrial School for Girls in Lancaster, Massachusetts, the first state reform school for girls in the United States, revealed the growing disillusionment in the mid- to late-nineteenth century regarding training schools. Intended as a model reform effort, Lancaster was the first "family-style" institution on this continent and embodied new theories about the reformation of youths. But an "examination of a reform institution during the second half of the nineteenth century reveals the evolution from reformist visions and optimistic goals at mid-century to pessimism and 'scientific' determinism at the century's close." Brenzel added that "the mid-century ideal of rehabilitative care changed to the principle of rigid training and custodial care by the 1880s and remained so into the early twentieth century."[6]

Twentieth-Century Changes

Several significant changes occurred in juvenile institutionalization during the first several decades of the twentieth century. One change was that reformers advocated treatment on several fronts. Case studies were used to prescribe treatment plans for residents; reception units were developed to diagnose and classify new admissions; individual therapies, such as psychotherapy and behavior modification, were used; and group therapies, such as guided group interaction, became popular means of transforming the inmate subculture. Institutional programs also became more diverse. Confined juveniles could graduate from state-accredited high school programs; home furloughs and work release programs were permitted in many training schools to include printing, barbering, welding, and automobile repair. Furthermore, the types of juvenile correctional facilities increased to include ranches and forestry camps, as well as the traditional prison-like training schools. Finally, there were several experimental forms of training schools developed that offered the promise of changing juvenile corrections; see Treatment Intervention 17.1 for examples of experimental training schools.

TREATMENT INTERVENTION 17.1

Experimental Training Schools

The George Junior Republic in Freeville, New York, and the Whittier State Reform School in Whittier, California, were two innovative and experimental reform schools during the first half of the twentieth century.

THE GEORGE JUNIOR REPUBLIC

William "Daddy" George was probably the most known innovator in juvenile corrections in the early twentieth century. His educational ideas and conservative economic principles in the Juvenile Republic in Freeville, New York won him a large following in both the United States and eventually throughout the Western world.

The basic organizational feature of the Junior Republic was inmate self-government. In an attempt to recreate the democratic political structure of the United States, inmates were elected as president, senator, and representative, and the residents' day-to-day life was regulated by this peer leadership. The Junior Republic also established such community institutions as banks, stores, police, and a judiciary to resolve conflicts. The Junior Republic further issued its own money and expected every resident to earn his keep.

The moral principle of "nothing without labor" undergirded the legal framework of the Junior Republic. George offered residents regular opportunities to earn a sufficient income to pay for basic food and lodging and to accumulate savings. This pioneer did not hesitate to punish sloth and foolishness. The "nothing without labor" principle did not result in starvation or exposure for uncooperative or lazy residents, but it did mean that residents would be sentenced to the Junior Republic's jail, which would be followed by a symbolic "repayment" for upkeep by being forced to crush stones.

WHITTIER STATE REFORM SCHOOL

Whittier, California's principal correctional institution for delinquent boys, was known for its attempt to implement the individual treatment ideal. In 1912, Fred Nelles, a Los Angeles businessman, was appointed as superintendent at Whittier. Nelles first rebuilt the institution according to the cottage rather than the congregate design. As was true with private training schools in both the United States and Europe, Nelles exerted considerable control over admissions. He was able to exclude boys over the age of sixteen and those who scored low on intelligence tests.

Nelles made clinical diagnosis of residents' behavior problems the centerpiece of his treatment plans. With the participation of the psychology departments at UCLA and Stanford, Nelles developed his own research departments to provide extensive psychological testing and, to a lessor extent, psychiatric counseling of residents. The research department's prime objectives were to formulate individual treatment plans that took into consideration residents' special needs and to pursue scientific studies into the causes and cures of delinquent behavior.

Residents had minimal restraints on their movements within the institution. They rarely marched in formation. No fences or guards prevented escape. The boys wore their own clothing, rather than institutional uniforms. Academic school, vocational training, and experience in teamwork, especially through athletics, were the main vehicles through which Nelles sought to transform residents' character. Whittier even sponsored a thriving Boy Scouts program. Corporal punishment was prohibited. The most severe and rarely used punishment was the assignment to a room in the lost-privilege cottage. But even here, residents received normal food provisions and were frequently interviewed to determine whether they were ready to resume regular activities.

How was responsibility at the very heart of the Junior Republic's model of institutional care? What is your evaluation of George's model of juvenile institutionalization? How did Nelles' view of the delinquent differ from that of George? What is your evaluation of Nelles' model of juvenile institutionalization? What is your design of how juveniles should be handled in long-term institutional care?

Source: Steven Schlossman, "Delinquent Children: The Juvenile Reform School," in *The Oxford History of the Prison: The Practice of Punishment in Western Society* (New York: Oxford University Press, 1995), pp. 377–381.

In spite of the improvements in many reform schools, as well as the truly experimental efforts in a few, the story of the twentieth-century training school is one of scaled-down prisons for juveniles.[7] In the 1960s and 1970s, reformers began to accuse training schools of being violent, inhumane, and criminogenic.[8]

The widespread criticisms of training schools, along with court decisions and pressure groups in the legislature, led to a number of reforms in the mid- and late-1970s. These innovations included no longer confining status offenders with delinquents in training schools, an increase in staff training programs, the growing acceptance of grievance procedures for residents, and the establishment of coeducational facilities.

In the late 1980s and 1990s, a number of disturbing changes took place in juvenile institutionalization. Training schools became overcrowded and more violent. Members of minorities made up a greater proportion of the population of juvenile correctional institutions, especially for drug offenses. Status offenders, as well as juveniles who had committed non-serious delinquent acts, continued to be committed to private training schools, but private placements also began to admit youngsters who had committed serious delinquent offenses. More youths were transferred to adult court for violent crimes and received long-term prison sentences (see Table 17.1, Time Line of Juvenile Institutionalization).

The Types of Institutional Placement for Juveniles

Reception centers, ranches and forestry camps, boot camps, and training schools are the main forms of juvenile correctional institutions. In the final decades of the twentieth century, juveniles were also increasingly sent to adult prisons. Private facilities play a significant role in the long-term custody of juveniles. In fact, there are more than twice as many privately operated juvenile facilities as there are publicly operated facilities. Yet private facilities hold less than half as many confined offenders as are held in public institutions.[9]

The newest information on juveniles in custody is drawn from the Census of Juveniles in Residential Placement (CJRP). Administered for the first time in 1997 by the Bureau of the Census for the Office of Juvenile Justice and Delinquency Prevention (OJJDP), the CJRP replaced the Census of Public and Private Juvenile Detention, Correctional, and

TABLE 17.1

Time Line of Juvenile Institutionalization

Date	Event
1825	New York House of Refuge was opened.
1854	Cottage system was introduced.
1850s and 1960s	Juvenile facilities were called training schools or industrial schools.
1880–1899	The public was disillusioned, realizing that training schools were primarily custodial institutions.
1900–1950	Training schools underwent a period of reform, especially with the introduction of varied forms of treatment.
1960s and 1970s	Training schools came under great criticism.
Late 1970S	Training schools underwent another period of reform.
Late 1980s and 1990s	Training schools became overcrowded, more violent, and confined increased numbers of minority youths.

Shelter Facilities (better known as the Children in Custody (CIC) Census), which had been conducted since the early 1970s.[10]

On October 29, 1997, 125,805 young persons were assigned beds in 1,121 public and 2,310 private facilities in the United States. Of these, 105,790 (84 percent) met the criteria for the census (under age 21, assigned a bed on October 29, 1997, charged with an offense or court-adjudicated for an offense, and placed in residential placement because of that offense). Figure 17.2 lists the numbers and percentages of juveniles in public and private facilities in 1997.

Reception and Diagnostic Centers

The purpose of **reception and diagnostic centers,** which are under the sponsorship of either public or private jurisdictions, is to determine which treatment plan suits each adjudicated youth and which training school is the best placement. In 1990, 21,591 youths were admitted to reception centers, 86 percent of whom had committed delinquent offenses.[11]

The evaluation of each resident used to take four to six weeks, but the process has been condensed today to an average length of thirty-four days. Evaluations are normally done by a psychiatrist, a clinical psychologist, a social worker, academic staff, and a chaplain. The psychiatrist does a psychiatric evaluation and the psychologist administers a battery of psychological tests measuring intelligence, attitude, maturity, and emotional problems. The social worker, meanwhile, develops a social case study of each youth. The academic staff during this orientation period determines the proper school placement and attempts to identify any debilitating learning problems. Physical and dental examinations also typically are given to the youth at this time. Finally, child-care workers in living units evaluate institutional adjustment and peer relationships. When all the reports have been prepared, a case conference is held on each resident to summarize that youth's needs and attitudes and recommend the best institutional placement.

In large youth commissions or departments of youth services, the recommendation must be approved by an institutional coordinator. After it is approved, the youth is transferred to the selected institution, accompanied by the diagnostic report. Because many training schools have their own orientation programs, however, it is not unusual for the report to receive little attention and for the youth to undergo nearly the same process again in the reception cottage.

Ranches and Forestry Camps

Minimum-security institutions, such as ranches and forestry camps, are typically reserved for youths who have committed minor crimes and for those who have been committed to the youth authority or private corrections for the first time. **Forestry camps** are popular in a number of states. Of the sixty-four camps in the United States in 1992, sixteen were in Florida; fourteen in New York; six in South Carolina; five each in Alabama, California, Missouri, and North Carolina; and four each in Maryland and Oregon.[12] Residents usually do conservation work in a state park, including cleaning up, cutting grass and weeds, and general maintenance. Treatment programs usually consist of group therapy, individual contacts with social workers and the child-care staff, and one or two home visits a month. Residents also may be taken to a nearby town on a regular basis to make purchases and to attend community events. Escapes are a constant problem because of the nonsecure nature of these facilities.

Private and county **ranches** are especially widely used in California and several other states. In 1990, ranches admitted 17,606 youths, or 13 percent of the confined juveniles. The average length of stay was 6.5 months (194 days), which was only one month less than the average length of stay in training schools (7.5 months, or 225 days). Significantly, 32 percent of African Americans were confined to ranches, compared with 47 percent in training schools.[13]

Nationally, 74% of juveniles are held in public facilities in the state where they committed their offense, 24% are held in in-state private facilities, and 2% are held in out-of-state private facilities.

State*	Juveniles in custody	In-state Public facilities	In-state Private facilities	Out-of-state private facilities	State*	Juveniles in custody	In-state Public facilities	In-state Private facilities	Out-of-state private facilities
U.S. total	105,790	74%	24%	2%	Missouri	1,401	81%	19%	0%
Alabama	1,685	54	46	0	Montana	302	56	14	29
Alaska	352	75	25	0	Nebraska	741	69	22	10
Arizona	1,868	86	13	1	Nevada	857	97	3	0
Arkansas	603	59	41	0	New Hampshire	186	65	30	5
California	19,899	91	8	1	New Jersey	2,251	97	3	0
Colorado	1,748	48	40	12	New Mexico	778	95	4	1
Connecticut	1,326	74	24	2	New York	4,661	56	44	1
Delaware	311	67	5	28	North Carolina	1,204	89	10	0
Dist. of Columbia	265	65	32	3	North Dakota	272	36	58	6
Florida	5,975	50	48	2	Ohio	4,318	91	8	1
Georgia	3,622	85	15	0	Oklahoma	808	65	34	0
Hawaii	134	84	9	7	Oregon	1,462	80	20	0
Idaho	242	70	14	17	Pennsylvania	3,962	37	58	5
Illinois	3,425	93	5	2	Rhode Island	426	79	20	0
Indiana	2,485	66	31	2	South Carolina	1,583	88	12	0
Iowa	1,064	38	60	3	South Dakota	528	83	16	1
Kansas	1,242	67	32	0	Tennessee	2,118	57	43	0
Kentucky	1,079	75	25	0	Texas	6,898	86	13	0
Louisiana	2,776	63	36	0	Utah	768	52	42	6
Maine	318	80	16	4	Vermont	49	44	36	20
Maryland	1,498	51	48	1	Virginia	2,879	93	7	0
Massachusetts	1,065	35	64	0	Washington	2,216	94	6	0
Michigan	3,710	53	42	5	West Virginia	398	54	28	18
Minnesota	1,522	58	34	8	Wisconsin	2,013	70	30	0
Mississippi	756	99	0	1	Wyoming	340	50	49	1

Percent of juveniles held in public in-state facilities

- Mississippi placed the largest proportion of juveniles in public in-state facilities (99%).

- Massachusetts placed the largest proportion of juveniles in private in-state facilities (64%).

- Montana placed the largest proportion of juveniles in out-of-state private facilities (29%).

- Among states placing juveniles in out-of-state private facilities, most placed more juveniles in private in-state facilities. The exceptions were Delaware, Idaho, and Montana: each placed more juveniles in out-of-state private facilities than in in-state private facilities.

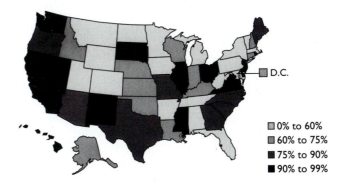

D.C.

■ 0% to 60%
■ 60% to 75%
■ 75% to 90%
■ 90% to 99%

FIGURE 17.2 Residential Placement of Juveniles in Public and Private Facilities

*State where the offense occurred.

Note: U.S. total includes 3,401 juveniles in private facilities for whom state of offense was not reported and 91 juveniles in out-of-state public facilities.

Source: Howard N. Snyder and Melissa Sickmund, *Juvenile Offenders and Victims: 1999 National Report* (Washington, D.C.: National Center for Juvenile Justice, 1999), p. 191. Authors' analysis of data from OJJDP's *Census of Juveniles in Residential Placement 1997* [machine-readable data file].

A resident in the Hennepin County Day School is spending some time with two horses. Riding horses and canoeing on a lake on the grounds are two of the activities that make this placement very different from most institutional settings.

Horseback riding is a popular recreational activity on ranches, but work details usually consist of taking care of the livestock, working in the garden, and performing general maintenance duties. Guided group interaction is the most widely used treatment, and one or two home visits a month give residents an opportunity to reintegrate themselves into community living.

Residents are generally much more positive about a placement at a forestry camp or ranch than about placement at a training school. They like both the more relaxed approach to security and the more frequent community contact. Residents also respond to the generally shorter stays at these minimum-security institutions, and, given the looser atmosphere of these settings, it is not surprising that they have better relations with staff members here than in training schools. Yet some youths who are homesick or are victimized by peers cannot handle these settings and repeatedly run away until they are transferred to more secure institutions. For a description of the Hennepin County Home School, see Treatment Intervention 17.2.

Boot Camps

Boot camps for youthful offenders, like those for adult offenders, are a relatively recent phenomenon. Emphasizing military discipline, physical training, and regimented activity for periods typically ranging from 30 to 120 days, the intent of these programs is to shock juvenile delinquents from committing further crimes.

The rationale for juvenile boot camps is consistent with the juvenile justice system's historical emphasis on rehabilitation, usually incorporating explicit assumptions about the needs of delinquent youths and providing remedial, counseling, and aftercare programs necessary to address these needs.[14] All the programs employ military customs and courtesies, including uniformed drill instructors, a platoon structure, and summary punishment of participants, including group punishment under some circumstances. Although there are differences in emphasis, with Denver creating the most militaristic environment, juvenile boot camp programs have generally discovered that they must tailor their environment to participants' maturity levels.[15]

TREATMENT INTERVENTION 17.2

Hennepin County Home School

The Hennepin County Home School (HCHS), is a state licensed residential institution for juvenile males and females between the ages of 13 and 18 who have been committed by the Hennepin County Juvenile Court. This innovative facility, which combines features of camps and ranches, is located on a beautiful 167-acre wooded site in Minnetonka, Minnesota approximately seventeen miles from downtown Minneapolis. The campus includes seven 24-bed residential cottages, a school facility with a full gymnasium, an administration and services building with a 16-bed secure internal support unit, a new 16-bed transitional living unit (TLU) and a horse barn and arena. The campus also includes playfields and is on a lake. The County Home School is licensed for 168 open and 16 secure beds.

The Adolescent Male Treatment Program (Cottages 5, 6, and 7) is a corrective treatment program with development specialization for residents who have committed major property offenses and crimes against persons. The length of commitment is determined by the juvenile court and ranges from 10 to 13 months, including a 45-day transition and a 2-month furlough component during which time the juvenile returns to the community at the conclusion of his institutional stay. The Female Offender Program (Cottage 2) is a corrective treatment program for property and person offenders. The length of the commitment is determined by the juvenile court and ranges from 10 to 13 months with a specialized 45-day transition and a minimum 2-month furlough. The Juvenile Sex Offender Program (Cottage 3) is a corrective treatment program for boys who have committed sexual offenses. The length of the commitment is indeterminate, with a furlough option after 12 months. The Beta Program (Cottage 1) is for less serious offenders. The length of stay is three to six weeks and the focus of the program's activities is on work for repayment of court-ordered restitution and public service projects.

One of the exciting new programs is the Intensive Aftercare Program. Residents are offered a continuum of services to meet their full range of needs, including successful community reintegration and aftercare. This continuum of care model reflects the Intensive Community Based Aftercare Model (IAP) developed by the Office of Juvenile Justice and Delinquency Prevention (OJJDP). The County School's IAP model includes six interwined phases: Assessment, case planning, institutional treatment, pre-release, transition, and community reintegration.

Superintendent Theresa E. Wise had this to say about County School:

> The value of Hennepin County School is that we provide a safe and secure environment where the youth has an opportunity to look at himself or herself. Some youth are afraid at home and school, and we want them to be and feel safe here. This institution believes that a safe and secure environment helps youth internalize change. We are also concerned about the whole youth, and, therefore, we attempt to partner with the external community and work with families.

What does the photograph of the resident and the horses suggest about this school? How does this facility seem to be different from the average public or private training school? Why is the continuum of care model such an important program?

Source: Information received in brochures, other materials developed by the Hennepin County Home School, and the Web page of the County Home School. Interview conducted in January 2002.

Boot camps for juveniles are generally reserved for midrange offenders, those who have failed with lesser sanctions such as probation but who are not yet hardened delinquents. The shock aspect of the boot camp experience includes incarceration as the environment within which the program takes place.[16] These programs typically focus on youths in their mid to late teens and exclude sex offenders, armed robbers, and violent offenders. Yet only a few programs limit themselves to nonviolent youths who have

A teen participant is having some problems with a sergeant in a boot camp program. Recent charges of abusive treatment is resulting in several states reassessing the value of boot camp programs.

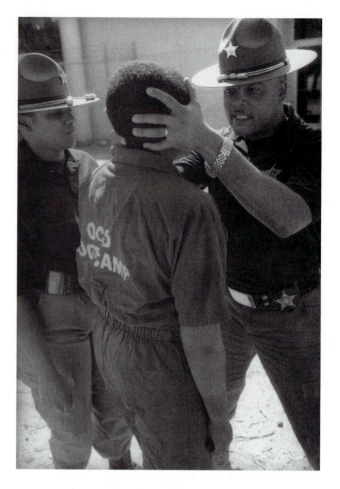

committed their first serious offense, or are being confined for the first time. For example, the Orleans Parish program accepts anyone who is sentenced by the juvenile judge.[17]

As of 1999, ten states had implemented about 50 boot camps which housed about 4,500 juvenile offenders nationwide. The oldest program was established in Orleans Parish, Louisiana, in 1985. Three of the newer programs—located in Cleveland, Denver, and Mobile—are funded through the Office of Juvenile Justice and Delinquency Prevention (OJJDP), which launched a three-site study of boot camps for youthful offenders in 1991.

The program guidelines of these three experimental programs identified six key components to maximize their effectiveness: education and job training and placement, community service, substance abuse counseling and treatment, health and mental health care, individualized and continuous case management, and intensive aftercare services. The 1994 evaluation of the three sites found that the sites were unable to implement the program guidelines fully. Each program "experienced considerable instability and staff turnover" and was unable to "implement and sustain stable, well-developed aftercare services."[18]

Boot camps for juveniles include some type of work detail; most allocate more than half the day to educational and counseling activities and most include some form of drug and alcohol counseling. In addition, most of the boot camp programs assign graduates to a period of intensive community supervision.[19]

A fair assessment may be that the quality of boot camps depends largely on how much they tailor their programs to participants' maturity levels and how effective they are in implementing and sustaining effective aftercare services. Doris McKenzie and colleagues recently completed a study of twenty-six juvenile boot camps, comparing them with traditional facilities (the experiences of 2,668 juveniles in twenty-six boot camps were compared to 1,848 juveniles in twenty-two traditional facilities).[20] They found that over all, juveniles in boot camps perceived their environments as more positive or therapeutic, less hostile or dangerous, and more structured than juveniles in traditional facilities perceived their environments. Moreover, this study revealed that over time, youths in boot camps became less antisocial and less depressed than youths in traditional facilities.[21]

Other follow-ups on juvenile boot camps have almost all found recidivism rates of boot camps to be slightly higher or about the same as those of traditional juvenile facilities.[22] Charges of abuse in boot camps have taken place in Arizona, Maryland, South Dakota, and Georgia. In the summer of 1999, a 14-year-old girl in South Dakota died from dehydration during a long-distance run.[23] In July 1, 2001, Anthony Haynes, a 14-year-old boy from Arizona, died at a boot camp where troubled juveniles were allegedly kicked and forced to eat mud. In this camp, the regimen includes forced marches, in-your-face discipline, and a daily diet of an apple, a carrot, and a bowl of beans.[24]

The combined disappointing recidivism results, as well as the charges of abuse, have prompted Georgia, Maryland, Arizona, and South Dakota to shut down or reevaluate the get tough with juveniles approach popularized in the early 1990s. Arizona removed fifty juveniles from the boot camp in which Haynes died. Maryland shut down one boot camp and suspended the military regimens at its other two facilities after reports of systematic assaults. In Maryland, the charges of abuse led to the ouster of the state's top five juvenile justice officials.[25]

Panaceas die hard in juvenile corrections, and this highly acclaimed approach of the past two decades will continue to be used across the nation. Its recent criticisms and disappointing recidivism data probably will result in fewer new programs being established and more scrutiny of the existing programs.

Public and Private Training Schools

Some training schools look like prisons. Others resemble college campuses, and still others have a home-like atmosphere. Yet, regardless of what they look like, training schools are used more today than they were in the 1970s and 1980s. Crowding has been one of the consequences of this growth in juvenile institutionalization. In 1995, more than 70 percent of long-term juvenile facilities were considered crowded (over capacity), compared with 62 percent in 1991.[26]

Training schools represent an extremely expensive way for a state to handle delinquent youths. In constant 1994 dollars, the total operational expenditures for juvenile facilities in the United States increased from $2.4 billion in 1975 to $3.8 billion in 1994, which is more than a 50 percent increase in the real cost of incarcerating juveniles. The average yearly per-resident operating costs for public juvenile facilities increased only 3 percent from 1975 to 1995, from $31,590 to $32,488. But private juvenile facilities skyrocketed in cost per resident from $21,215 in 1975 to $45,710 in 1995, nearly a 75 percent increase.[27]

The increase in population of juveniles in custody from 1975 to 1997 is almost entirely attributable to an increase in the number of males held in custody. On October 29, 1997, 86 percent of juveniles in residential placement were male. Minority males, as previously suggested, make up an increasingly larger segment of juveniles held in custody. On December 31, 1979, 13,752 African American juveniles were in custody, whereas on February 15, 1995, there were 43,268, more than a threefold increase. For Hispanic juveniles, the corresponding increase was from 4,395 in 1979 to 18,653 in 1995, more than a fourfold increase. In 1997, the proportion of minority youngsters in custody had exploded to 40 percent African American and 18 percent Hispanic.[28] See Table 17.2 for the percentage of minorities in residential placement and their offenses in 1997.

Juvenile males and females varied somewhat in the offenses for which they were held in custody in 1995. Person offenders accounted for 25 percent and property offenders for 30 percent of those juveniles in custody. States varied in the offense profile of juveniles in residential placement (See Figure 17.3).

TABLE 17.2

Percentage of Minorities Confined in Residential Placements and Their Charges in 1997

| Most serious offense | Total | Percentage of juvenile offenders in residential placement on October 29, 1997 | | | | |
		White	Black	Hispanic	American Indian	Asian
TOTAL JUVENILES IN RESIDENTIAL PLACEMENT	100%	37%	40%	18%	2%	2%
DELINQUENCY	100	36	41	19	1	2
Person	100	31	43	21	1	3
Criminal homicide	100	19	44	30	2	5
Sexual assault	100	51	33	12	2	1
Robbery	100	16	55	24	1	3
Aggravated assault	100	26	41	26	2	4
Simple assault	100	41	38	16	2	2
Other person	100	41	40	15	1	2
Property	100	43	35	17	2	2
Burglary	100	46	32	18	2	2
Theft	100	45	37	15	1	1
Auto theft	100	36	38	20	2	3
Arson	100	52	29	17	1	1
Other property	100	42	38	16	1	2
Drug	100	23	56	19	1	1
Trafficking	100	14	64	21	<1	1
Other drug	100	26	54	18	1	1
Public order	100	38	38	20	2	2
Weapons	100	24	45	27	1	3
Other public order	100	48	33	15	2	2
Technical violation	100	40	37	19	2	1
*Violent Crime Index**	100	27	45	23	1	3
*Property Crime Index***	100	43	35	17	2	2
STATUS OFFENSE	100	59	30	7	2	1

- Non-Hispanic black juveniles accounted for more than 6 in 10 juveniles in residential placement for drug trafficking and more than 5 in 10 in residential placement for other drug offenses.
- Non-Hispanic white juveniles accounted for the majority of juveniles in residential placement for sexual assault, arson, and status offenses

Note: Race proportions do not include persons of Hispanic ethnicity. Detail may not total 100% because of rounding.
*Includes criminal homicide, sexual assault, robbery, and aggravated assault.
**Includes burglary, theft, auto theft, and arson.

Source: Howard N. Snyder and Melissa Sickmund, *Juvenile Offenders and Victims: 1999 National Report* (Washington, D.C.: National Center for Juvenile Justice, 1999), p. 195. Authors' analysis of OJJDP's *Census of Juveniles in Residential Placement 1997* [machine-readable data file].

Youth gangs are becoming a serious problem in some training schools. In California Youth Authority, for example, gangs dominate daily life in bulging dormitories, in crowded cafeterias, and on the recreational fields.[29] In Steve Lerner's study on violence at Preston, he concluded that "the open dorms at the Youth Authority have become so vicious with the increasingly dense overcrowding that many inmates feel they have to join a gang in order to purchase protection."[30] The gang organization that is present in the California Youth Authority is relatively absent in training schools

The offense profile of juveniles in residential placement varies considerably from state to state.

State*	Person Violent	Other person	Property	Drugs	Public order	Status	State*	Person Violent	Other person	Property	Drugs	Public order	Status
U.S. total	25%	8%	30%	9%	21%	7%	Missouri	18%	6%	38%	7%	15%	16%
Alabama	11	7	35	7	29	12	Montana	17	12	29	6	23	14
Alaska	19	15	24	1	36	5	Nebraska	8	12	50	6	16	9
Arizona	16	8	36	10	27	4	Nevada	16	8	33	15	28	<1
Arkansas	16	13	38	5	20	7	New Hampshire	11	37	28	5	10	10
California	38	5	27	7	22	1	New Jersey	23	4	17	21	32	3
Colorado	22	13	32	6	24	3	New Mexico	24	11	35	5	24	1
Connecticut	16	11	19	24	26	5	New York	23	10	23	13	11	20
Delaware	23	9	33	12	23	<1	North Carolina	23	11	43	6	12	4
Dist. of Columbia	23	5	19	34	16	3	North Dakota	8	12	28	5	11	36
Florida	22	10	37	9	21	1	Ohio	25	8	34	7	22	4
Georgia	20	11	30	8	28	3	Oklahoma	31	7	35	4	18	6
Hawaii	22	19	27	1	22	9	Oregon	41	7	37	4	8	2
Idaho	14	12	36	2	37	0	Pennsylvania	20	10	27	11	22	10
Illinois	33	4	25	13	25	1	Rhode Island	28	12	23	15	20	2
Indiana	11	13	31	7	21	17	South Carolina	19	9	27	5	36	4
Iowa	16	11	36	10	14	13	South Dakota	14	12	28	7	27	13
Kansas	23	9	30	7	14	19	Tennessee	19	6	22	6	19	28
Kentucky	22	13	32	6	18	10	Texas	28	9	33	8	21	2
Louisiana	26	8	38	13	10	5	Utah	16	4	28	6	37	11
Maine	19	12	46	2	12	8	Vermont	6	29	31	2	16	16
Maryland	17	9	32	24	16	2	Virginia	20	9	26	7	34	5
Massachusetts	41	15	25	8	11	<1	Washington	32	8	33	5	20	1
Michigan	27	9	31	7	16	11	West Virginia	22	10	34	11	10	14
Minnesota	18	13	33	4	22	11	Wisconsin	16	13	34	8	23	6
Mississippi	21	3	40	9	25	1	Wyoming	8	11	33	13	16	20

Percent of juveniles held for Violent Crime Index offenses

- Nationally, 25% of the juveniles in residential facilities were charged with Violent Crime Index offenses. States with the highest proportions of Violent Crime Index offenders were Massachusetts (41%), Oregon (41%), and California (38%). Vermont (6%), Nebraska (8%), North Dakota (8%), and Wyoming (8%), had the lowest proportions.

- Most States had a large population of property offenders. Nebraska led he Nation with 50%. New Jersey and the District of Columbia were the only jurisdictions with less than 20% property offenders.

- The proportion of juveniles held for drug offenses ranged from 34% in the District of Columbia to 1% in Alaska and Hawaii.

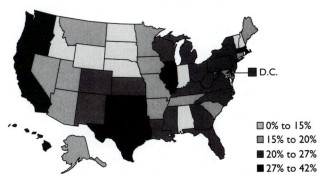

- D.C.

☐ 0% to 15%
■ 15% to 20%
■ 20% to 27%
■ 27% to 42%

FIGURE 17.3 Offense Profile of Juveniles in Residential Placement

*State where the offense occurred.

Note: U.S. total includes 3,401 juveniles in private facilities for whom state of offense was not reported.

Source: Howard N. Snyder and Melissa Sickmund, *Juvenile Offenders and Victims: 1999 National Report* (Washington, D.C.: National Center for Juvenile Justice, 1999), p. 190. Authors' analysis of data from OJJDP's *Census of Juveniles in Residential Placement 1997* [machine-readable data file].

elsewhere, but gang members are increasingly being sentenced to public training schools in other states.

L. Thomas Winfree Jr. and G. Larry Mays's study of three juvenile institutions in New Mexico revealed that up to 33 percent of those confined were gang members or had pro-gang attitudes.[31] The National Gang Crime Research Center's national survey of 1,015 gang members found that two juvenile correctional institutions in Ohio confined 268 gang youths, and a juvenile facility in Michigan confined sixty-one gang youths.[32] In addition, the Maclaren Training School in Portland, Oregon, the Ethan Allen School in Wales, Wisconsin, and the School for Boys in Eldora, Iowa have found it necessary to develop treatment programs for their increasingly expanding numbers of gang members.[33]

The larger states, such as California, Illinois, Michigan, and New York, have several training schools each.[34] Smaller states commonly have one training school for boys and another for girls. Massachusetts and Vermont have no training schools. Coeducational institutions gained some acceptance in the 1970s, when several states opened one or more coeducational campuses, but that trend seems to have passed.

The physical structure of training schools ranges from the homelike atmosphere of small cottages, to open dormitories that provide little privacy, to fortresslike facilities that have individual cells and fences. The level of security is usually higher for public than for private facilities because a larger proportion of the public facilities are detention centers designed to control residents' movement through staff monitoring and physical restrictions, such as fences.[35] See Figure 17.4 for the increase in security measures for public and private facilities from 1979 to 1995.

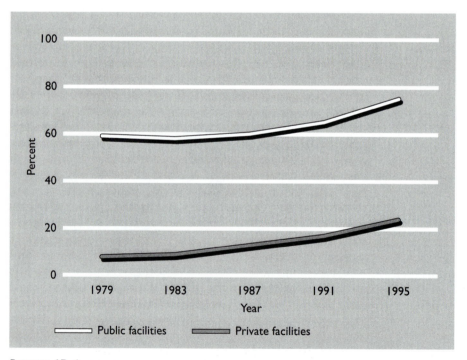

FIGURE 17.4 The Percentage of Public and Private Facilities, in which the Movement of Residents Is Controlled through Staff Monitoring of Entrances and Exits or through Locks, Bars, and Fences, Has Steadily Increased from 1979 to 1995.

Source: Office of Juvenile Justice and Delinquency Prevention, *Children in Custody, 1985–1995: Census of Public and Private Juvenile Detention, Correctional, and Shelter Facilities* (Washington, D.C.: Office of Justice Programs, 1999), Tables 25 and 26.

The programs that public and private training schools offer are superior to those of other juvenile institutions. The medical and dental services that residents receive tend to be very good. Most larger training schools have a full-time nurse on duty during the day and a physician who visits one or more days a week. Although institutionalized delinquents typically are unhappy with the medical and dental care they receive, most youths still receive far better medical and dental care than they did before they were confined.

The educational program is usually accredited by the state and is able to grant a high school diploma. According to the 1991 survey of juvenile facilities across the United States, the majority of training schools offer classes to prepare residents for the general equivalency diploma (GED) examination (63 percent). College preparation classes are also provided in an increasing number of training schools (19 percent). Furthermore, basic education classes are usually available, consisting of a review of the basic skills for reading, writing, and mathematics (95 percent). Special education (81 percent) and literacy or remedial reading (84 percent) are also provided in most of this nation's training schools.[36] Classes tend to be small, and students are permitted to progress at a rate that fits their needs. Yet a visit to a typical classroom in a training school does not produce a favorable impression; many students are bored, and a few may even be asleep.

According to a 1991 survey of juvenile facilities, vocational training provided by training schools consists of such courses as auto shop/engine repair (12 percent), carpentry/building trades (67 percent), cosmetology (12 percent), computer training (39 percent), food services (55 percent), electrical trades (21 percent), secretarial trades (18 percent), retail/sales (10 percent), printing (30 percent), forestry/agriculture (35 percent), and laundry services (17 percent).[37] Vocational training is generally not helpful in finding future employment. Residents have difficulty being admitted to the necessary labor unions after release, but a few residents do leave the institution and find excellent jobs with the skills they have learned.

The rehabilitation of juvenile delinquents remains the established purpose of most training schools. In the twentieth century, every conceivable method has been used in the effort to rehabilitate residents so they will refrain from unlawful behavior. The treatment technologies that are still in use include classification systems, treatment modalities, skill development, and prerelease programs. The most widely used treatment modalities are transactional analysis, reality therapy, psychotherapy, behavior modification, guided group interaction, positive peer culture, and drug and alcohol treatment. Rational therapy, sometimes called the "errors-in-thinking modality" or Cognitive Thinking Skills Program (CTSP), is the new treatment modality in juvenile corrections and recently has been implemented in a number of private and public training schools across the nation.

Mark W. Lipsey, David B. Wilson, and Lynn Cothern, in their meta-analysis of eighty-three studies on interventions with institutionalized offenders, found that seventy-four involved youthful offenders in the custody of juvenile justice institutions and nine involved residential institutions that were administered by mental health or private agencies. All juveniles in these placements had committed serious delinquencies that warranted confinement or close supervision in an institutional setting.[38] Table 17.3 reveals treatment types in order of effectiveness with both noninstitutionalized and institutionalized offenders.

One of the serious shortcomings of programming in many training schools is the lack of attention given to the needs of the adjudicated female offenders. The 1992 Amendment to the 1974 Juvenile Justice and Delinquency Prevention Act addressed the issue of gender bias, as it required states to analyze the need, types, and delivery of gender-specific services. As an example of gender bias treatment, a comparative study of 348 violent juvenile females and a similar number of males found that half the males were admitted to rehabilitative or alternative programs, but only 29.5 percent of females received treatment in any form.[39]

Recreation has always been emphasized in training schools. Male residents are usually offered such competitive sports as softball, volleyball, flag football, basketball, and sometimes even boxing or wrestling. Cottages may compete against each other, and the institution may have a team that competes against other institutional teams. Other

TABLE 17.3

A Comparison of Treatment Types in Order of Effectiveness

Types of Treatment Used with Noninstitutionalized Offenders	Types of Treatment Used with Institutionalized Offenders
Positive effects, consistent evidence	
Individual counseling	Interpersonal skills
Interpersonal skills	Teaching family homes
Behavioral programs	
Positive effects, less consistent evidence	
Multiple services	Behavioral programs
Restitution, probation/parole	Community residential
	Multiple services
Mixed but generally positive effects, inconsistent evidence	
Employment related training	Individual counseling
Academic programs	Guilded group counseling
Advocacy/casework	Group counseling
Family counseling	
Group Counseling	
Weak or no effects, inconsistent evidence	
Reduced caseload, probation/parole	Employment related training
	Drug abstinence
	Wilderness/challenge
Weak or no effects, consistent evidence	
Wilderness/challenge	Milieu therapy
Early release, probation/parole	
Deterrence programs	
Vocational programs	

Source: Mark W. Lipsey, David B. Wilson, and Lynn Cothern, "Effective Intervention for Serious Juvenile Offenders (Washington, D.C.: Juvenile Justice Bulletin; Office of Juvenile Justice and Delinquency Prevention, 2000), p. 5.

popular recreational activities include attending weekly movies; building model cars; participating in talent shows, dramatics, and choir; decorating the cottage during holidays; and playing ping pong, pool, and chess. Some training schools offer sailing or canoeing for residents, some have swimming pools, and some sponsor dances with residents of nearby training schools.

Religious instruction and services are always provided in state training schools. A full-time Protestant chaplain and a part-time Roman Catholic chaplain are available in most schools. Religious services that are offered include Sunday Mass and morning worship, confession, baptism, instruction for church membership, choir, and religious counseling. Usually few residents respond to these religious services—unless attendance is compulsory, and then residents respond with considerable resistance.

The punishment of misbehaving residents varies from school to school. Fortunately, blatant staff brutality has disappeared from most schools. Adult correctional systems have had enough problems with the federal courts that state governments do not want confinement conditions in their juvenile institutions to be declared unconstitutional. The amount of time residents spend in solitary confinement, or maximum isolation, is also generally less than it was a decade ago. The 1991 survey of juvenile facilities found that 20 percent of training schools do not permit isolation, 34 percent restrict isolation to twenty-four hours or less, 15 percent permit two to three days, 14 percent allow up to four or five days, and 6 percent allow six to ten days. Only 7 percent of training schools permit one month of isolation, and 4 percent have no limit on how long a juvenile can be isolated.[40]

The use of force and mechanical restraints in training schools has increased recently. According to a 1991 survey, 98 percent of training schools used handcuffs, 66 percent used anklets, 31 percent used security belts, 18 percent used four-point ties, and 5 percent used straitjackets.[41] The notion that restraints are needed to control residents appears to have contributed to their increased use. The danger is that improperly applied restraints or mechanical restraints that are applied for excessively long periods of time can result in serious physical injury or emotional trauma to a juvenile.

One of the debates that has raged for years concerns the comparison of private and public training schools. Privately administered training schools are usually better known to the public than are state institutions because private institutions' soliciting of funds has kept them in the public eye. Proponents of private institutions claim that they are more effective than public training schools because they have a limited intake policy, which allows them to chose whom they want to admit, and they can be more flexible and innovative.

A real problem of evaluating **private juvenile placements** is that few studies have examined the accuracy of these claims or the effects of institutional life on residents. Peter W. Greenwood, Susan Turner, and Kathy Rosenblatt's evaluation of the Paint Creek Youth Center (PCYC) in southern Ohio is probably the most positive evaluation of a private institutional placement for juveniles.[42] Their evaluation claimed that this program is different from the traditional training school because it is small (thirty-three beds); because it features a comprehensive and integrated therapeutic approach that emphasizes accountability, social learning, and positive peer culture; and because it has been able to implement family therapy and intensive aftercare services.[43]

Using a control group of youths who supposedly were randomly assigned to PCYC, to Training Institution, Central Ohio (TICO), or to other Department of Youth Services (DYS) institutions, Greenwood and colleagues found that the experimentals (those who had been assigned to PCYC) were less likely to have been recommitted to a correctional institution on new charges than were the controls (who had been assigned to TICO and other DYS facilities).[44]

Glen Mills is an impressive private residential school for court-adjudicated male delinquents between fifteen and eighteen years of age. Founded in 1826 as the Philadelphia House of Refuge, Glen Mills has provided services continuously for 175 years. Situated on nearly eight hundred acres in Delaware County, Pennsylvania, it has been at its present location for over 100 years. See Treatment Intervention 17.3, which describes the programs and facilities of Glen Mills.

David Shichor and Clemens Bartollas' examination of the patterns of public and private juvenile placements in one of the larger probation departments in southern California revealed that relatively few differences were apparent between juveniles who were sent to private and public placements. Although youths who were placed in private facilities had more personal problems and those in public institutions appeared to be somewhat more delinquent, the two populations did not vary markedly. Several other claims made by advocates of private placements also were not documented by this study, especially the claims that private placements provide more professional and treatment services to juveniles than do public placements and that private placements have lower staff/client ratios than do public placements. Furthermore, this study found that hard-core delinquents in private placements were not separated from those who had committed more minor offenses.[45]

A fair assessment of private placements is that, with some glaring exceptions, private training schools are usually more flexible and innovative than state facilities. The smaller size of private training schools is somewhat balanced by the fact that one-half of them still house 100 or more residents, numbers that are too large for effective work with institutionalized juveniles. Perhaps the old adage is right after all: The best institutions are private ones, and the worst juvenile institutional placements are also private ones.

TREATMENT INTERVENTION 17.3

Glen Mills School

Cosimo D. Ferrainola was selected as Executive Director in 1975 and remains director of this private training school. Glen Mills currently provides services to more than 1,000 students. In its impressive facilities, Glen Mills students have access to 15 different vocations, contemporary educational amenities, and five state of the art athletic facilities. There is also a library, a learning center, a computer lab, and a biology lab. To demonstrate the quality of its education program, in the Class of '99, 75 students earned a Glen Mills High School diploma, 294 earned a G.E.D., 235 took the A.C.T. (155 scoring above 17 and 91 scoring 20 or above), and 70 have enrolled in college.

Athletic programs at Glen Mills include JV football, varsity football, cross country, golf, soccer, basketball, wrestling, indoor and outdoor track, swimming, bowling, baseball, volleyball, tennis, and lacrosse. Facilities used for these sports consist of a natatorium, Hayes Recreation Center, Harrison Gymnasium, a campus field house, and a stadium locker room and weight room.

Staff widely uses the confrontation process at Glen Mills, both in and outside of the guided group interaction (GGI) treatment groups. Yet physical and emotional abuse of residents is not permitted by either staff members or other residents. In a book-length evaluation of Glen Mills, the authors conclude by saying:

Glen Mills is a world apart.... Where undeveloped potential flourishes in the rich soil of staff encouragement, competent and individualized instruction, varied programs, excellent facilities, and positive peer pressure. Where status and self-esteem can never be secured in service to Aggression and Manipulation,

the twin gods of the delinquent subculture, but rather are built with every step, however modest, toward self-improvement. Where students take pride in and accept responsibility for themselves and the community. Where boredom yields to a full daily schedule of educational and recreational activities rather than to that staple of the institutional environment, the television set. Where staff and students regard one another as allies. Where all are entitled to the basics of respect, safety, good food, and clean living quarters, and no reward is beyond the reach of a student willing to invest talents he possesses on his own and his peers' behalf.

But at the same time that staff give students respect and expect students to accept responsibility for themselves and not to harm each other, staff "take no nonsense" from students. In spite of the sizable number of students (up to 1,000 in 2001), staff are definitely in control.

How does Glen Mills seem to be different from most training schools? What are the dangers of a confrontational approach? Do you believe it is possible to overcome the negative effects of the delinquent peer culture? Would you like to work in such an institution?

Sources: Interviews with Glen Mills Schools staff in 2001; the pamphlet, "Glen Mills Schools: Service to Youth Since 1826; and Grant R. Grissom and William L. Dubnov, *Locks and Bars: Reforming Our Reform Schools* (Westport, Conn.: Praeger, 1989), p. 212.

Adult Prisons

Adult correctional institutions are a world apart from nearly all training schools. They are much larger, some containing several thousand inmates, and cover acres of ground. Life on the inside is typically austere, crowded, and dangerous. The violent and exploitative relationships that are found in adult correctional institutions make this disposition a very hard one for a juvenile. Institutionalized juveniles are particularly subject to sexual victimization and physical assault.[46] In 1996, 5,599 under-eighteen youths were admitted to state prison systems. Florida and New York, the two states with the most admissions of juveniles in 1996, had decreases between 1992 and 1996. See Table 17.4 for the number of under-eighteen youths admitted to state prison systems.

TABLE 17.4

Youth under Age Eighteen Admitted to State Adult Correctional Systems in 1996

State	Number newly admitted in 1996	Proportion of 1996 admissions	Percent change 1992–1996
ALL REPORTING STATES*	5,599	2.3%	−6%
Upper age 15			
New York	624	3.5	−10
North Carolina	378	3.6	−51
Upper age 16			
Illinois*	460	2.7	29
South Carolina	353	5.3	56
Michigan	295	3.7	29
Georgia	219	2.3	99
Wisconsin†	196	4.1	165
Missouri	180	2.4	53
Louisiana	138	2.0	24
New Hampshire	6	1.1	—
Upper age 17			
Florida	773	4.1	−21
California	394	0.8	116
Youth Authority only	286	39.6	81
Mississippi*	217	4.4	117
Ohio	206	1.6	94
Alabama*	172	3.1	66
Oregon	141	5.7	—
Maryland	139	1.8	−5
Colorado	125	3.0	—
Washington	86	1.7	146
Pennsylvania	76	1.4	69
Virginia	71	0.9	18
Iowa	56	1.8	93
Nevada	54	1.9	—
Minnesota	52	2.1	—
Nebraska	50	3.6	67
New Jersey	49	0.5	32
Arkansas	27	3.6	−85
Utah	22	1.7	—
South Dakota	11	1.6	—
Tennessee	10	0.2	—
Kentucky	10	0.2	—
North Dakota	5	1.3	—
Oklahoma	5	1.0	—
Maine	1	0.2	—
Hawaii	0	0.0	—
West Virginia	0	0.0	—

*Count has been adjusted for admissions that were missing age data, based on admissions that had age data.
†In 1996, Wisconsin changed its upper age of juvenile jurisdiction from 17 to 16.
—Too few cases to calculate a reliable percentage.

Source: Howard N. Snyder and Melissa Sickmund, *Juvenile Offenders and Victims: 1999 National Report* (Washington, D.C.: National Center for Juvenile Justice, 1999), p. 210. Authors' analysis of the Bureau of Justice Statistics' *National Corrections Reporting Program 1992–1996* [machine-readable data files].

Some variations on the practice of confining juveniles in adult institutions exist among the states. In some jurisdictions, states have no alternative but to place juveniles in adult institutions if the courts require incarceration. Some states, under special circumstances, can place youths in either juvenile or adult institutions, and other states can refer juveniles back to juvenile court for disposition. In some instances, youthful offenders are sent to juvenile facilities but then are transferred to adult institutions when they come of age.[47]

In October of 2000, Indiana stopped sending juveniles convicted of adult crimes into the general prison population. Those with lesser offenses are held at the medium-security Plainfield Correctional Facility or the minimum-security Medaryville Correctional Facility. But those juveniles who committed violent or serious offenses are sent to Wabash Valley, a maximum-security facility.[48]

Robert Ohlemiller, the deputy director of the Department of Corrections, explained that the move was intended to address state lawmakers' concern about juveniles in adult prison. He described the program as both responsive to the needs of youthful inmates and a responsible use of tax dollars.[49]

Kelly Dedel found that thirteen states permit the transfer of juveniles to adult facilities: California, Colorado, Hawaii, Indiana, Kentucky, Massachusetts, New Jersey, New York, Rhode Island, South Carolina, Texas, Washington, and Wisconsin. The court has authority to make such transfers in one-third of these states, the commitment agency has authority in one-third, and the transfer decision is a joint decision between two authorities (e.g., agency and court or juvenile and adult agency), in one-third. The reasons for such transfers include the age of the offender, seriousness of the offense, failure to benefit from the program, and poor institutional adjustment.[50] A violent attack on a staff member by an older resident with a serious committing offense, for example, would be the type of case most likely leading to a transfer from a juvenile facility to an adult prison.

The Quality of Residential Life in a Training School

The nature of the residential social system is an important factor in appraising the quality of inmate life in a training school. The many empirical studies on the **residential social system** have consistently challenged the efficacy of juvenile institutionalization. Too many of these studies present a frightening picture of what a juvenile experiences during confinement. These studies also have found that there are more similarities than differences in residential life in single-sex and coeducational institutions.

Training Schools for Boys

With few exceptions, studies of training schools for boys show an inmate society in which the strong take advantage of the weak. In their 1959 study of the State Industrial School for Boys in Golden, Colorado, Gordon E. Barker and W. Thomas Adams found two types of residential leaders: One held power through brute force, and the other ruled through charisma. According to these researchers, residents were involved in an unending battle for dominance and control.[51]

In the early 1960s, Howard W. Polsky studied a cottage in a residential treatment center in New York supported by the Jewish Board of Guardians and devoted to individual psychoanalytic treatment of emotionally disturbed children. The staff in Cottage Six were unable to keep residential leaders from exploiting peers. The social hierarchy that developed in this cottage had the following pecking order: leaders, their associates, "con artists," "quiet types," "busboys," and "scapegoats." The tougher the youth, the higher he ranked in the social order. Polsky also found that boys in higher classes in the hierarchy used ranking, scapegoating, aggression, "threat-gestures," and deviant skills and activities to keep lower-status boys in place. Those at the bottom of the status hierarchy found life so debilitating that most of them ended up in mental hospitals.[52]

Sethard Fisher, who studied a small training school in California, identified victimization and patronage as two of the major behaviors taking place. He defined *victimization* as "a predatory practice whereby inmates of superior strength and knowledge of inmate lore prey on weaker and less knowledgeable inmates."[53] *Patronage* referred to youths building "protective and ingratiating relationships with others more advantageously situated on the prestige ladder." Fisher also saw victimization as being made up of physical attack, agitation, and exploitation, with agitation a form of verbal harassment, and exploitation "a process whereby an inmate will attempt to coerce another by means of threat and duress."[54]

Clemens Bartollas, Stuart J. Miller, and Simon Dinitz's *Juvenile Victimization: The Institutional Paradox,* published in 1976, examined the culture that end-of-the-line delinquents established in a maximum-security institution in Columbus, Ohio. In this "jungle"—as residents frequently called the training school—dominant youths exploited submissive ones in every way possible. Ninety percent of the 150 residents were involved in this exploitation matrix: 19 percent were exploiters who were never themselves exploited, 34 percent were exploiters and victims at different times, 21 percent were occasionally victims and never exploiters, 17 percent were chronic victims, and 10 percent were neither victims nor exploiters.[55]

Bartollas and colleagues drew this conclusion about the lawless environment of this training school:

> The training school receives the worst of the labeled—the losers, the unwanted, the outsiders. These young men consider themselves to be among the toughest, most masculine and virile of their counterparts and they have the societal credentials to prove it. Yet, in much the same way that they themselves are processed, they create, import, and maintain a system which is as brutalizing as the one through which they passed. If anything, the internal environment and the organization and the interaction at TICO are less fair, less just, less humane, and less decent than the worst aspects of the criminal justice system on the outside. Brute force, manipulation, institutional sophistication carry the day, and set the standards which ultimately prevail. Remove the staff, and a feudal structure will emerge which will make the dark ages seem very enlightened.[56]

In a fifteen-year follow-up evaluation of this training school, Miller, Bartollas, and Dinitz found that the negative youth culture described in the 1976 study still thrives and that the strong still victimize the weak. Staff members were more disillusioned than they were at the time of the first study. They also are more fearful of victimization from residents.[57]

Training Schools for Girls and Coeducational Institutions

Until 1960, studies about confined juvenile girls were as numerous as those about incarcerated adult females. The early studies found that girls in training school became involved in varying degrees of lesbian alliances and pseudo-family relationships. In the past twenty years, only two major studies have been done on the female's adjustment to training school: Rose Giallombardo's *The Social World of Imprisoned Girls* and Alice Propper's *Prison Homosexuality: Myth and Reality.*[58]

Giallombardo examined three **training schools for girls** in various parts of the United States and found that a kinship system existed, with some variation, in each of the training schools. Pseudo-family membership organization was pervasive in all three institutions, whether called the "racket," the "sillies," or "chick business." It embraced 84 percent of the girls at the eastern institution, 83 percent at the central, and 94 percent at the western. Some of the social roles identified were "true butches," "true fems," "trust-to-be butches," "trust-to-be fems," "jive time butches," "jive time fems," "straights," "squealers," "pimps," "foxes," "cops," and "popcorns."[59]

The "parents," the leaders of these families, had considerable authority vested in their role. One resident explained the deference to the "parents": "The mother and the father—they're the ones that have the say. If they say, 'Don't go to school,' you say you have cramps, a backache, a stomachache, anything, but you don't go."[60]

Propper's *Prison Homosexuality* examined three coeducational and four girls' training schools scattered through the east, midwest, and south, of which five were public and two were private Catholic training schools. Residents reported homosexual behavior involving from 6 to 29 percent of the inmates in the various institutions. Propper found that the best indicator of homosexual participation during the present term of institutionalization was previous homosexuality. Only 12 percent of those who had never had a homosexual experience before entering the institution admitted engaging in homosexuality, compared with 71 percent of those with previous homosexual experience. In contrast to previously held assumptions, Propper found very little overlap between pseudo-family roles and homosexual behavior. Participation in homosexuality and make-believe families was just as prevalent in coeducational as in single-sex institutions, and homosexuality was as prevalent in treatment-oriented as in custody-oriented facilities. She also reported that residents sometimes continued homosexual experiences when they were released, even when their first experience was as the unhappy victim of a homosexual rape.[61]

Bartollas and Christopher M. Sieverdes's study of six coeducational institutions in a southeastern state drew the following conclusions: Females adhered more strongly to inmate groups and peer relationships than did males. Females felt more victimized by peers than did males, but they did not harass or manipulate staff as much as males did. They also were more satisfied with institutional life than were males.[62] Pseudo-families existed among girls, but they were based much less on homosexual alliances than were those in all-girls training schools.[63] Status offenders, who made up 70 percent of the girls and 30 percent of the boys, were the worst victims in these training schools and had the most difficulty adjusting to institutional life.[64] White males and females experienced high rates of personal intimidation and victimization by African American and American Indian youths.[65]

The Rights of Confined Juveniles

The rights of institutionalized juveniles have been examined by the federal courts and the Civil Rights of Institutionalized Persons Act (CRIPA). CRIPA gives the Civil Rights Division of the U.S. Department of Justice (DOJ) the power to bring actions against state or local governments for violating the civil rights of institutionalized persons.

The Courts

The courts have paid less attention to juvenile institutions because they are assumed to be more humane and to infringe less upon the constitutional rights of offenders than adult prisons. Yet the recent deteriorating conditions in juvenile correctional facilities, including overcrowded living conditions, the frequency of assaults among residents and against staff, and the growing presence of gang youths, have led to a wave of litigation. The courts have currently mandated two major rights: the right to treatment and the right to be free from cruel and unusual punishment.

RIGHT TO TREATMENT Several court decisions have held that a juvenile has a right to treatment when he or she is committed to a juvenile institution. The *White v. Reid* (1954) decision held that juveniles could not be kept in facilities that did not provide for their rehabilitation.[66] The *Inmates of the Boy's Training School v. Affeck* (1972) decision also held that juveniles have a right to treatment because rehabilitation is the true purpose of the juvenile court.[67] The Indiana Seventh Circuit's decision in *Nelson v. Heyne* (1973) agreed with the district court that residents of the Indiana Boys' School had a right to rehabilitative treatment.[68]

In the *Morales v. Turman* decision (1973), the U.S. District Court for the Eastern District of Texas issued the most extensive order ever justified by a child's right to treatment.[69] The court held that the State of Texas had to follow a number of criteria to ensure that proper treatment would be provided to confined juveniles. Among these criteria were minimum standards for assessing and testing children committed to the state; minimum standards for assessing educational skills and handicaps and for providing programs aimed at advancing a child's education; minimum standards for delivering vocational education and medical and psychiatric care; and minimum standards for providing a humane institutional environment. But the order was vacated by the Fifth Circuit Appeals Court on the grounds that a three-judge court should have been convened to hear the case. On *certiorari* to the U.S. Supreme Court, that Court reversed the Court of Appeals and remanded the case. Whether the order of the District Court can withstand the assault against it may affect future considerations of confined juveniles' right to treatment.[70]

RIGHT TO BE FREE FROM CRUEL AND UNUSUAL PUNISHMENT   Considerable case law has also been established ensuring confined juveniles the right to be free from cruel and unusual punishment. The *Pena v. New York State Division for Youth* decision (1976) held that the use of isolation, hand restraints, and tranquilizing drugs at Goshen Annex Center was punitive and antitherapeutic and therefore violated the Fourteenth Amendment right to treatment and the Eighth Amendment right to protection against cruel and unusual punishment.[71] The court in the case of *Inmates of the Boys' Training School v. Affeck* (1972) condemned such practices as solitary confinement and strip-cells, as well as the lack of educational opportunities, and established a number of minimum standards for youths who were confined at the training school.[72]

In *Morales v. Turman* (1973), the court found numerous instances of physical brutality and abuse, including hazing by staff and inmates, staff-administered beatings and tear gassings, homosexual attacks, extensive use of solitary confinement, and minimal clinical services.[73] In *Morgan v. Sproat* (1977), the court found youths confined in padded cells with no windows or furnishings and only flush holes for toilets, and denied access to all services or programs except a Bible.[74] In *State v. Werner* (1978), the court found that residents were locked in solitary confinement, beaten, kicked, slapped, and sprayed with mace by staff members, required to scrub floors with a toothbrush, and subjected to such punishments as standing and sitting for prolonged periods without changing position.[75] Federal courts have also held that extended periods of solitary confinement and the use of Thorazine and other medications for the purpose of control represent cruel and unusual punishment.[76] In a 1995 case, *Alexander v. Boyd and South Carolina Department of Juvenile Justice,* the district court ruled that the use of gas in three training schools to punish juveniles for disciplinary infractions violated the juveniles' due process rights. In its decision, the court noted that the use of gas irritates the mucous membranes of those who are exposed to it and causes instant pain and spasms in the eyelids, breathing problems, and coughing fits.[77]

CRIPA and Juvenile Correctional Facilities

As of November 1997, the Civil Rights Division had investigated 300 institutions under CRIPA. Seventy-three of these institutions, or about 25 percent, were juvenile detention and correctional facilities. The Civil Rights Division is presently monitoring conditions in thirty-four juvenile correctional facilities through consent decrees in Kentucky, New Jersey, and Puerto Rico. The consent decree filed in Kentucky includes all thirteen juvenile facilities in the state, the decree in New Jersey is with one facility, and in Puerto Rico with twenty facilities.[78]

The decree in Kentucky requires the state "to take a number of steps to protect juveniles from abuse, mistreatment, and injury; to ensure adequate medical and mental health care; and to provide adequate educational, vocational, and aftercare services."[79] The consent degree in Puerto Rico addressed life-threatening conditions including "juveniles committing and attempting suicide without staff intervention or treatment, widespread infection control problems caused by rats and other vermin, and defective plumbing that forced juveniles to drink from their toilet bowls."[80]

How Long-Term Juvenile Placements Need to Be Changed

On balance, it is difficult to dispute that some juveniles need confinement to get their behavior under control and that the community deserves protection from youths who repeatedly commit property and personal crimes. Yet everything must be done to ensure that training schools do as little harm as possible to residents. The "strong shall survive" inmate culture that is found in many maximum-security training schools is a travesty in a free and democratic society. In the lawless society of some training schools, characterized by intimidation, force, and victimization, male residents do not feel safe and, indeed, are not safe in these settings. Also, little good can be said about the disproportionate numbers of minority youths found in training schools or the number of youths who choose to withdraw through running away, drugs, mental breakdown, and suicide.[81] Dr. Jerome Miller has long been one of the sharpest critics of juvenile institutionalization; some of his reactions to training schools are found in Social Policy 17.4.

The old argument that juvenile institutions are "schools of crime" is much too simplistic, but there is convincing evidence that the recidivism rates are very high among those who have been confined in training schools. A 1989 review of the rearrest rates of juveniles in several jurisdictions that rely heavily on institutions demonstrated that rearrest rates ranged from a low of 51 percent to a high of 70 percent.[82] An analysis of youths released from state correctional and private facilities in 1985 and 1991 in Minnesota found that between 53 percent and 77 percent continued their criminal careers into adulthood.[83] Peter Greenwood and Franklin Zimring add that most state training schools "fail to reform . . . [and] make no appreciable reductions in the very high recidivism rates, on the order of 70 to 80 percent, that are expected for chronic offenders."[84]

The example of Glen Mills School that was cited earlier shows that it is possible to provide a quality program for juveniles who are confined in long-term institutions. It requires a varied program that is individualized for residents, committed staff members who are well trained, and facilities that do not reflect a prison-like setting. There is also the need to carry forth the positive gains made in institutional programming to life beyond the institution. Thus, unless there is an improved transition between the institution and community living, what takes place in long-term institutions will likely have little effect on community adjustment for residents.

Another important consideration in improving juvenile facilities is to extend institutional care beyond sixteen years of age. North Carolina was one of the first states to develop Youthful Offenders Camps for sixteen- to eighteen-year-old males. In the 1990s, Colorado, Florida, New Mexico, Minnesota, and Texas also developed intermediate, or transitional, systems between the juvenile and adult systems.[85] Thus, intermediate sentencing for youthful offenders that bridges the juvenile and adult systems is a positive way to keep some juveniles out of adult prisons.

SOCIAL POLICY 17.4

Close Down All Training Schools

Jerome Miller, director of the Division of Youth Services (DYS) in Massachusetts, was appalled in the early 1970s at what he termed the "sadistic discipline" found in the training schools of that state. Residents at Shirley Training School informed him that they had to drink from toilets or kneel for hours on the stone floor with a pencil under their knees.

One day, Miller received from an anonymous staff member of Shirley Training School a file containing summaries for male residents in Cottage Nine, the disciplinary cottage. It included the following, shocking information:

Donald, 16, beaten on the soles of his bare feet with straps. Walter, 16, handcuffed for 22 days and nights when returned from escape. Charles, 17, padlocked to water pipe, given a cold shower for six minutes.

Miller also discovered that one resident of this cottage had his feet strapped to a bed frame and was beaten on the bare soles with wooden paddles or the wooden backs of floor brushes. If all this was not enough, the DYS commissioner was informed why the escape rate at Shirley was so low—after a runaway was returned to the institution, "the escapee's ring finger was bent back across the top of his left hand until the finger broke."

In a 1991 publication, Miller defines training schools as "impervious to reform." According to Miller, training schools have a hidden task of holding a society together, which makes leaders of society reluctant to embark boldly on a policy of mass deinstitutionalization. Miller states: "Reform schools neither reform nor rehabilitate. The longer you lock up a kid in them, the less they protect society. They're useless, they're futile, they're rotten."

In a 2002 publication, Miller contributes another biting critique of U.S. training schools when he charges:

I think that what we are seeing today is a movement back to institutions. It is a system now driven by race. Teenagers who are diverted from institutions to smaller programs or specialized foster situations tend to be disproportionately Caucasian. Neglected state institutions are increasingly reserved for black kids. In the process they have grown more punitive and uncaring. This is happening across the county.

What are the actual criticisms that Miller makes of training schools? How representative are his criticisms of the training school or schools in your state?

Source: Jerome G. Miller, *Last One Over the Wall: The Massachusetts Experience in Closing Reform Schools* (Columbus: The Ohio State University Press, 1991), pp. 3, 95, and 96; and Clemens Bartollas, *Invitation to Corrections* (Boston: Allyn & Bacon, 2002), p. 391.

SUMMARY

This chapter summarizes the history and status of long-term institutional placements for juveniles. These long-term institutions consist of camps and ranches, reception centers, boot camps, training schools, and prisons. Although the proportion of juveniles who are sent to long-term facilities is small, these institutions of last resort are an integral part of society's control of law-violating juveniles.

An analysis of these placements for juveniles reveals the influence of a changing social context. Early in the nineteenth century, reformers established the training school as a means to protect children from the harsh treatment of adult facilities. Early in the twentieth century, discouraged by the custodial nature of juvenile institutionalization, reformers implemented the diversification of training schools' programs and structures and attempted to make juvenile placements more treatment-oriented. In the 1970s, with the publication of several devastating critiques of juvenile institutionalization, another major period of reform of training schools was initiated. Status offenders were deinstitutionalized, staff brutality was nearly eliminated, and youth correctional systems were held responsible for minimum standards of institutional care. With the increased use of training schools in the past two decades, fueled at least in part by a "get tough posture" with juvenile criminals, reformers no longer seem greatly interested in doing serious study on what goes on in juvenile institutionalization. Accordingly, the lack of up-to-date studies make it difficult to draw firm conclusions about the contemporary quality of institutional life for juveniles.

What we do know is that reception and diagnostic centers usually do a good job of evaluating the problems of residents, but their recommended treatment plans frequently are not implemented when youths are transferred to a camp or training school. Some camps and ranches provide an open setting and good staff support for offenders, but opponents of these institutions argue that most of these youths could function as well in community programs. Boot camps, the newest panacea in juvenile corrections, offer a disciplined and regimented setting. Whether this type of military discipline, with sometimes a little programming added, has long-term effects on many residents is still open to question. Private and public training schools vary so much that generalizations are difficult. The good training schools can provide positive impact on those youths receptive to change in their lives; the bad training schools can cause damage that will affect youths for as long as they live. Adult prisons are also no placement for a juvenile, but the recent outbursts of violent crimes among high-risk juveniles have resulted in increasing numbers of youths being sent to adult correctional institutions.

Unquestionably, hard-core delinquents pose a problem for the juvenile justice system; and given the present mood of the public, these youths will continue to be confined in long-term institutions. The task now is to design facilities, provide programs, and train staff that will ensure these offenders a humane and, if they choose, beneficial stay while they are confined for their socially unacceptable behavior.

KEY TERMS

boot camps, p. 508
cottage system, p. 508
forestry camps, p. 506
private juvenile placements, p. 517
ranches, p. 506

reception and diagnostic center, p. 506
residential social system, p. 520
training school, p. 503
training school for girls, p. 521

CRITICAL THINKING QUESTIONS

1. What experiences is a juvenile likely to have in each of the types of correctional institutions?
2. Compare private and state training schools.
3. Evaluate the quality of life in training schools.
4. Evaluate the effectiveness of training schools. What can be done to make training schools more effective?

WEB DESTINATIONS

Read about Hennepin County Home School at their Web site.
http://www.co.hennepin.mn.us/welcome.html

Learn more about Glen Mills School at their home page.
http://www.glenmillsschool.org/leftnar.html

Learn more about the characteristics of George Junior Republic's residents at this site.
http://theboojum.com/childrens_rights/z-ch09.htm

For information and links on the various types of boot camps, type OJJDP Boot Camps for Juveniles into your search engine.

To view sources on Juvenile Correctional Facilities, simply type Juvenile Correctional Facilities into your search engine.

NOTES

1. Hastings Hart, *Preventive Treatment of Neglected Children* (New York: Charities Publication Committee, 1910), p. 12.

2. David J. Rothman, *The Discovery of the Asylum* (Boston: Little, Brown & Company, 1971), pp. 53–54.

3. Steven Schlossman, "Delinquent Children: The Juvenile Reform School," in *The Oxford History of the Prison*, edited by Norval Morris and David J. Rothman (New York: Oxford University Press, 1995), p. 365.

4. Rothman, *The Discovery of the Asylum*, p. 65.

5. Ibid., pp. 225–227.

6. Barbara M. Brenzel, *Daughters of the State* (Cambridge, Mass.: MIT Press, 1983), pp. 1, 4–5. See also Alexander W. Pisciotta, "Saving the Children: The Promise and Practice of Parens Patriae, 1838–1898," *Crime and Delinquency* 28 (1982), pp. 410–425; Alexander W. Pisciotta, "Treatment on Trial: The Rhetoric and Reality of the New York House of Refuge, 1857–1935," *American Journal of Legal History* 29 (1985), pp. 151–181.

7. Schlossman, "Delinquent Children," p. 348.

8. See Howard Polsky, *Cottage Six: The Social System of Delinquent Boys in Residential Treatment* (New York: Russell Sage Foundation, 1963); Clemens Bartollas, Stuart J. Miller, and Simon Dinitz, *Juvenile Victimization: The Institutional Paradox* (New York: Halsted Press, 1976); Barry C. Feld, *Neutralizing Inmate Violence: The Juvenile Offender in Institutions* (Cambridge, Mass.: Ballinger, 1977); and Kenneth Wooden, *Weeping in the Playtime of Others: America's Incarcerated Children* (New York: McGraw-Hill, 1976).

9. Howard N. Snyder and Melissa Sickmund, *Juvenile Offenders and Victims: 1999 National Report* (Washington, D.C.: National Center for Juvenile Justice, 1999), p. 185.

10. Ibid., p. 186.

11. Parent, et al., *Conditions of Confinement*, p. 22.

12. *Corrections Compendium* (Lincoln, Neb.: CEGA Publishing, July 1992), pp. 12–14.

13. Parent, et al., *Conditions of Confinement*, pp. 22, 23, 32.

14. Jean Bottcher, "Evaluating the Youth Authority's Boot Camp: The First Five Months." Paper delivered to Western Society of Criminology, Monterey, California, February 1993; Institute for Criminological Research and American Institute for Research, *Boot Camp for Juvenile Offenders: Constructive Intervention and Early Support—Implementation Evaluation Final Report* (New Brunswick, N.J.: Rutgers University, 1992).

15. Roberta C. Cronin, *Boot Camps for Adult and Juvenile Offenders: Overview and Update*. A Final Summary Report Presented to the National Institute of Justice, 1994), p. 37.

16. Anthony W. Salerno, "Boot Camps: A Critique and a Proposed Alternative," *Journal of Offender Rehabilitation* 20 (1994), p. 149.

17. Ibid., p. 37.

18. Michael Peters, David Thomas, Christopher Zamberlan, and Caliber Associates, *Boot Camps for Juvenile Offenders: Program Summary* (Washington, D.C.: Office of Juvenile Justice and Delinquency Prevention, 1997), p. 3, 25.

19. Ibid.

20. Doris Layton MacKenzie, David B. Wilson, Gaylene Styve Armstrong, and Angela R. Gover, "The Impact of Boot Camps and Traditional Institutions on Juvenile Residents: Perceptions, Adjustment, and Change," *Journal of Research in Crime and Delinquency* 38 (August 2000), pp. 279–313.

21. Ibid., p. 279.

22. Brent Zaehringer, *Koch Crime Institute White Paper Report Juvenile Boot Camps: Cost and Effectiveness vs. Residential Facilities*, http://www.kci.org/publication/whitepaper/bootcamp/introduction.htm

23. Alexandra Marks, "States Fall Out of (Tough) Love with Boot Camps," *The Christian Science Monitor*, December 27, 1999, p. 1.

24. Associated Press, "Teen Dies at Boot Camp for Troubled Kids," *Milwaukee Times*, 4 July, 2001. For an article that suggests that what takes place at boot camps may be considered cruel and unusual and give rise to costly inmate litigation, see Faith E. Lutze and David C. Brody, "Mental Abuse as Cruel and Unusual Punishment: Do Boot Camp Prisons Violate the Eighth Amendment?," *Crime and Delinquency* 45 (April 1999), pp. 242-255.

25. Marks, "States Fall Out of (Tough) Love with Boot Camps," p. 1.

26. Melissa Sickmund, Howard N. Snyder, and Eileen Poe-Yamagata, *Juvenile Offenders and Victims 1997 Update on Violence* (Washington, D.C.: Office of Juvenile Justice and Delinquency Prevention, 1997), p. 41.

27. Ibid.

28. Bradford Smith, "Children in Custody: 20–year Trends in Juvenile Detention, Correctional, and Shelter Facilities," *Crime and Delinquency* 44 (October 1998), p. 533.

29. Steve Lerner, *Bodily Harm: The Pattern of Fear and Violence at the California Youth Authority* (Bolinas, Calif.: Common Knowledge Press, 1986).

30. Ibid., p. 12.

31. See L. Thomas Winfree Jr. and G. Larry Mays, "Family and Peer Influences on Gang Involvement: A Comparison of Institutionalized and Free-World Youths in a Southeastern State." Paper presented to the Annual Meeting of the American Society of Criminology in Boston, Massachusetts (November 1994); and L. Thomas Winfree Jr., G. Larry Mays, and Teresa Vigil-Backstrom, "Youth Gangs and Incarcerated Delinquents: Exploring the Ties between Gang Membership, Delinquency and Social Learning Theory," *Justice Quarterly* 11 (June 1994), pp. 229–256.

32. Task Force Report of the National Gang Crime Research Center, "The Economics of Gang Life." Paper presented at the Annual Meeting of the Academy of Criminal Justice Sciences, Boston, Massachusetts (March 1995), p. 24.

33. Catherine H. Conley, *Street Gangs: Current Knowledge and Strategies* (Washington, D.C.: U.S. Department of Justice, 1993), p. 55.

34. For the diverse forms of state juvenile institutionalization, see Kelly Dedel, "National Profile of the Organization of Juvenile Correctional Systems," p. 509.

35. Smith, "Children in Custody," p. 531.

36. Parent, et al., *Conditions of Confinement*, p. 134.

37. Ibid., p. 138.

38. Mark W. Lipsey, David B. Wilson, and Lynn Cothern, *Effective Intervention for Serious Juvenile Offenders: Juvenile*

Justice Bulletin (Washington, D.C.: Office of Juvenile Justice and Delinquency Prevention, 2000), p. 5.

39. Randall G. Sheldon and Sharon Tracey, "Violent Female Juvenile Offender: An Ignored Minority with the Juvenile Justice System," *Juvenile and Family Court Journal* 43 (1992), pp. 33–40.

40. Parent, et al., *Conditions of Confinement*, p. 182. The present author's experience with confined youths reveals that few can tolerate isolation for more than a couple of weeks.

41. Ibid., p. 185.

42. Peter W. Greenwood, Susan Turner, and Kathy Rosenblatt, *Evaluation of Paint Creek Youth Center: Preliminary Results* (Santa Monica, Calif.: Rand, 1989).

43. Ibid., p. 3.

44. Ibid., p. 58.

45. David Shichor and Clemens Bartollas, "Private and Public Placements: Is There a Difference?" *Crime and Delinquency* 36 (April 1990), pp. 289–299.

46. The author received a letter in the summer of 1992 from an inmate in an adult prison telling how he looked forward to sexually victimizing juveniles being sent to the facility.

47. Donna Hamparian, et al., "Youth in Adult Court: Between Two Worlds," *Major Issues in Juvenile Justice Information and Training* (Columbus, Ohio: Academy for Contemporary Problems, 1981).

48. Vic Rychaert, "15 Youths Doing Time with State's Meanest," *Indianapolis Star,* 30 April 2001, A1.

49. Ibid.

50. Dedel, "National Profile of the Organization of State Juvenile Correctional Systems," p. 515.

51. Gordon E. Barker and W. Thomas Adams, "The Social Structure of a Correctional Institution," *Journal of Criminal Law, Criminology and Police Science 49* (1959), pp. 417–499.

52. Howard Polsky, *Cottage Six: The Social System of Delinquent Boys in Residential Treatment* (New York: Russell Sage Foundation, 1963), pp. 69–88.

53. Sethard Fisher, "Social Organization in a Correction Residence," *Pacific Sociological Review* 5 (Fall 1961), p. 89.

54. Ibid., pp. 89–90.

55. Clemens Bartollas, Stuart J. Miller, and Simon Dinitz, *Juvenile Victimization: The Institutional Paradox* (New York: Halsted Press, 1976), pp. 131–150.

56. Ibid., p. 271.

57. Stuart J. Miller, Clemens Bartollas, and Simon Dinitz, *Juvenile Victimization Revisited: A Fifteen-Year Follow-Up at TICO* (unpublished manuscript).

58. Rose Giallombardo, *The Social World of Imprisoned Girls: A Comparative Study of Institutions for Juvenile Delinquents* (New York: John Wiley & Sons, 1974); Alice Propper, *Prison Homosexuality: Myth and Reality* (Lexington, Mass.: D. C. Heath & Company, 1981).

59. Giallombardo, *Social World of Imprisoned Girls,* pp. 145–211.

60. Ibid., p. 210.

61. Propper, *Prison Homosexuality.*

62. Christopher M. Sieverdes and Clemens Bartollas, "Institutional Adjustment among Female Delinquents," in *Administrative Issues in Criminal Justice,* edited by Alvin W. Cohn and Ben Ward (Beverly Hills, Calif.: Sage Publication, 1981), pp. 91–103.

63. Ibid.

64. Clemens Bartollas and Christopher M. Sieverdes, "The Victimized White in Juvenile Correctional System," *Crime and Delinquency* 34 (October 1981), pp. 534–543.

65. Ibid., p. 540.

66. *White v. Reid,* 125 F. Supp. (D.D.C.) 1954.

67. *Inmates of the Boys' Training School v. Affeck,* 346 F. Supp. 1354 (D. R. I. 1972).

68. *Nelson v. Heyne,* 355 F. Supp. 451 (N. D. Ind. 1973).

69. *Morales v. Turman,* 364 F. Supp. 166 (E. D. Tex. 1973).

70. Adrienne Volnik, "Right to Treatment: Case Development in Juvenile Law," *Justice System Journal* 3 (Spring 1973), pp. 303–304.

71. *Pena v. New York State Division for Youth,* 419 F. Supp. 203 (S. D. N. Y. 1976).

72. 346 F. Supp. 1354 (D.R.I. 1972), p. 1343.

73. *Morales v. Turman.*

74. *Morgan v. Sproat,* 432 F. Supp. 1130 (S. D. Miss. 1977).

75. *State v. Werner,* 242 S.E.2d 907 (W.Va. 1978).

76. See *Lollis v. New York State Dept. of Social Services,* 322 F. Supp. 473 (S. D. N. Y. 1970); *U.S. ex. rel. Stewart* v. *Coughlin,* No. C. 1793 (N. D. 111, November 22, 1971).

77. *Alexander v. Boys and South Carolina Department of Juvenile Justice,* 876 F. Supp. 773 (1995).

78. Patricia Puritz and Mary Ann Scali, *Beyond the Walls: Improving Conditions of Confinement for Youth in Custody: Report* (Washington, D.C.: Office of Juvenile Justice and Delinquency Prevention, 1998), pp. 4–5.

79. Ibid., p. 5.

80. Ibid.

81. For an empirical examination of these coping adaptations, see Bartollas, Miller, and Dinitz, *Juvenile Victimization,* pp. 169–179.

82. Barry Krisberg, James Austin, and Patricia Steele, *Unlocking Juvenile Corrections: Evaluating the Massachusetts Department of Youth Services* (San Francisco: Calif.: The National Council on Crime and Delinquency 6, 1989), pp. 26–32.

83. Minnesota Legislative Auditor, *Residential Facilities for Juvenile Offenders* (St. Paul, Minn.: State of Minnesota, 1995), pp. 71–73.

84. Peter Greenwood and Franklin Zimring, *One More Chance: the Pursuit of Promising Intervention Strategies for Chronic Juvenile Offenders* (Santa Monica, Calif.: Rand Corp, 1985), p. 40.

85. *Combating Violence and Dangerous Delinquency: the National Juvenile Justice Action Plan: Report* (Washington, D.C.: Coordinating Council on Juvenile Justice and Delinquency Prevention, 1996), p. 27.

Glossary

adjudication The process whereby a juvenile court judge decides, during an adjudicatory hearing, whether a child is a delinquent, a status offender, or a dependent or whether the allegations in the petition can be sustained.

adjudicatory hearing This stage of the juvenile court's proceedings usually includes the child's plea, the presentation of evidence by the prosecution and by the defense, cross-examination of witnesses, and the finding by the judge as to whether the allegations in the petition can be sustained.

adjustment model The emphasis of this rehabilative philosophy is to help delinquents demonstrate responsible behavior.

adolescence This term defines the life interval between childhood and adulthood, usually the period between the ages of twelve and eighteen years.

adult court Juveniles who have committed serious crimes can be waived to the adult court. In some states the adult court has jurisdiction over juveniles who commit certain offenses.

adversary system The juvenile justice system, like the adult justice system, is characterized by an adversarial relationship between the defense and prosecution. The judge acts as arbiter of the legal rules. For the judge to determine guilt, the prosecution must prove the charges beyond a reasonable doubt.

aftercare Supervision of juveniles who are released from correctional institutions so that they can make an optimal adjustment to community living.

aftercare officer Juvenile justice worker who supervises juveniles after their release from institutional care.

alcohol This is a drug that relaxes inhibitions, and adolescents participate in risky behavior under its influence.

alternative school A facility that provides an alternative educational experience, usually in a different location, for youths who are not doing satisfactory work in the public school setting.

amphetamines This drug is a stimulant and is used by adolescents in a variety of forms.

anomie Robert K. Merton states that a state of anomie, or normlessness, occurs when the integration between cultural goals and institutional means are lacking in a society.

appeal Review of juvenile court proceedings by a higher court. Although no constitutional right of appeal exists for juveniles, this right has been established by statute in some states.

appellate review A higher court that reviews the decision of a juvenile court proceeding. Decisions by appellate courts, including the U.S. Supreme Court, have greatly affected the development of juvenile court law.

arrest The process of taking a juvenile into custody for an alleged violation of the law. Juveniles who are under arrest have nearly all the due process safeguards accorded to adults.

attention home An innovative form of detention facility, found in several locations across the nation, that is characterized by an open setting.

bail The payment of a stipulated amount of money for an individual to be released from pretrial detention. Juveniles do not have a constitutional right to bail as do adults.

balanced and restorative model An integrative model that seeks to reconcile the interests of victims, offenders, and the community through programs and supervision practices.

behavior modification A treatment technology that rewards appropriate behavior positively, immediately, and systematically and assumes that rewards increase the occurrence of desired behavior.

beyond a reasonable doubt The degree of proof needed for a juvenile to be adjudicated a delinquent by the juvenile court during the adjudicatory stage of the court's proceedings.

bifurcated hearing Split adjudication and disposition hearings, which are the present trend of the juvenile court.

binding over The process of transferring (also called *certifying*) juveniles to the adult court. Binding over takes place after a judicial hearing on a juvenile's amenability to treatment or his or her threat to public safety.

biological positivism The belief that juveniles' biological limitations drive them to delinquent behavior.

blocked opportunity theory The theory that blocked or limited opportunity influences the involvement of both males and females in delinquent behavior.

body-type theory William Sheldon, Sheldon Glueck and Eleanor Glueck, and others found that youths with the mesomorphic (bony, muscular, and athletic) body type are more likely to be delinquent than are those with the endormorphic (soft, round, and fat) and ectomorphic (tall, thin, and fragile) body types.

booking The record of an arrest made in police stations. In some jurisdictions, photographing and fingerprinting juveniles are part of booking.

boot camps A military-style facility used as an alternative to prison in order to deal with prison crowding and public demands for severe punishment.

born criminal Lombroso claimed that some criminals are atavistic, or a reversion to an earlier evolutionary level, and thus, are born criminals.

Breed v. Jones (1995) The U.S. Supreme Court ruled that Breed's case did constitute double jeopardy; a juvenile court cannot adjudicate a case and then transfer the case over to the criminal court for adult processing of the same offense.

chancery court The philosophy of *parens patriae* was developed from the chancery court in England.

Chicago Areas Project A community organization project developed by Clifford R. Shaw and Henry D. McKay in the 1930s in Chicago.

child abuse Physical abuse is intentional behavior directed toward a child by the parents or caregiver to cause pain, injury, or death. Emotional abuse involves a disregard of a child's psychological needs. Sexual abuse, or incest, has to do with any sexual activity that involves physical contact or sexual arousal between members of a family who are not married to one another.

child neglect Disregarding the physical, emotional, or moral needs of children. Child neglect involves the failure of the parent or caregiver to provide nutritious food, adequate clothing and sleeping arrangements, essential medical care, sufficient supervision, access to education, and normal experiences that produce feelings of being loved, wanted, secure, and worthy.

children's rights movement Efforts of interest groups during the 1960s and 1970s to extend the rights of children.

"chivalry" factor Contends that the justice system treats adolescent females and women more leniently because of their gender.

chronic juvenile offender The Philadelphia cohort studies defined chronic offenders as youths who had committed five or more delinquent offenses. Other studies use this term to refer to a youth involved in serious and repetitive offenses.

citation A summons to appear in juvenile court.

classical school of criminology The basic theoretical constructs of this school are developed from the writings of Cesare Beccaria and Jeremy Bentham and view human beings as rational creatures who, being free to choose their actions, can be held responsible for their behavior.

cocaine A drug that creates mood elevation, elation, grandiose feelings, and heightened physical prowess.

cohort study Research usually including all individuals who were born in a particular year in a particular city or county and following them through part or all of their lives.

commitment Determination by a juvenile judge at the disposition stage of a juvenile court proceeding that a juvenile be sent to a juvenile correctional institution.

commitment to delinquency David Matza used this phrase to refer to the attachment that a juvenile may have to delinquent identity and values.

commitment to the social bond Travis Hirschi used this phrase to refer to the attachment that a juvenile has to conventional institutions and activities.

community-based corrections Probation, residential and day treatment programs, and parole (aftercare) are the basic forms of community-based corrections. The nature of the linkages between community programs and their social environments is the most distinguishing feature of community-based corrections. As frequency, duration, and quality of community relationships increase, the programs become more community based.

community corrections acts State-based acts through which counties that participate receive subsidies for diverting minor offenders from training schools.

community service project Court-required restitution in which a juvenile spends a certain number of hours working in a community project.

community volunteer An individual who donates his or her time to work with delinquents in the community.

complaint The charge made to an intake officer of the juvenile court that an offense has been committed.

concentric zone theory Robert Burgess's theory that urban areas grow in concentric circles was used by Clifford R. Shaw and Henry D. McKay to measure delinquency rates in Chicago and elsewhere. Shaw and McKay found that the delinquency rates decreased the further the zones were from the central city.

conflict theory The theory that delinquency is explained by socioeconomic class, by power and authority relationships, and by group and cultural differences.

consensual model A model of society that views the social order as a persistent stable structure that is well integrated and that is based on a consensus of values.

consent decree Formal agreement between a juvenile and the court in which the juvenile is placed under the court's supervision without a formal finding of delinquency.

constitutionalists Twentieth-century reformers who advocated that juveniles deserve due process protections when they appear before the juvenile court.

containment theory Walter C. Reckless's containment theory contends that strong inner containment and reinforcing external containment provide insulation against delinquent and criminal behavior.

contextual perspective A method of analysis found in delinquency studies that uses the interrelationships of two or more social, cultural, or political contexts to understand delinquent behavior as well as suggests means to prevent and control delinquent behavior.

control theory Control theories agree on the fundamental point that human beings must be held in check, or somehow be controlled, if delinquent tendencies are to be repressed.

cottage system A widely used treatment practice that places small groups of training school residents into cottages.

crack A less expensive and more potent version of cocaine.

crime control model Supporters of this model, such as James Q. Wilson, Ernest van den Haag, and others, believe that discipline and punishment are the most effective means of deterring youth crime.

criminal opportunity theory Philip J. Cook's theory claims that criminals tend to be attracted to targets that offer a high payoff with little risk of legal consequences.

criminogenic influences Characteristics of a society or an institution that lead to youth or adult crime.

critical theory Combines Marxist theory with the insights of later theorists, such as Sigmund Freud.

cruel and unusual punishment The Eighth Amendment to the U.S. Constitution guarantees freedom from cruel and unusual punishment while juveniles and adults are in correctional custody.

cultural conflict theory Thorsten Sellin, the best-known proponent of this perspective, holds that delinquency or crime arises because individuals are members of a subculture that has its own particular conduct norms.

cultural deviance theory Clifford R. Shaw and Henry D. McKay, as well as Walter B. Miller, view delinquent behavior as an expression of conformity to cultural values and norms that are in opposition to those of the larger U.S. society.

cultural transmission theories These theories contend that areas of concentrated crime maintain their high rates over a long period, even when the composition of the population changes rapidly.

culture The customs, beliefs, values, knowledge, and skills that guide an individual's behavior.

day treatment programs Court-mandated, community-based corrections programs that juveniles attend in the morning and afternoon. They return home in the evening.

decriminalization This term, as used in juvenile corrections, refers to the process of no longer regarding status offenses as delinquent (criminal) offenses.

deinstitutionalization The process of closing long-term institutions and moving residents to community-based corrections facilities. *Deincarceration* is another term used to describe this process.

Deinstitutionalization of Status Offenders Project (DSO) A project that evaluated the effects of deinstitutionalization of status offenders in eight states and prompted a national evaluation.

delinquency prevention Three levels of delinquency prevention have been identified. *Primary prevention* focuses on modifying conditions in the physical and social environment that lead to delinquency. *Secondary prevention* refers to intervention in the lives of juveniles or groups that have been identified as being in circumstances disposing toward delinquency. *Tertiary prevention* is directed at the prevention of recidivism.

delinquent act An act committed by a minor that violates the penal code of the government that has authority over the area in which the act occurred. If committed by an adult, this act could be prosecuted in a criminal court.

delinquent career Delinquents who repeatedly commit offenses and who appear to be committed to deviant values are sometimes said to be involved in a career.

delinquent subcultures Albert K. Cohen and others have defined delinquent subcultures as comprising lower-class juveniles who are experiencing strain or alienation from the larger culture.

dependency Legal status of a youth over whom the juvenile court has assumed jurisdiction because of inadequate care by parents or caretakers.

desistance Termination of a delinquent career or behavior.

detention Temporary restraint of a juvenile in a secure facility because he or she is acknowledged to be dangerous either to self or to others.

detention center Detention homes, also called juvenile halls and detention centers, were established at the end of the nineteenth century as an alternative to jails for juveniles.

detention facility A facility, also known as a *detention center* or *home*, that provides custodial care of juveniles during juvenile court proceedings.

detention hearing A hearing, usually conducted by an intake officer of the juvenile court, during which the decision is made as to whether a juvenile will be released to his or her parents or be detained in a detention facility.

determinate sentencing A form of sentencing that provides fixed forms of sentences for offenses. The terms of these sentences are generally set by the legislature rather than determined by judicial discretion.

determinism A philosophical position that suggests that individuals are driven into delinquent or criminal behavior.

deterrence The assumption that delinquency can be prevented by the threat of legal sanctions. Utilitarian punishment philosophy or proponents of the crime control model particularly advocate this belief.

differential association theory A perspective based on the belief that delinquent behavior is expected of individuals who have internalized a preponderance of definitions that are favorable to law violations.

differential identification theory Daniel Glaser's modification of differential association theory.

dispositional hearing The stage of the juvenile court proceedings in which the juvenile judge decides the most appropriate placement for a juvenile who has been adjudicated a delinquent, a status offender, or a dependent.

diversion The referral of juveniles to dispositional alternatives outside the formal juvenile justice system.

double jeopardy The *Breed v. Jones* decision (1975) ruled that juveniles cannot be tried in juvenile court and then be referred to the adult court. This would constitute double jeopardy and, according to the Fifth Amendment to the

U.S. Constitution, no person may be subject to being put in jeopardy of life or limb for the same offense twice.

drift theory According to David Matza, juveniles neutralize themselves from the moral bounds of the law and drift into delinquent behavior.

dropout A public or private school pupil who of his or her own volition no longer attends school.

drug addiction The excessive use of a drug, which is frequently accompanied by physical and/or psychological dependence.

drug and alcohol abuse intervention A treatment modality in which drug abusing juveniles are usually treated in a group context.

due process rights Constitutional rights that are guaranteed to citizens—whether adult or juvenile—during their contacts with the police, their proceedings in court, and their interactions with the public school.

Ecstasy A form of amphetamine, ecstasy began to be used by adolescents in the United States in the 1980's and 1990's.

ego The ego, according to Sigmund Freud, mediates between the id and the superego and is important in the socialization of the child.

electronic monitoring The use of electronic equipment to verify that an offender is at home or in a community correctional center during specified hours.

emerging gangs Gangs that formed in the late 1980s across the nation to traffick in crack cocaine.

emotionally disturbed offenders A broad category of youths whose emotional problems interfere with their everyday functioning and whose behaviors bring them into the juvenile justice system.

escalation of offenses The increase in the severity of delinquent offenses from one age to the next.

family court In some jurisdictions, such as New York, the family court hears all matters pertaining to juveniles, including delinquency and status offenses.

family therapy Treating an entire family is a widely used method of dealing with a delinquent's socially unacceptable behavior.

felicific calculus A theory that holds that human beings are oriented toward obtaining a favorable balance of pleasure and pain.

felony Criminal offense punishable by death or by incarceration in a state or federal correctional institution, usually for one year or more.

feminist theory of delinquency Meda Chesney-Lind argues that adolescent females' victimization at home and the relationship between that experience and their crimes have been systematically ignored.

financial restitution A court-ordered condition of probation in which a juvenile is required to make financial restitution to the victim of his or her crime.

fingerprinting Following arrest, juveniles and adults are fingerprinted as a form of pre-trial identification.

focal concerns Walter B. Miller contends that lower-class youths have different values or focal concerns (toughness, smartness, excitement, fate, and autonomy) from those of middle-class youths.

forestry camps Residents usually do conservation work in state parks, including cleaning up, cutting grass and weeds, and doing general maintenance.

foster care The foster home provides a setting for juveniles who must be removed from their natural homes.

free will Proponents of the classical school of criminology, as well as advocates of crime control or the justice model, believe that juveniles are rational creatures who, being free to choose their actions, can be held responsible for their behavior.

friendship patterns The relationships that exist in a teenage culture.

gang A youth gang is bound together by mutual interests, has identifiable leadership, and acts in concert to achieve a specific purpose that generally includes the conduct of illegal activity.

gang unit A specialized unit that is found in some police departments to intervene with gangs.

gender roles Societal expectations of what is masculine and what is feminine behavior.

general deterrence The threat and use of punishment to prevent illegal behavior among the population in general.

generation gap The widely accepted belief in the 1960s that there was a difference in the values of juveniles and of adults; that is, a gap between generations.

gentlemen reformers The reformers who advocated the development of houses of refuge, or juvenile institutions, in the early part of the nineteenth century as a means to deal with problem youths.

group delinquency Research has generally found that most delinquent behavior takes place with peers and is group related.

group home A placement for youths who have been adjudicated by the court—called a *group residence, halfway house, or attention home*—that serves a group of about thirteen to twenty-five youths as an alternative to institutionalization.

group home model A form of residential program in the community that has had some success with youthful offenders.

guided group interaction (GGI) Interaction that, whether it occurs in the community or in an institution, places youthful offenders in an intensive group environment under the direction of an adult leader. The guided-group-interaction process substitutes a whole new structure of beliefs, values, and behaviors for the values of delinquent peer subcultures.

halfway house A residential setting for adjudicated delinquents, usually those who need a period of readjustment to the community after an institutional confinement.

hard-line approach A desire to get tough with juvenile criminals that is currently found among some policymakers and the public.

heroin A refined form of morphine that was introduced about the turn of the twentieth century.

hidden delinquency Unobserved or unreported delinquency.

home detention A form of detention that is used in some jurisdictions in which the juvenile remains at home but receives intensive supervision by staff of the probation department.

houses of refuge Institutions that were designed by eighteenth-century reformers to provide an orderly disciplined environment similar to that of the "ideal" Puritan family.

id Sigmund Freud's theory of the personality refers to the id as the raw instincts and primitive drives. The id wants immediate gratification of its needs and, therefore, tends to be primitive and savage.

incidence of delinquency The frequency with which delinquent behavior takes place.

indeterminate sentencing This type of sentencing is used in most jurisdictions other than those that have mandatory or determinate sentencing. The juvenile judge has wide descretion and can commit a juvenile to the department of corrections or youth authority until correctional staff make the decision to release the juvenile.

index offenses The most serious offenses reported by the FBI in the *Uniform Crime Reports,* including murder and nonnegligent manslaughter, forcible rape, robbery, aggravated assault, burglary, larceny-theft, motor vehicle theft, and arson.

informal adjustment The attempt to handle a youthful offender outside of the formal structures of the juvenile justice system.

informal probation Instead of being adjudicated as a delinquent and placed on probation, a youth is informally assigned to the supervision of a probation officer.

inhalants Volatile liquids that give off a vapor, which is inhaled, producing short-term excitement and euphoria followed by a period of disorientation.

in loco parentis A guardian or an agency is given the rights, duties, and responsibilities of a parent.

In re Gault (1967) This case brought due process and constitutional procedures into juvenile courts.

In re Winship (1970) In Winship, the Supreme Court decided that juveniles are entitled to proof beyond a reasonable doubt during the adjudication proceedings.

instrumentalist Marxists The members of this group view the entire apparatus of crime control as the tool or instrument of the ruling class.

intake The first stage of juvenile court proceedings, in which the decision is made whether to divert the referral or to file a petition in juvenile court.

interstate compact Procedures for transferring a youth on probation or aftercare/parole from one state to another.

jail Juveniles are sometimes confined in county jails or police lockups. These adult facilities have few services to offer juveniles.

judicial waiver The process of relinquishing a juvenile to the adult court; also known as *certifying* or *binding over to the adult court.*

jury trial Juveniles do not have a constitutional right to a jury trial, but several jurisdictions permit juveniles to choose a jury trial.

just desserts This pivotal philosophical basis of the justice model holds that juveniles deserve to be punished if they violate the law; the punishment must be proportionate to the seriousness of the offense or the social harm inflicted on society.

justice as fairness The justice-as-fairness perspective, as David Fogel calls his justice model, advocates that it is necessary to be fair, reasonable, humane, and constitutional in the implementation of justice.

juvenile aftercare Concerned with the supervision of juveniles released from training school.

juvenile court officer Some probation departments refer to probation officers as juvenile court officers.

justice model A model of corrections based on the belief that individuals have free will and are responsible for their decisions and thus deserve to be punished if they violate the law, and the punishment they receive should be proportionate to the offense or the harm done.

juvenile drug courts These courts are designed for nonviolent offenders with substance abuse problems who require integrated sanctions and services such as mandatory drug testing, substance abuse treatment, supervised release, and aftercare.

Juvenile Justice and Delinquency Prevention Act of 1974 This federal law established a juvenile justice office within the Law Enforcement Assistance Administration to provide funds for the prevention and control of youth crime.

juvenile justice standards Jointly sponsored by the Institute of Judicial Administration and the American Bar Association, this project proposes that juveniles' sentences be based on the seriousness of crime rather than on the "needs" of the child.

juvenile officer A position for which some police departments provide specialized training so that police officers can work effectively with juveniles.

Kadi justice The kadi is a Molsem judge who sits in the marketplace and makes decisions without any apparent reference to rules and norms.

Kent v. United States (1966) The Kent decision, the first in which the U.S. Supreme Court dealt with a juvenile court case, concerned the matter of transfer.

labeling theory The labeling perspective claims that society creates the delinquent by labeling those who are apprehended as "different" from other youth, when in reality they are different only because they have been "tagged" with a deviant label.

law-and-order perspective This "get tough with criminals" approach became popular in juvenile corrections in the mid and late 1970s.

Law Enforcement Assistance Administration (LEAA) The Omnibus Crime Control and Safe Streets Act of 1968 established this unit in the U.S. Department of Justice to administer grants and provide guidance for crime prevention projects. Until funding ended for LEAA in the late 1970s, LEAA's grants permitted the expansion of community-based programs throughout the nation.

learning disabilities (LD) Children with special learning problems exhibit a disorder in one or more of the basic psychological processes involved in understanding or using spoken or written language. Some support exists for a theorized link between juvenile delinquency and learning disabilities.

least-restrictive model A model based on the assumption that a juvenile's penetration into the justice system should be minimized as much as possible.

legislative waiver This legislative act narrows juvenile court jurisdiction, excluding from juvenile courts those youths charged with certain offenses.

locura A state of mind in a Mexican American street gang denoting a type of craziness or wildness.

logical consequences model Advocates of this model believe that delinquent behavior should exact a cost and that youthful offenders should be made aware of the consequences of their socially unacceptable behavior.

mandatory sentencing Some states require that juveniles who commit certain offenses should receive a specified length of confinement.

Marijuana The most frequently used illicit drug. Is usually smoked.

Marxist orientation This position argues that crime and delinquency in capitalist society emerge because of the efforts of the powerful to maintain their power at all costs.

masculinity hypothesis Several studies of female delinquents propose that as girls become more boylike and acquire more "masculine" traits, they become more delinquent.

McKeiver v. Pennsylvania (1971) Denies juveniles the right to have jury trials.

medicalization of deviance Pertains to the role of the medical profession in creating deviance designations.

medical model Proponents of the medical model believe that delinquency is caused by factors that can be identified, isolated, treated, and cured.

minor A person who is under the age of legal consent.

Miranda v. Arizona A famous 1966 case in which the Supreme Court ruled that suspects taken into police custody must, before any questioning can take place, be informed that they have the right to remain silent, that anything they say may be used against them, and that they have the right to counsel.

Miranda warning Arrested subjects must be advised of three rights before interrogation: the right to remain silent, the right to consult with an attorney, and the right to court-appointed counsel if the suspect cannot afford private counsel. Juveniles also have these rights when they are taken into custody.

misdemeanor An offense that is punishable by incarceration for not more than one year in jail.

National Council of Crime and Delinquency This council, which publishes *Crime and Delinquency,* has long supported deinstitutionalization and the due process model in juvenile corrections.

neutralization Gresham M. Sykes and David Matza's theory of neutralization contends that youngsters attempt to rationalize their responsibility for delinquent acts.

New Jersey v. T.L.O. In this case, the Supreme Court examined the issue of whether Fourth Amendment rights against unreasonable searches and seizures apply to the school setting.

nonjudicial agencies Diversion programs that are outside the formal juvenile justice system.

norms The guidelines individuals follow in their relations with one another; shared standards of desirable behavior.

"nothing works" Robert Martinson and colleagues claimed in the mid 1970s that correctional treatment is ineffective in reducing recidivism of correctional clients.

Office of Juvenile Justice Delinquency Prevention (OJJDP) This office was established with the passage of the 1974 Juvenile Justice and Delinquency Prevention Act to deinstitutionalize status offenders.

Omnibus Crime Bill of 1978 (New York State) This bill, commonly known as the "juvenile offender law," stripped the family court of jurisdiction of thirteen-year-olds who have been accused of murder and fourteen-year-olds who have been accused of murder, attempted murder, and other violent offenses.

onset of delinquency The age at which a child begins to commit delinquent acts.

orthomolecular imbalances Chemical imbalances in the body, resulting from poor nutrition, allergies, and exposure to lead and certain other substances, which are said to lead to delinquency.

Outward Bound A wilderness-type survival program that is popular in many states as an alternative to institutionalization.

panaceas An easy answer to a complex problem.

parens patriae This medieval English doctrine sanctioned the right of the Crown to intervene in natural family relations whenever a child's welfare was threatened. The philosophy of the juvenile court is based on this legal concept.

People and Folks The major Chicago street gangs have divided themselves into these two supergangs.

petition A document filed in juvenile court by the intake unit asking that the court assume jurisdiction over a juvenile.

plea bargaining In urban courts, the defense counsel and the prosecution frequently agree that the juvenile will plead guilty in exchange for a reduction of the charges.

police discretion The choice between two or more possible means of handling a nonreviewable situation confronting a police officer.

police interrogation The process of interviewing a person who has been arrested with the expressed purpose of obtaining a confession.

positive peer culture This group modality, like its parent model, guided group interaction, is a group approach for building positive youth subcultures, and encompasses a strategy that extends to all aspects of daily life.

positivism This view has been the dominant philosophical perspective of juvenile justice since the juvenile court was established at the beginning of the twentieth century. It holds that, just as laws operate in the medical, biological, and physical sciences, laws govern human behavior, and these can be understood and used. The causes of human behavior, once discovered, can be modified to eliminate many of society's problems, such as delinquency.

power control thesis John Hagan and associates view the relationship between gender and delinquency as linked to power and control.

pretrial identification practices Photographing and placing juveniles in lineups are two of the most widely used pretrial identification practices.

prevalence of delinquency The percentage of the juvenile population who are involved in delinquent behavior.

primary deviation According to labeling theory, primary deviation represents the initial act committed by the deviant.

primary prevention Focuses on modifying conditions in the physical and social environment that lead to delinquency.

private training schools Juvenile courts frequently commit juveniles to training schools that are under private auspices; the county then pays the school a per diem rate for the care of these youths.

probation A court sentence under which the juvenile's freedom in the community is continued or only briefly interrupted, but the person is subject to supervision by a probation officer and the conditions imposed by the court.

probation officer An officer of the court who is expected to provide social history investigations, to supervise individuals who have been placed on probation, to maintain case files, to advise probationers on the conditions of their sentences, to perform any other probationary services that a judge may request, and to inform the court when persons on probation have violated the terms of that probation.

probation subsidies Financial assistance provided to local probation systems that are willing to comply with state standards.

process of becoming deviant Labeling theory contends that the process of acquiring a delinquent identity takes place in a number of steps.

Progressive Era During this era (the period from around 1890 to 1920) the wave of optimism that swept through U.S. society led to the acceptance of positivism. The doctrines of the emerging social sciences assured reformers that through positivism their problems could be solved.

proletariat Karl Marx contended that, with capitalism, society splits into two great opposing classes: the bourgeoisie (capitalist class) and the proletariat (working class).

prosecutor The representative of the state in court proceedings. Also called *county's attorney, district attorney,* or *state attorney.*

psychoanalytic theory Sigmund Freud contributed three insights that have helped shape the handling of juvenile delinquents: (1) personality is made up of three components—id, ego, and superego; (2) all normal children pass through three psychosexual stages of development—oral, anal, and phallic; and (3) a person's personality traits are developed in early childhood.

psychopath or sociopath This personality disorder type is frequently acknowledged as that of hard-core juvenile criminals. The claim is made that the psychopath or sociopath is the unwanted, rejected child who grows up but remains an undomesticated child and never develops trust or loyalty to an adult.

psychotherapy A treatment method in which various adaptations of Freudian therapy are used by psychiatrists, clinical psychologists, and psychiatric social workers to encourage delinquents to talk about past conflicts that cause them to express emotional problems through aggressive or antisocial behavior.

ranches and forestry camps Public and private juvenile correctional institutions that are usually less secure than training schools and have a more normalizing atmosphere.

rationality The quality or condition of being reasonable or rational or the possession or use of reason. Juveniles, according to rational choice theory, have free will and rationally calculate the cost of lawbreaking.

reality therapy William Glasser and G. L. Harrington base this treatment modality on the principle that individuals must accept responsibility for their behavior.

reception and diagnostic centers Juveniles who are committed to juvenile institutions frequently are sent first to these centers, which diagnose their problems and develop a treatment plan.

recidivism The repetition of delinquent behavior by a youth who has been released from probation status or from training school.

referee Many juvenile courts employ the services of these juvenile justice personnel, who may or may not be members of the bar. Their basic responsibility is to assist judges in processing youths through the courts.

reference group The group with which a juvenile identifies or to which he or she aspires to belong.

rehabilitation model The medical, the adjustment, and the reintegration models are parts of the more inclusive rehabilitative model because they are all committed to changing the offender.

rehabilitative philosophy The goal of this philosophy is to change an offender's character, attitudes, or behavior patterns so as to diminish his or her delinquent propensities.

reinforcement theory This theory states that behavior is governed by its consequent rewards and punishments.

reintegration model The idea that offenders' problems must be solved in the community in which they occur and community-based organizations can help offenders readjust to community life.

reliability The extent to which a questionnaire or interview yields the same answers from the same juveniles when they are questioned two or more times.

"representing" Secret handshakes and hand signs, unique to each gang.

residential programs Within community-based and institutional settings, these programs are conducted for the rehabilitation of youth.

residential social system The social hierarchy that is established by residents in an institution.

respondent Defense attorney

restitution Financial restitution and community service are widely used conditions of juvenile probation.

revocation of aftercare When juveniles on aftercare commit another offense or violate the conditions of parole, they may have their aftercare revoked and be returned to an institution.

right to treatment Several court decisions have held that a juvenile has a right to treatment on being committed to a training school.

routine activity approach Lawrence E. Cohen and Marcus Felson, who developed this approach, contend that crime rate trends and cycles are affected by the routine activity structure of U.S. society.

runaway behavior Usually defined as being away from home for twenty-four or more hours without permission of parents or caregivers.

school searches A process of searching students and their lockers to determine whether drugs or weapons are present.

search and seizure Juveniles, like adults, have constitutional safeguards to protect them against unauthorized police searches and seizures. To search a person or location, the Constitution requires a lawfully obtained search warrant.

secondary deviation According to labeling theory, secondary deviation represents societal reaction to the initial delinquent act.

secondary prevention Refers to intervention in the lives of juveniles in circumstances that dispose them toward delinquency.

sedatives These drugs are taken orally and affect the user by depressing the nervous system.

self-reflexive human beings Some theorists propose that delinquent behavior is not merely the product or consequence of societal and community forces but is also the creation of symbol-using, self-reflexive human beings.

sexual abuse, or incest Any sexual activity that involves physical contact or sexual arousal between members of a family who are not married to one another.

shelter care facilities Shelters are used primarily to provide short-term care for status offenders and for dependent or neglected children.

skill-development programs Programs that teach communication, decision-making, daily living, educational advancement, vocational, and career skills.

social class A term used to describe people who have similar incomes, educational achievements, and occupational prestige.

social control theory This perspective, according to Travis Hirschi and others, states that delinquent acts result when a juvenile's bond to society is weak or broken.

social development model This model, based on the integration of social control and cultural learning theories, proposes that the development of attachments to parents will lead to attachments to school and a commitment to education as well as a belief in and commitment to conventional behavior and the law.

social disorganization theory Juvenile delinquency, according to Shaw and McKay and others, results from the breakdown of social control among the traditional primary groups, such as the family and the neighborhood, because of the social disorganization of the community.

social history report A written report of a juvenile's social background that probation officers prepare for a juvenile judge to assist the court in making a disposition of a youth who has been ruled delinquent.

social injustice Many criminologists claim that social injustice is present in the juvenile justice system because poor youths tend to be disproportionately represented, because female status offenders are subjected to sexist treatment, and because racism is present and minorities are dealt with more harshly than whites.

socialization The process by which individuals internalize their culture; from this process an individual learns the norms, sanctions, and expectations of being a member of a particular society.

social process theories These theories examine the interactions between individuals and their environments that influence them to become involved in delinquent behavior.

social structure theories These theories suggest that the setting for delinquency is the social and cultural environment in which adolescents grow up or the subcultural groups with which they choose to become involved.

sociobiology An expression of biological positivism that stresses the interaction between the biological factors within an individual and the influence of their particular environment.

sociopath An emotionally deprived child who frequently becomes a hard-core juvenile delinquent.

soft determinism David Matza claimed that the concept of soft determinism contains the best resolution of the free will and positivism debate; that is, delinquents are neither wholly free nor wholly constrained but fall somewhere in between.

soft-line approach The lenient treatment of those youths who pose little threat to the social order.

specialization The act of a juvenile being repeatedly involved in one type of delinquency during the course of his or her offending.

specific deterrence Using threats and punishment to prevent illegal behavior by specific persons who have already broken the law.

state training school A long-term juvenile correctional facility that is operated by the department of corrections or youth commission of state government.

station adjustment One of several disposition options available to a police officer whereby a juvenile is taken to the police station following a complaint, the contact is recorded and the juvenile is given an official reprimand and then is released to his or her parents.

status offender A juvenile who commits a minor act that is considered illegal only because he or she is underage. Various terms are used to refer to status offenders including MINS (minors in need of supervision), CHINS (children in need of supervision), CHINA (children in need of assistance), PINS (persons in need of supervision), FINS (families in need of supervision), and JINS (juveniles in need of supervision).

strain theory A theory that proposes that the pressure that the social structure exerts on youths who cannot attain the cultural goal of success will push them to engage in nonconforming behavior.

structural Marxists A group that argues that the form of the legal system can work to reproduce capitalist social relations.

superego According to Freud, the superego, or the conscience, internalizes the rules of society.

supremacy of parental rights A presumption for parental autonomy in childrearing and the philosophy that coercive intervention is appropriate only in the face of serious harm to the child.

surveillance Probation officers make certain that probationers comply with the conditions of probation and that they do not break the law.

symbolic interactionist theory This theory in social psychology stresses the process of interaction among human beings at the symbolic level and has influenced the development of several social process theories of delinquent behavior.

taking into custody The process of arresting a juvenile for socially unacceptable behavior.

teaching-family group model A community-based residential program that has had some success with delinquent youth.

teen courts Teen courts, also know as youth courts, are a means of diversion that keeps juveniles out of the formal justice system.

tertiary prevention Directed at the prevention of recidivism among youthful offenders.

therapeutic community The purpose of this treatment modality is to create a total environment that is supportive of socially acceptable behavior. The modality is based on reducing role differences between the keepers and the kept and giving offenders every opportunity to analyze and take responsibility for their own behaviors.

tracking system A method to classify students according to their perceived abilities in public and private schools.

training school A correctional facility for long-term placement of juvenile delinquents.

transactional analysis (TA) A therapy, based on interpreting and evaluating personal relationships, that has proved to be of immediate value to many delinquents. Using catchy language, TA promises delinquents who feel "not OK" that several easy steps can make them "OK."

transfer The process of certifying a youth over to the adult court; it takes place by judicial waiver and legislative waiver.

underclass Individuals who appear to be permanently trapped in poverty and whose children are at high risk for delinquent behaviors.

Uniform Crime Reports The Federal Bureau of Investigation's annual report of crimes committed in the United States.

utilitarian punishment philosophy James Q. Wilson and Ernest van den Haag, leading spokespeople for this position, contend that punishment is necessary to deter youthful offenders and to protect society from crime.

validity A serious question concerning self-report studies rests with whether researchers can be certain that juveniles are being truthful when they fill out self-report questionnaires.

values Common ideas among individuals about what is good or bad, right or wrong, desirable and undesirable.

Vernonia School District 47J v. Acton The U.S. Supreme Court extended schools' authority to search by legalizing a random drug-testing policy for student athletes.

victimization surveys An ongoing survey of individuals in the United States conducted by the Bureau of Justice Statistics to determine the extent of crime.

volunteer programs Using volunteers to assist probation officers in a variety of ways.

women's liberation movement Freda Adler has argued that this movement has influenced females to commit crimes traditionally committed only by males.

youth service bureau (YSB) An agency outside the juvenile justice system that was designed to divert children and youths from the justice system by (1) mobilizing community resources to solve youth problems, (2) strengthening existing youth resources and developing new ones, and (3) promoting positive programs to remedy delinquency-prone conditions in the environment.

youth shelter A facility that is usually used to handle status offenders who need detention services.

Name Index

Subject Index